BIG IDEAS MATH®
Modeling Real Life

Grade 1

Volume 2

Common Core Edition

TEACHING EDITION

Ron Larson
Laurie Boswell

Big Ideas Learning™
Erie, Pennsylvania
BigIdeasLearning.com

Big Ideas Learning, LLC
1762 Norcross Road
Erie, PA 16510-3838
USA

For product information and customer support, contact Big Ideas Learning
at **1-877-552-7766** or visit us at ***BigIdeasLearning.com***.

Cover Image:
Valdis Torms, bgblue/DigitalVision Vectors/Getty Images

Printed in the U.S.A.

ISBN 13: 978-1-63708-532-5

2 3 4 5 6 7 8 9 10—25 24 23 22 21

One Voice from Kindergarten Through Algebra 2

Written by renowned authors, Dr. Ron Larson and Dr. Laurie Boswell, *Big Ideas Math* offers a seamless math pedagogy from elementary through high school. Together, Ron and Laurie provide a consistent voice that encourages students to make connections through cohesive progressions and clear instruction. Since 1992, Ron and Laurie have authored over 50 mathematics programs.

Each time Laurie and I start working on a new program, we spend time putting ourselves in the position of the reader. How old is the reader? What is the reader's experience with mathematics? The answers to these questions become our writing guides. Our goal is to make the learning targets understandable and to develop these targets in a clear path that leads to student success.

Ron Larson

Ron Larson, Ph.D., is well known as lead author of a comprehensive and widely used mathematics program that ranges from elementary school through college. He holds the distinction of Professor Emeritus from Penn State Erie, The Behrend College, where he taught for nearly 40 years. He received his Ph.D. in mathematics from the University of Colorado. Dr. Larson engages in the latest research and advancements in mathematics education and consistently incorporates key pedagogical elements to ensure focus, coherence, rigor, and student self-reflection.

My passion and goal in writing is to provide an essential resource for exploring and making sense of mathematics. Our program is guided by research around the learning and teaching of mathematics in the hopes of improving the achievement of all students. May this be a successful year for you!

Laurie Boswell, Ed.D., is the former Head of School at Riverside School in Lyndonville, Vermont. In addition to authoring textbooks, she provides mathematics consulting and embedded coaching sessions. Dr. Boswell received her Ed.D. from the University of Vermont in 2010. She is a recipient of the Presidential Award for Excellence in Mathematics Teaching and later served as president of CPAM. Laurie has taught math to students at all levels, elementary through college. In addition, Laurie has served on the NCTM Board of Directors and as a Regional Director for NCSM. Along with Ron, Laurie has co-authored numerous math programs and has become a popular national speaker.

Contributors, Reviewers, and Research

Big Ideas Learning would like to express our gratitude to the mathematics education and instruction experts who served as our advisory panel, contributing specialists, and reviewers during the writing of *Big Ideas Math: Modeling Real Life*. Their input was an invaluable asset during the development of this program.

Contributing Specialists and Reviewers

- **Sophie Murphy**, Ph.D. Candidate, Melbourne School of Education, Melbourne, Australia
  Learning Targets and Success Criteria Specialist and Visible Learning Reviewer
- **Linda Hall**, Mathematics Educational Consultant, Edmond, OK
  Advisory Panel
- **Michael McDowell**, Ed.D., Superintendent, Ross, CA
  Project-Based Learning Specialist
- **Kelly Byrne**, Math Supervisor and Coordinator of Data Analysis, Downingtown, PA
  Advisory Panel
- **Jean Carwin**, Math Specialist/TOSA, Snohomish, WA
  Advisory Panel
- **Nancy Siddens**, Independent Language Teaching Consultant, Las Cruces, NM
  English Language Learner Specialist
- **Kristen Karbon**, Curriculum and Assessment Coordinator, Troy, MI
  Advisory Panel
- **Kery Obradovich**, K–8 Math/Science Coordinator, Northbrook, IL
  Advisory Panel
- **Jennifer Rollins**, Math Curriculum Content Specialist, Golden, CO
  Advisory Panel
- **Becky Walker**, Ph.D., School Improvement Services Director, Green Bay, WI
  Advisory Panel and Content Reviewer
- **Deborah Donovan**, Mathematics Consultant, Lexington, SC
  Content Reviewer
- **Tom Muchlinski**, Ph.D., Mathematics Consultant, Plymouth, MN
  Content Reviewer and Teaching Edition Contributor
- **Mary Goetz**, Elementary School Teacher, Troy, MI
  Content Reviewer
- **Nanci N. Smith**, Ph.D., International Curriculum and Instruction Consultant, Peoria, AZ
  Teaching Edition Contributor
- **Robyn Seifert-Decker**, Mathematics Consultant, Grand Haven, MI
  Teaching Edition Contributor
- **Bonnie Spence**, Mathematics Education Specialist, Missoula, MT
  Teaching Edition Contributor
- **Suzy Gagnon**, Adjunct Instructor, University of New Hampshire, Portsmouth, NH
  Teaching Edition Contributor
- **Art Johnson**, Ed.D., Professor of Mathematics Education, Warwick, RI
  Teaching Edition Contributor
- **Anthony Smith**, Ph.D., Associate Professor, Associate Dean, University of Washington Bothell, Seattle, WA
  Reading and Writing Reviewer
- **Brianna Raygor**, Music Teacher, Fridley, MN
  Music Reviewer
- **Nicole Dimich Vagle**, Educator, Author, and Consultant, Hopkins, MN
  Assessment Reviewer
- **Janet Graham**, District Math Specialist, Manassas, VA
  Response to Intervention and Differentiated Instruction Reviewer
- **Sharon Huber**, Director of Elementary Mathematics, Chesapeake, VA
  Universal Design for Learning Reviewer

Student Reviewers

- T.J. Morin
- Alayna Morin
- Ethan Bauer
- Emery Bauer
- Emma Gaeta
- Ryan Gaeta
- Benjamin SanFrotello
- Bailey SanFrotello
- Samantha Grygier
- Robert Grygier IV
- Jacob Grygier
- Jessica Urso
- Ike Patton
- Jake Lobaugh
- Adam Fried
- Caroline Naser
- Charlotte Naser

Research

Ron Larson and Laurie Boswell used the latest in educational research, along with the body of knowledge collected from expert mathematics instructors, to develop the *Modeling Real Life* series. By implementing the work of renowned researchers from across the world, *Big Ideas Math* offers at least a full year's growth within a full year's learning while also encouraging a growth mindset in students and teachers. Students take their learning from surface-level to deep-level, then transfer that learning by modeling real-life situations. For more information on how this program uses learning targets and success criteria to enhance teacher clarity, see pages xiv–xv. The pedagogical approach used in this program follows the best practices outlined in the most prominent and widely accepted educational research, including:

- *Visible Learning*, John Hattie © 2009
- *Visible Learning for Teachers*
John Hattie © 2012
- *Visible Learning for Mathematics*
John Hattie © 2017
- *Principles to Actions: Ensuring Mathematical Success for All*
NCTM © 2014
- *Adding It Up: Helping Children Learn Mathematics*
National Research Council © 2001
- *Mathematical Mindsets: Unleashing Students' Potential through Creative Math, Inspiring Messages and Innovative Teaching*
Jo Boaler © 2015
- *What Works in Schools: Translating Research into Action*
Robert Marzano © 2003
- *Classroom Instruction That Works: Research-Based Strategies for Increasing Student Achievement*
Marzano, Pickering, and Pollock © 2001
- *Principles and Standards for School Mathematics*
NCTM © 2000
- *Rigorous PBL by Design: Three Shifts for Developing Confident and Competent Learners*
Michael McDowell © 2017
- Common Core State Standards for Mathematics
National Governors Association Center for Best Practices and Council of Chief State School Officers © 2010
- *Universal Design for Learning Guidelines*
CAST © 2011
- Rigor/Relevance Framework®
International Center for Leadership in Education
- *Understanding by Design*
Grant Wiggins and Jay McTighe © 2005
- Achieve, ACT, and The College Board
- *Elementary and Middle School Mathematics: Teaching Developmentally*
John A. Van de Walle and Karen S. Karp © 2015
- *Evaluating the Quality of Learning: The SOLO Taxonomy*
John B. Biggs & Kevin F. Collis © 1982
- *Unlocking Formative Assessment: Practical Strategies for Enhancing Students' Learning in the Primary and Intermediate Classroom*
Shirley Clarke, Helen Timperley, and John Hattie © 2004
- *Formative Assessment in the Secondary Classroom*
Shirley Clarke © 2005
- *Improving Student Achievement: A Practical Guide to Assessment for Learning*
Toni Glasson © 2009

Focus and Coherence from

Instructional Design

A single authorship team from Kindergarten through Algebra 2 results in a logical progression of focused topics with meaningful coherence from course to course.

FOCUS

A focused program dedicates lessons, activities, and assessments to grade-level standards while simultaneously supporting and engaging students in the major work of the course.

The **Learning Targets** in the Student Edition and the **Success Criteria** in the Teaching Edition focus the learning for each lesson into manageable chunks, with clear teaching text and examples.

Learning Target: Write related addition and subtraction equations to complete a fact family.

Laurie's Notes

Preparing to Teach

Students have heard about time and the language of time. Most students do not understand time or know how to tell time on an analog clock. In this lesson, students are introduced to telling time to the hour. They learn about the hour hand and telling time as o'clock.

Laurie's Notes prepare you for the math concepts in each chapter and lesson and make connections to the threads of major topics for the course.

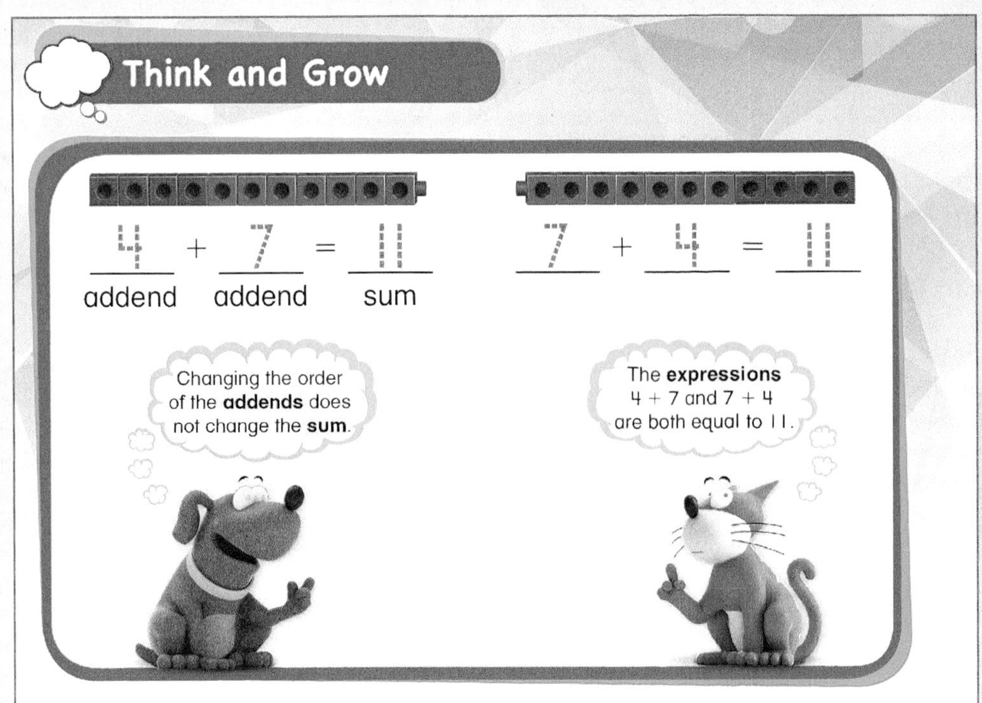

Think and Grow
4 + 7 = 11
addend addend sum
7 + 4 = 11
Changing the order of the addends does not change the sum.
The expressions 4 + 7 and 7 + 4 are both equal to 11.

a Single Authorship Team

COHERENCE

A single authorship team built a coherent program that has intentional progression of content within each grade and between grade levels. Your students will build new understanding on foundations from prior grades and connect concepts throughout the course.

The authors developed content that progresses from prior chapters and grades to future ones. In addition to charts like this one, Laurie's Notes give you insights about where your students have come from and where they are going in their learning progression.

Through the Grades		
Kindergarten	**Grade 1**	**Grade 2**
• Represent addition and subtraction with various models and strategies. • Solve addition and subtraction word problems within 10. • Fluently add and subtract within 5.	• Solve addition and subtraction word problems within 20. • Fluently add and subtract within 10. • Determine the unknown number to complete addition and subtraction equations.	• Solve addition and subtraction word problems within 100. • Solve word problems involving length and money. • Solve one- and two-step word problems. • Fluently add and subtract within 20.

One author team thoughtfully wrote each course, creating a seamless progression of content from Kindergarten to Algebra 2.

See pages xxx and xxxi for K-8 Progressions chart.

			Grade 2	Grade 3	Grade 4	Grade 5	Grade 6	
					Number and Operations – Base Ten		The Number System	
Number and Quantity	gain foundations for place value. *Chapter 8*	ence. Use place value and properties of operations to add and subtract. *Chapters 6–9*	Use place value and properties of operations to add and subtract. *Chapters 2–10, 14*	Use place value and properties of operations to perform multi-digit arithmetic. *Chapters 7–9, 12*	Generalize place value understanding for multi-digit whole numbers. Use place value and properties of operations to perform multi-digit arithmetic. *Chapters 1–5*	Understand the place value system. Perform operations with multi-digit whole numbers and with decimals to hundredths. *Chapters 1, 3–7*	Perform operations with multi-digit numbers and find common factors and multiples. *Chapter 1* Divide fractions by fractions. *Chapter 2* Extend understanding of numbers to the rational number system. *Chapter 8*	Perfor ration Chapt
				Num. and Oper. – Fractions	Number and Operations – Fractions		Ratios and Proportional Relation	
				Understand fractions as numbers. *Chapters 10, 11, 14*	Extend understanding of fraction equivalence and ordering. Build fractions from unit mal notation d compare	Add, subtract, multiply, and divide fractions. *Chapters 6, 8–11*	Use ratios to solve problems. *Chapters 3, 4*	Use pr to solv Chapt

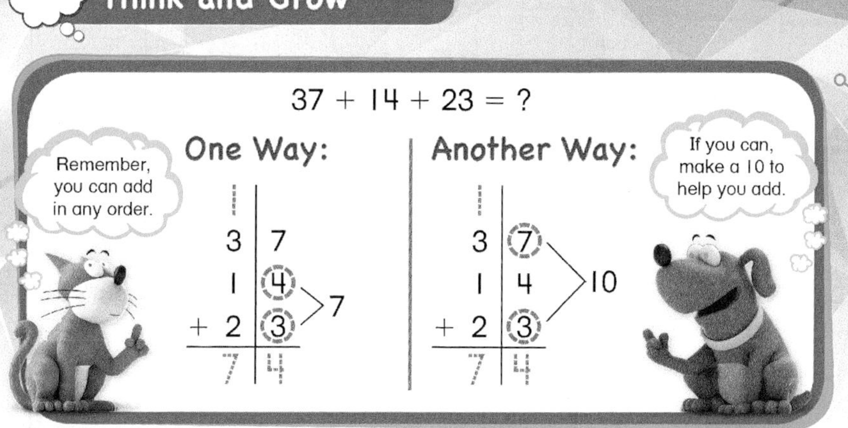

Throughout each course, lessons build on prior learning as new concepts are introduced. Here students are reminded of addition rules and strategies that they already know.

Rigor in Math: A Balanced Approach

Instructional Design

The authors wrote each chapter and every lesson to provide a meaningful balance of rigorous instruction.

RIGOR

A rigorous program provides a balance of three important building blocks.

- **Conceptual Understanding**
  Discovering why
- **Procedural Fluency**
  Learning how
- **Application**
  Knowing when to apply

Conceptual Understanding
Students have the opportunity to develop foundational concepts central to the *Learning Target* in each *Explore and Grow* by experimenting with new concepts, talking with peers, and asking questions.

Conceptual Thinking
Ask students to think deeply with conceptual questions.

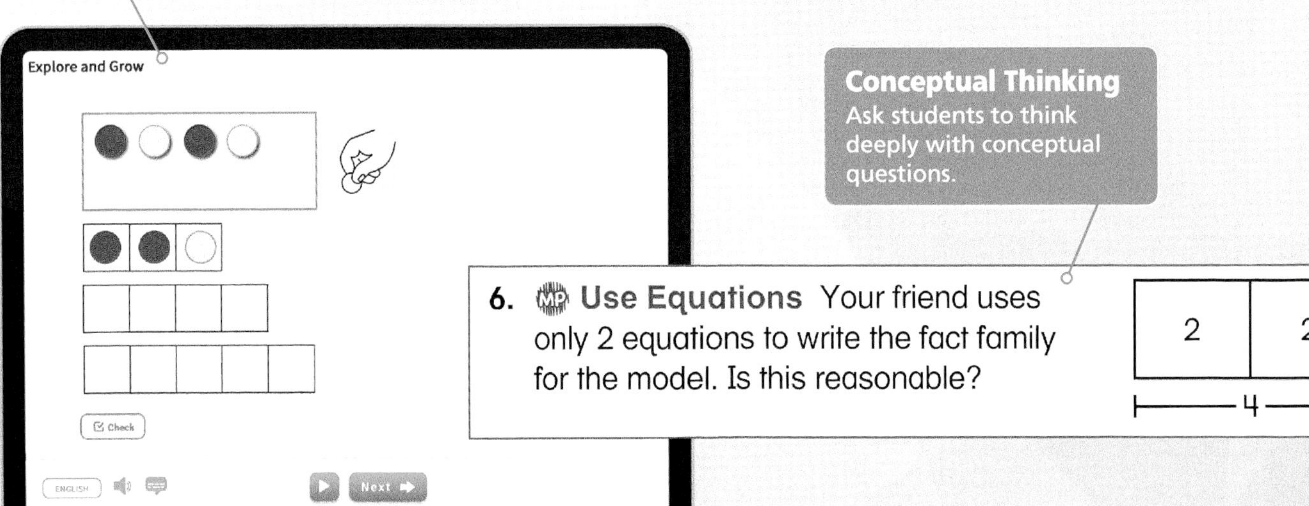

6. Use Equations Your friend uses only 2 equations to write the fact family for the model. Is this reasonable?

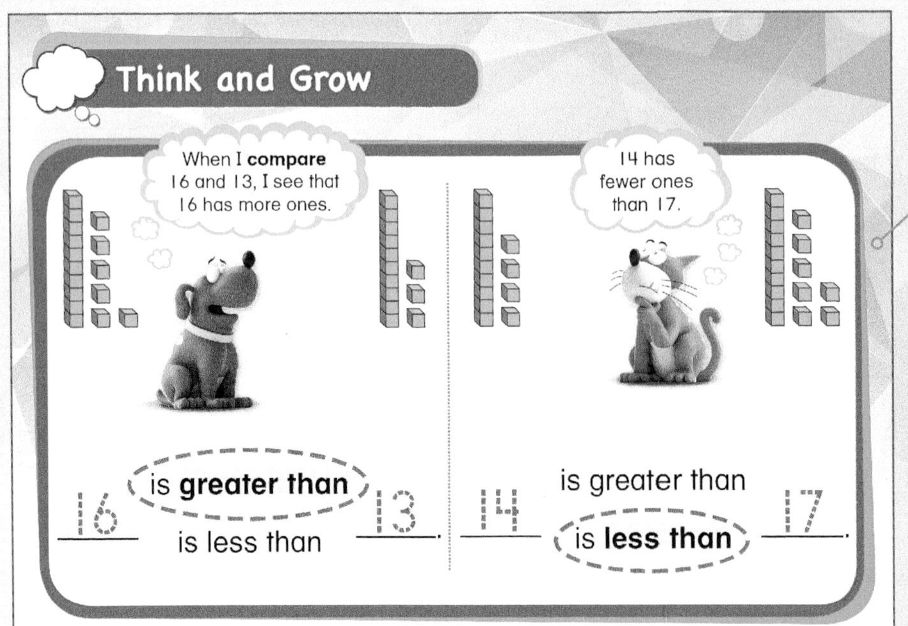

Think and Grow
When I compare 16 and 13, I see that 16 has more ones.
14 has fewer ones than 17.
16 is greater than 13
is less than
14 is greater than 17
is less than

Procedural Fluency
Solidify learning with clear, stepped-out teaching in *Think and Grow* examples.

Then shift conceptual understanding into procedural fluency with *Show and Grow*, *Apply and Grow*, *Practice*, and *Review & Refresh*.

5

Subtract Numbers within 20

- What do bees make?
- How many bees do you see? 7 of them fly away. How many bees are left?

Chapter Learning Target:
Understand subtraction strategies.

Chapter Success Criteria:
- I can identify counting back strategies.
- I can describe subtraction equations.
- I can explain the subtraction strategy I used.
- I can compare addition and subtraction strategies.

Connecting to Real Life
Students begin every chapter thinking about the world around them. Students then apply what they learn in the chapter with a related *Performance Task*.

Name ____________

Performance Task 5

1. You keep track of the number of honeybees and bumblebees you see.

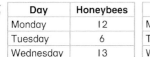

Day	Honeybees
Monday	12
Tuesday	6
Wednesday	13

Day	Bumblebees
Monday	5
Tuesday	14
Wednesday	

a. How many more honeybees did you see on Monday than on Tuesday?

____ more honeybees

Daily Application Practice
Modeling Real Life, *Dig Deeper*, and other non-routine problems help students apply surface-level skills to gain a deeper understanding. These problems lead students to independent problem-solving.

15. **Modeling Real Life** Your magic book has 163 tricks. Your friend's magic book has 100 more tricks than yours. How many tricks does your friend's magic book have?

_____ tricks

16. **DIG DEEPER!** You have 624 songs. Newton has 100 fewer than you. Descartes has 10 more than Newton. How many songs does Descartes have?

_____ songs

Problem-Solving Plan
Walk students through the Problem-Solving Plan, featured in many *Think and Grow* examples, to help them make sense of problems with confidence.

THE PROBLEM-SOLVING PLAN

1. **Understand the Problem**
   Think about what the problem is asking. Circle what you know and underline what you need to find.
2. **Make a Plan**
   Plan your solution pathway before jumping in to solve. Identify any relationships and decide on a problem-solving strategy.
3. **Solve and Check**
   As you solve the problem, be sure to evaluate your progress and check your answers. Throughout the problem-solving process, you must continually ask, "Does this make sense?" and be willing to change course if necessary.

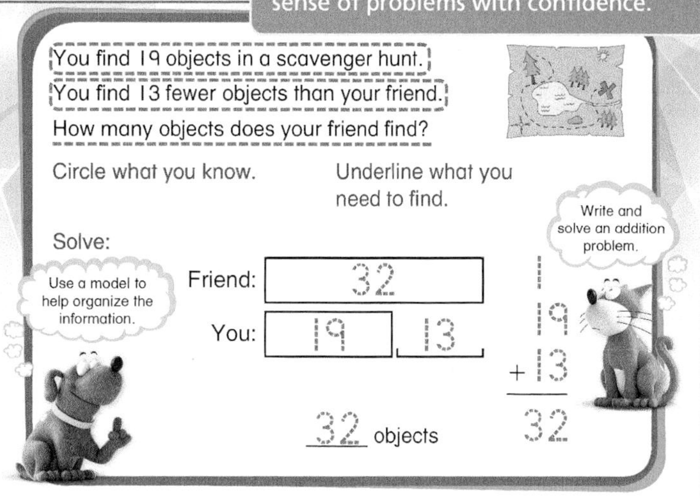

Embedded Mathematical Practices

Encouraging Mathematical Mindsets

Developing proficiency in the **Mathematical Practices** is about becoming a mathematical thinker. Students learn to ask why, and to reason and communicate with others as they learn. Use this guide to identify opportunities in the classroom for students to develop proficiency in mathematical practices.

1

One way to **Make Sense of Problems and Persevere in Solving Them** is to use the Problem-Solving Plan. Students take time to analyze the given information and what the problem is asking to help them plan a solution pathway.

Look for labels such as:

- Find Entry Points
- Analyze a Problem
- Interpret a Solution
- Make a Plan
- Use a Similar Problem
- Check Your Work

There are 33 students on a bus. 10 more get on. How many students are on the bus now?

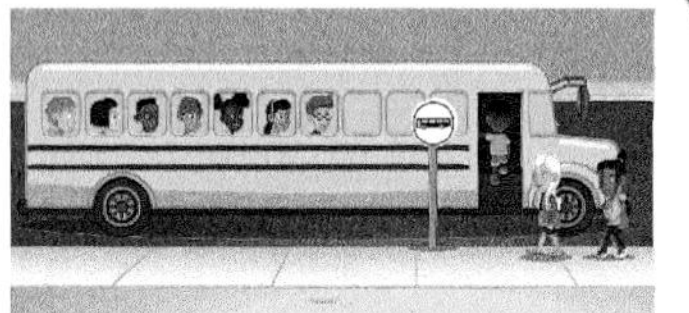

Addition equation:

MP Check Your Work When adding 10, should the digit in the tens place or the ones place change?

____ students

5. MP **Analyze a Problem** Use the numbers shown to write two addition equations.

8 10 2

____ + ____ = ____

____ + ____ = ____

2

Students **Reason Abstractly** when they explore an example using numbers and models to represent the problem. Other times, students **Reason Quantitatively** when they see relationships in numbers or models and draw conclusions about the problem.

Look for labels such as:

- Reasoning
- Number Sense
- Use Equations
- Use Expressions

7. MP **Reasoning** The minute hand points to the 7. What number will it point to in 10 minutes?

3. MP **Number Sense** Which numbers can you subtract from 55 without regrouping?

15 49 33 24

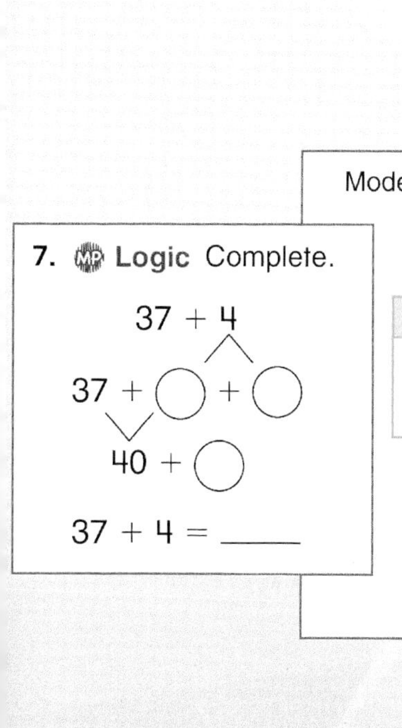

Model 27 two ways.

Tens	Ones

____ tens and ____ ones is ____.

____ tens and ____ ones is ____.

Construct an Argument Can you model 27 using only tens? Why or why not?

3

When students **Construct Viable Arguments and Critique the Reasoning of Others**, they make and justify conclusions and decide whether others' arguments are correct or flawed.

Look for labels such as:

- Construct an Argument
- You Be the Teacher
- Logic
- Make a Conjecture
- Justify a Result
- Compare Arguments

7. **Graph Data** Complete the weather chart to show an equal number of sunny days and rainy days. Write an equation to show how many sunny days and rainy days there are in all.

SUN	MON	TUE	WED	THU	FRI	SAT

___ + ___ = ___

Think and Grow: Modeling Real Life

Will the scissors fit inside a pencil case that is 7 color tiles long?

Circle: Yes No

Tell how you know:

Does It Make Sense? To fit inside, should the scissors be shorter or longer than the case?

4

To **Model with Mathematics**, students apply the math they learned to a real-life problem and interpret mathematical results in the context of the situation.

Look for labels such as:

- Modeling Real Life
- Graph Data
- Analyze a Relationship
- Does It Make Sense?

BUILDING TO FULL UNDERSTANDING

Throughout each course, students have opportunities to demonstrate specific aspects of the mathematical practices. Labels throughout the book indicate gateways to those aspects. Collectively, these opportunities will lead to a full understanding of each mathematical practice. Developing these mindsets and habits will give meaning to the mathematics students learn.

Embedded Mathematical Practices (continued

5

To Use **Appropriate Tools Strategically**, students need to know what tools are available and think about how each tool might help them solve a mathematical problem. Remind students that some tools may have limitations.

Look for labels such as:
- Choose Tools
- Use Math Tools
- Use Technology

8. **Choose Tools** Would you measure the length of a bus with a centimeter ruler or a meter stick? Why?

Use Math Tools How can you use a drawing to help organize the information given?

11. **DIG DEEPER!** There are 63 people in a theater, 21 people in the lobby, and 10 people in the parking lot. How many more people are in the theater than in both the lobby and the parking lot?

_____ more people

6

When students **Attend to Precision**, they are developing a habit of being careful in how they talk about concepts, label work, and write answers.

7. **DIG DEEPER!** Complete the model and the equation to match.

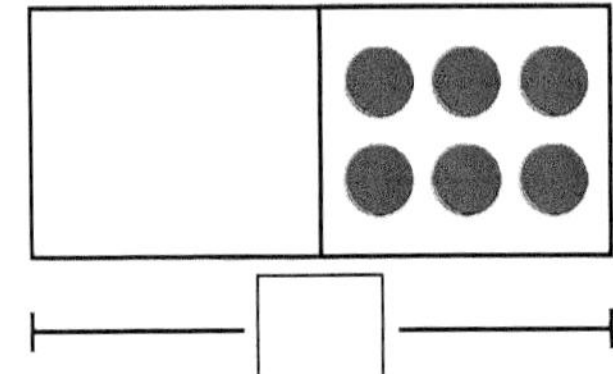

___ + ___ = 8

Communicate Clearly In the model, what shows the addends? the sum?

Look for labels such as:
- Precision
- Communicate Clearly
- Maintain Accuracy

5. **Precision** Which picture shows the correct way to measure the straw?

6. MP **Patterns** Find the sums. Think: What do you notice?

$4 + 5 =$ ____

$4 + 4 =$ ____

$5 + 5 =$ ____

	Tens	Ones
	☐	
	3	8
+	2	4

$38 + 24 =$ ____

MP **Structure** What step did you use to find 38 + 24 that you would not use to find 31 + 24? Why?

7

Students **Look For and Make Use of Structure** by looking closely to see structure within a mathematical statement, or stepping back for an overview to see how individual parts make one single object.

Look for labels such as:

- Structure
- Patterns

8. MP **Repeated Reasoning** What other shape has the same number of surfaces, vertices, and edges as a rectangular prism? How is that shape different from a rectangular prism?

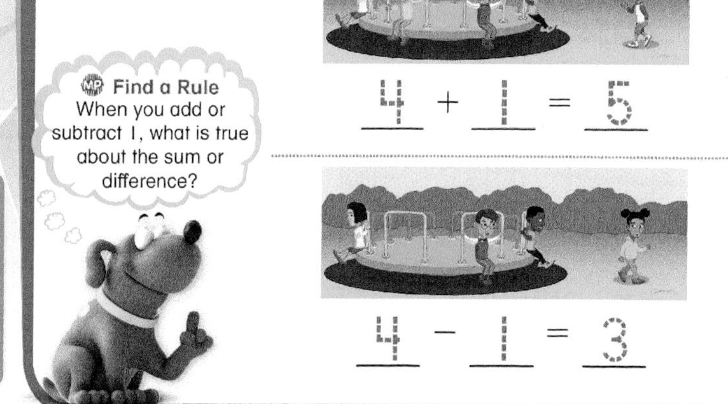

MP Find a Rule
When you add or subtract 1, what is true about the sum or difference?
4 + 1 = 5
4 - 1 = 3

8

When students **Look For and Express Regularity in Repeated Reasoning**, they can notice patterns and make generalizations. Remind students to focus on the goal of a problem, which will help them evaluate reasonableness of answers along the way.

Look for labels such as:

- Repeated Reasoning
- Find a Rule

Visible Learning Through Learning Targets,

Making Learning Visible

Knowing the learning intention of a chapter or lesson helps students focus on the purpose of an activity, rather than simply completing it in isolation. This program supports visible learning through the consistent use of Learning Targets and Success Criteria to ensure positive outcomes for all students.

Every chapter shows a **Learning Target** and four related **Success Criteria**. These are incorporated throughout the chapter content to help guide students in their learning.

Chapter Learning Target: Understand place value.

Chapter Success Criteria:

- I can identify different numbers.
- I can explain the values of numbers.
- I can model and write numbers.
- I can represent numbers in different ways.

Every lesson shows a **Learning Target** that is purposefully integrated into each carefully written lesson.

Name ______________________

Represent Numbers in Different Ways 7.5

Learning Target: Represent numbers in different ways.

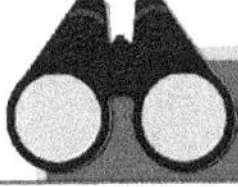

Explore and Grow

Review the learning target. "Today we learned how to add and subtract 1. Turn to your partner and discuss how to add 1 to any number. What does this have to do with counting? Now discuss how to subtract 1 from any number. What does this have to do with counting?"

Students can access the **Learning Target** and **Success Criteria** on every page of the Dynamic Student Edition.

Icons throughout **Laurie's Notes** suggest ways to target where students are in their learning.

MENU 7.5 Represent Numbers in Different Ways

LEARNING TARGET MATH TOOLS

Think and Grow

Show 123 two ways.

Hundreds	Tens	Ones
1	2	3

Hundreds	Tens	Ones
0	12	3

Learning Target

Represent numbers in different ways.

Success Criteria

- I can draw a quick sketch to model a three-digit number.
- I can tell the value of the digit in each place value.
- I can show two ways to model and write a number.

Click-Through Example

QUESTIONS FOR LEARNERS

As students progress through a lesson, they should be able to answer the following questions.

- What are you learning?
- Why are you learning this?
- Where are you in your learning?
- How will you know when you have learned it?
- Where are you going next?

Success Criteria, and Self-Assessment

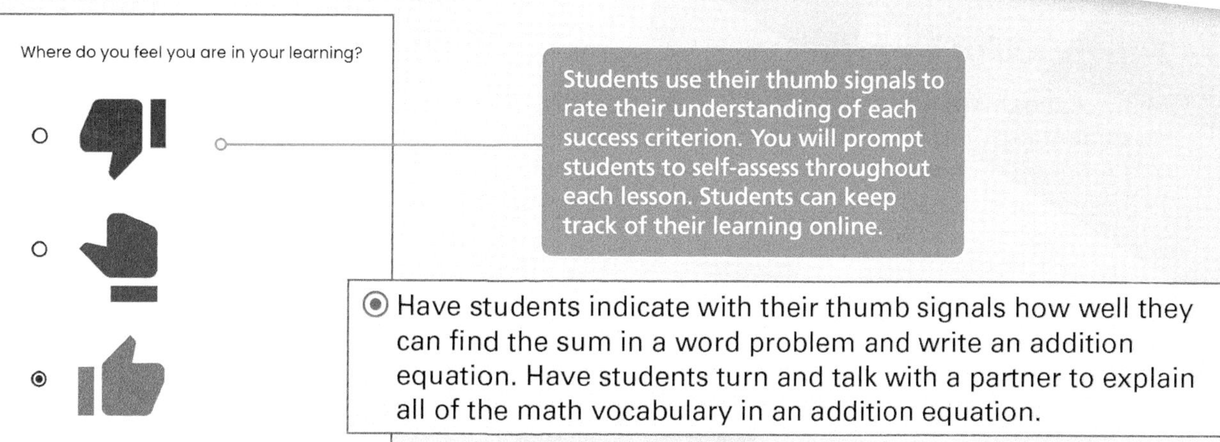

Where do you feel you are in your learning?

Students use their thumb signals to rate their understanding of each success criterion. You will prompt students to self-assess throughout each lesson. Students can keep track of their learning online.

Have students indicate with their thumb signals how well they can find the sum in a word problem and write an addition equation. Have students turn and talk with a partner to explain all of the math vocabulary in an addition equation.

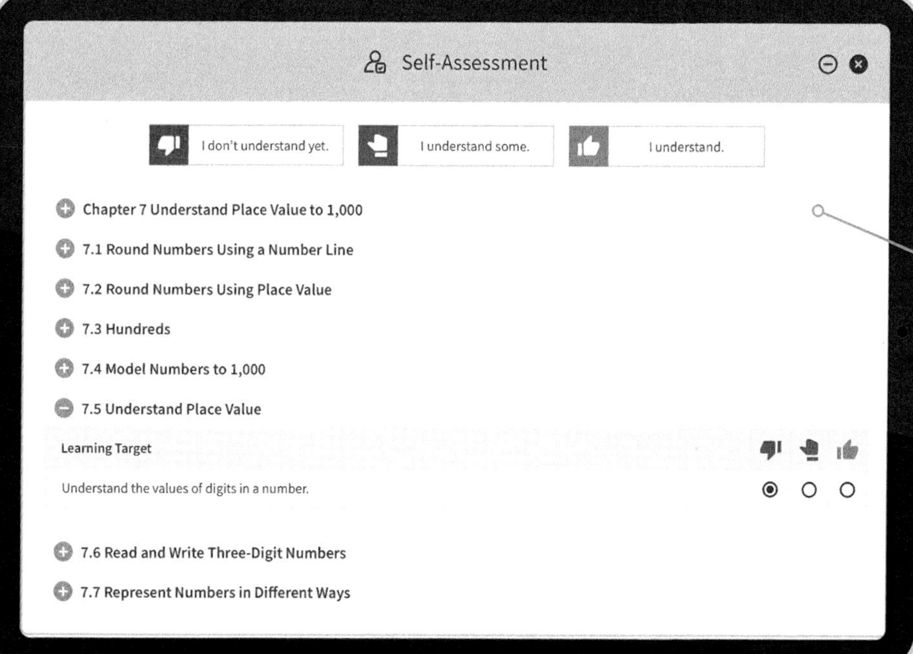

Self-Assessments are included throughout every lesson, and in the **Chapter Review**, to help students take ownership of their learning and think about where to go next.

Ensuring Positive Outcomes

John Hattie's *Visible Learning* research consistently shows that using Learning Targets and Success Criteria can result in two years' growth in one year, ensuring positive outcomes for student learning and achievement.

Sophie Murphy, M.Ed., wrote the chapter-level Learning Targets and Success Criteria for this program. Sophie is currently completing her Ph.D. at the University of Melbourne in Australia with Professor John Hattie as her leading supervisor. Sophie completed her Master's thesis with Professor John Hattie in 2015. Sophie has over 20 years of experience as a teacher and school leader in private and public school settings in Australia.

High-Impact Strategies

Purposeful Focus

Many of the things we do as educators have a positive effect on student learning, but which ones have the greatest impact? This program purposefully integrates **five key strategies** proven to have some of the highest impact on student achievement.

TEACHER CLARITY

Before starting a new topic, make the Learning Target clear. As students explore and learn, continue to connect their experiences back to the Success Criteria so they know where they are in their learning.

"The key to today's work is to find the value of each side of the equal sign, and see if they are the same. Everyone think of the value of 13 − 6 and hold it inside. Use any of your strategies. Who will suggest another expression for us to decide if it would make a true equation or not?" As a student gives an expression, ask if it would make a true equation or not. Then ask the student if he or she agrees with the decision.

"Let's use our thumb signals to tell how we are doing. How well can you count by tens and then by ones? How well can you write the numbers you have counted? How well can you write the numbers between 100 and 120?"

FEEDBACK

Actively listen as you probe for student understanding, being mindful of the feedback that you provide. When students provide you with feedback, you see where they are in their learning and make instructional decisions for where to go next.

? "Talk to your group or partner. What are some addition strategies you remember? Can you think of a problem you would use that strategy for?"

CLASSROOM DISCUSSION

Encourage your students to talk together! This solidifies understanding while honing their ability to reason and construct arguments. Students benefit from hearing the reasoning of classmates and hearing peers critique their own reasoning.

Daily Support from a Master Educator

In Laurie's Notes, master educator Laurie Boswell uses her professional training and years of experience to help you guide your students to better understanding.

Laurie studied Professor John Hattie's research on *Visible Learning* and met with Hattie on multiple occasions to ensure she was interpreting his research accurately and embedding it effectively. Laurie's expertise continues with an ongoing collaboration with Sophie Murphy, who is pursuing her Ph.D. under Professor Hattie.

for Student Achievement

DIRECT INSTRUCTION
Follow exploration and discovery with explicit instruction to build procedural skill and fluency. Teach with clear examples that have been carefully designed to ensure your students meet the success criteria of each lesson.

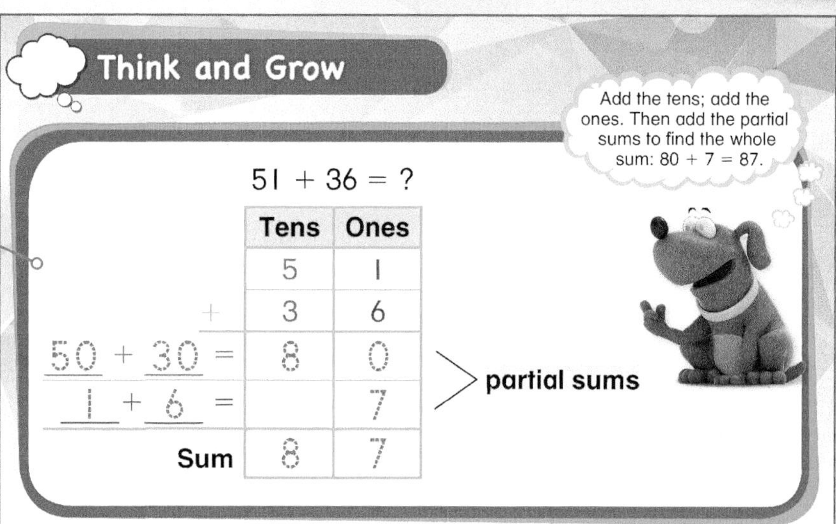

SPACED PRACTICE
Effective practice does not just focus on a single topic of new learning; students must revisit concepts over time so deeper learning occurs. This program cohesively offers multiple opportunities for students to build their conceptual understanding by intentionally revisiting and applying concepts throughout subsequent lessons and chapters. *Review & Refresh* exercises in every lesson also provide continual practice on the major topics.

Review & Refresh

Is the equation true or false?

6. $4 + 9 \stackrel{?}{=} 2 + 3 + 5$

True False

7. $5 + 3 \stackrel{?}{=} 4 + 4$

True False

We focus on **STRATEGIES** with some of the **HIGHEST IMPACT** on student achievement—up to 2 years of learning for a year of input.

Five Strategies for Purposeful Focus

Professor John Hattie, in his *Visible Learning* network, identified more than 250 influences on student learning, and developed a way of ranking them. He conducted meta-analyses and compared the influences by their **effect size**—the impact the factor had on student learning.

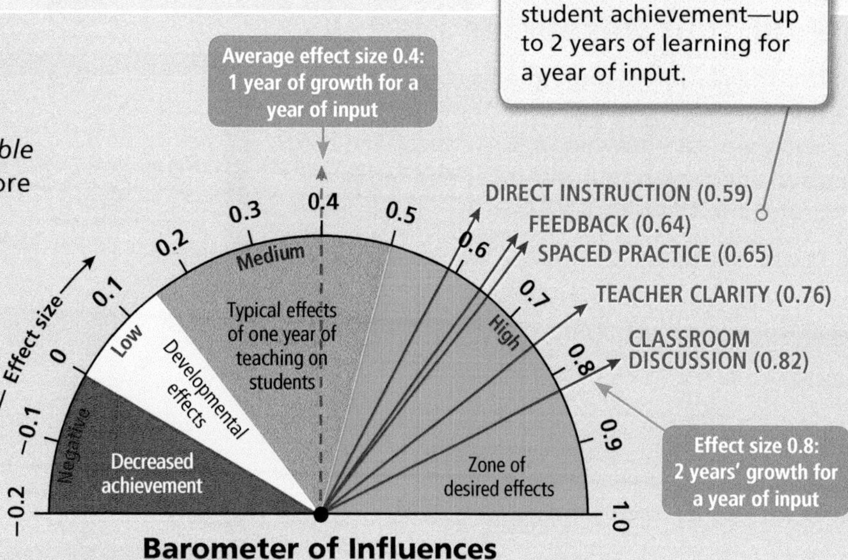

Barometer of Influences

How to Use This Program: Plan

Taking Advantage of Your Resources

You play an indispensable role in your students' learning. This program provides rich resources for learners of all levels to help you **Plan**, **Teach**, and **Assess**.

Laurie's Overview

About the Math

Earlier this year students learned strategies to develop addition
fluency w
to 1,000.
numbers
connects
numbers

Students who demonst
understanding of place
within 1,000. Students

Plan every chapter and lesson with tools in the Teaching Edition such as **Suggested Pacing, Progression Tables,** and math **Overviews** written by Laurie Boswell.

	Through the Chapter								
Standard	**6.1**	**6.2**	**6.3**	**6.4**	**6.5**	**6.6**	**6.7**	**6.8**	**6.9**
1.NBT.A.1 Count to 120, starting at any number less than 120. In this range, read and write numerals and represent a number of objects with a written numeral.	●	●							●
1.NBT.B.2 Understand that the two digits of a two-digit number represent amounts of tens and ones.			●	●	●	●	●	●	●
1.NBT.B.2a 10 can be thought of as a bundle of ten ones – called a "ten."			●	●	●	●	●	●	●
1.NBT.B.2b The numbers from 11 to 19 are composed of a ten and one, two, three, four, five, six, seven, eight, or nine ones.			●						
1.NBT.B.2c The numbers 10, 20, 30, 40, 50, 60, 70, 80, 90 refer to one, two, three, four, five, six, seven, eight, or nine tens (and 0 ones).				●	●	●	●	●	●

Key: ▲ = Preparing ● = Learning ★ = Complete

Find Your Resources Digitally

Use the resources page that is available on your *BigIdeasMath.com* dashboard. Here, you can download, customize, and print these planning resources and many more. Use the filters to view resources specific to a chapter or lesson.

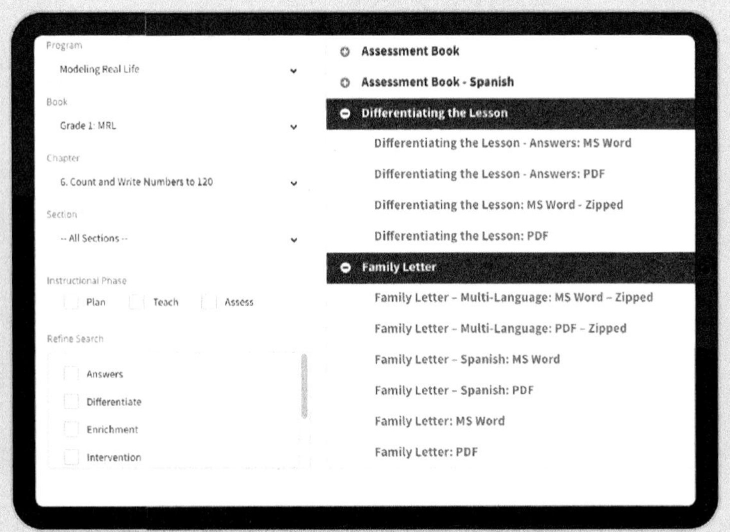

LEARNING TARGET | MATH TOOLS | MY NOTES | LAURIE'S NOTES

Think and Grow

Getting Started

- Students will use bar models to solve word problems as they did yesterday. If students continue to use linking cubes to model the problems, be sure they can correlate the steps with the cubes and filling in the bar models.

Teaching Notes

- Read the sand castle word problem. Have students explain the bar model, noting who has the shorter and longer bars and why. What do we know?

? Model: "What is the *given group* (known)?" My friend builds 6 sand castles. "Notice the 6 in the Friend bar. Why is it in the longer bar? Fill it in. What else do we know?" I build 4 fewer. "The 4 is already in the bracket for us."

Model: "How can we determine how many sand castles you build?" Have students respond with their strategies. As they describe addition and subtraction strategies, point out the corresponding equations. Have students fill in the equations as they are discussed.

- In the same way that *more* does not always mean to add (as discussed in yesterday's lesson), *fewer* also does not always mean to subtract. Students will not encounter

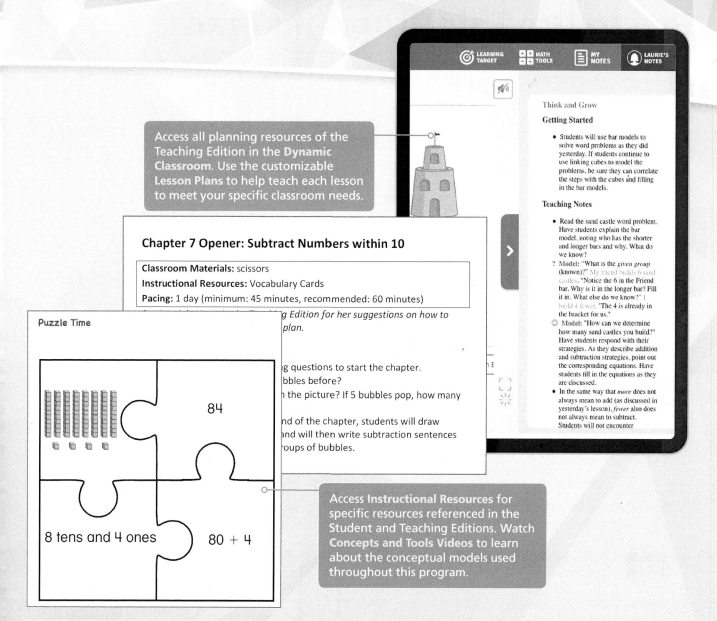

Access all planning resources of the Teaching Edition in the **Dynamic Classroom.** Use the customizable **Lesson Plans** to help teach each lesson to meet your specific classroom needs.

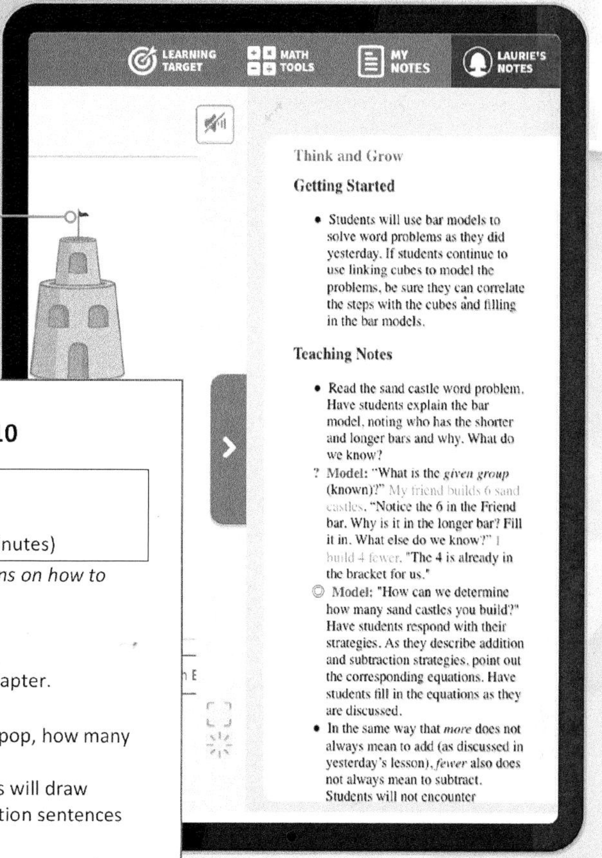

Chapter 7 Opener: Subtract Numbers within 10

Classroom Materials: scissors
Instructional Resources: Vocabulary Cards
Pacing: 1 day (minimum: 45 minutes, recommended: 60 minutes)

g Edition for her suggestions on how to
plan.

g questions to start the chapter.
bbles before?
n the picture? If 5 bubbles pop, how many

nd of the chapter, students will draw
and will then write subtraction sentences
oups of bubbles.

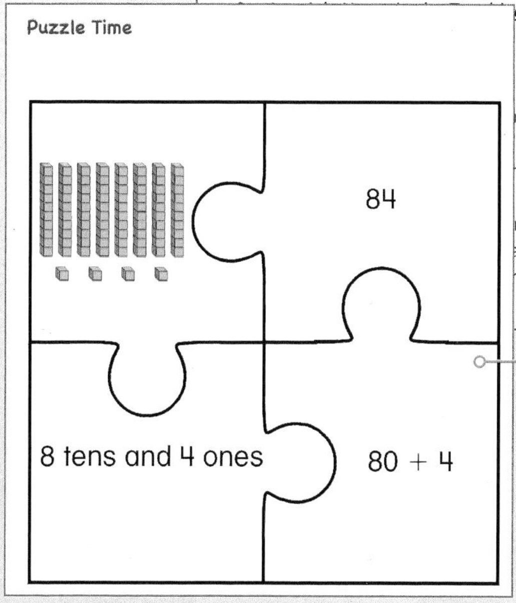

Puzzle Time

	84
8 tens and 4 ones	80 + 4

Access **Instructional Resources** for specific resources referenced in the Student and Teaching Editions. Watch **Concepts and Tools Videos** to learn about the conceptual models used throughout this program.

Plan Online

As you are planning, remember that the *Dynamic Classroom* has the same interactive tools, such as the digital *Sketchpad*, that students will use to model concepts. Plan ahead by practicing these tools to guide students as they use these manipulatives and models.

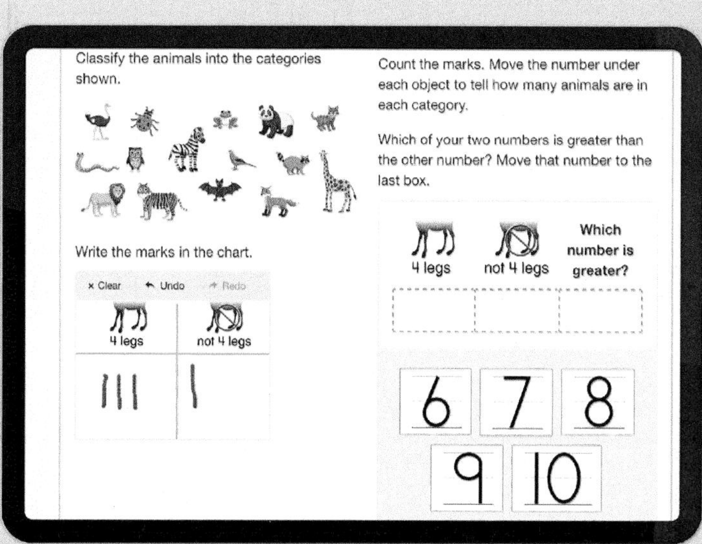

How to Use This Program: Teach

Multiple Pathways for Instruction

Everything you need to make the best instructional choices for your students is at your fingertips.

Present all content digitally using the **Dynamic Classroom.** Send students a page link on the fly with **Flip-To** to direct where you want your students to go.

Have students **Thinking Ahead** about chapter concepts in the world around them. Then, students will apply their learning in the **Performance Task** at the end of the chapter.

Chapter 10 - Measure and Compare Lengths

Performance Task

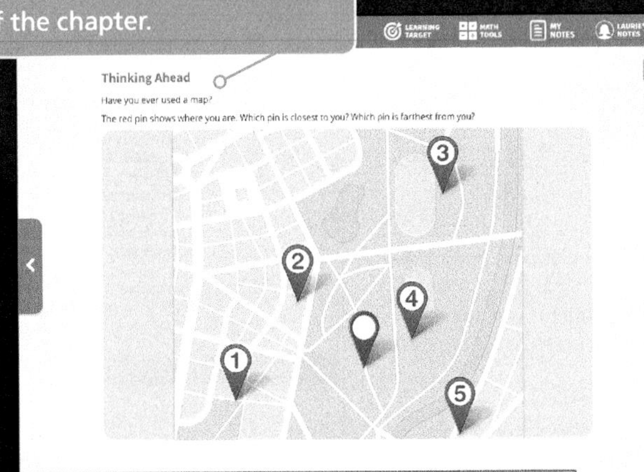

Dig In (Circle Time)

- "We have used the *count on* strategy in order to add many times. Who can model what it means to *count on* using the addition problem 5 + 3?"
- Set up the Large Number Line, using 0–20. Have students add by standing on the first addend, then walking the additional number of steps for the second addend.
- **Model:** "We also used number lines to help us count on. Who remembers using a number line? Let's model 3 + 6 on the number line." Have a student stand on the 3 on the Large Number Line. Remind students that they do not count 3 as one of the spaces we count. 3 is where we are starting. Have the student count on 6 times stepping to each next number as all students count on 4, 5, 6, 7, 8, 9.

  As students are counting on, show tally marks or hold up fingers to show how many times you are counting on in order to keep track of adding 6.

- "Sometimes it is hard to keep track of how many numbers we are counting on. We can keep track with our fingers, or make tallies. If we are drawing on a number line, we can count the hops we are drawing until we draw the right number, then we can see where we land on the number line."
- "Today we are going to use this strategy to add numbers up to 20. Let's try some together. I am going to show the number line movements on the chart paper while we walk them on the floor." Show the Number Line 0–20 and model the starting addend with a dot on the number line, then draw the "hops" along the number line for the second addend. Give several examples that have sums between 11 and 20, such as 5 + 7, 8 + 6, etc. Show counting the hops in addition to *counting on.*
- "Today we are counting on to find sums. Who can explain how we can find sums by *counting on* with or without a number line?"

Engage students with a creative hook at the beginning of each lesson with **Dig In.** This activity, written by master educator Laurie Boswell, provides a conceptual introduction to the lesson. Then encourage mathematical discovery in **Explore and Grow.**

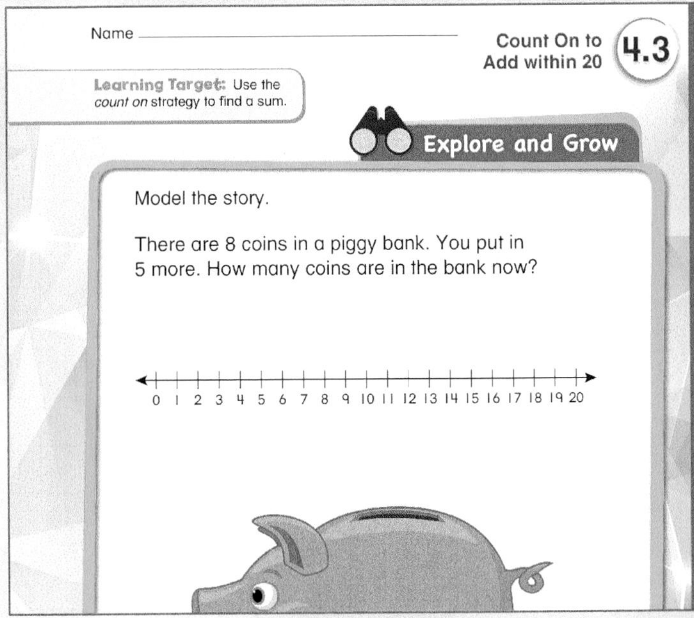

Lead students to procedural fluency with clear **Think and Grow** examples, followed by **Show and Grow** and **Apply and Grow** exercises which provide opportunities for students to try concepts on their own.

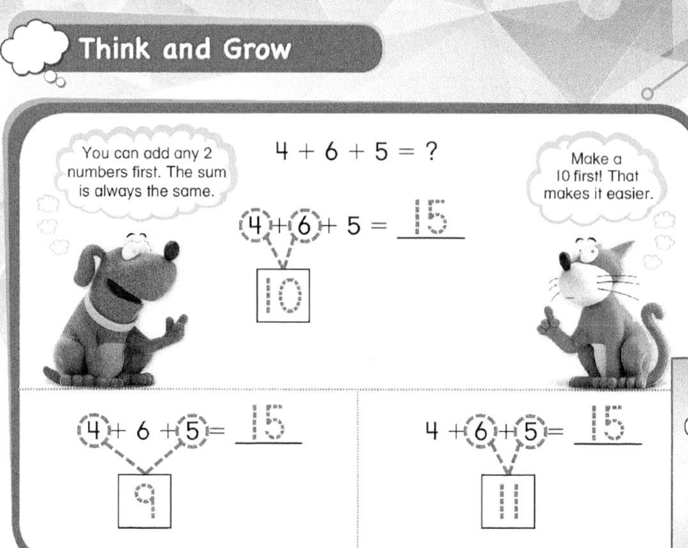

Think and Grow
You can add any 2 numbers first. The sum is always the same.
4 + 6 + 5 = ?
Make a 10 first! That makes it easier.
4 + 6 + 5 = 15
10
4 + 6 + 5 = 15
9
4 + 6 + 5 = 15
11

Help students apply and problem solve with **Modeling Real Life** applications, **Dig Deeper** problems, and **Mathematical Practice** conceptual problems.

Think and Grow: Modeling Real Life

Are there more state parks in North Carolina and Kentucky or in Kentucky and South Carolina?

State Parks	
State	**Number of State Parks**
North Carolina	29
Kentucky	38
South Carolina	43

Addition equations:

Compare: _____ ○ _____

There are more state parks in _________ and _________.

EMERGING students may not have their number facts mastered. Help them with discovering strategies to add the numbers.

- **Exercises 5–13:** Remind students that they do not have to add from left to right or top to bottom. Ask them which two numbers are easiest to add to begin. Students may need help drawing the branches and/or box for the sum.
- **Exercise 14:** Decompose the sum using a drawing.

5

1 | 4

PROFICIENT students are able to add the three numbers and know their addition facts.

- **Exercises 5–13:** Students work in small groups. Challenge students to think about which two numbers would be easiest to add first. Have them explain their choice.
- **Exercise 14:** Ask students to share and compare their strategies for finding the missing addend.

Let **Laurie's Notes** guide your teaching and scaffolding decisions at every step to support and deepen all students' learning. You may want to group students differently as they move in and out of these levels with each skill and concept. Student self-assessment and feedback help guide your instructional decisions about how and when to layer support.

Name ____________________

Lesson 2.6 **Extra Practice**

1. 4 + 5 = _____

9 − 5 = _____

2. 7 + 3 = _____

10 − 3 = _____

Differentiate and support your students with **Differentiating the Lesson, Resources by Chapter, English Language Support**, and much more.

How to Use This Program: Assess

Powerful Assessment Tools

Gain insight into your students' learning with these powerful formative and summative assessment tools tailored to every learning target and standard.

Access real-time data and navigate easily through student responses with **Formative Check.**

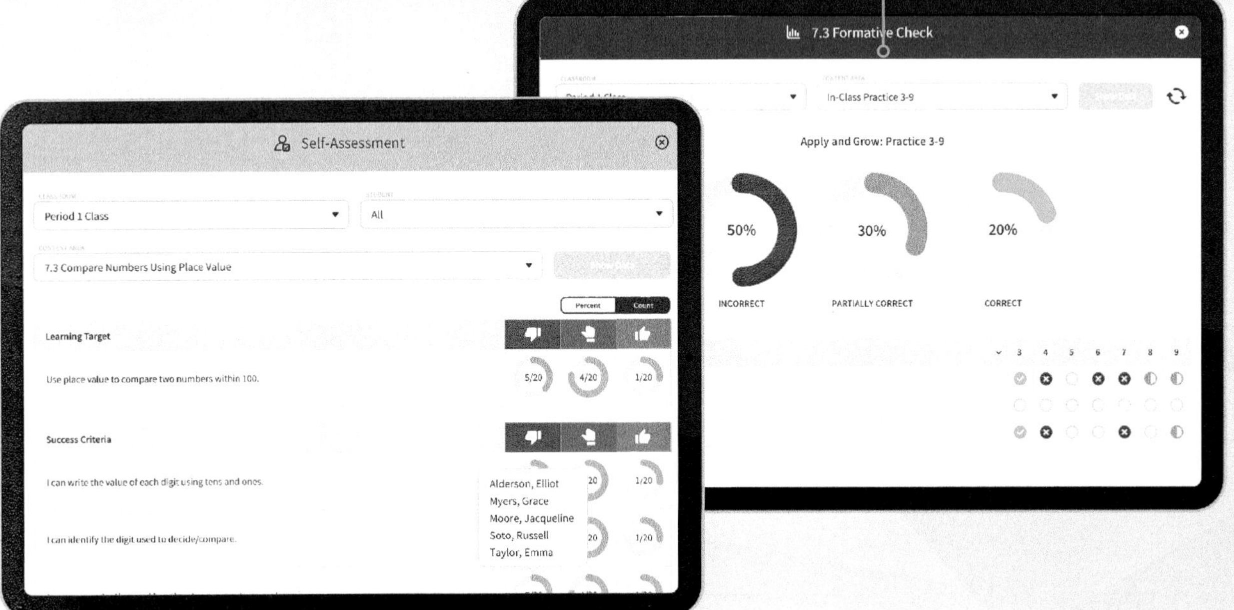

Assign print or digital versions of **Practice** to support all students in their learning progression. Assign additional exercises and revisit concepts with spaced practice to move every student toward proficiency with grade-level standards.

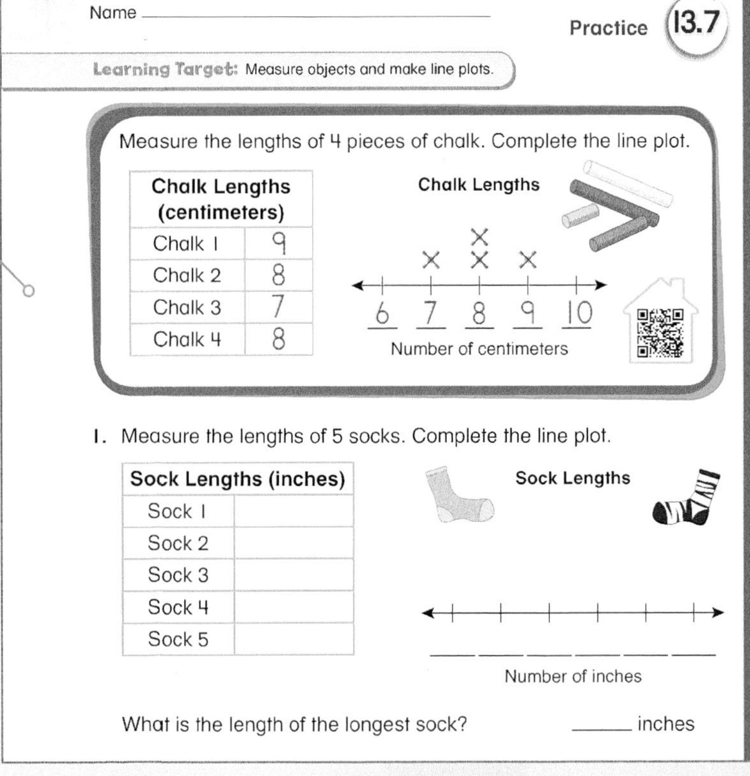

Name ____________________

Practice 13.7

Learning Target: Measure objects and make line plots.

Measure the lengths of 4 pieces of chalk. Complete the line plot.

Chalk Lengths (centimeters)	
Chalk 1	9
Chalk 2	8
Chalk 3	7
Chalk 4	8

1. Measure the lengths of 5 socks. Complete the line plot.

Sock Lengths (inches)	
Sock 1	
Sock 2	
Sock 3	
Sock 4	
Sock 5	

What is the length of the longest sock? _____ inches

Assign **Chapter Tests** to assess understanding of chapter content, or use **Alternative Assessments** and **Performance Tasks** in the Teaching Edition, which include scoring rubrics.

Name____________________________________

Chapter 12 **Test A**

Write the time shown by the hour hand.

1\.

_____ o'clock

2\.

half past _____

What time is shown on the clock?

3\.

_____ o'clock

4\.

half past _____

Name____________________________________

Grade 1 **Course Benchmark 2**

For use after Chapter 7

1\. There are 6 cats.

3 cats leave.

How many cats are left?

_____ cats

2\. $10 - 5 = ?$

5	

10

Think, 5 + _____ = 10.

So, 10 – 5 = _____.

Assess student learning of standards throughout the year with cumulative **Course Benchmark Tests**. Use the results to help plan instruction and intervention.

Measure learning across grades with adaptive **Progression Benchmark Tests.**

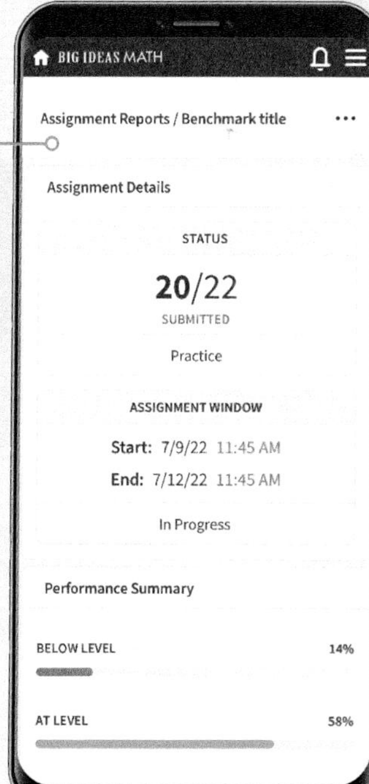

Use the **Assignment Builder** to assign digital versions of the print **Chapter Tests and Course Benchmark Tests.** Receive immediate feedback through robust reporting.

Assessment item point values are weighted. You can customize an item's total point value to fit your needs.

Strategic Support for All Learners

Support for English Language Learners

Support your English Language Learners (ELLs) with a blend of print and digital resources available in Spanish. Look to your Teaching Edition for opportunities to support all students with the language development needed for mathematical understanding.

Students' WIDA scores are a starting point. As the year progresses and students' language skills change and grow, students may move in and out of language levels with varying demands of content languages.

Clarify, Connect, and Scaffold

- Clarify language that may be difficult or confusing for ELLs
- Connect new learning to something students already know
- Differentiate student comprehension while completing practice exercises
- Target Beginner, Intermediate, and Advanced ELLs, which correspond to **WIDA** reading, writing, speaking, and listening language mastery levels

Practice Language and Content

- Practice math while improving language skills
- Use language as a resource to develop procedural fluency

Assess Understanding

- Check for development of mathematical reasoning
- Informally assess student comprehension of concepts

ELL Support

After reviewing the example, have students work in groups to discuss and complete Exercises 1–3. Expect students to perform according to their language proficiency level.

WIDA 1: Entering
WIDA 2: Emerging

Beginner students may model the process by drawing and writing out the math.

WIDA 3: Developing
WIDA 4: Expanding

Intermediate students may describe using simple sentences.

WIDA 5: Bridging
WIDA 6: Reaching

Advanced students may describe using detailed sentences that help guide discussion.

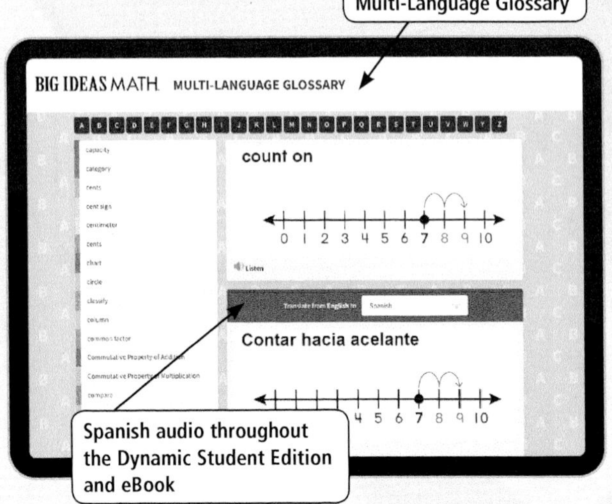

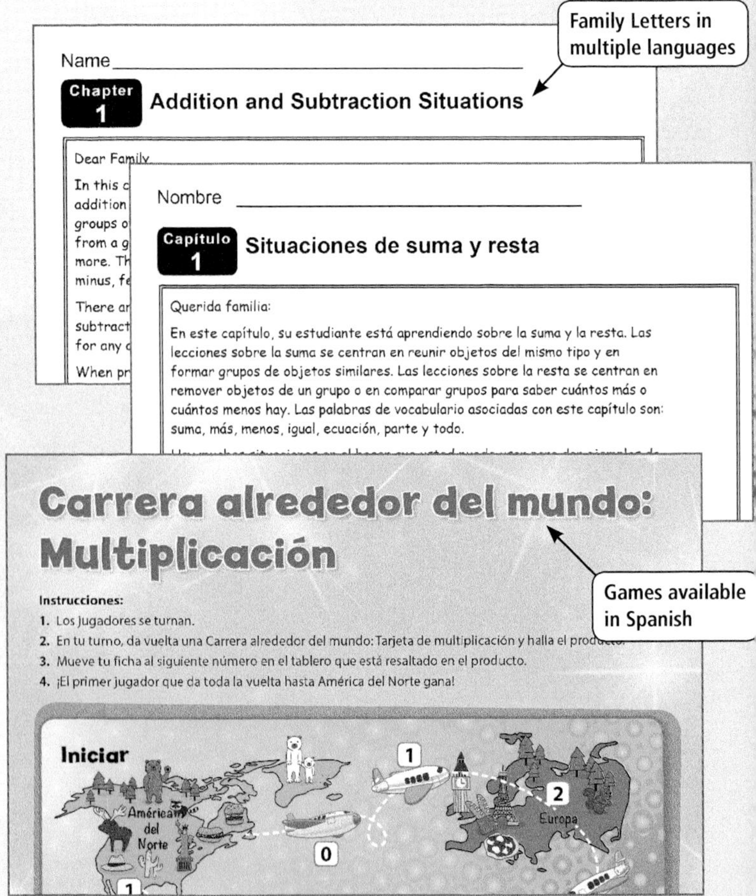

Students Get the Support They Need, When They Need It

There will be times throughout this course when students may need help. Whether students missed a lesson, did not understand the content, or just want to review, they can take advantage of the resources provided in the *Dynamic Student Edition*.

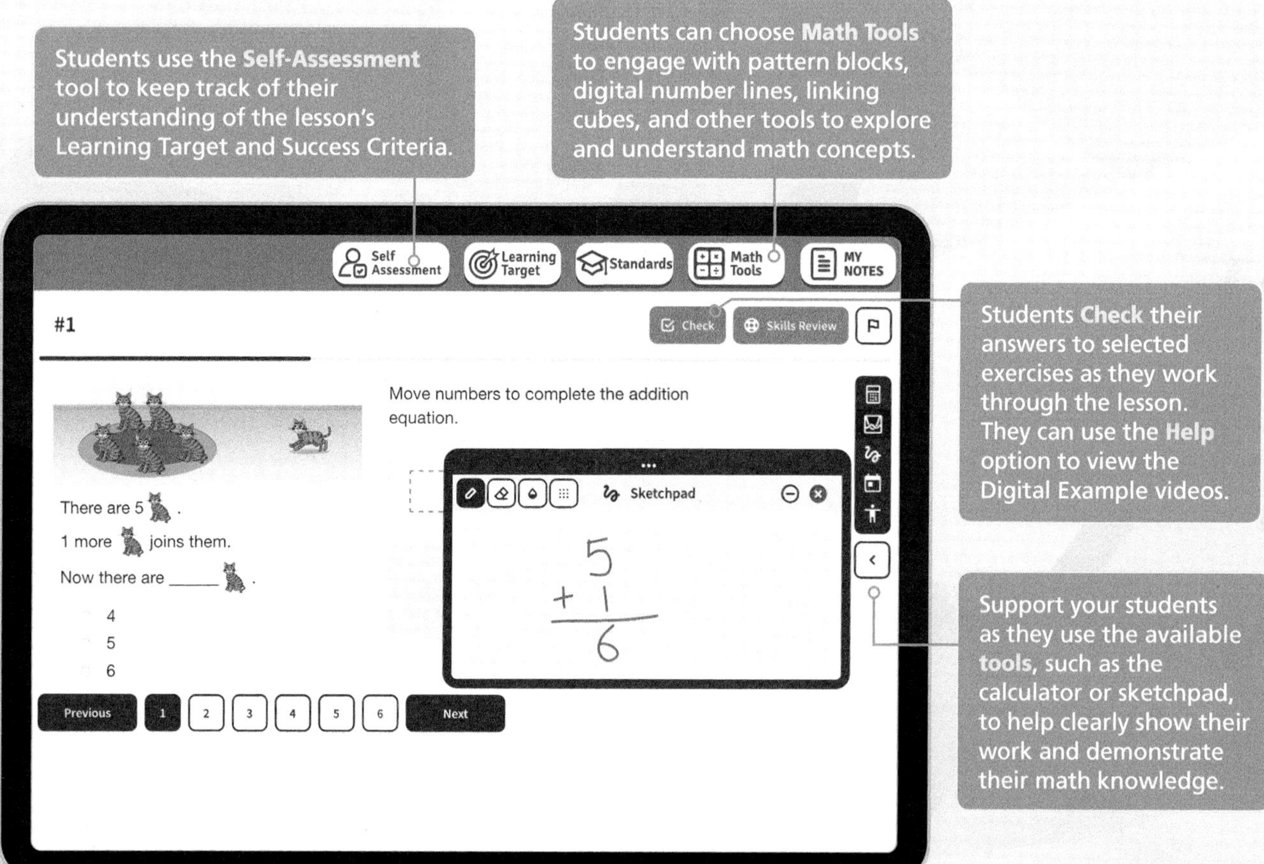

Students use the **Self-Assessment** tool to keep track of their understanding of the lesson's Learning Target and Success Criteria.
Students can choose **Math Tools** to engage with pattern blocks, digital number lines, linking cubes, and other tools to explore and understand math concepts.
Self Assessment
Learning Target
Standards
Math Tools
MY NOTES
#1
Check
Skills Review
Students **Check** their answers to selected exercises as they work through the lesson. They can use the **Help** option to view the Digital Example videos.
Move numbers to complete the addition equation.
Sketchpad
There are 5
1 more joins them.
Now there are ______
4
5
6
Previous
1
2
3
4
5
6
Next
Support your students as they use the available **tools**, such as the calculator or sketchpad, to help clearly show their work and demonstrate their math knowledge.

USE THESE QR CODES TO EXPLORE ADDITIONAL RESOURCES

Multi-Language Glossary
View definitions and examples of vocabulary words

Skills Trainer
Practice previously learned skills

Interactive Tools
Visualize mathematical concepts

Skills Review Handbook
A collection of review topics

Learning with Newton and Descartes

Who are Newton and Descartes?

Newton and Descartes are helpful math assistants who encourage students to think deeply about concepts and develop strong mathematical mindsets with student-facing Mathematical Practice questions.

MP **Check Your Work**
How can you use the addition facts to check that the differences are correct?

MP **Precision**
Which unit of measure did you use in your answer? Why?

Support for Social and Emotional Learning (SEL)

Students tap into rich characters, relationships, and emotions with *Math Musicals*, providing a landscape for social and emotional learning skills.

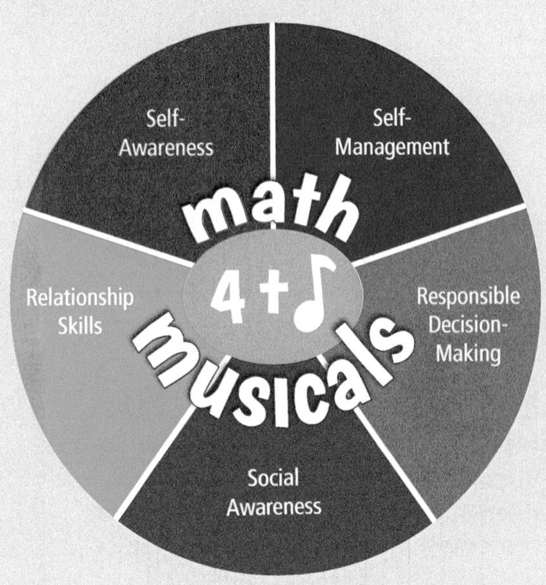

I don't like the way the bridge is swinging.

Descartes meowed, "Just close your eyes and take a deep breath, Newton. I'll guide you across the bridge. You can trust me. I am your best buddy, remember?"

Newton finally agreed to take Descartes's advice. "Alright, Tikal, you lead the way. Descartes, will you stay behind me? When I get scared, I feel so klutzy. I may not make it across without your help."

"Okay, carefully hold onto the rope as you walk, Newton. You can do this," meowed

...zzie, Koko, Agacio, and Cassandra.

...s swinging," moaned Newton.

...ed Descartes.

...de it across the rope bridge, including Newton.

..." woofed Newton proudly.

...e back. "You toughed it out, Newton. Good job!"

Self-Awareness
Newton is afraid of heights. He doesn't want to cross a hanging bridge in the Belize jungle. His friends give him the self-confidence he needs to successfully walk across the bridge.

Newton & Descartes's Math Musicals with Differentiated Rich Math Tasks

Math Musicals offer an engaging connection between math, literature, and music! Newton and Descartes team up in these educational stories and songs to bring mathematics to life!

Differentiated Rich Math Tasks encourage students to make sense of and extend the ideas presented in the stories and songs of *Newton & Descartes's Math Musicals.*

Math Musicals animation and story

Sheet Music

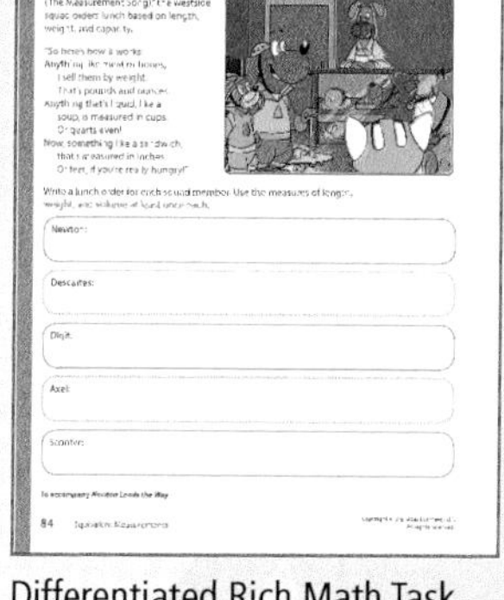
Differentiated Rich Math Task

Newton and Descartes said goodbye to Randy and Sly and continued on their way home. Before long, they made it through the park and were walking on the sidewalk. Both of them were a bit remorseful that they had taken the shortcut through the park.

Finally, Descartes meowed, "What are you thinking about, Newton?"

"Oh," woofed Newton. "I am just feeling a little sad that I got mud all over my autographed basketball jersey. I keep wondering if things would have turned out better if I hadn't suggested that we take the shortcut through the park."

"Come on, buddy," meowed Descartes. "You know what they say, 'Hindsight is 20-20.'"

"What does that mean?" woofed Newton.

"It means that we can see clearly *after* something has already

"Okay, I see that," barked Newton. "But what should we do abo autographed for us? I hope they're not ruined."

"We'll just have to put them in the washing machine and hope autograph doesn't," meowed Descartes.

142

Responsible Decision-Making
On the way home from meeting a famous basketball player, the two friends get mud all over their signed basketball jerseys. Newton is sad and thinks about his decision to take a shortcut home. But, Descartes suggests that they can wash the jerseys and save the autographs.

Relationship Skills
Descartes and some friends meet Hilde, a movie star. Hilde explains how being a movie star can be lonely and friendless. Mary tells Hilde that they would be happy to be friends with her.

Descartes, Mary, Cuisine, and Hilde dashed into the café.

Hilde moaned, "It is always like this. Even when I try to be as low-key as possible, it turns into a disaster. It is not easy being a famous movie star. I have *no* privacy and hardly any friends. Honestly, I am not sure who my true friends are."

Mary replied, "We would like to be your friends, Hilde."

With that, Hilde swirled her mane of fur around and barked, "You are such dears. I adore your company."

"Let's ditch this café and escape to somewhere really private," suggested Cuisine. "There is an awesome tree house in my backyard. We can order take out lunch and dine in the tree house. How about that?"

"That sounds like an adventure I cannot refuse," remarked Hilde. "But, how vill vee sneak past the paparazzi?"

Mary offered, "There is a back door. We can sneak out that way through the alley. Follow me."

They grabbed their take out containers and followed Mary.

160

Meeting the Needs of All Learners

Resources at Your Fingertips

This robust, innovative program utilizes a mixture of print and digital resources that allow for a variety of instructional approaches. The program encompasses hands-on activities, interactive explorations, videos, scaffolded instruction, learning support, and many more resources that appeal to students and teachers alike.

PRINT RESOURCES

Student Edition

Teaching Edition

Resources by Chapter
- Family Letter
- Warm-Ups
- Extra Practice
- Reteach
- Enrichment and Extension

Assessment Book
- Prerequisite Skills Practice
- Pre- and Post-Course Tests
- Course Benchmark Tests
- Chapter Tests

Instructional Resources
- Vocabulary Cards
- Activities
- Blackline Masters

Skills Review Handbook

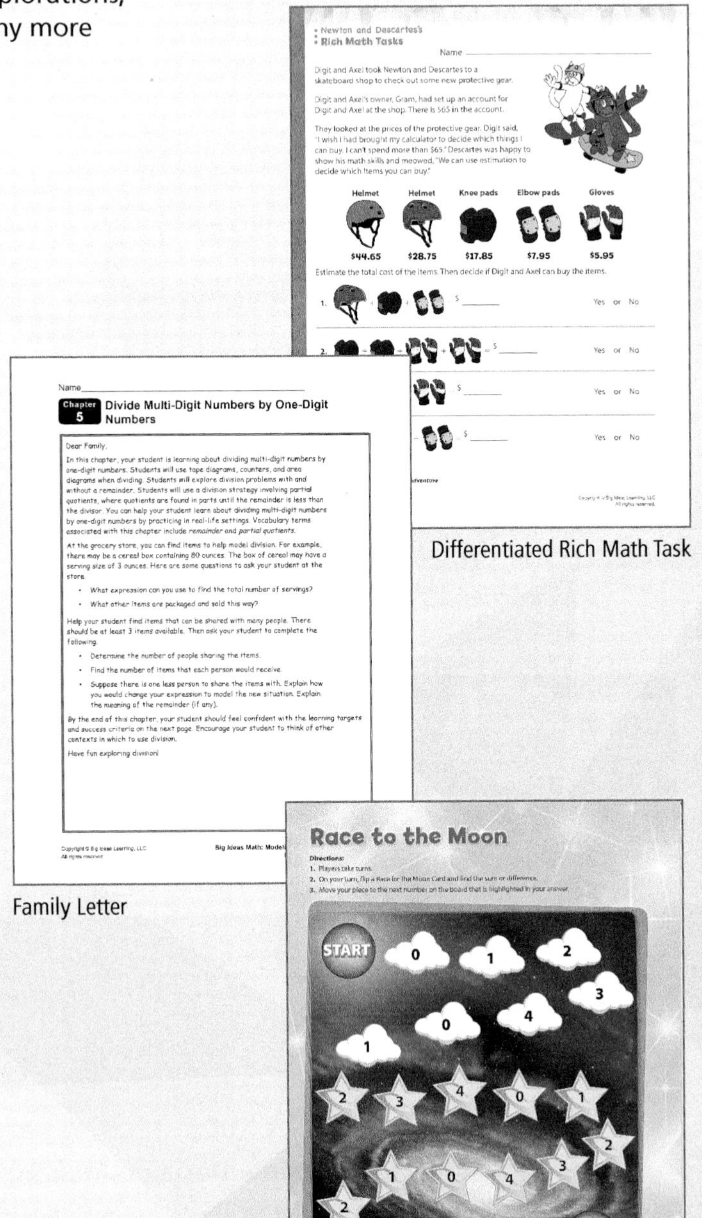

Newton and Descartes's Rich Math Tasks

Name ______

Digit and Axel took Newton and Descartes to a skateboard shop to check out some new protective gear.

Digit and Axel's owner, Gram, had set up an account for Digit and Axel at the shop. There is $65 in the account.

They looked at the prices of the protective gear. Digit said, "I wish I had brought my calculator to decide which things I can buy. I can't spend more than $65." Descartes was happy to show his math skills and meowed, "We can use estimation to decide which items you can buy."

Helmet	Helmet	Knee pads	Elbow pads	Gloves
$44.65	$28.75	$17.85	$7.95	$5.95

Estimate the total cost of the items. Then decide if Digit and Axel can buy the items.

1. \+ \+ = $ ______ Yes or No

2. \+ \+ \+ = $ ______ Yes or No

Differentiated Rich Math Task

Name ______

Chapter 5 Divide Multi-Digit Numbers by One-Digit Numbers

Dear Family,

In this chapter, your student is learning about dividing multi-digit numbers by one-digit numbers. Students will use tape diagrams, counters, and area diagrams when dividing. Students will explore division problems with and without a remainder. Students will use a division strategy involving partial quotients, where quotients are found in parts until the remainder is less than the divisor. You can help your student learn about dividing multi-digit numbers by one-digit numbers by practicing in real-life settings. Vocabulary terms associated with this chapter include *remainder* and *partial quotients*.

At the grocery store, you can find items to help model division. For example, there may be a cereal box containing 80 ounces. The box of cereal may have a serving size of 3 ounces. Here are some questions to ask your student at the store.

- What expression can you use to find the total number of servings?
- What other items are packaged and sold this way?

Help your student find items that can be shared with many people. There should be at least 3 items available. Then ask your student to complete the following.

- Determine the number of people sharing the items.
- Find the number of items that each person would receive.
- Suppose there is one less person to share the items with. Explain how you would change your expression to model the new situation. Explain the meaning of the remainder (if any).

By the end of this chapter, your student should feel confident with the learning targets and success criteria on the next page. Encourage your student to think of other contexts in which to use division.

Have fun exploring division!

Family Letter

Game (in the Student Edition)

ADDITIONAL RESOURCES

Manipulative Kits

Literature Kits

Newton & Descartes's Math Musicals with Differentiated Rich Math Tasks

Newton and Descartes Puppet Set

Through Program Resouces

TECHNOLOGY RESOURCES

Dynamic Student Edition
- Interactive Tools
- Interactive Explorations
- Digital Examples
- Self-Assessments

Dynamic Classroom
- Laurie's Notes
- Interactive Tools
- Interactive Explorations
- Digital Examples with PowerPoints
- Formative Check
- Self-Assessment
- Flip-To
- Digital Warm-Ups and Closures

Resources
- Skills Trainer
- Vocabulary Flash Cards
- Game Library
- Multi-Language Glossary
- Lesson Plans
- Differentiating the Lesson
- Graphic Organizers
- Pacing Guides
- Math Tool Paper
- Family Letters
- Homework App
- Skills Review Handbook

Dynamic Assessment System
- Practice
- Assessments
- Progression Benchmark Tests
- Detailed Reports

Video Support for Teachers
- Life on Earth Videos
- Professional Development Videos
- Concepts and Tools Videos

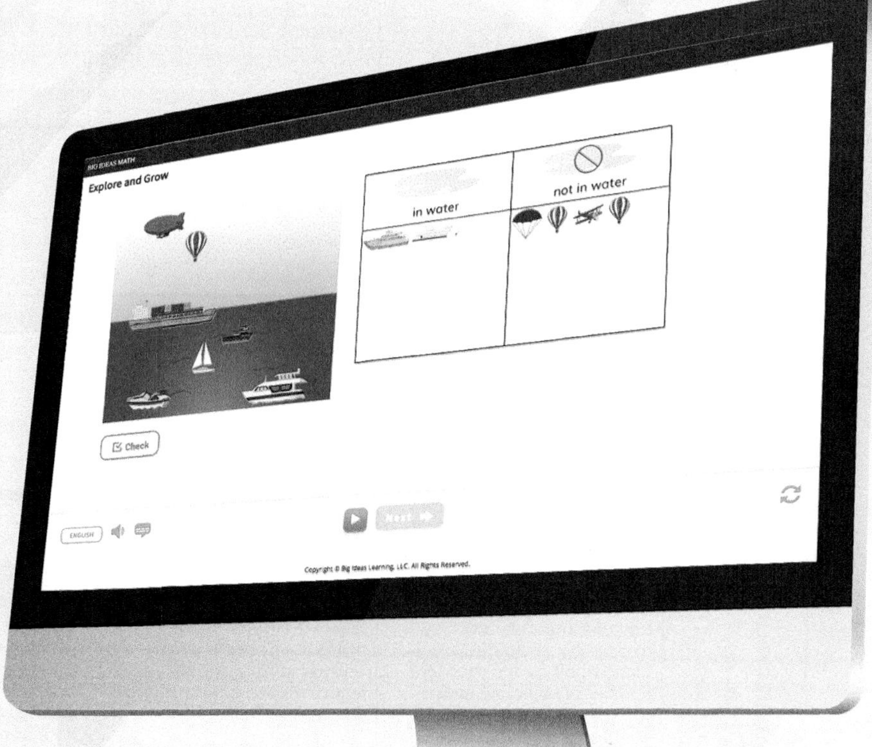

Cohesive Progressions

	Grade K	Grade 1	Grade 2	Grade 3
Number and Quantity	**Counting and Cardinality**			
	Know number names and the count sequence. Count to tell the number of objects. Compare numbers. *Chapters 1–4, 6, 8–10*			
	Number and Operations – Base Ten			
	Work with numbers 11–19 to gain foundations for place value. *Chapter 8*	Extend the counting sequence. Use place value and properties of operations to add and subtract. *Chapters 6–9*	Use place value and properties of operations to add and subtract. *Chapters 2–10, 14*	Use place value and properties of operations to perform multi-digit arithmetic. *Chapters 7–9, 12*
				Num. and Oper. – Fractions
				Understand fractions as numbers. *Chapters 10, 11, 14*
Algebra and Functions	**Operations and Algebraic Thinking**			
	Understand addition as putting together and adding to, and understand subtraction as taking apart and taking from. *Chapters 5–7*	Solve problems involving addition and subtraction within 20. Apply properties of operations. Work with addition and subtraction equations. *Chapters 1–5, 10, 11*	Solve problems involving addition and subtraction within 20. Work with equal groups of objects. *Chapters 1–6, 15*	Solve problems involving multiplication and division within 100. Apply properties of multiplication. Solve problems involving the four operations, and identify and explain patterns in arithmetic. *Chapters 1–5, 8, 9, and 14*
Geometry	**Geometry**			
	Identify and describe shapes. Analyze, compare, create, and compose shapes. *Chapters 11, 12*	Reason with shapes and their attributes. *Chapters 12, 14*	Reason with shapes and their attributes. *Chapter 15*	Reason with shapes and their attributes. *Chapters 10, 13*
Measurement, Data, and Probability	**Measurement and Data**			
	Describe and compare measurable attributes. Classify objects and count the number of objects in each category. *Chapters 4, 11, 13*	Measure lengths indirectly and by iterating length units. Tell and write time. Represent and interpret data. *Chapters 10–12*	Measure and estimate lengths in standard units. Relate addition and subtraction to length. Work with time and money. Represent and interpret data. *Chapters 11–14*	Solve problems involving measurement and estimation of intervals of time, liquid volumes, and masses of objects. Represent and interpret data. Understand the concepts of area and perimeter. *Chapters 6, 12, 14, 15*

Through the Grades

Grade 4	Grade 5	Grade 6	Grade 7	Grade 8
Number and Operations – Base Ten		**The Number System**		
Generalize place value understanding for multi-digit whole numbers. Use place value and properties of operations to perform multi-digit arithmetic. *Chapters 1–5*	Understand the place value system. Perform operations with multi-digit whole numbers and with decimals to hundredths. *Chapters 1, 3–7*	Perform operations with multi-digit numbers and find common factors and multiples. *Chapter 1* Divide fractions by fractions. *Chapter 2* Extend understanding of numbers to the rational number system. *Chapter 8*	Perform operations with rational numbers. *Chapters 1, 2*	Extend understanding of numbers to the real number system. *Chapter 9*
Number and Operations – Fractions		**Ratios and Proportional Relationships**		
Extend understanding of fraction equivalence and ordering. Build fractions from unit fractions. Understand decimal notation for fractions, and compare decimal fractions. *Chapters 7–11*	Add, subtract, multiply, and divide fractions. *Chapters 6, 8–11*	Use ratios to solve problems. *Chapters 3, 4*	Use proportional relationships to solve problems. *Chapters 5, 6*	
Operations and Algebraic Thinking		**Expressions and Equations**		
Use the four operations with whole numbers to solve problems. Understand factors and multiples. Generate and analyze patterns. *Chapters 2–6, 12*	Write and interpret numerical expressions. Analyze patterns and relationships. *Chapters 2, 12*	Perform arithmetic with algebraic expressions. *Chapter 5* Solve one-variable equations and inequalities. *Chapters 6, 8* Analyze relationships between dependent and independent variables. *Chapter 6*	Write equivalent expressions. *Chapter 3* Use numerical and algebraic expressions, equations, and inequalities to solve problems. *Chapters 3, 4, 6*	Understand the connections between proportional relationships, lines, and linear equations. *Chapter 4* Solve linear equations and systems of linear equations. *Chapters 1, 5* Work with radicals and integer exponents. *Chapters 8, 9*
				Functions
				Define, evaluate, and compare functions, and use functions to model relationships between quantities. *Chapter 7*
Geometry				
Draw and identify lines and angles, and classify shapes by properties of their lines and angles. *Chapters 13, 14*	Graph points on the coordinate plane. Classify two-dimensional figures into categories based on their properties. *Chapters 12, 14*	Solve real-world and mathematical problems involving area, surface area, and volume. *Chapter 7*	Draw, construct, and describe geometrical figures and describe the relationships between them. *Chapters 5, 9, 10* Solve problems involving angle measure, area, surface area, and volume. *Chapters 9, 10*	Understand congruence and similarity. *Chapters 2, 3* Use the Pythagorean Theorem. *Chapter 9* Solve problems involving volumes of cylinders, cones, and spheres. *Chapter 10*
Measurement and Data		**Statistics and Probability**		
Solve problems involving measurement and conversion of measurements from a larger unit to a smaller unit. Represent and interpret data. Understand angles and measure angles. *Chapters 10–13*	Convert measurement units within a given measurement system. Represent and interpret data. Understand volume. *Chapters 11, 13*	Develop understanding of statistical variability and summarize and describe distributions. *Chapters 9, 10*	Make inferences about a population, compare two populations, and use probability models. *Chapters 7, 8*	Investigate patterns of association in bivariate data. *Chapter 6*

Common Core State Standards for

Standard Code	Standard	Grade 1
Operations and Algebraic Thinking		
1.OA.A.1	Use addition and subtraction within 20 to solve word problems involving situations of adding to, taking from, putting together, taking apart, and comparing, with unknowns in all positions, e.g., by using objects, drawings, and equations with a symbol for the unknown number to represent the problem.	**1.1, 1.2, 1.3, 1.4, 1.5, 1.6, 1.7, 1.8, 1.9, 2.1, 2.2, 2.3, 2.4, 2.5, 2.6, 2.7, 2.8, 2.9, 3.1, 3.2, 3.3, 3.4, 3.5, 3.6, 3.7, 3.8, 4.1, 4.2, 4.3, 4.4, 4.5, 4.6, 4.7, 4.8, 5.1, 5.2, 5.3, 5.4, 5.5, 5.6, 5.7**, 7.1, **10.5**, 11.4, **11.5**, 13.8
1.OA.A.2	Solve word problems that call for addition of three whole numbers whose sum is less than or equal to 20, e.g., by using objects, drawings, and equations with a symbol for the unknown number to represent the problem.	**4.4, 4.5**, 4.8, **11.5**
1.OA.B.3	Apply properties of operations as strategies to add and subtract. *Examples: If 8 + 3 = 11 is known, then 3 + 8 = 11 is also known. (Commutative property of addition.) To add 2 + 6 + 4, the second two numbers can be added to make a ten, so 2 + 6 + 4 = 2 + 10 = 12. (Associative property of addition.)*	**2.1, 2.2, 2.6, 4.4, 4.5, 4.6, 4.7, 4.8, 5.3, 5.4**, 9.3
1.OA.B.4	Understand subtraction as an unknown-addend problem. *For example, subtract 10 – 8 by finding the number that makes 10 when added to 8.*	**2.9, 3.5, 5.2, 8.7**
1.OA.C.5	Relate counting to addition and subtraction (e.g., by counting on 2 to add 2).	**2.3, 2.7, 2.8, 2.9, 3.1, 3.3, 4.3, 5.1, 5.2**
1.OA.C.6	Add and subtract within 20, demonstrating fluency for addition and subtraction within 10. Use strategies such as counting on; making ten (e.g., 8 + 6 = 8 + 2 + 4 = 10 + 4 = 14); decomposing a number leading to a ten (e.g., 13 − 4 = 13 − 3 − 1 = 10 − 1 = 9); using the relationship between addition and subtraction (e.g., knowing that 8 + 4 = 12, one knows 12 − 8 = 4); and creating equivalent but easier or known sums (e.g., adding 6 + 7 by creating the known equivalent 6 + 6 + 1 = 12 + 1 = 13).	**1.1, 1.2, 1.3, 1.4, 1.5, 1.6, 1.7, 1.8, 1.9, 2.1, 2.2, 2.3, 2.4, 2.5, 2.6, 2.7, 2.8, 2.9, 3.1, 3.2, 3.3, 3.4, 3.5, 3.6, 3.7, 3.8, 4.1, 4.2, 4.3, 4.4, 4.5, 4.6, 4.7, 4.8, 5.1, 5.2, 5.3, 5.4, 5.5, 5.6, 5.7**

Boldface indicates a lesson in which the standard is a primary focus.

Mathematical Content Correlated to Grade 1

Standard Code	Standard	Grade 1
1.OA.D.7	Understand the meaning of the equal sign, and determine if equations involving addition and subtraction are true or false. *For example, which of the following equations are true and which are false?* $6 = 6$, $7 = 8 - 1$, $5 + 2 = 2 + 5$, $4 + 1 = 5 + 2$.	**1.2, 2.6, 3.6, 5.5, 5.6**
1.OA.D.8	Determine the unknown whole number in an addition or subtraction equation relating to three whole numbers. *For example, determine the unknown number that makes the equation true in each of the equations* $8 + ? = 11$, $5 = \square - 3$, $6 + 6 = \square$.	**1.1, 1.2, 1.3, 1.4, 1.5, 1.6, 1.7, 1.8, 1.9, 2.1, 2.2, 2.3, 2.4, 2.5, 2.6, 2.7, 2.8, 2.9, 3.1, 3.2, 3.3, 3.4, 3.5, 3.6, 3.7, 3.8, 4.1, 4.2, 4.3, 4.6, 4.7,** 4.8, **5.1, 5.2, 5.3, 5.4,** 5.7, 8.1, 8.2, 8.3, 8.4, 8.5, 8.6, 8.7, 8.8, 9.1, 9.2, 9.3, 9.4, 9.5
Number and Operations in Base Ten		
1.NBT.A.1	Count to 120, starting at any number less than 120. In this range, read and write numerals and represent a number of objects with a written numeral.	**6.1, 6.2,** 6.3, 6.4, **6.9**
1.NBT.B.2	Understand that the two digits of a two-digit number represent amounts of tens and ones. Understand the following as special cases:	7.2, 7.3, 7.4, 7.5, 7.6, 9.3
	a. 10 can be thought of as a bundle of ten ones — called a "ten."	**6.3, 6.4, 6.5, 6.6, 6.7, 6.8, 6.9,** 7.1, **8.1, 8.2, 9.1, 9.2, 9.3, 9.4, 9.5, 9.6**
	b. The numbers from 11 to 19 are composed of a ten and one, two, three, four, five, six, seven, eight, or nine ones.	6.3, 6.8, **7.1, 9.1, 9.2, 9.4, 9.5, 9.6**
	c. The numbers 10, 20, 30, 40, 50, 60, 70, 80, 90 refer to one, two, three, four, five, six, seven, eight, or nine tens (and 0 ones).	6.2, **6.4, 6.5, 6.6, 6.7, 6.8, 6.9,** 7.1, **8.3, 8.4, 8.5, 8.6, 8.7, 8.8, 9.1, 9.2, 9.4, 9.5, 9.6**

Boldface indicates a lesson in which the standard is a primary focus.

Common Core State Standards for

Standard Code	Standard	Grade 1
1.NBT.B.3	Compare two two-digit numbers based on meanings of the tens and ones digits, recording the results of comparisons with the symbols >, =, and <.	1.3, 1.4, 4.3, 4.4, 4.5, 4.6, 4.7, 5.5, **7.1, 7.2, 7.3, 7.4, 7.5, 7.6,** 8.6, 8.8, 9.6, 11.1, 11.2, 11.3
1.NBT.C.4	Add within 100, including adding a two-digit number and a one-digit number, and adding a two-digit number and a multiple of 10, using concrete models or drawings and strategies based on place value, properties of operations, and/or the relationship between addition and subtraction; relate the strategy to a written method and explain the reasoning used. Understand that in adding two-digit numbers, one adds tens and tens, ones and ones; and sometimes it is necessary to compose a ten.	**8.1, 8.3, 8.4, 8.7, 8.8, 9.1, 9.2, 9.3, 9.4, 9.5, 9.6**
1.NBT.C.5	Given a two-digit number, mentally find 10 more or 10 less than the number, without having to count; explain the reasoning used.	**8.1, 8.2**
1.NBT.C.6	Subtract multiples of 10 in the range 10–90 from multiples of 10 in the range 10–90 (positive or zero differences), using concrete models or drawings and strategies based on place value, properties of operations, and/or the relationship between addition and subtraction; relate the strategy to a written method and explain the reasoning used.	**8.5, 8.6, 8.7**
Measurement and Data		
1.MD.A.1	Order three objects by length; compare the lengths of two objects indirectly by using a third object.	**10.1, 10.2, 10.4, 10.5**
1.MD.A.2	Express the length of an object as a whole number of length units, by laying multiple copies of a shorter object (the length unit) end to end; understand that the length measurement of an object is the number of same-size length units that span it with no gaps or overlaps. *Limit to contexts where the object being measured is spanned by a whole number of length units with no gaps or overlaps.*	**10.3, 10.4, 10.5**
1.MD.B.3	Tell and write time in hours and half-hours using analog and digital clocks.	**12.1, 12.2, 12.3, 12.4**

Boldface indicates a lesson in which the standard is a primary focus.

Mathematical Content Correlated to Grade 1

Standard Code	Standard	Grade 1
1.MD.C.4	Organize, represent, and interpret data with up to three categories; ask and answer questions about the total number of data points, how many in each category, and how many more or less are in one category than in another.	**11.1, 11.2, 11.3, 11.4, 11.5**
Geometry		
1.G.A.1	Distinguish between defining attributes (e.g., triangles are closed and three-sided) versus non-defining attributes (e.g., color, orientation, overall size); build and draw shapes to possess defining attributes.	**13.1, 13.2, 13.6, 13.7**
1.G.A.2	Compose two-dimensional shapes (rectangles, squares, trapezoids, triangles, half-circles, and quarter-circles) or three-dimensional shapes (cubes, right rectangular prisms, right circular cones, and right circular cylinders) to create a composite shape, and compose new shapes from the composite shape.	**13.3, 13.4, 13.5, 13.8, 13.9**
1.G.A.3	Partition circles and rectangles into two and four equal shares, describe the shares using the words *halves*, *fourths*, and *quarters*, and use the phrases *half of*, *fourth of*, and *quarter of*. Describe the whole as two of, or four of the shares. Understand for these examples that decomposing into more equal shares creates smaller shares.	**14.1, 14.2, 14.3**

Boldface indicates a lesson in which the standard is a primary focus.

Suggested Pacing

Chapters 1–14	152 Days

Chapter 1 (13 Days)

Chapter Opener	1 Day
Lesson 1.1	1 Day
Lesson 1.2	1 Day
Lesson 1.3	1 Day
Lesson 1.4	1 Day
Lesson 1.5	1 Day
Lesson 1.6	1 Day
Lesson 1.7	1 Day
Lesson 1.8	1 Day
Lesson 1.9	1 Day
Connect and Grow	2 Days
Chapter Assessment	1 Day
Year-To-Date	**13 Days**

Chapter 2 (13 Days)

Chapter Opener	1 Day
Lesson 2.1	1 Day
Lesson 2.2	1 Day
Lesson 2.3	1 Day
Lesson 2.4	1 Day
Lesson 2.5	1 Day
Lesson 2.6	1 Day
Lesson 2.7	1 Day
Lesson 2.8	1 Day
Lesson 2.9	1 Day
Connect and Grow	2 Days
Chapter Assessment	1 Day
Year-To-Date	**26 Days**

Chapter 3 (12 Days)

Chapter Opener	1 Day
Lesson 3.1	1 Day
Lesson 3.2	1 Day
Lesson 3.3	1 Day
Lesson 3.4	1 Day
Lesson 3.5	1 Day
Lesson 3.6	1 Day
Lesson 3.7	1 Day
Lesson 3.8	1 Day
Connect and Grow	2 Days
Chapter Assessment	1 Day
Year-To-Date	**38 Days**

Chapter 4 (12 Days)

Chapter Opener	1 Day
Lesson 4.1	1 Day
Lesson 4.2	1 Day
Lesson 4.3	1 Day
Lesson 4.4	1 Day
Lesson 4.5	1 Day
Lesson 4.6	1 Day
Lesson 4.7	1 Day
Lesson 4.8	1 Day
Connect and Grow	2 Days
Chapter Assessment	1 Day
Year-To-Date	**50 Days**

Chapter 5 (11 Days)

Chapter Opener	1 Day
Lesson 5.1	1 Day
Lesson 5.2	1 Day
Lesson 5.3	1 Day
Lesson 5.4	1 Day
Lesson 5.5	1 Day
Lesson 5.6	1 Day
Lesson 5.7	1 Day
Connect and Grow	2 Days
Chapter Assessment	1 Day
Year-To-Date	**61 Days**

Chapter 6 (13 Days)

Chapter Opener	1 Day
Lesson 6.1	1 Day
Lesson 6.2	1 Day
Lesson 6.3	1 Day
Lesson 6.4	1 Day
Lesson 6.5	1 Day
Lesson 6.6	1 Day
Lesson 6.7	1 Day
Lesson 6.8	1 Day
Lesson 6.9	1 Day
Connect and Grow	2 Days
Chapter Assessment	1 Day
Year-To-Date	**74 Days**

Chapter 7 (10 Days)

Chapter Opener	1 Day
Lesson 7.1	1 Day
Lesson 7.2	1 Day
Lesson 7.3	1 Day
Lesson 7.4	1 Day
Lesson 7.5	1 Day
Lesson 7.6	1 Day
Connect and Grow	2 Days
Chapter Assessment	1 Day
Year-To-Date	**84 Days**

Chapter 8 (12 Days)

Chapter Opener	1 Day
Lesson 8.1	1 Day
Lesson 8.2	1 Day
Lesson 8.3	1 Day
Lesson 8.4	1 Day
Lesson 8.5	1 Day
Lesson 8.6	1 Day
Lesson 8.7	1 Day
Lesson 8.8	1 Day
Connect and Grow	2 Days
Chapter Assessment	1 Day
Year-To-Date	**96 Days**

Chapter 9 (10 Days)

Chapter Opener	1 Day
Lesson 9.1	1 Day
Lesson 9.2	1 Day
Lesson 9.3	1 Day
Lesson 9.4	1 Day
Lesson 9.5	1 Day
Lesson 9.6	1 Day
Connect and Grow	2 Days
Chapter Assessment	1 Day
Year-To-Date	**106 Days**

Chapter 10 (9 Days)

Chapter Opener	1 Day
Lesson 10.1	1 Day
Lesson 10.2	1 Day
Lesson 10.3	1 Day
Lesson 10.4	1 Day
Lesson 10.5	1 Day
Connect and Grow	2 Days
Chapter Assessment	1 Day
Year-To-Date	**115 Days**

Chapter 11 (9 Days)

Chapter Opener	1 Day
Lesson 11.1	1 Day
Lesson 11.2	1 Day
Lesson 11.3	1 Day
Lesson 11.4	1 Day
Lesson 11.5	1 Day
Connect and Grow	2 Days
Chapter Assessment	1 Day
Year-To-Date	**124 Days**

Chapter 12 (8 Days)

Chapter Opener	1 Day
Lesson 12.1	1 Day
Lesson 12.2	1 Day
Lesson 12.3	1 Day
Lesson 12.4	1 Day
Connect and Grow	2 Days
Chapter Assessment	1 Day
Year-To-Date	**132 Days**

Chapter 13 (13 Days)

Chapter Opener	1 Day
Lesson 13.1	1 Day
Lesson 13.2	1 Day
Lesson 13.3	1 Day
Lesson 13.4	1 Day
Lesson 13.5	1 Day
Lesson 13.6	1 Day
Lesson 13.7	1 Day
Lesson 13.8	1 Day
Lesson 13.9	1 Day
Connect and Grow	2 Days
Chapter Assessment	1 Day
Year-To-Date	**145 Days**

Chapter 14 (7 Days)

Chapter Opener	1 Day
Lesson 14.1	1 Day
Lesson 14.2	1 Day
Lesson 14.3	1 Day
Connect and Grow	2 Days
Chapter Assessment	1 Day
Year-To-Date	**152 Days**

An editable version of the Pacing Guide is available at *BigIdeasMath.com*.

1 Addition and Subtraction Situations

2 Fluency and Strategies within 10

Major Topic
Supporting Topic
Additional Topic

3 More Addition and Subtraction Situations

Number Land

To Play: Put the Addition and Subtraction Cards in a pile. Start at Newton. Take turns drawing a card and moving your piece to the missing number in the equation. Repeat this process until a player gets back to Newton.

Add Numbers within 20

Subtract Numbers within 20

- Major Topic
- Supporting Topic
- Additional Topic

6 Count and Write Numbers to 120

7 Compare Two-Digit Numbers

Let's learn how to compare two-digit numbers!

Add and Subtract Tens

Add Two-Digit Numbers

- Major Topic
- Supporting Topic
- Additional Topic

10 Measure and Compare Lengths

Think and Grow
Use color tiles to **measure** lengths of objects.
Do not leave gaps or overlap the tiles.
length unit
about 4 color tiles

Represent and Interpret Data

Tell Time

■ Major Topic
■ Supporting Topic
■ Additional Topic

13 Two- and Three-Dimensional Shapes

14 Equal Shares

Let's learn about equal shares!

8 Add and Subtract Tens

Chapter Overview

Lesson	Learning Target	Success Criteria
8.1 Mental Math: 10 More	Use mental math to add 10.	• Add 10 to a number and write the sum. • Explain what changes when you add 10 to a number.
8.2 Mental Math: 10 Less	Use mental math to subtract 10.	• Subtract 10 from a number and write the difference. • Explain what changes when you subtract 10 from a number.
8.3 Add Tens	Add tens.	• Use models to add tens. • Tell how many tens are in the model. • Write the addition equation that matches the model.
8.4 Add Tens Using a Number Line	Use an open number line to add tens.	• Use an open number line to show my starting number. • Draw hops to show each ten I add. • Write the sum.
8.5 Subtract Tens	Subtract tens.	• Use models to subtract tens. • Tell how many tens are left in the model. • Write the subtraction equation that matches the model.
8.6 Subtract Tens Using a Number Line	Use an open number line to subtract tens.	• Use an open number line to show my starting number. • Draw hops to show each ten I subtract. • Write the difference.
8.7 Use Addition to Subtract Tens	Use addition to subtract tens.	• Write an addition equation with a missing addend. • Count on to find the missing addend. • Use the missing addend to write the difference.
8.8 Add Tens to a Number	Add tens to a number.	• Use a model to count on by tens from a two-digit number. • Write the sum.

Chapter Learning Target:
Understand adding and subtracting tens.

Chapter Success Criteria:
- Identify the number ten.
- Describe what changes when adding or subtracting ten.
- Model adding and subtracting tens.
- Use a number line to show adding and subtracting tens.

Progressions

Through the Grades		
Kindergarten	**Grade 1**	**Grade 2**
• Understand the numbers 11 to 19 as a group of 10 ones and some more ones. • Represent addition and subtraction with various models and strategies. • Add and subtract within 10. • Fluently add and subtract within 5.	• Understand the value of each digit in a two-digit number. • Understand a group of 10 ones as a ten. • Use models, properties, and strategies to add within 100. • Mentally find 10 more or 10 less than a two-digit number. • Use models, properties, and strategies to subtract a decade number from a two-digit number.	• Understand the value of each digit in a three-digit number. • Understand a group of 10 tens as a hundred. • Use strategies to fluently add and subtract within 100. • Use models, properties, and strategies to add and subtract within 1,000.

	Through the Chapter							
Standard	**8.1**	**8.2**	**8.3**	**8.4**	**8.5**	**8.6**	**8.7**	**8.8**
1.NBT.B.2 Understand that the two digits of a two-digit number represent amounts of tens and ones.	●	●	●	●	●	●	●	●
1.NBT.B.2a 10 can be thought of as a bundle of ten ones – called a "ten."	●	●						
1.NBT.B.2c The numbers 10, 20, 30, 40, 50, 60, 70, 80, 90 refer to one, two, three, four, five, six, seven, eight, or nine tens.			●	●	●	●	●	●
1.NBT.C.4 Add within 100, including adding a two-digit number and a one-digit number, and adding a two-digit number and a multiple of 10, using concrete models or drawings and strategies based on place value, properties of operations, and/or the relationship between addition and subtraction; relate the strategy to a written method and explain the reasoning used. Understand that in adding two-digit numbers, one adds tens and tens, ones and ones; and sometimes it is necessary to compose a ten.	●		●	●			●	●
1.NBT.C.5 Given a two-digit number, mentally find 10 more or 10 less than the number, without having to count; explain the reasoning used.	●	★						
1.NBT.C.6 Subtract multiples of 10 in the range 10–90 from multiples of 10 in the range 10–90, using concrete models or drawings and strategies based on place value, properties of operations, and/or the relationship between addition and subtraction; relate the strategy to a written method and explain the reasoning used.					●	●	★	
1.OA.B.4 Understand subtraction as an unknown-addend problem.							★	

Key: ▲ = Preparing ● = Learning ★ = Complete

Laurie's Overview

About the Math

First grade students like to collect. They may have collections of rocks or small collectibles, or anything! Most likely students can tell you how many they have of something. As they collect more, addition becomes a natural way to tell how many they have. Imagine if you had to start counting from 1 every time.

Chapter 8 begins with the important learning of adding two-digit numbers based on place value. Addition and subtraction are linked together with place value in learning. Some research suggests that understanding place value is a prerequisite for addition and subtraction, while other research suggests that addition and subtraction contexts offer an opportunity to make sense of place value. What is clear is that if students only think of addition and subtraction as a manipulation of some kind with numbers and do not think of the value of the digits in the numbers, they make more errors and are not able to evaluate the reasonableness of their answers.

This chapter introduces or extends the following big ideas:

- Flexible methods for addition and subtraction involve decomposing and composing numbers based on place value.
- The location of a digit in a number determines its value.
- In addition and subtraction, tens are added or subtracted with tens, and ones with ones.
- Different models can show how place value and addition work together. These models can be used interchangeably.

These important concepts form the basis of Chapter 8 as students add or subtract groups of tens. They are continued through Chapter 9 as students progress to adding any two two-digit numbers.

Throughout the lessons in this chapter, students will need to think of the two-digit numbers in terms of tens and ones. This may still be difficult for some students. One structure that we used in Chapter 6, which may be helpful to bring back in this chapter, is a tens and ones chart. We continue to use base ten blocks or quick sketches. Using these on top of the tens and ones chart, along with writing the digits of the number in the chart, can serve to solidify the place value understanding needed for addition and subtraction with two-digit numbers.

Tens	Ones
2	3

Models

We continue to use the models students are familiar with in this chapter. The primary models that are used are base ten blocks or quick sketches, the hundred or 120 chart, and number lines. The use of number lines are extended to include an open number line.

- **Base Ten Blocks and Quick Sketches:** As stated above, students may still not have a solid understanding of place value. Emerging students may still be operating on a counting basis for numbers and addition. As students add groups of tens together, or groups of tens to any two-digit number, they see that adding tens is the same process as adding ones. The only difference is paying attention to the values of what is being added: adding ten rods can have a total of 5 rods, but that has a value of 50, not 5. Additionally, students recognize that rods are only added to rods and cubes will only be combined with cubes (Chapter 9).
- **120 Chart or Hundred Chart:** A number chart is used in almost all lessons and could be used for all lessons if students show greater understanding with it. Students add within 100 in first grade, so you do not need the larger chart. More advanced students may appreciate the challenge of greater numbers and using it will reinforce the counting to 120. In this chapter, we use movement down a column of numbers to show addition of tens, and up a column of numbers to show subtraction of tens. In Lesson 8.7 where students use the "addition to subtract" strategy, we show both movements in the same column side-by-side to model the thinking required for the strategy and inverse relationship of the operations.

1	2	3	4	5	6	7	8	9	10
11	2	13	14	15	16	17	18	19	20
21	22	23	24	25	26	27	28	29	30
31	32	33	34	35	36	37	38	39	40
41	42	43	44	45	46	47	48	49	50
51	52	53	54	55	56	57	58	59	60
61	62	63	64	65	66	67	68	69	70
71	72	73	74	75	76	77	78	79	80
81	82	83	84	85	86	87	88	89	90
91	92	93	94	95	96	97	98	99	100

- **Open Number Line:** Students have had limited exposure to number lines, primarily with the "count on" and "count back" strategies and comparing numbers. In this chapter, we introduce an open number line. Students learn that a number line can begin and end with any number, and that not every number must be shown with tick marks between numbers. They use the number line to show "hops" which are addition or subtraction of a group of 10 in one move, rather than the individual hops from Chapters 4 and 5. When using the "hops" students will count on by tens to fill in the numbers on the number line. We do not show an arching hop for the total of hops (as shown below) in lessons as this becomes crowded and might be confusing. Instead, students count by tens for the total hops added or subtracted. You may want to show the arching total of hops (+30 or −20 in the example below) for explicit instruction.

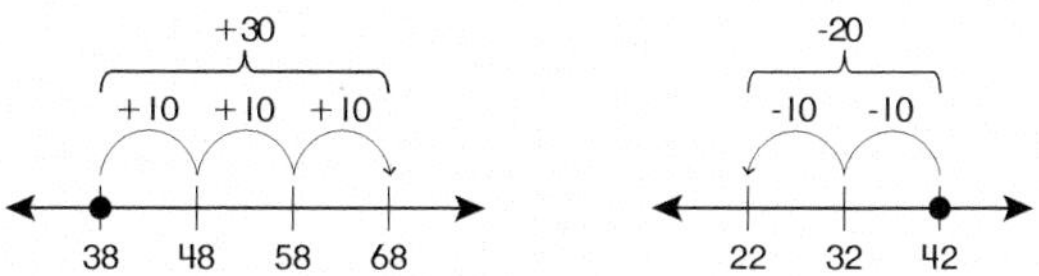

In Chapter 8, many of the addition and subtraction strategies used with single digit and teen numbers are brought back to add and subtract two-digit numbers. We use many of the same activities and Dig In times to ensure that students make the connections to previous work and do not think of addition and subtraction with tens as anything new or different. As students make these connections, number sense is developed and schema is formed.

This chapter lays the foundation for adding any two-digit numbers together based on place value. It is important that students are allowed to use multiple representations and strategies as they make sense of the connections between place value and operations. These will all be used as well in the next chapter.

Check out the
virtual manipulatives.
BigIdeasMath.com

Chapter Materials and Resources

The primary materials and resources needed for this chapter are listed below. Other materials may be needed for the additional support ideas provided throughout the chapter.

Classroom Materials	Chapter Opener	8.1	8.2	8.3	8.4	8.5	8.6	8.7	8.8	Connect and Grow
scissors	•									
base ten blocks		*	*	•		•			*	
whiteboards								•	•	
die										•
two-color counters										•
beads										•
string										•
bags										•
buttons										•

Instructional Resources	Chapter Opener	8.1	8.2	8.3	8.4	8.5	8.6	8.7	8.8	Connect and Grow
Vocabulary Cards	•				+					
120 Chart		*	*	*		*		•	*	
Large Number Line					+		+			

• class set + teacher only * per pair/group

Suggested Pacing

Day 1	Chapter Opener	Performance Task Preview		Vocabulary			
Day 2	Lesson 8.1	Warm-Up	Dig In	Explore	Think	Apply: Practice	Think: Modeling Real Life
Day 3	Lesson 8.2	Warm-Up	Dig In	Explore	Think	Apply: Practice	Think: Modeling Real Life
Day 4	Lesson 8.3	Warm-Up	Dig In	Explore	Think	Apply: Practice	Think: Modeling Real Life
Day 5	Lesson 8.4	Warm-Up	Dig In	Explore	Think	Apply: Practice	Think: Modeling Real Life
Day 6	Lesson 8.5	Warm-Up	Dig In	Explore	Think	Apply: Practice	Think: Modeling Real Life
Day 7	Lesson 8.6	Warm-Up	Dig In	Explore	Think	Apply: Practice	Think: Modeling Real Life
Day 8	Lesson 8.7	Warm-Up	Dig In	Explore	Think	Apply: Practice	Think: Modeling Real Life
Day 9	Lesson 8.8	Warm-Up	Dig In	Explore	Think	Apply: Practice	Think: Modeling Real Life
Day 10	Connect And Grow	Performance Task		Activity		Chapter Practice	
Day 11		Centers					
Day 12	Chapter Assessment	Chapter Assessment					

Year-to-Date: 96 Days

Mathematical Practices

Students have opportunities to develop aspects of the mathematical practices throughout the chapter. Here are some examples.

1. **Make Sense of Problems and Persevere in Solving Them**
   8.1 Think and Grow: Modeling Real Life, *p. 406*
2. **Reason Abstractly and Quantitatively**
   8.5 Explore and Grow, *p. 427*
3. **Construct Viable Arguments and Critique the Reasoning of Others**
   8.2 Apply and Grow: Practice Exercise 19, *p. 411*
4. **Model with Mathematics**
   8.4 Practice Exercise 5, *p. 426*
5. **Use Appropriate Tools Strategically**
   8.6 Practice Exercise 5, *p. 438*
6. **Attend to Precision**
   8.2 Practice Exercise 13, *p. 414*
7. **Look for and Make Use of Structure**
   8.7 Apply and Grow: Practice Exercise 6, *p. 441*
8. **Look for and Express Regularity in Repeated Reasoning**
   8.6 Explore and Grow: *p. 433*

Laurie's Notes

Performance Task Preview

- Preview the page to gauge students' prior knowledge about how objects move. In science, students may have learned that an object is in motion when its position is changing.

? "How do pinwheels move?" pinwheels move in a circle

? "The pinwheels in the picture spin 40 times. Then it spins 20 more times. How many times does it spin in all?" The pinwheel spins 60 times.

- In the Performance Task at the end of the chapter, students will add and subtract tens to count the number of seconds a pinwheel spins.

8 Add and Subtract Tens

- How do pinwheels move?
- A pinwheel spins 40 times. Then it spins 20 more times. How many times does it spin in all?

Chapter Learning Target:
Understand adding and subtracting tens.

Chapter Success Criteria:
- I can identify the number ten.
- I can describe what changes when adding or subtracting ten.
- I can model adding and subtracting tens.
- I can use a number line to show adding and subtracting tens.

Check out the digital flash cards.
BigIdeasMath.com

Laurie's Notes

ELL Support

Review the terms *decade numbers* and *digits*. The term *decade numbers* is related to multiples of 10. However, in everyday language *decade* refers to ten years. The word *digit* refers to one number within a number that has more than one place value. In everyday language the word *digits* may refer to fingers and toes.

Vocabulary Review

? **Preview:** "What numbers do you see in the blue column?" 10, 20, 30, 40, 50, 60, 70, 80, 90, 100, 110, and 120

- Have students say each review word out loud. Have students discuss how the words are related.

? "What do we call the numbers in the blue column?" decade numbers "What are the 1 and 6 in the number 16?" digits

- Direct students to the lower half of the page. Have students use their vocabulary card to go over the new word.
- **Extension:** Have students relate the new word and the review words. Can the tick on the number line start with a decade number? What about any digit?

Chapter 8 Vocabulary

Activity

- **Echo:** Say a vocabulary word and then pass an "echo ball" to a student. The student echos, or repeats, the word and then passes the echo ball back to you. Students need to listen carefully to repeat the word correctly. Consider challenging the students by having them define the words after they echo them.
  Teaching Tip: Decide how you are going to have your students pass the ball before you begin. Silent and gentle hand passes are recommended.
  Note: Due to this chapter only having one new vocabulary word, consider saying this word multiple times in different voices.

Newton & Descartes's Math Musicals

with Differentiated Rich Math Tasks

Newton and Descartes team up in these educational stories and songs to bring mathematics to life! Use the Newton and Descartes hand puppets to act out the stories. Encourage students to sing the songs to take full advantage of the power of music to learn math. Visit *www.MathMusicals.com* to access all the adventures, songs, and activities available!

Name ______________________

8 Vocabulary

Review Words
decade numbers
digits

Organize It

Use the review words to complete the graphic organizer.

decade numbers

1	2	3	4	5	6	7	8	9	10
11	12	13	14	15	16	17	18	19	20
21	22	23	24	25	26	27	28	29	30
31	32	33	34	35	36	37	38	39	40
41	42	43	44	45	46	47	48	49	50
51	52	53	54	55	56	57	58	59	60
61	62	63	64	65	66	67	68	69	70
71	72	73	74	75	76	77	78	79	80
81	82	83	84	85	86	87	88	89	90
91	92	93	94	95	96	97	98	99	100
101	102	103	104	105	106	107	108	109	110
111	112	113	114	115	116	117	118	119	120

The digits of 16 are 1 and 6.

Define It

What am I?

←——→

$13 - 3 = B$ $6 - 4 = M$ $4 + 4 = P$ $12 - 8 = R$
$5 + 1 = O$ $1 + 2 = E$ $3 + 2 = L$ $10 - 3 = U$
$5 + 4 = I$ $9 - 8 = N$

6	8	3	1		1	7	2	10	3	4		5	9	1	3
O	P	E	N		N	U	M	B	E	R		L	I	N	E

Chapter 8 Vocabulary Cards

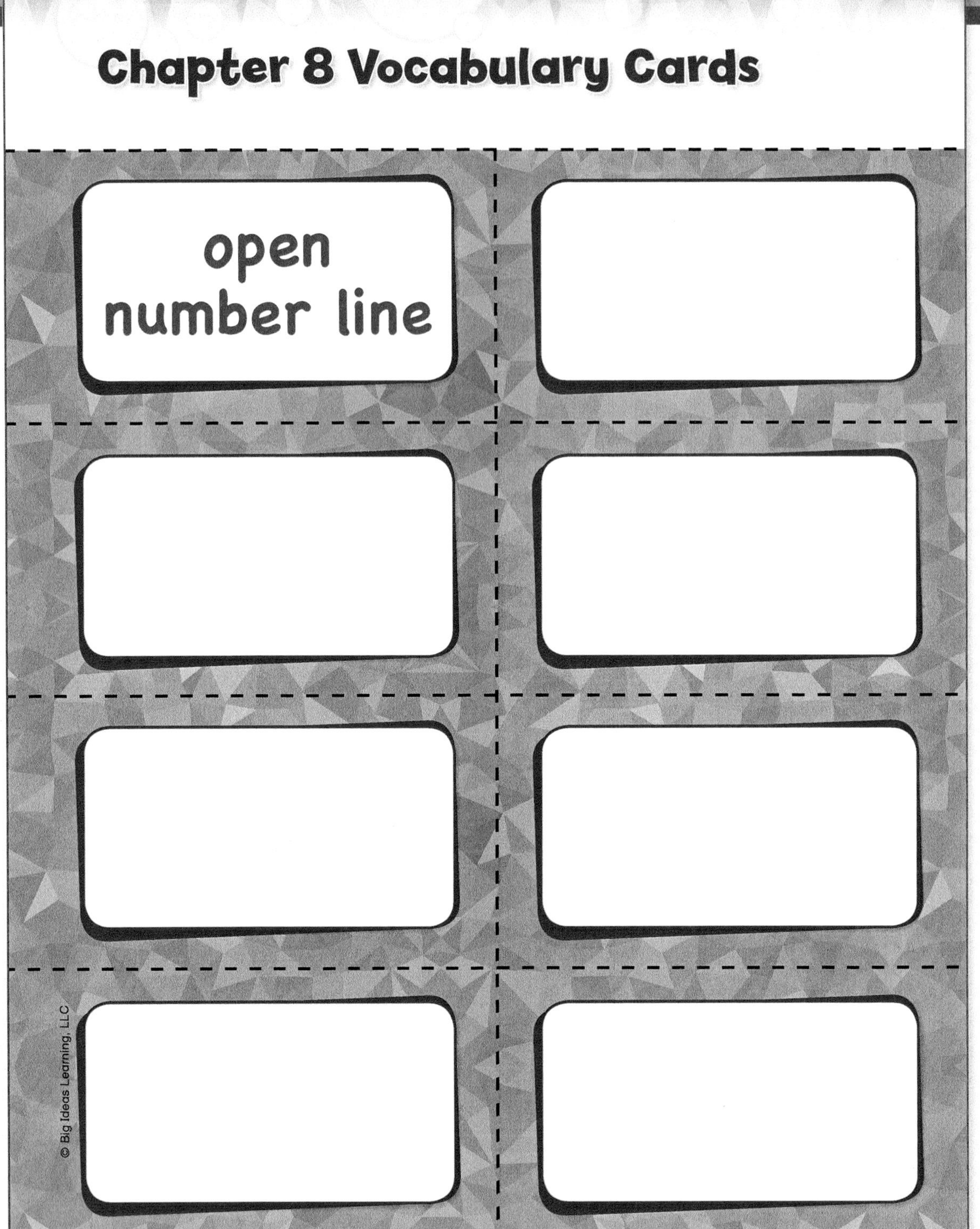

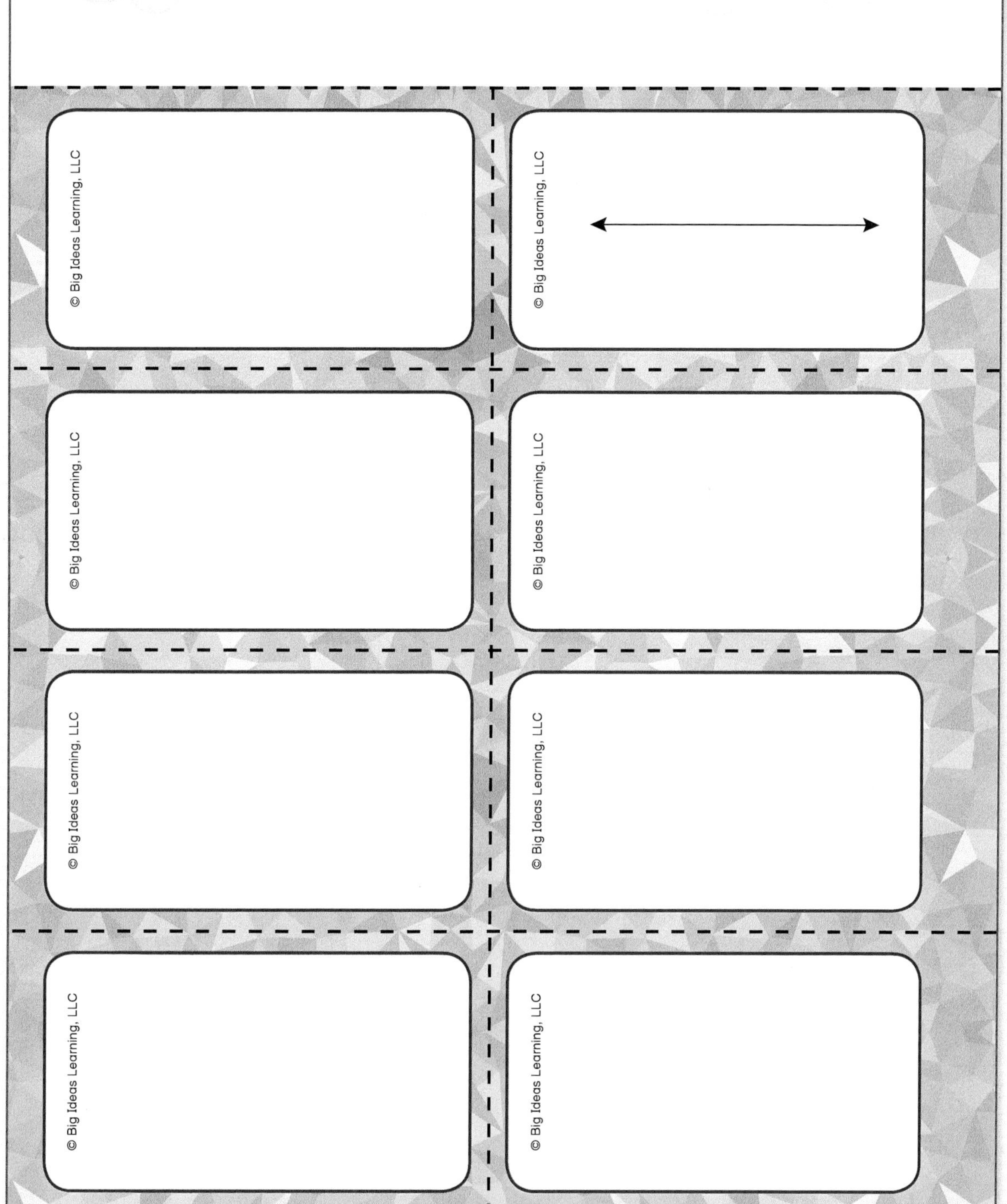
© Big Ideas Learning, LLC
© Big Ideas Learning, LLC
© Big Ideas Learning, LLC
© Big Ideas Learning, LLC
© Big Ideas Learning, LLC
© Big Ideas Learning, LLC
© Big Ideas Learning, LLC
© Big Ideas Learning, LLC

8.1

Check out the
Dynamic Classroom.

BigIdeasMath.com

Laurie's Notes

COMMON CORE **STATE STANDARDS**
1.NBT.B.2a, 1.NBT.C.4, 1.NBT.C.5

Learning Target

Use mental math to add 10.

Success Criteria

- Add 10 to a number and write the sum.
- Explain what changes when you add 10 to a number.

Warm-Up

Practice opportunities for the following are available in the Resources by Chapter or at *BigIdeasMath.com.*

- Daily skills
- Vocabulary
- Prerequisite skills

ELL Support

Explain that the word *mental* refers to thoughts within the mind. When you do mental math, you think through math problems in your mind without writing them out. If there are Spanish speakers, point out that the word *mente* means "mind," and it sounds similar. This can provide a helpful reminder of the meaning of the word *mental*.

Preparing to Teach

Today we build on students understanding of place value to add 10 mentally. This is the beginning lesson that will build through Chapters 8 and 9 culminating in adding two-digit numbers.

Materials

- 120 Chart*
- base ten blocks

**Found in the Instructional Resources*

Dig In (Circle Time)

In Circle Time we review adding 10 to a number using the 120 or hundred chart and base ten blocks. Each set of partners should have a 120 Chart and some base ten blocks. Students will use the resources, describe how adding ten changes the digits of the number, then practice visualizing the same problem to give a sum.

- To begin Circle Time, explain to students that today they will continue to add 10 to any number. Have students tell the strategies they have developed so far for adding ten to a number. Have them describe what happens to the digits of a number when they add ten. Listen for students to explain that the digit in the tens place of the addend goes up by 1.

? "Let's add 53 + 10. One of you model 53 + 10 with base ten blocks, and the other partner show 53 + 10 on the 120 Chart. Did you both get the same answer? How are the digits in the sum different from 53?"

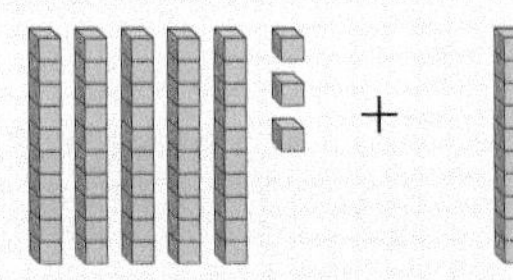

◉ "Now I want everyone to close their eyes. Imagine 53 in your mind. It can be on the chart, in base ten blocks or just the number. Now add 10 to it. What is the sum?" Have students share how they imagined adding 10 and finding the sum.

- "When you think of adding 10 to a number, you might picture it on the hundred chart and seeing in your mind the number just below. You might think of the base ten blocks, and adding another rod to the number. You might think of taking the ten digit and adding one to the digit, which adds a total of ten to the number."
- Repeat the process with 87 + 10. Have partners change who uses blocks and the chart. Then have them close their eyes and do the problem mentally.
- Have students share their strategies for adding ten in their minds. They should describe what they imagine or see mentally.

◉ "Today we will be adding 10 to a number in our minds. Let's try one more without any modeling. What is 29 + 10?"

? Teaching Prompt ◉ Learning Target

Name ______________________________

Learning Target: Use mental math to add 10.

Explore and Grow

Find each sum. What do you notice?

13 + 10 = 23

39 + 10 = 49

52 + 10 = 62

Add the tens digits. Keep the ones digits unchanged.

Explore and Grow

- Have students model each of the addition problems with base ten blocks and with the 120 Chart. You can continue to use partners and have them exchange the models as in the Dig In.
- Let students write the sums without using models if they are able.

? **MP7 Look for and Make Use of Structure:** "How did you find these sums? What do you notice about the sums for these exercises?"

◉ Have students who did not use models share how they added 10 mentally.

ELL Support

Discuss the example. Point out that when you add ten, you add 1 to the tens place value to find the sum. This is demonstrated by moving from row to row in the hundred chart. Have students work in pairs as they practice language while completing Exercise 1–8. Have one student ask the other, "What is the sum?" Then have them alternate roles for the other exercises.

Beginner students may answer with a number.

Intermediate and **Advanced** students may answer stating the addition sentence and its sum.

Laurie's Notes

Think and Grow

Getting Started

- Students will now add 10 mentally. A hundred chart is provided for support for students who might need it.

Teaching Notes

? **Model:** "We want to add 27 + 10. Newton suggests that you think of the hundred chart and find 27, then move down a row. Tell your partner how moving down 1 is adding 10 on the hundred chart. What number is below 27? Fill in the sum."

- **Model:** "We want to try to add 10 in our minds. We have practiced adding 10 in many different ways. You can imagine any method in your mind to add 10. If you need to look at the hundred chart, you can. Try to imagine it though and think what number would be below."
- **Model:** "Everyone think of 14 + 10. Write in the sum. Compare your sum with your partner. Tell each other how you thought of the sum."
- Have students continue to add 10 for Exercises 2–4, and then check in. Students should share their strategies for adding 10 in their minds, and share their sums.

? **MP8 Look for and Express Regularity in Repeated Reasoning:** "How do the digits in the first addend change when you add 10? Discuss this with your partner. How can this pattern help you know how to add 10 to a number easily?"

- Students should be progressing toward thinking about the tens digit increasing by one, rather than thinking about the entire number and adding 10 more to it. This place value reasoning will continue to be developed through this and the next chapter.
- **Supporting Learners:** Students can refer to the hundred chart as needed. Each time they do, ask how the digits in the addend and the sum compare. Help them express that the digits in the tens place is one more in the sum than in the addend.
- **Extension:** Have students ask a partner (number) + 10 problems. The partner asking should look at the hundred chart to be sure the sum is correct. Switch roles.

Think and Grow

27 + 10 = 37

1	2	3	4	5	6	7	8	9	10
11	12	13	14	15	16	17	18	19	20
21	22	23	24	25	26	27	28	29	30
31	32	33	34	35	36	37	38	39	40
41	42	43	44	45	46	47	48	49	50
51	52	53	54	55	56	57	58	59	60
61	62	63	64	65	66	67	68	69	70
71	72	73	74	75	76	77	78	79	80
81	82	83	84	85	86	87	88	89	90
91	92	93	94	95	96	97	98	99	100

Think of moving
down 1 row on a
hundred chart.

Show and Grow *I can do it!*

Use mental math.

1. 14 + 10 = 24
2. 46 + 10 = 56
3. 83 + 10 = 93
4. 75 + 10 = 85
5. 21 + 10 = 31
6. 60 + 10 = 70
7. 10 + 89 = 99
8. 10 + 68 = 78

Scaffold instruction to support all students in their learning. Learning is individualized and you may want to group students differently as they move in and out of these levels with each skill and concept. Student self-assessment and feedback help guide your instructional decisions about how and when to layer support for all students to become proficient learners.

Meeting the needs of all learners.

Laurie's Notes

Apply and Grow: Practice

SCAFFOLDING INSTRUCTION

Students continue to add 10 mentally. Exercises go from adding 10 to an addend, to 10 plus an addend, to finally finding a missing addend.

EMERGING students can find a sum when adding 10, but need a model or chart to find the sum. They do not understand place value yet, so each addition exercise seems to be new.

- **Exercises 9–14:** Observe how students are adding 10. Do they recognize any patterns yet?
- **Exercises 15–18:** Students now add a number to 10, instead of adding 10 to a number. Remind students that we learned that the order that you add the addends does not matter. So, for each of these exercises, they can switch the order of the addends and still think about adding 10.
- **Exercises 19 and 20:** These exercises have students find a missing addend. Have students look at the pattern of the tens place between the sum and the given addend. See if they recognize the pattern of adding a 10.
- **Exercise 21:** For the first equation, ask if they see two numbers in the list that if you add 10 to one of them, they get the other. Have them cross those off the number list. How do the remaining numbers make an equation that will sum to 96?

PROFICIENT students can add 10 mentally using various strategies.

- **Exercises 9–14:** Students are able to fill in sums.
- **Exercises 15–18:** Remind students that two addends can be added in any order. Ask how they can think about these exercises in the same way as Exercises 9–14. Have them explain why this is true.
- **Exercises 19 and 20:** Students find the missing addend. Ask students what pattern they notice that could let them know what is the missing addend.
- **Exercise 21:** Have students wrestle with the equations.

Additional Support

- Students continue to look at the hundred chart to solve the exercises. They explain how the ten digit changes with each sum.

Extension: Adding Rigor

- Students pick a number, and place it on one of the blanks in the equation _____ + 10 = _____. Tell what the missing number should be.

Name

Apply and Grow: Practice

Use mental math.

9. 16 + 10 = 26

10. 63 + 10 = 73

11. 8 + 10 = 18

12. 44 + 10 = 54

13. 19 + 10 = 29

14. 59 + 10 = 69

15. 10 + 22 = 32

16. 10 + 50 = 60

17. 10 + 71 = 81

18. 10 + 38 = 48

19. 55 + 10 = 65

20. 87 + 10 = 97

21. DIG DEEPER! Use each number once to complete the equations.

86 76 10 66

66 + 10 = 76

86 + 10 = 96

ELL Support

Check for understanding of Lesson 8.1. Read the example aloud as students follow along. Clarify unknown vocabulary if necessary. Allow time to complete the exercise. Have students respond to the following questions by writing answers and holding them up for your review.

1. How many total students are on the bus?
2. How many total tents are in the campground?

Laurie's Notes

Think and Grow: Modeling Real Life

Today's applications provide a story where students will add ten to find a new sum.

- ? **Preview:** "We have another bus story today. How many of you ride a bus? How many students do you think are on the bus?"
- Discuss the story. "There are 33 students on the bus. 10 more students get on the bus. What do we need to do to find out how many students are on the bus altogether? Please write the equation $33 + 10 = \_\_\_$."
- Have students tell a partner how they could add 33 and 10 mentally. Share strategies for adding $33 + 10$. Fill in the sum for their equations.
- Introduce Exercise 22. Have students say what they need to add and write the equation down. Next, have them add mentally and write their sum.
- ◉ "Use your thumb signals to show how well you can add 10 to a number in your head. How well do you think you recognize when 10 has been added to a number?"

Closure

- Have students tell a partner what happens to a number when 10 is added to it. Call on several different students to share.
- Have students share their favorite way to add 10 mentally.
- Play "Sum Now!" Tell students that you will give them a number to which they will add 10. You will count quietly to 5, then say "Sum Now!" and everyone will shout out the sum. Play several rounds. You can have a "girls only" round, "boys only" round, "blue eyes only" round, etc.

Think and Grow: Modeling Real Life

There are 33 students on a bus. 10 more get on. How many students are on the bus now?

Addition equation:

$$33 + 10 = 43$$

Check Your Work When adding 10, should the digit in the tens place or the ones place change?

43 students

Show and Grow *I can think deeper!*

22. There are 61 tents at a campground. 10 more are put up. How many tents are at the campground now?

Addition equation:

$$61 + 10 = 71$$

71 tents

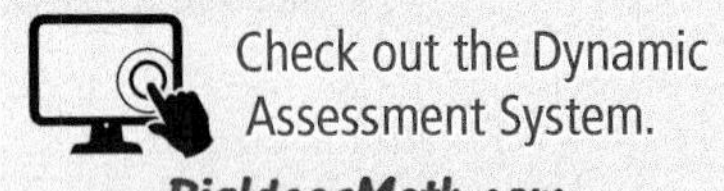
Check out the Dynamic Assessment System.
BigIdeasMath.com

Scaffold assignments to support all students in their learning progression. Revisit with spaced practice to move every student toward proficiency.

Connect and Extend Learning

Practice Notes

- Provide students with base ten blocks or a hundred chart for support.

Prior Skills

- **Exercises 17 and 18:** Grade 1, Finding 10 Less, Finding 1 Less

Cross-Curricular Connections

Physical Education

- Show ___ + 10 = ___ on the board where all students can see. Write several numbers from 1 to 89 on sheets of paper. Have two students stand up next to each other. Hold one of the sheets of paper over the first blank of the equation on the board. The first student to find the sum correctly stays standing up and plays the next round against the next student. Continue until all the number cards are used or all students have played at least once.

Name ____________________

Learning Target: Use mental math to add 10.

Think of moving down 1 row on a hundred chart.

$74 + 10 =$ 84

61	62	63	64	65	66	67	68	69	70
71	72	73	74	75	76	77	78	79	80
81	82	83	(84)	85	86	87	88	89	90
91	92	93	94	95	96	97	98	99	100

Use mental math.

1. $30 + 10 =$ 40
2. $81 + 10 =$ 91
3. $6 + 10 =$ 16
4. $57 + 10 =$ 67
5. $48 + 10 =$ 58
6. $26 + 10 =$ 36
7. $10 + 43 =$ 53
8. $10 + 65 =$ 75
9. $10 + 82 =$ 92
10. $10 + 79 =$ 89

Connect and Extend Learning

Extend Student Learning

Visual-Spatial

- Provide pairs of students with a deck of cards, using only the cards for 1–8. Have students shuffle their deck and divide the cards evenly between them. Each student flips over one card and places it in the middle, forming a two-digit number. The student who successfully adds 10 to the number first keeps both cards. For example, if one student flips over a 6 and the other flips over a 2, the two-digit number is 62. The first student to call out 72 (62 + 10) takes the 6 and 2 cards. Play until all cards are used or time is up.

Lesson Resources	
Surface Level	**Deep Level**
Resources by Chapter • Extra Practice • Reteach Differentiating the Lesson Skills Review Handbook Skills Trainer	Resources by Chapter • Enrichment and Extension Graphic Organizers Dynamic Assessment System • Lesson Practice

Use mental math.

11. 22 + 10 = 32

12. 85 + 10 = 95

13. 64 + 10 = 74

14. 41 + 10 = 51

15. DIG DEEPER! Use each number once to complete the equations.

25 10 15 35

10 + 15 = 25

25 + 10 = 35

16. MP **Modeling Real Life** There are 42 teachers at a school. The school hires 10 more. How many teachers are there now?

42 + 10 = 52

52 teachers

Review & Refresh

17.

10 less than 87 is 77.

18.

1 less than 33 is 32.

8.2

Check out the
Dynamic Classroom.

BigIdeasMath.com

Laurie's Notes

STATE STANDARDS
1.NBT.B.2a, 1.NBT.C.5

Learning Target

Use mental math to subtract 10.

Success Criteria

- Subtract 10 from a number and write the difference.
- Explain what changes when you subtract 10 from a number.

Warm-Up

Practice opportunities for the following are available in the Resources by Chapter or at *BigIdeasMath.com.*

- Daily skills
- Vocabulary
- Prerequisite skills

ELL Support

Point out the key words *less, subtract,* and *difference* all signal subtraction. Explain to students that scanning the page for these words helps them predict what will happen. The words *less* and *subtract* describe the process of subtraction, and the word *difference* describes the result.

Preparing to Teach

Today will be just like yesterday's lesson, only with subtraction. We repeat the same thinking and modeling so that students realize that this is not really anything new. We want students to understand that adding 10 and subtracting 10 are not very different and follow the same pattern and thinking.

Materials

- 120 Chart*
- base ten blocks

**Found in the Instructional Resources*

Dig In (Circle Time)

In Circle Time we review subtracting 10 from a number using the 120 Chart and base ten blocks. Each set of partners should have a 120 Chart and some base ten blocks. Students will use the resources, describe how subtracting 10 changes the digits of the number, then practice visualizing the problem to find the difference.

- To begin Circle Time, explain to students that today they will subtract 10 from a number. Have students tell the strategies they have developed for subtracting 10 from a number. Have them describe what happens to the digits of a number when they subtract 10. Listen for students to explain that the digit in the tens place of the addend goes down by 1.
- ? "Let's subtract 39 − 10. One of you model 39 − 10 with base ten blocks, and the other partner show 39 − 10 on the 120 Chart. Did you both get the same answer? How are the digits in the difference different from 39? What stayed the same?"
- ◉ "Now I want everyone to close their eyes. Imagine 39 in your mind. It can be on the chart, in base ten blocks or just the number. Now subtract 10 from it. What is the difference?" Have students share how they imagined subtracting 10 and finding the difference.
- "When you think of subtracting 10 from a number, you might picture it on the hundred chart and seeing in your mind the number just above. You might think of the base ten blocks, and taking one of the ten rods from the number. Or, you might think of taking the ten digit and subtracting one from it, which is the same as subtracting 10."
- Repeat the process with 46 − 10. Have partners change who uses blocks and the chart. Then have them close their eyes and do the problem mentally.
- Have students share their strategies for subtracting 10 in their minds. They should describe what they imagine or see mentally.
- ◉ "Today we will be subtracting 10 from a number in our minds. Let's try one more without any modeling. What is 88 − 10?"

? Teaching Prompt ◉ Learning Target

Name ______________________

Mental Math: 10 Less **8.2**

Learning Target: Use mental math to subtract 10.

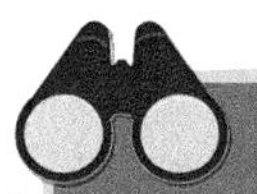

Explore and Grow

Find each difference. What do you notice?

33 − 10 = 23

67 − 10 = 57

82 − 10 = 72

Subtract one from each tens digit. Keep the ones digit unchanged.

Explore and Grow

- Have students model each of the subtraction problems with base ten blocks and with the 120 Chart. You can continue to use partners and have them exchange the models as in the Dig In.
- Let students write the differences without using models if they are able.

? **MP7 Look for and Make Use of Structure:** "How did you find these differences? What do you notice about the differences for these exercises?"

◉ Have students who did not use models share how they subtracted 10 mentally.

ELL Support

Discuss the example. Point out that when you subtract 10, you subtract 1 from the tens place value to find the difference. This is demonstrated by moving back from row to row in the hundred chart. Have students work in pairs as they practice language while completing Exercises 1–6. Have one student ask the other, "What is the difference?" Then have them alternate roles for the other exercises.

Beginner students may answer with a number.

Intermediate and **Advanced** students may answer stating the subtraction sentence and its difference.

Laurie's Notes

Think and Grow

Getting Started

- Students will now subtract 10 mentally. A hundred chart is provided for support for students who might need it.

Teaching Notes

? **Model**: "Descartes is subtracting 36 − 10. He suggests that you think of the hundred chart and find 36, then move up a row. Tell your partner how moving up one is subtracting 10 on the hundred chart. What number is above 36? Fill in the difference."

- **Model**: "We want to subtract 10 in our minds. We have subtracted 10 in many different ways. You can imagine any method in your mind. If you need to look at the hundred chart, you can. Try to imagine it though, and think what number would be above."
- **Model**: "Everyone think of 55. We want to subtract 10. Write in the difference. Compare your answer with your partner. Tell each other how you thought of the difference."
- Have students continue to subtract 10 for Exercises 2–3 and then check in. Students should share their strategies for subtracting 10 in their minds, and share their differences.

? **MP8 Look for and Express Regularity in Repeated Reasoning:** "How do the digits in the number (minuend) change when you subtract 10? Discuss this with your partner. How is this different than adding 10? How can this pattern help you know how to subtract 10 from a number easily?"

- Students should be thinking about the tens digit decreasing by one, rather than thinking about the entire number and subtracting 10 from it. This place value reasoning is the foundation to multi-digit addition and subtraction.
- **Supporting Learners:** Students can refer to the hundred chart as needed. Each time they do, ask how the digits in the number and the sum compare. Help them express that the digits in the tens place is one more in the sum than in the addend.
- **Extension:** Have students ask a partner (number) − 10 problems. The partner asking should look at the hundreds chart to be sure the difference is correct. Switch roles.

Think and Grow

36 − 10 = 26

1	2	3	4	5	6	7	8	9	10
11	12	13	14	15	16	17	18	19	20
21	22	23	24	25	26	27	28	29	30
31	32	33	34	35	36	37	38	39	40
41	42	43	44	45	46	47	48	49	50
51	52	53	54	55	56	57	58	59	60
61	62	63	64	65	66	67	68	69	70
71	72	73	74	75	76	77	78	79	80
81	82	83	84	85	86	87	88	89	90
91	92	93	94	95	96	97	98	99	100

Think of moving up 1 row on a hundred chart.

Show and Grow *I can do it!*

Use mental math.

1. 55 − 10 = 45
2. 21 − 10 = 11
3. 18 − 10 = 8
4. 74 − 10 = 64
5. 89 − 10 = 79
6. 72 − 10 = 62

Scaffold instruction to support all students in their learning. Learning is individualized and you may want to group students differently as they move in and out of these levels with each skill and concept. Student self-assessment and feedback help guide your instructional decisions about how and when to layer support for all students to become proficient learners.

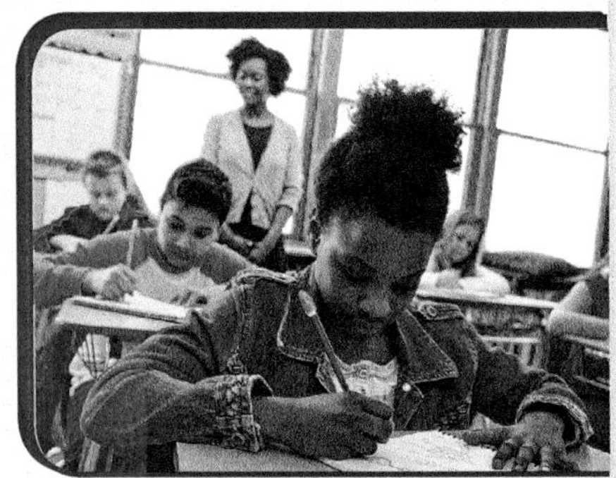

Meeting the needs of all learners.

Laurie's Notes

Apply and Grow: Practice

SCAFFOLDING INSTRUCTION

Students continue to subtract 10 mentally. Generally, subtraction is more difficult than addition for students. Although this lesson seems to be a simple step from yesterday, it may not be. Exercises go from subtracting ten from a number to finding the number from which 10 has been subtracted.

EMERGING students can find a difference when subtracting 10, but need a model or chart to do so. They may get confused and add by accident. They may still not fully understand place value, so each exercise seems to be new.

- **Exercises 7–16:** Observe how students are subtracting 10. Do they recognize and use the tens pattern, or are they using the chart?
- **Exercises 17 and 18:** Students now find the number (minuend) from which 10 is subtracted. They can "think addition" as a hint.
- **Exercise 19:** Students need to show how they know Newton's subtraction is correct. They can show a base ten quick sketch, the number above 94 in a hundred chart, or explain the ten digit.

PROFICIENT students can subtract 10 mentally using various strategies.

- **Exercises 7–16:** Students are able to fill in the differences using mental strategies.
- **Exercises 17 and 18:** Ask students to brainstorm ways they have found the missing minuend in the past. Refer them to the subtraction chart made in Lesson 5.7 if available. If not, remind them of the "think addition" strategy.
- **Exercise 19:** Students should brainstorm with a partner how they can show Newton is correct. Challenge them to think of more than one way.

Additional Support

- Students continue to look at the hundred chart to solve the exercises. They explain how the tens digit changes each time until the pattern becomes automatic.

Extension: Adding Rigor

- Students pick a number and place it on one of the blanks in the equation _____ − 10 = _____. Then they tell what the missing number should be.

Name ___________________________

Apply and Grow: Practice

Use mental math.

7. 60 − 10 = 50	**8.** 45 − 10 = 35
9. 50 − 10 = 40	**10.** 34 − 10 = 24
11. 51 − 10 = 41	**12.** 86 − 10 = 76
13. 64 − 10 = 54	**14.** 97 − 10 = 87
15. 28 − 10 = 18	**16.** 73 − 10 = 63
17. 32 − 10 = 22	**18.** 90 − 10 = 80

19. MP YOU BE THE TEACHER Is Newton correct? Explain.

yes; Find 94 on the hundred chart,

move up 1 row.

ELL Support

Check for understanding of Lesson 8.2. Read the example aloud as students follow along. Point out that the word *ride* can name a thing (noun) or an action (verb). Clarify any confusion or unknown vocabulary. Allow time to complete the exercise. Have students respond to the following questions by writing answers and holding them up for your review.

1. How many rides are left?
2. How many flavors are left?

Laurie's Notes

Think and Grow: Modeling Real Life

Today's applications provide a story where students will subtract 10 to find a new sum.

- ? **Preview**: "How many of you have been to an amusement park? Do you like roller coasters? What are your favorite rides?"
- Discuss the story. "There are 47 rides at the part, and you have only ridden 10. What do we need to do to find out how many more rides there are? Please write the equation 47 − 10 = ___ ."
- Have students tell a partner how they would subtract 10 from 47 mentally. Share strategies for subtracting 10. Then students fill in the difference for their equations.
- Introduce Exercise 20. Have students say what they need to subtract and write the equation down. Watch for students who write 10 − 65 instead of 65 − 10. Next, have them subtract mentally and write the difference.
- ◉ "Use your thumb signals to show how well you can subtract 10 from a number in your head. How well do you think you recognize when 10 has been subtracted from a number?"

Closure

- Have students tell a partner what happens to a number when 10 is subtracted from it. Call on several different students to share.
- Have students share their favorite way to subtract 10 mentally.
- Play "Difference Now!" Tell students that you will give them a number from which they will subtract 10. You will count quietly to 5, then say "Difference Now!" and everyone will shout out the difference. Play several rounds. Play some specialty rounds (ride the bus, have a cat for a pet, etc.) for fun.

Think and Grow: Modeling Real Life

You want to ride all 47 rides at an amusement park. You ride 10 of them. How many rides are left?

Subtraction equation:

$$47 - 10 = 37$$

37 rides

Show and Grow *I can think deeper!*

20. You want to try all 65 flavors at a frozen yogurt shop. You try 10 of them. How many flavors are left?

Subtraction equation:

$$65 - 10 = 55$$

55 flavors

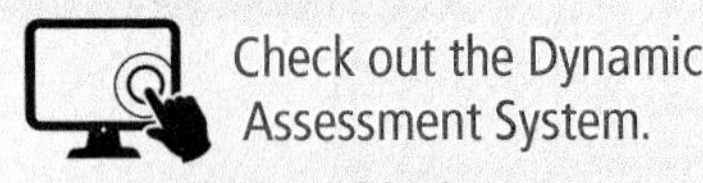
Check out the Dynamic
Assessment System.
BigIdeasMath.com

Scaffold assignments to support all students in their learning progression. Revisit with spaced practice to move every student toward proficiency.

Connect and Extend Learning

Practice Notes

- Provide students with base ten blocks or a hundred chart for support.

Prior Skills

- **Exercise 14:** Grade 1, Solving *Take From* Problems with Start Unknown

Cross-Curricular Connections

Physical Education

- Show ___ + 10 = ___ and ___ − 10 = ___ on the board where all students can see. Write several numbers from 11 to 89 on sheets of paper. Have two students stand up next to each other. Hold one of the sheets of paper over the first blank of either equation on the board. Go back and forth from adding 10 to subtracting 10 regularly through the activity. The first student to find the sum or difference correctly stays standing up and plays the next round against the next student. Continue until all the number cards are used or all students have played at least once.

Name ______________________

Practice 8.2

Learning Target: Use mental math to subtract 10.

Think of moving up 1 row on a hundred chart.

83 − 10 = 73

61	62	63	64	65	66	67	68	69	70
71	72	73	74	75	76	77	78	79	80
81	82	83	84	85	86	87	88	89	90
91	92	93	94	95	96	97	98	99	100

Use mental math.

1. 12 − 10 = 2

2. 49 − 10 = 39

3. 37 − 10 = 27

4. 26 − 10 = 16

5. 40 − 10 = 30

6. 62 − 10 = 52

7. 88 − 10 = 78

8. 91 − 10 = 81

9. 25 − 10 = 15

10. 87 − 10 = 77

Connect and Extend Learning

Extend Student Learning

Visual-Spatial

- Provide pairs of students with a deck of cards, using only the cards for 1–9. Have students shuffle their deck and divide the cards evenly between them. Each student flips over one card and places it in the middle, forming a two-digit number. The student who successfully subtracts 10 from the number first keeps both cards. For example, if one student flips over a 3 and the other flips over a 7, the two-digit number is 37. The first student to call out 27 (37 − 10) takes the 3 and 7 cards. Play until all cards are used or time is up.

Lesson Resources	
Surface Level	**Deep Level**
Resources by Chapter • Extra Practice • Reteach Differentiating the Lesson Skills Review Handbook Skills Trainer	Resources by Chapter • Enrichment and Extension Graphic Organizers Dynamic Assessment System • Lesson Practice

11. MP **YOU BE THE TEACHER** Is Descartes correct? Explain.

no; 40 − 10 = 30; Find 40 on the hundred chart and move up 1 row.

12. MP **Modeling Real Life** There are 99 levels in a video game. You complete 10 of them. How many are left?

99 − 10 = 89

89 levels

13. MP **Communicate Clearly** How is subtracting 10 similar to adding 10? How is it different?

Sample answer: To add or subtract 10, move 1 row on a hundred chart. To add, move down 1 row below the number being added to. To subtract, move up 1 row above the number you are subtracting from.

Review & Refresh

14. A group of students are at the arcade. 4 of them leave. There are 5 left. How many students were there to start?

9 students

8.3

Check out the
Dynamic Classroom.

BigIdeasMath.com

Laurie's Notes

Learning Target

Add tens.

Success Criteria

- Use models to add tens.
- Tell how many tens are in the model.
- Write the addition equation that matches the model.

Warm-Up

Practice opportunities for the following are available in the Resources by Chapter or at *BigIdeasMath.com*.

- Daily skills
- Vocabulary
- Prerequisite skills

ELL Support

Discuss the word *alike*. Explain that this word means same or similar. It is not the word *like*, which can be used to describe how someone feels toward something, or someone.

COMMON CORE STATE STANDARDS
1.NBT.B.2c, 1.NBT.C.4

Preparing to Teach

Today we continue to use place value as a strategy for addition by adding decade numbers. They will recognize that adding decade numbers, for example 30 + 40 has the same reasoning as 3 + 4 if place value is understood.

Materials

- 120 Chart*
- base ten blocks

**Found in the Instructional Resources*

Dig In (Circle Time)

In Circle Time we review decade numbers with base ten blocks and the 120 Chart. Students will use these tools to add decade numbers. Continue to have one partner work on the 120 Chart and the other with base ten blocks, then switch tools for the next example.

? "Who remembers what a decade number is? Tell your partner where the decade numbers are located on the 120 Chart. What is special about a decade number?" There are 0 ones.

◉ "Tell your partner how many tens are in the number 30. Tell your partner how many tens are in the number 80. Tell how many tens are in the number 50. Tell your partner how you know how many tens are in a decade number."

? "Today we are going to add decade numbers. We want to add 40 + 20. Show 40 with base ten blocks and find 40 on the 120 Chart. Now add 20 more with rods and move down twice on the chart. What sum do you get?"

◉ **MP2 Reason Abstractly and Quantitatively:** "How many tens are in 40? How many tens are in 20? How many tens are in 60? Does anyone suspect a pattern?"

- Repeat the process with 60 + 30. Have partners change who uses blocks and the chart. Discuss the number of tens in 60, 30, and 90.
- To have students reason about adding tens, liken it to adding ones in the following way: Have 4 students stand in pairs in the center of the circle. Give one pair of students 3 unit cubes and 5 unit cubes. Give the other pair 3 ten rods and 5 ten rods. Have the pair of students with unit cubes join their cubes together and say their sum. Have the students with rods join their rods together and first say how many rods they have, and then the value of 8 rods, or 80.
- If time, repeat with other numbers of cubes and rods.
- Have students share their hypothesis about adding tens so far.

◉ "Today we will add groups of tens. We will find out that knowing place value and decade numbers will help us know how."

? Teaching Prompt ◉ Learning Target

Name ______________________

Add Tens **8.3**

Learning Target: Add tens.

Explore and Grow

Model each problem. How are the problems alike? How are they different?

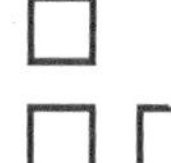

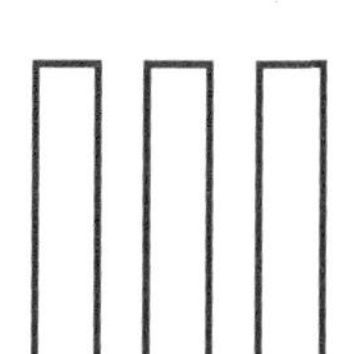
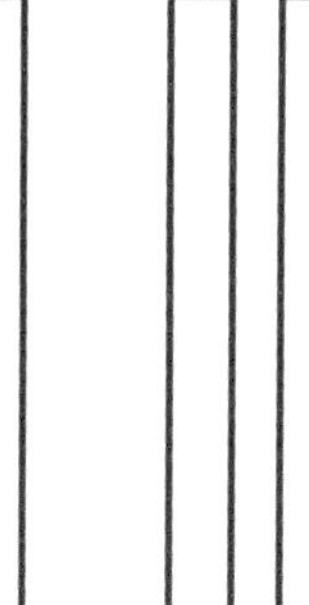

The sum of 3 and 2 is 5 in both problems;The first problem is adding ones digits and the second problem is adding tens digits.

$3 + 2 = \underline{5}$

$30 + 20 = \underline{50}$

Explore and Grow

- Tell students to use base ten blocks to model the two equations side-by-side in the space above the equations. Have students discuss each question with their partners.

? **MP2 Reason Abstractly and Quantitatively**: "How does knowing the sum of 3 + 2 help us know the sum of 30 + 20? Why is this correct?"

◉ Have students explain how the role of place value affects 3 + 2 and 20 + 20.

Laurie's Notes

ELL Support

Model the example. Then have students practice language in groups as they complete Exercises 1 and 2. Have groups discuss the following questions: "How many tens are in each number? How many tens are there when you add?" Monitor discussion and expect students to perform according to their language proficiency level.

Beginner students may state numbers.

Intermediate students may state numbers and phrases and read aloud the completed sentences in the book.

Advanced students may describe the process used to answer the questions.

Think and Grow

Getting Started

- We now formalize the role of place value when adding tens. Students will recognize that when adding the decade numbers, they are adding groups of tens together.

Teaching Notes

? **Model:** "Let's begin by looking at the addition equation and model. 20 + 50. How many tens are in 20? Draw in the model of 2 ten rods. How many tens are in 50? Draw in the model of 5 ten rods."

- **MP3 Critique the Reasoning of Others:** "Newton is adding the number of tens that he sees. Instead of adding 20 + 50, he is thinking that 2 groups of ten and 5 more groups of ten are 7 tens. Do you think this is a good strategy? Fill in the equation 2 tens + 5 tens = 7 tens."
- **Model:** "Descartes agrees with Newton's reasoning, but thinks that is not the final answer. We were supposed to add 20 + 50. So Descartes takes the next step. He realizes that 7 tens is 70. So, 20 + 50 = 70. Fill in the sum."
- Walk students through Exercise 1 together by asking how many tens are in 40, and fill in the 4 tens. Repeat with 50, and the sum.
- Watch as students complete Exercise 2.

? **MP2 Reason Abstractly and Quantitatively:** "How do the digits in the tens place show the sum of decade numbers?"

- **Supporting Learners:** Have students draw a quick sketch of the exercise, or model with base ten blocks.
- **Supporting Learners:** Students can refer to the hundred chart and count down the column for each ten.
- **Extension:** Have students use base ten blocks or the hundred chart to pose decade addition equations to a partner. Partners give the sums as decade numbers without the intermediate step of adding tens. Students alternate roles of posing and answering equations.

Think and Grow

Look at the tens digits. 2 + 5 = 7, so 2 tens + 5 tens = 7 tens.

20 + 50 = ?

7 tens is 70.

2 tens + 5 tens = 7 tens

So, 20 + 50 = 70.

Show and Grow *I can do it!*

1. 40 + 50 = ?

4 tens + 5 tens = 9 tens

So, 40 + 50 = 90.

2. 30 + 30 = ?

3 tens + 3 tens = 6 tens

So, 30 + 30 = 60.

Laurie's Notes

Scaffold instruction to support all students in their learning. Learning is individualized and you may want to group students differently as they move in and out of these levels with each skill and concept. Student self-assessment and feedback help guide your instructional decisions about how and when to layer support for all students to become proficient learners.

Meeting the needs of all learners.

Apply and Grow: Practice

SCAFFOLDING INSTRUCTION

Students add decade numbers by thinking of groups of ten. They develop the reasoning using the ten digits to add groups of tens without modeling. They should be able to add the tens digits to get the sum of tens, and unpack the tens for the sum. Students should be able to explain this process in their own words demonstrating place value understanding, and not a rote procedure.

EMERGING students can add the tens digits and most can write the sum. However, they may not be able to fully explain the role of place value or demonstrate understanding of why they add the tens digits.

- **Exercises 3 and 4:** Observe students as they fill in the place values. Do they correctly identify each decade number with the number of groups of ten? Do they make the connections between the sum of the number of tens and the actual sum?
- **Exercises 5–8:** Students add decade numbers without intermediate steps. Have students say how many groups of ten are in each number and add those numbers of groups to find the sum.
- **Exercises 9 and 10:** Students find the missing addend. Remind students of the strategies previously used to find missing addends. They need to reason about groups of tens.
- **Exercise 11:** Let students know there are multiple correct answers.

PROFICIENT students can add groups of ten and explain their reasoning.

- **Exercises 5–8:** Students can make the transition to adding decade numbers without showing groups of tens.
- **Exercises 9 and 10:** Students may need to be reminded of strategies for finding a missing addend.
- **Exercise 11:** Students select all of the correct answers for the model, and defend why they are correct. They explain what is wrong with the incorrect answer.

Additional Support

- Encourage students to draw quick sketches or use base ten blocks to reinforce groups of ten.

Extension: Adding Rigor

- Students pose addition problems of any two-digit number plus a decade number to partners. They should use a hundred chart or base ten blocks to confirm the sum.

Name ________________

Apply and Grow: Practice

3. 20 + 40 = ?

2 tens + 4 tens = 6 tens

So, 20 + 40 = 60.

4. 50 + 30 = ?

5 tens + 3 tens = 8 tens

So, 50 + 30 = 80.

5. 40 + 10 = 50

6. 70 + 20 = 90

7. 30 + 40 = 70

8. 20 + 60 = 80

9. 30 + 10 = 40

10. 30 + 60 = 90

11. DIG DEEPER! Which choices match the model?

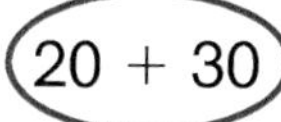

50 (circled)

20 + 30 (circled)

2 tens + 3 ones

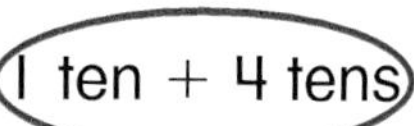

1 ten + 4 tens (circled)

ELL Support

Check for understanding of Lesson 8.3. Read the example aloud as students follow along. You may want to discuss the food pictured and ask if students are familiar with each. Clarify any unknown vocabulary. Allow time to complete the exercise. Have students respond to the following questions by writing answers and holding them up for your review.

1. How many total meatballs are there?
2. How many total bags of pretzels are there?

Laurie's Notes

Think and Grow: Modeling Real Life

Today's applications provide a story where students will add tens to find a sum.

? **MP1 Make Sense of Problems:** Discuss the story. "There are 20 meatballs on a tray. How would we model 20? Sketch 2 rods for 20 meatballs. Another tray has the same number of meatballs, so how many meatballs are on that tray? Draw the model for another 20. What equation does our model represent? Write it below."

- Have students suggest strategies for adding 20 + 20. They will suggest adding 2 tens and 2 tens. Remind students that they may also want to use doubles to find the number of groups of tens.
- Introduce Exercise 12. Students should follow the model given in the previous exercise.

◉ "Use your thumb signals to show how well you can add decade numbers. How well can you say the number of groups of ten in each decade number? How well can you tell the number represented by some groups of ten? How well can you add decade numbers without modeling groups of ten?"

Closure

- Have students sit back-to-back with a partner. Each student should have a whiteboard.
- Give partners an addition expression to solve. One partner will add using a model, either a quick sketch or by writing (number 1) tens + (number 2) tens = (sum) tens. The other partner will write the sum.
- When partners have had enough time to write their sums, cue students to turn around and compare their answers. Are they equivalent? If not, can they find an error?

Think and Grow: Modeling Real Life

One tray has 20 meatballs. Another tray has the same number of meatballs. How many meatballs are there in all?

Model:

Addition equation:

20 + 20 = 40

40 meatballs

Show and Grow *I can think deeper!*

12. One box has 40 bags of pretzels. Another box has the same number of bags. How many bags are there in all?

Model:

Addition equation:

40 + 40 = 80

80 bags

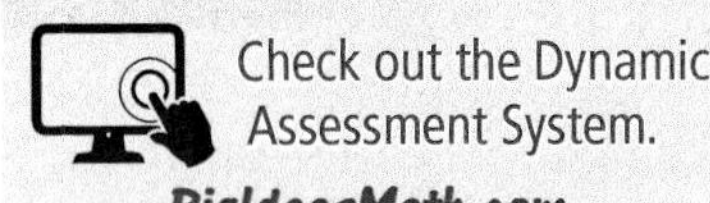
Check out the Dynamic Assessment System.
BigIdeasMath.com

Scaffold assignments to support all students in their learning progression. Revisit with spaced practice to move every student toward proficiency.

Connect and Extend Learning

Practice Notes

- **Exercises 5 and 6:** Point out that these equations have a missing addend.
- **Exercise 9:** Remind students that there may be more than one correct choice.

Prior Skills

- **Exercises 11–14:** Grade 1, Adding within 20

Cross-Curricular Connections

Music

- Write "+20" or "−20" on several index cards and place around the classroom. Give each student a piece of paper with a decade number from 20 to 70 written on it. While playing music, have students walk around the room. When the music stops, students go to the nearest index card and either add or subtract 20 from their number. Repeat using different starting numbers or different numbers on the index cards.

Name ______________________

Practice 8.3

Learning Target: Add tens.

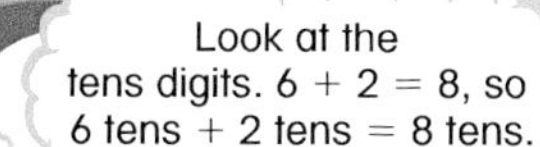
Look at the
tens digits. 6 + 2 = 8, so
6 tens + 2 tens = 8 tens.

60 + 20 = ?

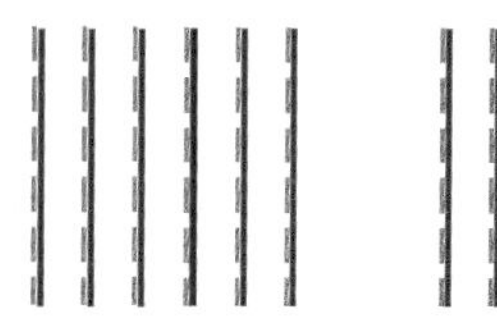

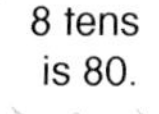
8 tens
is 80.

6 tens + 2 tens = 8 tens

So, 60 + 20 = 80.

1. 20 + 70 = ?

2 tens + 7 tens = 9 tens

So, 20 + 70 = 90.

2. 50 + 30 = ?

5 tens + 3 tens = 8 tens

So, 50 + 30 = 80.

3. 60 + 20 = 80

4. 40 + 40 = 80

Chapter 8 | Lesson 3 **419**

Connect and Extend Learning

Extend Student Learning

Bodily-Kinesthetic

- Use masking tape or pieces of paper to make a game board on the floor. Place a ten in each space. Have two students each toss a beanbag onto the board. Students work together to find the sum of the numbers the beanbags land on. Alternatively, create a board on a piece of paper and have students toss counters.

30	10	4 tens	||
||||	20	50	2 tens
2 tens	3 tens	|||	10

Lesson Resources	
Surface Level	**Deep Level**
Resources by Chapter • Extra Practice • Reteach Differentiating the Lesson Skills Review Handbook Skills Trainer Math Musicals	Resources by Chapter • Enrichment and Extension Graphic Organizers Math Musicals Dynamic Assessment System • Lesson Practice

5. 10 + 40 = 50

6. 30 + 30 = 60

7. 50 + 20 = 70

8. 40 + 50 = 90

9. DIG DEEPER! Which choices match the model?

3 tens + 4 ones

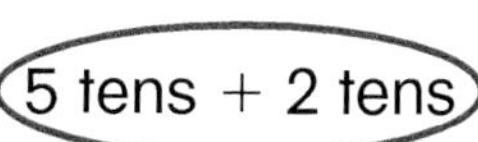

5 tens + 2 tens

60

30 + 40

10. MP **Modeling Real Life** One magic set has 30 pieces. Another set has the same number of pieces. How many pieces are there in all?

30 + 30 = 60

60 pieces

Review & Refresh

11. 11 = 6 + 5

12. 20 = 3 + 17

13. 16 = 11 + 5

14. 14 = 5 + 9

8.4

Laurie's Notes

COMMON CORE STATE STANDARDS 1.NBT.B.2c, 1.NBT.C.4

Learning Target

Use an open number line to add tens.

Success Criteria

- Use an open number line to show my starting number.
- Draw hops to show each ten I add.
- Write the sum.

Warm-Up

Practice opportunities for the following are available in the Resources by Chapter or at *BigIdeasMath.com.*

- Daily skills
- Vocabulary
- Prerequisite skills

ELL Support

When you hop you jump over things. When you move on a number line by groups of ten, you hop over ten numbers. Students may be familiar with the word hopping in the context of playing on a playground, or the way a rabbit or frog moves.

Preparing to Teach

Students have added decade numbers and explained sums in terms of groups of tens. Today students will use another model to show the addition of groups of ten: an open number line. The open number line is an efficient strategy for adding any multi-digit numbers.

Materials

- Large Number Line*

**Found in the Instructional Resources*

Dig In (Circle Time)

Students will add decade numbers, and coordinate their addition with walking an open number line. Prepare 11 Large Number Lines and label each as a unit of 10. For example, one sheet will be 0, the next 10, the next for 20, etc. with the last showing 100. This number line is the same idea as was used in Lesson 2.7 Dig In. Save this to use again in Lesson 8.6.

- "We have used number lines many times this year. We have used 0–10 number lines, and 0–20, and recently we learned that you can use a number line and show any starting and ending numbers you want. Today we will use the number line in another way. Look at the large number line in the center of our circle. What do you notice?" Students should say that the numbers are in tens, not ones.
- Draw a similar number line on chart paper. Use this to explain that between each number would be ten ones, but we are not drawing all of the ones in.
- ◉ "Today we are going to add decade numbers on the number line. Let's begin by adding 50 + 40. Tell your partner the sum."
- "Now we will walk it on the number line." Have a student stand at 50, then step four times ending at 90.
- We can draw this on the number line as well. Show a point on 50, then draw 4 hops to 60, 70, 80, and 90. Ask students to explain why you did not have to draw 40 hops. To clarify that each hop was equal to 10, write a small "+10" above each hop.

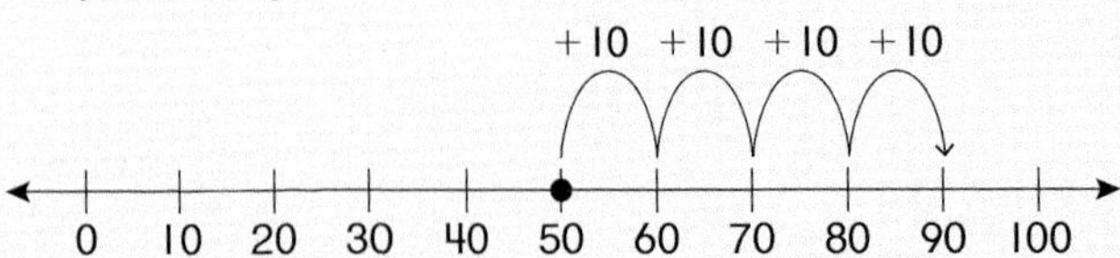

- ? **MP2 Reason Abstractly and Quantitatively:** "How is walking the number line or showing the hops like adding the number of tens like we did yesterday? How is it like using base ten blocks?"
- Repeat with additional problems. Have a different student walk the number line, and then sketch hops on the chart paper number line.
- ◉ "Today we will add groups of tens. We will find out that knowing place value and decade numbers will help us know how."

? Teaching Prompt ◉ Learning Target

Name ______________________

Add Tens Using a Number Line 8.4

Learning Target: Use an open number line to add tens.

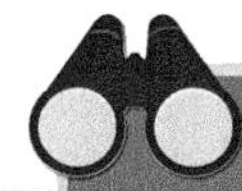

Explore and Grow

Write the missing numbers. How do the hops help you solve?

30 + 20 = 50

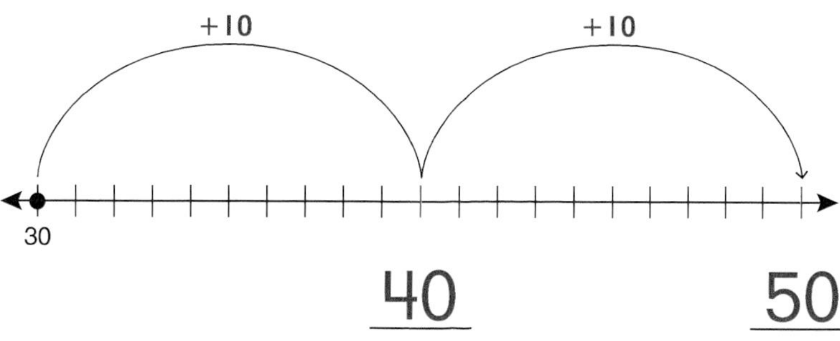

Each hop represents a jump of 10.

Explore and Grow

- "We are adding 30 + 20. Notice we started the number line at 30 and not 0. Remember that we can start and end a number line wherever we want."
- Have students count the tick marks within the first hop. Have them suggest what number is on the number line after the first hop. Students write in 40.
- ? "When we went from 30 to 40, what number was added? Write a small +10 on top of the first hop."
- Repeat this conversation for the second hop, and then write in the sum.
- ◉ "Tell your partners how the number line shows that 30 + 20 = 50."

Laurie's Notes

ELL Support

Model the example. Point out that the digit in the tens place of the second number tells them how many hops they must make on the line. Then have students practice verbal language in pairs using Exercises 1 and 2. Have one student ask another, "How many hops did you move? What is your sum?" Then have them alternate roles for other exercises.

Beginner students may answer only with numbers.

Intermediate students may answer using simple sentences, such as, "I moved three hops."

Advanced students may answer using complex sentences and a detailed description of their process.

Think and Grow

Getting Started

- We now move to adding on an **open number line**. Students will be given the starting point on the line, and will then draw hops to represent adding a ten. They fill in the values on the number line, and write the sum.

Teaching Notes

- ? **Model:** "Newton and Descartes are adding 40 + 30. Newton starts at 40 because it is the first addend. Notice that Newton does not draw a mark for every number, like 41, 42, 43.... He draws a big hop on the number line to show 10. Draw Newton's first hop of 10, and write +10 above it. Now draw another hop of ten and write +10 above it, and the final hop of ten and write +10 above it. How does Newton know to only draw three hops?"
- **Model:** "Descartes knows that 30 is the same as 3 tens. To fill in the numbers on the number line, start at 40 and count by tens. Fill in 50, 60, and 70. So now we know that 40 + 30 = 70."
- Have students anticipate how they will complete Exercise 1. Have them tell their partners how many tens are in 40, and as a result, how many hops they will show on the number line. Have students draw the hops and label +10 above each hop.
- Once the hops are drawn and labeled, have students count by tens to fill in the numbers on the number line for each hop. This may be challenging for first grade students as they begin. Finally, they can fill in the sum.
- Watch as students complete Exercise 2. Identify areas of difficulty. It is not a concern if students are having dexterity problems with drawing the hops. However, if students do not understand a hop as a representation of ten, or are not able to label the number line based on hops, this shows potential misconceptions and needs to be addressed. Students showing a lack of understanding or possible misconceptions should be grouped to work through Exercise 3 and possibly Exercise 4, to solidify learning.
- **Supporting Learners:** Have students model the problem with base ten blocks. They draw a large hop for each rod added. They can count by tens with each rod added to label the number line.
- **Extension:** Give students a starting point and an ending point for the number line. Students determine how many hops are needed (missing addend) to reach the sum, and then write the equation.

Think and Grow

Start at 40 on an **open number line**.

40 + 30 = 70

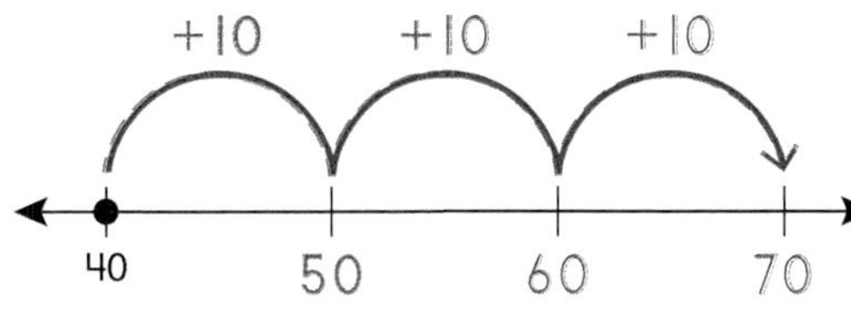

30 is the same as 3 tens. So, count on by 3 tens.

Show and Grow *I can do it!*

1. 50 + 40 = 90

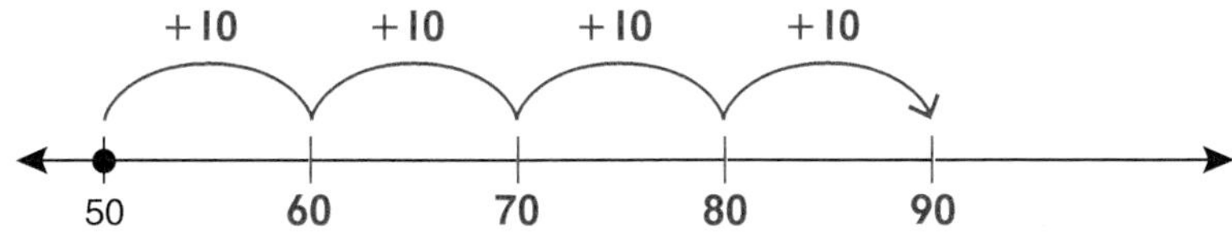

2. 60 + 20 = 80

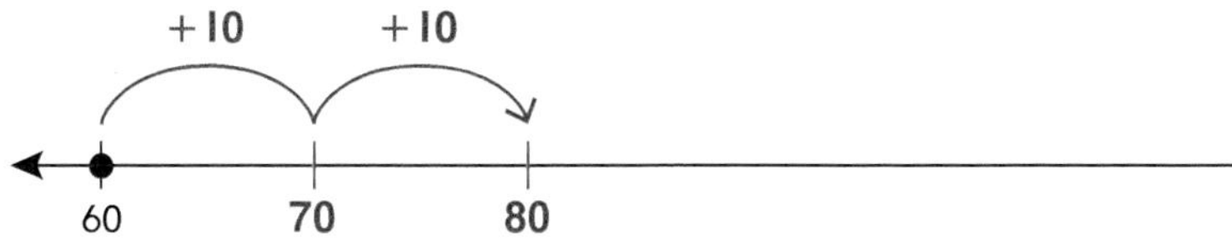

Laurie's Notes

Scaffold instruction to support all students in their learning. Learning is individualized and you may want to group students differently as they move in and out of these levels with each skill and concept. Student self-assessment and feedback help guide your instructional decisions about how and when to layer support for all students to become proficient learners.

Meeting the needs of all learners.

Apply and Grow: Practice

SCAFFOLDING INSTRUCTION

Students add on open number lines, including labeling the first addend as the starting point on the number line.

EMERGING students can add tens from yesterday's work, but the open number line may not be a model that they can use easily. Emerging students may still draw miscellaneous hops instead of understanding that each hop correlates to a plus 10. Having a number line that does not begin at zero, and does not show tick marks equal to one, may also be a source of confusion.

- **Exercise 3:** This exercise is the same as Exercises 1 and 2, and can be used for re-teaching.
- **Exercises 4–6:** These number lines do not provide the starting point. Watch to see if students place the first addend at the beginning of the number line, or if they place it elsewhere. This could be a misconception about the number line starting at 0.
- **Exercise 7:** Students may need to look at prior models to determine where the addends and sum can be found on the number line. Students may write $70 + 80 = 90$, pulling the numbers from the number line. Instead, remind students that they want to find how many tens need to be added to the start to get to the end. Ask them what the $+10$ on each hop represents.

PROFICIENT students can show the addition on the open number line and explain how each hop is adding one group of ten.

- **Exercises 4–6**: Watch to see if students' fine motor skills are a source of difficulty in solving problems. Students may understand this process but may not be able to draw the hops evenly or well. Encourage students that practice will make the drawing easier.
- **Exercise 7**: Students should be able to write the correct equation. Have them explain why 80 is not used when writing the equation.

Additional Support

- Encourage students to draw quick sketches or use base ten blocks to reinforce groups of ten.

Extension: Adding Rigor

- Students use an open number line to add a decade number to any two-digit number. Remind students of finding 10 more than any number. They use a hundred chart to help if needed.

Name ____________________

Apply and Grow: Practice

3. 40 + 20 = 60

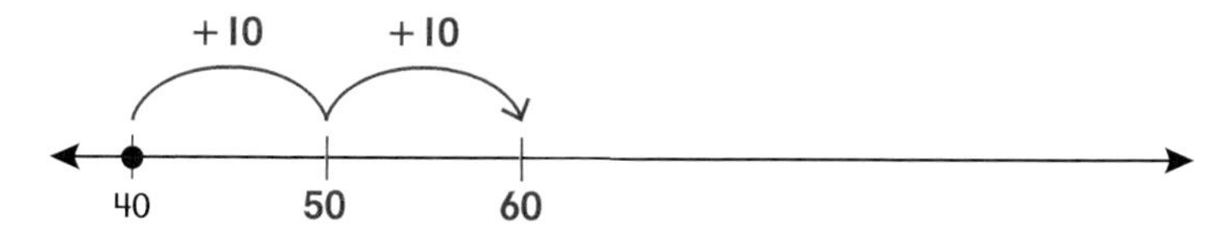

4. 50 + 30 = 80

+10 +10 +10

50 60 70 80

5. 60 + 40 = 100

+10 +10 +10 +10

60 70 80 90 100

6. 20 + 50 = 70

+10 +10 +10 +10 +10

20 30 40 50 60 70

7. **Structure** Write an equation that matches the number line.

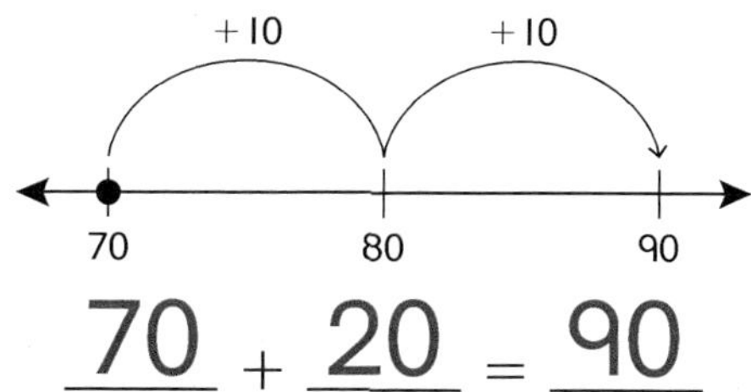

70 + 20 = 90

Chapter 8 | Lesson 4 **423**

Laurie's Notes

ELL Support

Check for understanding of Lesson 8.4. Read the example aloud as students follow along. Point out that the word *can* may refer to a thing or to the ability to do something. Ask if students are familiar with paper airplanes and fold an example if needed. Allow time to complete the exercise. Ask the following questions and have students display answers on a whiteboard or with a thumbs up or down signal to answer yes/no questions.

1. To add cans, where do you begin on the number line?
2. How many hops do you move?
3. How many cans do you collect?
4. Do you collect more cans than your friend?
5. To add paper airplanes, where do you begin on the number line?
6. How many hops do you move?
7. How many airplanes does your friend's class make?
8. Does your class make more airplanes?

Think and Grow: Modeling Real Life

The application stories today involve two steps to solve. Students will also need to make a comparison of the two numbers in the story. A number line is provided to both add the decade numbers in the story, and it can also be used to compare the numbers as was done in Lesson 7.5, although they should be able to compare digits in the two numbers.

? Discuss the story. "How can I find out how many total cans you collect? You have 20, and collect 20 more. Let's show 20 + 20 on the number line."

- "Your friend has 45 cans. Where on the number line is 45? Show 5 little lines for each number after 40 to show 45. Based on the number line, which number is greater, 40 or 45? What is the symbol to use? Fill in 45 > 40." Note that 40 < 45 is also correct, but might be confusing for students to answer the question based on who has more cans.

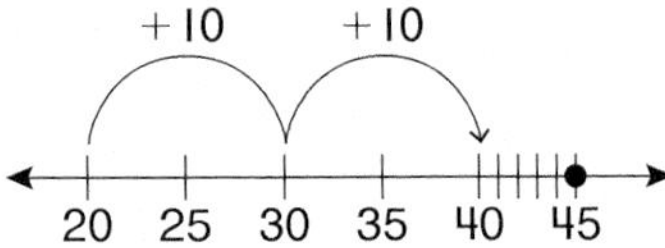

- Remind students that they did not have to use the number line to compare the numbers. They can also look at the tens digit, which in this case are both 4, and then look at the ones digit to compare. Any students who are still confused about comparing numbers could model with base ten blocks.
- Introduce Exercise 8. Have students clarify their thinking about which numbers are added, and which numbers should be compared to answer the question. Once you talk through the process with students, let them work on the problem independently.

◉ "I want to know how it is going for you with using an open number line to add. There are a lot of steps. How you are doing with drawing the starting point on an open number line? How are you doing with drawing the correct number of hops and labeling them +10? How are you doing with showing the numbers on the number line? How are you doing with finding the sum?"

Closure

- Have students sit with a partner and share one whiteboard and one marker. Tell students that they will trade back and forth to complete the problem 60 + 20.
  - Partner 1 draws an open number line and label the starting point.
  - Partner 2 draws hops and label +10.
  - Partner 1 writes the numbers on the number line.
  - Partner 2 writes the equation (60 + 20 = 80).

Think and Grow: Modeling Real Life

You have 20 cans. You collect 20 more cans. Your friend collects 45 cans in all. Who collects more cans?

Model:

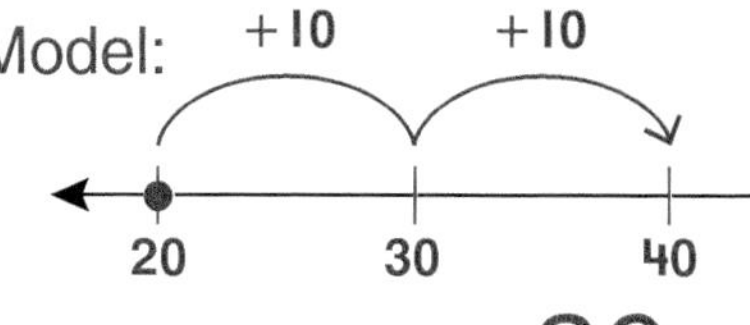

Addition equation: 20 + 20 = 40

Compare: 40 < 45

Who collects more cans? You (Friend)

Show and Grow *I can think deeper!*

8. Your class makes 62 paper airplanes. Your friend's class makes 30 small airplanes and 30 large airplanes. Whose class makes more airplanes?

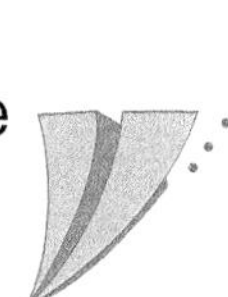

Model:

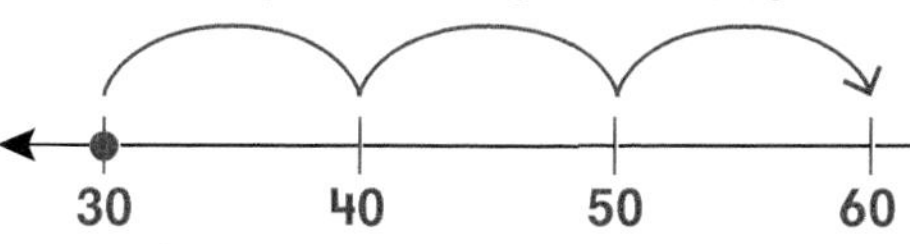

Addition equation: 30 + 30 = 60

Compare: 62 > 60

Whose class makes more airplanes?

Friend's class

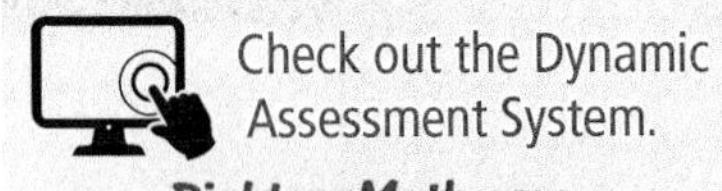
Check out the Dynamic Assessment System.
BigIdeasMath.com

Scaffold assignments to support all students in their learning progression. Revisit with spaced practice to move every student toward proficiency.

Connect and Extend Learning

Practice Notes

- Provide open number lines or base ten blocks for support.

Prior Skills

- **Exercise 7:** Grade 1, Counting to 120 by Tens

Cross-Curricular Connections

Language Arts

- *One is a Snail, Ten is a Crab: A Counting by Feet Book;* by April Pulley Sayre and Jeff Sayre; Read the book aloud to students, stopping and counting the legs of crabs by 10s. Use a floor number line for students to model the sum of 3 crabs and 5 crabs by crab-walking across the number line. Repeat with different combination of crabs.

Name ________________

Practice 8.4

Learning Target: Use an open number line to add tens.

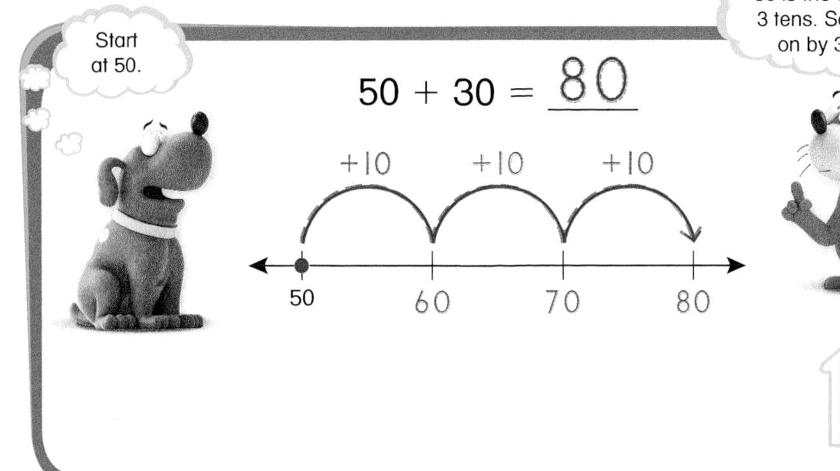

1. 60 + 30 = 90

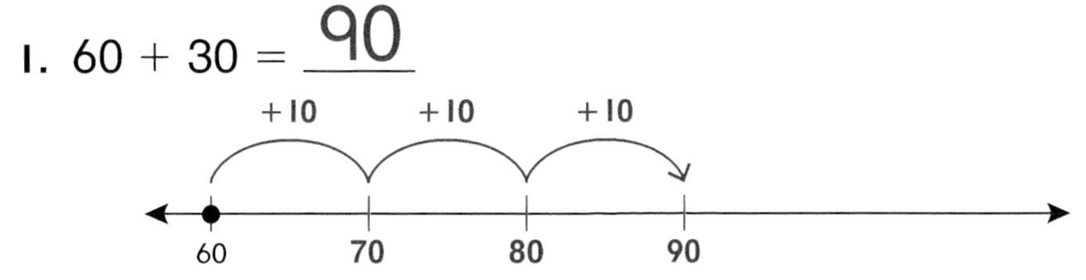

2. 20 + 20 = 40

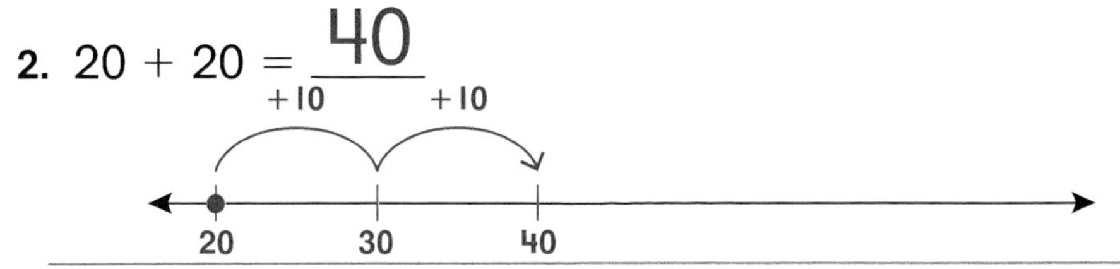

3. 30 + 70 = 100

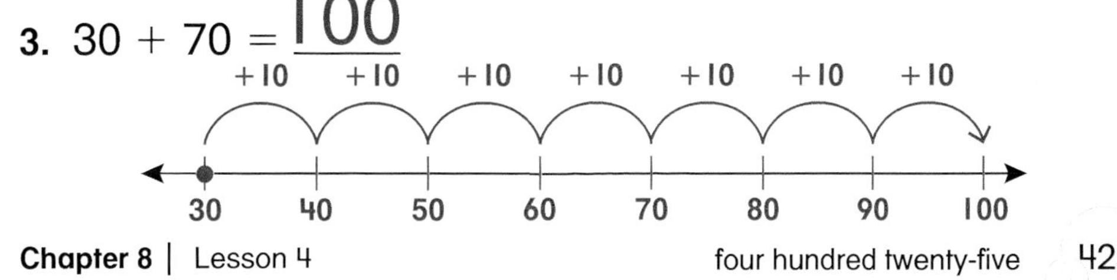

Connect and Extend Learning

Extend Student Learning

Visual-Spatial

- Use masking tape to cover the 6 on several dice. Give each student two dice. Students roll the dice and use the numbers to create addition problems with tens. For example, if a student rolls a 3 and a 4, they write the problem 30 + 40. Have students use a number line to find the sum.

Lesson Resources	
Surface Level	**Deep Level**
Resources by Chapter • Extra Practice • Reteach Differentiating the Lesson Skills Review Handbook Skills Trainer	Resources by Chapter • Enrichment and Extension Graphic Organizers Dynamic Assessment System • Lesson Practice

4. **Structure** Write an equation that matches the number line.

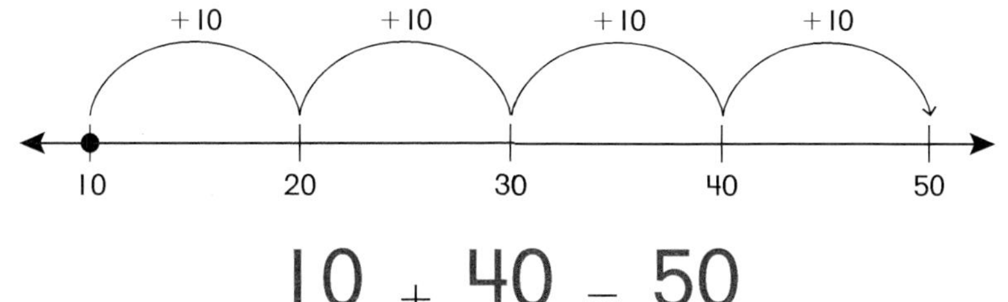

10 + 40 = 50

---

5. **Modeling Real Life** You make 39 snow bricks. Your friend makes 20 small snow bricks and 30 large snow bricks. Who makes more snow bricks? 20 + 30 = 50

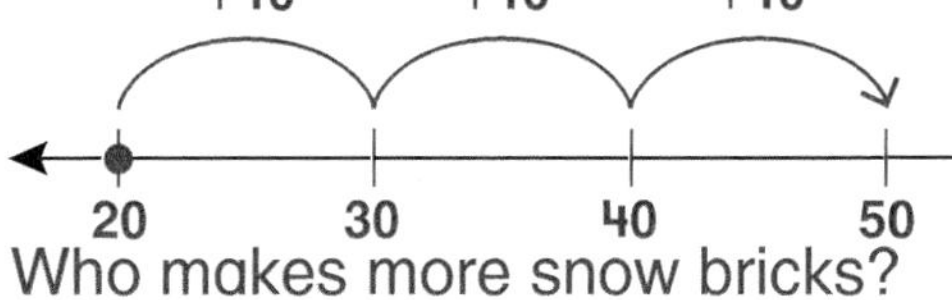

39 < 50

Who makes more snow bricks? You (Friend)

---

6. **DIG DEEPER!** Write an equation with a sum of 60. *Sample answer:*

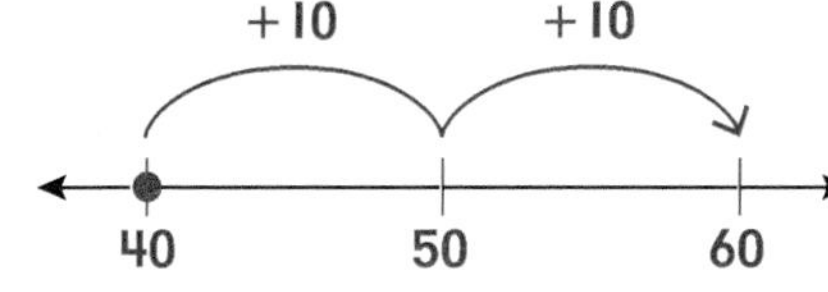

40 + 20 = 60

Review & Refresh

7. Count by tens to write the missing numbers.

49, 59, 69, 79, 89, 99

8.5

Check out the
Dynamic Classroom.

BigIdeasMath.com

Laurie's Notes

Learning Target

Subtract tens.

Success Criteria

- Use models to subtract tens.
- Tell how many tens are left in the model.
- Write the subtraction equation that matches the model.

Warm-Up

Practice opportunities for the following are available in the Resources by Chapter or at *BigIdeasMath.com.*

- Daily skills
- Vocabulary
- Prerequisite skills

ELL Support

The directions ask how models are alike and different. Ask students which words are opposites in the directions. Check their understanding by asking them to describe what each word means, using synonymous words or phrases, such as *similar/same* and *not the same/unlike.*

COMMON CORE **STATE STANDARDS**
1.NBT.B.2c, 1.NBT.C.6

Preparing to Teach

Today we use place value as a strategy for subtracting decade numbers. This lesson mirrors 8.3 with addition. We repeat the same thinking and modeling from 8.3 so that students realize that this is not really anything new. We want students to understand that adding tens and subtracting tens are not very different and follow the same reasoning.

Materials

- 120 Chart*
- base ten blocks

**Found in the Instructional Resources*

Dig In (Circle Time)

In Circle Time we briefly review adding decade numbers with base ten blocks and the 120 Chart. Students will use these tools to subtract decade numbers. Have one partner work with the 120 Chart and the other with base ten blocks, then switch tools for the next example.

- "I want to review adding 20 + 40. If you are holding the 120 Chart, show your partner how to use the chart to add. If you have base ten blocks, show your partner how to use them to add."
- "What if I want to subtract? Let's subtract 50 − 10. Show your partners how to model 50 − 10 with your tools. Why do you move up the column when using the 120 Chart to subtract 10?"
- ? "Today we are going to subtract decade numbers. We want to subtract 60 − 20. Show 60 with base ten blocks (6 rods). To subtract 20, remove or take away 20 (2 rods). What difference do you get?"
- ? "We want to do the same problem again using the 120 Chart. Find 60 on the 120 Chart. To subtract 20 on the 120 Chart, we move up the column twice on the chart. What difference do you get?"
- ◉ **MP2 Reason Abstractly and Quantitatively:** "How many tens are in 60? How many tens are in 20? How many tens are in 40? Does anyone suspect a pattern?" Repeat the process with 40 − 30. Have partners change who uses blocks and the chart. Discuss the numbers of tens in 40, 30, and 10.
- Connect subtracting tens to subtracting ones. Have 2 pairs of students stand in the center of the circle. Give one pair of students 8 unit cubes and the other pair 8 ten rods. Have the first pair of students show how to subtract 5 and say the difference. Have the second pair show how to subtract 5 rods and first say how many rods they have, and then the value of 3 rods, or 30. Repeat with more examples.
- Have students share their guess about how to subtract tens.
- ◉ "Today we will subtract groups of tens. We will see that it is not very different than adding groups of tens."

? Teaching Prompt ◉ Learning Target

Name ________________________

Learning Target: Subtract tens.

Explore and Grow

Model each problem. How are the problems alike? How are they different?

The difference of 5 and 2 is 3 in both problems; The first problem is subtracting ones digits and the second problem is subtracting tens digits.

$5 - 2 = \underline{3}$

Reasoning How does knowing the difference of 5 − 2 help you know the difference of 50 − 20?

$50 - 20 = \underline{30}$

Explore and Grow

- Tell students to use base ten blocks to model the two equations side-by-side in the space above the equations. Have students discuss each equation with their partners.
- Have students explain how the role of place value affects 5 − 2 and 50 − 20. Tell your partner how this is like using place value when adding decade numbers.

ELL Support

Model the example. Then have students practice language in groups as they complete Exercises 1 and 2. Have groups discuss the following questions: "How many tens are in each number? What is the difference?" Monitor discussion and expect students to perform according to their language proficiency level.

Beginner students may state numbers.

Intermediate students may state numbers and phrases, and read aloud the completed sentences in the book.

Advanced students may describe the process used to answer the questions.

Laurie's Notes

Think and Grow

Getting Started

- We now formalize the role of place value when subtracting tens. In the same way that students recognized adding groups of ten, they will apply the same reasoning to subtracting groups of tens.

Teaching Notes

? **Model:** "Let's begin by looking at the subtraction equation and model. 60 − 40. How many tens are in 60? Draw in the model of 6 ten rods. How many tens are in 40? Notice for subtraction, you circle the group of 4 ten rods and cross them out."

- **MP3 Critique the Reasoning of Others:** "Newton is subtracting the number of tens that he sees. Instead of subtracting 60 − 40, he is thinking that 6 groups of ten minus 4 groups of ten are 2 groups of ten. Do you think this is a good strategy? Fill in the equation 6 tens − 4 tens = 2 tens."
- **Model:** "Descartes agrees with Newton's reasoning, but thinks that is not the final answer. We were supposed to subtract 60 − 40. So Descartes takes the next step. He realizes that 2 tens is 20. So, 60 − 40 = 20. Fill in the difference."
- Walk students through Exercise 1 together by asking how many tens are in 70, and fill in 7 tens. Repeat with 30, and the difference of 4 tens. Ask what 70 − 30 is equal to.
- Watch as students complete Exercise 2.

? **MP2 Reason Abstractly and Quantitatively:** "How do the digits in the tens place show the difference of decade numbers?"

- **Supporting Learners:** Have students draw a quick sketch of the problem, or model with base ten blocks.
- **Supporting Learners:** Students can refer to the hundred chart and count up the column for each ten.
- **Extension:** Have students use base ten blocks or the hundred chart to pose decade subtraction equations to a partner. Partners give the differences as decade numbers without the intermediate step of subtracting tens. Students alternate roles of posing and answering equations.

Think and Grow

Look at the tens digits.
6 − 4 = 2, so
6 tens − 4 tens = 2 tens.

60 − 40 = ?

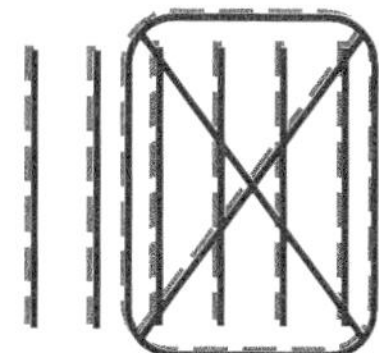

6 tens − 4 tens = 2 tens

So, 60 − 40 = 20.

Show and Grow *I can do it!*

1. 70 − 30 = ?

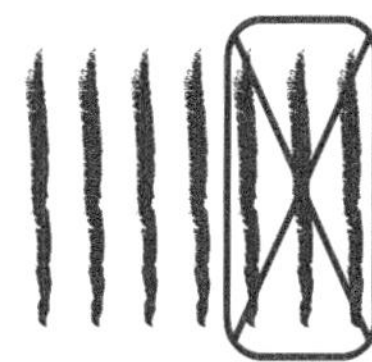

7 tens − 3 tens = 4 tens

So, 70 − 30 = 40.

2. 40 − 20 = 20

4 tens − 2 tens = 2 tens

So, 40 − 20 = 20.

Scaffold instruction to support all students in their learning. Learning is individualized and you may want to group students differently as they move in and out of these levels with each skill and concept. Student self-assessment and feedback help guide your instructional decisions about how and when to layer support for all students to become proficient learners.

Meeting the needs of all learners.

Laurie's Notes

Apply and Grow: Practice

SCAFFOLDING INSTRUCTION

Students subtract decade numbers by thinking of groups of ten. They develop the reasoning using the tens digit to subtract groups of tens without modeling. They should be able to subtract the tens digits to get the difference of the groups of ten and then name the number for the difference. Students should be able to explain this process in their own words demonstrating place value understanding, and not a rote procedure.

EMERGING students can subtract the tens digits and most can write the difference. However, they may not be able to fully explain the role of place value or demonstrate understanding of why they subtract the tens digits.

- **Exercises 3 and 4:** Observe students as they fill in the place values. Do they correctly identify each decade number with the number of groups of ten? Do they make the connections between the difference of the number of tens and the actual difference?
- **Exercises 5–8:** Students subtract decade numbers without intermediate steps. Have students say how many groups of ten are in each number and subtract those numbers of groups to find the difference.
- **Exercises 9 and 10:** Students find the missing change (subtrahend). Remind students of the *think addition* strategy if they need a hint.
- **Exercise 11:** Let students know there are multiple correct answers.

PROFICIENT students can subtract groups of ten and explain their reasoning.

- **Exercises 5–8:** Students can make the transition to subtracting decade numbers without showing groups of tens.
- **Exercises 9 and 10:** Students may need to be reminded of strategies for finding the missing change.
- **Exercise 11:** Students select all of the correct answers for the model, and defend why they are correct. They explain what is wrong with the incorrect answer.

Additional Support

- Encourage students to draw quick sketches or use base ten blocks to reinforce groups of ten.

Extension: Adding Rigor

- Students pose subtraction problems of any two-digit number minus a decade number to partners.

Name ______

Apply and Grow: Practice

3. 90 − 30 = ?

9 tens − 3 tens = 6 tens

So, 90 − 30 = 60.

4. 50 − 10 = ?

5 tens − 1 ten = 4 tens

So, 50 − 10 = 40.

5. 30 − 20 = 10

6. 40 − 40 = 0

7. 80 − 50 = 30

8. 90 − 70 = 20

9. 20 − 10 = 10

10. 50 − 30 = 20

11. DIG DEEPER! Which choices match the model?

50 − 30

80 − 30

5 tens − 3 tens

8 tens − 3 tens

Chapter 8 | Lesson 5 429

ELL Support

Check for understanding of Lesson 8.5. Read the example aloud as students follow along. You may want to discuss the school activities mentioned. Allow time to complete the exercise. Have students respond to the following questions by writing answers and holding them up for your review.

1. How many spelling words do you have?
2. What is your subtraction sentence?
3. How many students are on the football team?
4. What is your subtraction sentence?

Laurie's Notes

Think and Grow: Modeling Real Life

Today's applications provide a story where students will subtract tens to find a difference.

? Discuss the story. "There are 80 math problems. Good thing we don't really have that many, huh? How would we model 80? Sketch 8 rods for 80 math problems. You have 40 fewer spelling words. Circle or box 40 in your model and cross them out. What equation does our model represent? Write it below."

- Have students suggest strategies for subtracting 80 − 40. They may say to look at the remaining rods from the model, or think 8 − 4. They may think of counting back, etc.
- Introduce Exercise 12. Students should follow the model given in the previous exercise.

◉ "Use your thumb signals to show how well you can subtract decade numbers. How well can you say the number of groups of ten in each decade number? How well can you tell the number represented by some groups of ten? How well can you subtract decade numbers without modeling groups of ten?"

Closure

- Have students sit back-to-back with a partner. Each student should have a whiteboard.
- Give partners a subtraction expression to solve. One partner will subtract using a model, either a quick sketch or by writing (number 1) tens − (number 2) tens = (difference) tens. The other partner will write the equation with the difference without a model.
- When partners have had enough time to work, cue students to turn around and compare their answers. Are they equivalent? If not, can they find an error?
- Repeat the activity with students switching roles.

Think and Grow: Modeling Real Life

You have 80 math problems. You have 40 fewer spelling words. How many spelling words do you have?

3+1=4 2+7=4
2+3=5 1+4=5
1+8=9 2+9=11
3+6=9 3+4=7
2+1=3 1+3=4

Model:

Subtraction equation:

80 − 40 = 40

40 spelling words

Show and Grow *I can think deeper!*

12. There are 60 students in a play. A football team has 30 fewer students. How many students are on the football team?

Model:

Subtraction equation:

60 − 30 = 30

30 students

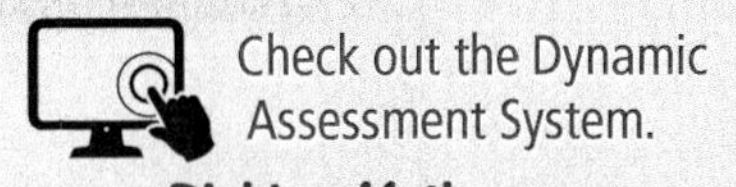
Check out the Dynamic Assessment System.

BigIdeasMath.com

Scaffold assignments to support all students in their learning progression. Revisit with spaced practice to move every student toward proficiency.

Connect and Extend Learning

Practice Notes

- Consider providing tens rods or hundreds charts for students to work with.
- **Exercises 5–8:** Point out that the difference is provided in these exercises.

Prior Skills

- **Exercises 11–14:** Grade 1, Subtracting within 20

Cross-Curricular Connections

Music

- Have students count down by 10s, using the tune of 99 Bottles on the Wall:

  90 bubbles up in the air
  90 bubbles – oh!
  10 go "pop, poppity-pop"
  Now there are….. 80 bubbles up in the air

Name ____________________

Practice 8.5

Learning Target: Subtract tens.

Look at the tens digits.
9 − 6 = 3, so
9 tens − 6 tens = 3 tens.

90 − 60 = ?

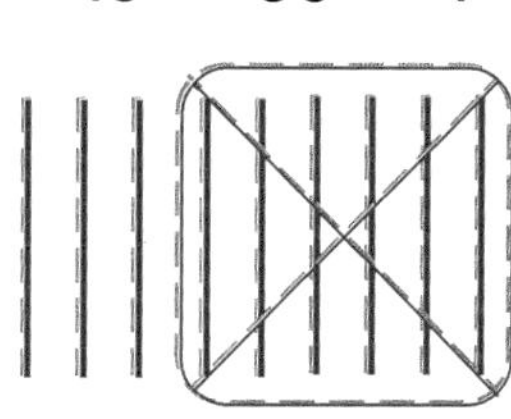

3 tens
is 30.

9 tens − 6 tens = 3 tens

So, 90 − 60 = 30.

1. 70 − 50 = ?

7 tens − 5 tens = 2 tens

So, 70 − 50 = 20.

2. 60 − 20 = ?

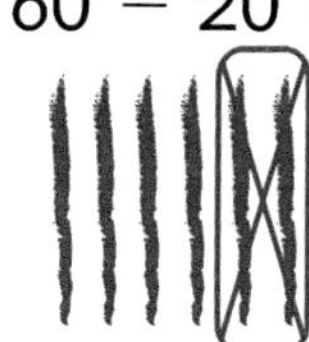

6 tens − 2 tens = 4 tens

So, 60 − 20 = 40.

3. 60 − 60 = 0

4. 30 − 10 = 20

Connect and Extend Learning

Extend Student Learning

Bodily-Kinesthetic

- Have students represent subtraction equations using fingers. Call a group of students up to the front. Ask them to hold up all ten fingers. Ask the class, "How many fingers do we see?" Then ask some of the students to sit down. Ask the class, "How many fingers just left to go sit down?" Listen for the answer, then ask, "How many fingers are left up here with me?" Write the equation out on the board. Repeat with different students and different numbers.

Lesson Resources	
Surface Level	**Deep Level**
Resources by Chapter • Extra Practice • Reteach Differentiating the Lesson Skills Review Handbook Skills Trainer	Resources by Chapter • Enrichment and Extension Graphic Organizers Dynamic Assessment System • Lesson Practice

5. 70 − 70 = 0

6. 50 − 10 = 40

7. 40 − 20 = 20

8. 90 − 40 = 50

9. DIG DEEPER! Which choices match the model?

(90 − 50) circled

40 − 5

4 tens − 5 ones

(9 tens − 5 tens) circled

10. MP **Modeling Real Life** There are 40 chairs in the library. There are 30 fewer tables than chairs. How many tables are there?

40 − 30 = 10

10 tables

Review & Refresh

11. 11 − 7 = 4

12. 16 − 8 = 8

13. 15 − 8 = 7

14. 18 − 9 = 9

8.6

Check out the
Dynamic Classroom.

BigIdeasMath.com

Laurie's Notes

COMMON CORE STATE STANDARDS 1.NBT.B.2c, 1.NBT.C.6

Learning Target

Use an open number line to subtract tens.

Success Criteria

- Use an open number line to show my starting number.
- Draw hops to show each ten I subtract.
- Write the difference.

Warm-Up

Practice opportunities for the following are available in the Resources by Chapter or at *BigIdeasMath.com.*

- Daily skills
- Vocabulary
- Prerequisite skills

ELL Support

Explain that an open number line can help you do subtraction as well as addition. Ask students how subtraction and addition on a number line are alike. Then ask how they are different. Clarify that a key difference is that one moves to the right for addition and to the left for subtraction.

Preparing to Teach

Students have now subtracted decade numbers and explained differences in terms of groups of tens. Just as with addition, today students will use an open number line to model subtraction. This lesson mirrors 8.4 with adding decade numbers. We repeat the same thinking and modelling from 8.4 so that students realize that, again, this is not anything new.

Materials

- Large Number Line*

**Found in the Instructional Resources*

Dig In (Circle Time)

Students will subtract decade numbers, and coordinate the subtraction with walking an open number line. Use the Large Number Line from Lesson 8.4.

- "You have used an open number line to add decade numbers. Tell your partner what you remember about using an open number line." Have several students share.
- "Notice that we have our large number line in the circle again, and I have a smaller open number line on chart paper. We will use both to subtract."
- ◉ "Let's begin by subtracting 90 − 40. Tell your partner the difference, and how you know."
- "Now we will walk it on the number line." Have a student stand at 90, then walk back four times ending at 50.
- "We can draw this on the open number line as well. With subtraction, this works in the opposite way than addition does. We start with 90, which will be on the right end of the number line." Show a point at 90, then draw 4 hops back down the line. Write −10 above each hop.

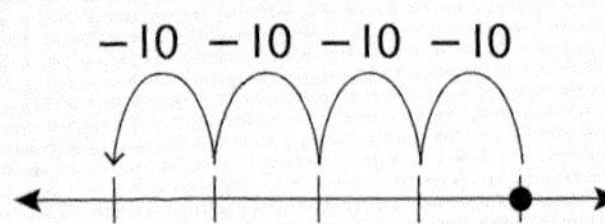

−10 −10 −10 −10

- "We need to figure out what number each hop lands on. Let's count back from 90 by tens." As students say each number, fill in the number line.
- ? **MP2 Reasoning Abstractly and Quantitatively**: "How is walking the number line or showing the hops like subtracting the number of tens like we did yesterday? How is it like using base ten blocks?"
- Repeat with additional problems. Have a student walk the number line, and then sketch hops on the open number line.
- ◉ "Today we will subtract groups of tens. We will see that it is really just like adding groups of tens. We can look at the digits in the tens place to know how to subtract the groups of tens."

? Teaching Prompt ◉ Learning Target

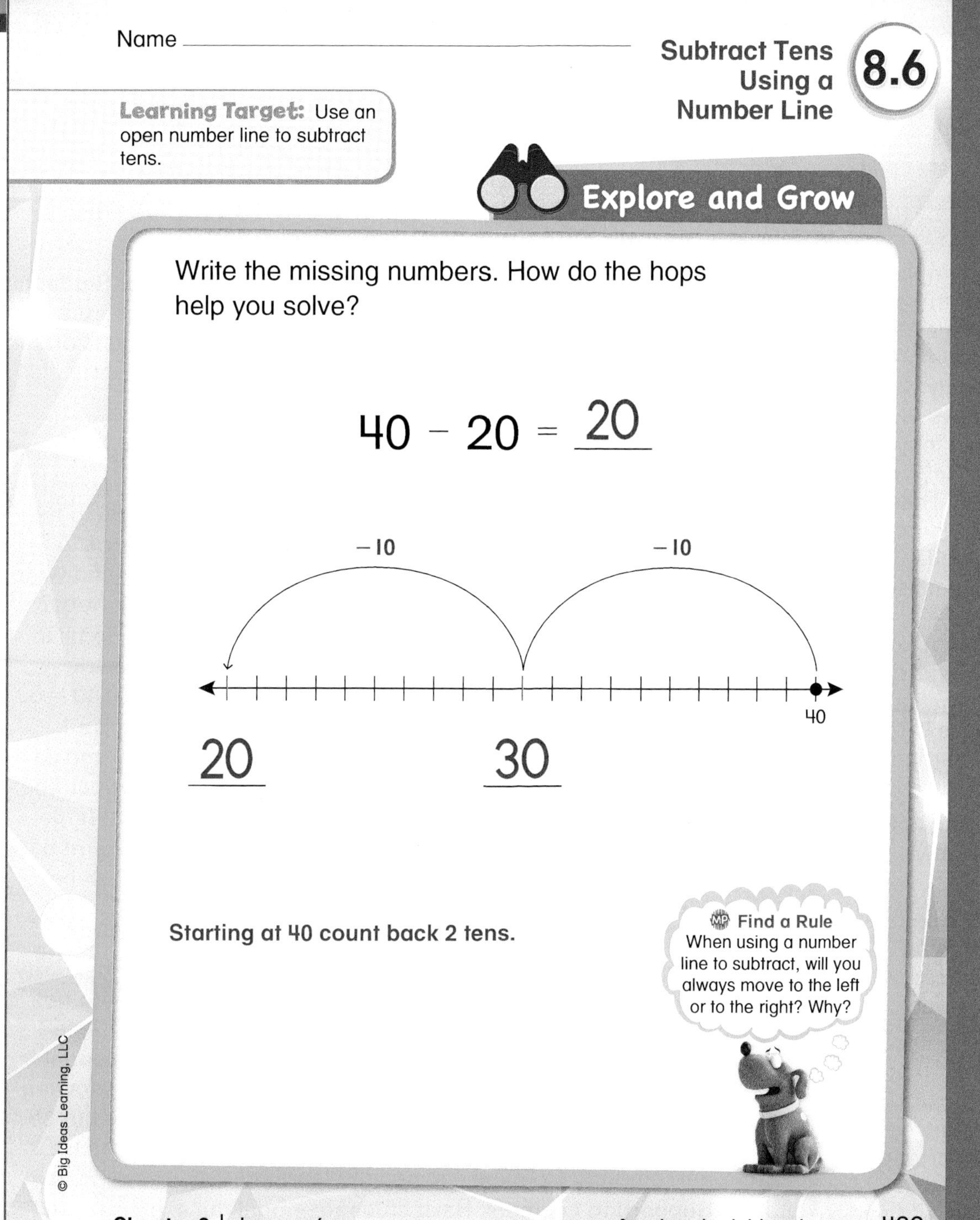

Name
Subtract Tens Using a Number Line
8.6
Learning Target: Use an open number line to subtract tens.
Explore and Grow
Write the missing numbers. How do the hops help you solve?
40 - 20 = 20
-10
-10
40
20
30
Starting at 40 count back 2 tens.
Find a Rule
When using a number line to subtract, will you always move to the left or to the right? Why?
© Big Ideas Learning, LLC
Chapter 8 | Lesson 6
four hundred thirty-three
433

Explore and Grow

- "We are subtracting 40 − 20. Point to the 40 and tell your partner why it is there."
- "Subtraction is opposite of addition, so we go from right to left. Tell what number is on the number line after the first hop. How do you know?" Students write in 30.
- "When we went from 40 to 30, what number was subtracted? Write a small −10 on top of the first hop."
- Repeat this conversation for the second hop, and then write in the difference.
- ◉ "Tell your partners how the number line shows that 40 − 20 = 20."

ELL Support

Model the example. Point out that the digit in the tens place of the second number tells them how many hops they must make on the line. Since they are subtracting, they will hop to the left. Then have students practice verbal language in pairs using Exercises 1 and 2. Have one student ask another, "How many hops did you move? What is your difference?" Then have them alternate roles for other exercises.

Beginner students may answer only with numbers.

Intermediate students may answer using simple sentences, such as, "I moved three hops."

Advanced students may answer using complex sentences and a detailed description of their process.

Laurie's Notes

Think and Grow

Getting Started

- We now move to subtracting on an open number line. Students will be given the starting point on the line, and will then draw hops to represent subtracting a ten. They fill in the values on the number line, and write the difference.

Teaching Notes

- ? **Model:** "Newton and Descartes are subtracting 90 − 40. Newton starts at 90 because it is the number from which we subtract. Notice that Newton draws a big hop on the number line to the left to show he subtracted 10. Draw Newton's first hop of 10, and write −10 above it. Now draw 3 more hops of ten and write −10 above each. How does Newton know to draw four hops?"
- **Model:** "Descartes knows that 40 is the same as 4 tens. To fill in the numbers on the number line, start at 90 and count back by tens. Fill in 80, 70, 60, and 50. So now we know that 90 − 40 = 50."
- Have students anticipate how they will complete Exercise 1. Have them tell their partners how many tens are in 50, and as a result, how many hops back they will show on the number line. Have students draw the hops and label −10 above each hop.
- Once the hops are drawn and labeled, have students count back by tens to fill in the numbers on the number line for each hop. Finally, they can fill in the difference.
- Watch as students complete Exercise 2. Identify areas of difficulty. It is not a concern if students are still having dexterity problems with drawing the hops. However, if students do not understand a hop as a representation of ten, or are not able to label the number line based on hops, this shows potential misconceptions and needs to be addressed. Students showing a lack of understanding or possible misconceptions should be grouped to work through Apply and Grow: Practice Exercise 3 and possibly Exercise 4 to solidify learning.
- **Supporting Learners:** Have students model the exercise with base ten blocks. They draw a large hop for each rod subtracted. They can count back by tens with each rod removed to label the number line.
- **Extension:** Give students a starting point and an ending point for the number line. Students determine how many hops are needed (missing change) to reach the difference, and then write the equation.

Think and Grow

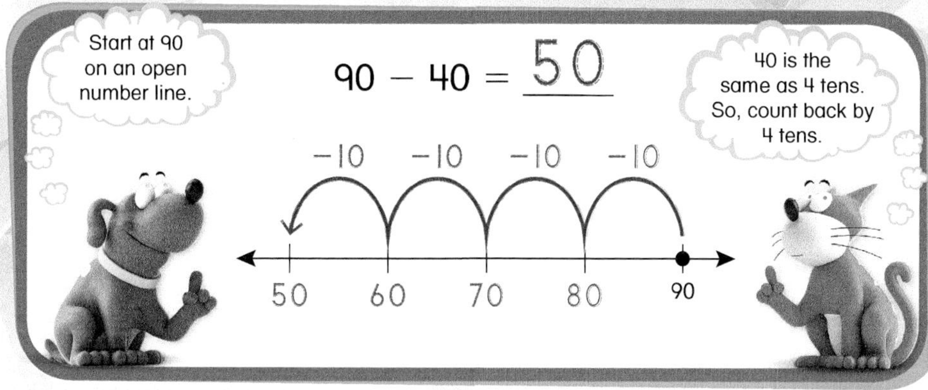

Show and Grow *I can do it!*

1. 80 − 50 = 30

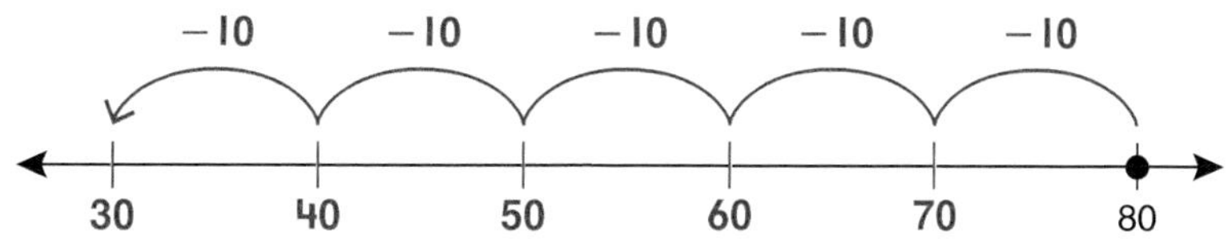

2. 70 − 30 = 40

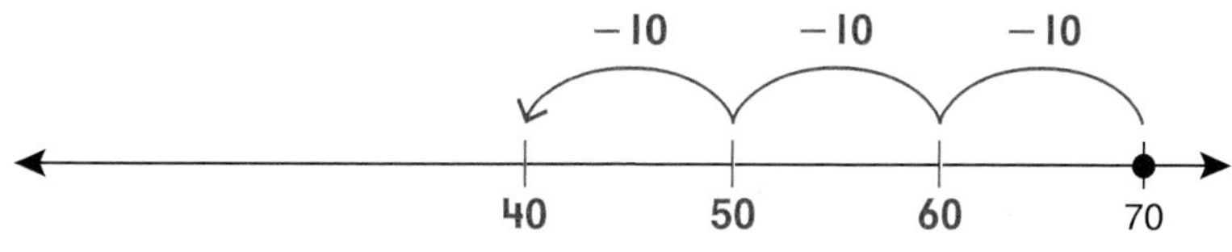

Scaffold instruction to support all students in their learning. Learning is individualized and you may want to group students differently as they move in and out of these levels with each skill and concept. Student self-assessment and feedback help guide your instructional decisions about how and when to layer support for all students to become proficient learners.

Meeting the needs of all learners.

Laurie's Notes

Apply and Grow: Practice

SCAFFOLDING INSTRUCTION

Students subtract on open number lines, including labeling the minuend as the starting point on the number line. Watch to see that students place the minuend at the far right of the number line as this will not be their habit.

EMERGING students can add subtract tens from previous work, but the open number line may still cause confusion, especially moving from right to left.

- **Exercise 3:** This exercise is the same as 1 and 2, and can be used for re-teaching.
- **Exercises 4–6:** These number lines do not provide the starting point. Watch to see if students place the start value at the end (far right) of the number line, or if they place it elsewhere. This could be a misconception about the number line or subtraction.
- **Exercise 7:** Students may need to look at prior models to determine where the minuend (start), subtrahend (change) and difference can be found on the number line. Students may write 40 − 80 or some other strange combination, pulling the numbers from the number line at random. Remind students that they want to find how many tens need to be subtracted from the greatest number to get to the end. Ask them what the −10 on each hop represents.

PROFICIENT students can show the subtraction on the open number line and explain how each hop is subtracting one group of ten.

- **Exercises 4–6:** Students may confuse how to start the work on the number line. Watch to see if students' fine motor skills are a source of difficulty in solving problems. Students may understand this process but may not be able to draw the hops evenly or well. Encourage students that practice will make the drawing easier.
- **Exercise 7:** Students should be able to write the correct equation. Have them explain why 40 is not used when writing the equation.

Additional Support

- Encourage students to draw quick sketches or use base ten blocks to reinforce groups of ten, following yesterday's lesson.

Extension: Adding Rigor

- Students use an open number line to subtract a decade to any two-digit number. This could lead to 37 − 50 however, so monitor it closely.

Name ___

Apply and Grow: Practice

3. 60 − 20 = 40

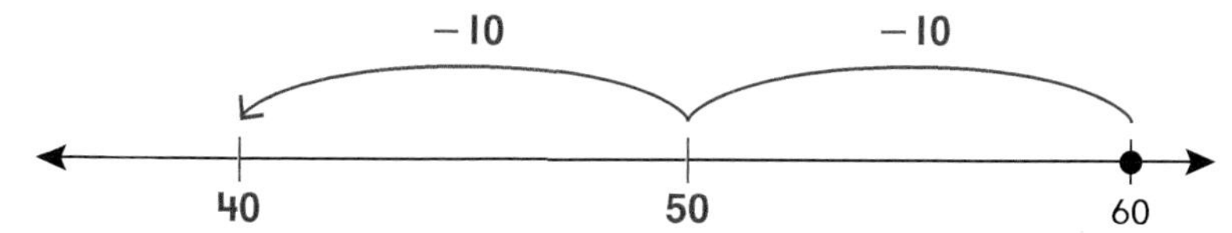

4. 40 − 30 = 10

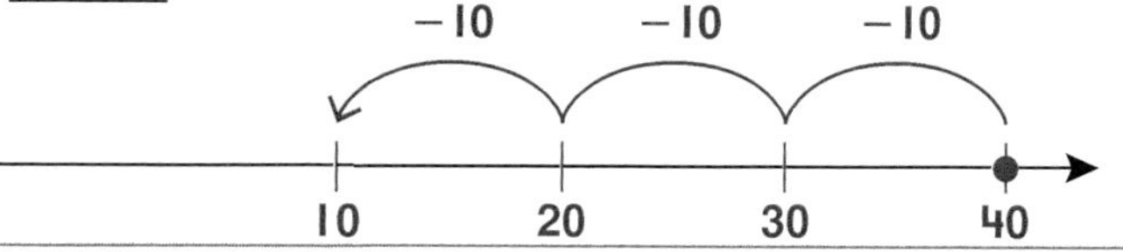

5. 90 − 40 = 50

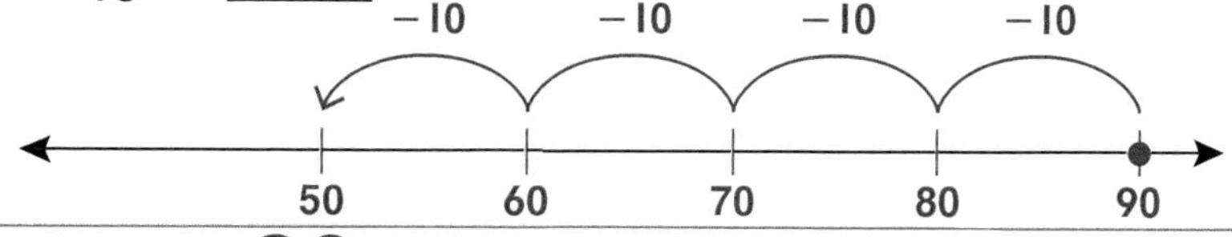

6. 90 − 70 = 20

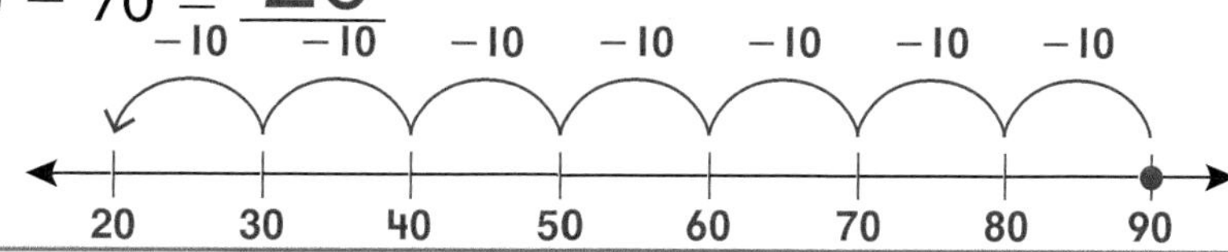

7. **Structure** Write the equation that matches the number line.

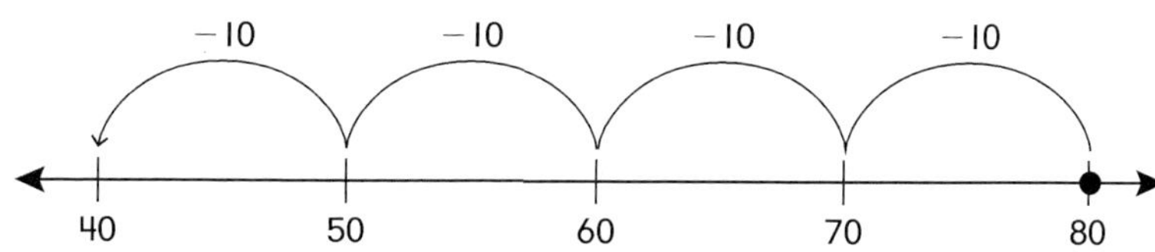

80 − 40 = 40

ELL Support

Check for understanding of Lesson 8.6. Read the example aloud as students follow along. Clarify any unknown vocabulary. Allow time to complete the exercise. Ask the following questions and have students display answers on a whiteboard or with a thumbs up or down signal to answer yes/no questions.

1. To subtract golf balls, where do you begin on the number line?
2. How many hops do you move?
3. How many golf balls are left?
4. Do you have more golf balls than your friend?
5. To subtract batteries, where do you begin on the number line?
6. How many hops do you move?
7. How many batteries are left?
8. Does Pack A have more batteries than Pack B?

Laurie's Notes

Think and Grow: Modeling Real Life

The application stories today involve two steps to solve. Students will also need to make a comparison of the difference and another number in the story. A number line is provided to subtract the numbers in the story, and it can also be used to compare. These applications follow Lesson 8.4's applications with the exception of subtraction.

? Discuss the story. "How can I find out how many golf balls you have left? You have 80 and hit 60 of them. Let's show $80 - 60$ on the number line."

- "Your friend has 28 golf balls left. Where on the number line is 28? Show 8 little lines for each number after 20 to show 28. Based on the number line, which number is greater, 20 or 28? What is the symbol to use? Fill in $28 > 20$." Note that $20 < 28$ is also correct, but might be confusing for students to answer the question based on who has more golf balls.
- Remind students that they did not have to use the number line to compare the numbers. They can also look at the tens digit, which in this case are both 2, and then look at the ones digit to compare. Any students who are still confused about comparing numbers could model with base ten blocks.
- Introduce Exercise 8. Have students clarify their thinking about which numbers are subtracted, and which numbers should be compared to answer the question. Once you talk through the process with students, let them work on the problem independently.

◉ "Use your thumb signals to show how you are doing with drawing the starting point on an open number line? How are you doing with drawing the correct number of hops moving down the number line and labelling them -10? How are you doing with showing the numbers on the number line? How are you doing with finding the difference?"

Closure

- Have students sit with a partner and share one whiteboard and one marker. Tell students that they will trade back and forth to complete the problem $60 - 20$.
  - Partner 1 draws an open number line and label the starting point.
  - Partner 2 draws hops and label -10.
  - Partner 1 writes the numbers on the number line.
  - Partner 2 writes the equation ($60 - 20 = 40$).

Think and Grow: Modeling Real Life

You have a bucket of 80 golf balls. You hit 60 of them. Your friend has 28 golf balls left. Who has more golf balls left?

Model:

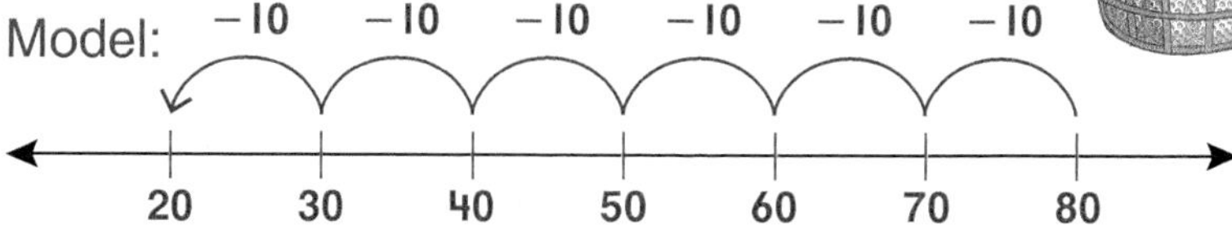

20 30 40 50 60 70 80

Subtraction equation: 80 − 60 = 20

Compare: 20 < 28

Who has more golf balls left? You (Friend)

Show and Grow *I can think deeper!*

8. Pack A has 50 batteries. 40 of them have been used. Pack B has 15 batteries. Which pack has more batteries left?

Model:

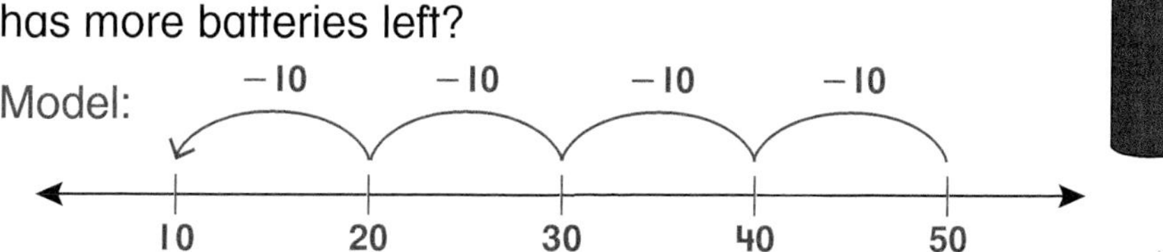

10 20 30 40 50

Subtraction equation: 50 − 40 = 10

Compare: 10 < 15

Which pack has more batteries left? Pack A (Pack B)

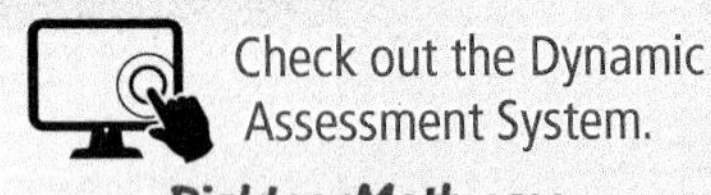
Check out the Dynamic Assessment System.
BigIdeasMath.com

Scaffold assignments to support all students in their learning progression. Revisit with spaced practice to move every student toward proficiency.

Connect and Extend Learning

Practice Notes

- **Exercise 6:** Preview the question with students. Ask them to identify which words signal that it is a subtraction problem. Then ask students to explain what steps they need to take to answer the question.

Prior Skills

- **Exercises 7 and 8:** Grade 1, Using Addition to Subtract within 20

Cross-Curricular Connections

Physical Education

- Use 3 partially-filled water bottles as bowling pins. Students start with a score of 90 and roll a soft small ball towards the pins to knock down as many as possible. Each pin that is knocked down subtracts 10 from the students' score. Have students use a floor number line to hop backwards to show the change in their score. Students take turns and get 3 attempts to knock down the pins. For example, if a student knocks down 2 pins on the first roll, 1 on the second roll, and 3 on the third roll, then they would show $90 - 20 = 70$, $70 - 10 = 60$, and $60 - 30 = 30$. Tell students the goal is to get as close to zero as possible.

Name ______________________

Learning Target: Use an open number line to subtract tens.

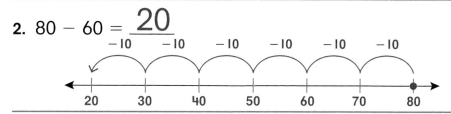

$70 - 40 = \underline{30}$

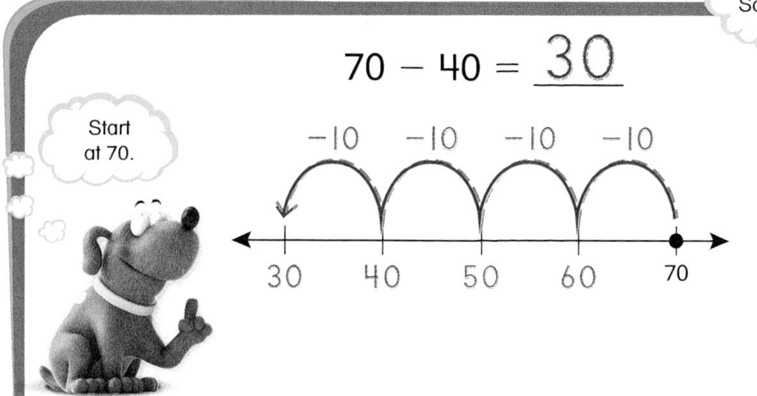

1. $50 - 30 = \underline{20}$

−10 −10 −10

20 30 40 50

2. $80 - 60 = \underline{20}$

−10 −10 −10 −10 −10 −10

20 30 40 50 60 70 80

3. $90 - 20 = \underline{70}$

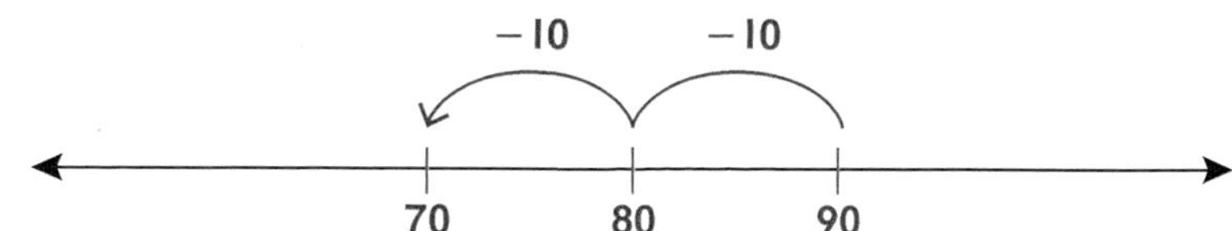

−10 −10

70 80 90

Connect and Extend Learning

Extend Student Learning

Interpersonal

- Assign each student a decade number from 10 to 90. Have students hold a piece of paper in front of themselves with their number written on it. Some numbers will be repeated. Call two students up to the front and have them show their numbers to the class. Say to the class, "We want to write a subtraction sentence with these numbers. Who has a number that will complete the sentence?" Volunteers write the sentence using the two given numbers and their number. For example, if you call on two students with numbers 50 and 30, a student with 20 can write $50 - 30 = 20$, or a student with 80 can write $80 - 50 = 30$. Repeat with different pairs of students.

Lesson Resources	
Surface Level	**Deep Level**
Resources by Chapter • Extra Practice • Reteach Differentiating the Lesson Skills Review Handbook Skills Trainer	Resources by Chapter • Enrichment and Extension Graphic Organizers Dynamic Assessment System • Lesson Practice

4. **Structure** Write the equation that matches the number line.

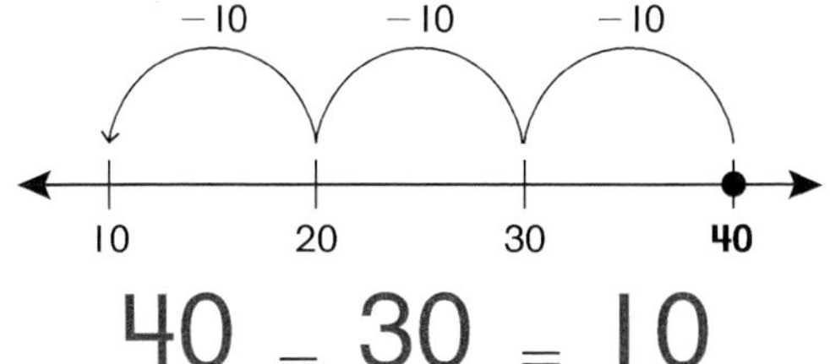

40 − 30 = 10

5. **Choose Tools** Do you prefer to use models or a number line to subtract tens? Explain.

Check students' work.

6. **Modeling Real Life** You have 80 raffle tickets and give away 30 of them. Your friend has 47 raffle tickets. Who has more raffle tickets?

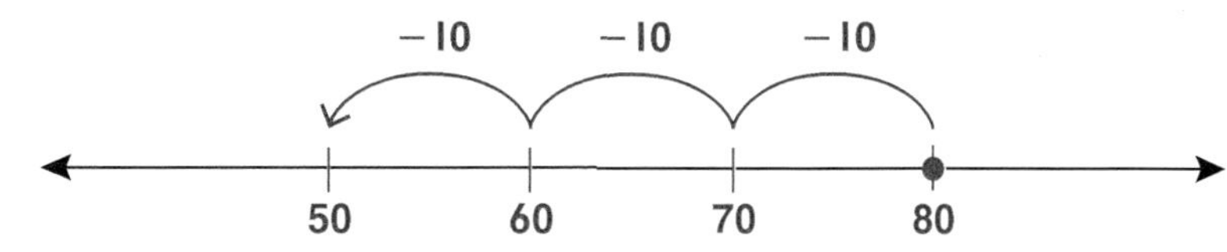

80 − 30 = 50   50 > 47

Who has more raffle tickets?  Friend

Review & Refresh

7. 13 − 8 = ?

Think 8 + 5 = 13.

So, 13 − 8 = 5.

8. 15 − 7 = ?

Think 7 + 8 = 15.

So, 15 − 7 = 8.

Check out the
Dynamic Classroom.
BigIdeasMath.com

Laurie's Notes

Learning Target

Use addition to subtract tens.

Success Criteria

- Write an addition equation with a missing addend.
- Count on to find the missing addend.
- Use the missing addend to write the difference.

COMMON CORE

STATE STANDARDS
1.OA.B.4, 1.NBT.B.2c, 1.NBT.C.4, 1.NBT.C.6

Preparing to Teach

We continue our work with adding and subtracting decade numbers. In today's lesson we will revisit the strategy for subtraction introduced in Lesson 2.9, add to subtract. The tools we will use are the 120 Chart and open number line.

Materials

- 120 Chart*
- whiteboards

**Found in the Instructional Resources*

Warm-Up

Practice opportunities for the following are available in the Resources by Chapter or at *BigIdeasMath.com*.

- Daily skills
- Vocabulary
- Prerequisite skills

Dig In (Circle Time)

Dig In time will begin by recalling the *think addition to subtract* strategy. We will practice moving from a subtraction equation to a missing addend equation. We will see how both subtraction and missing addend can be solved using a 120 Chart and open number line.

- "We have used a lot of strategies to subtract this year. Name as many as you can. All of these strategies can be used to subtract any numbers, including the decade numbers with which we have been working."
- ◉ "Today we are going to use the *add to subtract* strategy. Let's review. If I want to subtract 19 − 15, I can think, 'what do I need to add to 15 to reach 19?'" Write on chart paper: 19 − 15 = _____ and 15 + ____ = 19.
- Have students tell why the answer to both equations are 4. Have students share their strategies for finding 4. Check to see if students remember and can use the strategy before moving forward.
- "Let's try subtracting 60 − 40. Tell your partner what the addition equation should be."
- **MP5 Use Appropriate Tools Strategically:** Explain that we can still use the 120 Chart as we have been doing to add and subtract decade numbers. Highlight 60 and 40 on the chart. Show how you can count back by tens from 60 to 40, but also *count on* by tens to 60.

1	2	3	4	5	6	7	8	9	10
11	2	13	14	15	16	17	18	19	20
21	22	23	24	25	26	27	28	29	30
31	32	33	34	35	36	37	38	39	40
41	42	43	44	45	46	47	48	49	50
51	52	53	54	55	56	57	58	59	60
61	62	63	64	65	66	67	68	69	70
71	72	73	74	75	76	77	78	79	80
81	82	83	84	85	86	87	88	89	90
91	92	93	94	95	96	97	98	99	100

−10 −10 +10 +10

- Next, use an open number line. Show the beginning at 40, and then hop and count on by tens to 60. Remind students that 2 hops of ten is adding 20.
- ◉ Give additional problems. All students write the missing addend equation. One partner draws a part of the hundred chart, and the other draws an open number line. Switch roles.
- ◉ "Today we will subtract groups of tens by thinking addition. It is not really new – we know the strategy and have used the tools!"

ELL Support

Explain that the operations of addition and subtraction are opposites. To explain the actions of doing each operation, you use the action words (verbs) *add* and *subtract*. These are opposite actions. To describe the operations, you use the names (nouns) *addition* and *subtraction*, which are also opposites.

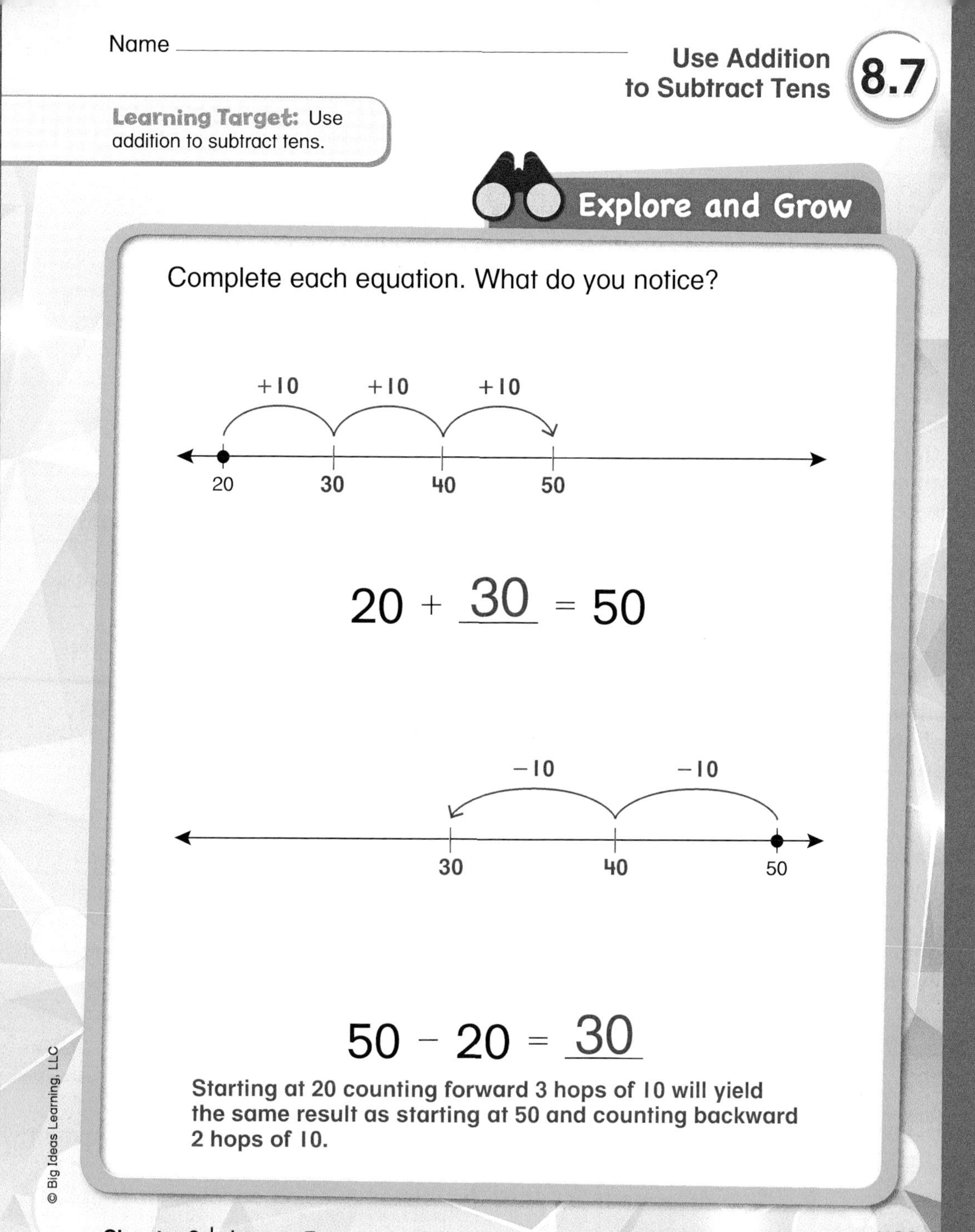

Name
Use Addition to Subtract Tens
8.7
Learning Target: Use addition to subtract tens.
Explore and Grow
Complete each equation. What do you notice?
+10
+10
+10
20
30
40
50
20 + 30 = 50
−10
−10
30
40
50
50 − 20 = 30
Starting at 20 counting forward 3 hops of 10 will yield the same result as starting at 50 and counting backward 2 hops of 10.
© Big Ideas Learning, LLC
Chapter 8 | Lesson 7
four hundred thirty-nine
439

Explore and Grow

- Have students solve the two equations using the open number lines. This should be review from previous lessons. Watch as students complete the exercise as a formative assessment. Which students need support in using the number lines?
- Discuss what students notice from the exercise. same answer, same number of hops, opposite directions
- Use student responses to show that you can use addition to subtract. Ask if students think using addition is easier than subtraction. That is why we use the strategy.

◉ "Tell your partners how to use *think addition to subtract* strategy."

ELL Support

Explain that when adding to subtract, you plot two numbers on the number line. Then you count how many hops it takes to move between the two numbers. The number of hops tells you how many tens are needed. Model the example. Have students practice verbal language in pairs using Exercises 1 and 2. Have one student ask another, "What two numbers do you plot? How many spaces do you move? What is the difference?" Then have them alternate roles for other exercises.

Beginner students may answer only with numbers.

Intermediate students may answer using simple sentences, such as, "I plotted 80 and 50."

Advanced students may answer using complex sentences and a detailed description of their process.

Laurie's Notes

Think and Grow

Getting Started

- Students are supported in using the *add to subtract* strategy. They are given the missing addend equation and the starting point on the number line. They fill in the values on the number line and in the equations as in previous lessons.

Teaching Notes

- ? **Model:** "Newton and Descartes are subtracting 80 − 50. Newton says to start at 50. What must Newton be thinking to start at 50? Notice the equation below the number line. Tell your partner how the equation will solve 80 − 50."
- **Model:** "Descartes says to count by tens to get to 80. Decide with your partner why he will stop at 80."
- **Model:** "Draw in the hops and count by tens with me as we count on from 50 to 80."
- **MP6 Attend to Precision:** Have students tell their partners when they will know to stop drawing hops for Exercise 1. Have students draw the hops and label +10 above each hop, and the numbers along the number line.
- Students fill in the equations based on the number line.
- Watch as students complete Exercise 2. Identify areas of difficulty. Students should be more able to draw and label hops on the number line now. Students showing a lack of understanding or possible misconceptions should be grouped to work through Apply and Grow: Practice Exercise 3 and possibly Exercise 4 to solidify learning.
- **Supporting Learners:** Have students refer to the hundred chart and draw hops down the column. They transfer these hops to the number line.
- **Extension:** Play "Add to Subtract" with a partner. One student writes a subtraction problem (without the difference), and the other partner writes the related missing addend equation.

Think and Grow

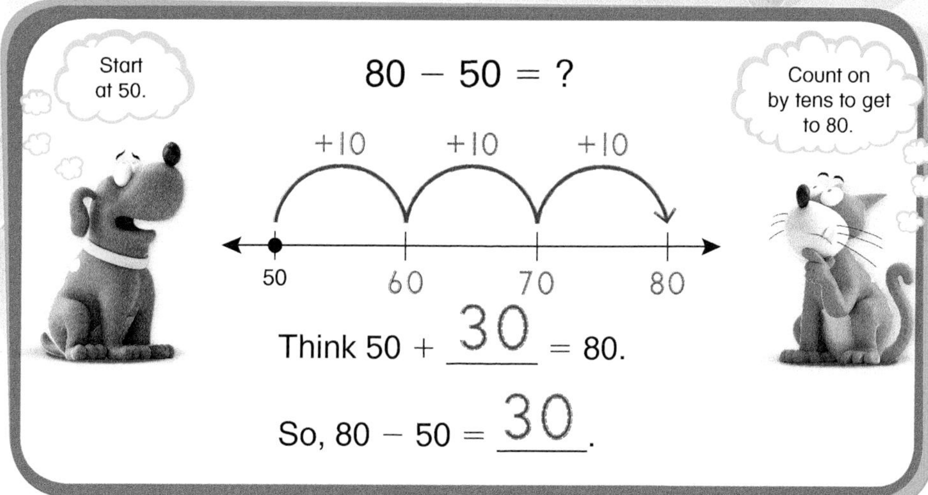

Think 50 + 30 = 80.

So, 80 − 50 = 30.

Show and Grow *I can do it!*

1. 90 − 70 = ?

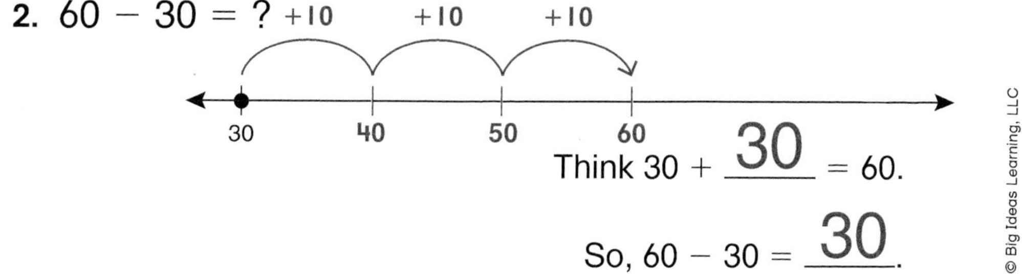

Think 70 + 20 = 90.

So, 90 − 70 = 20.

2. 60 − 30 = ?

+10 +10 +10

30 40 50 60

Think 30 + 30 = 60.

So, 60 − 30 = 30.

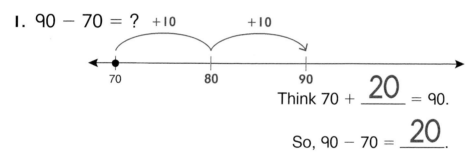

Scaffold instruction to support all students in their learning. Learning is individualized and you may want to group students differently as they move in and out of these levels with each skill and concept. Student self-assessment and feedback help guide your instructional decisions about how and when to layer support for all students to become proficient learners.

Meeting the needs of all learners.

Laurie's Notes

Apply and Grow: Practice

SCAFFOLDING INSTRUCTION

Students continue to add on an open number line with the related missing addend equations provided. Watch to see that students are using the number line to add, and not subtract, to practice the strategy. Let students who show subtraction know that is correct, but ask what would happen if they reversed the direction of the hops.

EMERGING students may not be secure in using the open number line to for solving equations. They may confuse the direction of hops, left-to-right or right-to-left based on addition or subtraction. Reinforce the operation and direction with students as well as the group of 10 for each hop.

- **Exercise 3:** This exercise is the same as 1 and 2, and can be used for re-teaching.
- **Exercises 4 and 5:** These number lines do not provide the starting point. Be sure that students notice the missing addend equations that are provided if they are unsure of where to start the number line. Based on the missing addend equation, have students say where they begin the number line, and at what number they should quit drawing hops. It will help students to count by tens from the beginning number to the ending number before drawing.
- **Exercise 6:** This exercise is to check if students understand the relationship of addition and subtraction. Can they explain why the equations go together, or are they matching the numbers within each equation (for example, 70, 60 and 10)?

PROFICIENT students understand the relationship of addition and subtraction, and can use the number lines to model both.

- **Exercises 4 and 5:** Errors are due to carelessness rather than misconceptions.
- **Exercise 6:** Students can explain the relationship of addition and subtraction when matching equations.

Additional Support

- Students count by tens before using the number line and use the hundred chart for reference.

Extension: Adding Rigor

- "Create a Fact Family Triangle for Exercises 1 and 2. Tell your partner how *think addition to subtract* is like thinking about a fact family."

Name ______

Apply and Grow: Practice

3. 50 − 30 = ?

+10 +10

30 40 50

Think 30 + 20 = 50. So, 50 − 30 = 20.

4. 70 − 20 = ?

+10 +10 +10 +10 +10

20 30 40 50 60 70

Think 20 + 50 = 70. So, 70 − 20 = 50.

5. 90 − 50 = ?

+10 +10 +10 +10

50 60 70 80 90

Think 50 + 40 = 90. So, 90 − 50 = 40.

6. MP **Structure** Match the related addition and subtraction equations.

60 + 10 = 70	70 − 50 = 20
50 + 10 = 60	70 − 60 = 10
50 + 20 = 70	60 − 50 = 10

Laurie's Notes

ELL Support

Check for understanding of Lesson 8.7. Read the example aloud as students follow along. Clarify any unknown vocabulary. Allow time to complete the exercise. Ask the following questions and have students display answers on a whiteboard or with a thumbs up or down signal to answer yes/no questions.

1. To find the number of toothbrushes, what two numbers do you plot on the number line?
2. How many hops do you move?
3. How many toothbrushes are left?
4. To find the number of bottles of glitter, what two numbers do you plot on the number line?
5. How many hops do you move?
6. How many bottles are left?

Think and Grow: Modeling Real Life

The application stories today continue subtracting decade numbers. A number line is provided to use as students wish – either with addition or subtraction. The missing addend equations are not provided. Students will write the subtraction equation that has been solved and fill in the final answer.

? Discuss the story. "How can I find out how many toothbrushes are left? I will need to subtract. What is the subtraction equation? Write it in below the number line."

- "We can use the number line to show subtraction, or we can use it to show the related addition. I prefer to add, so I need to think of where I will start and end. I want to know what should be added to 20 to get to 40. I will start at 20, and draw hops to get to 40. Count by tens with me." Have students count the total hops, and tell how many toothbrushes are left.
- Take time to have students offer other methods they could use to solve the application.
- Introduce Exercise 7. Have students tell their partner what the subtraction equation is, and write it on the sheet.
- Have students tell their partner what strategy they will use. When using addition, where will they start and end on the number line? Once you talk through the process with students, let them work on the exercise independently.
- **MP4 Model with Mathematics**: Once students have solved, ask them to determine whether their answer makes sense. Students should realize that their answer should be less than 70 bottles because 30 bottles have been used.

◉ "Use your thumb signals to show how you are doing using addition to subtract. How are you at knowing where to start on the number line and where to end when adding to subtract? How are you at telling a missing addend equation from subtraction?"

Closure

- "To see how each of us are doing, please show how to model addition on an open number line to solve 70 − 30 = ____. For extra challenge, see if you can write the missing addend equation."

Think and Grow: Modeling Real Life

A dentist has 40 toothbrushes. She gives away 20 of them. How many toothbrushes does she have left?

Model:

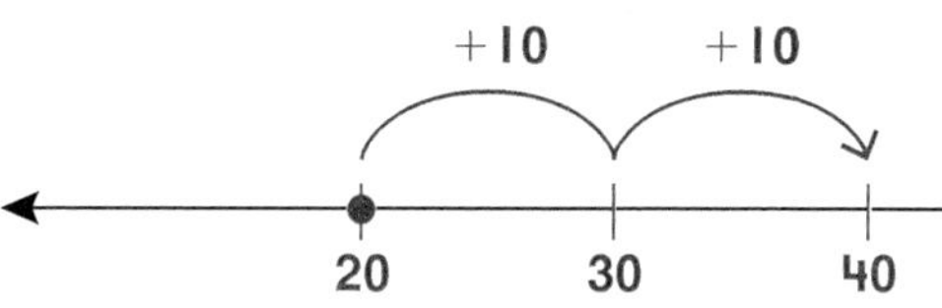

Subtraction equation:

40 − 20 = 20

20 toothbrushes

Show and Grow *I can think deeper!*

7. An art room has 70 bottles of glitter. 30 have been used. How many bottles are left?

Model:

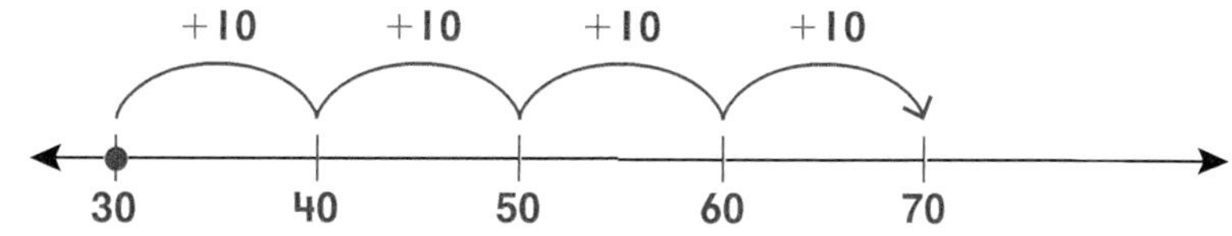

Subtraction equation:

70 − 30 = 40

40 bottles

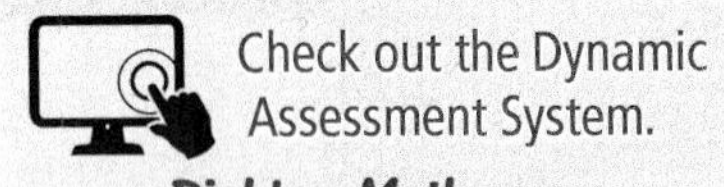
Check out the Dynamic Assessment System.
BigIdeasMath.com

Scaffold assignments to support all students in their learning progression. Revisit with spaced practice to move every student toward proficiency.

Connect and Extend Learning

Practice Notes

- **Exercise 3:** Students who need support may benefit from using base ten blocks to represent the equations.
- **Exercise 4:** Consider discussing what it means to deliver a newspaper. Many students may not be aware of the practice of receiving a daily newspaper at home.

Prior Skills

- **Exercise 6:** Grade 1, Comparing Numbers

Cross-Curricular Connections

Language Arts

- Have students use a large piece of construction paper and markers to make a poster about using addition to subtract tens. Ask students to pick a subtraction equation, using tens, and write it in large print at the top of their paper. For example: $50 - 30 =$ _____. Under the equation, have them draw a number line to show how to solve the problem. Under the number line, have them copy and complete the following sentences.

  Think _______ plus _______ equals _______.
  So _______ minus _______ equals _______.

  Next to the sentences, have them write each equation.

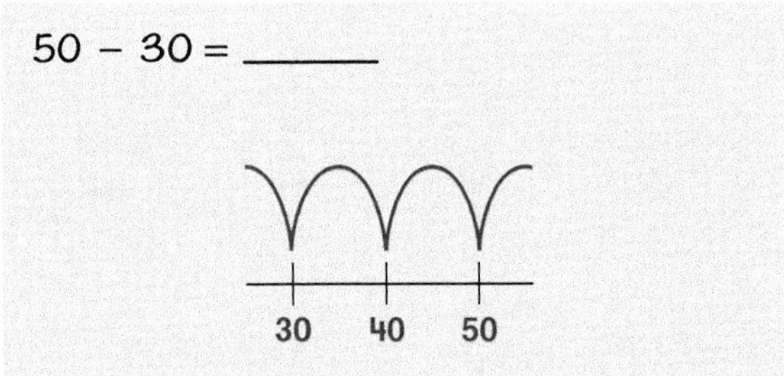
50 − 30 = ______
30
40
50
Think 30 plus 20 equals 50.
30 + 20 = 50
So 50 minus 30 equals 20.
50 − 30 = 20

Name ____________________

Practice 8.7

Learning Target: Use addition to subtract tens.

Start at 20. Count on by tens to get to 60.

60 − 20 = ?

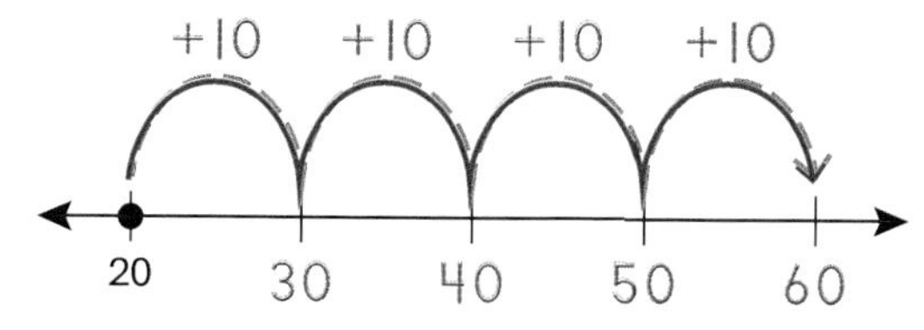

Think 20 + 40 = 60.

So, 60 − 20 = 40.

1. 70 − 40 = ?

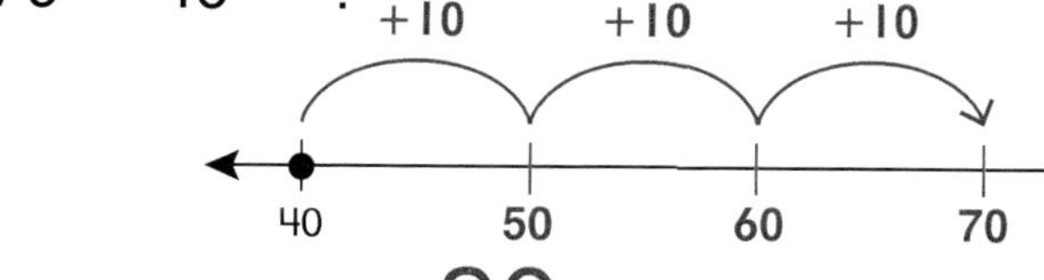

Think 40 + 30 = 70. So, 70 − 40 = 30.

2. 90 − 30 = ?

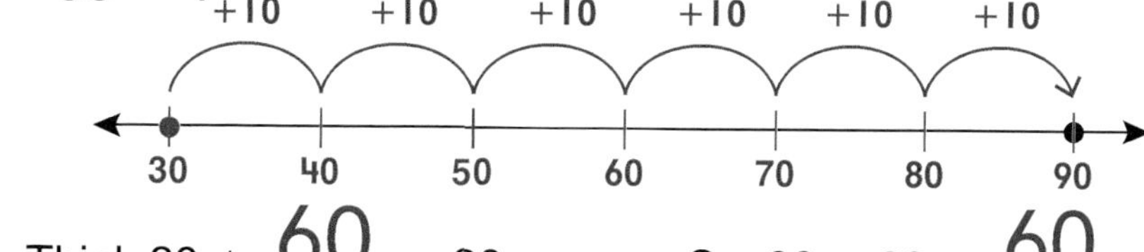

Think 30 + 60 = 90. So, 90 − 30 = 60.

Connect and Extend Learning

Extend Student Learning

Logical-Mathematical

- Have students write the decade numbers 10 through 90 in a 3×3 array in any order, using each number once. Students start at the top left and determine how much to add or subtract to produce the number to the right. Continue around the array until students reach the middle square last. Students can write their equations on a separate paper, or draw them on the same page using arrows. This activity can also be done outside and created with chalk. Students can hop from one square to another saying what operation and number they are adding or subtracting.

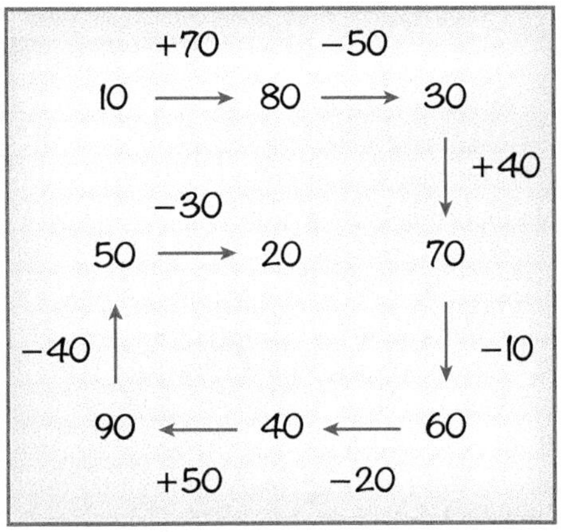

+70 −50
10 → 80 → 30
+40 (30 ↓ 70)
−30
50 → 20 70
−40 (90 ↑ 50) −10 (70 ↓ 60)
90 ← 40 ← 60
+50 −20

Lesson Resources	
Surface Level	**Deep Level**
Resources by Chapter • Extra Practice • Reteach Differentiating the Lesson Skills Review Handbook Skills Trainer	Resources by Chapter • Enrichment and Extension Graphic Organizers Dynamic Assessment System • Lesson Practice

3. **Structure** Match the related addition and subtraction equations.

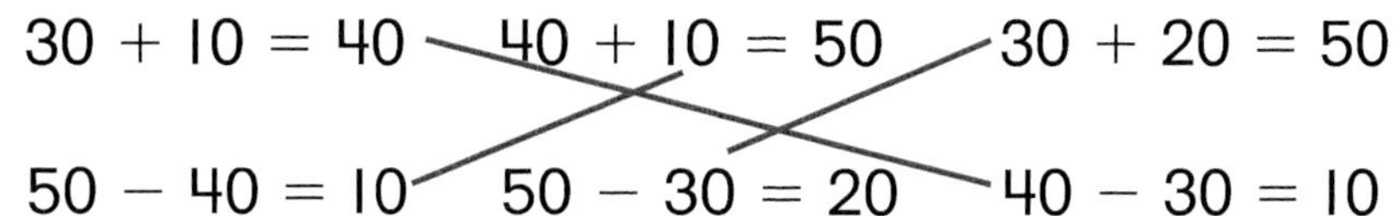

30 + 10 = 40 40 + 10 = 50 30 + 20 = 50

50 − 40 = 10 50 − 30 = 20 40 − 30 = 10

4. **Modeling Real Life** Newton has 80 newspapers to deliver. He delivers 50 of them. How many newspapers does he have left?

+10 +10 +10

50 60 70 80

80 − 50 = 30

30 newspapers

5. **DIG DEEPER!** Write the missing number.

60 −  = 10

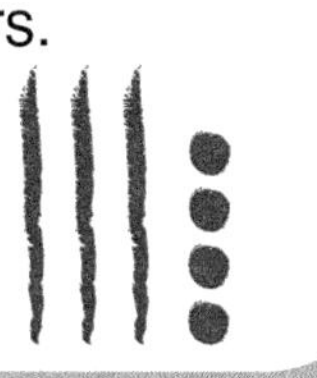 − 40 = 40

− = 30

Review & Refresh

6. Make quick sketches to compare the numbers.

43 is greater than / is less than 34.

Laurie's Notes

BigIdeasMath.com

STATE STANDARDS
1.NBT.B.2c, 1.NBT.C.4

Learning Target

Add tens to a number.

Success Criteria

- Use a model to count on by tens from a two-digit number.
- Write the sum.

Warm-Up

Practice opportunities for the following are available in the Resources by Chapter or at *BigIdeasMath.com.*

- Daily skills
- Vocabulary
- Prerequisite skills

ELL Support

Point out the word *notice* in the directions. Explain that *What do you notice?* is asking what you see or recognize when you add each multiple of ten. Explain that the word *notice* can be an action word (verb), as it is used here. It can also be used to name something (as a noun). A notice is a written announcement or public sign that provides information or a warning.

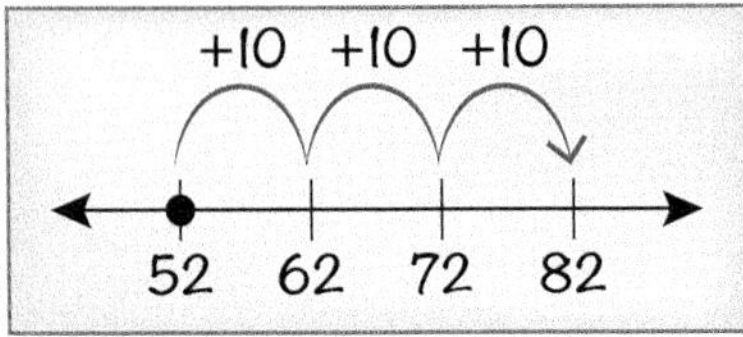

Preparing to Teach

Today we conclude the chapter by adding tens to any two-digit number. We use the same models in this lesson as previous in order to show that adding tens to any two-digit number is no different than adding decade numbers.

Materials

- whiteboards
- 120 Chart*
- base ten blocks

**Found in the Instructional Resources*

Dig In (Circle Time)

In Circle Time we review adding decade numbers with base ten blocks and the 120 Chart. Students will use these tools to add tens to any two-digit number. Continue to have one partner work on the 120 Chart and the other with base ten blocks, then switch tools for the next example.

- "Let's warm up by adding 30 + 20. Share with your partner how you used your tool to find the sum."
- "We have also added 10 to any number. Let's practice those. Tell your partner what is 10 more than 18. Tell what is 57 + 10." Have students share how they find the sums.
- "Today we will combine both of these ideas and add groups of ten to any two-digit number. Suppose instead of 30 + 20, I want to add 34 + 20. Whisper to your partner what you think the sum is."

? "If you have the base ten blocks, build 34. If you have the chart, find 34. How do we add 20 with the blocks? on the chart? What is the sum?"

1	2	3	4	5	6	7	8	9	10
11	2	13	14	15	16	17	18	19	20
21	22	23	24	25	26	27	28	29	30
31	32	33	34	35	36	37	38	39	40
41	42	43	44	45	46	47	48	49	50
51	52	53	54	55	56	57	58	59	60
61	62	63	64	65	66	67	68	69	70
71	72	73	74	75	76	77	78	79	80
81	82	83	84	85	86	87	88	89	90
91	92	93	94	95	96	97	98	99	100

- Have students trade tools and repeat with 46 + 30.

? **MP2 Reason Abstractly and Quantitatively:** "What pattern do you notice when adding tens to another two-digit number? How is this like adding groups of tens?"

- Have students add 52 + 30. Demonstrate how to use an open number line. Remind students that you can start and end a number line at any place. Begin the number line with 52. Have students tell you how many hops of 10 to take to add 30.

? **MP2 Reason Abstractly and Quantitatively:** "How is adding 52 + 30 on the open number line like what we have been doing? How is it different?"

- Repeat with 2 more examples using all three models.

◉ "Today we will add groups of tens to any two-digit number."

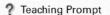

? Teaching Prompt ◉ Learning Target

Name ________________

Learning Target: Add tens to a number.

Explore and Grow

Find each sum. What do you notice?

1	2	3	4	5	6	7	8	9	10
11	12	13	14	15	16	17	18	19	20
21	22	23	24	25	26	27	28	29	30
31	32	33	34	35	36	37	38	39	40
41	42	43	44	45	46	47	48	49	50
51	52	53	54	55	56	57	58	59	60

Add the tens digit and keep the ones digit the same.

15 + 10 = 25 27 + 10 = 37

15 + 20 = 35 27 + 20 = 47

15 + 30 = 45 27 + 30 = 57

Explore and Grow

- Remind students of how the number chart has been used to add tens. So far they have only added decade numbers, and used the last column for the addition. Today, they will add tens in any column, based on the first addend.
- Have students find the sums. Observe if students are using the chart or if they can find sums without it.
- Discuss the patterns they notice.
- Have students tell their partners why the ones digit does not change. Tell the pattern of the tens digit in the sum. Explain why this is true using place value.

Laurie's Notes

ELL Support

Model the example. Have students practice verbal language in groups using Exercises 1 and 2. Lead groups to explore both models for completing the exercises as they discuss the following questions: "How do we draw groups of tens and ones? What is the sum? On a number line, what two numbers do we plot? How many spaces do we move?" Monitor discussion and expect students to perform according to their language proficiency level.

Beginner students may answer with short phrases, such as, "one ten and six ones."

Intermediate students may answer using sentences, such as, "Draw a group of one ten and six ones and another group of three tens."

Advanced students may answer using complex sentences and a detailed description of the process.

Think and Grow

Getting Started

- Students will continue to add using quick sketches and open number lines. Continue to have students explain the process of adding in terms of place value. Can students explain *why* the ones digit does not change, and *why* you can add the tens digits?

Teaching Notes

- **Model:** "Newton and Descartes are adding 16 + 30. Newton is using a quick sketch. Make a quick sketch of 16. Now sketch the 30 he adds."
- **Model:** "Notice that Newton circles all the ten rods. You can only add tens with tens and ones with ones. The tens are circled because those are what can be added together. Circle the tens. Now tell your partner what is the sum. Fill in 46."
- **Model:** "Descartes wants to use the open number line to add. He knows you can start a number line with any number. He starts with 16. Tell your partner how many hops he needs to take to add 30. Fill in the hops and +10 above each hop."
- Have students count by tens from 16 and fill in the number line.
- Discuss Exercise 1 with students. With what number should the open number line begin if students are using that method?
- Observe the method students are choosing to use. They may draw a quick sketch, draw an open number line, or even show the column of a number chart.
- Watch as students complete Exercise 2. Challenge students to try a different model from the one they used in Exercise 1 if they are able.

? **MP2 Reason Abstractly and Quantitatively:** "How do the different models all show adding tens? What is the same and what is different?"

- **Supporting Learners:** If students have difficulty with one model for adding, suggest a different model.
- **Supporting Learners:** Provide base ten blocks to manipulate instead of using a quick sketch. Be sure students have a hundred chart on which to draw.
- **Extension:** Have students solve similar equations in teams of two or three. Each student will use one of the three models to solve and then compare answers. They then rotate models.

Think and Grow

$16 + 30 =$ 46

Add the tens. Keep 6 for the ones digit.

One Way: Make a quick sketch.

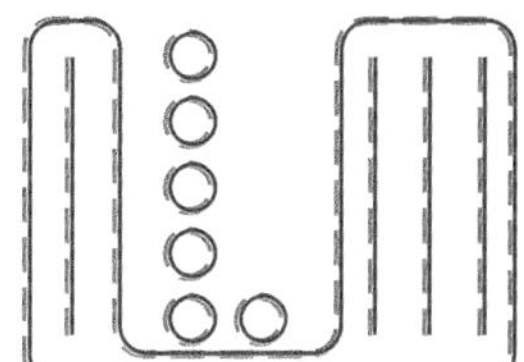

Another Way: Use an open number line.

Start at 16. Count on by 3 tens.

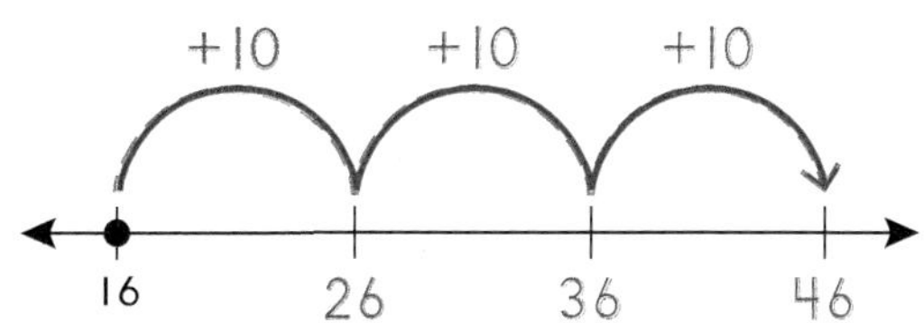

Show and Grow *I can do it!*

1. $23 + 50 =$ 73

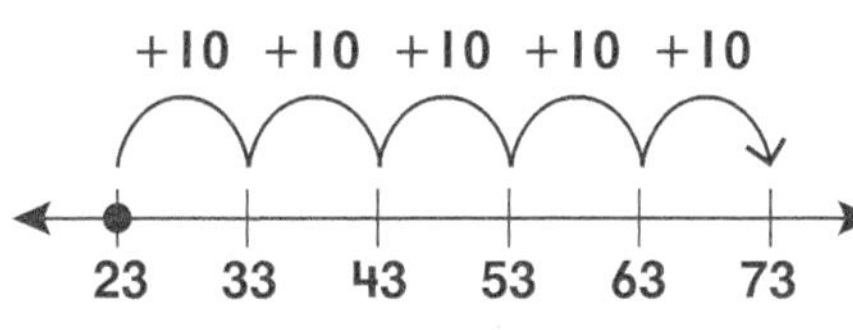

2. $6 + 70 =$ 76

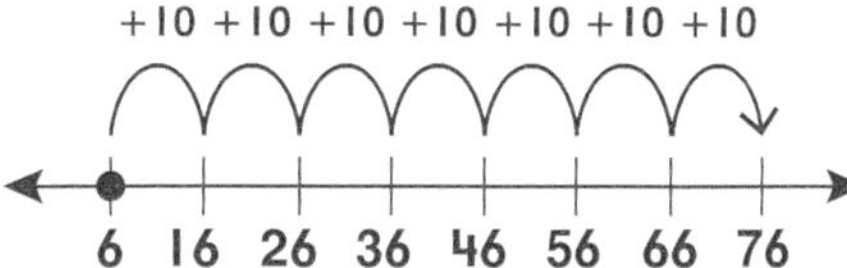

Scaffold instruction to support all students in their learning. Learning is individualized and you may want to group students differently as they move in and out of these levels with each skill and concept. Student self-assessment and feedback help guide your instructional decisions about how and when to layer support for all students to become proficient learners.

Meeting the needs of all learners.

Laurie's Notes

Apply and Grow: Practice

SCAFFOLDING INSTRUCTION

Students continue to practice adding tens to any other number. They may use any model, however encourage them to try different models.

EMERGING students model with base ten blocks, but may struggle with other representations. Concrete materials will help students reason about place value and adding tens.

- **Exercises 3–6:** Observe if students are struggling with the concept or a specific model. Suggest other models, or gather small groups of students to model different exercises. Try modeling Exercise 3, and have them try 4, etc.
- **Exercises 7 and 8:** Have students say what is different about these equations. Does it matter which side the sum is on? Remind students that these exercises are not any different from the others.
- **Exercise 9:** Students can build the equation with base ten blocks, and compare their model to Newton's quick sketch. They should explain in their own way that Newton grouped the tens together and added correctly. The ones do not change because no ones were added.

PROFICIENT students can add groups of ten to any number and explain their reasoning. They may be most comfortable with one model and should be encouraged to stretch and try others.

- **Exercises 3–6:** Students correctly show the addition of tens with no change in the ones.
- **Exercises 7 and 8:** Students may need to be reminded that equations can be written with the sum first as they have not seen this form of an equation recently. Ask them about other forms they remember (vertical).
- **Exercise 9:** Students explain the role of place value when adding in their own way to explain why Newton is correct. If they only say his model is correct, ask what the model shows. Push for them to reason about place value.

Additional Support

- Have students choose the model with which they are most comfortable and stay with that model until more comfortable.

Extension: Adding Rigor

- Students add any 2 two-digit numbers. They use any model to find the sum.

Name ______

Apply and Grow: Practice

3. 27 + 40 = 67

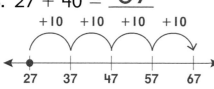

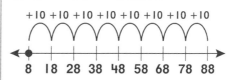

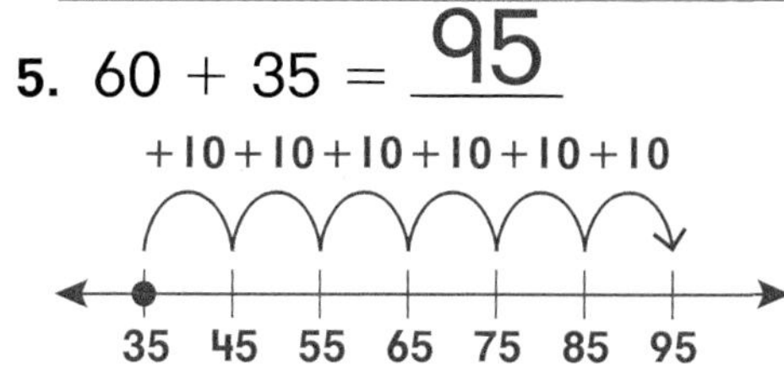

4. 8 + 80 = 88

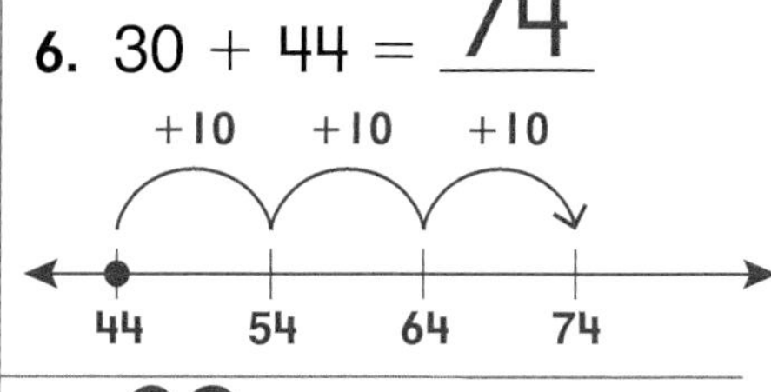

5. 60 + 35 = 95

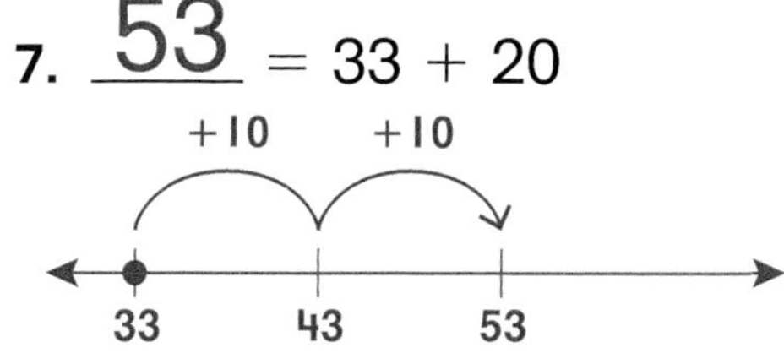

6. 30 + 44 = 74

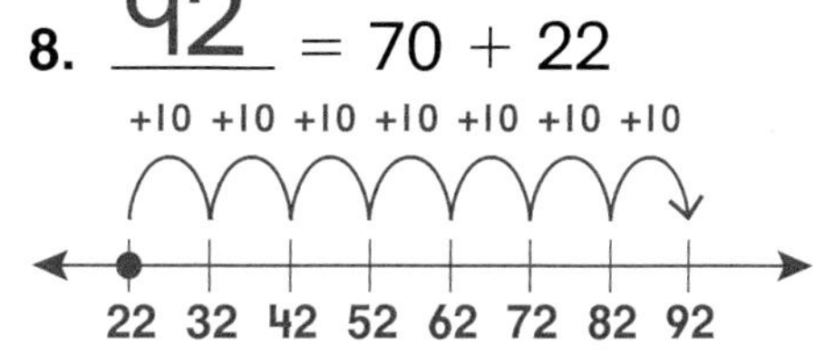

7. 53 = 33 + 20

+10 +10

33 43 53

8. 92 = 70 + 22

+10 +10 +10 +10 +10 +10 +10

22 32 42 52 62 72 82 92

9. MP YOU BE THE TEACHER Is Newton correct? Explain.

yes; Add the tens and keep 6 for the ones digit.

Laurie's Notes

ELL Support

Check for understanding of Lesson 8.8. Read the example aloud as students follow along. You may want to discuss snowballs with students who are unfamiliar with snow. Ask them to share their experiences if they have them. Allow time to complete the exercise. Ask the following questions and have students display answers on a whiteboard or with a thumbs up or down signal to answer yes/no questions.

1. How many birds do you count?
2. Do you count more birds than your friend?
3. How many snowballs does your friend make?
4. Do you make more snowballs than your friend?

Think and Grow: Modeling Real Life

The application stories today involve two steps to solve. Students will also need to make a comparison of the two numbers in the story. These are similar to the applications in Lesson 8.4.

- ? **Preview:** "When you are outside, do you ever try to count anything? What do you count?"
- Discuss the story. Have students tell partners how to determine how many birds you counted in all. Write the equation. Students can add 8 and 40 in any way.
- ? "If you count 48 birds and your friend counts 45 birds, who counted more? How do you know? Which is the correct symbol to use?" Finally, answer the question.
- As you discuss Exercise 10, students may wonder if the size of the snowball matters. Do not let them worry about the size of the snowball but how many snowballs get made.
- Students can talk to their partners to share which numbers they should add together, and how they are choosing to add.
- ⦿ "Today we will use fist to five to describe how you are doing in adding tens to any two-digit number. If you are totally confused, show your fist. If you are excellent, show five. You can be anywhere in between as well. How are you at adding tens to a two-digit number using base ten blocks? using a quick sketch? using a 120 Chart? using an open number line? not using any model?"

Closure

- Have students find a partner who likes to use a different model than they like, and sit back-to-back. Each student should have a whiteboard.
- Give partners an addition expression to solve, such as 28 + 60. Students use their favorite model or strategy to solve.
- When partners have had enough time to work, cue students to turn around and compare their answers. Are they the same? If not, can they find an error?
- ? "Suppose you are just adding the numbers and have no tools or models. How could you add 28 + 60 just based on the digits? Share ideas with your partners."

Think and Grow: Modeling Real Life

You count 8 birds on your way to school. You count 40 more on your way home. Your friend counts 45 birds in all. Who counts more birds?

Sample answer:

Model: [4 tens, 8 ones]

Addition equation: 40 + 8 = 48

Compare: 48 (>) 45

Who counts more birds? (You) Friend

Show and Grow *I can think deeper!*

10. You make 21 snowballs. Your friend makes 11 small snowballs and 20 large snowballs. Who makes more snowballs?

Sample answer:

Model: [3 tens, 1 one]

Addition equation: 11 + 20 = 31

Compare: 21 (<) 31

Who makes more snowballs? You (Friend)

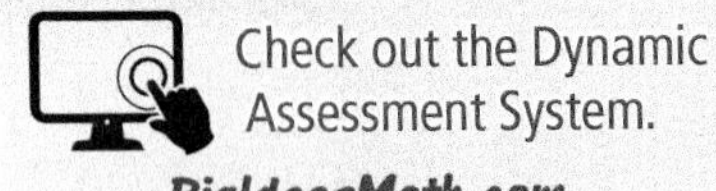
Check out the Dynamic Assessment System.
BigIdeasMath.com

Scaffold assignments to support all students in their learning progression. Revisit with spaced practice to move every student toward proficiency.

Connect and Extend Learning

Practice Notes

- Provide number lines or base ten blocks for support.

Prior Skills

- **Exercise 7:** Kindergarten, Describing Three-Dimensional Shapes

Cross-Curricular Connections

Physical Education

- Divide the class into equal groups, such as groups of 5. Line the groups up at a starting line a short distance away from the board. Across from each group, write a row of numbers on the board, one for each student in the group. Give one student in each group a marker or piece of chalk to write on the board. When you say "Go!" the first student from each group runs to the board, adds 10 to the first number in the row, writes the sum, runs back to their group, and hands the marker to the next student. Then the second student runs to the board, adds 20 to the second number in the row, writes the sum, runs back to their group, and hands the marker to the next student. The third, fourth, and fifth members of the group should repeat this adding 30, 40, and 50, respectively. The first team to finish all five sums wins.

Name ____________________

Practice 8.8

Learning Target: Add tens to a number.

12 + 20 = 32

Add the tens. Keep 2 for the ones digit.

One Way: Make a quick sketch.

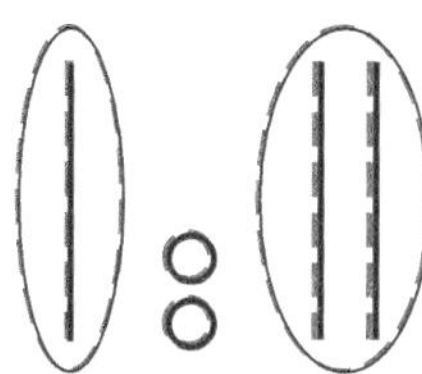

Another Way: Use an open number line.

Start at 12. Count on by 2 tens.

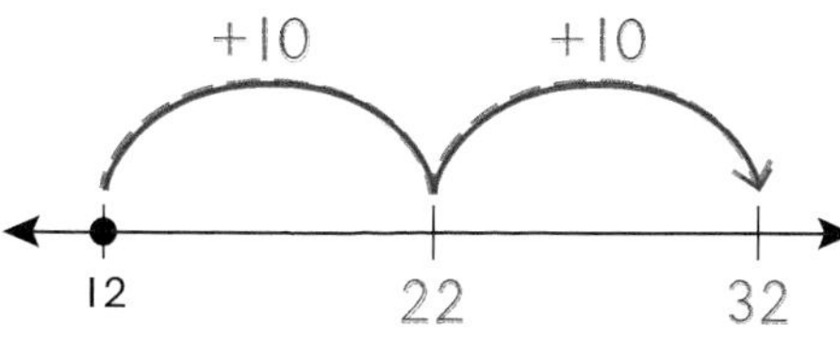

1. 19 + 40 = 59

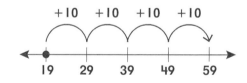

+10 +10 +10 +10

19 29 39 49 59

2. 60 + 23 = 83

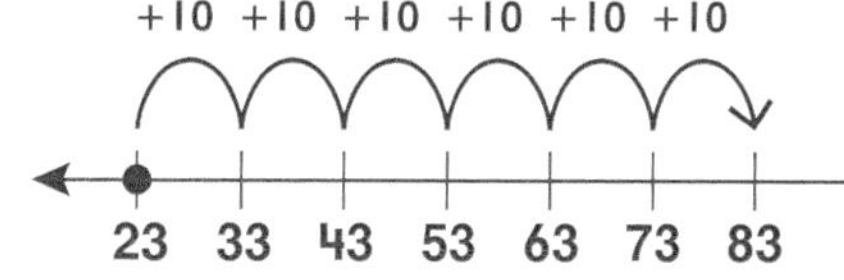

Connect and Extend Learning

Extend Student Learning

Intrapersonal

- Give each student a bowl of beads. Explain that they will play "Musical Beads." Play a song for a short period of time and have students count out beads one by one until the song stops. Have students write down the total number of beads they counted. Then, instruct the class to add 20. Have students write and solve the equation. Play multiple rounds, varying how long you play the music and the decade number students add.

Lesson Resources	
Surface Level	**Deep Level**
Resources by Chapter • Extra Practice • Reteach Differentiating the Lesson Skills Review Handbook Skills Trainer	Resources by Chapter • Enrichment and Extension Graphic Organizers Dynamic Assessment System • Lesson Practice

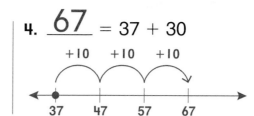

3. 95 = 5 + 90

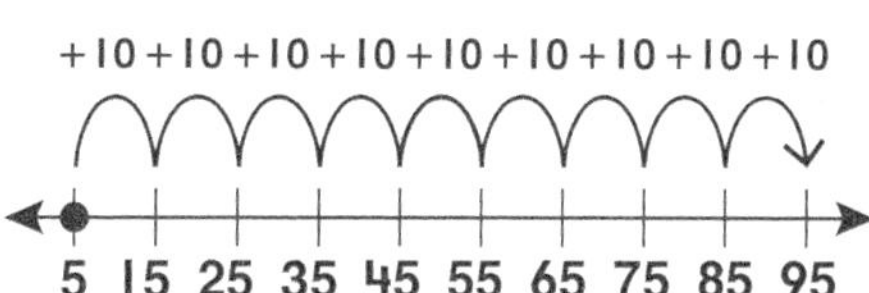

4. 67 = 37 + 30

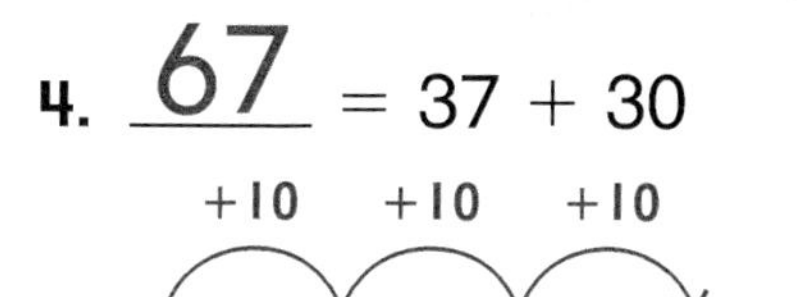

5. **Modeling Real Life** You have 24 glow sticks and buy 40 more. Your friend has 66 glow sticks. Who has more glow sticks?

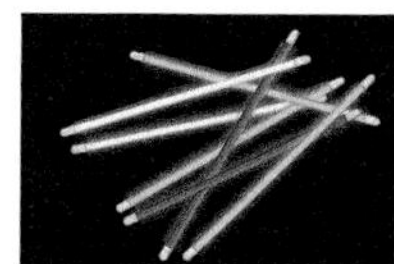

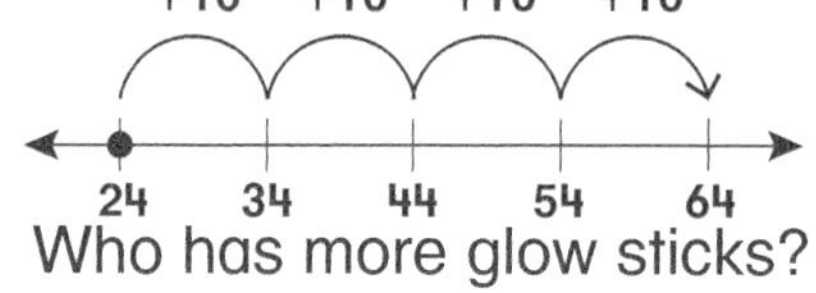

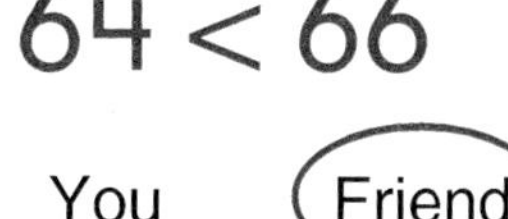

Who has more glow sticks? You (Friend)

6. **Modeling Real Life** You earn 54 points in a video game. Your friend earns some points. You and your friend have a total of 94 points. How many points does your friend earn?

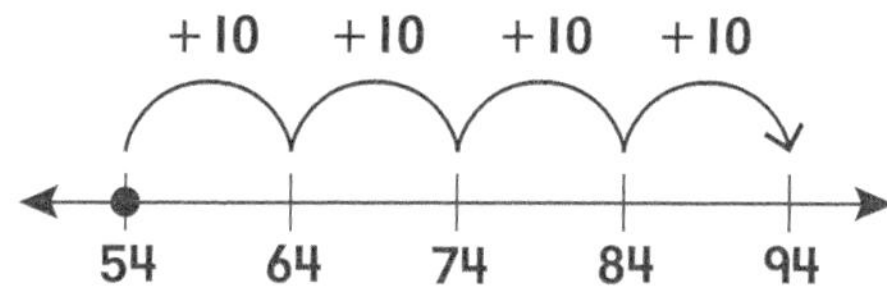

40 points

Review & Refresh

7. Circle the solid shapes that stack.

Laurie's Notes

Performance Task

In this task, students will add and subtract tens using spinning pinwheels and tops. Students learn about objects in motion in first grade science. In part (a) of Exercise 1, students may be able to use mental math to solve, but encourage them to write the equation. In parts (b) and (c), students can use addition or subtraction to solve. Use student responses to gauge their understanding about adding and subtracting tens.

- Decide ahead of time whether students will be working independently, in pairs, or in groups.
- Pause between direction lines for students to complete each step.
- Have students share their work and thinking with others. Discuss as a class.

Exercise	Answers and Notes	Points
1a	10 seconds	2
1b	70 seconds	3
1c	60 seconds	3
1d	Yellow	4
	Total	12

ELL Support

Have students practice verbal language by working in groups. Have Intermediate and Advanced students alternate reading sections aloud within their groups. Clarify any language that they do not understand. You may want to demonstrate spinning a top and a pinwheel if you have them available, or ask students to share experiences with each. Beginners will focus only on questions and answers. Circulate to monitor their language. Expect students to perform according to their proficiency level.

Beginner students may use single words, such as numbers.

Intermediate students may answer using phrases, such as, "ten seconds."

Advanced students may answer using sentences, such as, "The yellow top spins ten more seconds than the red pinwheel."

Name ______________________

Performance Task 8

1. The tables show the numbers of seconds 3 pinwheels and 3 tops spin.

Pinwheel	Seconds
Red	40
Yellow	90
Blue	60

Top	Seconds
Red	70
Yellow	50
Blue	36

a. How many more seconds does the yellow top spin than the red pinwheel?

$50 - 40 = 10$

10 seconds

b. The red pinwheel spins 30 fewer seconds than the red top. How long does the red top spin?

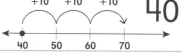

+10 +10 +10

40 50 60 70

$40 + 30 = 70$

70 seconds

c. The blue pinwheel and the blue top spin for 96 seconds in all. How long does the blue pinwheel spin?

$96 - 36 = 60$

60 seconds

d. Which pinwheel spins the longest?

Red  Blue

Check out the interactive version in the Game Library.
BigIdeasMath.com

Laurie's Notes

10 More or 10 Less

Materials

- 1 die per pair
- two-color counters

10 More or 10 Less allows students to mentally add 10 or subtract 10 from a number. Students will first identify a two-digit number by rolling a single die to find out how many tens the number is. Students will decide to add 10 more or subtract 10 from that number. They will cover their total with a counter on the board. The person to have the most counters on the board wins.

? "Can you tell me what 6 tens is?" 60 "How do you know?" I can picture it in my head; I can count out loud. "What is 10 more from that number?" 70 "I roll a 1. What is 1 ten?" 10 "What is 10 less than that number?" 0

- "Today you will be playing 10 More or 10 Less. You need to roll a die to see how many tens you have. Then you can decide to add ten to your number or subtract ten from your number. Cover your total on the game board. The player with the most counters on the board, wins!"
- Read the directions to students. Model how to roll a die and then decide to add ten or subtract ten from that number. Then show what to do if you cannot place a counter on the board.
- Partner students and distribute materials. Have students begin playing.
- While students play, look for students solving problems mentally. Allow students to use markers and whiteboards to make quick sketches to help them determine their numbers.
- **Supporting Learners:** Have a place value mat and base ten blocks available for students who need to build their numbers.

Closure

? "What equations can you write to help you play this game?"

10 More or 10 Less

To Play: Players take turns. On your turn, roll a die to see how many tens you have. Decide whether you want to add 10 to your number or subtract 10 from your number. Place a counter on your sum or difference. Once the board is covered, clear the board and play again.

Learning Target Correlation

Lesson	Learning Target	Exercises
8.1	Use mental math to add 10.	1–8
8.2	Use mental math to subtract 10.	9–14
8.3	Add tens.	15–17
8.4	Use an open number line to add tens.	18, 19
8.5	Subtract tens.	20–22
8.6	Use an open number line to subtract tens.	23, 24
8.7	Use addition to subtract tens.	25, 26
8.8	Add tens to a number.	27, 28

Name ______________________

Chapter 8 Practice

8.1 Mental Math: 10 More

Use mental math.

1. 58 + 10 = 68
2. 15 + 10 = 25
3. 29 + 10 = 39
4. 41 + 10 = 51
5. 10 + 7 = 17
6. 10 + 36 = 46
7. 84 + 10 = 94
8. 47 + 10 = 57

8.2 Mental Math: 10 Less

Use mental math.

9. 24 − 10 = 14
10. 78 − 10 = 68
11. 31 − 10 = 21
12. 95 − 10 = 85
13. 17 − 10 = 7
14. 53 − 10 = 43

Chapter Resources		
Surface Level	**Deep Level**	**Transfer Level**
Resources by Chapter • Extra Practice • Reteach Differentiating the Lesson Skills Review Handbook Skills Trainer Game Library Math Musicals	Resources by Chapter • Enrichment and Extension Graphic Organizers Game Library Math Musicals	Dynamic Assessment System • Chapter Test Assessment Book • Chapter Tests A and B

8.3 Add Tens

15. 60 + 20 = ?

6 tens + 2 tens = 8 tens

So, 60 + 20 = 80.

16. 30 + 50 = 80

17. 60 + 30 = 90

8.4 Add Tens Using a Number Line

18. 50 + 40 = 90

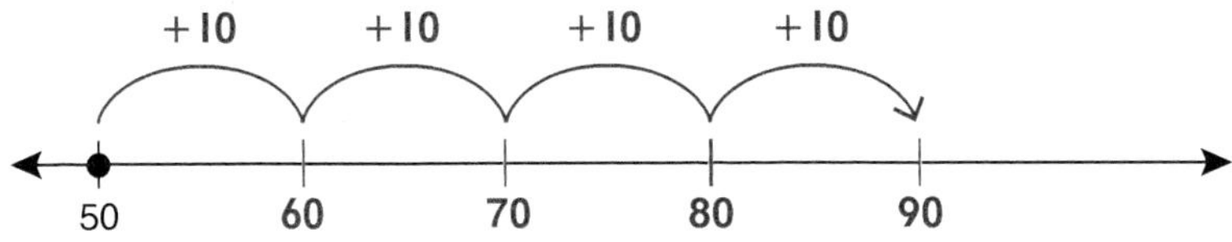

19. Structure Write an equation that matches the number line.

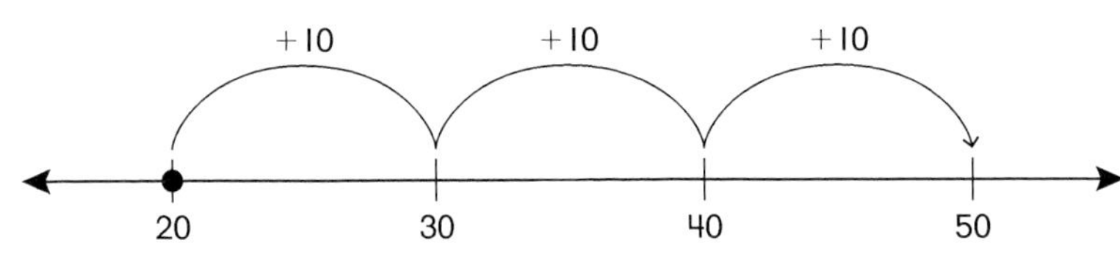

20 + 30 = 50

8.5 Subtract Tens

20. 90 − 40 = ?

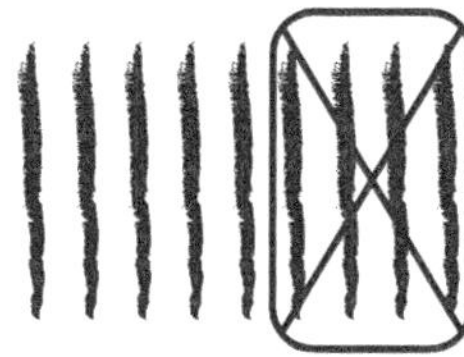

9 tens − 4 tens = 5 tens

So, 90 − 40 = 50.

21. 70 − 40 = 30

22. 80 − 20 = 60

8.6 Subtract Tens Using a Number Line

23.

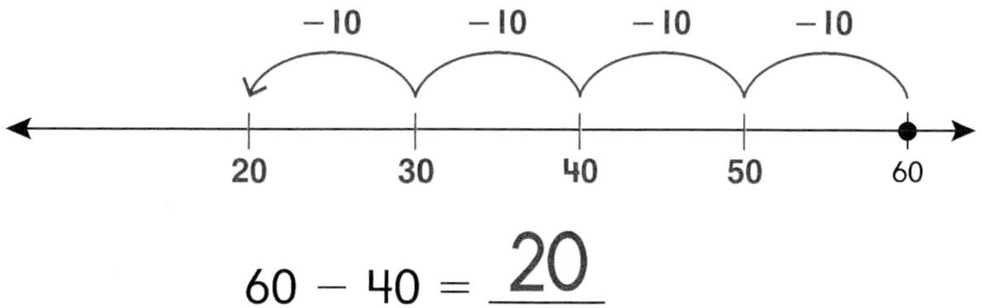

60 − 40 = 20

24. Structure Write the equation that matches the number line.

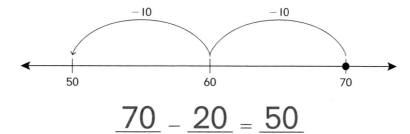

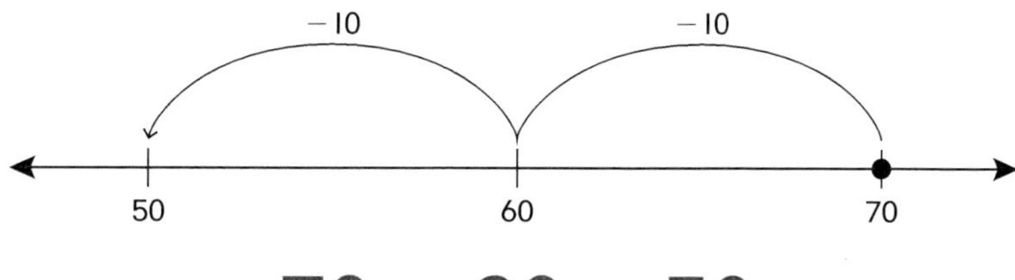

70 − 20 = 50

8.7 Use Addition to Subtract Tens

25. 80 − 60 = ?

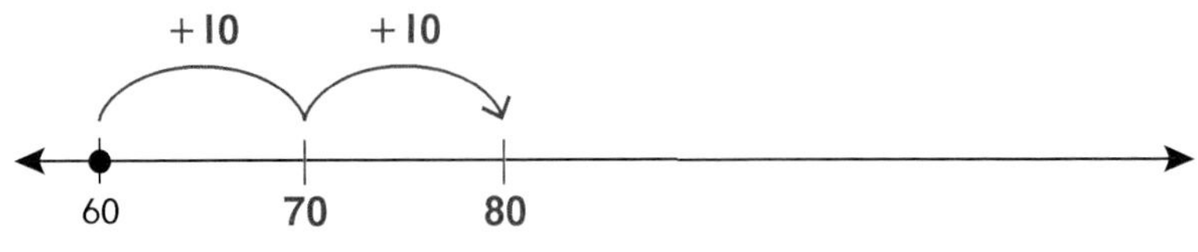

Think 60 + 20 = 80. So, 80 − 60 = 20.

26. **Modeling Real Life** A mail carrier has 90 packages to deliver. She delivers 60 of them. How many packages are left?

+10 +10 +10

60 70 80 90

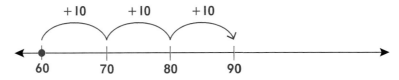

90 − 60 = 30

30 packages

8.8 Add Tens to a Number

27. 27 + 50 = 77

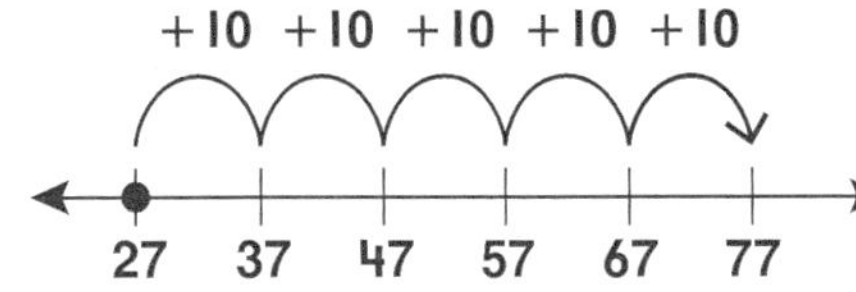

28. 92 = 80 + 12

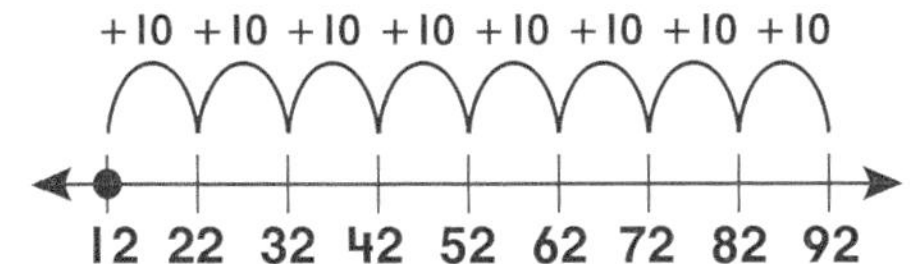

Centers

Center 1: 10 More or 10 Less

Materials: Student Edition page 452, 1 die per pair, two-color counters

Have students complete the activity. See page T-452 for the directions.

Center 2: Skills Trainer

Materials: computers or devices with Internet access

Have students go to *BigIdeasMath.com* to access the Skills Trainer.

Center 3: Tens Beads

Materials: beads, string

Provide each student with a string and access to beads. Ask each student place 10, 20, 30, or 40 beads on the string. Have students find a partner. One student writes an equation for the sum of the beads, the other writes an equation for the difference. Students trade equations with their partner, and model the equation using an open number line.

Center 4: Roll On Addition

Materials: 2 dice

Students roll both dice to create a two-digit number. On their first roll, students use a strategy of their choice (open number line, base ten blocks, or hundred chart) to add 10 more to the number rolled. On their next roll, students should instead add 20 more to the number rolled. Students should repeat this two more times adding 30 and 40 to the number rolled. Have students record their addition equations on a sheet of paper.

Center 5: Adding Change

Materials: bags, buttons, counters

Place a number of buttons in a bag. Label counters with decade numbers and place in another bag. Have students grab a handful of buttons and write the number of buttons. Have students choose a counter and add that number to the number of buttons. Repeat several times.

Chapter Assessment Guide

Chapter tests are available in the Assessment Book.
An alternative assessment option is listed below.

Linguistic

Call students over individually and provide them with a two-digit number between 10 and 89. Have students add a decade number to the starting number using a strategy of their choice (open number line, mental math, hundred chart, base ten blocks, quick sketch of base ten blocks). Ask the student to verbally explain how they used the strategy to add the decade number. Provide students with a two-digit number between 11 and 99. Have students subtract a decade number from the starting number using a different strategy than they used in the previous exercise. Ask the student to verbally explain how they used the strategy to subtract a decade number.

Task	Points
Use addition strategy to correctly find the sum	2 points
Correctly explain addition strategy	2 points
Use a different subtraction strategy to correctly find the difference (give partial credit for correctly using the same strategy as for addition)	2 points
Correctly explain subtraction strategy (do not give points if a different strategy was not used)	2 points
Total	8 points

My Thoughts on the Chapter

What worked...

Teacher Tip

Not allowed to write in your teaching edition? Use sticky notes to record your thoughts.

What did not work...

What I would do differently...

9 Add Two-Digit Numbers

Chapter Overview

Lesson	Learning Target	Success Criteria
9.1 Add Tens and Ones	Add two numbers by adding the tens and adding the ones.	• Use quick sketches to model adding two numbers. • Add the tens and add the ones. • Write the sum.
9.2 Add Tens and Ones Using a Number Line	Use a number line to add two numbers.	• Use an open number line to count on by tens and ones from the starting number. • Write the sum.
9.3 Make a 10 to Add	Make a 10 to add a one-digit number and a two-digit number.	• Make a quick sketch to show both numbers. • Tell whether I can make a 10. • Add the tens and count on the ones.
9.4 Add Two-Digit Numbers	Use place value to add two numbers.	• Make a quick sketch to show both numbers. • Tell whether I can make a 10. • Add the tens and count on the ones.
9.5 Practice Addition Strategies	Choose a strategy to add two numbers.	• Choose a strategy to add two numbers. • Explain the strategy I used. • Add the numbers and write the sum.
9.6 Problem Solving: Addition	Solve addition word problems.	• Identify what information is given in the word problem. • Identify what the question is asking. • Choose a strategy to solve. • Explain the strategy I used to solve.

Chapter Learning Target:
Understand adding two-digit numbers.

Chapter Success Criteria:
- Identify two-digit numbers.
- Describe an addition strategy.
- Write a sum.
- Explain the strategy and the sum.

Progressions

Through the Grades		
Kindergarten	**Grade 1**	**Grade 2**
• Understand the numbers 11 to 19 as a group of 10 ones and some more ones. • Represent addition and subtraction with various models and strategies. • Add and subtract within 10. • Fluently add and subtract within 5.	• Understand the value of each digit in a two-digit number. • Understand a group of 10 ones as a ten. • Use models, properties, and strategies to add within 100.	• Understand the value of each digit in a three-digit number. • Understand a group of 10 tens as a hundred. • Use strategies to fluently add and subtract within 100. • Use models, properties, and strategies to add and subtract within 1000.

	Through the Chapter					
Standard	**9.1**	**9.2**	**9.3**	**9.4**	**9.5**	**9.6**
1.NBT.B.2 Understand that the two digits of a two-digit number represent amounts of tens and ones.	●	●	●	●	●	★
1.NBT.B.2a 10 can be thought of as a bundle of ten ones – called a "ten."	●	●	●	●	●	★
1.NBT.B.2b The numbers from 11 to 19 are composed of a ten and one, two, three, four, five, six, seven, eight, or nine ones.	●	●		●	●	★
1.NBT.B.2c The numbers 10, 20, 30, 40, 50, 60, 70, 80, 90 refer to one, two, three, four, five, six, seven, eight, or nine tens.	●	●		●	●	★
1.NBT.C.4 Add within 100, including adding a two-digit number and a one-digit number, and adding a two-digit number and a multiple of 10, using concrete models or drawings and strategies based on place value, properties of operations, and/or the relationship between addition and subtraction; relate the strategy to a written method and explain the reasoning used. Understand that in adding two-digit numbers, one adds tens and tens, ones and ones; and sometimes it is necessary to compose a ten.	●	●	●	●	●	★

Key: ▲ = Preparing ● = Learning ★ = Complete

Laurie's Overview

About the Math

Chapter 9 continues adding two-digit numbers based on place value. Students will use multiple strategies and models to add. Beginning in Lesson 9.3, students come to understand that sometimes the ones in a sum will need to be regrouped to form a ten. The same big ideas from Chapter 8 are extended in this chapter:

- Flexible methods for addition and subtraction involve decomposing and composing numbers based on place value.
- The location of a digit in a number determines its value.
- In addition and subtraction, tens are added or subtracted with tens, and ones with ones.
- Different models can show how place value and addition work together. These models can be used interchangeably.

Students continue to think of numbers in terms of place value in every lesson in this chapter. Repeatedly they add the tens together and the ones together to find a sum. Some students may still be confusing place value. This will become very apparent as regrouping of ones becomes necessary. For example, when adding 68 + 23, students may write the sum as 811, showing 8 tens and 11 ones. Continue to reinforce regrouping with concrete manipulatives (base ten blocks or other) to show the role of the digits. Writing a number in the place value mat and building all ones, then grouping and exchanging ten cubes for a rod will help students solidify their thinking of place value. It is typical for some first-grade students to continue to need this reinforcement of place value. Try not to let students resort to memorization of the names "tens" and "ones" as this will not serve them well in reasoning and number sense.

Models

We continue to use the models from chapter 8 with which students are familiar. The primary models that are used are base ten blocks or quick sketches, the hundred chart or 120 chart, and open number lines. The place value mat is brought back to clarify place value and regrouping with base ten blocks and quick sketches. Students will also use a place value chart to write the digits of the addends and sum.

- **Base Ten Blocks and Quick Sketches:** Students have been working with these two models, and should be comfortable with them. As students start to regroup ones, have them make the exchange of cubes for a rod to understand what the digits in the sum mean – for example, 68 + 23 = 91, not 811 as stated above. With quick sketches, students circle groups of ten ones to represent another ten. When counting or recording the number of tens and ones for the sum, some students will benefit from crossing out the group of ten ones and drawing in a new ten rod. It is recommended to have all students do this, especially as they are learning about regrouping. Other students will be able to count the ten rods from the addends and the group of ten ones that are circled for the total number of tens without confusion.

- **120 Chart or Hundred Chart:** We continue to use a hundred chart or 120 chart for addition, moving vertically to add tens and horizontally to add ones within an equation. The hundred chart can be thought of as a series of stacked number lines. Students will see that adding the ones and then the tens results in the same sum as adding the tens and then the ones. A new strategy that students can use is to show the movement within a hundred chart by arrows, ↓ for + 10, ↑ for − 10, → for +1 and ← for −1. This results in thinking very much like an open number line. The numbers below the arrows show the student count, but normally are not written.

$68 + 23 = 91$

68 ↓ ↓ → → →
(78)(88)(89)(90)(91)

- **Open Number Line:** Students continue to use an open number line to add any two numbers. This strategy will become many students' favorite strategy. In Lesson 9.6, it is used to find missing addends in applications.
- **Place Value Chart:** The place value chart becomes an explicit strategy in this chapter. Students progress from using it as a tool for modeling addends, grouping, and finding a sum with both base ten blocks and quick sketches, to writing the digits of the addends and sum into the same chart. In first grade, these two representations are used side-by-side. The explicit count of the tens and ones matches the digits in the addend, and after regrouping the digits of the sum. You will notice that the numeric place value chart looks like the vertical form of the standard algorithm for addition. We do not teach students how to "carry" a ten or perform the algorithm at this stage. We are still building the conceptual development of addition and place value. Students will record their sums in a vertical format as well, tying all three representations together. They will find their sums from working with the models, and not manipulating the numbers through the algorithm.

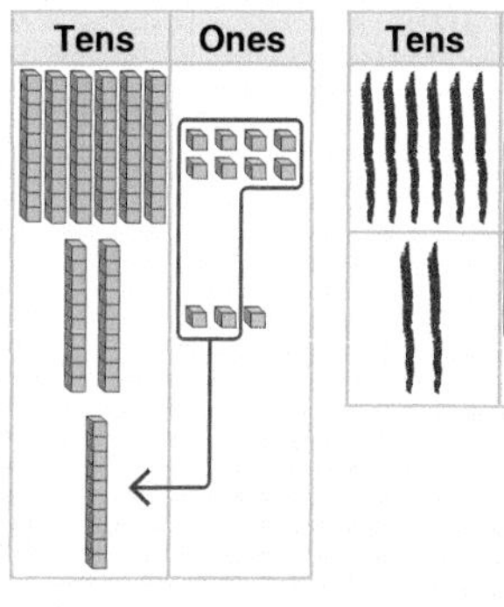

Tens	Ones
6 2	8 3
9	1

Chapter 9 continues to show that students' initial learning of strategies and models for addition are not for any particular group of numbers or situations. All the strategies and models can be used for any addition situation. One specific example is Lesson 9.6 where students solve multiple addition application stories using any strategy they choose. In this lesson, missing addend contexts come back for the first time in a little while. They should connect this to the *add to subtract strategy* that has been used recently. These strategies form the basis for mental math and estimation. The more comfortable they are with a strategy, the more sense they can make with mental strategies. Instead of seeing an algorithm in their heads for addition, they think add tens, gather ones, see it on a hundred chart, etc. Try some mental math problems with your students throughout the day.

Many of the lessons have students explaining their thinking or choice of a strategy as a success criteria. Places to have students tell their thinking to a partner or share out loud for discussion are embedded into lessons. Even so, the more often students "speak math" and explain their thinking, the more proficient mathematicians they become. Having students present their work, answer questions, and model ideas are essential in their mathematics journey. Be sure to find time to let your students be stars!

Check out the
virtual manipulatives.
BigIdeasMath.com

Chapter Materials and Resources

The primary materials and resources needed for this chapter are listed below. Other materials may be needed for the additional support ideas provided throughout the chapter.

Classroom Materials	Chapter Opener	9.1	9.2	9.3	9.4	9.5	9.6	Connect and Grow
base ten blocks		•		•	•	•		•
colored pencils or crayons		•						
whiteboards			*			•		
2 dice								*
scissors								*
paper clips								•

Instructional Resources	Chapter Opener	9.1	9.2	9.3	9.4	9.5	9.6	Connect and Grow
Hundred Chart			*			•		
Part-Part-Whole Mat for Manipulatives				•				
Place Value Mat		•			•			
Go Fish Nature Cards								*
Addition Spinners								•

• class set + teacher only * per pair/group

Suggested Pacing

<table>
<tr><td>Day 1</td><td>Chapter Opener</td><td colspan="2">Performance Task Preview</td><td colspan="4">Vocabulary</td></tr>
<tr><td>Day 2</td><td>Lesson 9.1</td><td>Warm-Up</td><td>Dig In</td><td>Explore</td><td>Think</td><td>Apply: Practice</td><td>Think: Modeling Real Life</td></tr>
<tr><td>Day 3</td><td>Lesson 9.2</td><td>Warm-Up</td><td>Dig In</td><td>Explore</td><td>Think</td><td>Apply: Practice</td><td>Think: Modeling Real Life</td></tr>
<tr><td>Day 4</td><td>Lesson 9.3</td><td>Warm-Up</td><td>Dig In</td><td>Explore</td><td>Think</td><td>Apply: Practice</td><td>Think: Modeling Real Life</td></tr>
<tr><td>Day 5</td><td>Lesson 9.4</td><td>Warm-Up</td><td>Dig In</td><td>Explore</td><td>Think</td><td>Apply: Practice</td><td>Think: Modeling Real Life</td></tr>
<tr><td>Day 6</td><td>Lesson 9.5</td><td>Warm-Up</td><td>Dig In</td><td>Explore</td><td>Think</td><td>Apply: Practice</td><td>Think: Modeling Real Life</td></tr>
<tr><td>Day 7</td><td>Lesson 9.6</td><td>Warm-Up</td><td>Dig In</td><td>Explore</td><td>Think</td><td>Apply: Practice</td><td>Think: Modeling Real Life</td></tr>
<tr><td>Day 8</td><td rowspan="2">Connect And Grow</td><td colspan="2">Performance Task</td><td colspan="2">Activity</td><td colspan="2">Chapter Practice</td></tr>
<tr><td>Day 9</td><td colspan="6">Centers</td></tr>
<tr><td>Day 10</td><td>Chapter Assessment</td><td colspan="6">Chapter Assessment</td></tr>
</table>

Year-to-Date: 106 Days

Mathematical Practices

Students have opportunities to develop aspects of the mathematical practices throughout the chapter. Here are some examples.

1. **Make Sense of Problems and Persevere in Solving Them**
   9.3 Think and Grow, *p. 472*
2. **Reason Abstractly and Quantitatively**
   9.1 Apply and Grow: Practice Exercise 11, *p. 461*
3. **Construct Viable Arguments and Critique the Reasoning of Others**
   9.3 Practice Exercise 7, *p. 476*
4. **Model with Mathematics**
   9.4 Practice Exercise 5, *p. 482*
5. **Use Appropriate Tools Strategically**
   9.2 Practice Exercise 6, *p. 470*
6. **Attend to Precision**
   9.3 Explore and Grow, *p. 471*
7. **Look for and Make Use of Structure**
   9.2 Apply and Grow: Practice Exercise 6, *p. 467*
8. **Look for and Express Regularity in Repeated Reasoning**
   9.5 Apply and Grow: Practice, *p. 485*

Laurie's Notes

Performance Task Preview

- Preview the page to gauge students' prior knowledge about playing sports and adding two-digit numbers.
- ? "What are your favorite sports?" Listen for student responses about playing sports and games.
- ? "You dribble a basketball 18 times with your right hand and 32 times with your left hand. How many times do you dribble the basketball in all?" 50 times
- In the Performance Task at the end of the chapter, students add two-digit numbers to find the number of points collected in a game.

9 Add Two-Digit Numbers

Chapter Learning Target:
Understand adding two-digit numbers.

Chapter Success Criteria:
- I can identify two-digit numbers.
- I can describe an addition strategy.
- I can write a sum.
- I can explain the strategy and the sum.

- What are your favorite sports?
- You dribble a basketball 18 times with your right hand and 32 times with your left hand. How many times do you dribble the basketball in all?

Check out the
digital flash cards.
BigIdeasMath.com

Laurie's Notes

Vocabulary Review

- ? **Preview:** "What type of chart do you see?" place value chart
- Have students say each Review Word out loud. Have students explain how the words are related.
- Have students identify which column is the tens and which column is the ones.
- Direct students to the lower half of the page. Have students use the remaining review words to complete the crossword puzzle. Inform students that although there is a space in "120 chart," they will skip the space when writing it in the crossword puzzle.
- **Supporting Learners:** Some students may be overwhelmed by the boxes. Explain that they are able to compare the number of boxes to the number of letters in the word.

ELL Support

Explain that the directions instruct you to complete the graphic organizer. Review with students that a chart is composed of rows and columns and point out examples of each on a sample chart. Explain that a graphic organizer is a visual way to present information in a way that is helpful for understanding. Other types of graphic organizers include graphs, tables, diagrams, and arrows that indicate flow of information.

Newton & Descartes's Math Musicals

with Differentiated Rich Math Tasks

Newton and Descartes team up in these educational stories and songs to bring mathematics to life! Use the Newton and Descartes hand puppets to act out the stories. Encourage students to sing the songs to take full advantage of the power of music to learn math. Visit *www.MathMusicals.com* to access all the adventures, songs, and activities available!

Name ______________________________

9 Vocabulary

Review Words
120 chart
column
ones
row
tens

Organize It

Use the review words to complete the graphic organizer.

tens	ones

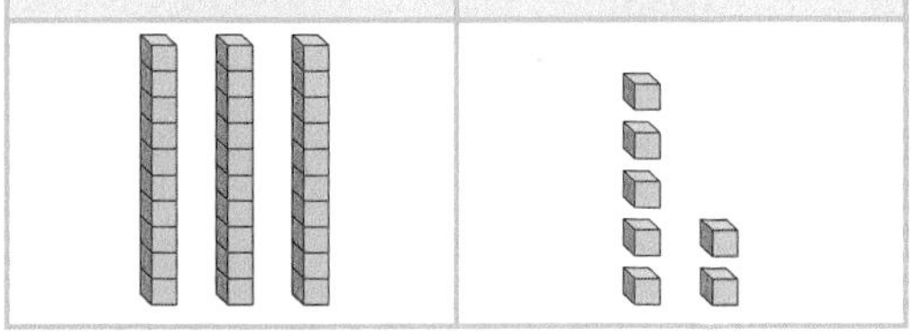

Define It

Use the review words to complete the puzzle.

Across

1.

1	2	3	4	5	6	7	8	9	10
11	12	13	14	15	16	17	18	19	20
21	22	23	24	25	26	27	28	29	30
31	32	33	34	35	36	37	38	39	40
41	42	43	44	45	46	47	48	49	50
51	52	53	54	55	56	57	58	59	60
61	62	63	64	65	66	67	68	69	70
71	72	73	74	75	76	77	78	79	80
81	82	83	84	85	86	87	88	89	90
91	92	93	94	95	96	97	98	99	100
101	102	103	104	105	106	107	108	109	110
111	112	113	114	115	116	117	118	119	120

Down

2.

1	2	3	4	5	6
11	12	13	14	15	16
21	22	23	24	25	26
31	32	33	34	35	36

3.

1	2	3	4	5
11	12	13	14	15
21	22	23	24	25
31	32	33	34	35

[1] 1	2	0	[2] c	h	a	[3] r	t
			o			o	
			l			w	
			u				
			m				
			n				

9.1

Check out the
Dynamic Classroom.
BigIdeasMath.com

Laurie's Notes

COMMON CORE

STATE STANDARDS
1.NBT.B.2a, 1.NBT.B.2b, 1.NBT.B.2c, 1.NBT.C.4

Learning Target

Add two numbers by adding the tens and adding the ones.

Success Criteria

- Use quick sketches to model adding two numbers.
- Add the tens and add the ones.
- Write the sum.

Warm-Up

Practice opportunities for the following are available in the Resources by Chapter or at *BigIdeasMath.com*.

- Daily skills
- Vocabulary
- Prerequisite skills

ELL Support

Explain that the directions instruct students to use a model. Remind them that a model is a way to show how something looks, like a fashion model wears clothes to show how clothes look. When using a model in math, students show how math operations look. Here students will use base ten blocks to show how tens and ones look when they are added.

Preparing to Teach

We continue to build students' understanding of place value and addition as we add any two-digit numbers. Students will use base ten blocks and quick sketches to decompose the addends into tens and ones, and join the ones together and then the tens together for the sum.

Materials

- base ten blocks
- colored pencils or crayons
- Place Value Mat*

**Found in the Instructional Resources*

Dig In (Circle Time)

In Circle Time we review adding decade numbers to any two-digit number with base ten block as a foundation before adding any two two-digit numbers. Students will work with a partner to build the addends. One partner will gather the tens and the other the ones to form the sum.

- "Let's warm up by adding 43 + 50. Work with your partner to find the sum using any of the methods or tools we have used." Have students share their strategies.
- ? "Let's talk about the number 43. How many tens are in 43? How many ones? How about 50? How many tens? How many ones? When you add them together, how many tens are in the sum? How many ones? Do you see any pattern of tens and ones so far?"
- ◉ "Today, we are going to add any two-digit numbers together. To add numbers, we need to add tens with tens and ones with ones."
- Have two students model adding 24 + 11 in the middle of the circle. Each student should build one of the addends with base ten blocks, holding rods in one hand and cubes in the other. Tell the students to swap rods and cubes so that one student has all the rods and the other has all the cubes. This is the sum. Have students all say the sum as they look at the rods and cubes.
- Students practice adding numbers using base 10 blocks with a partner. Each partner builds one of the addends. When addends are built, they should first push the blocks together to model joining the addends, then separate them into tens and ones to find the sum.
- After several examples, model how to use a quick sketch to add. Have students model 35 + 24. Draw a quick sketch of 35 and 24. As students rearrange the blocks to put the tens together and the ones together, circle the ones followed by the tens. Color coding will help students work with the quick sketch.
- ◉ **MP7 Look for and Make Use of Structure:** "Do you see a pattern in the tens and the ones when adding two-digit numbers?"
- ◉ "Today, we will keep adding any two numbers."

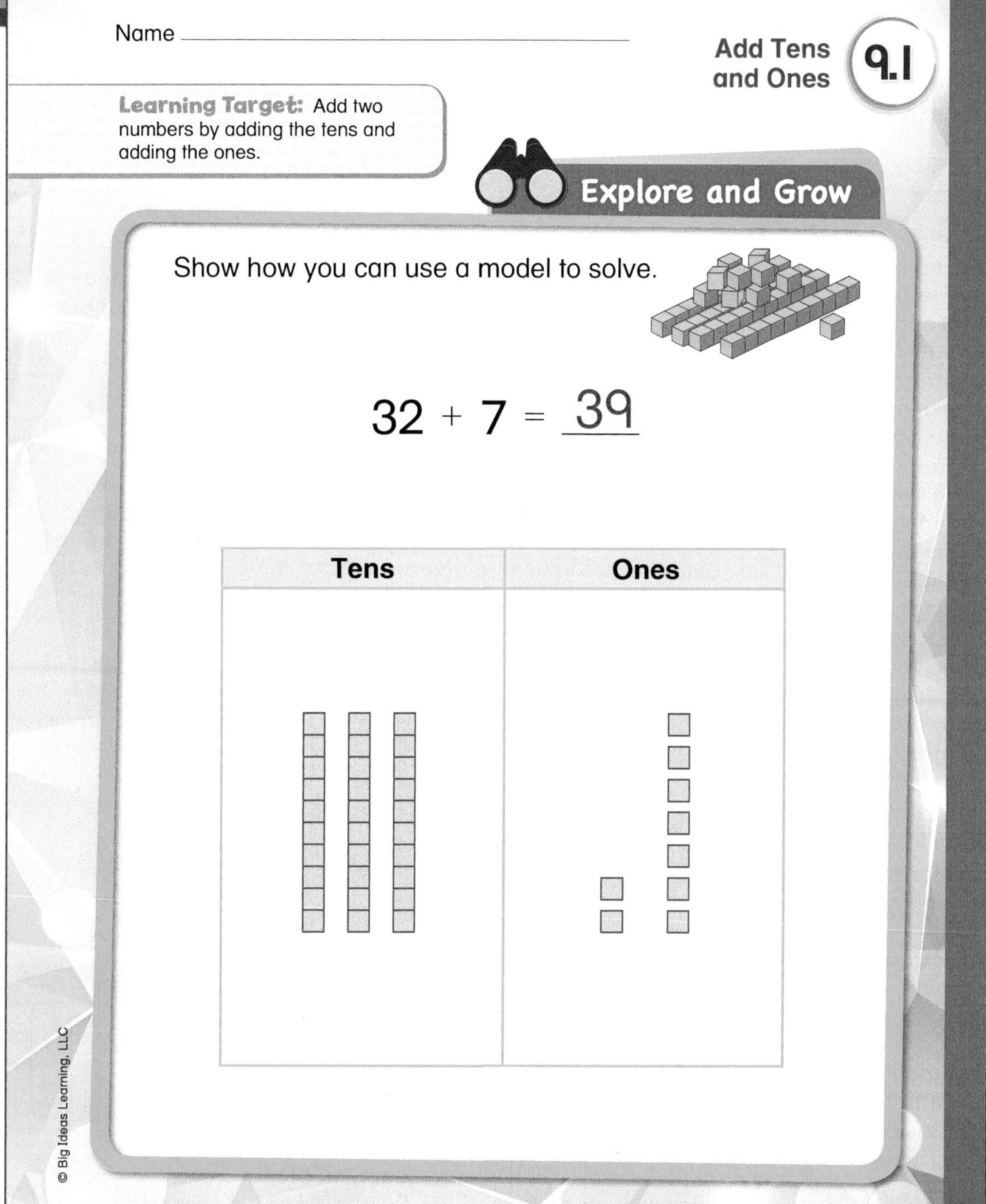

Name
Add Tens and Ones
9.1
Learning Target: Add two numbers by adding the tens and adding the ones.
Explore and Grow
Show how you can use a model to solve.
32 + 7 = 39
Tens
Ones
© Big Ideas Learning, LLC
Chapter 9 | Lesson 1
four hundred fifty-nine
459

Explore and Grow

- Have students model 32 with base ten blocks using the place value mat. Next, model 7 in the ones column underneath the 2 from 32. Students should be able to see the two addends separately.
- Students combine the ones together. Ask students if there are any tens to combine. Since there are not tens to combine, the two ten rods don't change.
- Have students say the sum and write it in.
- Have students tell their partners why the tens digit does not change. Tell the pattern of the ones digit in the sum. Explain why this is true using place value.

ELL Support

Discuss the example. Point out that each line models 10 and each circle models 1. When they count, the number of lines is written in the tens place and the number of circles in the ones place. Have students work in pairs as they practice language while completing Exercises 1–4. Have one student ask the other, "How many tens are there? How many ones? What is the answer?" Then have them alternate roles for the other exercises.

Beginner students may answer with numbers.
Intermediate students may answer with phrases, such as, "four tens."
Advanced students may answer with sentences, such as, "There are four tens."

Laurie's Notes

Think and Grow

Getting Started

- Students will add numbers using quick sketches. Continue to have students explain the process of adding in terms of place value. Encourage students to use one color to circle ones and another color to circle tens.

Teaching Notes

- **Model**: "Descartes is adding 31 + 14. He is using a quick sketch." Point to the sketch of 31. Point to 14.
- **Model**: "Descartes is going to circle the rods together and the cubes together because you add tens with tens and ones with ones. Circle all of the ones. Now circle all of the tens in a different color. Do you agree that the sum is 45? Write in the sum."
- Discuss Exercise 1 with students. Have them point to each of the addends. Have students circle the ones first followed by the tens. This does not make any mathematical difference, however, when students need to regroup ones in lesson 9.3, it is easier to have grouped the ones before the tens.
- Have students write in the sum.
- Watch as students complete Exercise 2. If students have difficulty, determine if it is an error in counting or an error with place value. If needed, reteach with Exercise 3 and have students try Exercise 4 independently.

? **MP2 Reason Abstractly and Quantitatively**: "How do the digits in the addends determine the digits in the sum?"

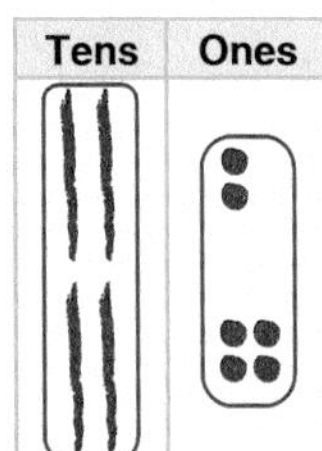

- **Supporting Learners**: Provide base ten blocks to manipulate instead of using a quick sketch. Provide a Place Value Mat for modeling.
- **Extension**: Have students draw numbers out of a bag to add. They can use base ten blocks, quick sketches, or add the digits if they understand the pattern.

Think and Grow

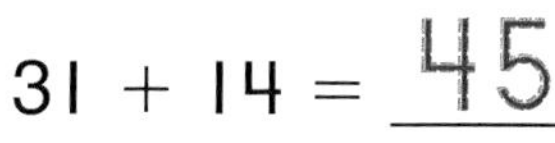

31 + 14 = 45

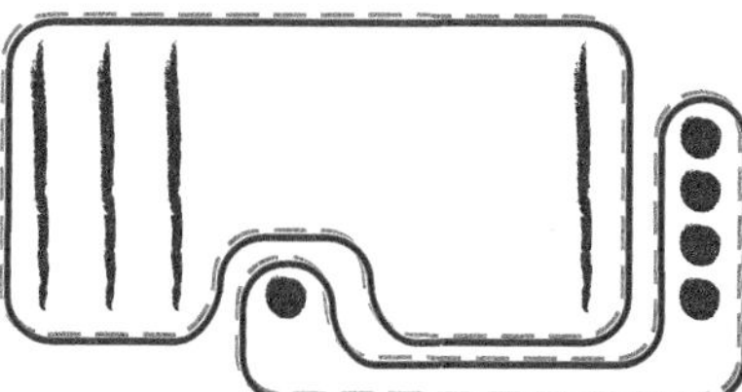

Add the ones. Then add the tens.

Show and Grow I can do it!

1. 25 + 12 = 37

2. 36 + 3 = 39

3. 21 + 8 = 29

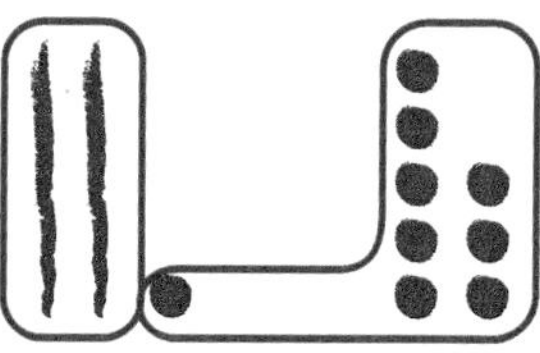

4. 22 + 24 = 46

Scaffold instruction to support all students in their learning. Learning is individualized and you may want to group students differently as they move in and out of these levels with each skill and concept. Student self-assessment and feedback help guide your instructional decisions about how and when to layer support for all students to become proficient learners.

Meeting the needs of all learners.

Laurie's Notes

Apply and Grow: Practice

SCAFFOLDING INSTRUCTION

Students continue to add numbers combining tens and ones. They can build with base ten blocks, draw quick sketches, or add digits.

EMERGING students need to continue to model with base ten blocks. They may be able to correctly circle tens and ones with provided quick sketches but not be able to sketch their own. This indicates they have not mastered place value. Watch to see if students can name the places and the values of the digits in a number.

- **Exercises 5 and 6:** Students continue to work with provided quick sketches. Watch to see that they combine place values correctly. Encourage students to color code throughout.
- **Exercises 7–10:** Students need to model the addition for each exercise. Allow students to use the base ten blocks, rather than a quick sketch, or a Place Value Mat.
- **Exercise 11:** Students choose the addend to complete the addition equation. Ask students to name the digit that changed from the addend to the sum to help.

PROFICIENT students can add groups of tens and ones to any number and explain their reasoning. They may be ready to start adding without a model, but this is not expected right now.

- **Exercises 5 and 6:** Students may not need to circle tens and ones, but simply count from the model to find the sum.
- **Exercises 7–10:** Students can quick sketch numbers and circle or count the tens and ones. They may not need a model.
- **Exercise 11:** Students choose the correct addend to complete the equation. Have them explain how they know which is correct.

Additional Support

- Have students quick sketch the numbers vertically rather than horizontally, and "stack" the tens and the ones units.

Extension: Adding Rigor

- Students roll 3 dice to make a two-digit and a one-digit number. Add these numbers.

Name ______________________________

Apply and Grow: Practice

5. 34 + 4 = <u>38</u>

6. 43 + 15 = <u>58</u>

7. 71 + 20 = <u>91</u>

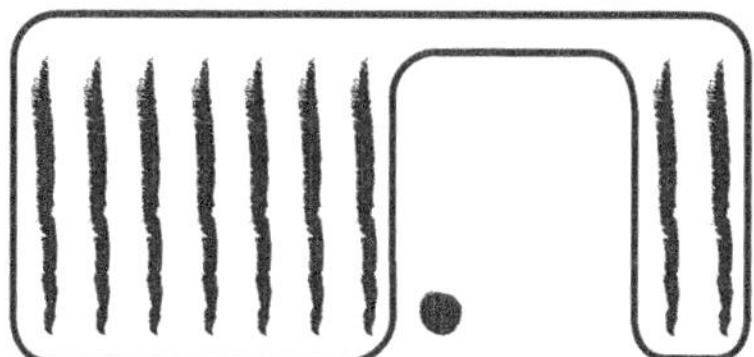

8. 93 + 6 = <u>99</u>

9. 55 + 23 = <u>78</u>

10. 62 + 32 = <u>94</u>

11. MP **Reasoning** Circle the number to complete the equation.

41 + _____ = 46

(5)   50

ELL Support

Check for understanding of Lesson 9.1. Read each story aloud as students follow along. Clarify unknown vocabulary if necessary. You may want to demonstrate a jumping jack. Allow time to complete each exercise. Have students respond to the following questions by writing answers and holding them up for your review.

1. How many tens do you draw for the number of minutes?
2. How many ones do you draw?
3. What is the total number of minutes?
4. How many tens do you draw for the number of jumping jacks?
5. How many ones do you draw?
6. What is the total number of jumping jacks?

Laurie's Notes

Think and Grow: Modeling Real Life

Today's applications involve adding two two-digit numbers. Students will write the addition equation and use any model they like to solve.

- **Preview:** "About how many minutes do you think you spend watching TV a day?" Note, this might be hard as first-grade students do not know how to tell time yet!
- Discuss the story. Have students tell partners how to find the total number of minutes. Write the equation. Have students suggest how to model the addition. For your model, use a quick sketch and circle tens and ones.
- Have students tell you the total number of minutes and fill in the blank.
- Discuss Exercise 12. They may want to model jumping jacks or share how many they have done in PE. Students can either model the addition and then write the equation or vice versa.
- Students can talk to their partners to share which numbers they should add together, and how they are modeling the addition.
- ◉ "Today, we added any two numbers. Using your thumb signals, how well can you model numbers with tens and ones? How well can you group tens and group ones from the addends? How well can you find the sum of any two numbers?"

Closure

- "We have been adding any two numbers. Tell your partner what is the most important thing to remember." add tens with tens and ones with ones
- "Practice! What is the sum of 32 + 41?" 73

Think and Grow: Modeling Real Life

You watch television for 24 minutes in the morning and 32 minutes at night. How many minutes do you spend watching television in all?

Addition equation:

24 + 32 = 56

Model:

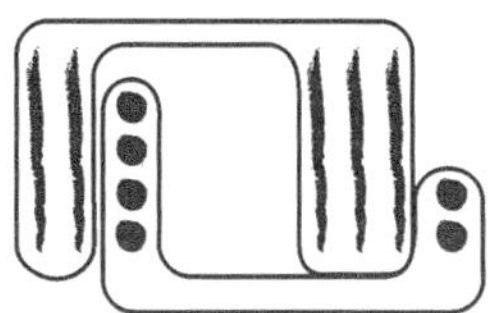

56 minutes

Show and Grow *I can think deeper!*

12. You do 42 jumping jacks in the morning and 46 at night. How many jumping jacks do you do in all?

Addition equation:

42 + 46 = 88

Model:

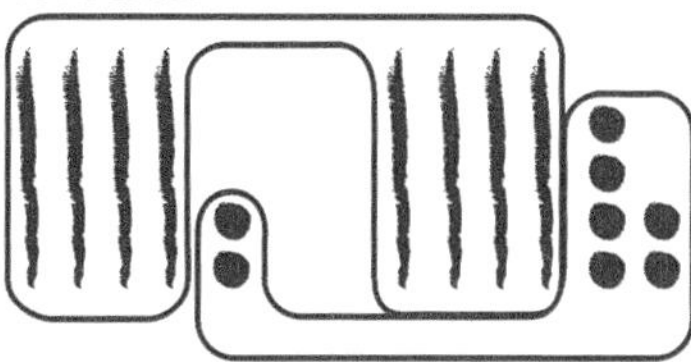

88 jumping jacks

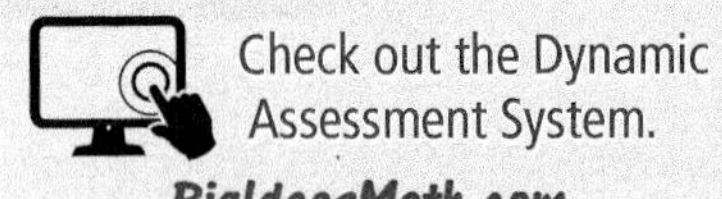
Check out the Dynamic Assessment System.
BigIdeasMath.com

Scaffold assignments to support all students in their learning progression. Revisit with spaced practice to move every student toward proficiency.

Connect and Extend Learning

Practice Notes

- Provide place value mats and base ten blocks for support, if needed.
- **Exercise 6:** Have students write an addition equation to model the problem.

Prior Skills

- **Exercises 8 and 9:** Grade 1, Counting Tens and Ones to Write Numbers

Cross-Curricular Connections

Language Arts

- Divide students into groups of four. Give two students in each group some rods and give the other two students some cubes. The group works together to write an addition equation represented by their base ten blocks. Have students create a word problem that can be modeled by their equation and share with the class.

Name ______________________

Practice 9.1

Learning Target: Add two numbers by adding the tens and adding the ones.

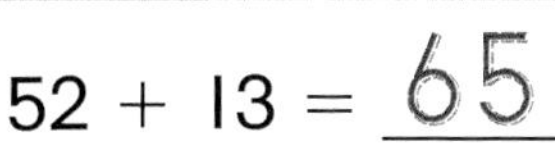

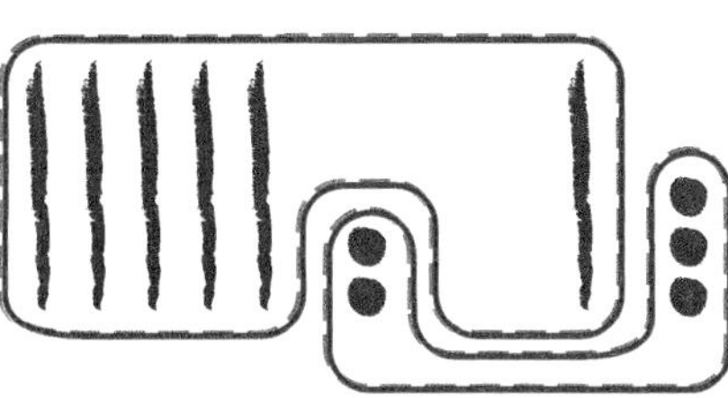

1. 42 + 7 = 49

2. 61 + 35 = 96

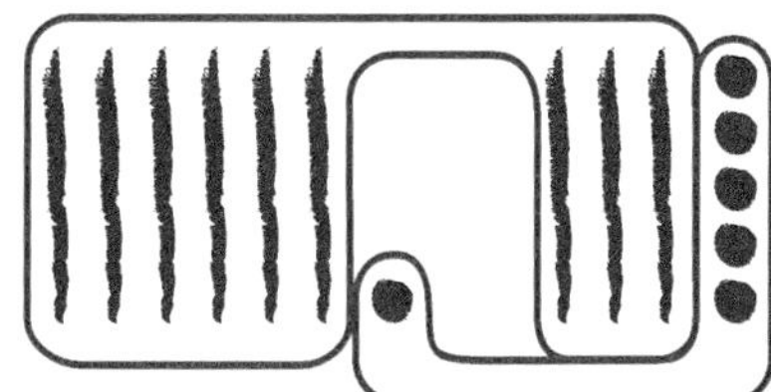

3. 74 + 11 = 85

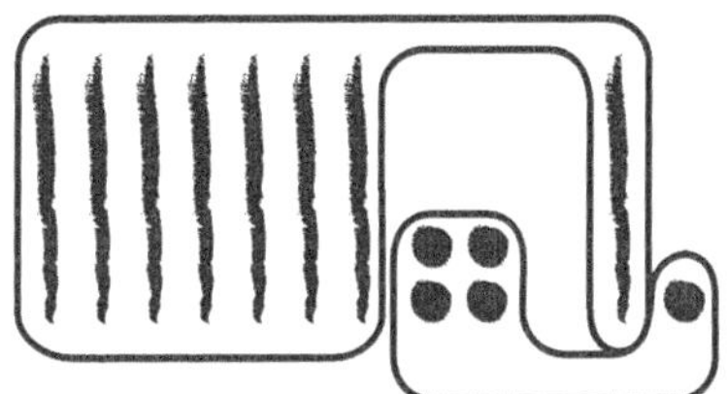

4. 86 + 2 = 88

Connect and Extend Learning

Extend Student Learning

Logical-Mathematical

- With the class, create a "shape code" that assigns a shape to each number. Use the code to write addition problems on the board and have students use base ten blocks to model and solve the problem. Students can also write their own problems and trade with a partner to solve.

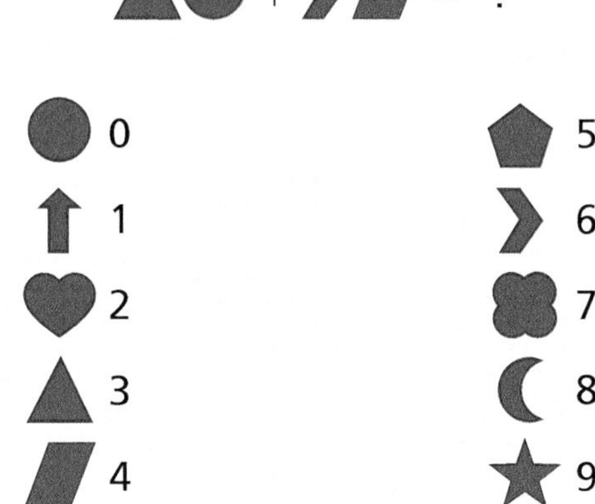

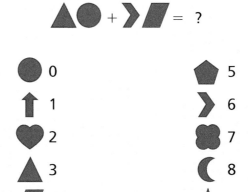

Lesson Resources	
Surface Level	**Deep Level**
Resources by Chapter • Extra Practice • Reteach Differentiating the Lesson Skills Review Handbook Skills Trainer	Resources by Chapter • Enrichment and Extension Graphic Organizers Dynamic Assessment System • Lesson Practice

5. MP **Reasoning** Circle the number to complete the equation.

$22 + \_\_\_\_ = 92$

7 (70)

6. MP **Modeling Real Life** You eat 33 grapes. Your friend eats 23 grapes. How many grapes do you and your friend eat in all?

$33 + 23 = 56$

56 grapes

7. DIG DEEPER! What is the greatest number of tens you can add to a two-digit number to get a sum of 35?

2 tens

Review & Refresh

8.

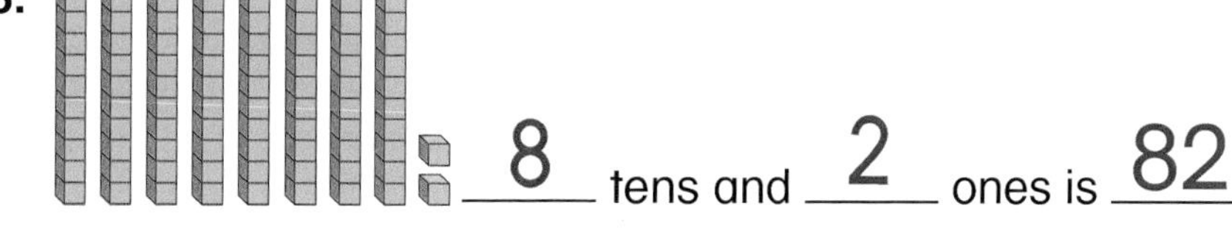

8 tens and 2 ones is 82.

9.

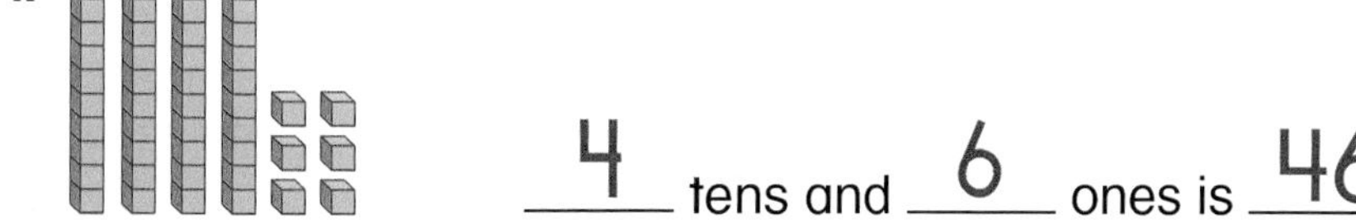

4 tens and 6 ones is 46.

9.2

Check out the
Dynamic Classroom.
BigIdeasMath.com

Laurie's Notes

Learning Target

Use a number line to add two numbers.

Success Criteria

- Use an open number line to count on by tens and ones from the starting number.
- Write the sum.

Warm-Up

Practice opportunities for the following are available in the Resources by Chapter or at *BigIdeasMath.com*.

- Daily skills
- Vocabulary
- Prerequisite skills

ELL Support

Explain that the directions ask students to show how to use the chart by coloring. Explain that moving down a column shows adding tens and moving across a row shows adding ones. Although the word *show* often means "an entertaining presentation" in everyday language, here it means a way to model or demonstrate while using the chart.

STATE STANDARDS
1.NBT.B.2a, 1.NBT.B.2b, 1.NBT.B.2c, 1.NBT.C.4

Preparing to Teach

Students will add two more models for adding two numbers. Today, students will use a hundred chart to add and an open number line. Students will see that adding tens and ones is the same as only adding tens or only adding ones with these tools. Students will also see that the order in which the place values are added does not make a difference to the sum.

Materials

- Hundred Chart*
- whiteboards

**Found in the Instructional Resources*

Dig In (Circle Time)

Students work with a partner to add two numbers. Partners will alternate using a hundred chart and an open number line. Give each pair of students a Hundred Chart and a whiteboard and marker.

- "Yesterday we used base ten blocks and quick sketches to add two numbers. Tell your partner what is very important to remember when adding any two numbers."
- ? **Model:** "Today, we are going to add two numbers using a hundred chart and using an open number line. Let's review adding on a hundred chart. To add ones, for example 23 + 4, how do you move on the chart? Moving across a row is the same as adding ones. To add tens, for example 23 + 30, how do you move on the chart? Moving down a column is the same as adding tens. To add both tens and ones, you will move across for the ones in the addend and down for the tens in the addend. It does not matter if you add the tens and then the ones, or the ones first and then the tens."
- ◉ Model adding 31 + 26 on a number line. Show that you can add the 20 to 31 first and then the 6, or add the 6 and then the 20. Have students work together to add 43 + 35.
- "Now let's look at the open number line." Show 31 + 26 on an open number line. Remind students to start the number line with the first addend. They can hop by tens first and then by ones, or vice versa. After modeling, have students work together to show 43 + 35 on an open number line on their whiteboards.
- Give students several problems to practice adding with both models, alternating who uses which model and comparing sums.
- ◉ "Today, we are continuing adding any two numbers. How is using the hundred chart, number line, and base ten blocks alike and different?"

? Teaching Prompt ◉ Learning Target

Name ________________________________

Add Tens and Ones Using a Number Line

9.2

Learning Target: Use a number line to add two numbers.

Explore and Grow

Color to show how you can use the hundred chart to find the sum.

23 + 34 = 57

1	2	3	4	5	6	7	8	9	10
11	12	13	14	15	16	17	18	19	20
21	22	23	24	25	26	27	28	29	30
31	32	33	34	35	36	37	38	39	40
41	42	43	44	45	46	47	48	49	50
51	52	53	54	55	56	57	58	59	60
61	62	63	64	65	66	67	68	69	70
71	72	73	74	75	76	77	78	79	80
81	82	83	84	85	86	87	88	89	90
91	92	93	94	95	96	97	98	99	100

Explore and Grow

- "We are adding 23 + 34. To begin, locate 23 on the chart. We want to add 34. Tell your partner how many tens and how many ones are in 34."
- "You can add either the tens or the ones first. Just remember to move down the column for tens and across the row for ones."
- Have students compare their sums with a partner. Did both students move the same way on the chart (tens or ones first)? The sum does not change.
- "We can add any two numbers with a hundred chart. Next we will use number lines."

ELL Support

Point out that moving by tens is the same as moving down a column in a hundred chart, and moving by ones is the same as moving across a row. After working with the examples, have students practice language as they work in groups to complete Exercises 1 and 2. As they work they should answer the following questions: "Where do we begin on the number line? How many tens do we move? How many ones do we move? What is the answer?" You may want to suggest that the group alternate using the models shown by Newton and Descartes to become familiar with both.

Beginner students may answer with numbers.
Intermediate may answer with sentences.
Advanced students may answer providing explanations of the processes used.

Laurie's Notes

Think and Grow

Getting Started

- We now move to adding on an open number line. Students will be given the starting point on the line, and will then draw hops to represent adding the second addend. Coordinating the hops to show adding ones and tens can be challenging for students. Filling in the values on the number line is also a challenge coordinating the ones and tens as well as with spacing.

Teaching Notes

- **Model**: "Newton and Descartes are adding 26 + 32. Newton starts at 26 and wants to add the tens in 32 first. He draws 3 big hops on the number line to show 30. Draw Newton's hops of 10, and write +10 above them. Next, Newton draws 2 small hops to show adding 2. The 2 is 2 ones, not 2 tens or 20. So, the hops are smaller and each small hop shows a +1. Trace the small hops and fill in +1 above them.
- ? **Model**: "Let's think about what Newton added, and the numbers on the number line. He started at 26 and added 10. What number is he at? Then he added another 10. What number? And a third ten. What number? Then Newton added 1. What number is he at now? And another one. What is the sum?"
- **Model**: "Descartes is also adding 26 + 32. He starts at 26 also, but he wants to add the ones first and then the tens. Fill in the small hops that Descartes makes to add 2, and write +1 above them. Now fill in Descartes's three hops of 10 to add 30 more. Write +10 above them."
- Have students fill in the numbers on the number line. Ask students what they notice about the two number lines. They should see that the sum is the same although the numbers on the number line are not the same based on what is added first.
- As students look at Exercise 1, ask what they notice about the second addend. Because they are adding 7, there will be no tens hops.
- Watch to see that students are adding 7 single hops, and numbering the number line accordingly. It is possible students will still add by 7 tens instead of by ones.
- Watch as students complete Exercise 2. If students confuse tens and ones hops, reteach a small group with Exercise 3.
- **Supporting Learners**: Have students circle the tens digit of the second addend in one color, and hop that number with the same color. Repeat with a different color for the ones.
- **Extension**: Give students a starting point and an ending point for the number line. Students determine how many hops are needed (missing addend) to reach the sum, and then write the equation.

Think and Grow

$26 + 32 = ?$

One Way:

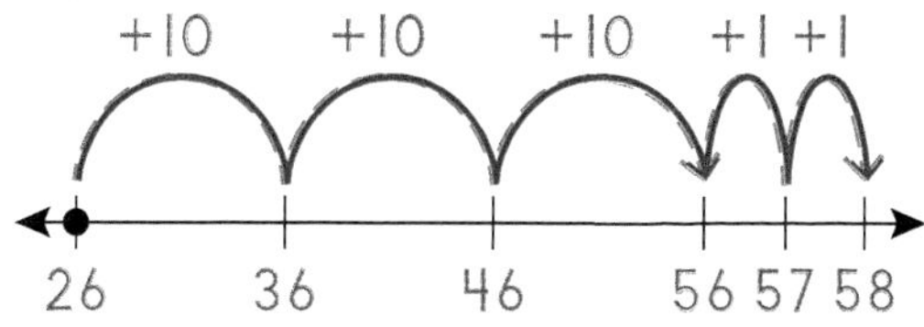

Start at 26.
Count by tens,
then by ones.

Another Way:

You can also count by
ones, then by tens.

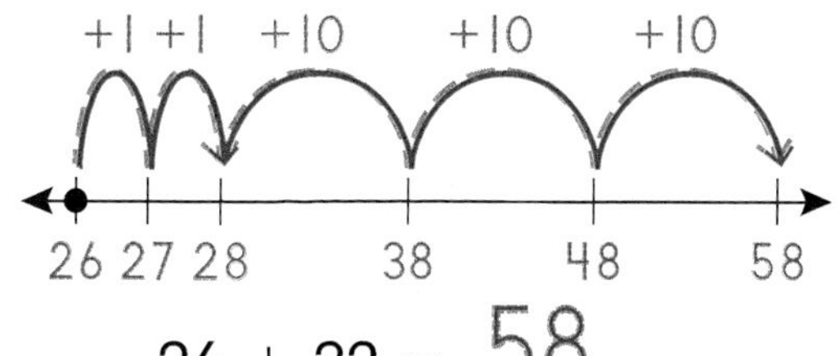

$26 + 32 =$ 58

Show and Grow *I can do it!*

1 and 2. Sample answers are given.

1. $22 + 7 =$ 29

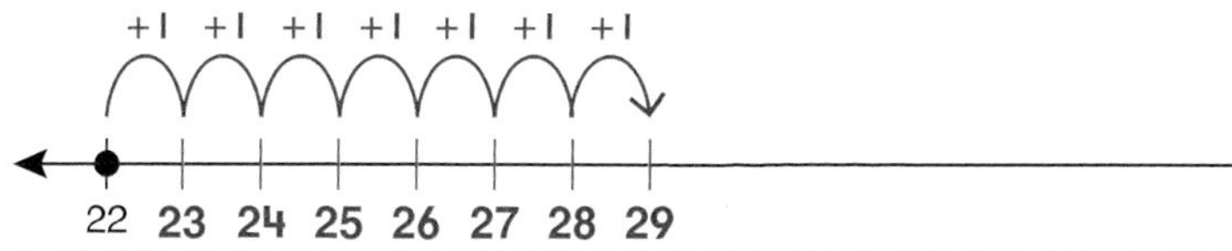

2. $35 + 41 =$ 76

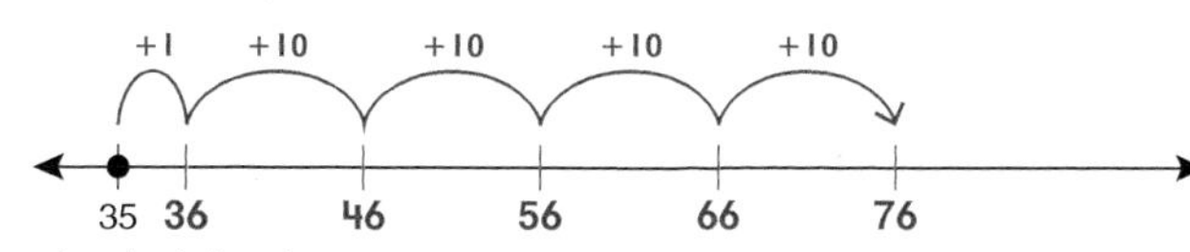

Scaffold instruction to support all students in their learning. Learning is individualized and you may want to group students differently as they move in and out of these levels with each skill and concept. Student self-assessment and feedback help guide your instructional decisions about how and when to layer support for all students to become proficient learners.

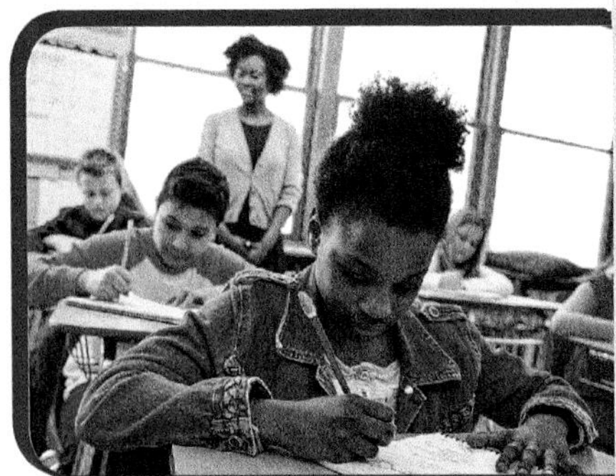

Meeting the needs of all learners.

Laurie's Notes

Apply and Grow: Practice

SCAFFOLDING INSTRUCTION

Students add on open number lines, including labeling the first addend as the starting point on the number line.

EMERGING students may draw miscellaneous hops now that the tens and ones are combined instead of understanding that each hop correlates to a plus ten or a plus one. The size of the hop may not correspond to the place value being added.

- **Exercise 3:** This exercise is the same as 1 and 2, and can be used for re-teaching.
- **Exercises 4 and 5:** These number lines do not provide the starting point. Watch to see if students recognize the starting addend and correctly decompose the second addend into tens and ones. The structure of the number line may be more difficult than the actual adding of the numbers. If students understand the addition with place value, the number line will come with more practice.
- **Exercise 6:** Focus students on the starting point on the number line, and the values of the hops being added. The numbers on the number line along the way may confuse emerging students.

PROFICIENT students can show the addition on the open number line and explain how each hop is adding either groups of ten or groups of one.

- **Exercises 4 and 5:** Have students explain the place value involved in their hops, and the numbers they write on the number line. This is to reinforce the addition of place value.
- **Exercise 6:** Students should be able to write the correct equation. Have them explain how they could determine the equation if the labels above the hops were not provided.

Additional Support

- Students can continue to use a Hundred Chart to see the numbers on the number line resulting from the tens and ones hops.

Extension: Adding Rigor

- Students add any 2 two-digit numbers on an open number line. One partner begins with showing hops of one, and the other hops of ten to compare their final answers.

Name ____________________

Apply and Grow: Practice

3. 53 + 40 = 93   **3–5. Sample answers are given.**

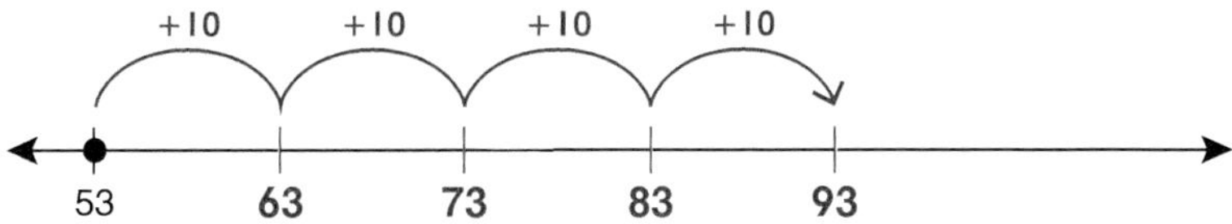

4. 82 + 12 = 94

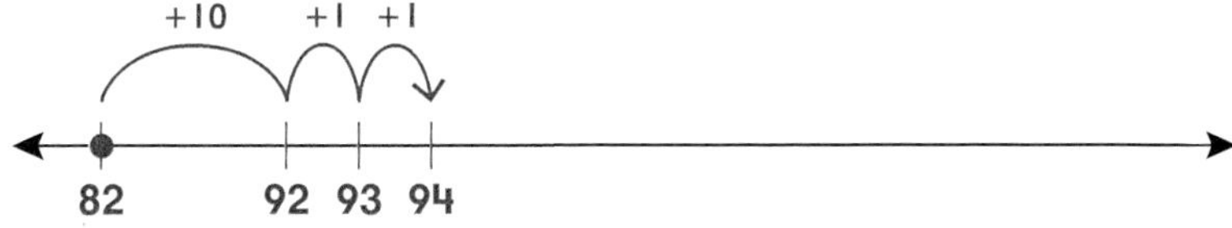

5. 48 + 31 = 79

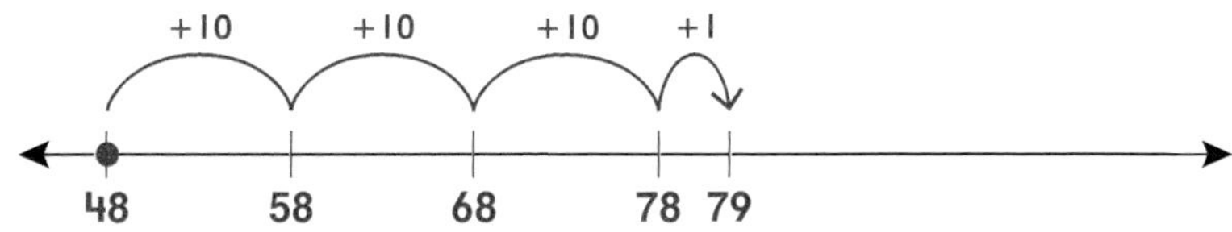

6. **Structure** Write an equation that matches the number line.

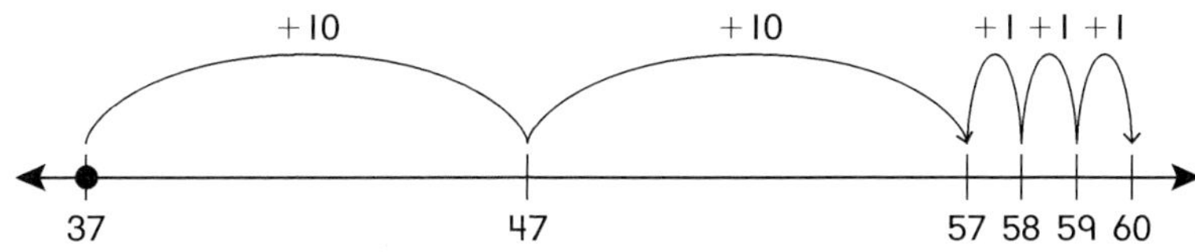

37 + 23 = 60

Laurie's Notes

ELL Support

Check for understanding of Lesson 9.2. Read each story aloud as students follow along. You may want to discuss the meanings of home team and visiting team. Clarify any confusion or unknown vocabulary. Allow time to complete each exercise. Have students respond to the following questions by writing answers and holding them up for your review.

1. In the example, where do you begin on the number line?
2. How many tens do you move?
3. How many ones do you move?
4. How many points does the visiting team score?
5. In Exercise 7, where do you begin on the number line?
6. How many tens do you move?
7. How many ones do you move?
8. How many points do you score?

Think and Grow: Modeling Real Life

The application problems today are phrased in the context of "more" in order to form an addition equation. An open number line is provided for the addition. Students can model the addition on the number line and then write an equation, or write the equation first and then model.

? **Preview:** "Who likes to watch basketball? Who is your favorite team? About how many points does a team score in a game?"

? Discuss the story. "Did the visiting or home team score more points? How can I find out how many total points the visiting team scores?"

- "The home team scores 37 points. I put 37 at the start of the number line because I will count on from there. I need to add 22 points. I am choosing to add the 20 first, and then 2. I need to add two hops of 10 for the twenty." Draw the hops, label +10 above each, and have students tell you what numbers to write on the number line.
- Next add the 2 hops. Remind students that we added two tens before, but these are two ones. Draw and label hops. Have the students tell you the numbers to write on the number line and how many points the visiting team scored.
- Introduce Exercise 7. Have students talk to their partners about the number and types of hops they will need to add 25. Watch as they complete the exercise.

◉ "I want to know how it is going for you with using an open number line to add any two numbers. How are you doing with determining the number of tens and ones to add? How are you doing with drawing the hops and labeling them? How are you doing with showing the numbers on the number line? How are you doing with finding the sum?"

Closure

- Have students sit with a partner and share one whiteboard and one marker. Tell students that they will trade back and forth to complete the problem 36 + 52.
  - Partner 1 draws an open number line and labels the starting point.
  - Partner 2 draws hops and labels them (tens or ones).
  - Partner 1 draws the rest of the hops and labels them (tens or ones).
  - Partner 2 labels the numbers on the number line.
  - Partner 1 writes the final equation.

Think and Grow: Modeling Real Life

The home team scores 37 points. The visiting team scores 22 more. How many points does the visiting team score?

Addition equation:

37 + 22 = 59

Model: ***Sample answer:***

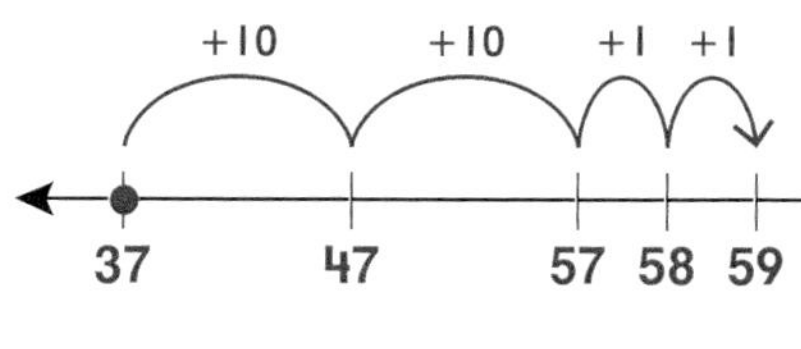

59 points

Show and Grow *I can think deeper!*

7. Your friend scores 63 points. You score 25 more than your friend. How many points do you score?

SPACE ATTACK!

Addition equation:

63 + 25 = 88

Model: ***Sample answer:***

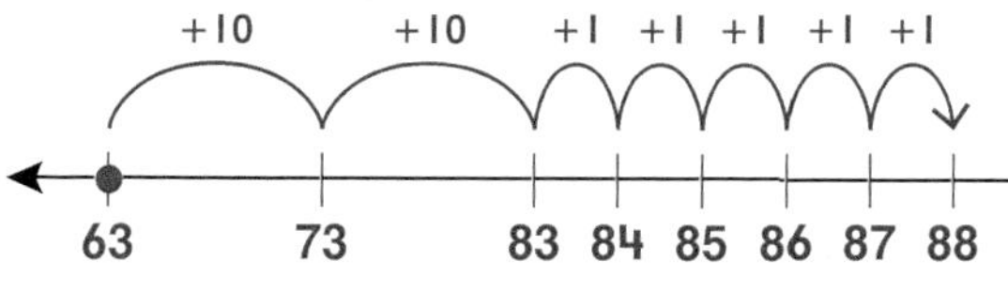

88 points

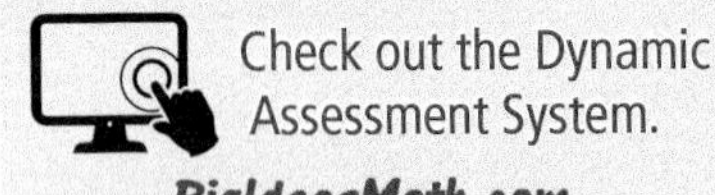
Check out the Dynamic Assessment System.
BigIdeasMath.com

Scaffold assignments to support all students in their learning progression. Revisit with spaced practice to move every student toward proficiency.

Connect and Extend Learning

Practice Notes

- Remind students that they can add the tens first or the ones first.
- **Extension:** In Exercise 5, have students find the total number of keys on a piano.

Prior Skills

- **Exercises 7 and 8:** Grade 1, Adding Three Numbers by Making a 10

Cross-Curricular Connections

Social Studies

- Using the numbers 1 to 50, number the states on the Map of The United States Instructional Resource. You may want to number states according to the order they became states. Project the map for the class to see. Have students find sums of pairs of states. Alternatively, have students choose two states they want to visit or have been to and find the sum.

Name ______________________

Practice 9.2

Learning Target: Use a number line to add two numbers.

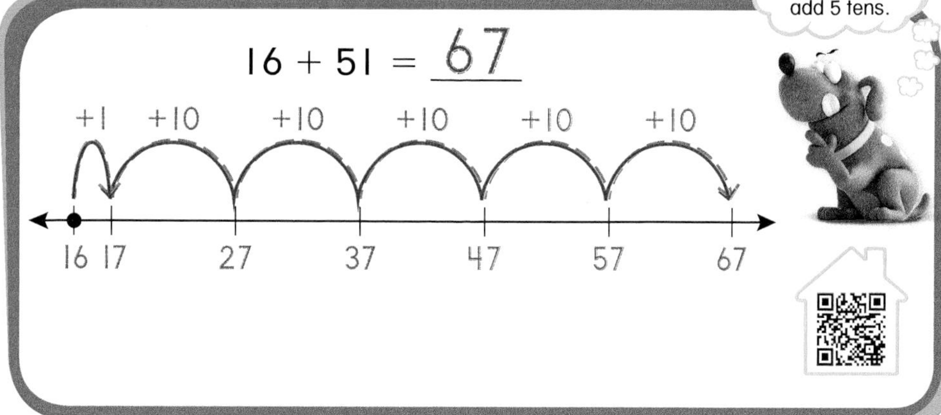

1. 13 + 60 = 73 **1–3. Sample answers are given.**

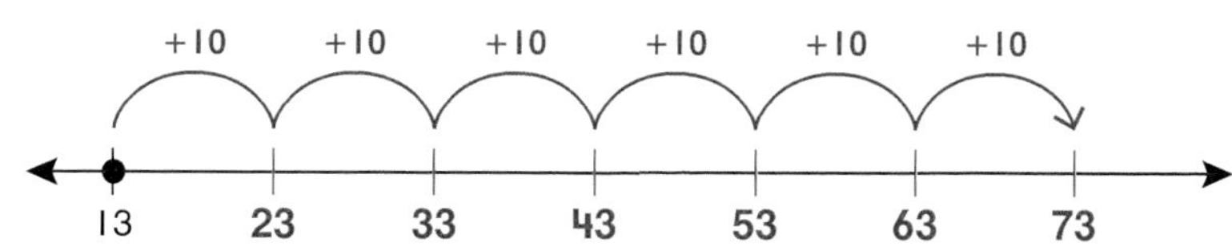

2. 81 + 18 = 99

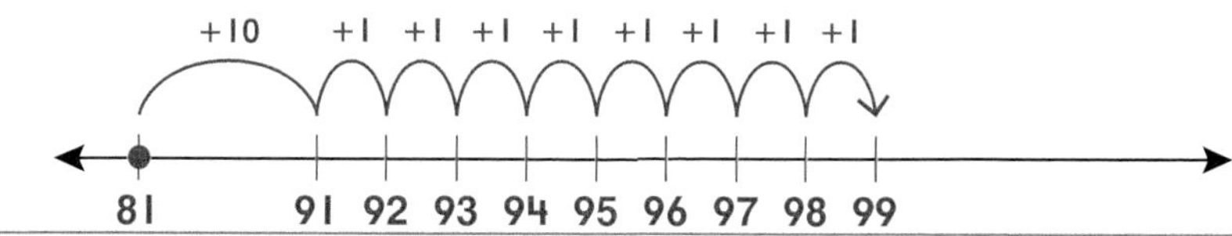

3. 56 + 42 = 98

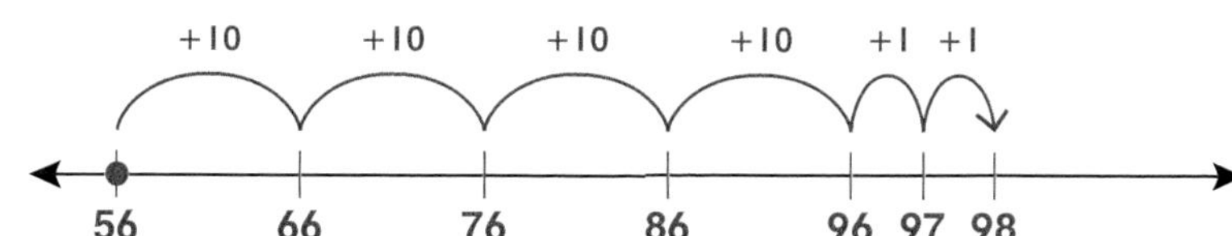

Connect and Extend Learning

Extend Student Learning

Bodily-Kinesthetic

- Divide students into groups and create an open number line on the floor for each group. Write a two-digit number on the board. Students in each group take turns rolling two dice to create a two-digit number, then model adding the number on the board to their number on the number line. For example, if the number on the board is 27 and a student rolls a 3 and a 4, they could model 34 + 27 or 43 + 27 by hopping along their number line. Use the same number on the board throughout the activity or use a new number for each round.

Lesson Resources	
Surface Level	**Deep Level**
Resources by Chapter • Extra Practice • Reteach Differentiating the Lesson Skills Review Handbook Skills Trainer Math Musicals	Resources by Chapter • Enrichment and Extension Graphic Organizers Math Musicals Dynamic Assessment System • Lesson Practice

4. **Structure** Write an equation that matches the number line.

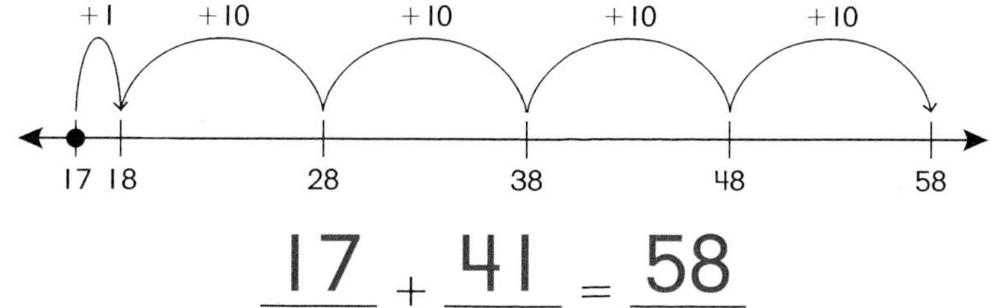

17 + 41 = 58

5. **Modeling Real Life** There are 36 black keys on a piano. There are 16 more white keys than black keys. How many white keys are there?

Sample answer: 36 + 16 = 52

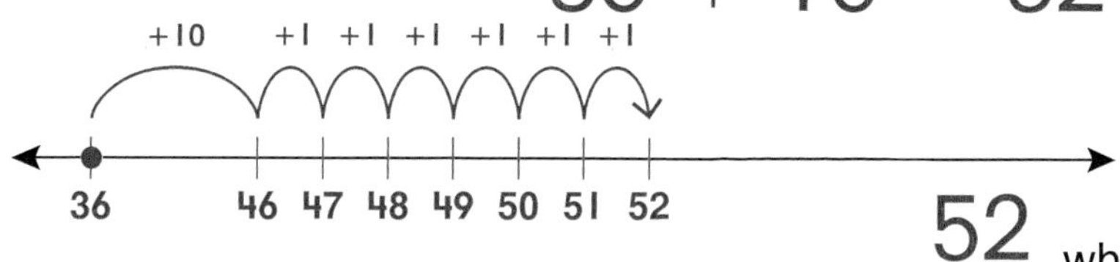

52 white keys

6. **Choose Tools** Do you prefer to use models or a number line to add two numbers? Explain.

Check students' work.

Review & Refresh

7. 3 + 7 + 4 = 14

8. 4 + 5 + 6 = 15

9.3

Check out the
Dynamic Classroom.

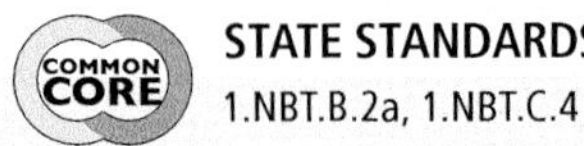
BigIdeasMath.com

Laurie's Notes

COMMON CORE **STATE STANDARDS** 1.NBT.B.2a, 1.NBT.C.4

Preparing to Teach

Yesterday students added two numbers by joining the tens and the ones. Today, students will add a two-digit and a one-digit number and determine whether a ten can be made after joining the ones. We build on the *make a 10* strategy from Lessons 4.5–4.7.

Materials

- base ten blocks
- Part-Part-Whole Mat for Manipulatives*

**Found in the Instructional Resources*

Dig In (Circle Time)

Students use base ten blocks to add two-digit and one-digit numbers. They determine if a ten can be made by joining the ones cubes and exchange them for a ten rod. They will model the single-digit number on the part-part-whole mat to illustrate making a ten.

- "Do you remember playing Make It 10? I'll say a number and you show me the number of fingers needed to add to make 10." Play several rounds.
- ◉ **Model:** "We are going to use the *make a 10* strategy that we used before." To review the strategy, have 8 students stand in the middle of the circle. Have another group of 4 students stand in another group. Tell students that we want to add 8 + 4. "How could we make one of the groups into 10?" Have 2 students move from the 4 to the 8 group. "How many students are there in all?"
- Show 8 + 4 on a Part-Part-Whole Mat for Manipulatives.
- ◉ **Model:** "Today, we are going to use this strategy with adding two-digit and one-digit numbers. Try 27 + 5. Build 27 + 5 with the base ten blocks. Now group the ones. How many cubes are there?"
- Have students regroup the cubes into groups of 10 and 2, and replace the 10 cubes with one rod. Tell the sum.
- ◉ **Model:** "Let's try 46 + 8. Build 46." Place 8 cubes in the Whole section of the Part-Part-Whole Mat for Manipulatives. "Look at the 6 cubes of 46. How many more cubes need to be added to have 10 cubes?" Place 4 cubes in the left part of the mat. Place the other 4 cubes in the right part of the mat. Exchange the 6 and 4 cubes in the left part of the mat for a rod and tell the sum.
- ◉ Have students model 61 + 3. Ask if they can make a 10. Explain that not all equations will regroup and that is the first decision to make.
- Have students model more equations with and without grouping as time permits.
- ◉ "Today, we are adding two numbers. We will decide if a 10 can be made from the ones units, and then how to make a 10 to find the sum.

Learning Target

Make a 10 to add a one-digit number and a two-digit number.

Success Criteria

- Make a quick sketch to show both numbers.
- Tell whether I can make a 10.
- Add the tens and count on the ones.

Warm-Up

Practice opportunities for the following are available in the Resources by Chapter or at *BigIdeasMath.com*.

- Daily skills
- Vocabulary
- Prerequisite skills

ELL Support

Point out that the words *one-digit* and *two-digit* are each made using two words with a line (hyphen) between them. These types of words are known as hyphenated words. Compound words are made using two words together without a hyphen. Each kind of word creates a single word that uses both meanings to express an idea.

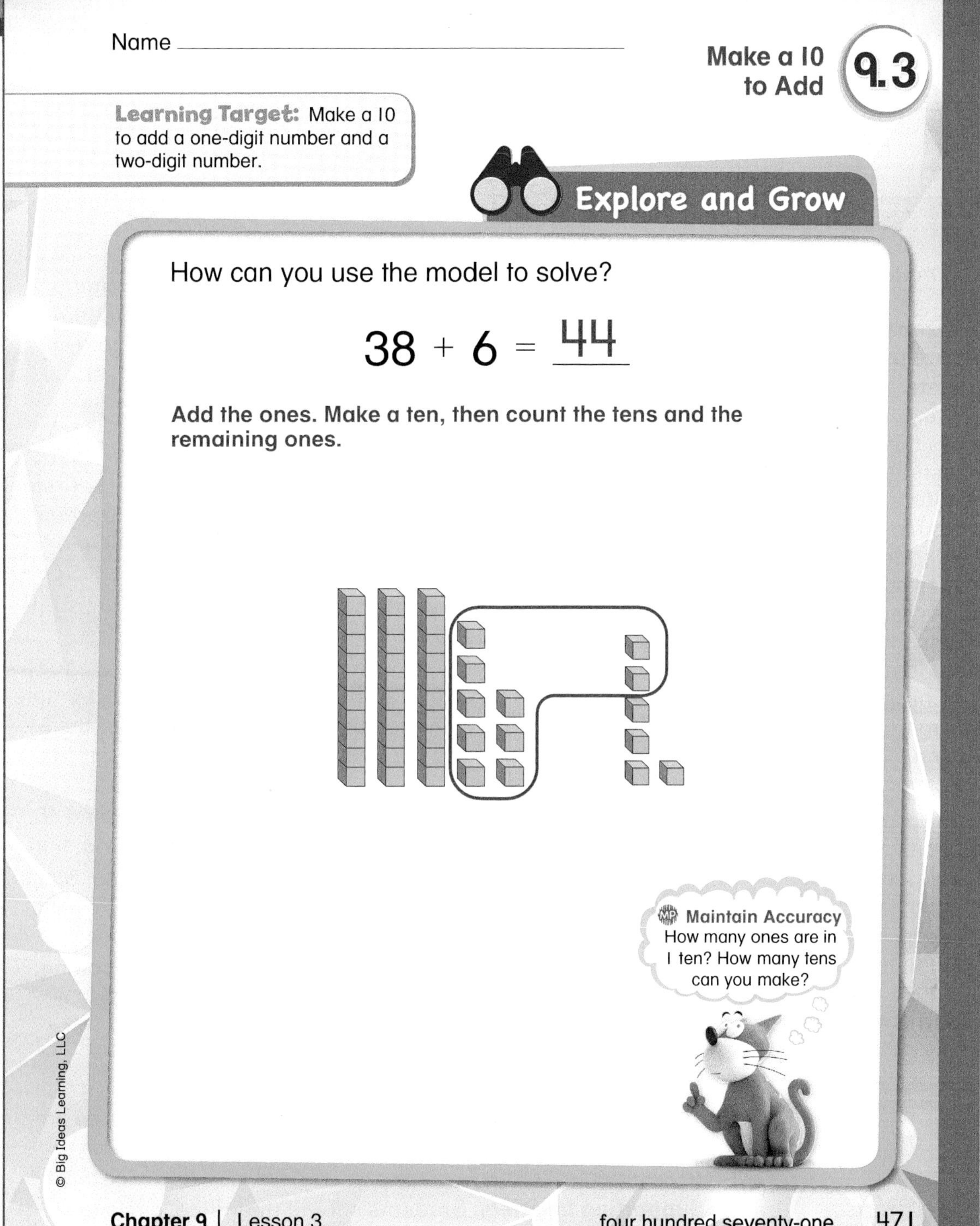

Name
Make a 10 to Add
9.3
Learning Target: Make a 10 to add a one-digit number and a two-digit number.
Explore and Grow
How can you use the model to solve?
38 + 6 = 44
Add the ones. Make a ten, then count the tens and the remaining ones.
Maintain Accuracy
How many ones are in 1 ten? How many tens can you make?
© Big Ideas Learning, LLC
Chapter 9 | Lesson 3
four hundred seventy-one
471

Explore and Grow

- Have students model 38 + 6 with base ten blocks and regroup the cubes as they did during the Dig In. Discuss what they did with the blocks.
- "We can use the quick sketch to show how you can group 10. Circle 10 cubes."
- To make it clear that the group of 10 cubes is now the same as a 10, they can cross the group out and draw a rod. Discuss how to count the model to find the sum.
- "Sometimes we will need to regroup the ones after adding because there will be more than 10 ones. We will need to make a group of ten to be counted with the other tens, and then count the ones."

Laurie's Notes

ELL Support

Model the example for the class, then have students practice language in groups as they complete Exercises 1 and 2. Have groups discuss the following questions: "How many tens are in the first number? Is another ten added? How many ones are left? What is the total?" Monitor discussion and expect students to perform according to their language proficiency level.

Beginner students may state one-word answers.
Intermediate students may state phrases or simple sentences.
Advanced students may describe the process used to answer the questions.

Think and Grow

Getting Started

- Students will use quick sketches for addition and determine if a ten can be made or not prior to finding the sum. Addition notation for the *make a 10* strategy using Part-Part-Whole is introduced in the first model, and will be used in the rest of the lesson.

Teaching Notes

- **Model:** "Descartes is adding 38 + 5. He looks at the ones first. Look at the model. Tell your partner if he can make a 10 when he adds the ones." Have students circle the group of 10 and circle Yes.
- ◉ **Model:** "Let's add the tens and count the ones to find the sum. 10, 20, 30, 40, 41, 42, 43."
- **Model:** "Descartes shows how he found partner numbers for 5 to show making a ten. Look at the how he used part-part-whole to show what he did with the quick sketch. He used 2 of the 5 to join with 38 and made 40. He still had 3 more ones left from the 5."
- Students will need this model to complete Exercises 9 and 10.
- ◉ **Model:** "Newton is also adding numbers. He adds 25 + 4. Tell your partner if he can make a 10 when he adds the ones. Since 5 + 4 = 9, there are not enough ones to make a ten. Circle No. We can look at the model and write the sum."
- **MP8 Look for and Express Regularity in Repeated Reasoning:** As students look at Exercise 1, ask how they can decide if a 10 can be made. Students should tell why they cannot make a group of ten. Do they recognize the addition of the ones digits yet?
- Watch as students complete Exercise 2. Notice if students are counting the model or looking at the ones digits. Are they regrouping correctly?
- **Supporting Learners:** Students should underline, circle or highlight the ones digits in the addends. This will help them determine if they can make a 10.
- **Supporting Learners:** Students should cross out the circled group of ten and draw in an extra rod to show the regrouping and sum more clearly.
- **Supporting Learners:** Provide base ten blocks and a Part-Part-Whole Mat for Manipulatives.
- **Extension:** Can students draw the numeric representation (as in Descartes's model) for these equations?

Think and Grow

38 + 5 = 43

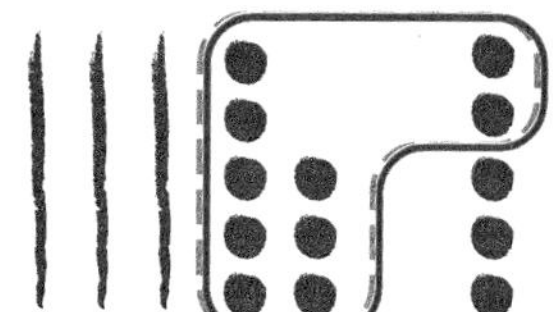

Make a 10? (Yes) No

When there are 10 or more ones, make a ten.

38 + 5

38 + 2 + 3

40 + 3

25 + 4 = 29

Make a 10? Yes (No)

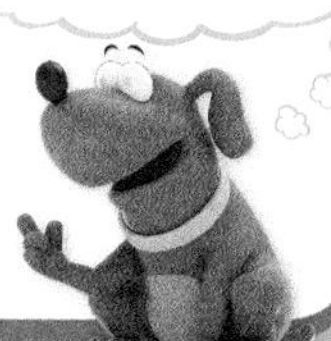

MP **Analyze a Problem** Why don't you need to make a 10 here?

Show and Grow *I can do it!*

1. 41 + 7 = 48

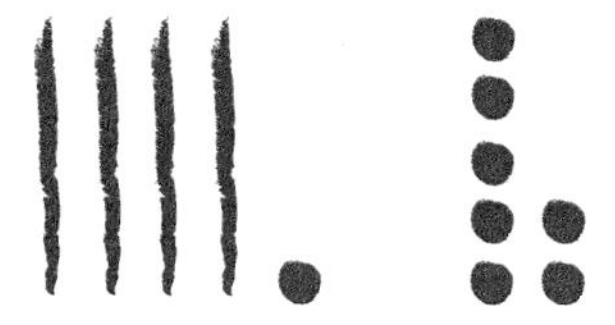

Make a 10? Yes (No)

2. 56 + 8 = 64

Make a 10? (Yes) No

Laurie's Notes

Scaffold instruction to support all students in their learning. Learning is individualized and you may want to group students differently as they move in and out of these levels with each skill and concept. Student self-assessment and feedback help guide your instructional decisions about how and when to layer support for all students to become proficient learners.

Meeting the needs of all learners.

Apply and Grow: Practice

SCAFFOLDING INSTRUCTION

Students progress from being provided a quick sketch with which to decide if a ten can be made and find the sum, to looking at the equations to decide if a ten can be made and finding the sum. Students should draw a quick sketch of the equations that require regrouping and not just count on from the first addend. The quick sketch and regrouping reinforces place value and will set up the thinking required in the following lessons.

EMERGING students will count the number of ones units in order to determine if a ten can be made. They may not remember to circle a group of ten. They may not count a group of ten as another ten rod when determining the sum.

- **Exercises 3 and 4:** These exercises are the same as 1 and 2. Exercise 3 can be used for re-teaching if needed.
- **Exercises 5–8:** Students should look at the ones digits in the addends to determine if a ten can be made. They will likely need to draw a quick sketch to determine the sums.
- **Exercises 9 and 10:** Students should draw a quick sketch of the equation. They will find partner numbers for the second addend so that one of the numbers makes a ten with the ones of the first addend. This prompt should help them start. This was modeled on the Think and Grow page.

PROFICIENT students tell whether a ten can be made by looking at the ones digits in the addends. They may need to continue to quick sketch to find sums.

- **Exercises 5–8:** If students do not model the addition, ask how they are finding the sum. Students who count on will not develop the necessary place value reasoning.
- **Exercises 9 and 10:** Students can fill in the model and explain how to make a ten.

Additional Support

- Provide base ten blocks. As students regroup the ones, they can see the partner numbers of the second addend that are needed to make a ten.

Extension: Adding Rigor

- Have students roll 3 dice to make a two-digit number and a one-digit number, and add. Model like Exercise 9 if possible.

Name ______________________________

Apply and Grow: Practice

3. 72 + 4 = 76

Make a 10? Yes (No)

4. 63 + 9 = 72

Make a 10? (Yes) No

5. 14 + 6 = 20

Make a 10? (Yes) No

6. 27 + 5 = 32

Make a 10? (Yes) No

7. 46 + 7 = 53

Make a 10? (Yes) No

8. 81 + 8 = 89

Make a 10? Yes (No)

Logic Complete.

9. 56 + 6

56 + (4) + (2)

60 + (2)

56 + 6 = 62

10. 39 + 9

39 + (1) + (8)

40 + (8)

39 + 9 = 48

ELL Support

Check for understanding of Lesson 9.3. Read each story aloud as students follow along. You may want to ask students to share experiences making puzzles. Explain that each shape on the map is a state in the country. Allow time to complete each exercise. Have students demonstrate understanding by responding to the following questions for each exercise. They may write answers on whiteboards and hold them up for your review or use a thumbs up or down signal for yes/no questions.

1. How many tens do you draw?
2. How many ones do you draw?
3. Do the ones make a ten?
4. How many extra ones are there?
5. What is the answer?

Laurie's Notes

Think and Grow: Modeling Real Life

The application problems continue addition of a two-digit and one-digit number. Students are asked to write the addition equation and to model. Encourage students to use a quick sketch or the equation showing part-part-whole of the second addend to show the regrouping of ones to a ten.

- ? **Preview**: "Have you ever put a jigsaw puzzle together? How does that work?" You can show a puzzle if desired.
- ? Discuss the story. "How can we find out how many puzzle pieces there are in all?"
- "You've put 17 of the pieces together. There are 7 left, and we assume no pieces are missing. Write the equation to show how many puzzle pieces there are in all. How should we model this?"
- Make a quick sketch of 17 and 7. Have students suggest how we might find the sum. Students should suggest that you group ones together to make a ten. Be prepared for students to suggest counting on. This will find the sum but not reinforce the regrouping of ten. Cross out the group of ten and draw an additional rod. Count the sum.
- Next to the quick sketch, show the equation with the second addend decomposed.
- Introduce Exercise 11. Have students tell their partners the numbers to add and if they think they will be able to make a ten or not. Students can model using either method. Use this problem as a formative assessment.
- ◉ "Let's use thumb signals to show how you are doing with your learning. How are you at deciding if a 10 can be made when adding? How are you at modeling and making a ten with a quick sketch? How are you at modeling and making a ten with partner numbers? How are you at finding the sum when you need to make a ten?"

Closure

- Show students 2 addition equations: $24 + 5 =$ ___ and $33 + 8 =$ ___. Have students select the equation that will make a ten. They model the equation using the model of their choice and find the sum on whiteboards. Challenge students to try to show both models if they think they can.

Think and Grow: Modeling Real Life

You put 17 puzzle pieces together. There are 7 left. How many puzzle pieces are there in all?

Addition equation:

$17 + 7 = 24$

Model:

Make a 10?  Yes No

24 puzzle pieces

Show and Grow *I can think deeper!*

11. You color 46 states. There are 4 left. How many states are there in all?

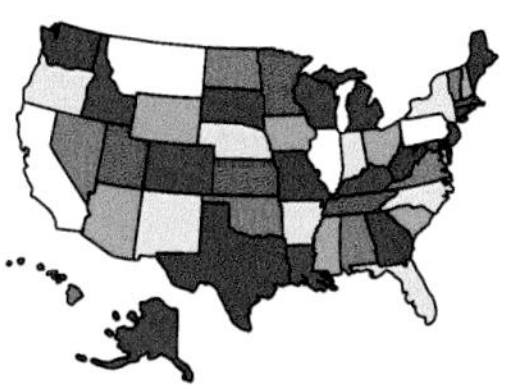

Addition equation:

$46 + 4 = 50$

Model:

Make a 10?  Yes No

50 states

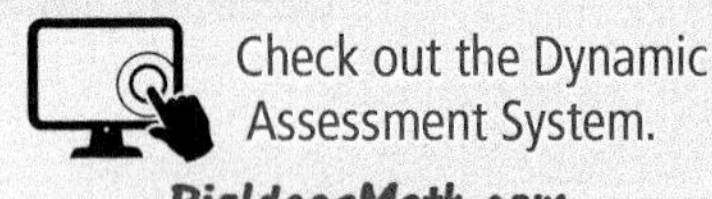
Check out the Dynamic
Assessment System.
BigIdeasMath.com

Scaffold assignments to support all students in their learning progression. Revisit with spaced practice to move every student toward proficiency.

Connect and Extend Learning

Practice Notes

- Provide base ten blocks for support, if needed.
- **Exercise 8**: You may want to discuss animals that lay eggs (reptiles, birds, fish, insects) and animals that do not (mammals).

Prior Skills

- **Exercise 10:** Kindergarten, Describing Two-Dimensional Shapes

Cross-Curricular Connections

Language Arts

- Write spelling or sight words on the board for students to copy. Have students write or circle the consonants using one color and the vowels using a different color. The total number of vowels should be a one-digit number and the total number of consonants should be a two-digit number. Students count the number of each and use the numbers as addends in an addition equation. You could use student names or write a sentence such as, "Adding two numbers is so much fun!" Alternatively, give students a collection of letter tiles to sort.

Name ________________________

Practice 9.3

Learning Target: Make a 10 to add a one-digit number and a two-digit number.

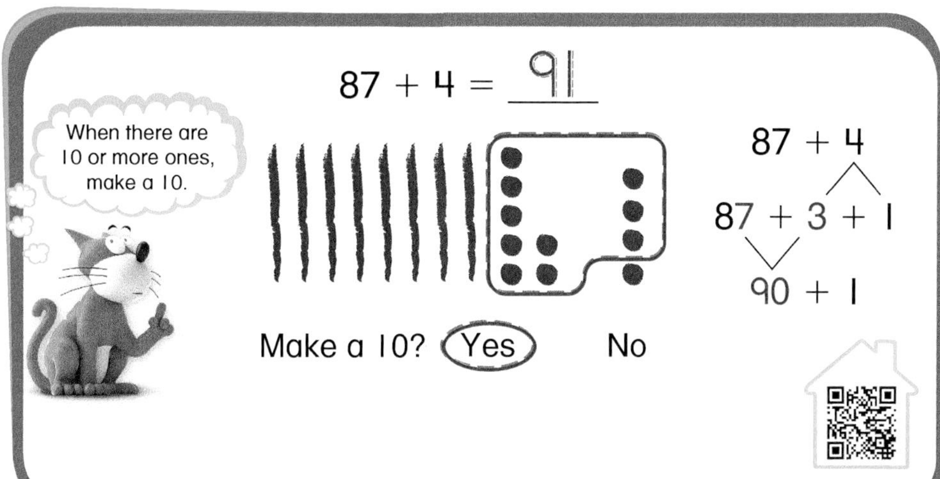

When there are 10 or more ones, make a 10.
87 + 4 = 91
Make a 10? Yes No
87 + 4
87 + 3 + 1
90 + 1

1. 66 + 5 = 71

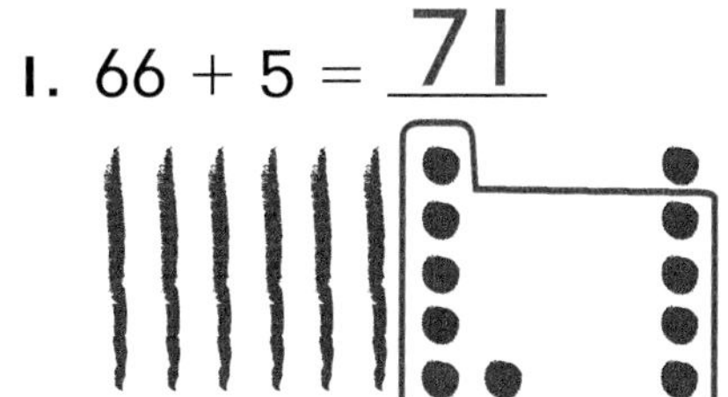

Make a 10? Yes No

2. 74 + 3 = 77

Make a 10? Yes 

3. 28 + 8 = 36

Make a 10?  No

4. 52 + 9 = 61

Make a 10?  No

Connect and Extend Learning

Extend Student Learning

Logical-Mathematical

- Give each student number cards 1 to 8 and have them use three cards to create a two-digit number and a one-digit number. Have students write an equation for the sum of their numbers and make a sketch of the problem, stating whether they make a 10 to add or not. Students can also work in pairs or small groups. Repeat with different numbers.

Lesson Resources	
Surface Level	**Deep Level**
Resources by Chapter • Extra Practice • Reteach Differentiating the Lesson Skills Review Handbook Skills Trainer	Resources by Chapter • Enrichment and Extension Graphic Organizers Dynamic Assessment System • Lesson Practice

5. 26 + 7 = 33

Make a 10?  Yes No

6. 41 + 6 = 47

Make a 10? Yes  No

7. Logic Complete.

37 + 4

37 + 3 + 1

40 + 1

37 + 4 = 41

8. Modeling Real Life
A snake lays 24 eggs.
Another snake lays 9 eggs.
How many eggs are there in all?

33 eggs

9. DIG DEEPER! Find the sums. What is similar about how you find the sums?

36 + 6 = 42

56 + 6 = 62

In both cases, I add 4 first to make a ten.

Review & Refresh

10. Color the shapes that have 4 vertices.

 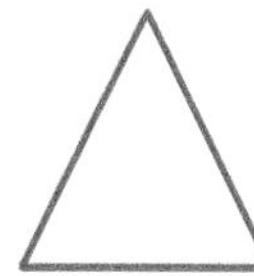  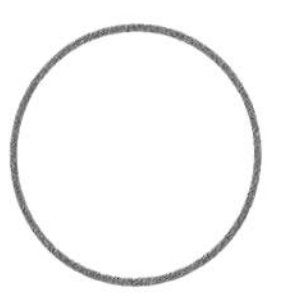

9.4

Check out the
Dynamic Classroom.
BigIdeasMath.com

Laurie's Notes

STATE STANDARDS
1.NBT.B.2a, 1.NBT.B.2b, 1.NBT.B.2c, 1.NBT.C.4

Learning Target

Use place value to add two numbers.

Success Criteria

- Make a quick sketch to show both numbers.
- Tell whether I can make a 10.
- Add the tens and count on the ones.

Warm-Up

Practice opportunities for the following are available in the Resources by Chapter or at *BigIdeasMath.com*.

- Daily skills
- Vocabulary
- Prerequisite skills

ELL Support

Review the meaning of *place value* and the values associated with each digit of a two-digit number. The word *value* refers to an amount. The digit farthest to the right represents ones. The digit to its left represents tens. The term *place value* refers to the value of each digit as determined by its place, or location, in a number.

Preparing to Teach

We continue adding two numbers by joining the tens and the ones, grouping and making a ten as appropriate. Today's addends will both be two-digit numbers. We model the numbers in a place value chart, setting up the vertical notation of the standard addition algorithm.

Materials

- base ten blocks
- Place Value Mat*

**Found in the Instructional Resources*

Dig In (Circle Time)

Students use base ten blocks to add two-digit numbers. They group ones and make an exchange for a ten within the chart.

- "We are going to continue adding numbers today and making a ten when necessary. Let's start by adding 56 + 7, just like we did yesterday. Use your Place Value Mat to model 56, and underneath model the 7."

? "How many of the 7 cubes do I need to add to the 6 to make a ten? Move 4 cubes up to join the 6. Count to see there are 10. Pick up the 10 cubes and trade them for a ten rod. Put the rod in the tens column. What is the sum?"

◉ **Model**: "Today we are going to continue adding. This time both addends will have two digits. Let's model 55 + 17. Can we make a ten?"

◉ Have students regroup the cubes into a group of 10 and a group of 2. They replace the 10 cubes with one rod, and place the rod in the Tens column. Tell the sum.

- Have students complete 2 additional equations: 39 + 26 and 47 + 38. Students should work with a partner repeating the process of modeling the addends, making an exchange, and telling the sum. Partner 1 should model the addends, Partner 2 makes the exchange, and Partner 1 tells the sum. Then switch roles.
- Have students tell their partners how what we are doing is the same as yesterday. How is it different?

◉ "Today, we are adding two-digit numbers. We will need to regroup ones to make a ten. That is what we learned to do yesterday. To find the sum, we will add the number of tens including the ten we made, and the rest of the ones."

? Teaching Prompt ◉ Learning Target

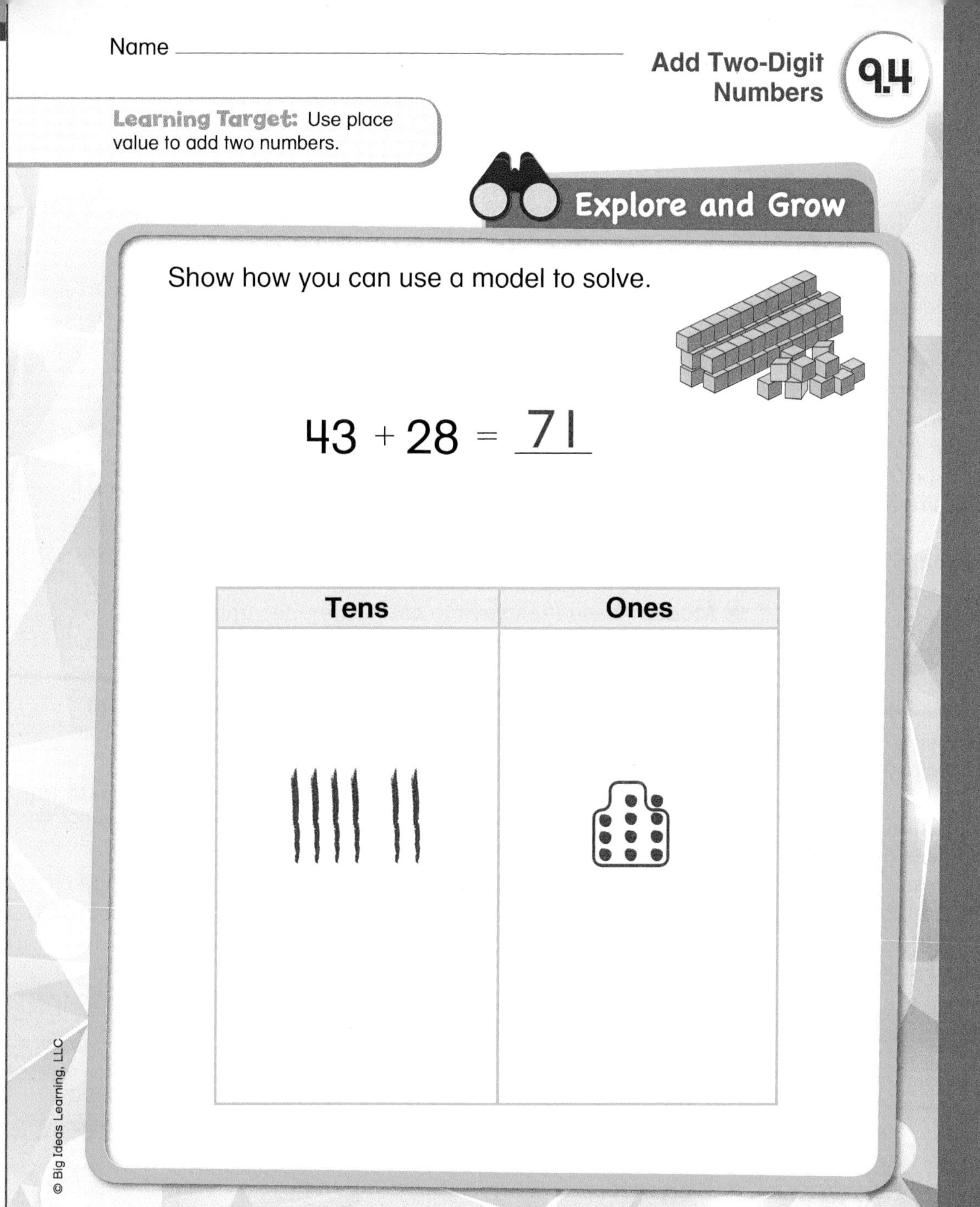
Name
Add Two-Digit Numbers
9.4
Learning Target: Use place value to add two numbers.
Explore and Grow
Show how you can use a model to solve.
43 + 28 = 71
Tens
Ones
© Big Ideas Learning, LLC
Chapter 9 | Lesson 4
four hundred seventy-seven
477

Explore and Grow

- Have students model 43 + 28 with base ten blocks. Tell them to show the addition and regroup ones as they need to. They should write in the sum.
- Watch to see if students exchange the unit cubes for a rod, or if they write the sum as 611 (6 rods and 11 cubes).
- "When we first added two-digit numbers we added the tens and the ones. There are 4 tens and 2 tens in the addends, but the sum has 7 tens. Tell your partner why."

ELL Support

Review the example. Then have students practice verbal language in pairs. Have one student ask another, "How many tens/ones are in the first number? How many tens/ones are in the second number? Is another ten added? How many ones are left? What is the total?" Have them alternate roles for other exercises.

Beginner students may state one-word answers.
Intermediate students may state phrases or simple sentences.
Advanced students may describe the process used to answer the questions.

Laurie's Notes

Think and Grow

Getting Started

- Students will use quick sketches within a place value chart for addition and regrouping. They will use digits in a place value chart to record the addition.

Teaching Notes

- **Model:** "Newton and Descartes are adding 26 + 28. Newton draws a quick sketch of the two addends. Trace the quick sketch. Newton has circled a group of ones. Tell your partner why."
- ◉ **Model:** "Newton says to count the number of 10 units by counting the rods and the group of 10 units. How many tens are in the sum? Write in the 5 below the quick sketch for 5 tens."
- ◉ **Model:** "Descartes says to count the ones units that are left. How many units are left? Be careful not to count any units that are part of the group of ten. Write in the 4 for the ones."
- Have students look at the chart to the right. "The addition problem has been written vertically into a place value chart. Do you see the tens and ones in 26 and 28 being added? The number of tens and ones are written at the bottom beneath the line meaning *equals* when you write the equation vertically. Fill in the 5 tens and the 4 ones in the place value chart."
- Have students quick sketch the addends in the place value chart. They circle a group of 10 ones. Have students tell their partner how many tens and how many ones are in the sum. Fill in the number of tens and ones in the bottom of the numeric place value chart and in the blanks below.
- **Supporting Learners:** Provide base ten blocks for students to manipulate.
- **Supporting Learners:** Students should cross out the circled group of ten and draw in an extra rod to show the regrouping and sum more clearly.
- **Extension:** Explain where the extra ten in the sum comes from based on the digits in the addends. They should look at the numeric place value chart.

Think and Grow

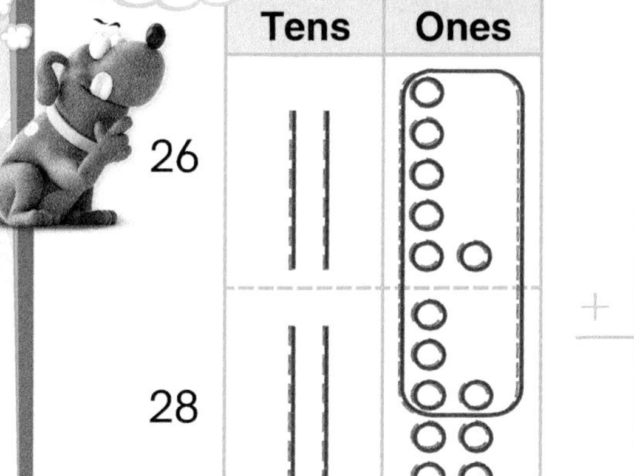
Find the number of tens by counting the rods and the group of 10 units.

Find the number of ones by counting the units that are left.

26 + 28 = ?

	Tens	Ones
26		
28		

	Tens	Ones
	2	6
+	2	8
	5	4

5 tens 4 ones

Show and Grow *I can do it!*

1. 39 + 45 = ?

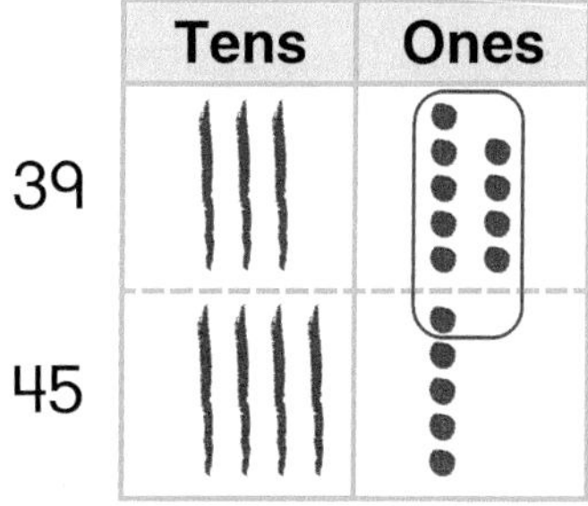

	Tens	Ones
39		
45		

	Tens	Ones
	3	9
+	4	5
	8	4

8 tens 4 ones

Scaffold instruction to support all students in their learning. Learning is individualized and you may want to group students differently as they move in and out of these levels with each skill and concept. Student self-assessment and feedback help guide your instructional decisions about how and when to layer support for all students to become proficient learners.

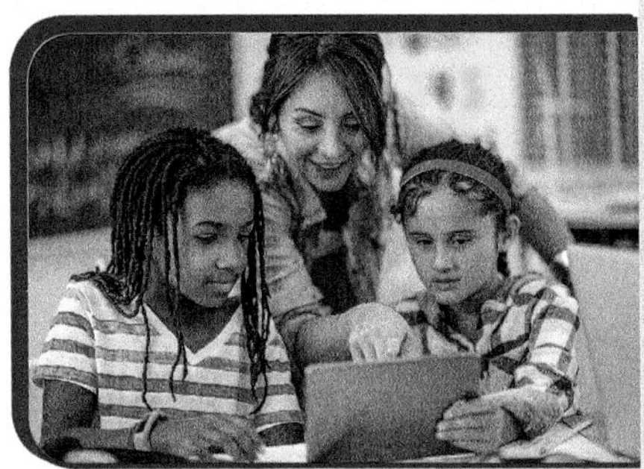

Meeting the needs of all learners.

Laurie's Notes

Apply and Grow: Practice

SCAFFOLDING INSTRUCTION

Students continue to use quick sketches in a place value chart to add two-digit numbers. They will write the sum in the vertical addition format.

EMERGING students may continue to need place value reinforcement. They may miss counting a group of ten ones with the tens. Having students cross out the group of ten ones and adding a rod will help with making sense of the sum.

- **Exercise 2:** This exercise is the same as Exercise 1. Watch students as they complete the exercise to see if anyone needs a small group re-teaching.
- **Exercises 3 and 4:** Students continue to quick sketch the addends and find the sum. They write the sum in the vertical equation.
- **Exercise 5:** This exercise shows one of the common mistakes students make at this stage. The addends are modeled correctly, and the ones are grouped. However, the sum does not reflect the circled group of ten ones. They should explain this in their own words.

PROFICIENT students can draw quick sketches, regroup, and tell the sums.

- **Exercises 3 and 4:** Students may need to be reminded about the vertical format of an equation as they have not worked with it recently.
- **Exercise 5:** Students may assume the sum is correct because the model is correct. If so, have them cover the sum in the equation and have them say the sum from the quick sketch model.

Additional Support

- Provide base ten blocks. Being able to regroup and exchange blocks will make the addition more visual.

Extension: Adding Rigor

- Have students roll 4 dice to make 2 two-digit numbers. They should quick sketch and add. Write a vertical equation for the numbers.

Name ___

Apply and Grow: Practice

2. 19 + 35 = ?

	Tens	Ones
19	|	•••••••••
35	|||	•••••

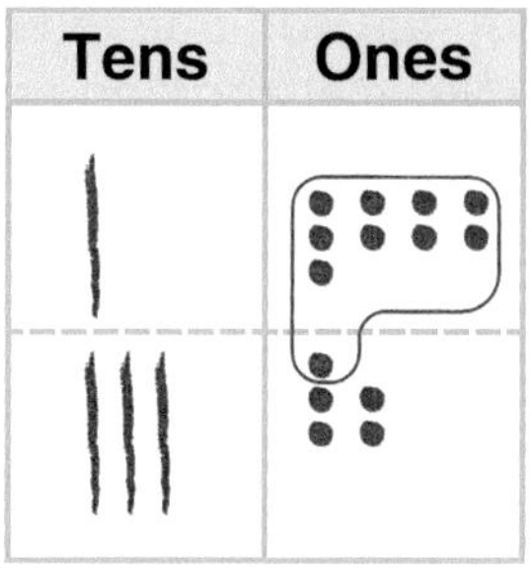

	Tens	Ones
	1	9
+	3	5
	5	4

5 tens 4 ones

3. 43 + 17

	Tens	Ones
	4	3
+	1	7
	6	0

4. 67 + 14

	Tens	Ones
	6	7
+	1	4
	8	1

5. MP YOU BE THE TEACHER Is the sum correct? Explain.

58
+ 28
76

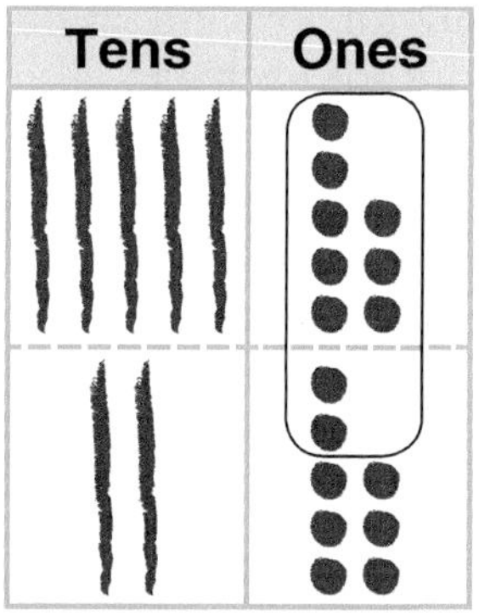

Tens	Ones
|||||	••••••••
||	••••••••

no; The ten made up of the circled ones was not added in.

ELL Support

Check for understanding of Lesson 9.4. Read each story aloud as students follow along. Clarify any misunderstanding. Point out that the word *read* describes an activity in the present and the past, but is pronounced differently in each time period. You may want to model the sentences "I will read today" and "I read yesterday" to demonstrate. Allow time to complete each exercise. Ask the following questions for each exercise and have students display answers on a whiteboard. Have them indicate yes/no answers with a thumbs up/down signal.

1. How many tens are in the first number?
2. How many ones are in the first number?
3. How many tens are in the second number?
4. How many ones are in the second number?
5. Do the ones make another ten?
6. How many extra ones are there?
7. What is the total?

Laurie's Notes

Think and Grow: Modeling Real Life

The application problems continue addition of two-digit numbers. Students are asked to write a vertical addition equation and to quick sketch in the place value chart.

- Discuss the story. Have students tell how many pages were read and what numbers need to be added. They write the equation vertically.
- Make a quick sketch of 34 and 37 in the place value chart. Have students suggest how to find the sum. Students should suggest that you group ones together to make a ten. Some students may need to cross out the group of ten and draw an additional rod.
- Students should determine the number of tens and ones in the sum and fill in the blanks. They write the sum in the vertical equation.
- **MP4 Model with Mathematics:** Discuss with students the number of stickers they will get. Some may want to say 71 stickers. Remind them that they get one sticker for every ten pages. They look at the number of tens to see that they will get 7 stickers. Ask students how many more pages they need to read to get another sticker.
- Discuss Exercise 6. Students follow the same thinking and example just completed. Remind students that they earn a coin for every 10 cans, not for each can.

◉ "Let's use thumb signals to show how you are doing with your learning. How are you at using the place value chart with quick sketches to find a sum? How are you at finding the tens and ones in the sum? How are you at writing in the sum in a vertical addition equation?"

Closure

- Show students a quick sketch of 37 + 38 in a place value chart. Students write a vertical equation including the sum.

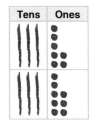

Tens	Ones

Think and Grow: Modeling Real Life

You earn a sticker for every 10 pages you read. You read 34 pages one week and 37 the next. How many stickers do you earn?

Addition problem:

$$\begin{array}{r} 34 \\ +37 \\ \hline \end{array}$$

Model:

Tens	Ones
|||	
|||	

Write the missing numbers:

7 tens 1 one

7 stickers

Show and Grow *I can think deeper!*

6. You earn a coin for every 10 cans you recycle. You recycle 18 cans one week and 25 the next. How many coins do you earn?

Addition problem:

$$\begin{array}{r} 18 \\ +25 \\ \hline \end{array}$$

Model:

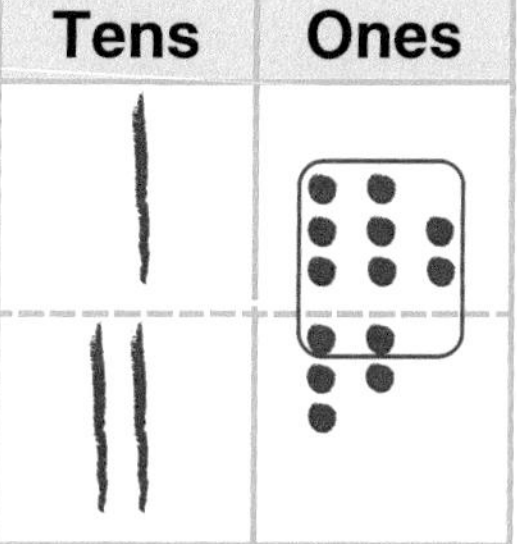

Tens	Ones
|	
||	

Write the missing numbers:

4 tens 3 ones

4 coins

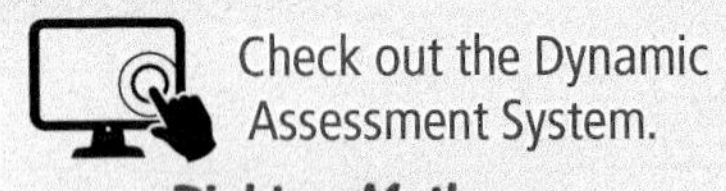
Check out the Dynamic
Assessment System.
BigIdeasMath.com

Scaffold assignments to support all students in their learning progression. Revisit with spaced practice to move every student toward proficiency.

Connect and Extend Learning

Practice Notes

- Provide Place Value Mats and base ten blocks for support, if needed.
- **Exercise 4**: Challenge students to answer without finding the sums.

Prior Skills

- **Exercise 6**: Grade 1, Identifying Whether an Equation is True or False

Cross-Curricular Connections

Language Arts

- *A Fair Bear Share* by Murphy, Stuart J; Read the book aloud to students. Have students find the sums, using two numbers at a time, as you go along. Have students show their work on Place Value Mats.

Name ______________________

Practice 9.4

Learning Target: Use place value to add two numbers.

$16 + 27 = ?$

Remember to make a 10 when there are 10 or more ones.

	Tens	Ones
16	|	○○○○○○
27	||	○○○○○○○

	Tens	Ones
	1	6
+	2	7
	4	3

4 tens 3 ones

1. $57 + 15 = ?$

	Tens	Ones
57	|||||	●●●●●●●
15	|	●●●●●

	Tens	Ones
	5	7
+	1	5
	7	2

7 tens 2 ones

Connect and Extend Learning

Extend Student Learning

Bodily-Kinesthetic

- Have students work with a partner. Have one partner do jumping jacks or another activity while the other partner counts the number completed. Set a timer or have them continue until the music stops, then have partners switch roles. Students add their numbers to find the total number of jumping jacks they did in all. Repeat with different activities or time limits.

Lesson Resources	
Surface Level	**Deep Level**
Resources by Chapter • Extra Practice • Reteach Differentiating the Lesson Skills Review Handbook Skills Trainer	Resources by Chapter • Enrichment and Extension Graphic Organizers Dynamic Assessment System • Lesson Practice

2. $\begin{array}{r} 40 \\ +\ 36 \\ \hline \end{array}$

	Tens	Ones
	4	0
+	3	6
	7	6

3. $\begin{array}{r} 29 \\ +\ 52 \\ \hline \end{array}$

	Tens	Ones
	2	9
+	5	2
	8	1

4. **DIG DEEPER!** Do you need to use the *make a 10* strategy to find each sum?

28 + 34 = ? (Yes) No 42 + 21 = ? Yes (No)

56 + 15 = ? (Yes) No 68 + 11 = ? Yes (No)

5. **Modeling Real Life** You need a box for every 10 muffins you make. You make 33 blueberry muffins and 47 banana muffins. How many boxes do you need?

8 boxes

Review & Refresh

6. Is the equation true or false?

$6 + 9 \stackrel{?}{=} 17 - 1$ 6 + 9: 17 − 1:

15 $\stackrel{?}{=}$ 16

True (False)

9.5

Laurie's Notes

Check out the
Dynamic Classroom.
BigIdeasMath.com

COMMON CORE

STATE STANDARDS
1.NBT.B.2a, 1.NBT.B.2b, 1.NBT.B.2c, 1.NBT.C.4

Learning Target

Choose a strategy to add two numbers.

Success Criteria

- Choose a strategy to add two numbers.
- Explain the strategy I used.
- Add the numbers and write the sum.

Warm-Up

Practice opportunities for the following are available in the Resources by Chapter or at *BigIdeasMath.com*.

- Daily skills
- Vocabulary
- Prerequisite skills

ELL Support

Explain that a strategy is a plan or approach used to accomplish something. Students have learned different ways to add numbers. Each way of adding is a strategy. When you develop more than one strategy for doing something, you expand your tools for learning and increase your chance for success.

Preparing to Teach

Today, we practice using a hundred chart, open number line, and quick sketches to add two-digit numbers with regrouping. Students will choose the strategy they want to use on a variety of problems. Encourage students to practice more than one strategy instead of only using one on all problems.

Materials

- whiteboards
- Hundred Chart*
- base ten blocks

**Found in the Instructional Resources*

Dig In (Circle Time)

Students will practice solving addition with regrouping using all of the strategies they have learned.

- "You may not realize it, but we have learned 5 different strategies to add two-digit numbers." Have students tell the strategies they remember. hundred chart; base ten blocks; quick sketch; open number line; place value chart with numbers (or quick sketch)
- ◉ **Model**: "Let's add 47 + 35." Model all 5 strategies for students to copy and review on their whiteboards.
- As you model each strategy, be sure to emphasize exchanging ten ones for one ten, and how to determine the sum.
- ◉ Divide students around the circle into 5 sections. For example, if you have 24 students, have first 5 students be group 1, etc. For each problem, assign a group a strategy to practice. After work time, students show their completed work to compare. Rotate strategies with each problem. Problems can be: 35 + 16; 44 + 27; 51 + 49; 73 + 18; 68 + 24
- To shorten the time for Dig In, eliminate base ten blocks and/or the Hundred Chart. Use 3 or 4 problems and rotate strategies.
- ◉ For a final problem, have students choose whichever strategy they want to use. Students share why they chose their strategy.
- ◉ "Today you will choose the strategy you want to use to solve the addition equations."

? Teaching Prompt ◉ Learning Target

Name ______________________

Learning Target: Choose a strategy to add two numbers.

Practice Addition Strategies **9.5**

Explore and Grow

Show two ways you can find the sum. *Sample answer:*

23 + 39 = 62

Tens	Ones
||	•••
|||	•••••••••

6 tens 2 ones

23 + 39 = 62

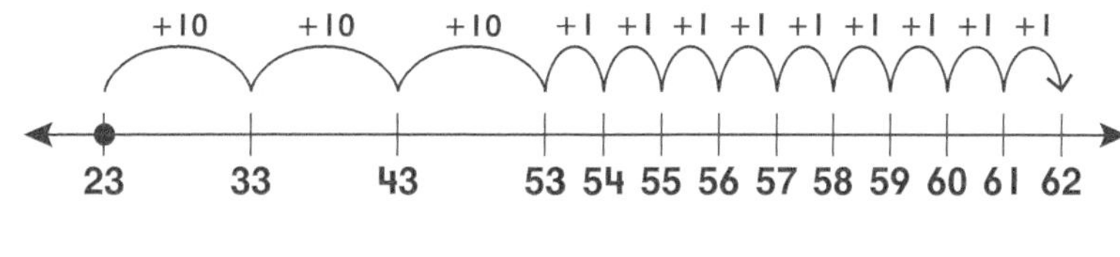

Explore and Grow

- Have students show two different ways to find the sum. Select students to share their strategies with the class, or partner students who have at least one different strategy to teach each other.
- Try to keep track of students' preferred strategies.
- "There is not a *right* strategy to use when adding. Sometimes a strategy might be easier to use depending on the numbers being added. Which strategies do you like to use, and why?"

ELL Support

Review the two strategies presented. Then have groups work together to complete Exercises 1 and 2. Have half of the students in each group use one strategy and half use another. Have groups discuss the following questions as they apply to each problem: "How many tens are in each number? How many ones? Do the ones create another ten? What is the answer?" Monitor discussion and expect students to perform according to their language proficiency level.

Beginner students may state one-word answers.
Intermediate students may state phrases and simple sentences.
Advanced students may describe the process used to answer the questions.

Laurie's Notes

Think and Grow

Getting Started

- Students will use an open number line and a quick sketch to add the same equation. These are two of many strategies that could be used.

Teaching Notes

- **Model**: "Newton is adding 29 + 36 in two different ways. At first he uses a quick sketch. Find the quick sketch of 29 and draw it in. Next find the quick sketch of 36 and draw it in."
- ◉ **Model**: "Newton notices that there are more than ten ones units when they are joined together. Notice the circle of ones units. Newton circled 10 ones because they should be grouped to make 1 ten unit. You can cross through all the ones and draw in an extra ten rod if that helps to see the sum. How many tens and how many ones are in the sum? Write in the sum."
- **Model**: "Newton also uses an open number line. He begins the number line with 29. Newton chooses to make six hops of +1 first. He could have added the ten hops first if he wanted, but it doesn't matter. After he hops six hops of +1, he makes the three +10 hops. Sketch in the hops."
- ◉ **Model**: "Draw in the hops on the number line, and the +1 and +10 above the hops. Let's count the numbers together from the hops. Now fill in the numbers on the number line and write in the sum."
- ? **MP6 Attend to Precision**: "Which of Newton's methods do you think shows the addition more clearly? Which one shows grouping 10 ones to make 1 ten better? Of these methods, which is easier for you to use and why?"
- Students choose any method (not just Newton's) to add the numbers in Exercises 1 and 2. Encourage them to try two different strategies for the two exercises.
- **Supporting Learners:** Provide base ten blocks for students to manipulate.
- **Supporting Learners:** Provide a Hundred Chart for students to trace the numbers along the chart to fill in the number line.
- **Supporting Learners:** Suggest a different strategy for students to try if the one they choose is difficult for them.
- **Extension:** Have students compare and contrast the two methods. How are they alike and how are they different? Choose a third method and show the sum. Is your method more like the quick sketch or the number line, and why?

Think and Grow

$29 + 36 = ?$

One Way:

$$\begin{array}{r} 29 \\ +\ 36 \\ \hline 65 \end{array}$$

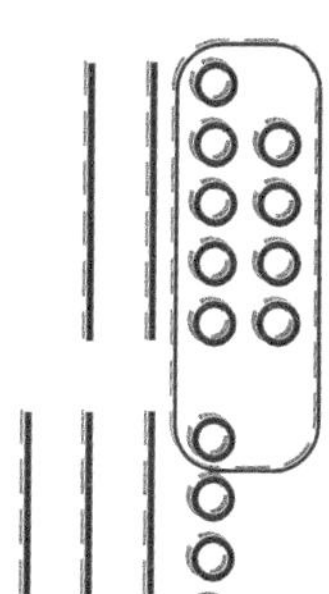

Another Way:

$29 + 36 = \underline{65}$

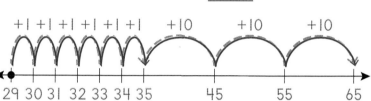

+1 +1 +1 +1 +1 +1 +10 +10 +10

29 30 31 32 33 34 35 45 55 65

Show and Grow *I can do it!*

1. $47 + 24 = \underline{71}$

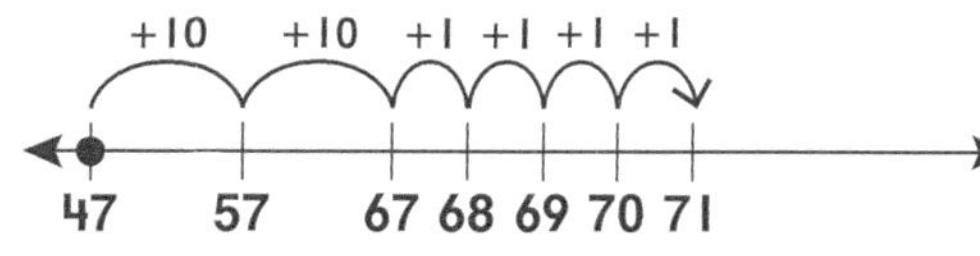

2. $38 + 43 = \underline{81}$

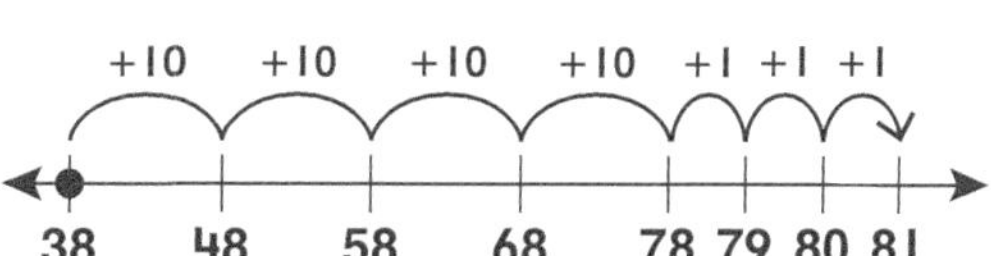

Scaffold instruction to support all students in their learning. Learning is individualized and you may want to group students differently as they move in and out of these levels with each skill and concept. Student self-assessment and feedback help guide your instructional decisions about how and when to layer support for all students to become proficient learners.

Meeting the needs of all learners.

Laurie's Notes

Apply and Grow: Practice

SCAFFOLDING INSTRUCTION

Students continue to add two-digit numbers using any method they choose. If a student uses a single strategy successfully, have them try a different strategy to stretch their learning.

EMERGING students may want to use only the base ten blocks or Hundred Chart as these can be the most concrete to use. Show students how base ten blocks can be shown by a quick sketch, and how the hundred chart can be shown on an open number line.

- **Exercises 3–6:** Students use a variety of strategies to add.
- **Exercise 6:** This equation does not require regrouping of ones into a ten. Watch to see if students count an "extra" ten in the sum anyway. Are they confused by not needing to regroup ones?
- **Exercise 7:** This exercise shows another common error of mistaken place value. Reinforce the value of the digits in 26, and have students look at the number line again.

PROFICIENT students can use multiple strategies for regrouping ones and finding the sum.

- **Exercises 2–6:** Students use multiple strategies. Have students explain why they chose the strategies they did. Are some strategies easier to use based on the addends?
- **Exercise 6:** Students are not confused by the ones digits and do not try to regroup in any way.
- **Exercise 7:** Have students explain the role of place value and correct the work. What problem does the number line show?

Additional Support

- Have students work with the two most comfortable strategies, as long as one of the strategies clearly shows how to regroup ones to a ten.

Extension: Adding Rigor

- Write the 5 strategies onto cards or slips of paper. Have students roll 4 dice to make 2 two-digit numbers and draw a strategy card. They add the numbers using the strategy on the card.

Name ______

Apply and Grow: Practice

3. 22 + 18 = 40

+10 +1 +1 +1 +1 +1 +1 +1 +1

22 32 33 34 35 36 37 38 39 40

4. 57 + 34 = 91

+10 +10 +10 +1 +1 +1 +1

57 67 77 87 88 89 90 91

5. 73 + 19 = 92

+10 +1 +1 +1 +1 +1 +1 +1 +1 +1

73 83 84 85 86 87 88 89 90 91 92

6. 81 + 11 = 92

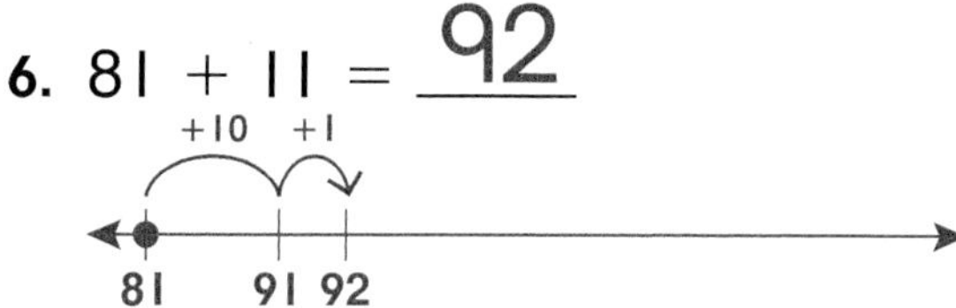

Repeated Reasoning Did you use the same strategy to solve each problem? Why or why not?

7. YOU BE THE TEACHER Is the sum correct? Explain.

17 + 26 ≟ 79

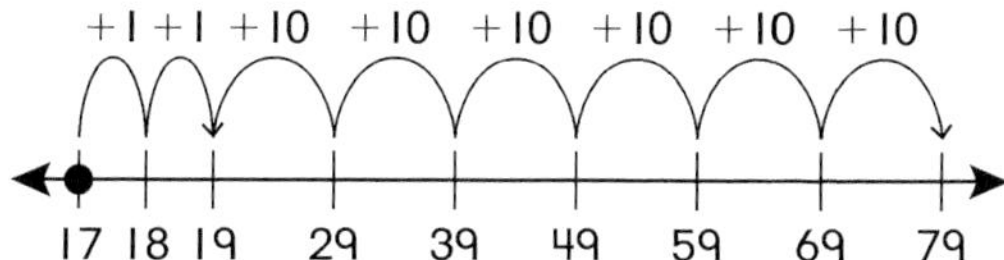

no; The ones are added as tens and the tens are added as ones.

Chapter 9 | Lesson 5 485

ELL Support

Check for understanding of Lesson 9.5. Read each story aloud as students follow along. Explain any unknown vocabulary or unfamiliar situations. Allow time to complete each exercise. Have students respond to the following questions by writing answers and holding them up for your review.

1. How many songs does your friend have?
2. How many candles do you sell?

Laurie's Notes

Think and Grow: Modeling Real Life

The application problems continue addition of two-digit numbers. Students are asked to write an addition equation and to model the addition in any way they choose.

- Discuss the story. Do students know anyone who has a playlist or a device that plays music?
- ? **MP1 Persevere in Solving Problems**: "If you have 48 songs, and your friend has 27 more than you, how can we figure out how many songs your friend has?"
- Write the addition equation. Have students vote on how to model the problem. For this teaching, model two different methods even though students only use one method on Exercise 8.
- Discuss Exercise 8. Have students discuss with a partner the numbers to be added and write the equation. For some partners, challenge them to use different strategies and compare their work for extra challenge.
- ◉ "Let's use a fist to five to show how you are doing with using different strategies for adding two-digit numbers and regrouping. We used 5 different strategies today: hundred chart; base ten blocks; quick sketch; open number line; place value chart with numbers (or quick sketch)." Have an example of each strategy for students to look at. "Show me a number, from fist meaning no strategy and 5 meaning all strategies, of how many strategies you feel you can use easily."

Closure

- Show students 57 + 34 on an open number line. On whiteboards, have students show the same problem using a different strategy.

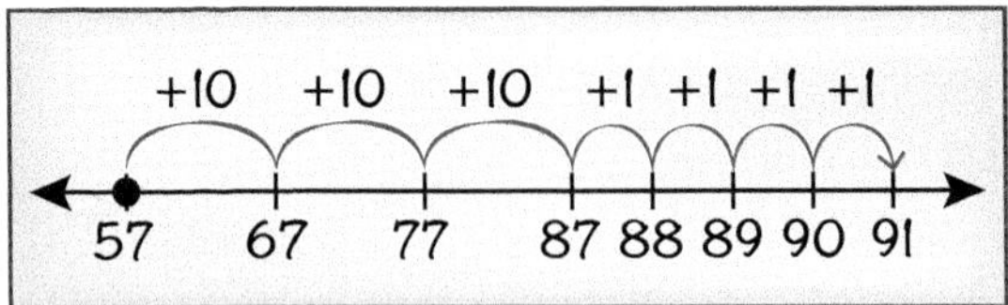

Think and Grow: Modeling Real Life

You have 48 songs. Your friend has 27 more than you. How many songs does your friend have?

Addition equation:

$48 + 27 = 75$

Model: ***Sample answer:***

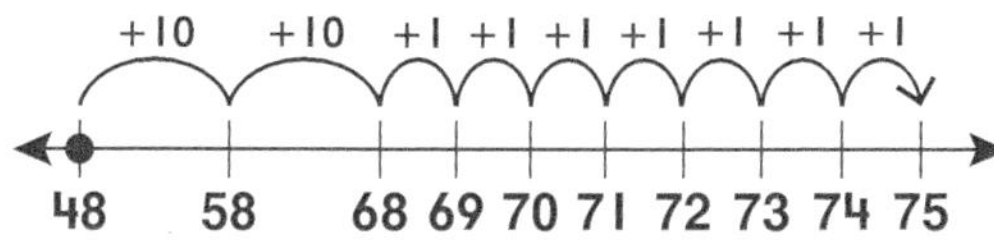

75 songs

Show and Grow *I can think deeper!*

8. Your friend sells 56 candles. You sell 35 more than your friend. How many candles do you sell?

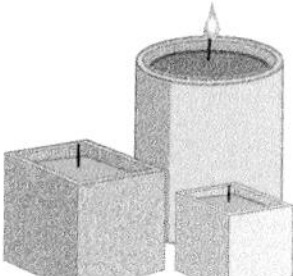

Addition equation:

$56 + 35 = 91$

Model: ***Sample answer:***

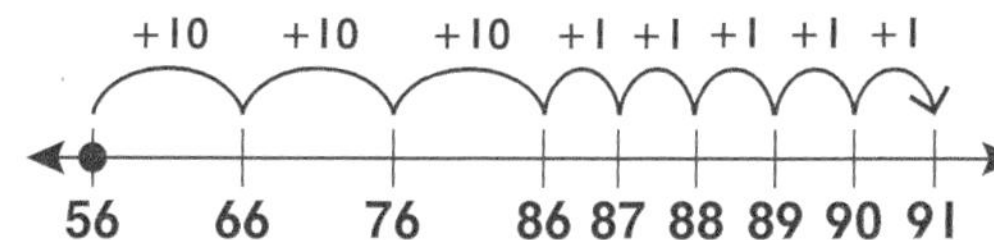

91 candles

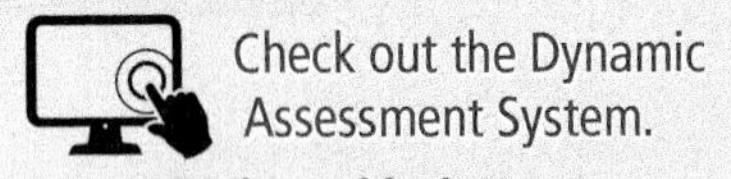
Check out the Dynamic
Assessment System.
BigIdeasMath.com

Scaffold assignments to support all students in their learning progression. Revisit with spaced practice to move every student toward proficiency.

Connect and Extend Learning

Practice Notes

- Remind students that they can use any strategy to solve.
- Provide models and manipulatives for support, if needed.
- **Exercise 5**: As an extension, ask students how many leaves you and your friend collect in all.

Prior Skills

- **Exercise 7**: Kindergarten, Describing Objects by Attributes

Cross-Curricular Connections

Art

- Have students create a poster about their favorite strategy for adding two numbers. Students should include an addition problem to model the strategy and draw a picture for the problem. Students can work in pairs or groups and then present their posters to the class.

Name ______________________

Learning Target: Choose a strategy to add two numbers.

$34 + 16 = ?$

One Way:

$$\begin{array}{r} 34 \\ +\ 16 \\ \hline 50 \end{array}$$

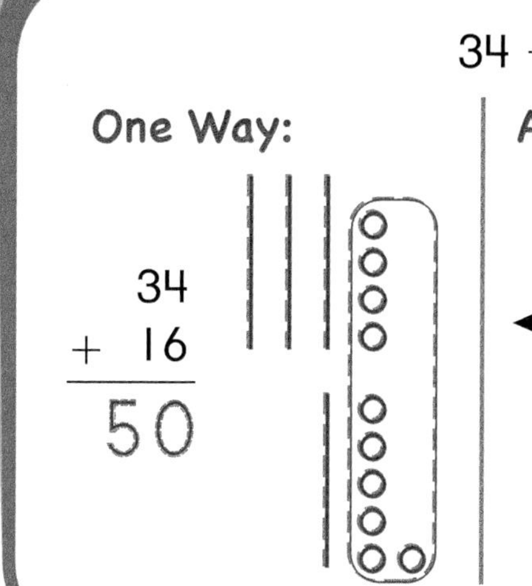

Another Way:

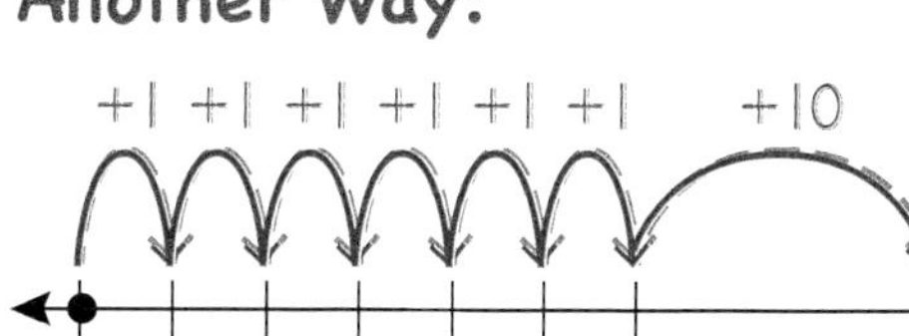

1. $62 + 29 =$ <u>91</u>

+10 +10 +1 +1 +1 +1 +1 +1 +1 +1 +1

62 72 82 83 84 85 86 87 88 89 90 91

2. $84 + 8 =$ <u>92</u>

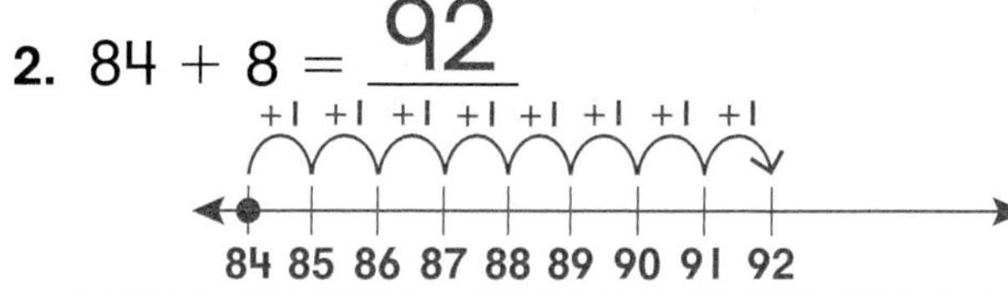

Communicate Clearly Which method do you prefer? Why?

3. $75 + 17 =$ <u>92</u>

+10 +1 +1 +1 +1 +1 +1 +1

75 85 86 87 88 89 90 91 92

Connect and Extend Learning

Extend Student Learning

Interpersonal

- Set up 5 bins or mark off 5 areas on the floor with tape. Label each bin or area with a different strategy. Write an addition problem on a whiteboard and then ask for a volunteer to toss a bean bag to determine the strategy for solving the equation. You can also divide students into groups and have one student from each group toss a bean bag. Repeat with different problems.

<table>
<tr><th colspan="2">Lesson Resources</th></tr>
<tr><th>Surface Level</th><th>Deep Level</th></tr>
<tr><td>Resources by Chapter
• Extra Practice
• Reteach
Differentiating the Lesson
Skills Review Handbook
Skills Trainer</td><td>Resources by Chapter
• Enrichment and Extension
Graphic Organizers
Dynamic Assessment System
• Lesson Practice</td></tr>
</table>

4. YOU BE THE TEACHER Is the sum correct? Explain.

$$\begin{array}{r} 58 \\ +\ 33 \\ \hline 91 \end{array}$$

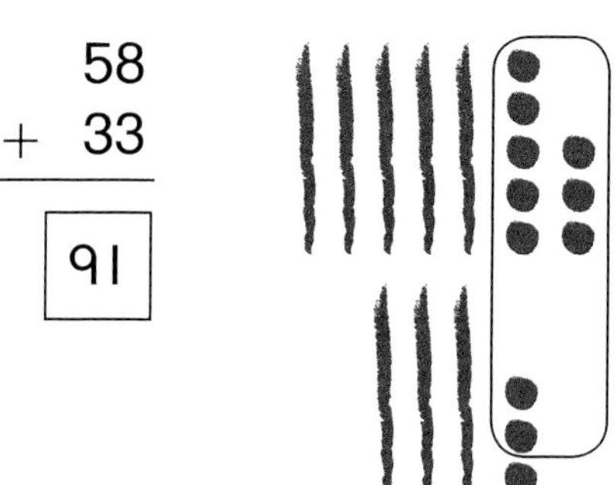

yes; 8 tens + 1 ten = 9 tens

9 tens + 1 one = 91

5. **Modeling Real Life** You collect 12 leaves. Your friend collects 26 more than you. How many leaves does your friend collect?

+10 +10 +1 +1 +1 +1 +1 +1

12 22 32 33 34 35 36 37 38

12 + 26 = 38

38 leaves

6. **Modeling Real Life** You pick 25 oranges. Newton picks 16 oranges and Descartes picks 7 oranges. Do you or Newton and Descartes together pick more oranges? How many more?

(You) Newton and Descartes 2 more oranges

Review & Refresh

7. Circle the measurable attributes of the table.

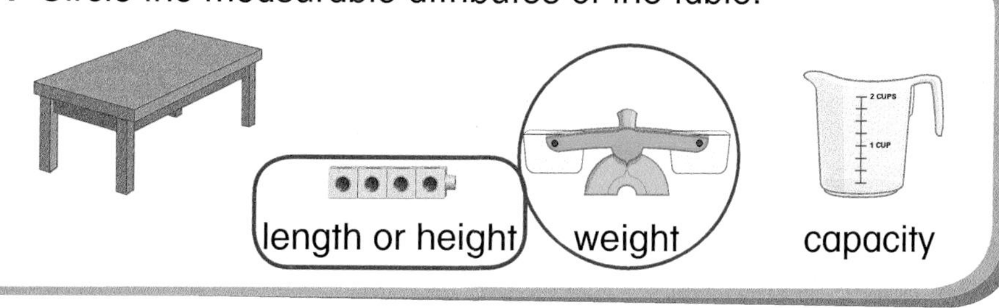

(length or height) (weight) capacity

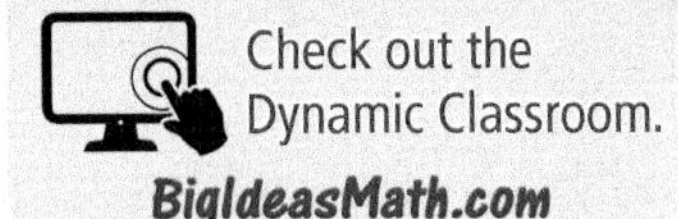
Check out the
Dynamic Classroom.
BigIdeasMath.com

Laurie's Notes

STATE STANDARDS
1.NBT.B.2a, 1.NBT.B.2b, 1.NBT.B.2c, 1.NBT.C.4

Preparing to Teach

Today's lesson has students solving real-world addition problems. They will circle the information they know from the story, and underline what they are to find out. This structure was used in Lesson 4.8. All of the exercises have space for students to solve the applications as they choose.

Dig In (Circle Time)

Students will practice solving addition applications. We review circling the information we know and underlining what we need to find. To remind students of their addition strategies, add to the list begun in Lesson 4.8 with the most recent strategies. Prepare two or three addition word problems on chart paper in advance, and have student circle the information and underline what we want to find.

- "We are going to solve lots of application stories today using all the strategies we have learned. We made a strategy chart for addition a while ago – today we will add to it with the strategies we have been using."
- Show the chart from Lesson 4.8. Add the strategies from yesterday to the chart or start a new chart.
- Use the following application stories. 1) Newton has 18 toys. Descartes gives him 13 more. How many toys does Newton have? 2) I have 47 pencils in boxes, and found 19 loose pencils. How many pencils do I have? 3) Our class has 37 rulers. I hope to get 15 more. How many rulers will we have?
- ◉ **Model:** For each story, discuss what we know. Have a student volunteer to come up and circle the information we know. Ask what we want to find out. Have another student come up and underline what we want to find out.
- Students should work alone or with a partner to solve the application. They may use whatever strategy they want.
- ◉ After each story, have several students share their strategy and why they chose to use it.
- ◉ "Today, you will choose the strategy you want to use to solve our application stories."

Learning Target

Solve addition word problems.

Success Criteria

- Identify what information is given in the word problem.
- Identify what the question is asking.
- Choose a strategy to solve.
- Explain the strategy I used to solve.

Warm-Up

Practice opportunities for the following are available in the Resources by Chapter or at *BigIdeasMath.com.*

- Daily skills
- Vocabulary
- Prerequisite skills

ELL Support

Explain that when a story involves performing a math operation, the story is called a word problem. Students will need to develop strategies for understanding what math is needed in order to solve a word problem. One strategy that may be helpful is to review in their vocabulary notebooks the vocabulary they have listed that signals addition.

? Teaching Prompt ◉ Learning Target

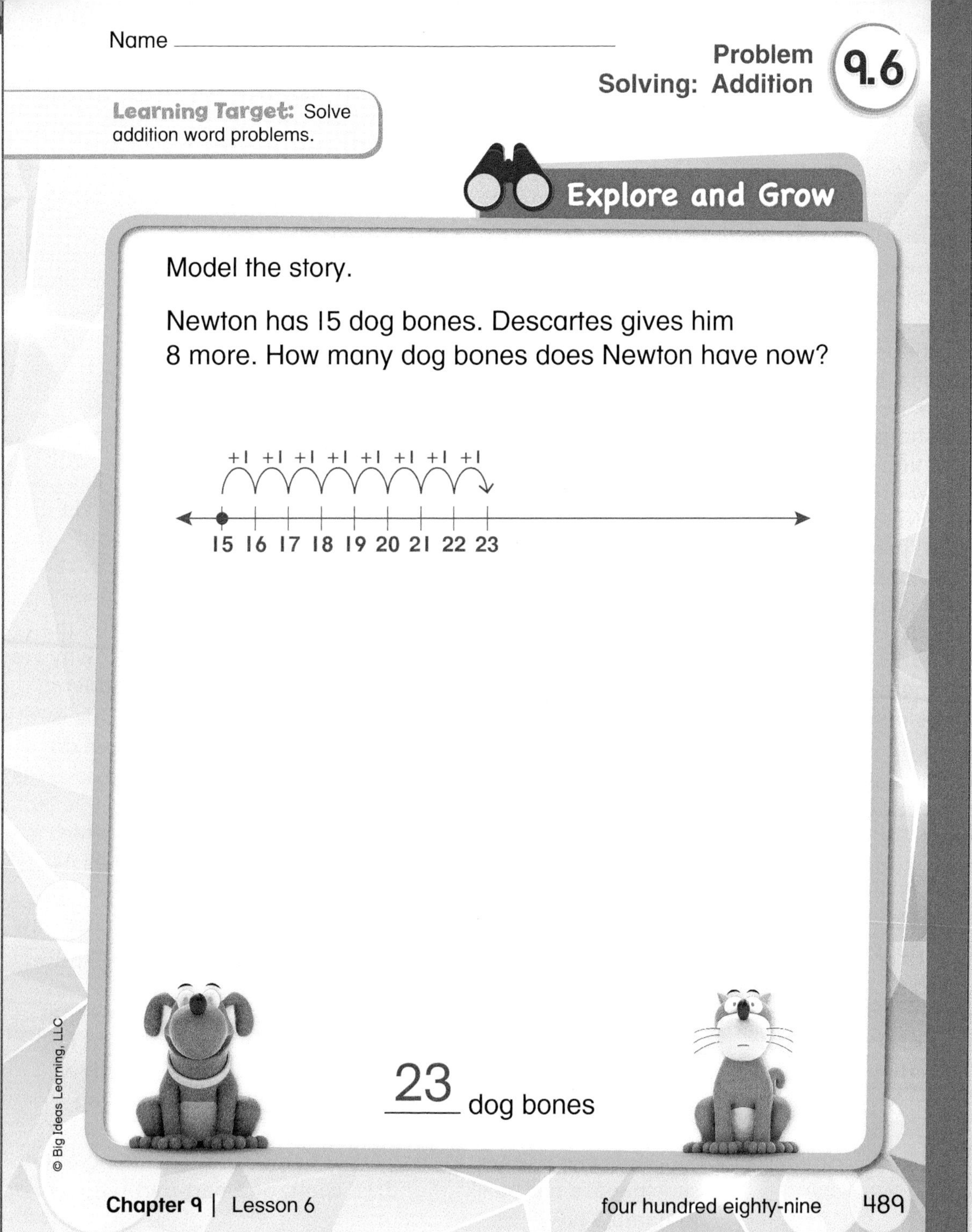

Name
Problem Solving: Addition
9.6
Learning Target: Solve addition word problems.
Explore and Grow
Model the story.
Newton has 15 dog bones. Descartes gives him 8 more. How many dog bones does Newton have now?
+1 +1 +1 +1 +1 +1 +1 +1
15 16 17 18 19 20 21 22 23
23 dog bones
© Big Ideas Learning, LLC
Chapter 9 | Lesson 6
four hundred eighty-nine 489

Explore and Grow

- Discuss the story with students. Have students suggest what we know and circle it. Have them underline what we want to find out.
- **MP3 Critique the Reasoning of Others:** Students can model and solve the story any way they want. Have some students share their strategies with the class. Have the other students determine whether each strategy makes sense and whether there is a more efficient way to solve.
- ◉ "Did anyone try a strategy that they do not usually use? Share it with us. Why did you decide to try that strategy?"

ELL Support

Model the example. Then have students practice verbal language in groups. For each exercise, have each group discuss the following questions: "What information do we circle? What do we underline? What is the equation? What is the answer?" Monitor discussion and provide support as needed. Expect students to perform at their language proficiency level.

Beginner students may use one word or simple phrases.
Intermediate students may use phrases or simple sentences.
Advanced students may use detailed sentences and describe the process needed.

Laurie's Notes

Think and Grow

Getting Started

- Students will continue to circle information that we know and underline what we want to find out in stories. They continue to choose the strategy they want to use to model and solve the stories.

Teaching Notes

- "We have another story to read." Have students read the story with a partner. "Who can tell the story in their own words?"
- ⦿ **Model**: "Tell your partner what we know in this story. Circle both sentences. Tell your partner what we want to find out. Underline it."
- **MP2 Reason Abstractly and Quantitatively**: "Notice that we know the first addend, and we know the sum. That is why the equation has a missing addend. Explain to your partner why we do not add 28 and 44. Explain why there is a missing addend."
- ⦿ **Model**: "Newton decides to use an open number line. This is different reasoning than we have used so far because we do not know what to add. We know we need to get to 44. Descartes starts at 28. He thinks, can I add 10? Yes, because 28 + 10 is 38. Can he add another 10? No, because that would be 48 which is greater than 44. So, Descartes adds ones until he reaches 44. Trace in the hops and the +10 and +1 for the size of the hop."
- **MP5 Use Appropriate Tools Strategically**: "Tell your partner how the number line shows the number of minutes you ride your scooter. Fill in the minutes."
- Exercise 1 is another missing addend story. Check to see that they have circled the information, underlined the need to find questions, and shown an equation. If students do not show an equation, check to see that they realize they are finding a missing addend.
- Students can use any strategy that helps them, including a quick sketch, base ten blocks, hundred chart, or a part-part-whole mat to name a few.
- **Supporting Learners**: Help students recognize the story as a missing addend situation. Suggest strategies for solving including the open number line (like the model), hundred chart, or base ten blocks.
- **Extension**: Have students compare and contrast their solution methods. Which method is easier to use with missing addend? Why?
- **Extension**: Try to prove your answer is correct by solving it another way.

Think and Grow

You ride your bike for 28 minutes. Then you ride your scooter. You ride for 44 minutes in all. How long do you ride your scooter?

Circle what you know. Underline what you need to find.

Solve: 28 + ? = 44

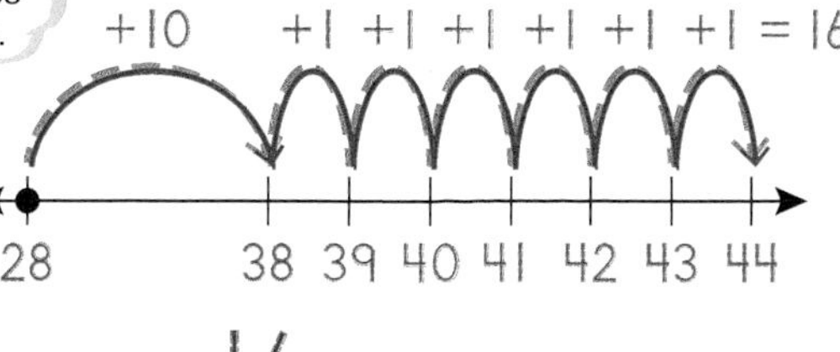

16 minutes

Show and Grow *I can do it!*

1. You have 49 toy soldiers. You buy some more. Now you have 84. How many toy soldiers did you buy?

Circle what you know: Underline what you need to find.

Solve: 49 + ? = 84

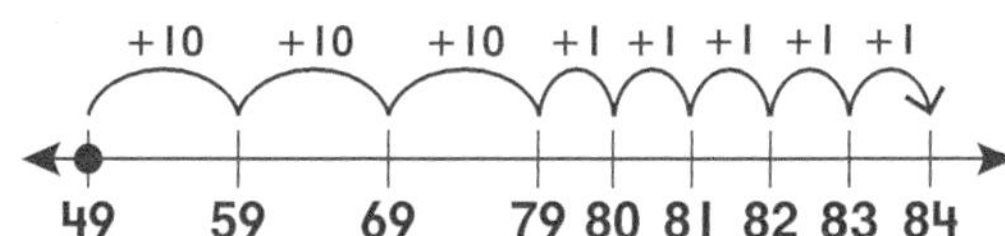

35 toy soldiers

Scaffold instruction to support all students in their learning. Learning is individualized and you may want to group students differently as they move in and out of these levels with each skill and concept. Student self-assessment and feedback help guide your instructional decisions about how and when to layer support for all students to become proficient learners.

Meeting the needs of all learners.

Laurie's Notes

Apply and Grow: Practice

SCAFFOLDING INSTRUCTION

Students continue to solve applications involving missing addends and a comparison addition problem. Students may need support recognizing the type of equation that will solve each situation. Students continue to use a strategy of their choosing.

EMERGING students are still mastering addition and regrouping with the variety of strategies. They will need support in using strategies to find missing addends as they have only been used to find sums previously.

- **Exercise 2:** This application is another missing addend situation.
- **Exercise 3:** This application is a joining situation, but is tricky in the wording. Try helping students rephrase it as "A teacher has 34 erasers. There are 46 more pencils than erasers. How many pencils are there?"
- **Exercise 4:** This exercise has students reason about numbers because it does not tell how many toys there are in all. Emerging students may need help realizing that any number that adds to a sum greater than 60 is correct. They might try to add each number. Instead, recommend that they find the number that will equal a sum of 60 and go from there.

PROFICIENT students can use multiple strategies to solve addition equations, but may need help in recognizing the addition context.

- **Exercise 2:** Have students compare this story to the ones on Think and Grow. They should see they have one addend and a sum. It is a missing addend story.
- **Exercise 3:** The wording of this story is tricky. If students do not recognize what to do, have them say how many more pencils there would be if the erasers are 46 fewer than the pencils.
- **Exercise 4:** Are students trying to add each number to see if the sum is greater than 60? Suggest they find the least number of toys the friend could have to equal 60.

Additional Support

- Help students understand how to set up an equation for each story and then let them solve using a strategy of their choosing.

Extension: Adding Rigor

- Have students find a partner who used a different strategy. They try to convince their partner that their strategy was the best to use.

Name ____________________

Apply and Grow: Practice

2. You have 55 pounds of dog food and some cat food. You have 63 pounds of pet food in all. How many pounds of cat food do you have?

Circle what you know.

Underline what you need to find.

Solve: 55 + ? = 63

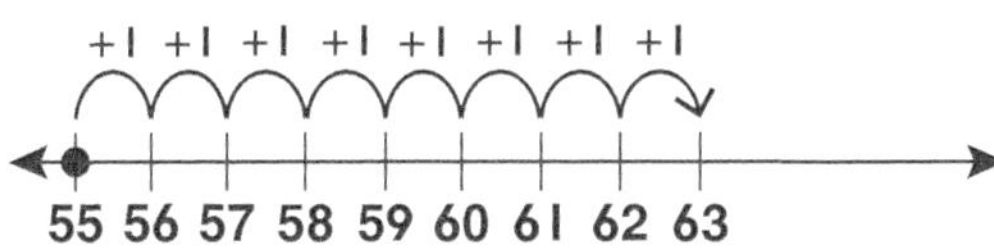

8 pounds

3. A teacher has 34 erasers. There are 46 fewer erasers than pencils. How many pencils are there?

34 + 46 = ?

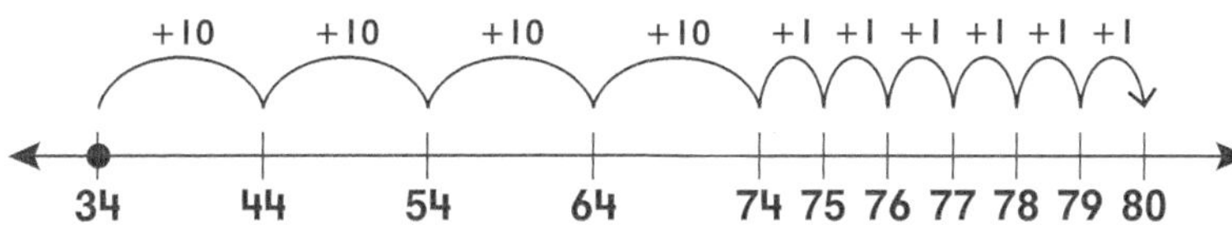

80 pencils

4. DIG DEEPER! You have 25 toys. Your friend has more than you. There are more than 60 toys in all. How many toys can your friend have?

29 33 24 38

ELL Support

Check for understanding of Lesson 9.6. Read each story aloud as students follow along. Clarify any unknown vocabulary. Have students work in pairs and write the equations needed to solve the problem on a whiteboard to hold up for your review. Ask the following yes/no questions and have students signal the answers with a thumbs up or thumbs down.

1. Do you have enough invitations?
2. Do you have enough bottles of water?

Laurie's Notes

Think and Grow: Modeling Real Life

The application stories continue with addition contexts. In these applications, students are asked if they have collected enough of the objects. Be sure students continue to circle the known information, including the number of items that are needed in each story, and underline what they need to find.

- Discuss the story. Have students tell what they know from the story. Be sure they include the number of invitations that are needed. They circle the known information. Have students underline what they need to find out.

? "How will we know how many invitations we have altogether? How do you want to show the addition?"

- Model the addition using a strategy students suggest. As you have watched students choose strategies, model a second strategy that students are not using.
- When the sum is found, point out that we need to compare 72 and 60 with the correct symbol. Students fill in 72 > 60 and answer Yes.
- Discuss Exercise 5. Have students discuss with a partner the numbers to be added, and to what number they will compare the sum. Students work through the application as the previous story was modeled.

◉ "Let's use our thumb signs to show how you are doing with using different strategies to solve applications. How are you doing with determining what needs to be added? How are you doing with finding missing addends? How are you doing with solving the stories?"

Closure

- Write an application story with students to be solved. Have them fill in the blanks to make the story: The first-grade students have ______ (two-digit number) ______ (plural noun). The second-grade students also have some. Altogether the first- and second-grade students have _____ (two-digit number greater than the first number) ______ (same plural noun). How many _____ (same plural noun) do the second-grade students have?
- Students solve their application story.

Think and Grow: Modeling Real Life

You need 60 invitations. You have 36 and buy 36 more. Do you have enough invitations?

Circle what you know.

Underline what you need to find.

Solve: 36 + 36 = 72

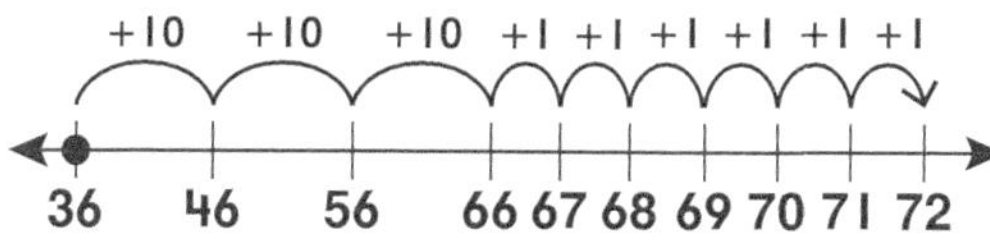

Compare: 72  > 60 Yes No

Show and Grow *I can think deeper!*

5. You need 84 bottles of water. You have 48 and buy 32 more. Do you have enough bottles of water?

Circle what you know.

Underline what you need to find.

Solve: 48 + 32 = 80

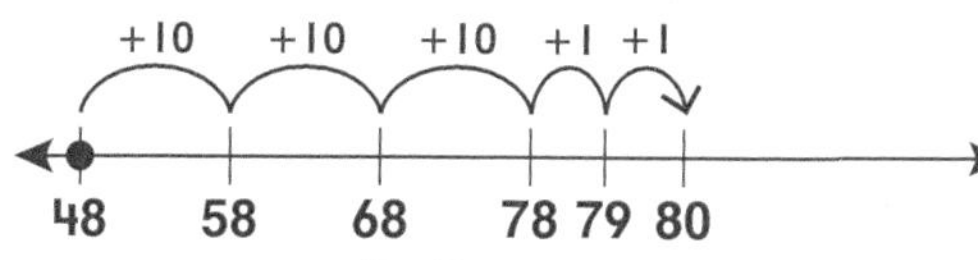

Compare: 80 < 84 Yes  No

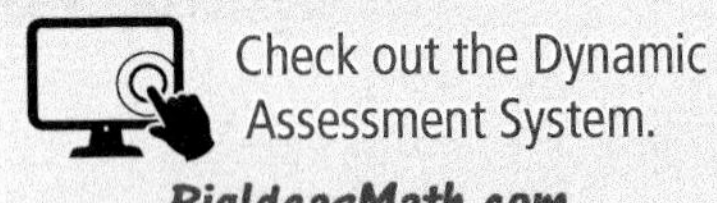
Check out the Dynamic Assessment System.
BigIdeasMath.com

Scaffold assignments to support all students in their learning progression. Revisit with spaced practice to move every student toward proficiency.

Connect and Extend Learning

Practice Notes

- **Exercise 2:** Students may think that because the word "fewer" is used, this is a subtraction exercise.
- **Exercise 3:** Explain to students that having exactly 60 toys is different than having more than 60 toys.

Prior Skills

- **Exercises 5 and 6:** Kindergarten, Comparing Lengths

Cross-Curricular Connections

Language Arts

- Divide students into pairs. Have one student tell the other a story (like the ones in this lesson) that includes two numbers to be used as addends or the sum in an equation. Have the other student write down the equation that arises from the story, then have the pair work together to solve the equation. Then let them switch roles, and have the other student tell a story for the first student to create an equation from.

Name ____________

Practice 9.6

Learning Target: Solve addition word problems.

You have 23 seashells. You find some more. Now you have 39. How many more seashells did you find?

Circle what you know.

Underline what you need to find.

Solve: 23 + ? = 39

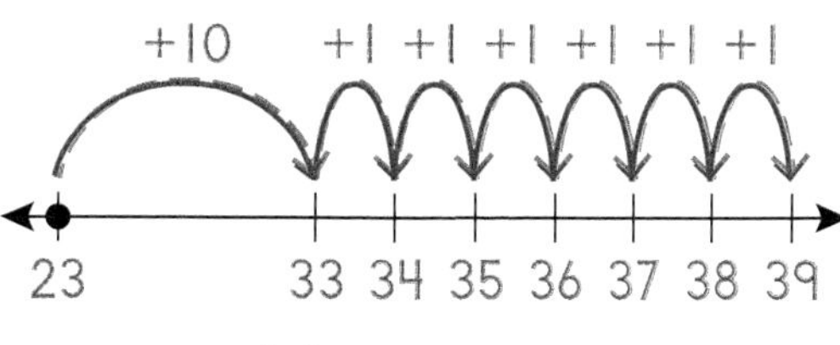

16 seashells

1. You have 31 stuffed animals. You and your friend have 60 stuffed animals in all. How many stuffed animals does your friend have?

31 + ? = 60

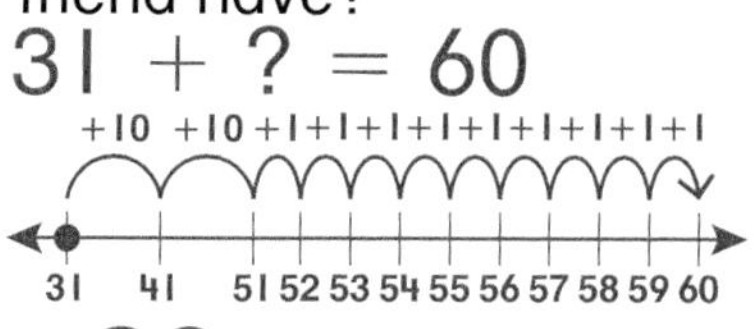

29 stuffed animals

2. A store has 56 shirts. There are 28 fewer shirts than pairs of pants. How many pairs of pants are there?

56 + 28 = 84

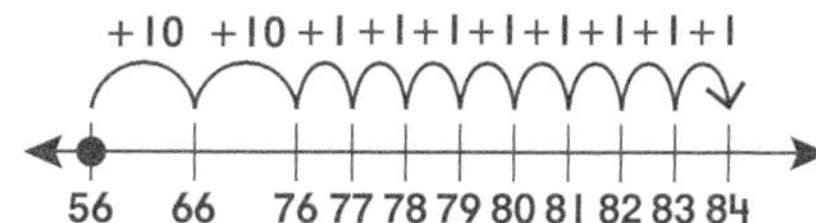

84 pairs of pants

Connect and Extend Learning

Extend Student Learning

Musical

- Teach the students the form of a song to the tune of "99 Bottles." Use these lyrics:

  33 cartons of milk in the fridge,
  33 cartons of milk
  Somebody put in 25 more
  How many cartons of milk are there now?

  Have the class solve this as a group. First have them say the equation and write it on the board. Ask the class what strategy they should use to solve the equation, then have them solve it as a group. Repeat with different numbers.

Lesson Resources	
Surface Level	**Deep Level**
Resources by Chapter • Extra Practice • Reteach Differentiating the Lesson Skills Review Handbook Skills Trainer	Resources by Chapter • Enrichment and Extension Graphic Organizers Dynamic Assessment System • Lesson Practice

3. DIG DEEPER! You have 46 toys. You and your friend have more than 60 toys in all. What is the fewest number of toys your friend can have? Explain.

13 14 (15) 16

46 + 13 = 59, 46 + 14 = 60, and 46 + 15 = 61. 61 is the fewest number of toys you can have and still have more than 60.

4.  **Modeling Real Life** Newton needs 90 chairs for a party. He has 51. He rents 39 more. Does Newton have enough chairs?

51 + 39 = 90 90 = 90

Circle: (Yes) No

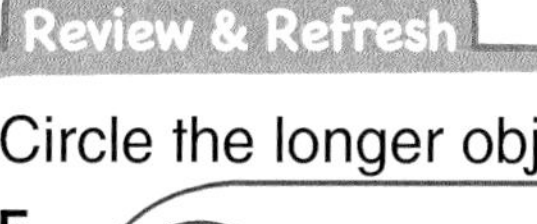

Circle the longer object.

5.

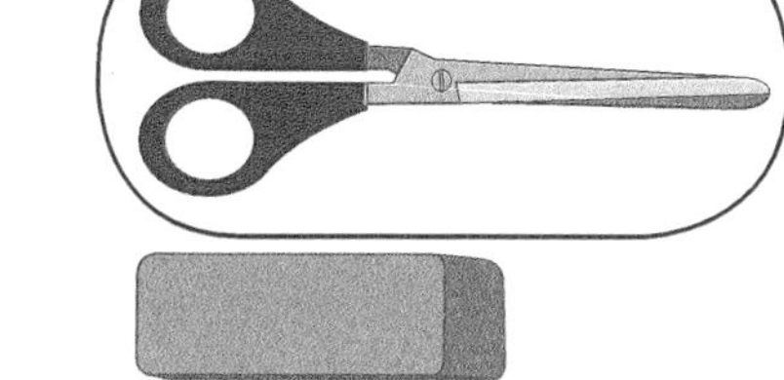

6.

ELL Support

Have students practice verbal language by working on Connect and Grow in groups. Have Intermediate and Advanced students alternate reading sections aloud within their groups. Beginners will focus only on questions and answers. Circulate to monitor their language. Expect students to perform according to their proficiency level.

Beginner students may use single words, such as numbers and yes or no answers.
Intermediate students may answer using phrases or sentences, such as "The red ball is worth more because...."
Advanced students may answer using sentences and guide the process used to find answers.

Laurie's Notes

Performance Task

In this task, students will count and demonstrate their understanding of adding two-digit numbers by adding the number of points collected during a game. Students can use any of the addition strategies learned in this chapter, including quick sketches and a number line. Use student responses to gauge their understanding about adding two-digit numbers.

- Decide ahead of time whether students will be working independently, in pairs, or in groups.
- Pause between direction lines for students to complete each step.
- Have students share their work and thinking with others. Discuss as a class.

Exercise	Answers and Notes	Points
1a	43 points; $30 + 13 = 43$	3
1b	62 points; $38 + 24 = 62$	3
1c	Yes; $43 + 62 = 105$, $105 > 100$	4
1d	*Sample answer:* The red ball is smaller.	2
	Total	12

Name ____________________

Performance Task

1. You play a game. Each red ball you collect is worth 10 points. Each yellow ball you collect is worth 1 point.

a. You collect 3 red balls and 13 yellow balls. How many points do you have?

30 + 13 = 43

43 points

b. Your teammates score 38 points and 24 points. How many points do your teammates have in all?

38 + 24 = 62

62 points

c. Your team wants to have 100 points. Does your team reach its goal?

43 + 62 = 105

105 > 100

(Yes) No

d. Why do you think a red ball is worth more points?

Sample answer: **The red ball is smaller.**

Check out the interactive version in the Game Library.

BigIdeasMath.com

Laurie's Notes

Race for 100

Materials

- 2 dice per group
- base ten blocks

Race for 100 requires students to add one- and two-digit numbers up to 100. Students will work to exchange 10 ones for a ten until reaching 100, which students will identify as 10 tens.

? "What do you see on the page?" a place value mat

- "Today you are going to use the place value mat to race for 100."

? "How many ones equal 10?" 10 "How many tens equal 100?" 10 "You will be working to exchange ones for tens until reaching 100."

- **Note:** This may be done on a Hundred Chart if students are still working to regroup.
- Review the directions while modeling how to play. Be sure to reinforce the exchange of 10 cubes for a rod.

? "How many rods do you need to reach 100?" 10 Review counting by tens to 100 if necessary.

- Partner students and distribute base ten blocks and dice.
- While students play, pay attention to whether students are counting their ones after every roll. Some students may be able to add 10, 11, and 12 to their mats using a rod and some cubes. Have these students explain their understanding to others in their group.
- When game play concludes, have students discuss how they knew when to exchange cubes for a rod.
- **Supporting Learners:** Some students may have difficulty exchanging ones for tens. Have students track their total on a Hundred Chart and compare their tens and ones to the number on their hundred chart.

Closure

- Write the number 38 on the board. Roll two dice. Have students add the sum of the dice to 38. Have students explain their strategy for solving.

Race for 100

To Play: Take turns. On your turn, roll the dice. Find the sum of the numbers and place that many cubes on your mat. If you have 10 or more cubes in the Ones column, exchange 10 cubes for a rod to place in your Tens column. Continue taking turns until someone reaches 100.

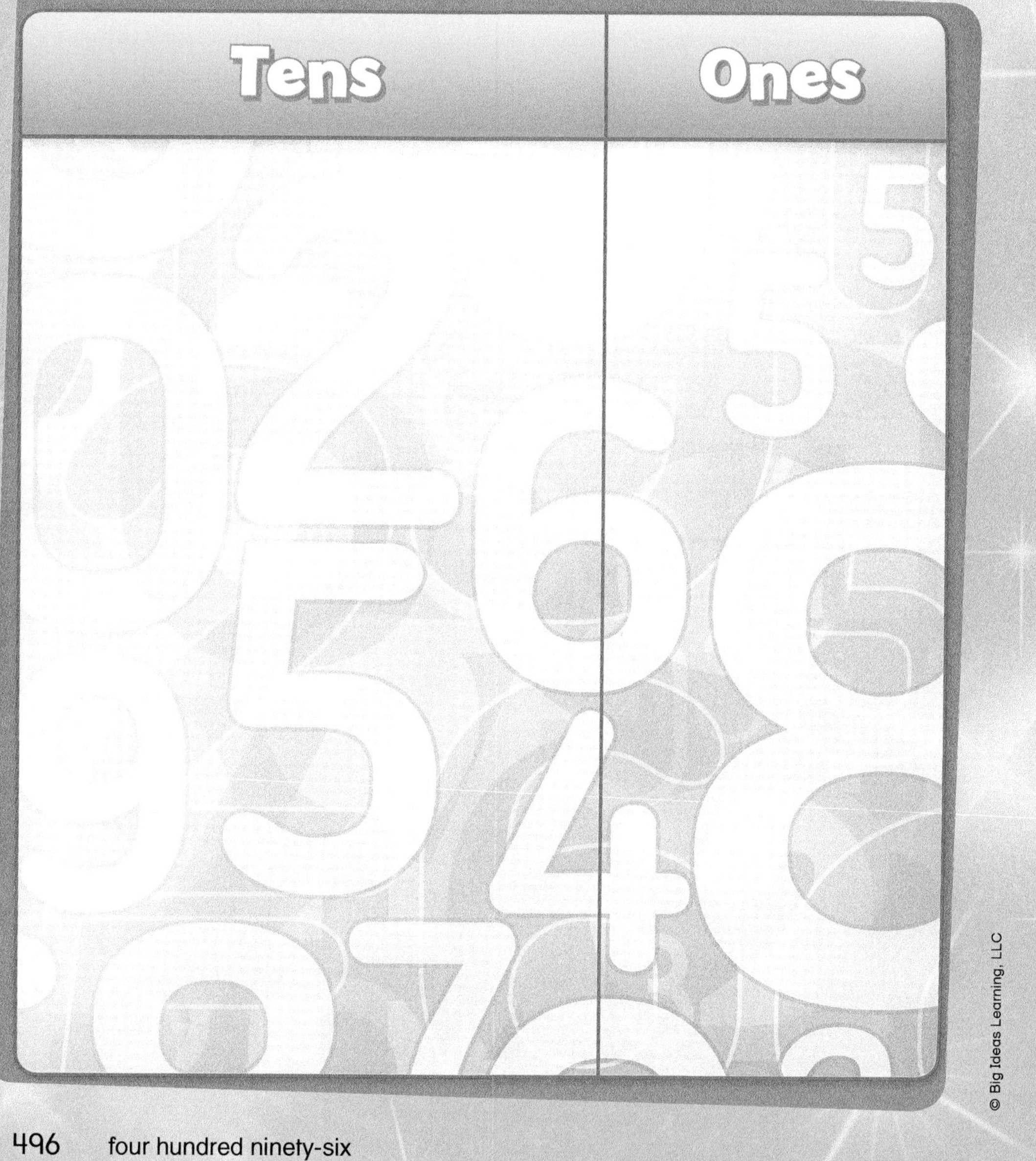

Learning Target Correlation

Lesson	Learning Target	Exercises
9.1	Add two numbers by adding the tens and adding the ones.	1, 2
9.2	Use a number line to add two numbers.	3–5
9.3	Make a 10 to add a one-digit number and a two-digit number.	6–9
9.4	Use place value to add two numbers.	10–12
9.5	Choose a strategy to add two numbers.	13, 14
9.6	Solve addition word problems.	15, 16

Name ____________________

Chapter Practice 9

9.1 Add Tens and Ones

1. 56 + 3 = 59

2. 22 + 54 = 76

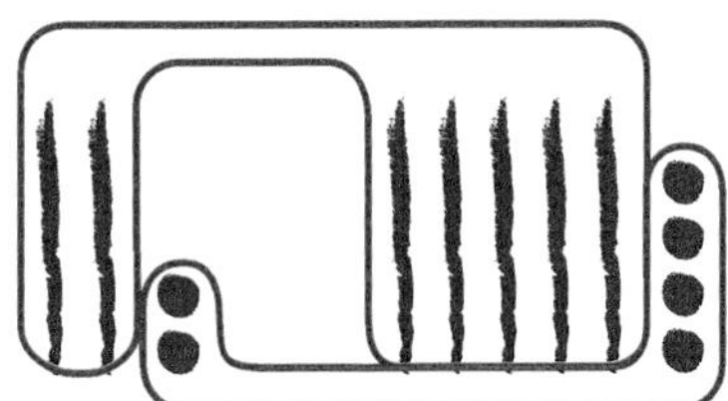

9.2 Add Tens and Ones Using a Number Line

3 and 4. Sample answers are given.

3. 62 + 25 = 87

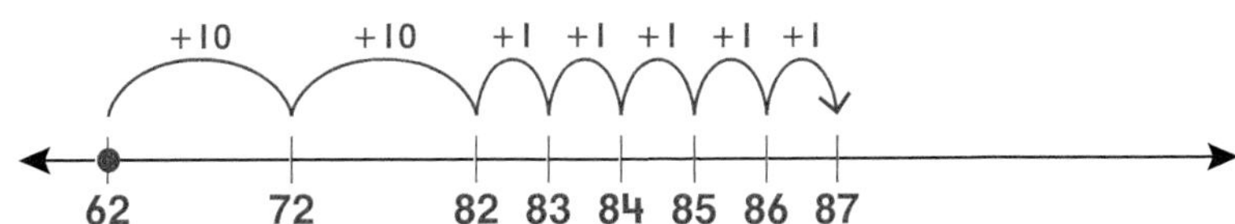

4. 38 + 51 = 89

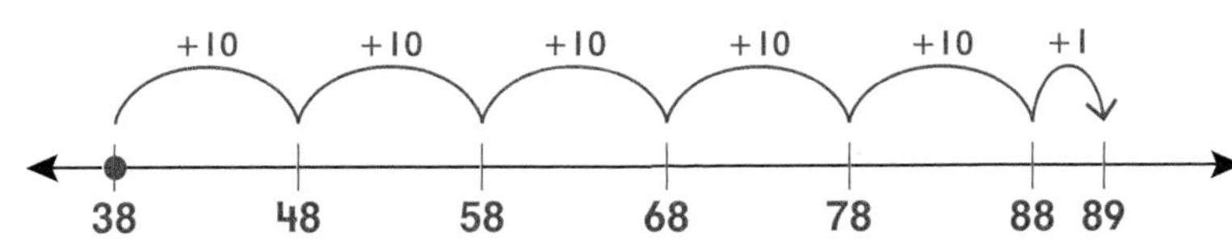

Chapter Resources		
Surface Level	**Deep Level**	**Transfer Level**
Resources by Chapter • Extra Practice • Reteach Differentiating the Lesson Skills Review Handbook Skills Trainer Game Library Math Musicals	Resources by Chapter • Enrichment and Extension Graphic Organizers Game Library Math Musicals	Dynamic Assessment System • Chapter Test Assessment Book • Chapter Tests A and B

5. **Structure** Write an equation that matches the number line.

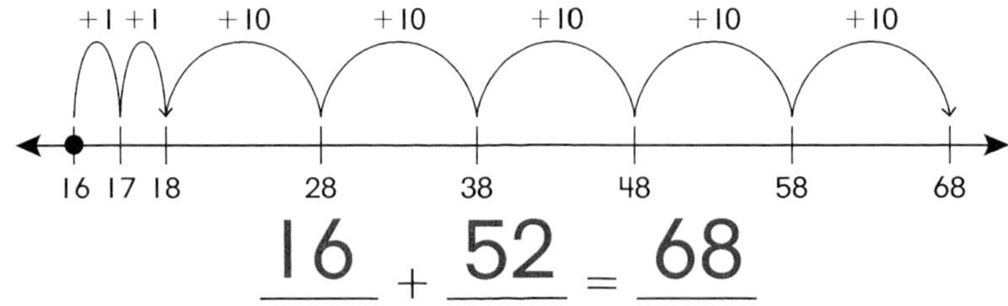

16 + 52 = 68

9.3 Make a 10 to Add

6. 42 + 6 = 48

Make a 10? Yes (No)

7. 27 + 7 = 34

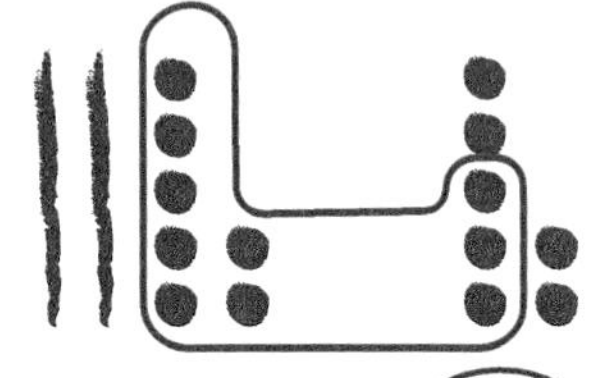

Make a 10? (Yes) No

Logic Complete.

8. 34 + 7

34 + (6) + (1)

40 + (1)

34 + 7 = 41

9. 59 + 8

59 + (1) + (7)

60 + (7)

59 + 8 = 67

9.4 Add Two-Digit Numbers

Make quick sketches to find the sum.

10. $\begin{array}{r} 28 \\ +\ 33 \\ \hline 61 \end{array}$

Tens	Ones

6 tens 1 one

11. $\begin{array}{r} 49 \\ +\ 24 \\ \hline 73 \end{array}$

Tens	Ones

7 tens 3 ones

12. **Modeling Real Life** Your club earns a badge for every 10 trees planted. Your club plants 25 trees in the fall and 25 in the spring. How many badges does your club earn?

$25 + 25 = 50$

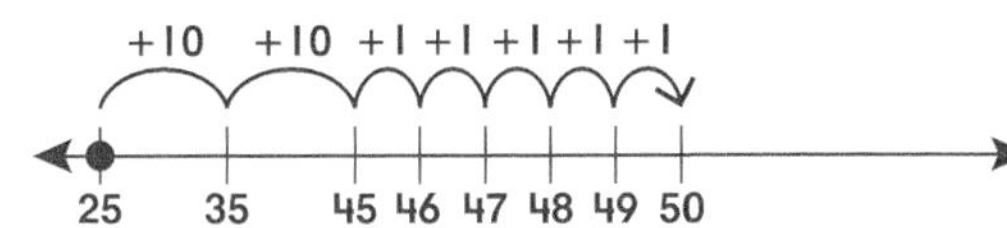

5 badges

9.5 Practice Addition Strategies

13. 19 + 43 = 62

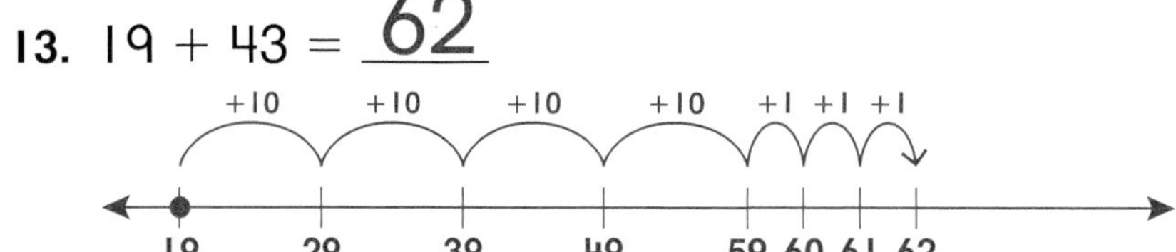

14. 66 + 28 = 94

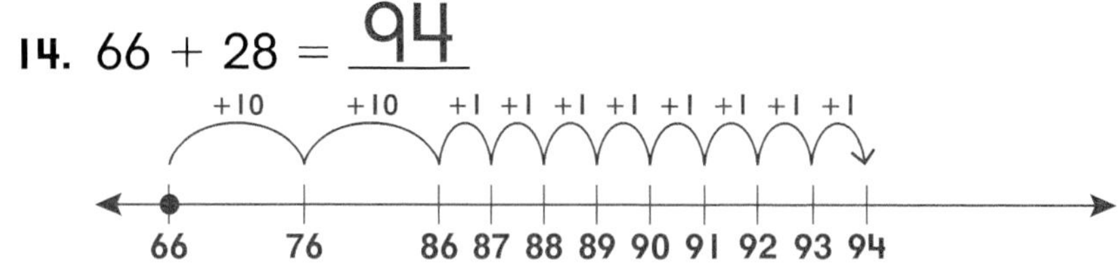

9.6 Problem Solving: Addition

15. Your friend has 59 marbles. You have 23 more than your friend. How many marbles do you have? 59 + 23 = 82

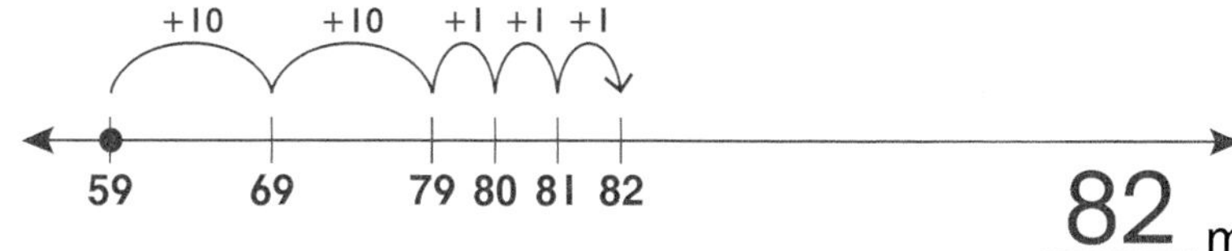

82 marbles

16. Modeling Real Life You need 50 party hats. You have 24. You buy 16 more. Do you have enough party hats?

26 + 16 = 40   40 < 50

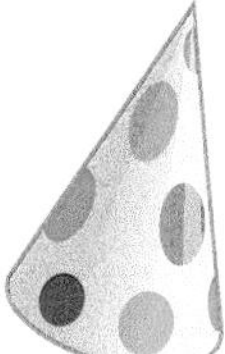

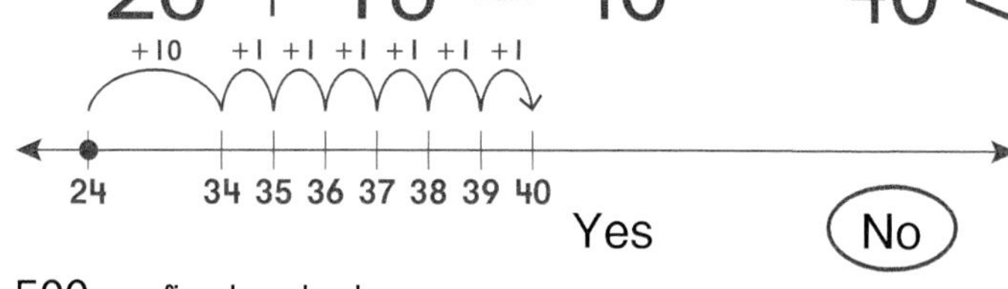

Yes   (No)

Centers

Center 1: Race for 100

Materials: Student Edition page 496, 2 dice per group, base ten blocks

Have students complete the activity. See page T-496 for the directions.

Center 2: Skills Trainer

Materials: computers or devices with Internet access

Have students go to *BigIdeasMath.com* to access the Skills Trainer.

Center 3: Go Fish Nature

Materials per pair: Go Fish Nature Cards*, scissors

Cut out the Go Fish Nature Cards and shuffle them. Deal five cards to each student and place the rest in a pile. When students have two of the same type of card, they write an equation using the numbers on the cards as addends and find the sum. Partners check each other's work. If the sum is correct, students set aside the pair of cards. If a student makes an error finding the sum, they place the cards at the bottom of the pile. Students take turns asking for cards by type, such as "Do you have any flowers?" and drawing from the pile as needed. Play until one student is out of cards or all cards are paired.

Center 4: Addition Spinners

Materials: Addition Spinners*, paper clips

Students spin both spinners and find the sum of the numbers. Have students write the equation and state the strategy they used to solve. Students can also work in pairs, comparing their sums and circling the one that is greater. Repeat several times.

**Found in the Instructional Resources*

Chapter Assessment Guide

Chapter tests are available in the Assessment Book.
An alternative assessment option is listed below.

Visual-Spatial

Have students make a booklet with one page for each of the addition strategies they learned in this chapter: hundred chart, base ten blocks, open number line, make a 10, and place value chart. Provide students with addition problems to model each strategy or have them create their own to solve. Give students a word problem and have them create an additional page solving the problem using the strategy of their choice.

Task	Points
Page showing each strategy	2 points each; 10 points total
Solving a problem using each strategy	1 point each; 5 points total
Solving a word problem	2 points
Total	17 points

My Thoughts on the Chapter

What worked...

Teacher Tip

Not allowed to write in your teaching edition? Use sticky notes to record your thoughts.

What did not work...

What I would do differently...

10 Measure and Compare Lengths

Chapter Overview

Lesson	Learning Target	Success Criteria
10.1 Order Objects by Length	Order objects by length.	• Identify the longest object. • Identify the shortest object. • Order objects from longest to shortest or from shortest to longest.
10.2 Compare Lengths Indirectly	Compare the lengths of two objects using a third object.	• Tell whether the first object is longer or shorter than the third object. • Tell whether the second object is longer or shorter than the third object. • Use the two comparisons to reason about the first and second object.
10.3 Measure Lengths	Use like objects to measure length.	• Start measuring at the beginning of the object and stop at the end. • Measure the length with no gaps or overlays. • Tell how many units long the object is.
10.4 Measure More Lengths	Measure an object in different ways.	• Start measuring at the beginning of the object and stop at the end. • Measure an object using one type of like unit. • Measure an object using another type of like unit. • Explain what happens when you measure an object in different ways.
10.5 Solve *Compare* Problems Involving Lengths	Solve *compare* word problems involving length.	• Identify what information is given in the word problem. • Identify what the question is asking. • Use a bar model to solve a comparison problem. • Explain the strategy I used to solve.

Chapter Learning Target:
Understand length.

Chapter Success Criteria:
- Identify the lengths of objects.
- Order objects from longest to shortest.
- Compare different lengths.
- Measure the length of objects.

Progressions

Through the Grades		
Kindergarten	**Grade 1**	**Grade 2**
• Describe attributes that can be measured. • Describe more than one attribute of an object. • Compare the measurable attributes of two objects. • Describe how the measurable attributes of two objects are different. • Solve addition and subtraction word problems within 10.	• Order three objects by length. • Indirectly compare the lengths of two objects. • Use same-size length units to measure the length of an object. • Measure an object with no gaps or overlays. • Solve addition and subtraction word problems within 20.	• Measure an object using tools. • Measure an object twice, using two different units. • Solve addition and subtraction word problems within 100. • Solve one- and two-step word problems.

	Through the Chapter				
Standard	**10.1**	**10.2**	**10.3**	**10.4**	**10.5**
1.MD.A.1 Order three objects by length; compare the lengths of two objects indirectly by using a third object.	●	●		●	★
1.MD.A.2 Express the length of an object as a whole number of length units, by laying multiple copies of a shorter object (the length unit) end to end; understand that the length measurement of an object is the number of same-size length units that span it with no gaps or overlaps. *Limit to contexts where the object being measured is spanned by a whole number of length units with no gaps or overlaps.*			●	●	★
1.OA.A.1 Use addition and subtraction within 20 to solve word problems involving situations of adding to, taking from, putting together, taking apart, and comparing, with unknowns in all positions e.g., by using objects, drawings, and equations with a symbol for the unknown number to represent the problem.					●

Key: ▲ = Preparing ● = Learning ★ = Complete

Laurie's Overview

About the Math

In kindergarten, students developed an understanding of what the word *attribute* means, a characteristic of the object. Hand children a group of objects to describe. If the objects are common objects versus geometric solids, students should use a variety of words to describe them. They are sharing the attributes of the objects. They often use *big* and *small* to reference relative size. They will also mention color, texture, and the names of objects, but these attributes are not measurable. In this chapter, we build on kindergarten's foundation and examine the measurable attribute of *length*.

Geometric measurement connects the strands of geometry and number. Fundamental concepts related to measurement are explored in this chapter. Before students can measure an attribute, they must identify and understand that attribute. For example, students may say they are the tallest in the room because they are standing on a chair. They might think one string is shorter than another because it is in a twisting pattern instead of stretched out. We begin the study of length and measurement by learning that length is found by locating where an object begins and ends when it is straight, and then determining how far it is between the two endpoints.

Measurement involves a comparison of an attribute of an object—say, length—with a unit that has the same attribute. Students begin their exploration in length measurement by using direct comparison of three objects, placing them side by side, and determining the longest, the shortest, and the one in the middle. "The green crayon is longer than the red. The orange crayon is longer than the green." An aspect of direct measurement that we need to be explicit about is that the objects must be aligned to compare their lengths.

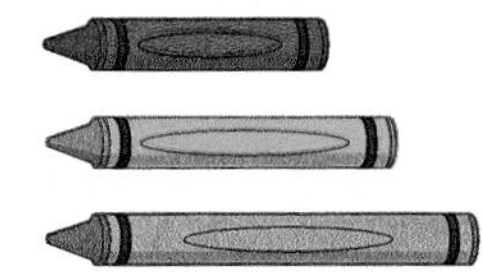

Sometimes objects cannot be placed side by side for comparison. In this case, another object can be used to make an indirect comparison. For example, the silk flower is longer than the string, and the toy dog is shorter than the string, therefore the silk flower is longer than the toy dog. This reasoning is called *transitive reasoning* in mathematics. It is often used in comparisons of quantities and measurement. In this chapter, students use a length of string to compare two objects and conclude which object is longer or shorter.

Once students have compared the length of objects directly and indirectly, we add the component of number to length using non-standard units to measure. Measurement is the process of assigning a number to the magnitude of an attribute, in this case length. Measurement is dependent on the unit being used. In this chapter, we use color tiles and large paper clips for units.

To measure length, units are laid end-to-end alongside the object until the distance is completely covered. This is called iterations of unit. When using units to measure any attribute, there are four important principles.

- Units must be equal to be used. That is, you cannot use an inch tile, a two-inch paper clip, and a toothpick to say something is three units long.
- Units must align with the length being measured—begin at the beginning of the length and end at the end. It seems simple, but alignment can be a challenge for first grade students.
- Units must be placed side by side without gaps, or you do not get a true measurement.
- Units also must not overlap when laid out or you do not get a true measurement.

Students will be reminded of and practice these principles as they practice measuring a wide variety of objects. They will measure with both tiles and paper clips in Lesson 10.4, and discover that the size of the unit being used to measure determines the number of units needed. For example, when measuring the same pencil, it will take fewer paper clips than tiles because the paper clip is longer. This is a foundational learning that prepares students for standard measurement and conversion within measurement systems.

The chapter culminates with students solving comparison length word problems. Students will review the use of the comparison bar model first introduced in Chapter 3, transfer the model to both addition and subtraction equations, and use any of the addition and subtraction strategies with which they have been working.

Models

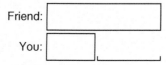

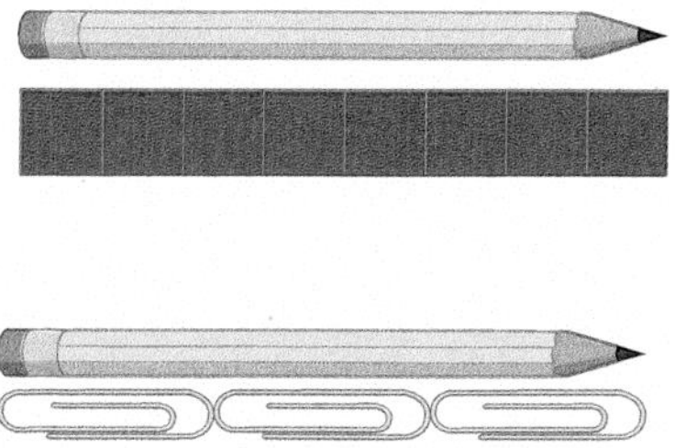

- In this chapter students begin to measure with color tiles. They describe lengths in terms of how many tiles it takes to fill the distance from beginning to end of the object. This allows them to connect number to length.
- Students will also use large paper clips as a unit of measure in the same way as the tiles.
- Students will discover that it takes fewer paper clips than tiles to measure the same object. This is because each paper clip is twice the length of a tile.
- A bar model is used for the final lesson in the chapter solving comparison length problems. This model was introduced in Chapter 3 and is used throughout the course.

Friend:

You:

Chapter 10 is a transition in the course from number to data, time, geometry, and foundational concepts in fractions. It is an active, hands-on chapter uniting students' intuition of attributes, more and less, and shapes with formal measurement.

Check out the
virtual manipulatives.
BigIdeasMath.com

Chapter Materials and Resources

The primary materials and resources needed for this chapter are listed below. Other materials may be needed for the additional support ideas provided throughout the chapter.

Classroom Materials	Chapter Opener	10.1	10.2	10.3	10.4	10.5	Connect and Grow
scissors	•						•
objects to compare lengths		•	•	•	•	•	
string			•				*
color tiles				•	•	•	*
large paper clips					•	•	*
small paper clips							*
crayons							•
construction paper		•					•

Instructional Resources	Chapter Opener	10.1	10.2	10.3	10.4	10.5	Connect and Grow
Vocabulary Cards	•	+		+			
Blank Bar Model						•	
Fish Measurement Cards							•
What Is Longer? Cards							•

• class set + teacher only * per pair/group

Suggested Pacing

Day 1	Chapter Opener	Performance Task Preview		Vocabulary			
Day 2	Lesson 10.1	Warm-Up	Dig In	Explore	Think	Apply: Practice	Think: Modeling Real Life
Day 3	Lesson 10.2	Warm-Up	Dig In	Explore	Think	Apply: Practice	Think: Modeling Real Life
Day 4	Lesson 10.3	Warm-Up	Dig In	Explore	Think	Apply: Practice	Think: Modeling Real Life
Day 5	Lesson 10.4	Warm-Up	Dig In	Explore	Think	Apply: Practice	Think: Modeling Real Life
Day 6	Lesson 10.5	Warm-Up	Dig In	Explore	Think	Apply: Practice	Think: Modeling Real Life
Day 7	Connect And Grow	Performance Task			Activity	Chapter Practice	
Day 8		Centers					
Day 9	Chapter Assessment	Chapter Assessment					

Year-to-Date: 115 Days

Laurie's Notes

Mathematical Practices

Students have opportunities to develop aspects of the mathematical practices throughout the chapter. Here are some examples.

1. **Make Sense of Problems and Persevere in Solving Them**
   10.1 Think and Grow: Modeling Real Life, *p. 506*
2. **Reason Abstractly and Quantitatively**
   10.3 Practice Exercise 4, *p. 520*
3. **Construct Viable Arguments and Critique the Reasoning of Others**
   10.1 Apply and Grow: Practice Exercise 5, *p. 505*
4. **Model with Mathematics**
   10.3 Think and Grow: Modeling Real Life, *p. 518*
5. **Use Appropriate Tools Strategically**
   10.2 Explore and Grow, *p. 509*
6. **Attend to Precision**
   10.1 Explore and Grow, *p. 503*
7. **Look for and Make Use of Structure**
   10.5 Explore and Grow, *p. 527*
8. **Look for and Express Regularity in Repeated Reasoning**
   10.1 Apply and Grow: Practice, *p. 505*

Performance Task Preview

- Preview the page to gauge students' prior knowledge about reading maps and comparing lengths.

? "Have you ever used a map?" Listen for student responses about using maps in their own town and when on a trip.

? "In the picture of the map, the red pin shows where you are. Which pin is closest to you? Which pin is farthest from you?"
4 is closest, 3 is farthest

- In the Performance Task at the end of the chapter, students will use a map of a neighborhood to measure and compare lengths, directly and indirectly.

Measure and Compare Lengths

- Have you ever used a map?
- The red pin shows where you are. Which pin is closest to you? Which pin is farthest from you?

Chapter Learning Target:
Understand length.

Chapter Success Criteria:
- I can identify the lengths of objects.
- I can order objects from longest to shortest.
- I can compare different lengths.
- I can measure the length of objects.

Check out the
digital flash cards.
BigIdeasMath.com

Laurie's Notes

Vocabulary Review

? **Preview:** "What do you notice about the dolphins?" *Sample answer:* one is longer than the other

- Have students say each review word out loud. Have students explain how the words are related.
- Have students identify which dolphin is longer and which is shorter.
- Direct students to the lower half of the page. Have students use their vocabulary cards to identify the words being modeled. Explain how to find the words in the word search.
- **Extension:** Have students write a story using the review words.

Chapter 10 Vocabulary

Activity

- **Ready, Set, Action!:** Say the vocabulary word and model the action. Have students repeat. Make sure to decide what action you are going to do for each vocabulary card ahead of time. For length, hold your hands open in front of you and slowly move them outward. Holding your thumb and index finger out, as if pinching something between them, can model length unit. Measure can be acted out by using the movement for length unit and moving it across your body as if measuring the length. Hold your arms out as far as they go to act out longest, and close together to act out shortest.
- **Supporting Learners:** Limit the number of cards the students lay out in front of them.

ELL Support

Explain that in this chapter students will compare lengths. When you compare objects, you use a word known as a comparative to describe what you are comparing. *Longer* and *shorter* are both comparatives. To make a comparative from an adjective, you may simply add the ending *-er*. Use *longer* in a sentence to demonstrate its use. Then ask students to create and share a sentence using *shorter*. Other examples are *taller*, *larger*, and *smaller*.

Newton & Descartes's Math Musicals

with Differentiated Rich Math Tasks

Newton and Descartes team up in these educational stories and songs to bring mathematics to life! Use the Newton and Descartes hand puppets to act out the stories. Encourage students to sing the songs to take full advantage of the power of music to learn math. Visit *www.MathMusicals.com* to access all the adventures, songs, and activities available!

Name ____________________

10 Vocabulary

Review Words
longer
shorter

Organize It

Use the review words to complete the graphic organizer.

longer

shorter

Define It

Use your vocabulary cards to identify the words. Find each word in the word search.

1. 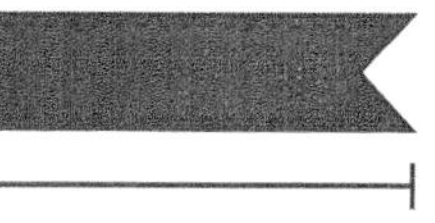

2. 

3.

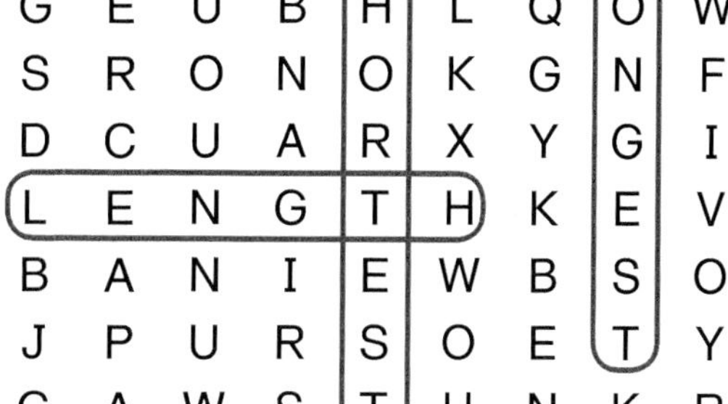

K	T	L	M	S	R	A	L	E
G	E	U	B	H	L	Q	O	W
S	R	O	N	O	K	G	N	F
D	C	U	A	R	X	Y	G	I
L	E	N	G	T	H	K	E	V
B	A	N	I	E	W	B	S	O
J	P	U	R	S	O	E	T	Y
C	A	W	S	T	U	N	K	R
L	O	M	E	A	S	U	R	E

Chapter 10 Vocabulary Cards

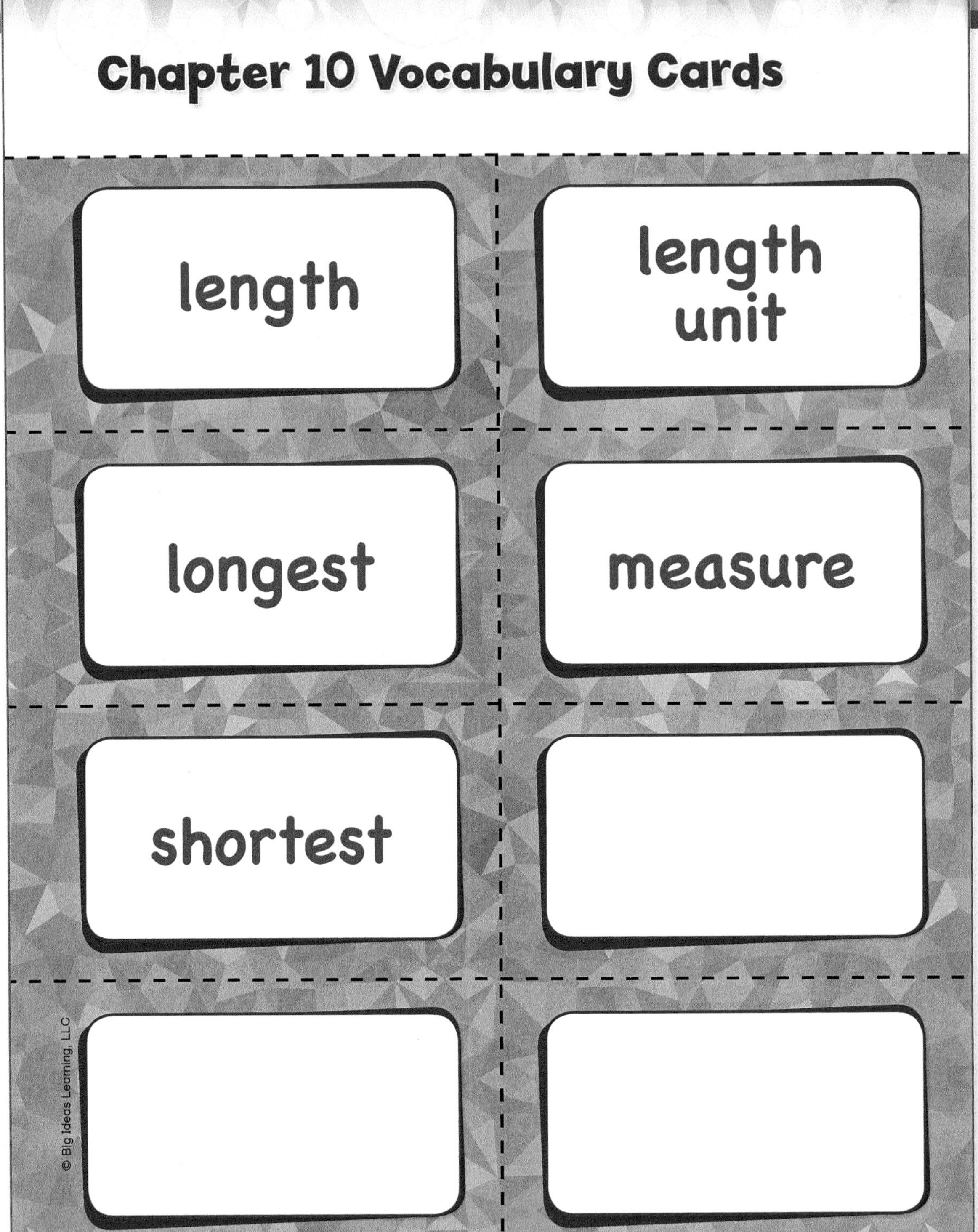

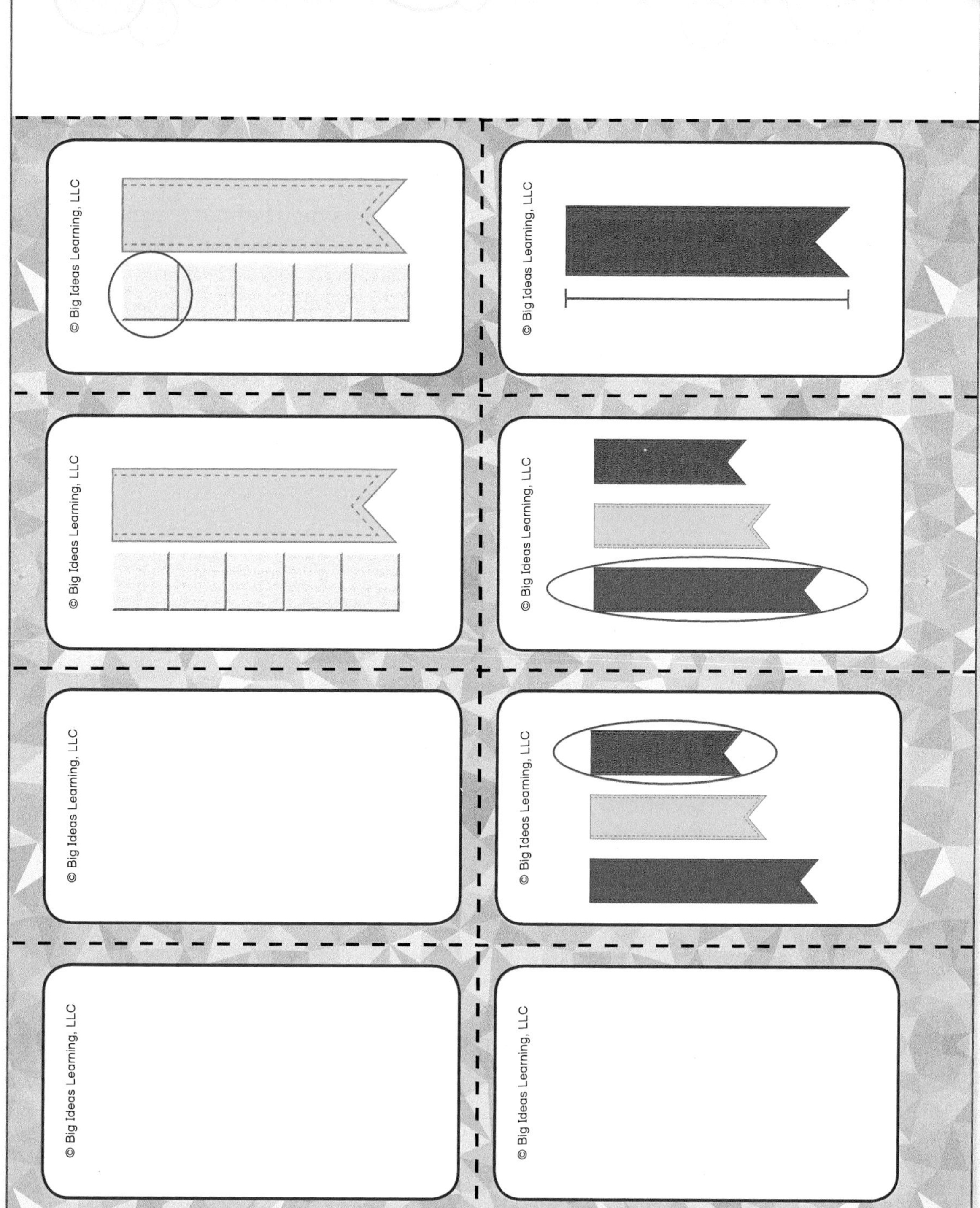
© Big Ideas Learning, LLC
© Big Ideas Learning, LLC
© Big Ideas Learning, LLC
© Big Ideas Learning, LLC
© Big Ideas Learning, LLC
© Big Ideas Learning, LLC
© Big Ideas Learning, LLC
© Big Ideas Learning, LLC

10.1

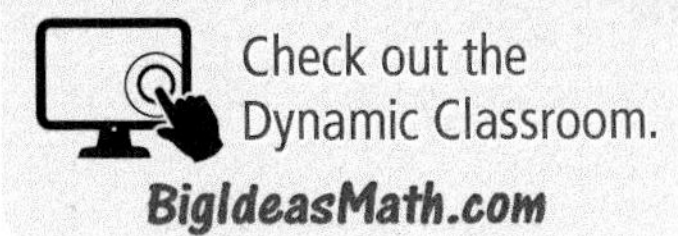
Check out the
Dynamic Classroom.

BigIdeasMath.com

Laurie's Notes

COMMON CORE STATE STANDARDS
1.MD.A.1

Learning Target

Order objects by length.

Success Criteria

- Identify the longest object.
- Identify the shortest object.
- Order objects from longest to shortest or from shortest to longest.

Warm-Up

Practice opportunities for the following are available in the Resources by Chapter or at *BigIdeasMath.com.*

- Daily skills
- Vocabulary
- Prerequisite skills

ELL Support

Explain that when comparing the length of two or more objects, the one that is longer than *all* of the others is the longest. The word *longest* is known as a superlative and it describes the object with the most of a specific characteristic. The *-est* ending is added to the adjective to make a superlative. Demonstrate the use of *longest* and *shortest* by comparing three objects.

Preparing to Teach

Students are familiar with comments made about length. "This piece of yarn is so long," or "My pencil is so short." They have a sense that *length* refers to a horizontal direction. In this lesson, our goal is for students to compare the length of three objects and tell the order of the objects from longest to shortest or from shortest to longest. The comparison is done directly. The objects are placed beside one another or students use eyesight to compare the lengths in a picture.

Materials

- objects to compare lengths
- construction paper

Dig In (Circle Time)

Students will compare and describe objects by using lengths. They have had experience with comparing two objects in kindergarten, so today's lesson will be an extension adding a middle length.

- Begin by having students name things they think are long. Then have them describe things that are short. This will refresh vocabulary and give you a sense of what they remember from kindergarten.
- ◉ "Today we are going to compare the lengths of three objects. When we compare, one will be longest, one will be shortest, and one will be in the middle."
- Call on three students to stand in the middle of the circle. Ask students to tell their partners whose hair is longest, whose hair is shortest, and whose hair is in the middle. "In order from longest to shortest hair, it is (name 1, name 2, and name 3). In order from shortest to longest hair, it is (name 3, name 2, and name 1)."
- Show a group of objects to compare lengths, such as pencils or pieces of yarn. "I have three pencils. Tell your partners which pencil is longest and which is shortest." Have students tell the order of the pencils from longest to shortest. Then have students tell the order from shortest to longest.
- Repeat with another set of objects.
- ? **MP7 Look for and Make Use of Structure**: "What do you notice about the order of the objects when you change from describing longest to shortest, to shortest to longest?" First and last objects switch, middle stays middle
- ◉ "Today we are going to compare the lengths of objects and describe them from longest to shortest, or from shortest to longest."

? Teaching Prompt ◉ Learning Target

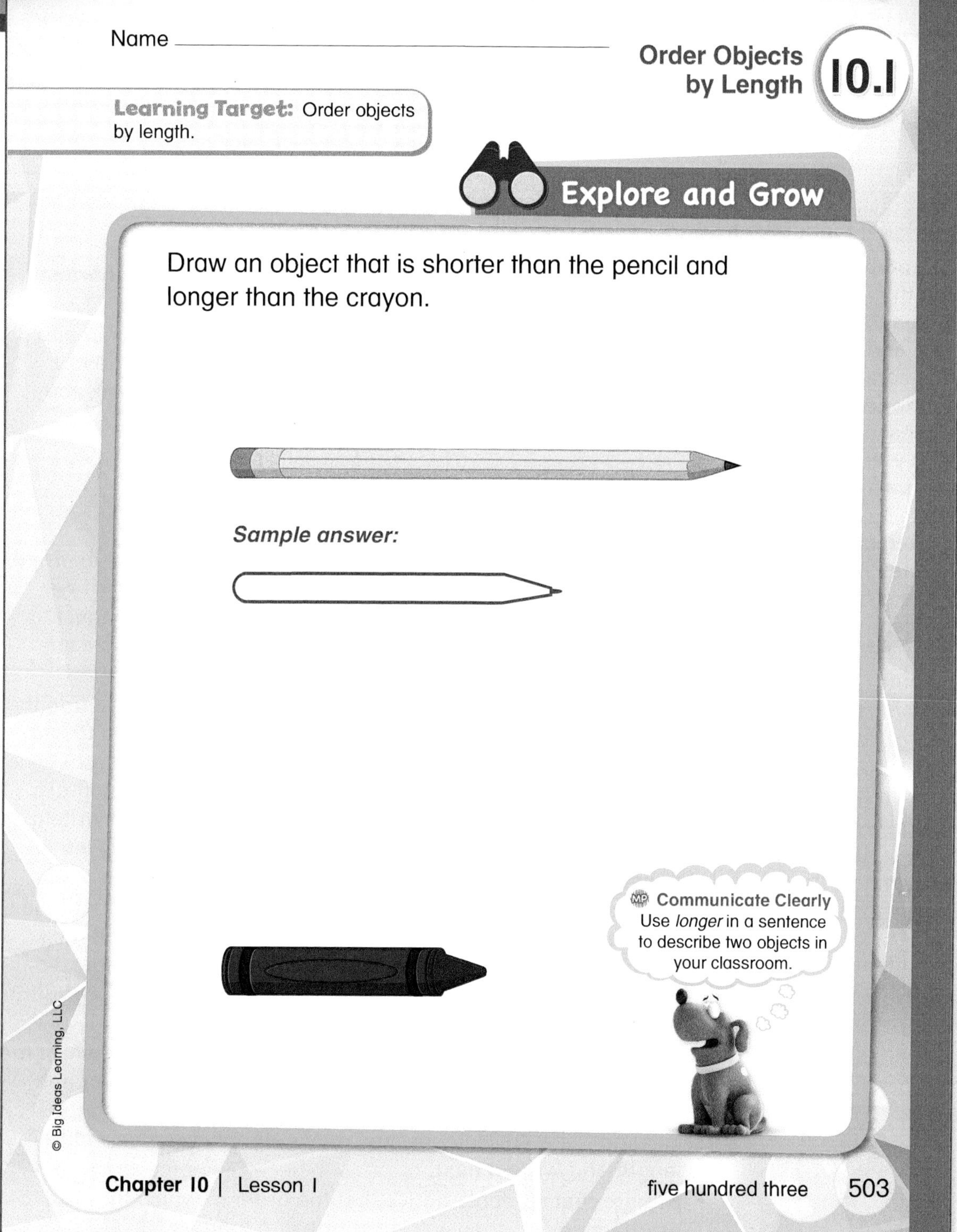

Name
Order Objects by Length 10.1
Learning Target: Order objects by length.
Explore and Grow
Draw an object that is shorter than the pencil and longer than the crayon.
Sample answer:
Communicate Clearly
Use *longer* in a sentence to describe two objects in your classroom.
© Big Ideas Learning, LLC
Chapter 10 | Lesson 1
five hundred three 503

Explore and Grow

- Discuss with students where an object shorter than the pencil would end. Be sure students understand that their object needs to start at the same starting point as the pencil and crayon.
- To help students begin the drawing at the correct place, show a dotted line vertically down the beginning of the pencil to the crayon.
- Have students show where an object longer than the crayon would end.
- Students can draw vertical dotted lines to show the end of the crayon and the end of the pencil for the range of their object if they want.

Laurie's Notes

ELL Support

Discuss the example. Point out that the word *order* means "put in order," and should not be confused with ordering food or online purchases. Have students work in pairs as they practice language while completing Exercises 1 and 2. Have one student ask the other, "Which is longest? Which is shortest?" Then have them alternate roles for each exercise.

Beginner students may answer with the name of a color.
Intermediate students may answer with phrases, such as, "the red snake."
Advanced students may answer with sentences, such as, "The red snake is longest."

Think and Grow

Getting Started

- Introduce the vocabulary terms **length**, **longest**, and **shortest**. Use objects to model the meaning of the words.
- In kindergarten students also worked with height. Height and length are similar and therefore easily confused. You do not usually talk about how long someone is, but you do talk about hair length.

Teaching Notes

◉ Students will order three objects from longest to shortest, or from shortest to longest.

- **Model:** "There are 3 snakes, a yellow, a red, and a brown. Read the direction line and tell your partner the order in which we want to list them– longest to shortest or shortest to longest. It is important to check and pay attention to the order we are supposed to use."
- **Model:** "To list the snakes from longest to shortest, first find the longest. Notice that you look at the tail end to the head to see the length." Point to the brown snake where it says length. "The red snake is longest, so write red on the first line. Sometimes it is easiest to find the shortest next—the yellow—and write it on the last line. Finally, we see the middle snake that is left is brown. Write brown on the middle line."

? **Model:** "Let's look at the snakes one more time. I can write the red snake first as longest. Now compare the brown and the yellow. Which is longer of those two? The brown is longer, so it would be written next. Finally, the yellow is shortest and written last. This is another way to think about ordering."

- For Exercise 1, have students tell partners the order in which the chalk is to be listed. Have them identify the longest color and write it on the first line. Students can either write the shortest last and fill the middle, or they may naturally see the middle length and write it next.
- Be sure that students notice that the order in which they are to list the paint brushes is from shortest to longest.
- **Supporting Learners:** Students may need additional experience with comparing the lengths of objects they can hold.
- **Supporting Learners:** Focus students on two objects at a time rather than all three.

◉ "Explain to your partner how to compare the length of three objects and write them in order." Pause. "Are you feeling good about using the words longest and shortest?"

Think and Grow

Order from longest to shortest.

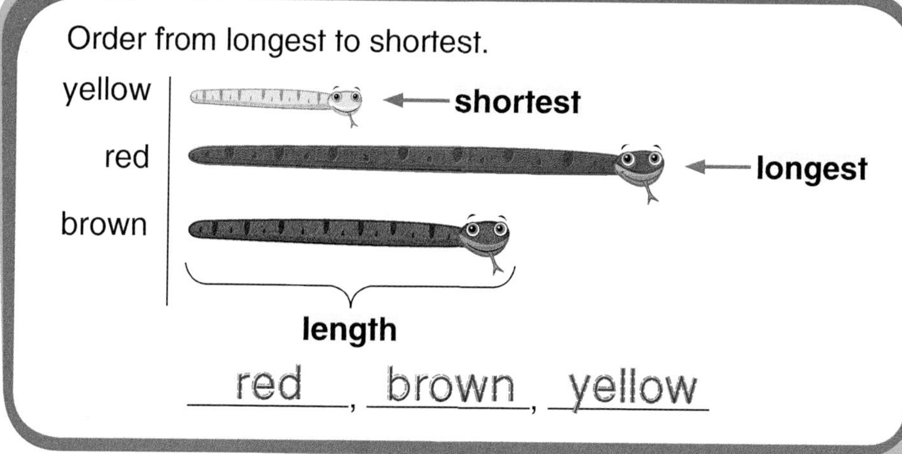

red, brown, yellow

Show and Grow *I can do it!*

1. Order from longest to shortest.

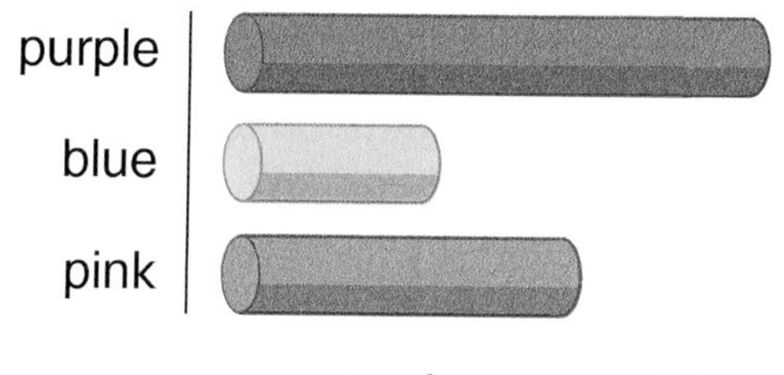

purple, pink, blue

---

2. Order from shortest to longest.

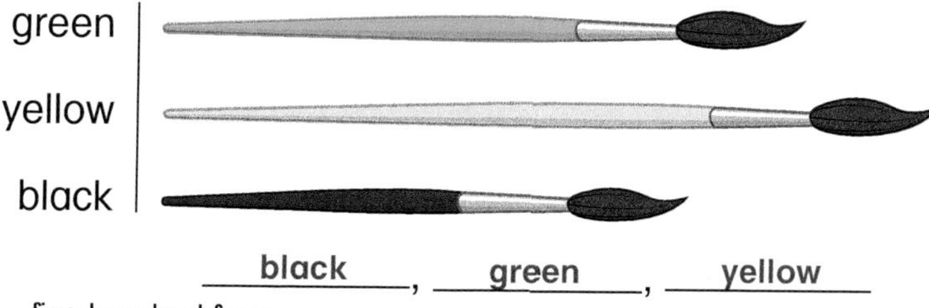

black, green, yellow

Scaffold instruction to support all students in their learning. Learning is individualized and you may want to group students differently as they move in and out of these levels with each skill and concept. Student self-assessment and feedback help guide your instructional decisions about how and when to layer support for all students to become proficient learners.

Meeting the needs of all learners.

Laurie's Notes

Apply and Grow: Practice

SCAFFOLDING INSTRUCTION

Exercises 3 and 4 continue to have students order three objects. Students will need to pay attention to the direction line to see if the order is to be longest to shortest, or shortest to longest.

EMERGING students may confuse ordering by length due to the third object. They may be able to spot the longest and the shortest, and think the middle length needs a name as well. Some may confuse length with height, which in these exercises relates to thickness, which will prevent ordering of any kind.

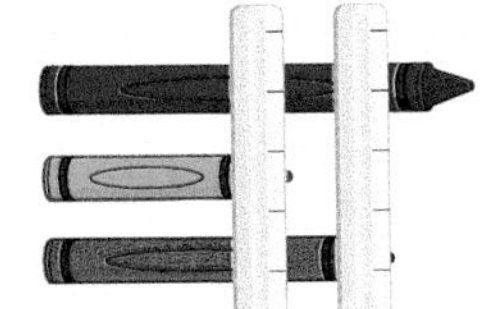

- **Exercises 3 and 4:** Students can use a straightedge or ruler to move across the objects. Demonstrate that you start at the far left end and move the straightedge across the objects. Which objects extends beyond the other? Use a second ruler to find the longest crayon or bar.
- **Exercise 5:** Students should pay attention to the required order. They can continue to use a straight edge if needed to help determine shortest and longest. For explanation, students can give the correct answer, suggest that the order was longest to shortest, or explain that yellow is longest not shortest, etc.

PROFICIENT students are generally accurate in identifying which object is longer or shorter by direct comparison or by using their eyesight. They can explain how they know they are correct and identify errors.

- **Exercises 3–5:** If errors are made, check to see that students paid attention to the required order: longest to shortest or shortest to longest.

Additional Support

- Students may need to hold and feel two objects to compare their lengths.

Extension: Adding Rigor

- Have students work in trios. Each student finds an object. They will compare their objects then stand in order as they determine: longest to shortest, shortest to longest, or both.

Name ________________

Apply and Grow: Practice

3. Order from longest to shortest.

purple

green

red

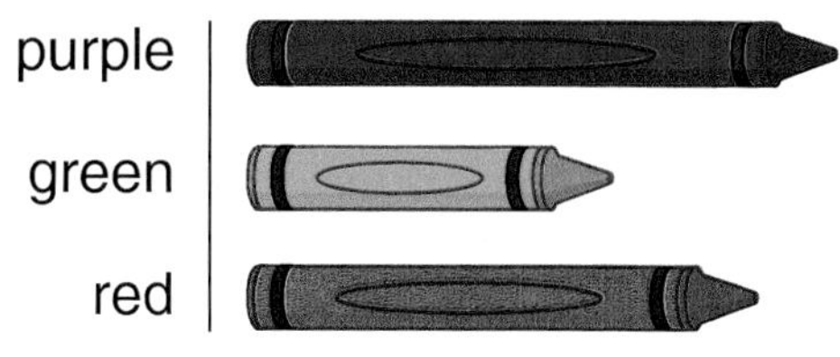

purple, red, green

4. Order from shortest to longest.

green

pink

blue

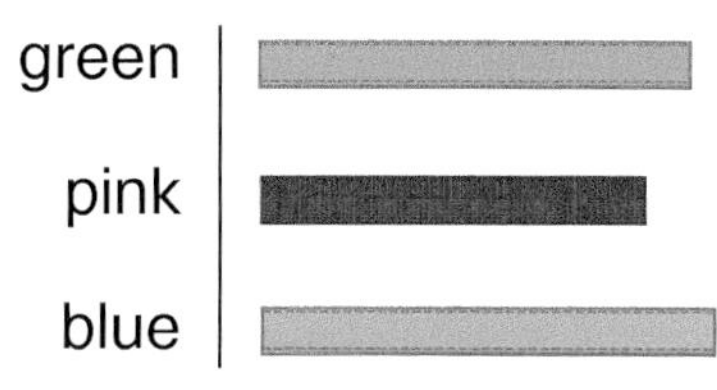

pink, green, blue

Repeated Reasoning
What is always true about the longest object?

5. YOU BE THE TEACHER Your friend ordered from shortest to longest. Is your friend correct? Explain.

yellow

red

green

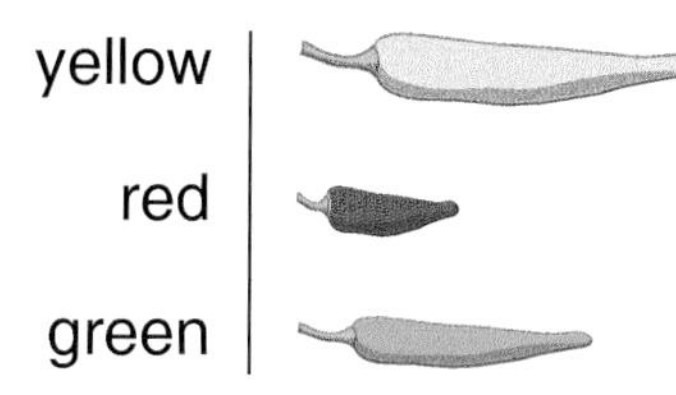

no; The shortest is red, the longest is yellow.

yellow, green, red

ELL Support

Check for understanding of Lesson 10.1. Read each story aloud as students follow along. Clarify unknown vocabulary if necessary. Have students make two cards with the names Newton and Descartes. Ask the following questions. If the correct answer is "you" have them raise their hand. If it is Newton or Descartes, have them hold up the appropriate card.

1. Who has the longest yarn?
2. Who has the shortest yarn?
3. Who has the longest pencil?
4. Who has the shortest pencil?

Laurie's Notes

Think and Grow: Modeling Real Life

These applications allow students to demonstrate their understanding of longest, middle, and shortest. They draw to problem solve and determine the longest or shortest in the different situations.

- Read and discuss the yarn example with students. Ask students to describe what they know and what they are trying to find out.
- **Model:** "We can't really compare all three yarn lengths at the same time. We can only work with two at a time. Look at the first line. Your yarn is longer than Newton's. Draw a line to show your yarn, and a line for Newton's yarn. Remember that your yarn is longer than Newton's so your line should be longer than Newton's." Pause "Next, Descartes's yarn is longer than Newton's and shorter than yours. Draw a line for Descartes's yarn that is longer than Newton's and shorter than yours." Pause and check. "Based on your drawings, who has the longest yarn? Circle the answer."
- Review the directions with students for Exercise 6. Have them tell their partners what they are trying to decide to be sure they understand the directions. Encourage students to model the story line by line. Be sure students pay attention to the question to be answered.
- **MP3 Construct Viable Arguments:** Have students order "your," Newton's and Descartes's yarn from longest to shortest and shortest to longest. Defend how they know. Repeat with pencils.
- ◉ "You have compared lengths of three objects and ordered them for longest to shortest or shortest to longest. Can you explain to your partner how to find the longest object? the shortest object? the one in the middle?"

Closure

- Cut varying lengths of construction paper strips and give one to each student.
- Students can mingle and move until you say "Freeze!" Students stop and form groups of three with students around them. Tell them either "longest to shortest" or "shortest to longest" randomly. Students line up in order based on their paper strips. Repeat several times.

Think and Grow: Modeling Real Life

Your yarn is longer than Newton's. Descartes's is longer than Newton's and shorter than yours. Who has the longest yarn?

Draw a picture:

You

Newton

Descartes

Make a Plan Whose yarn should you draw first?

Who has the longest yarn?

(You) Newton Descartes

Show and Grow *I can think deeper!*

6. Descartes's pencil is shorter than Newton's. Yours is shorter than Newton's and longer than Descartes's. Who has the shortest pencil?

Draw a picture:

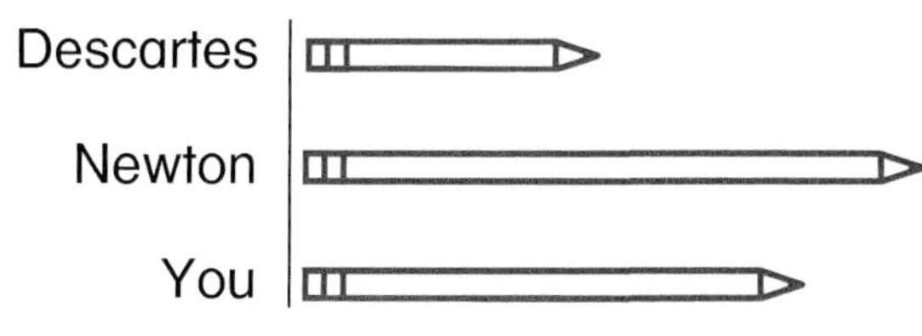

Who has the shortest pencil?

(Descartes) Newton You

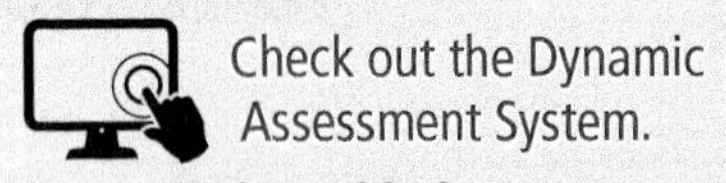
Check out the Dynamic Assessment System.
BigIdeasMath.com

Scaffold assignments to support all students in their learning progression. Revisit with spaced practice to move every student toward proficiency.

Connect and Extend Learning

Practice Notes

- **Exercises 1–3:** Use two straightedges or rulers to move across the objects.

Prior Skills

- **Exercises 6 and 7:** Grade 1, Comparing Numbers Using Symbols

Cross-Curricular Connections

Science

- Discuss how trees grow, what they need to survive, and how seasons and weather can affect them. Focus on the dropping of limbs and sticks. Go on a walk outside if you can, and have students each collect three sticks. Then have students order them from shortest to longest. If sticks are not available, use craft sticks, toothpicks, and rulers.

Name ____________________

Practice **10.1**

Learning Target: Order objects by length.

Order from longest to shortest.

purple

green

pink

purple, pink, green

Order from longest to shortest.

1. bat 1

bat 2

bat 3

bat 2, bat 1, bat 3

---

2. gold

red

blue

gold, blue, red

Connect and Extend Learning

Extend Student Learning

Bodily-Kinesthetic

- Prepare different-sized straws to give to students. After you give each student a straw, play music and have them walk around until it stops. They will then get into a group of three and stand according to their straw lengths. If lengths are the same size, then they link arms or sit down.

Lesson Resources	
Surface Level	**Deep Level**
Resources by Chapter • Extra Practice • Reteach Differentiating the Lesson Skills Review Handbook Skills Trainer	Resources by Chapter • Enrichment and Extension Graphic Organizers Dynamic Assessment System • Lesson Practice

3. Order from shortest to longest.

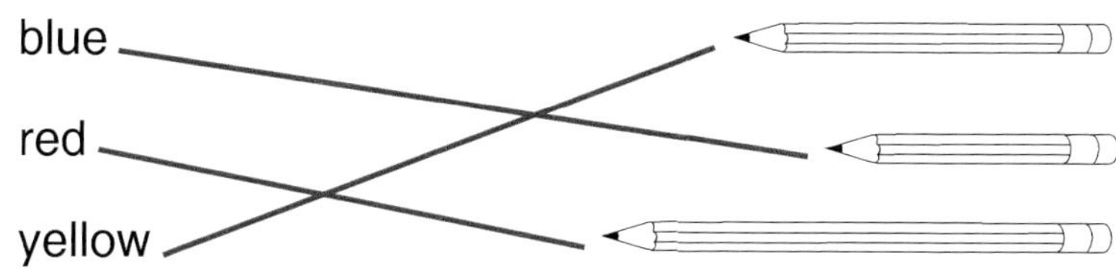

vine 3, vine 1, vine 2

4. **Analyze a Problem** Use the clues to match.
The red pencil is longer than the yellow pencil.
The shortest pencil is blue.

blue
red
yellow

---

5. **Modeling Real Life** Your jump rope is longer than Newton's. Descartes's is longer than Newton's and shorter than yours. Who has the longest jump rope?

You
Newton
Descartes

Who has the longest jump rope?

(You) Newton Descartes

Compare.

6. 25 (<) 52

7. 41 (<) 44

10.2

Laurie's Notes

Check out the
Dynamic Classroom.

BigIdeasMath.com

Learning Target

Compare the lengths of two objects using a third object.

Success Criteria

- Tell whether the first object is longer or shorter than the third object.
- Tell whether the second object is longer or shorter than the third object.
- Use the two comparisons to reason about the first and second object.

Warm-Up

Practice opportunities for the following are available in the Resources by Chapter or at *BigIdeasMath.com*.

- Daily skills
- Vocabulary
- Prerequisite skills

ELL Support

Write "indirectly" on the board with a slash after the prefix *in-* (in/directly). Say, "When *in-* is at the beginning of a word, it often means *not*. Comparing directly means you compare objects to each other. Comparing indirectly means you do *not* compare objects to each other, but use a measuring tool."

COMMON CORE STATE STANDARDS
1.MD.A.1

Preparing to Teach

Students will compare lengths of two objects and determine which object is longer or shorter than the other. Instead of using direct comparison, students will use a piece of string, or drawing of a piece of string, to make the comparison indirectly.

Materials

- string
- objects to compare lengths

Dig In (Circle Time)

Students will use their length of string to find an object longer and shorter than it. They will then say how the objects compare to each other based on the relationship to the piece of string.

◉ "Yesterday we compared the lengths of three objects by looking at which was longest and shortest. Today we are going to compare the lengths of two objects, but we won't be able to line them up to compare. Instead we are going to use a piece of string to make the comparison."

? Show a new pencil to the students. Take a piece of string (shorter than the pencil) and compare it to the pencil. "Which is longer? The pencil or the string?" Put the pencil to the side and show a pen or marker that is shorter than the string. Compare the string to the pen. "Which is longer the pen or the string?" Put the pen aside. Keep the string in sight.

- **MP2 Reason Abstractly and Quantitatively:** "The pencil was longer than my string. The pen was shorter than my string. Tell your partner if you think the pencil or the pen is longer, and why." Have several students explain their reasoning.
- Explain that if one object is longer than the string, and the other is shorter, then the longer must be longer than the shortest as well. Take out the pen and pencil and show them side-by-side. Repeat the reasoning that the pencil is longer than the string but the pen is shorter than the string. The pencil must be longer than the pen.
- **MP4 Model with Mathematics:** Give each student a piece of string. Students find one object longer and one object shorter than their string. They tell their partner the object that is longer and the object that is shorter than their string, and how the two objects compare to each other.

◉ "Today we are going to compare the lengths of two objects that we cannot line up to compare. Instead, we will use string to compare each object, then make a conclusion about longest and shortest."

? Teaching Prompt ◉ Learning Target

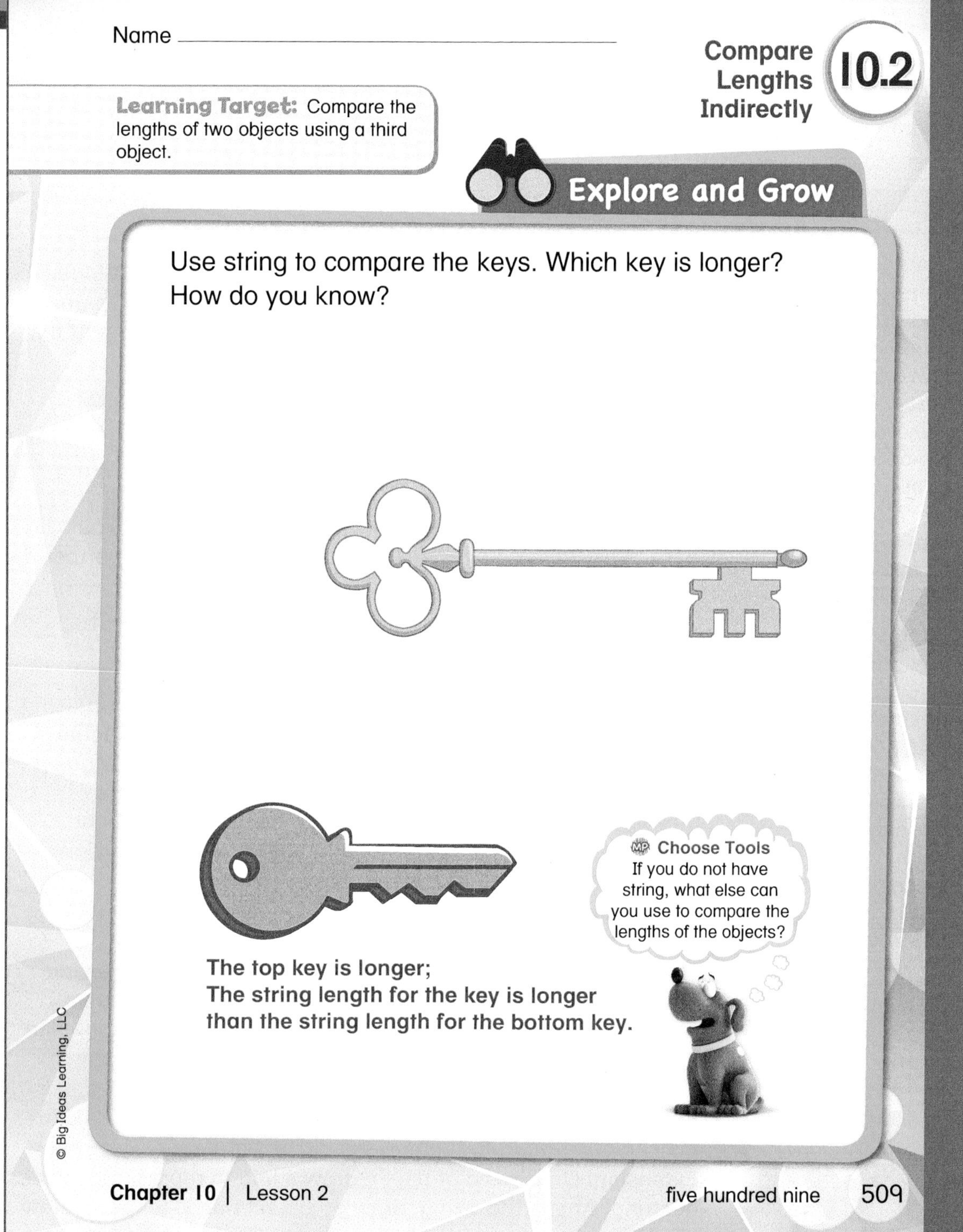

Name
Learning Target: Compare the lengths of two objects using a third object.
Compare Lengths Indirectly
10.2
Explore and Grow
Use string to compare the keys. Which key is longer? How do you know?
Choose Tools
If you do not have string, what else can you use to compare the lengths of the objects?
The top key is longer;
The string length for the key is longer than the string length for the bottom key.
© Big Ideas Learning, LLC
Chapter 10 | Lesson 2
five hundred nine 509

Explore and Grow

- **MP5 Use Appropriate Tools Strategically:** Ask students to explain why they need to use string to compare the keys instead of just comparing their lengths from the picture. The keys do not start at the same place, so we can't compare their lengths from the picture.
- Have students use their string to find the key that is longer than the string, and the key that is shorter than the string.
- Have students tell their partners how they know which key is longer.
- Have several students share their reasoning about the longer or shorter key. Listen for similar reasoning as described in the Dig In.

ELL Support

Discuss the example. Review the names of objects pictured in Exercises 1 and 2. Then have students work in pairs as they practice language. Have one student ask the other, "Which is longer? Which is shorter?" Then have them alternate roles for the other exercises.

Beginner students may answer with the name of an object. **Intermediate** students may answer with simple sentences, such as, "The stick is longer." **Advanced** students may answer with detailed sentences, such as, "The stick is longer than the frog."

Laurie's Notes

Think and Grow

Getting Started

- The exercises continue to use indirect measurement. A blue line is used to represent the same piece of string. It is shown under two different pictures. This is to simulate the measurement that was done with the keys.

Teaching Notes

- **Model:** "Newton and Descartes are comparing the length of the stick and the frog. They cannot move the stick to the frog to compare them, so they use a blue piece of string. Tell your partner how the stick compares to the string. Now tell your partner how the frog compares to the string. Tell your partner if the stick or the frog is longer, and how you know."
- Have several students explain their thinking about which object is longer. Have students circle the stick after several explanations are made.
- Students continue to make length comparisons based on using the drawing of the string. Notice that in Exercise 1, students circle the longer object as was modeled. In Exercise 2, students cross out the shorter object. Direction lines will give one of these two instructions: either circle the longer or cross out the shorter. Be sure students pay attention to each direction throughout the lesson.
- **Supporting Learners:** Give students a piece of string that is the same length as the blue line to use for measuring.
- **Supporting Learners:** Students may need support in drawing the conclusion about which object is longer. Show them another comparison (such as with the pencil and pen shown in the Dig In) with objects they can hold so they can see why the conclusion will be correct.
- **Extension:** Explain why you need string to compare the pictures instead of comparing them as we did yesterday.
- **Extension:** On a piece of paper, draw a line to represent a piece of string. Above the string, draw an object that is longer. Below the string draw an object that is shorter. Compare the two objects you drew.
- ◉ "Explain to your partner how a piece of string can be used to compare the lengths of two objects."

Think and Grow

Circle the longer object.

Use the string to compare the lengths.

The stick is longer than the string. The string is longer than the frog. So, the stick is longer than the frog.

Show and Grow *I can do it!*

1. Circle the longer object.

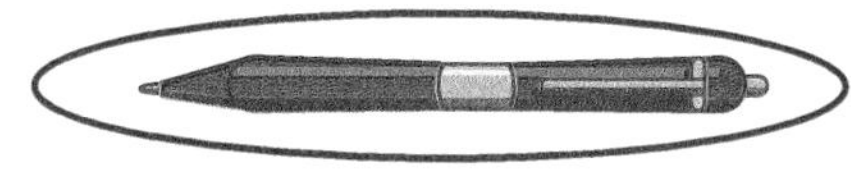

2. Draw a line through the shorter object.

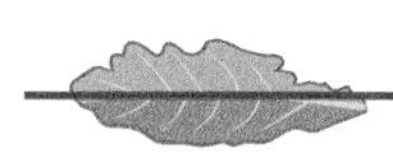

Scaffold instruction to support all students in their learning. Learning is individualized and you may want to group students differently as they move in and out of these levels with each skill and concept. Student self-assessment and feedback help guide your instructional decisions about how and when to layer support for all students to become proficient learners.

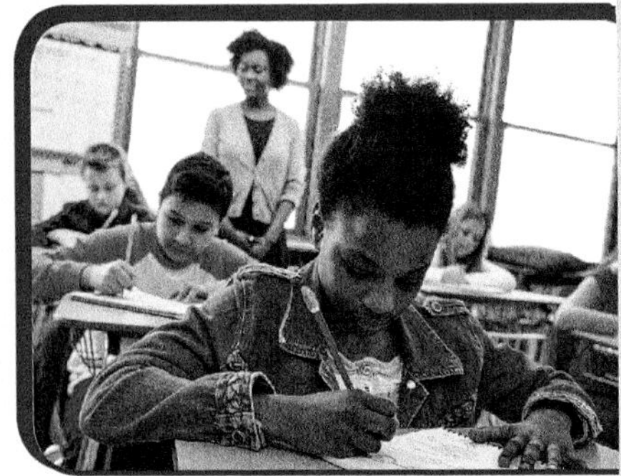

Meeting the needs of all learners.

Laurie's Notes

Apply and Grow: Practice

SCAFFOLDING INSTRUCTION

Exercises 3 and 4 continue to have students indirectly compare the lengths of two objects. They will need to pay attention to the direction line to see if they are to draw a line through the shorter object or circle the longer.

EMERGING students may have difficulty with the transitive reasoning that if the stapler is longer than the string, and the tape dispenser is shorter than the string, then the stapler is longer than the tape dispenser. They are most likely able to explain the individual relationships, such as the stapler is longer than the string.

- **Exercises 3 and 4:** Provide the actual objects, or similar, and a piece of string in a proportional length to have students transfer the concept from physical objects to the pictures.
- **Exercise 5:** Students who have memorized a pattern to answer these questions (such as A is longer than the string and B is shorter, therefore A is longer than B) will have difficulty with this exercise. Both the bookmark and the key are shorter than the string. Providing two objects that are shorter than a piece of string and comparing by how much they are shorter will help students reason about this answer. Students can also draw a vertical line from the end of each object to the string to compare how much string is left.

PROFICIENT students can explain how they know which object is longer or shorter than another using string. They may fall into a reasoning pattern and not think about *why* the pattern must be true.

- **Exercise 5:** Encourage students to explain the relationship in terms of the string (both objects are shorter than the string, the bookmark is much closer to the length of the string than the key) rather than using their eye sight to say, "You can see the bookmark is longer."

Extension: Adding Rigor

- Have students use indirect measurement of stationary objects in the room such as a width of a poster and a width of a desk.

Name ______________________________

Apply and Grow: Practice

3. Draw a line through the shorter object.

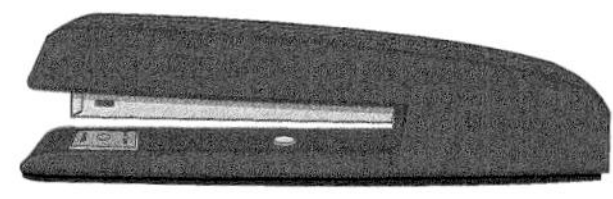

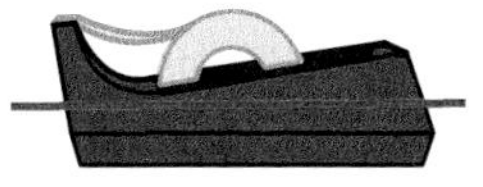

4. Circle the longer object.

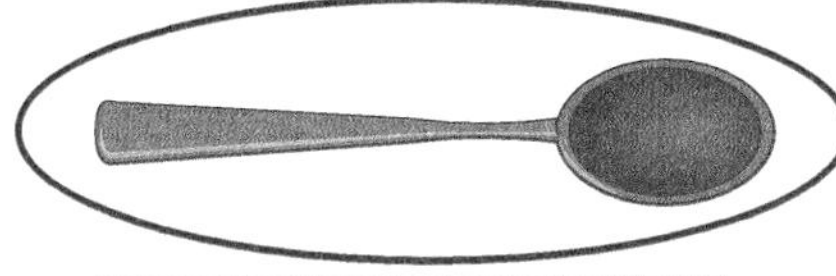

5. DIG DEEPER! Which object is longer? Explain.

Both objects are shorter than the string. The bookmark is closer to the length of the string than the key is.

ELL Support

Check for understanding of Lesson 10.2. Read each story aloud as students follow along. Clarify unknown vocabulary if necessary. Ask the following questions and have them answer using a thumbs up or thumbs down signal for *yes* or *no*.

1. Is the green crayon longer than the yellow crayon?
2. Is it shorter than the yellow crayon?
3. Is the yellow ribbon longer than the blue ribbon?
4. Is it shorter than the blue ribbon?

Laurie's Notes

Think and Grow: Modeling Real Life

These applications follow the same reasoning as yesterday's applications as students compare two different items to a third item. They draw to problem solve and determine if a given item is longer or shorter than another.

- Read and discuss the crayon example with students. Ask students to describe what they know and what they are trying to find out. You might ask students how crayons out of the same box could be different lengths.
- ? **Model:** "We are going to use the same strategy to solve these stories as we did yesterday. Let's start with the first sentence. Draw a line for the green crayon and a line for the blue crayon that is shorter than the green." Pause. "Now draw a line for the yellow crayon. The blue crayon is shorter than the yellow. So, will the yellow crayon be longer or shorter than the blue?" Pause. "Is the green crayon longer or shorter than the yellow?" Pause. "Circle shorter."
- Review the directions with students for Exercise 6. Have them tell their partners their strategy for solving the exercise before they begin. They should guess what the answer will be, and then draw the model to see if their guess was correct or not.
- ◉ **MP3 Construct Viable Arguments:** "Explain to your partners how you can tell if an object is longer or shorter than another just by using a piece of string. Tell what to do if both objects are longer or shorter than the string."

Closure

- **Guess and Check:** Choose pairs of items around the room that seem to be approximately the same length to compare using string.
  - Cut two pieces of string the same length.
  - Name two objects to compare.
  - Give a piece of string to two students to use to measure an object.
  - Have the class decide which of the objects is longer or shorter.
  - Repeat with various objects. Have some of the objects both be longer or shorter than the string length.

Think and Grow: Modeling Real Life

A green crayon is shorter than a blue crayon. The blue crayon is shorter than a yellow crayon. Is the green crayon longer than or shorter than the yellow crayon?

Draw a picture: green

blue

yellow

Longer   (Shorter)

Show and Grow *I can think deeper!*

6. A yellow ribbon is longer than a pink ribbon. The pink ribbon is longer than a blue ribbon. Is the yellow ribbon longer than or shorter than the blue ribbon?

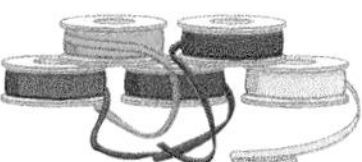

Draw a picture: yellow

pink

blue

(Longer)   Shorter

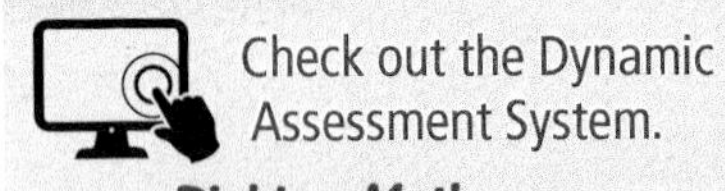
Check out the Dynamic Assessment System.
BigIdeasMath.com

Scaffold assignments to support all students in their learning progression. Revisit with spaced practice to move every student toward proficiency.

Connect and Extend Learning

Practice Notes

- **Exercises 1 and 2:** Remind students to pay attention to the direction lines to see if they are to draw a line through the shorter object or circle the longer object.
- **Exercise 4:** Have students explain how they know their answer is correct.

Prior Skills

- **Exercise 6:** Kindergarten, Describing Objects by Attributes

Cross-Curricular Connections

Language Arts

- *How Long?: Wacky Ways to Compare Length (Wacky Comparisons)* by Jessica Gunderson; Read the book aloud to students. Discuss with students what items they could measure in the classroom using colored tiles and paper clips. Then have students choose an item, measure it, draw a picture, and write a silly sentence that goes along with it.

Name ____________________

Learning Target: Compare the lengths of two objects using a third object.

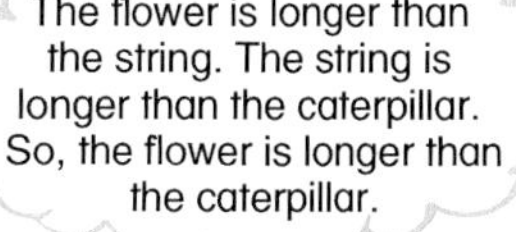

The flower is longer than the string. The string is longer than the caterpillar. So, the flower is longer than the caterpillar.

Circle the longer object.

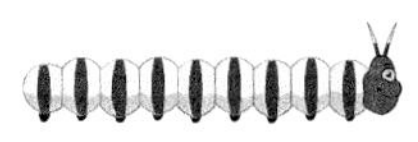

1. Circle the longer object.

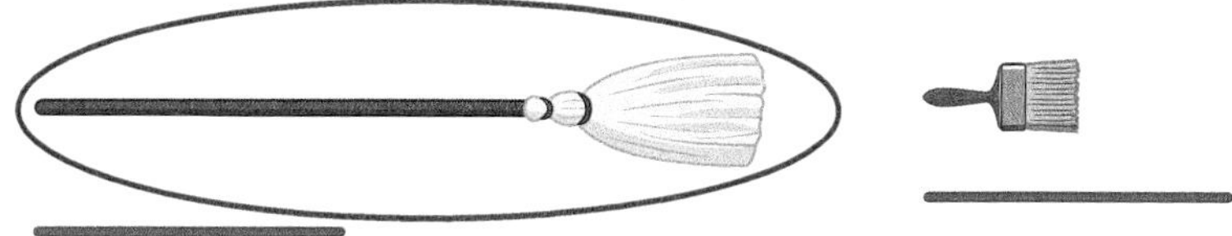

2. Draw a line through the shorter object.

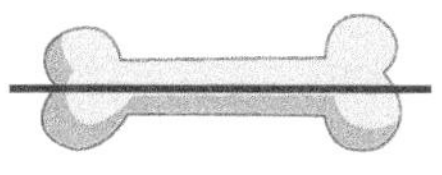

Connect and Extend Learning

Extend Student Learning

Visual-Spatial

- Post different length items such as sticky notes, notecards, construction paper (cut into strips), sentence strips, and string around the room. Then play with students "The Detective Sees..." by describing an item to students but not saying its name. Students will have to use the description to guess the item. Be sure to include length as part of your description. For instance, "The Detective sees an item that is shorter than the construction paper but longer than the sticky notes." Repeat with different objects. Students can also draw objects on the board to use in comparisons.

Lesson Resources	
Surface Level	**Deep Level**
Resources by Chapter • Extra Practice • Reteach Differentiating the Lesson Skills Review Handbook Skills Trainer	Resources by Chapter • Enrichment and Extension Graphic Organizers Dynamic Assessment System • Lesson Practice

3. Analyze a Problem Use the clues to match.
The blue string is longer than the orange string.
The purple string is shorter than the orange string.

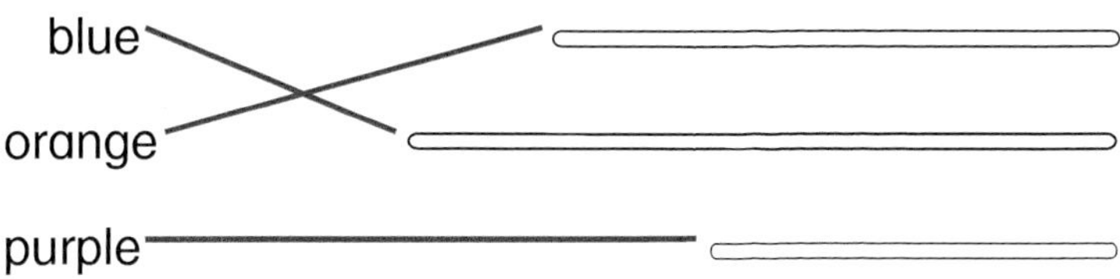

4. Modeling Real Life A kayak is shorter than a canoe. The canoe is shorter than a paddle board. Is the kayak longer than or shorter than the paddle board?

Longer  Shorter

5.  DIG DEEPER! A city bus is shorter than a tractor trailer. A van is shorter than a city bus. Compare the tractor trailer and the van.

The tractor trailer is longer than the van.

Review & Refresh

6. Circle the objects that have capacity as an attribute.

10.3

Check out the
Dynamic Classroom.

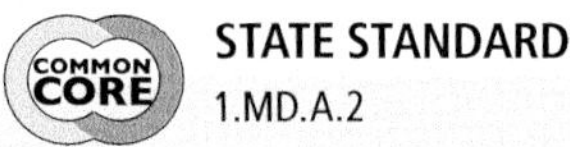
BigIdeasMath.com

Laurie's Notes

COMMON CORE STATE STANDARDS
1.MD.A.2

Learning Target

Use like objects to measure length.

Success Criteria

- Start measuring at the beginning of the object and stop at the end.
- Measure the length with no gaps or overlays.
- Tell how many units long the object is.

Warm-Up

Practice opportunities for the following are available in the Resources by Chapter or at *BigIdeasMath.com.*

- Daily skills
- Vocabulary
- Prerequisite skills

ELL Support

Point out that the learning target uses the phrase *like objects*. Students will be familiar with the word *like* as it is used to describe how someone feels toward something or someone. Here it means "the same or similar." Other words that could be used in place of *like* (synonyms) are *similar, comparable, alike,* or *identical.* They may want to include these words in their vocabulary notebooks.

Preparing to Teach

Students will use color tiles to measure lengths of objects. Students will learn to line up the start points of both the object and the tiles, and to align the tiles end-to-end without overlaps or gaps.

Materials

- color tiles
- objects to compare lengths

Dig In (Circle Time)

Students will use color tiles to measure a variety of objects. They will learn to line up the starting points, and not to overlap the tiles or have gaps between the tiles.

◉ "We have been comparing objects and determining which object is longest, and which is shortest. Today we want to find a way to describe how long an object is. Today we will be using color tiles to measure lengths."

- Show a pencil to the students. "I want to know how long my pencil is. I will use tiles to measure it. Watch how I measure with the tiles."
- Show students how to line up the tiles underneath the pencil. As you model, point out the essential skills of measuring: Begin at the same place. Do not overlap the tiles. Do not have gaps between the tiles. Count to show the pencil is about 8 tiles long.
- Model measuring a few more objects and counting to measure the length.
- Play "What Went Wrong?" Tell students that you are going to measure the pencil again, but this time you will do something wrong. Students give a thumbs up signal when they know what is wrong. When most students are ready, have them all say what is wrong together. Things to do wrong: Do not start at the beginning of the pencil, overlap the tiles, have gaps in the tiles.
- If time, have students measure an object with a partner using tiles.

◉ "Today we are going to measure objects using tiles. We will be very careful to start lining up our tiles at the beginning of the object. We will be very careful not to have any gaps between the tiles. We will be very careful not to overlap the tiles."

? Teaching Prompt ◉ Learning Target

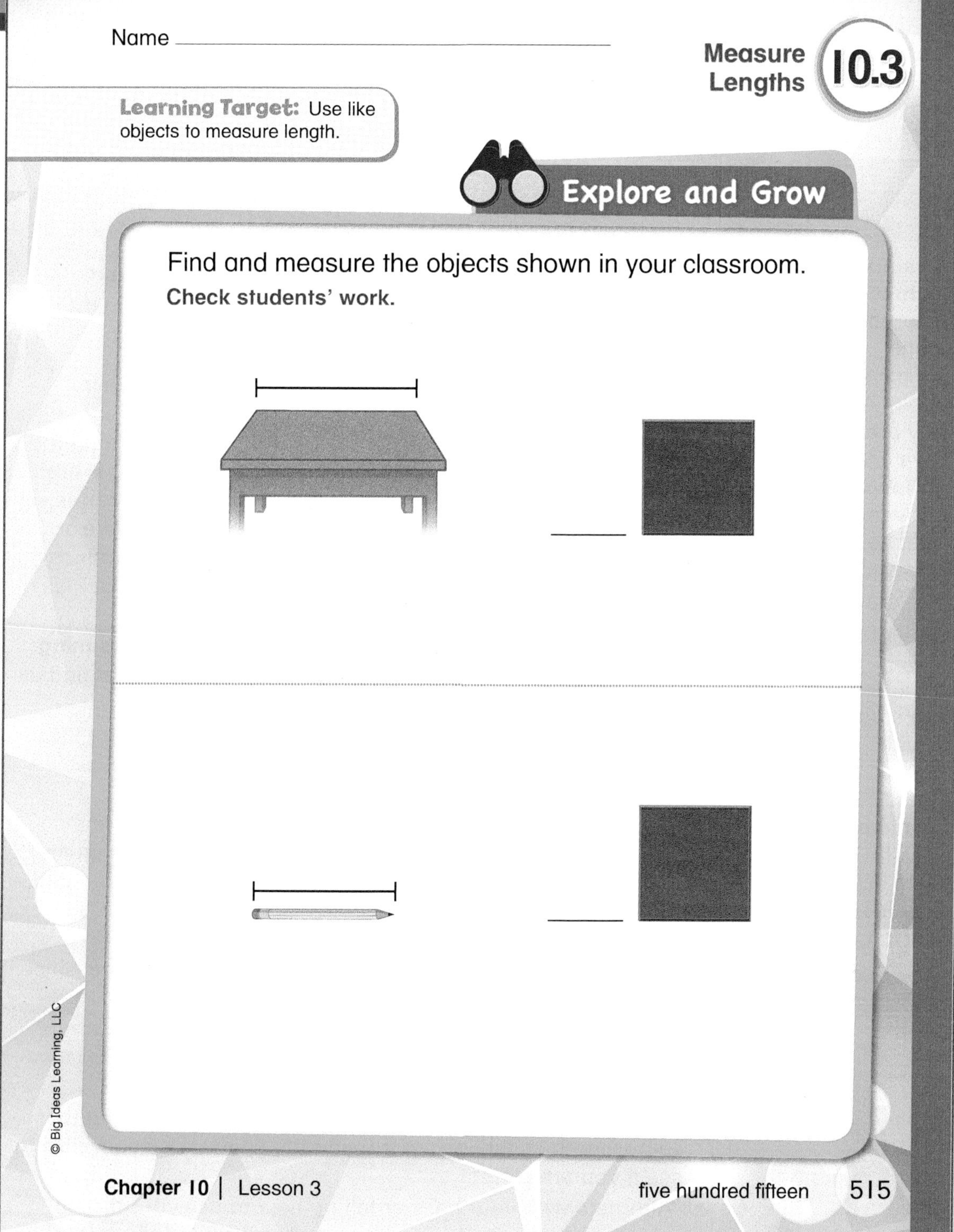

Name
Measure Lengths 10.3
Learning Target: Use like objects to measure length.
Explore and Grow
Find and measure the objects shown in your classroom.
Check students' work.
© Big Ideas Learning, LLC
Chapter 10 | Lesson 3
five hundred fifteen 515

Explore and Grow

- Students should use color tiles to measure the actual objects in your classroom, not the pictures.
- Observe how students are using the tiles. Do they align the side of the first tile with one end of the object? Are they aligning tiles correctly without gaps or overlaps?
- Do they count to tell the number of tiles as their measurement?

ELL Support

Explain the example. Review the names of objects pictured on this page and the next. Then have students work in groups as they practice language. Have groups discuss the following questions: "How many color tiles must be put on the line? How long is the (object)?"

Beginner students may answer with a number.
Intermediate students may answer with phrases, such as, "four color tiles."
Advanced students may answer with sentences, such as, "The paint tray is four color tiles long."

Laurie's Notes

Think and Grow

Getting Started

- Introduce the vocabulary cards **measure** and **length unit**.
- The exercises continue to use color tiles for measurement. Students will line up the tiles with the marked length of the object.

Teaching Notes

- **Model**: "Newton and Descartes are finding how long their paints are. They line up tiles to see how long their paints are. Place a tile in each of the boxes under the paints. Descartes says that we should use tiles to measure the length. Since we are using tiles, one tile would be a *length unit*. Newton reminds us that when we use tiles, we can't have gaps between the tiles or overlap the tiles."
- ? **MP8 Look for and Express Regularity in Repeated Reasoning:** "What tip about measurement did Newton forget to remind us about?" Start at the beginning of the object.
- Have students count how many tiles it takes to measure the paints. Fill in 4 in the answer. "Notice we say *about 4 tiles* because it is probably not exactly perfect."
- In Exercises 1 and 2, students use their tiles to measure the worm and spoon. Point out the line under each picture giving the length of the objects by showing their beginning and end. Students should line their tiles up under this length line rather than with the picture.
- Ask students if they know what kind of worm it must be, since it takes one color tile to measure. Inch worm
- **Supporting Learners:** Depending on fine motor skills, some students may need help lining up their tiles even though they know what they are supposed to do.
- **Extension:** Find other objects in the room that are about the same length as the inch worm and the spoon. Use your tiles to see if you are correct.
- ◉ "Alternate with your partner telling how to use your tiles to measure an object. Be sure to say what we need to be careful not to do also."

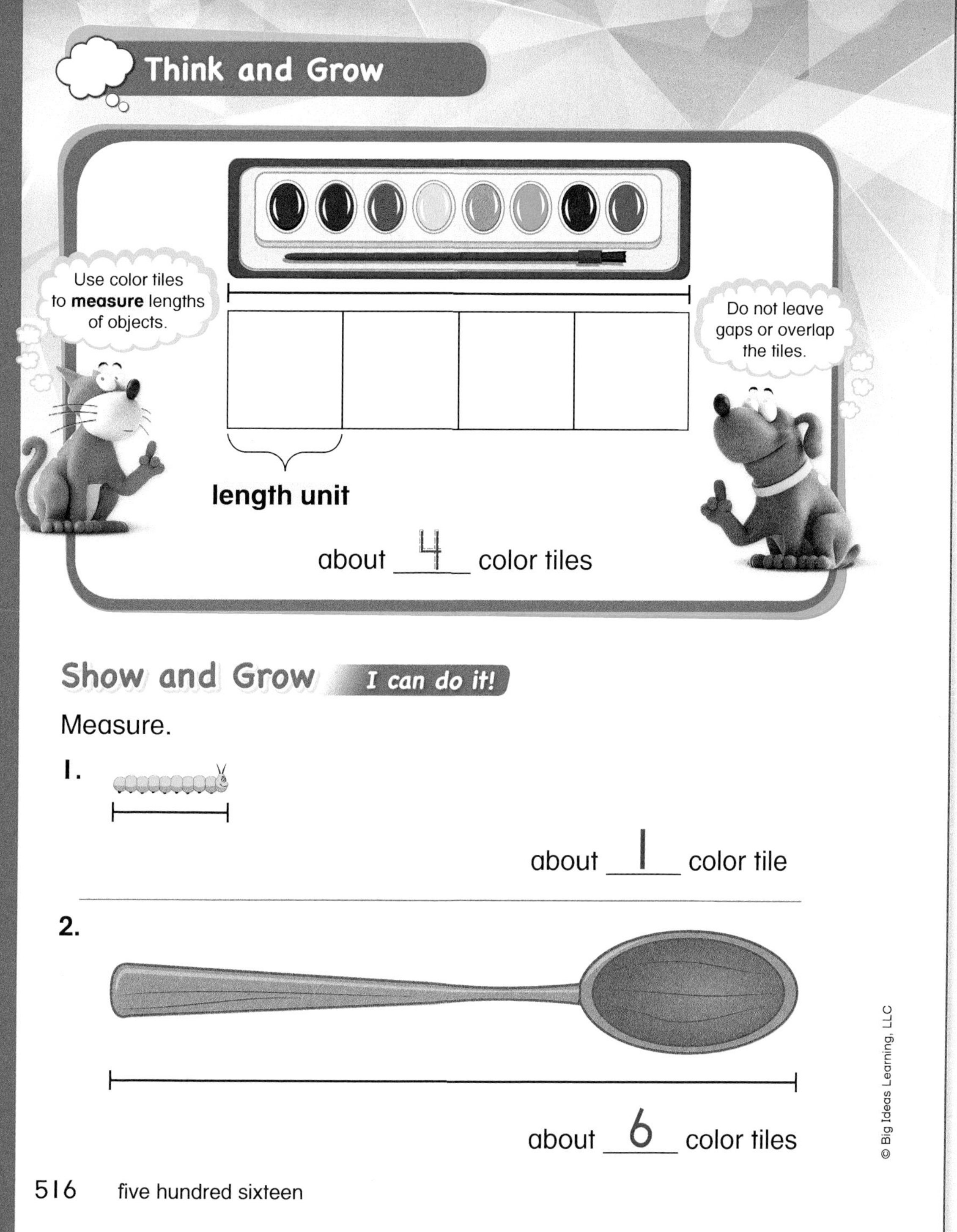

Think and Grow

Use color tiles to **measure** lengths of objects.

Do not leave gaps or overlap the tiles.

length unit

about 4 color tiles

Show and Grow I can do it!

Measure.

1.

about 1 color tile

2.

about 6 color tiles

Laurie's Notes

Scaffold instruction to support all students in their learning. Learning is individualized and you may want to group students differently as they move in and out of these levels with each skill and concept. Student self-assessment and feedback help guide your instructional decisions about how and when to layer support for all students to become proficient learners.

Meeting the needs of all learners.

Apply and Grow: Practice

SCAFFOLDING INSTRUCTION

Exercises 3 and 4 continue to have students measure lengths of objects by lining up tiles. They should continue to use the length line under each picture.

EMERGING students may not be connecting the number of tiles with how long each object is. They also may not be aligning the tiles correctly to show the length.

- **Exercises 3 and 4:** Continue to observe how students are aligning tiles. Are they counting the tiles to determine the length?
- **Exercise 5:** Students should recognize the correct way to line up tiles to measure a length. Have students tell partners why they did not select any of the other pictures.

PROFICIENT students understand that the number of tiles is telling how long an object is. They understand the correct way to align the tiles, and are able to do so.

- **Exercise 5:** Have students say what is wrong with each of the incorrect pictures.

Extension: Adding Rigor

- Have students estimate how long an object in the classroom is, and then check with their tiles. Have them record their work on a sheet of paper.

Name ______________________________

Apply and Grow: Practice

Measure.

3.

about 5 color tiles

4.

about 3 color tiles

5. Precision Which picture shows the correct way to measure the straw?

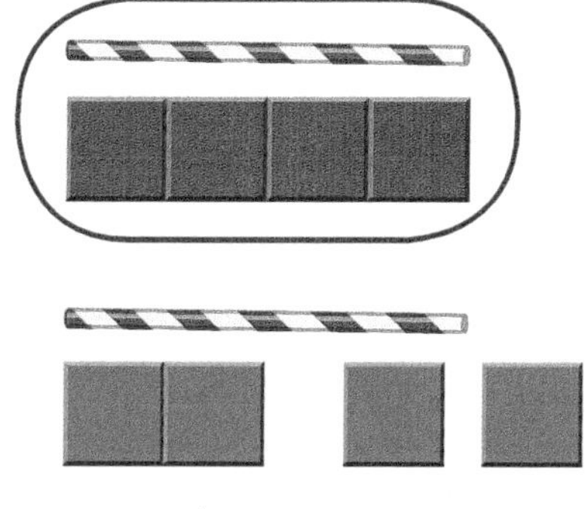

ELL Support

Check for understanding of Lesson 10.3. Read each question aloud as students follow along. Clarify unknown vocabulary if necessary. Have them answer using a thumbs up or thumbs down signal for *yes* or *no*.

Laurie's Notes

Think and Grow: Modeling Real Life

These applications allow students to demonstrate their understanding of using numbers to compare the lengths of two objects. In these applications, students will measure an object, and then determine if it will fit into a case that is a given specific length.

- ? **Preview:** "What do you see on this page? What are some things we put scissors in? Do your parents keep their cell phones in cases?" If you have a cell phone case, show how it fits.
- **MP1 Make Sense of Problems:** Read and discuss the scissor example with students. Ask students to describe what they know and what they are trying to find out. Ask students what the relationship of the scissors to the case would need to be if they are going to fit.
- ? **Model:** "Let's see how long the scissors are. Use your tiles to measure the scissors." Pause "The pencil case is 7 tiles long. Are the scissors longer or shorter than the case? Will they fit? How do you know?"
- Review the directions with students for Exercise 6. Have them tell their partners their strategy for solving the exercise before they begin. They can guess what the answer will be to practice estimating lengths.
- **MP3 Construct Viable Arguments:** Have several students share their explanations for Exercise 6.
- ◉ "We have been using tiles to measure the lengths of objects. Use your thumb signals to show how well you can measure the length of an object and tell the number of tiles long it is."

Closure

- Play "Yes or No?" Show students objects with tiles to show the measurement. Some should be measured correctly, and some incorrectly. Each time you show an object, and put the tiles beneath it to measure, say, "The pencil is 8 tiles long." Students say yes or no based on whether the tiles are lined correctly or not. For a very challenging turn, place the tiles correctly but give the wrong number of tiles to see if the students can catch your error.

Think and Grow: Modeling Real Life

Will the scissors fit inside a pencil case that is 7 color tiles long?

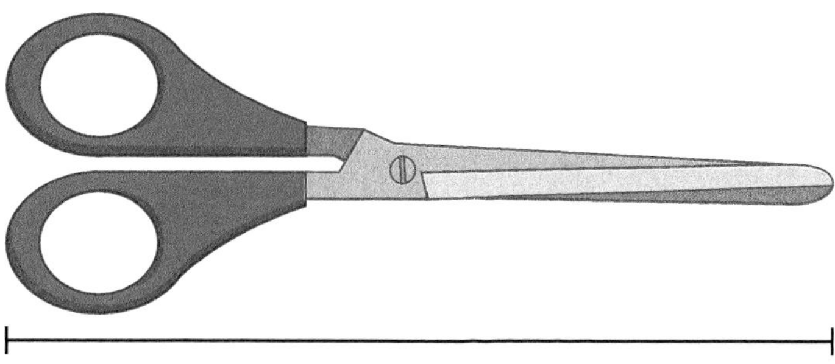

Circle: 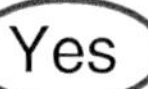 Yes No

Tell how you know: **The scissors are about 5 color tiles long. 5 is less than 7.**

Does It Make Sense? To fit inside, should the scissors be shorter or longer than the case?

Show and Grow *I can think deeper!*

6. Will the cell phone fit inside a case that is 5 color tiles long?

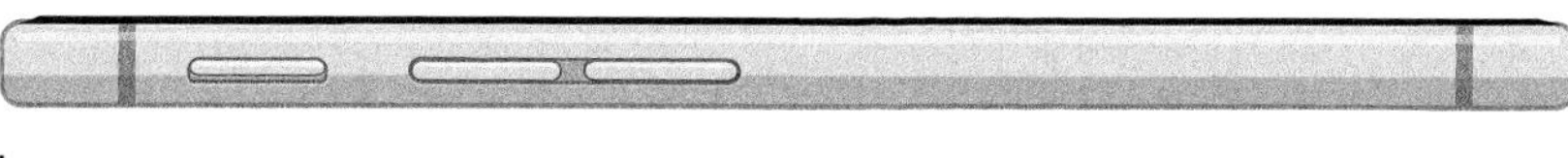

Circle: Yes  No

Tell how you know: **The cell phone is about 6 color tiles long. 6 is greater than 5.**

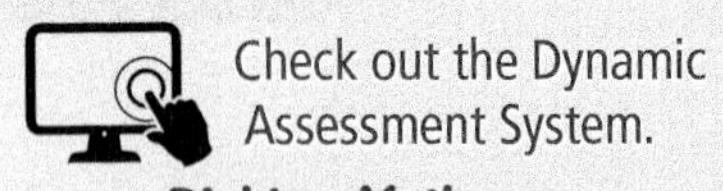
Check out the Dynamic Assessment System.
BigIdeasMath.com

Scaffold assignments to support all students in their learning progression. Revisit with spaced practice to move every student toward proficiency.

Connect and Extend Learning

Practice Notes

- Remind students to line up tiles correctly.
- **Exercise 5:** Be sure students explain how they know their answer is correct.

Prior Skills

- **Exercises 7 and 8:** Grade 1, Practicing Addition Strategies

Cross-Curricular Connections

Science

- Discuss the life cycle of a plant. Have students each grow a bean in a bag and take weekly observations on how their plant grows. Have them measure the height of their plants with color tiles.

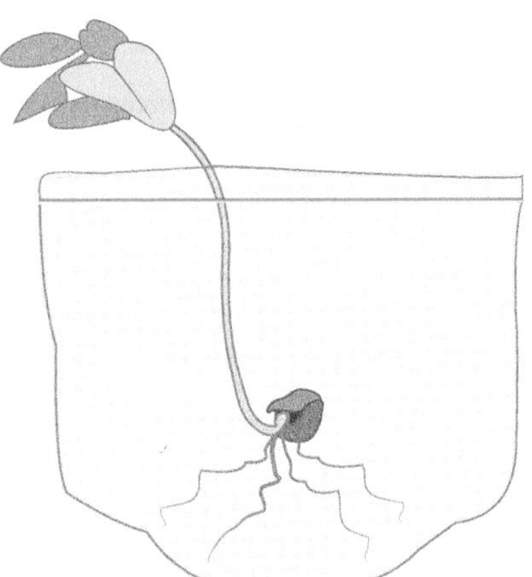

Name ______________________

Learning Target: Use like objects to measure length.

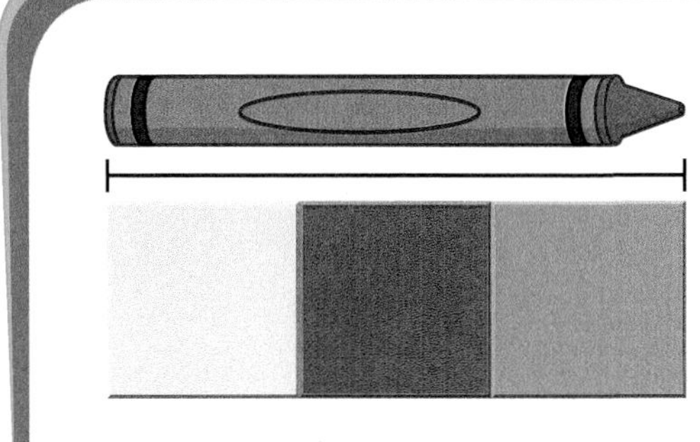

about 3 color tiles

Measure.

1. 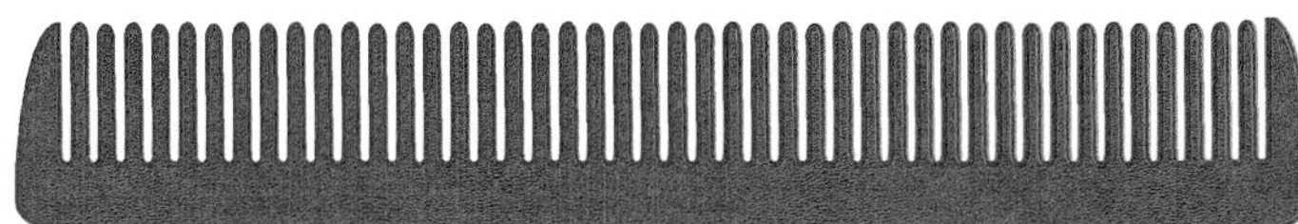

about 5 color tiles

2. 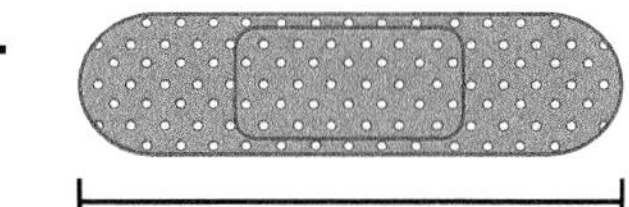

about 2 color tiles

3. 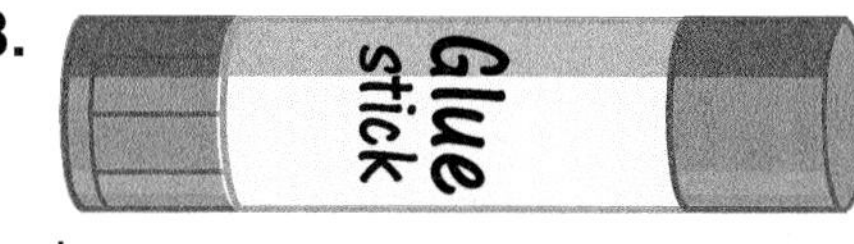

about 3 color tiles

Chapter 10 | Lesson 3 **519**

Connect and Extend Learning

Extend Student Learning

Interpersonal

- Set up a class interview with a carpenter or other professional that uses measurement as part of their job. Prompt students to prepare questions to ask the professional, especially questions having to do with what they are learning in math. Have the professional explain how he or she uses length, tools used to measure, and when he or she first learned about length. Allow time for students to ask questions. Once the interview is over, have students write a thank you card and include their favorite part of the interview.

Lesson Resources	
Surface Level	**Deep Level**
Resources by Chapter • Extra Practice • Reteach Differentiating the Lesson Skills Review Handbook Skills Trainer Math Musicals	Resources by Chapter • Enrichment and Extension Graphic Organizers Math Musicals Dynamic Assessment System • Lesson Practice

4. **Reasoning** The green yarn is about 3 color tiles long. How long is the blue yarn?

about 6 color tiles

5. **Modeling Real Life** Will the gift card fit inside an envelope that is 8 color tiles long?

Circle:  Yes No

Tell how you know:
The gift card is about 4 color tiles long. 4 is less than 8.

6. **DIG DEEPER!** Draw a bookmark that is 2 color tiles longer than the gift card in Exercise 5. Will it fit inside the envelope?

Check students' work.

Yes

Review & Refresh

7. $72 + 19 = $ 91

8. $54 + 9 = $ 63

10.4

Check out the Dynamic Classroom.
BigIdeasMath.com

Laurie's Notes

COMMON CORE

STATE STANDARDS
1.MD.A.1, 1.MD.A.2

Learning Target

Measure an object in different ways.

Success Criteria

- Start measuring at the beginning of the object and stop at the end.
- Measure an object using one type of like unit.
- Measure an object using another type of like unit.
- Explain what happens when you measure an object in different ways.

Warm-Up

Practice opportunities for the following are available in the Resources by Chapter or at *BigIdeasMath.com.*

- Daily skills
- Vocabulary
- Prerequisite skills

ELL Support

Point out that when you measure how long an object is, you measure its length. Length is a dimension. Explain that there are other dimensions, such as width and height. You may want to model these dimensions with an object in the classroom, such as a bookcase.

Preparing to Teach

Students will continue to measure objects using non-standard units. Today students will use both color tiles and large paper clips to measure the lengths of objects. Students will measure the same object in two different ways, and realize that the length of the unit determines how many units are needed.

Materials

- color tiles
- large paper clips
- objects to compare lengths

Dig In (Circle Time)

Students will use color tiles and large paper clips to measure a variety of objects. They will discuss why measuring the same object with the different units requires a different number of tiles than paper clips. All students should have tiles and large paper clips with which to work.

- "Yesterday we measured objects using color tiles. Tell your partner the three things we need to remember when measuring an object using tiles." start at beginning of object, no gaps, no overlaps
- ◉ "Today we are going to continue measuring objects with tiles, but we are also going to use large paper clips. Look at a tile and a paper clip. What do you notice?" paper clip is longer; tile is square
- "Yesterday we measured my pencil with tiles. It took (number) tiles. Tell your partner if you think it will take more or less paper clips to measure the same pencil. Why?"
- Show how to measure the pencil with paper clips. Reinforce the principles of starting at the beginning of the pencil, no gaps, and no overlaps. Linking the paper clips together would be an overlap, so do not let students do that.
- Model measuring a few more objects with both tiles and paper clips, and count to compare the number of each.
- Have students work with partners to measure a few objects. One partner should use tiles and the other paper clips.
- ? **MP2 Reason Abstractly and Quantitatively**: "Why do you think it takes less paper clips than tiles to measure the same object?"
- ◉ "Today we are going to measure more objects using both tiles and paper clips. We will be very careful to start lining up our units (tiles or paper clips) at the beginning of the object. We will be very careful not to have any gaps or overlap in our units."

? Teaching Prompt ◉ Learning Target

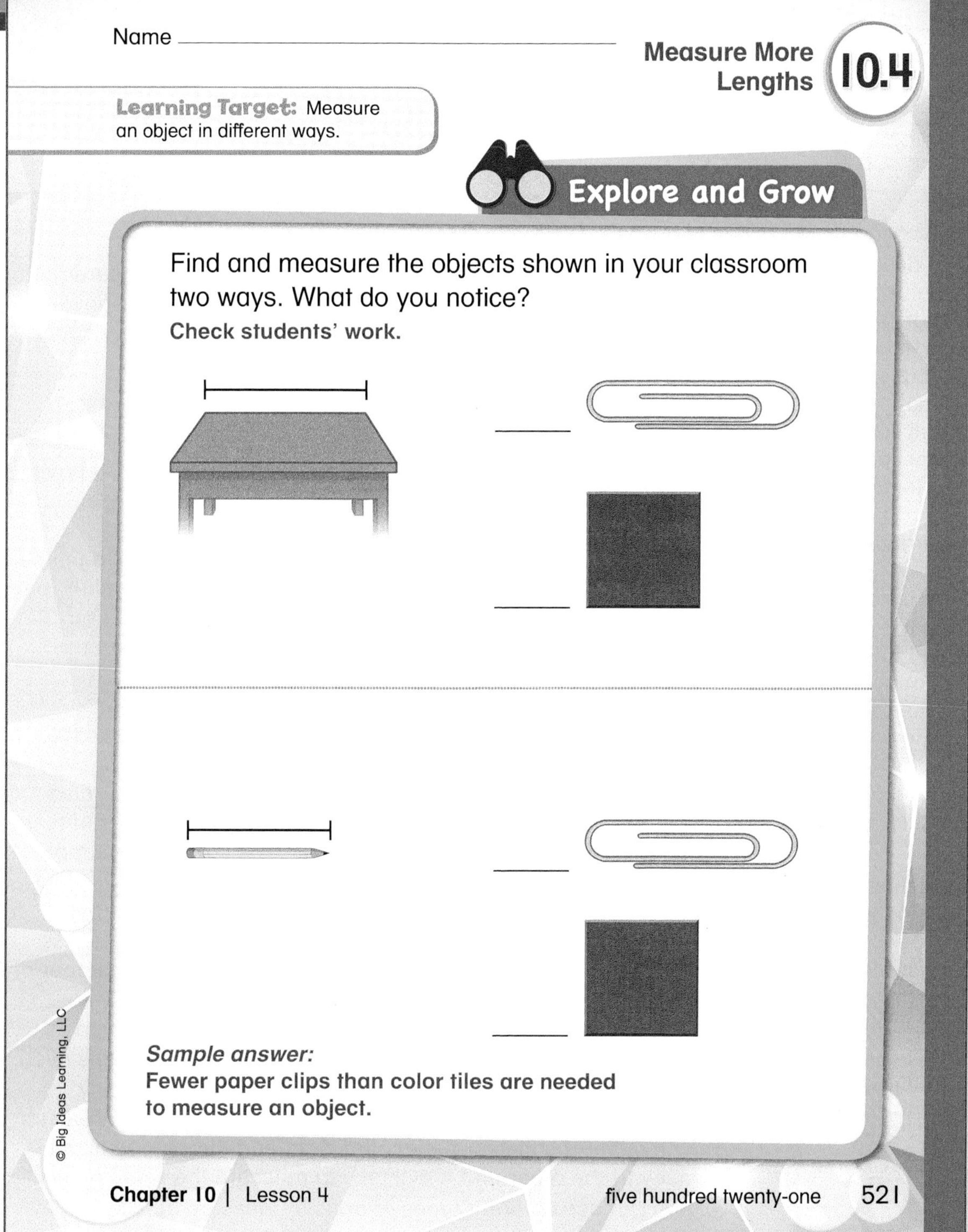

Name
Measure More Lengths 10.4
Learning Target: Measure an object in different ways.
Explore and Grow
Find and measure the objects shown in your classroom two ways. What do you notice?
Check students' work.
Sample answer:
Fewer paper clips than color tiles are needed to measure an object.
© Big Ideas Learning, LLC
Chapter 10 | Lesson 4
five hundred twenty-one 521

Explore and Grow

- Students should use tiles and paper clips to measure the actual objects in your classroom, not the pictures.
- Notice if students consistently use the measurement tools correctly and are counting to tell the number of paper clips and tiles needed to measure.
- Tell your partners what you notice about the number of paper clips and the number of tiles it takes to measure the same object.

ELL Support

Explain that to describe length, you can use different units of measurement. Review the example. Explain that the length of the carrot is either 6 color tiles or 3 paper clips. Then have students practice verbal language in pairs using Exercises 1 and 2. Review the names of the items shown if necessary. Have one student ask another, "How long is the carrot in color tiles? How long is it in paper clips?" Have them alternate roles for the other exercises.

Beginner students may answer using numbers.
Intermediate students may answer with phrases, such as, "six color tiles."
Advanced students may answer with sentences, such as, "The carrot is six color tiles long."

Laurie's Notes

Think and Grow

Getting Started

- Students continue to use tiles and paper clips for measurement. Students can line up the tiles above the line provided showing the length of the object, and the paper clips below. They could also measure with one tool at a time.

Teaching Notes

? **Model:** "We want to find out how long the carrot is. Let's use our tiles to see how long the carrot is by lining them up above the carrot. Fill in the squares with your tiles. How many tiles long is the carrot? Fill in 6 color tiles."

? **Model:** "Now let's find out how long the carrot is by using paper clips. Line them up below the carrot. How many paper clips long is the carrot? Fill in 3 paper clips."

- In Exercises 1 and 2, students use their tools to measure the toothbrush and skateboard. Point out the line under each picture giving the length of the objects by showing their beginning and end. Students can line their tiles up above the line and on top of the picture if they want, and the paper clips underneath the line. If it is easier, students can use their tiles below the line as they did yesterday, record the number of tiles, and then remove the tiles and measure in the same location using paper clips.
- Ask students if they are noticing a pattern with the number of tiles and paper clips. They probably notice that it takes less paper clips than tiles, but do they see it is double the number of tiles than paper clips?
- **Supporting Learners:** Depending on fine motor skills, some students may need help lining up the tiles and paper clips even though they know what they are supposed to do.
- **Extension:** Find other objects in the room to measure. Measure with either the tiles or paper clips first, and then guess how many of the other unit it will take to measure the same object.

◉ "We can use different types of units to measure objects. Today we are using a tile unit, and a paper clip unit. When we use different units, it may not take the same number of each kind to measure the same object. You have seen that it does not take the same number of paper clips as tiles to measure the same object. Tell your partner which unit is longer. Say which unit takes more to measure. Explain to your partner why this might be true. We will talk more about this later, so it might be a guess right now."

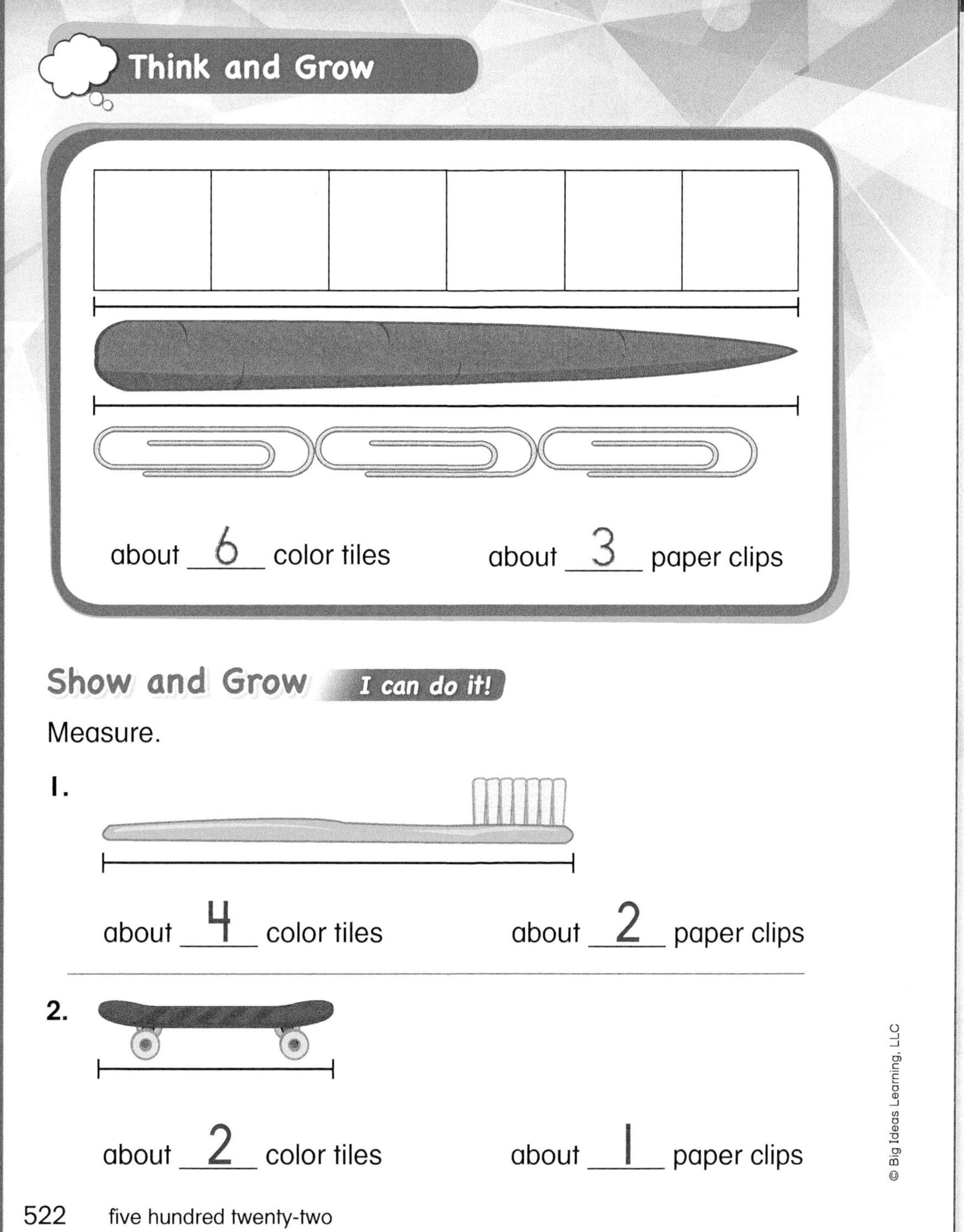

Think and Grow

about 6 color tiles about 3 paper clips

Show and Grow *I can do it!*

Measure.

1.

about 4 color tiles about 2 paper clips

2.

about 2 color tiles about 1 paper clips

Scaffold instruction to support all students in their learning. Learning is individualized and you may want to group students differently as they move in and out of these levels with each skill and concept. Student self-assessment and feedback help guide your instructional decisions about how and when to layer support for all students to become proficient learners.

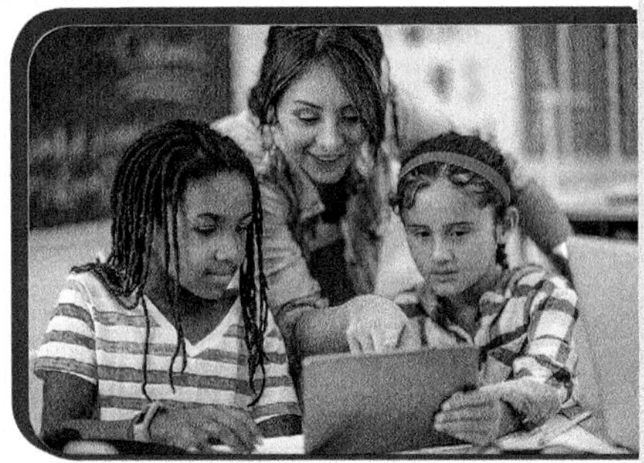

Meeting the needs of all learners.

Laurie's Notes

Apply and Grow: Practice

SCAFFOLDING INSTRUCTION

Exercises 3 and 4 continue to have students measure lengths of objects by using tiles and paper clips. They should continue to use the length line under each picture.

EMERGING students may not see the relationship between the number of tiles and number of paper clips needed to measure an object. If they notice that it always takes less paper clips, they may not understand why this would be true. They do not connect the length of the unit to the number of units needed.

- **Exercises 3 and 4:** Continue to observe how students are measuring. Do they understand that the number of tiles will not be the same as the number of paper clips?
- **Exercise 5:** Students can measure the pencil to find the answer, but it is hopeful that they would recognize that the number of paper clips is always less than the tiles.

PROFICIENT students understand that the number of tiles is always more than paper clips. They connect this fact to the length of the units and can explain that because the paper clips are longer it will take less to fill in the length of the object.

- **Exercise 5:** Have students explain why less paper clips are needed, and not be satisfied by saying that it always takes less paper clips than tiles.

Extension: Adding Rigor

- Have students estimate how long an object in the classroom is, and then check with their tiles or paper clips. They then guess how many of the other units long it is. Have them record their work on a sheet of paper. Have students find the relationship between the number of tiles and the number of paper clips needed to measure the same object. They can line up two tiles against one paper clip to check their guess.

Name ___

Apply and Grow: Practice

Measure.

3.

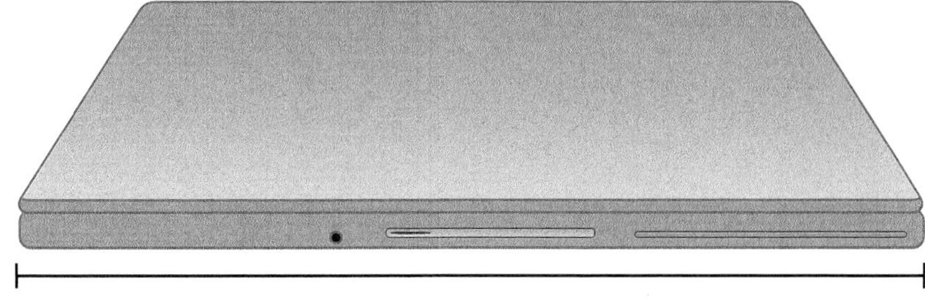

about 6 color tiles about 3 paper clips

4.

about 4 color tiles about 2 paper clips

5. YOU BE THE TEACHER Your friend says the pencil is more paper clips long than color tiles. Is your friend correct? Explain.

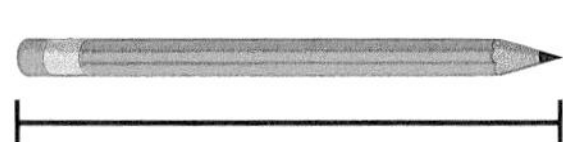

no; The pencil is about 2 color tiles long and about 1 paper clip long.

ELL Support

Check for understanding of Lesson 10.4. Read each exercise aloud as students follow along. Clarify any unknown vocabulary. Allow time to complete each exercise. Ask the following questions for each exercise and have students indicate *yes/no* answers with a thumbs up/down signal.

1. Is your guitar more than 33 paper clips long?
2. Is your mailbox more than 11 color tiles long?

Laurie's Notes

Think and Grow: Modeling Real Life

These applications allow students to demonstrate their understanding of using two different units for measurement. In these applications students are given the length of an object with either paper clips or tiles and need to say if the object is more or less than that number in the other unit.

- Discuss the tile and the paper clip pictures on the page. Have students discuss what they notice and already know from having worked with them in math today.
- Read and discuss the guitar story with students. Notice that the guitar is not in proportion to the paper clips and tiles. Have students describe how big a guitar is and if they have ever played a guitar or knows someone who does.
- ? **Model:** "Our story says that the real guitar is 33 color tiles long. Tell your partner if it will take more or less paper clips to measure. How do you know?" Have several students explain why it will take less paper clips to practice mathematical explanations.
- Review the directions with students for Exercise 6. Have them tell their partners how they will explain their answer.
- **MP3 Construct Viable Arguments:** Explain why it takes more tiles than paper clips to measure the same object. Listen to see if students explain that the shorter the unit, the more it will take to cover the length, and vice versa.
- ◉ "We have been using tiles and paper clips to measure the lengths of objects. Use your thumb signals to show how well you can measure the length of an object. How well can you tell if it will take more or less than the given unit to measure with the other unit?"

Closure

? Show a tile, a paper clip, and a new pencil. Tell students that you want to measure the length of your desk with each of these units. "Which unit will take the most? Which will take the least? Which will be in the middle? Why?"

Think and Grow: Modeling Real Life

Your guitar is 33 color tiles long. Is your guitar more than or less than 33 paper clips long?

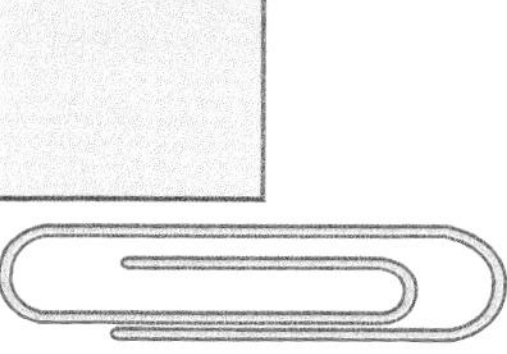

Circle: more than 33 **(less than 33)**

Tell how you know: **I color tile is shorter than I paper clip, so it takes fewer paper clips to measure the length of the guitar.**

Show and Grow *I can think deeper!*

6. Your mailbox is 11 paper clips long. Is your mailbox more than or less than 11 color tiles long?

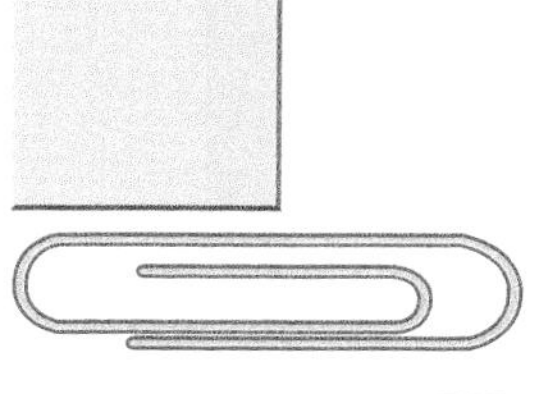

Circle: **(more than 11)** less than 11

Tell how you know: **I paper clip is longer than I color tile, so it takes more color tiles to measure the length of the mailbox.**

Check out the Dynamic
Assessment System.
BigIdeasMath.com

Scaffold assignments to support all students in their learning progression. Revisit with spaced practice to move every student toward proficiency.

Connect and Extend Learning

Practice Notes

- **Exercises 2–4:** If students are having difficulties, then have them use actual color tiles and paper clips to solve the problem. Be sure students explain how they know their answers are correct.

Prior Skills

- **Exercise 5:** Grade 1, Solving *Take From* Problems

Cross-Curricular Connections

Science

- Discuss the concept of force and motion with students. Set up an experiment involving a toy car going down a race track or ramp. Have students predict how far the car will go using certain units, like paper clips or color tiles. Conduct the experiment, then measure to see the results.

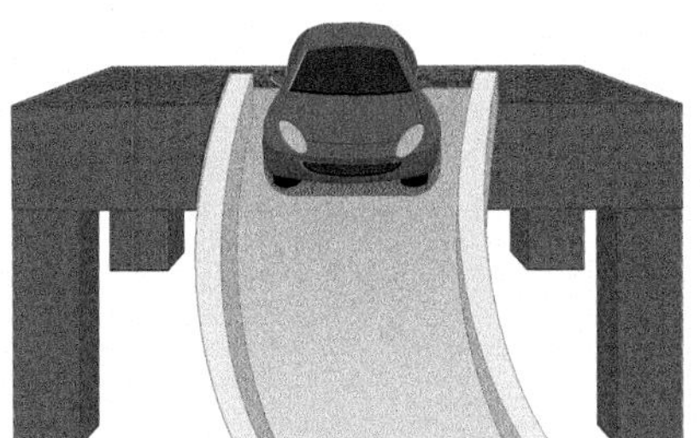

Name ____________________

Practice 10.4

Learning Target: Measure an object in different ways.

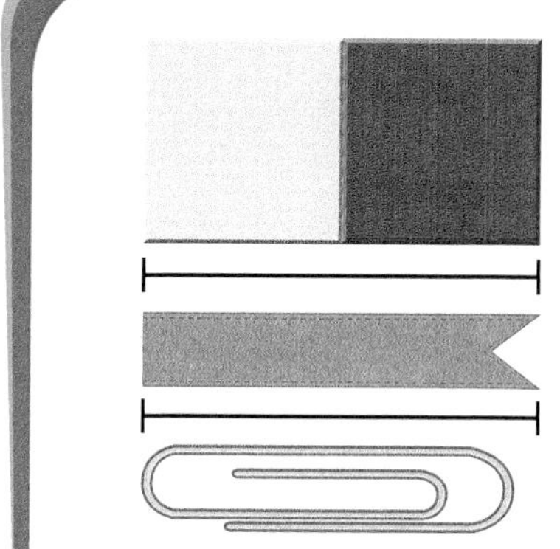

about 2 color tiles

about 1 paper clip

Measure.

1.

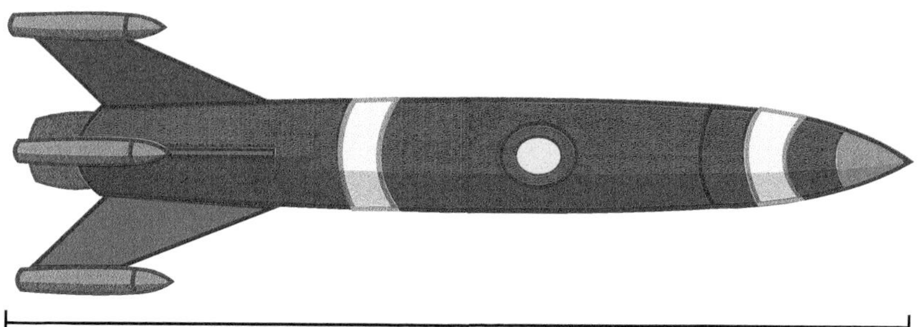

about 6 color tiles

about 3 paper clips

Connect and Extend Learning

Extend Student Learning

Visual-Spatial

- Set up a measurement scavenger hunt in your classroom. Prepare items ahead of time that are so many color tiles or paper clips long and place them around the room. Write their rough measurements on the board. Have students go around the room and start measuring. They can list any items that meet the measured requirements on paper and review them at the end.

Lesson Resources	
Surface Level	**Deep Level**
Resources by Chapter • Extra Practice • Reteach Differentiating the Lesson Skills Review Handbook Skills Trainer	Resources by Chapter • Enrichment and Extension Graphic Organizers Dynamic Assessment System • Lesson Practice

2. YOU BE THE TEACHER Your friend says the marker is more color tiles long than paper clips. Is your friend correct? Explain. **yes; The marker is about 8 color tiles long and less than 2 paper clips long.**

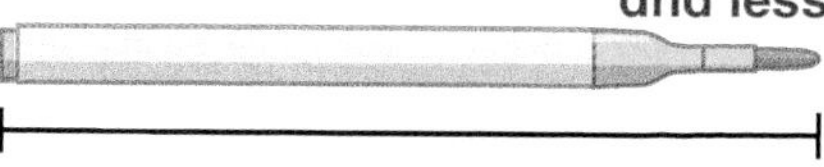

3. Modeling Real Life Your folder is 15 color tiles long. Is your folder more than or less than 15 paper clips long?

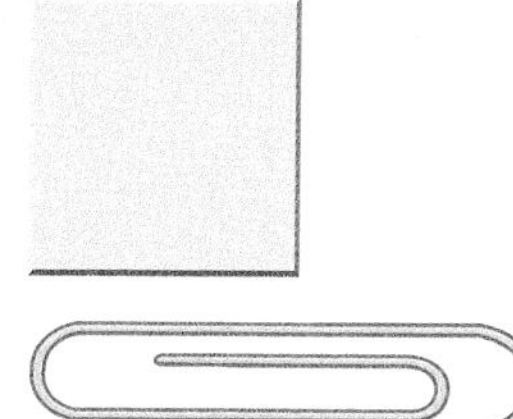

Circle: more than 15 less than 15

Tell how you know:
I color tile is shorter than I paper clip, so it takes fewer paper clips to measure the length of the folder.

4. DIG DEEPER! Your crayon is 4 color tiles long. About how many paper clips long is the crayon? Explain.
Sample answer: **about 2 paper clips; A paper clip is about double the size of a color tile; 4 = 2 + 2**

about 2 paper clips

Review & Refresh

5. 8 tigers swim.
5 tigers leave.
How many tigers are left?

8 − 5 = 3

3 tigers

10.5

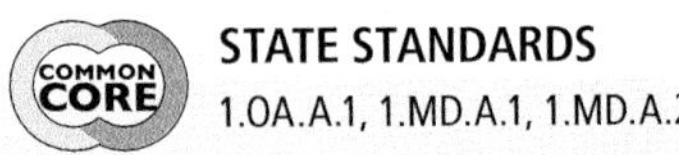

Laurie's Notes

COMMON CORE **STATE STANDARDS**
1.OA.A.1, 1.MD.A.1, 1.MD.A.2

Learning Target

Solve *compare* word problems involving length.

Success Criteria

- Identify what information is given in the word problem.
- Identify what the question is asking.
- Use a bar model to solve a comparison problem.
- Explain the strategy I used to solve.

Warm-Up

Practice opportunities for the following are available in the Resources by Chapter or at *BigIdeasMath.com.*

- Daily skills
- Vocabulary
- Prerequisite skills

ELL Support

Explain that when you compare the length of objects, you use a comparative adjective, such as *longer* or *shorter*. Comparative adjectives are often made by adding *-er* to the end of an adjective. You may want to have students practice the phrases *longer than* and *shorter than* in the context of sample sentences.

Preparing to Teach

Students will apply length measurement to application problems. They will find the number of units shorter or longer than a given length. This lesson will recall Lessons 3.4, 3.5, and 9.6 among many others.

Materials

- large paper clips
- color tiles
- Blank Bar Model*
- objects to compare lengths

**Found in the Instructional Resources*

Dig In (Circle Time)

Students will reason about measurement stories and use tiles and paper clips to solve the story problem. They will review and use a bar model to show their thinking. They will relate the bar model to addition and subtraction.

- "We have been measuring all kinds of objects. We compared lengths of objects to find which is longer and which is shorter. We've used tiles and paper clips to tell a number measurement for objects. Tell your partners something you know about measuring length."
- ◉ "Today we are going to use everything we have learned to solve measurement stories. We will also be using a strategy we learned back at the beginning of the year – the comparison bar model."
- **?** Bring two objects that can be measured and compared using paper clips or tiles. The example is written for two small baskets. "I have two baskets. One basket is 3 tiles long. The other basket is 5 tiles long. How much longer is the bigger basket? Tell your partner what you think."
- Have students share their answer and reasoning. Most students will think $5 - 3$ or $3 + \_\_\_ = 5$.
- "When we solve length stories, it is not different from all the other comparison stories we have solved through the year. We will still add or subtract. We will model the situation. Let's model this."
- **?** "Do you remember using a bar model to compare? The longer bar is for the longest object. The shorter bar is for the shortest object. The bracket holds the difference. So, for the basket, the longer basket is 5 (fill in 5 in the bar model) and the shorter is 3 (fill in 3). What is the difference? We can think addition (Write $3 + \_\_\_ = 5$), or we can subtract (Write $5 - 3 = \_\_\_$). The longer basket is 2 tiles longer. The shorter basket is 2 tiles shorter!"

5		$5 - 3 = \_\_$
3		$3 + \_\_ = 5$

- Repeat with one other example. Ask students to help you fill in the bar model, and write related addition and subtraction equations to solve.
- ◉ "Today we are going to solve many stories comparing the lengths of two objects. We will use a bar model, and write addition and subtraction equations."

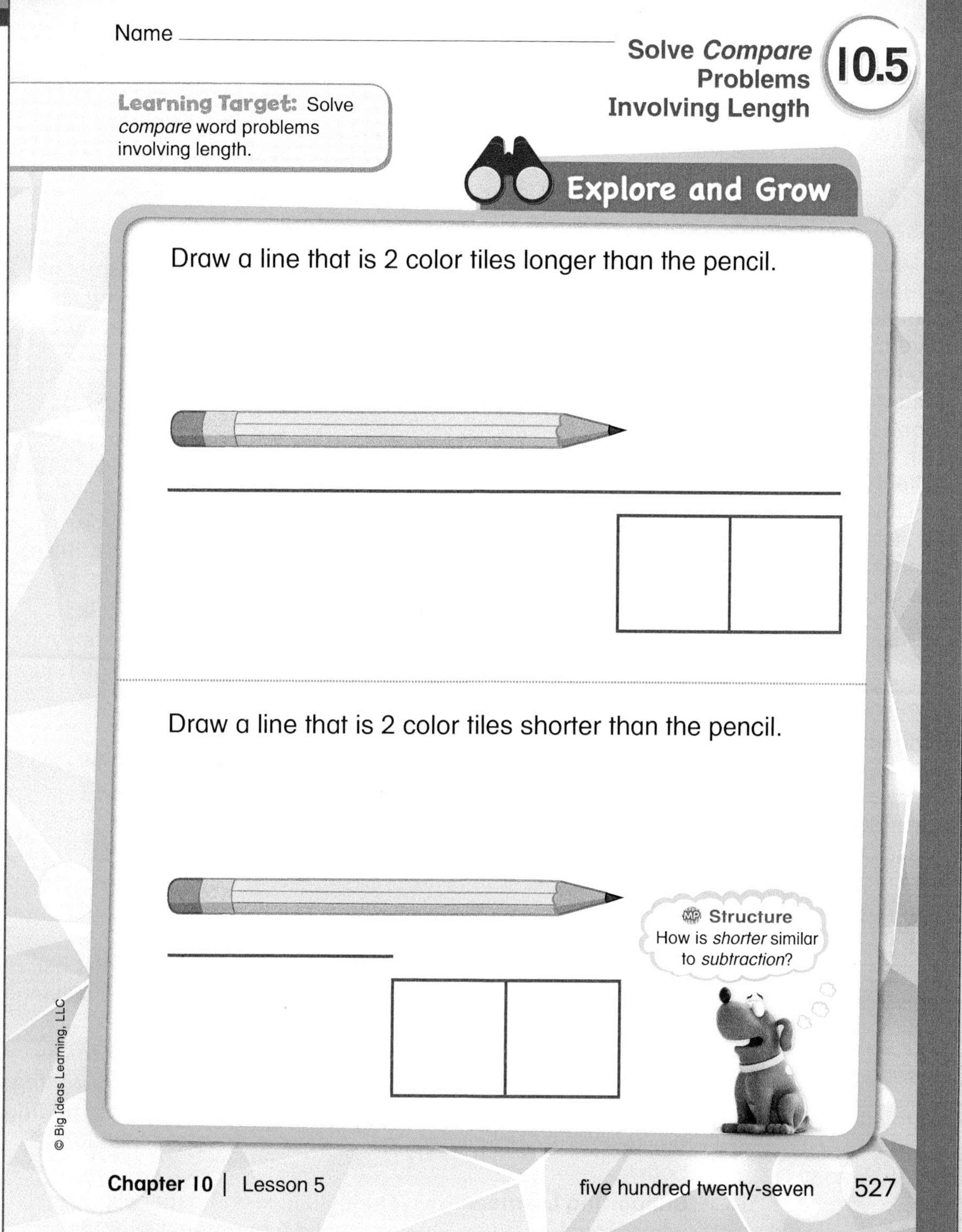

Name

Solve *Compare* Problems Involving Length **10.5**

Learning Target: Solve *compare* word problems involving length.

Explore and Grow

Draw a line that is 2 color tiles longer than the pencil.

Draw a line that is 2 color tiles shorter than the pencil.

Structure
How is *shorter* similar to *subtraction*?

Explore and Grow

- Discuss with students what they are trying to do. Have them identify and explain the key words that talk about length: longer and shorter.
- Students should be encouraged to find their own method to discover the correct length. Most students will line up tiles beneath the pencil, and then add or subtract 2 tiles. From this they will draw the line. Some students may want to draw a line that is the length of the pencil, then add tiles at the end to extend, or put tiles on the end of the line to erase.
- **MP6 Attend to Precision:** "Tell your partners how you found your line. Tell how you knew whether to add or subtract tiles. Circle the key words that told you what to do."

ELL Support

Review the example. Then have groups work together to complete Exercise 1. Have groups discuss the following questions: "How long is one item? How long is the other? What is the difference in length? How much longer/shorter is one than the other?" Monitor discussion and expect students to perform according to their language proficiency level.

Beginner students may state one-word answers.
Intermediate students may state phrases and simple sentences.
Advanced students may state detailed sentences.

Laurie's Notes

Think and Grow

Getting Started

- The exercises compare given lengths of two objects. Students use a bar model to show the comparison, and write both an addition and subtraction equation to solve for the difference in length.

Teaching Notes

- **Model**: "Let's talk about shoes. Do we all wear the same size shoe? Let's underline what we know and circle what we want to know. In our story, your shoe is 7 tiles long and your friend's is 9 tiles long. We want to know how many tiles shorter is your shoe. Begin by filling in the long bar with the longer number of tiles. Fill the shorter bar with the shorter number of tiles."
- ? **Model**: "You probably already know the answer. Let's talk about how we find the difference between the lengths. Tell your partner how we could think subtraction. Fill in the subtraction equation. What is 9 − 7? How do you know?" counted back, knew fact, etc. "Fill in 2."
- ? **Model**: "We can also think addition. Tell your partner how to think addition to find the difference. Fill in the addition equation. What plus 7 is 9? How do you know?" counted on, knew fact, etc. "Fill in 2."
- Fill in the 2 in the bar model, and answer line.
- Be sure to take the opportunity to review addition and subtraction strategies throughout this lesson.
- In Exercise 1, students repeat the process for filling in the bar model, writing subtraction and addition equations, and solving the comparison.
- Students have not used a bar model for a while. Watch to see if they remember how to use it, and if they are correctly writing the corresponding equations. Ask students how they are finding the answer. Are they using subtraction strategies? addition? both?
- **Supporting Learners:** Give students tiles and paper clips to use as manipulatives. They can build a bar model with the manipulatives to see the comparison.
- ◉ "We are using many of our strategies that we have developed throughout the year. How are you feeling so far about identifying what we know from the story? finding what we want to know? using a bar model?"

Think and Grow

Your shoe is 7 color tiles long. Your friend's is 9 color tiles long. How many tiles shorter is your shoe?

Friend: 9

You: 7 | 2

9 − 7 = 2

7 + 2 = 9

2 color tiles

Show and Grow *I can do it!*

1. Your lunch box is 6 paper clips long. Your friend's is 3 paper clips long. How many paper clips longer is your lunch box?

You: 6

Friend: 3 | 3

6 − 3 = 3

3 + 3 = 6

3 paper clips

Scaffold instruction to support all students in their learning. Learning is individualized and you may want to group students differently as they move in and out of these levels with each skill and concept. Student self-assessment and feedback help guide your instructional decisions about how and when to layer support for all students to become proficient learners.

Meeting the needs of all learners.

Laurie's Notes

Apply and Grow: Practice

SCAFFOLDING INSTRUCTION

Exercises 2 and 3 continue to have students use a bar model to solve a comparison length story. Encourage students to underline what they know and circle what they want to know, as they have done in the past.

EMERGING students may need support in using the bar model. Remind them to fill in the longer amount from the story in the top (longer) bar, and the shorter in the bottom bar. They may need to be reminded how to transfer the information into equations.

- **Exercise 3:** Students choose the equation they want to use to solve the story.
- **Exercise 4:** Students may benefit from drawing a bar model. Many students will be able to tell the difference because it is a basic number fact. Translating the numerical difference into the sentences may be more difficult. Have students tell you the difference in tiles. Then ask if your pencil is longer or shorter than your friend's. Help them fill the blanks in the first sentence in this way. They should be able to fill in the second sentence.

PROFICIENT students understand that the number of tiles is always more than paper clips. They connect this fact to the length of the units and can explain that because the paper clips are longer it will take less to fill in the length of the object.

- **Exercise 3:** Ask students why they chose the equation they did.
- **Exercise 4:** Students may need prompting as to what goes into the second blank. Remind them that they are comparing length, so they want length comparison words. Try not to supply "longer and shorter" for them, but give an example for them to describe to surface the words.

Extension: Adding Rigor

- Have students find two objects to measure. They say how long each is, and then make a bar model to solve for the difference. Have them write both an addition and a subtraction equation to solve.

Name ______

Apply and Grow: Practice

2. Your scarf is 10 paper clips long. Your friend's is 7 paper clips long. How many paper clips longer is your scarf?

You: 10

Friend: 7 | 3

10 − 7 = 3

7 + 3 = 10

3 paper clips

---

3. Your marker is 6 color tiles long. Your friend's is 7 color tiles long. How many tiles shorter is your marker?

Sample answer:

Friend: 7

You: 6 | 1

7 ⊖ 6 = 1

1 color tile

---

4. **Reasoning** Your pencil is 4 color tiles long. Your friend's is 2 color tiles long. Complete the sentences.

Your pencil is 2 color tiles longer than your friend's.

Your friend's pencil is 2 color tiles shorter than yours.

ELL Support

Check for understanding of Lesson 10.5. Read each story aloud as students follow along. Explain unknown vocabulary or unfamiliar situations. You could have students complete a hands-on activity by creating paper chains and airplanes as they work through the exercises. Have students respond to the following questions by holding up the appropriate number of fingers.

1. How many paper clips long is your friend's paper chain?
2. How many paper clips long is your paper airplane?

Laurie's Notes

Think and Grow: Modeling Real Life

These applications allow students to demonstrate their understanding of using bar models and either addition or subtraction to solve comparison stories. In these applications, one length and the comparison is given rather than both lengths.

? **Preview:** "What do you see on the page? Have you ever made paper chains? Have you made a paper airplane before? What do you think we might be comparing? Let's find out ..."

- Read and discuss the paper chain story with students. Have students tell you what we know and what we want to find out. Point out that this is the first story where we do not know both lengths. We know a difference and one of the lengths.

? **Model:** "Your friend's paper chain is 6 paper clips shorter than yours. Where in the bar model do we fill in the difference between lengths?" bracket "Fill in 6 in the bracket to show the difference in length. Is your chain longer or shorter than your friend's?" longer "Your chain is 12 clips long. Will 12 go into the top or bottom bar?" top bar

? **Model:** "How can we find how long your friend's chain is? There are two different equations we could use. Tell your partner an equation that we could use." $12 - 6 =$ ___ or $6 +$ ___ $= 12$

- Go over strategies with students for solving the equations. They may recognize doubles, count on or count back, make a 10, get to 10, etc.
- Review the directions with students for Exercise 5. Have them tell their partners what they know, and if it is two lengths or a length and a difference. Watch as they fill in the bar model and choose an equation.
- **MP3 Construct Viable Arguments:** Explain why solving a length comparison story is not really different from what we have been doing all year.

⦿ "We have been using bar models to solve comparison problems. We did this earlier in the year and from time to time. Use your thumb signals to show how confident you are at using bar models again. How confident are you at writing an equation from the model?"

Closure

- "My hand is about 3 paper clips long. My friend's is about 5. My friend drew this bar model to show how much bigger her hand is. She says 8 paper clips. What went wrong?"

(blank)	
5	3

$\underline{8} - 3 = 5$

$5 + 3 = \underline{8}$

Think and Grow: Modeling Real Life

Your friend's paper chain is 6 paper clips shorter than yours. Your chain is 12 paper clips long. How long is your friend's?

Model: You: 12

Friend: 6 | 6

Equation:

Sample answer:

$12 - 6 = 6$

6 paper clips long

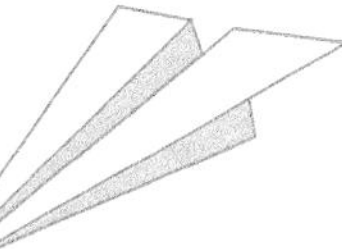

Show and Grow *I can think deeper!*

5. Your paper airplane is 9 color tiles shorter than your friend's. Your friend's paper airplane is 16 color tiles long. How long is yours?

Model: Friend: 16

You: 7 | 9

Equation:

Sample answer:

$16 - 9 = 7$

7 color tiles long

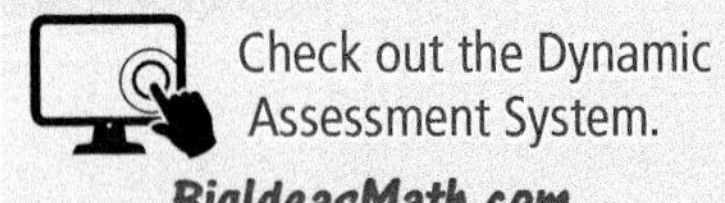
Check out the Dynamic
Assessment System.
BigIdeasMath.com

Scaffold assignments to support all students in their learning progression. Revisit with spaced practice to move every student toward proficiency.

Connect and Extend Learning

Practice Notes

- Review the different parts of the bar model with students.

Prior Skills

- **Exercises 5 and 6:** Grade 1, Adding Doubles from 1 to 5

Cross-Curricular Connections

Social Studies

- List state names on the board. Have students select one and create it using letter tiles. They will compare the length of their state name to their partner's by looking at the number of tiles each student used. They will then create a word problem by describing how many more tiles are used or whether they are the same amount.

Name ______________________

Learning Target: Solve *compare* word problems involving length.

Your book is 4 color tiles long. Your friend's is 6 color tiles long. How many tiles shorter is your book?

Friend: | 6 |

You: | 4 | 2

6 − 4 = 2

4 + 2 = 6

2 color tiles

1. Your backpack is 15 paper clips long. Your friend's is 12 paper clips long. How many paper clips longer is your backpack?

You: | 15 |

Friend: | 12 | 3

15 − 12 = 3

12 + 3 = 15

3 paper clips

Connect and Extend Learning

Extend Student Learning

Linguistic

- Create a story problem with missing numbers and words or use the one below.

  Your ____(a)____ is ____(b)____color tiles longer than your friend's. Your friend's ____(a)____ is 13 color tiles long. How long is yours?

  For (a) have students fill in a name of an object like a scarf or necklace. For (b) have students fill in about how long that object is and then fill in (a) again. Students can switch their problems with a partner and solve. Provide extra paper for them to use bar models on.

Lesson Resources	
Surface Level	**Deep Level**
Resources by Chapter • Extra Practice • Reteach Differentiating the Lesson Skills Review Handbook Skills Trainer	Resources by Chapter • Enrichment and Extension Graphic Organizers Dynamic Assessment System • Lesson Practice

2. **Reasoning** Your baseball mitt is 8 paper clips long. Your friend's is 7 paper clips long. Complete the sentences.

Your friend's baseball mitt is 1 paper clip **shorter** than yours.

Your baseball mitt is 1 paper clip **longer** than your friend's.

---

3. **Modeling Real Life** Your desk is 7 paper clips longer than your friend's. Your friend's desk is 14 paper clips long. How long is yours?

$14 + 7 = 21$

You: 21

Friend: 14 | 7

21 paper clips long

---

4. **DIG DEEPER!** In Exercise 3, your cousin's desk is longer than your friend's desk, but shorter than your desk. What is the greatest length that your cousin's desk could be? the shortest?

20 paper clips; 15 paper clips

Review & Refresh

5. $5 + 5 =$ 10

6. $2 + 2 =$ 4

Laurie's Notes

ELL Support

Have students practice verbal language by working on the Performance Task in groups. Have Intermediate and Advanced students alternate reading sections aloud within their groups. Guide them to use string to measure distances and copy string lengths on a piece of paper so they can compare. Explain that they must use the routes shown on the map, including corners, and cannot simply lay a string between two points. Beginners will focus only on questions and answers. Circulate to monitor their language. Expect students to perform according to their proficiency level.

Beginner students may use single words. **Intermediate** students may answer using phrases or simple sentences. **Advanced** students may answer using detailed sentences and help guide the process used to find answers.

Performance Task

In this task, students will use a map to demonstrate their understanding of measuring and comparing lengths. As students are measuring, be sure they measure along the road, not just by connecting the two points.

- Decide ahead of time whether students will be working independently, in pairs, or in groups.
- Pause between direction lines for students to complete each step.
- Have students share their work and thinking with others. Discuss as a class.

Exercise	Answers and Notes	Points
1	post office, library, school	3
2	Check students' work.	2
3a	park	2
3b	Check students' work.	3
	Total	10

Name ________________________

Performance Task 10

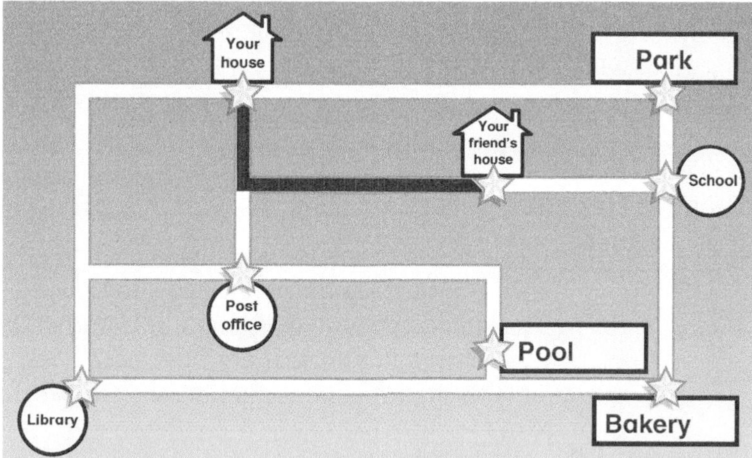

1. Use a piece of string to compare the routes from your house to the library, the post office, and the school. Order the routes from shortest to longest.

post office, library, school

2. Use a piece of string to measure the different routes from your house to your friend's house. Color the route you would use to ride your bike to your friend's house. **Sample answer shown above.**

3. a. The bakery is farther from your house than the pool. The park is closer to your house than the pool. Which place is closest to your house?

(Park) Bakery Pool

b. Label the park, bakery, and pool on the map.

Check out the interactive version in the Game Library.
BigIdeasMath.com

Laurie's Notes

Fish Measurement

Materials

- 1 set of Fish Measurement Cards* per student
- scissors

**Found in the Instructional Resources*

Fish Measurement has students compare the length of three fish at a time.

? "What do you notice about the table on the page?" *Sample answer:* There is a spot for shortest and longest. "What do you think goes in between shortest and longest?" *Sample answer:* The object with the length that is between the shortest and longest.

- "Today you are going to compare the lengths of fish."
- Review the directions while modeling how to play. Have students explain whether the cards are in order from shortest to longest and how they know.
- Explain that they will continue playing until all their cards have been used. Once they have gone through their cards once, they then shuffle their cards and restart, comparing different fish.
- Partner students and distribute the Fish Measurement Cards.
- While students play, be sure that they are lining up the ends of the fish to compare, not the ends of the cards.
- When game play concludes, have students discuss how they compared three fish at a time.
- **Extension:** Have students compare the lengths of different site words.
- **Supporting Learners:** Some students may have difficulty comparing three at a time. Have students flip two cards to compare instead of three.

Closure

- **Exit Ticket:** Hold up two objects. Have students explain how they would measure and compare the lengths of the objects.

Fish Measurement

To Play: Flip over 3 Fish Measurement Cards. Compare the lengths of the 3 fish. Place each card in the correct box. Discuss your answers with your partner.

Shortest

Longest

Learning Target Correlation

Lesson	Learning Target	Exercises
10.1	Order objects by length.	1, 2
10.2	Compare the lengths of two objects using a third object.	3–5
10.3	Use like objects to measure length.	6, 7
10.4	Measure an object in different ways.	8, 9
10.5	Solve *compare* word problems involving length.	10–12

Name ______________________________

Chapter Practice 10

10.1 Order Objects by Length

1. Order from longest to shortest.

shark 

fish 

lobster 

shark, lobster, fish

2. MP **Analyze a Problem** A green snake is shorter than a black snake. A brown snake is shorter than the black snake. Which snake is the longest?

green  black brown

10.2 Compare Lengths Indirectly

3. Circle the longer object.

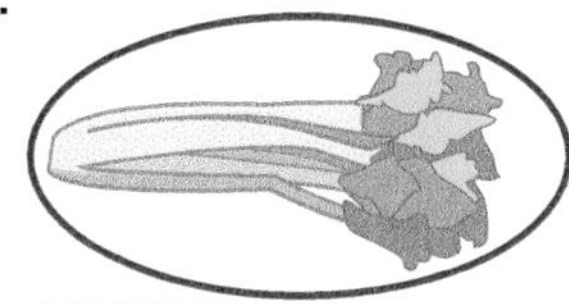

Chapter Resources		
Surface Level	**Deep Level**	**Transfer Level**
Resources by Chapter • Extra Practice • Reteach Differentiating the Lesson Skills Review Handbook Skills Trainer Game Library Math Musicals	Resources by Chapter • Enrichment and Extension Graphic Organizers Game Library Math Musicals	Dynamic Assessment System • Chapter Test Assessment Book • Chapter Tests A and B

4. Circle the longer object.

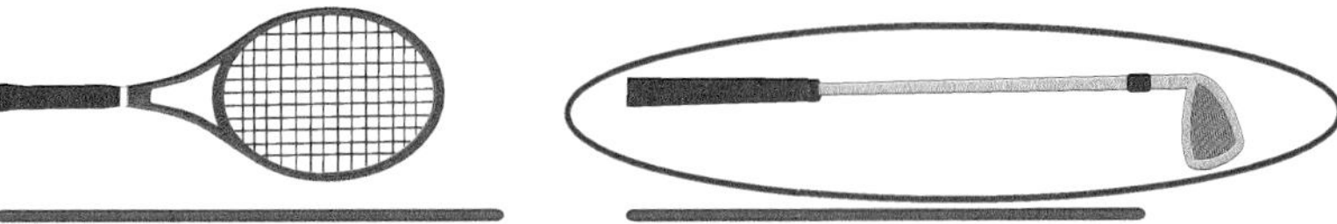

5. Draw a line through the shorter object.

10.3 Measure Lengths

Measure.

6.

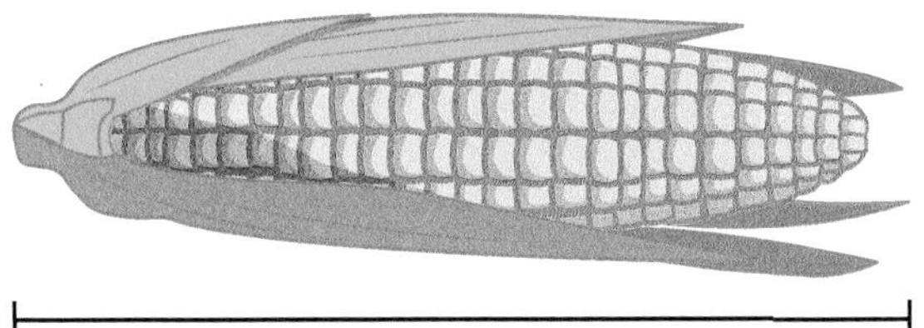

about 4 color tiles

7.

about 5 color tiles

10.4 Measure More Lengths

Measure.

8. MATH

about 4 color tiles   about 2 paper clips

9. **Modeling Real Life** Your hockey stick is 18 paper clips long. Is your hockey stick more than or less than 18 color tiles long?

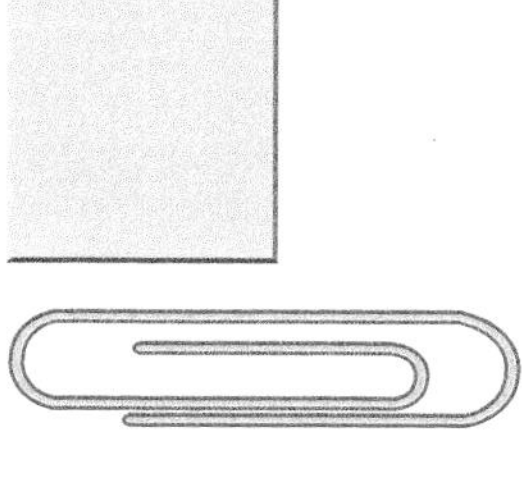

Circle: (more than 18)   less than 18

Tell how you know: **A paper clip is longer than a color tile, so it takes more color tiles to measure the length of the hockey stick.**

10.5 Solve *Compare* Problems Involving Length

10. Your water bottle is 5 paper clips long. Your friend's is 4 paper clips long. How many paper clips longer is your water bottle?

You: 5

Friend: 4 | 1

5 − 4 = 1

4 + 1 = 5

1 paper clip

---

11. Your bookshelf is 19 color tiles long. Your friend's is 15 color tiles long. How many tiles longer is your bookshelf?

Sample answer:

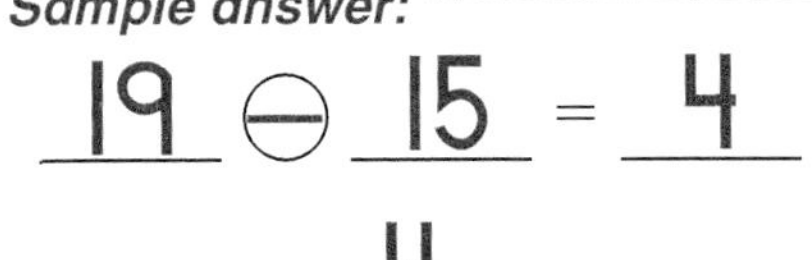

You: 19

Friend: 15 | 4

19 ⊖ 15 = 4

4 color tiles

---

12. MP **Reasoning** Your pencil is 6 color tiles long. Your friend's is 3 color tiles long. Complete the sentences.

Your pencil is 3 color tiles longer than your friend's.

Your friend's pencil is 3 color tiles shorter than yours.

Centers

Center 1: Fish Measurement

Materials per student: Student Edition page 534, 1 set of Fish Measurement Cards*, scissors

Have students complete the activity. See page T-534 for the directions.

Center 2: Skills Trainer

Materials: computers or devices with Internet access

Have students go to *BigIdeasMath.com* to access the Skills Trainer.

Center 3: Order Lengths

Materials per pair: strings, construction paper

Cut strings into many different lengths. Students pick three pieces of string and order them according to their length. They do this multiple times until all items have been selected from the pile. Then have students find three items in the classroom and write them down according to their length. Be sure they write whether it is from longest to shortest or shortest to longest.

Center 4: What is Longer?

Materials per pair: What is Longer? Cards*, scissors, color tiles, large paper clips, and small paper clips

Cut the What is Longer? Cards ahead of time and have them shuffled in a pile. Students will each draw a card and line up the number of manipulatives according to the card. They will then determine which one is longer when compared to their partner's line. The person with the card that made the longer line of manipulatives takes both cards. They repeat this process until all of the cards have been used.

Center 5: Cartoon

Materials per student: crayons, scissors, construction paper
Have students fold their paper into fourths then use the boxes to create a cartoon story about length. Be sure students include at least two different lengths of items and compare them. Students can have humor, silliness, and multiple characters in their cartoon stories. Suggest that students draw characters or items in their story on a different color construction paper, cut them out, and then glue them on their paper. Allow time for students to share their stories.

** Found in the Instructional Resources*

Chapter Assessment Guide

Chapter tests are available in the Assessment Book.
An alternative assessment option is listed below.

Visual-Spatial

Have students pretend they own their own scarf company. They are to draw and design two different scarves. They will then measure their scarves using paper clips or color tiles and create a word problem that compares the two. They will solve the word problem and show their work. After that, they will design a doll scarf option. They will then order the scarves and describe how they ordered. You can have students create other clothing items such as ties or leg warmers.

Task	Points
2 scarves are designed and measured	4 points
Word problem solved and shows work	3 points
Doll option designed	1 point
Scarves are described how they are ordered	2 points
Total	10 points

My Thoughts on the Chapter

What worked...

Teacher Tip

Not allowed to write in your teaching edition? Use sticky notes to record your thoughts.

What did not work...

What I would do differently...

11 Represent and Interpret Data

Chapter Overview

Lesson	Learning Target	Success Criteria
11.1 Sort and Organize Data	Make a tally chart to organize and understand data.	• Record data in a tally chart. • Use a tally chart to answer questions.
11.2 Read and Interpret Picture Graphs	Understand the data shown by a picture graph.	• Read the data in a picture graph to answer questions. • Compare the data in a picture graph.
11.3 Read and Interpret Bar Graphs	Understand the data shown by a bar graph.	• Read the data in a bar graph to answer questions. • Compare the data in a bar graph.
11.4 Represent Data	Make picture graphs and bar graphs.	• Count the tally marks in each category. • Represent the data using a tally chart. • Represent the data using a picture graph or bar graph.
11.5 Solve Problems Involving Data	Use data from graphs to answer questions.	• Read different types of graphs. • Compare amounts in each category. • Write a question that reading a graph will answer.

Chapter Learning Target:
Understand data.

Chapter Success Criteria:

- Record data on a tally chart.
- Use a tally chart.
- Compare data.
- Interpret data.

Progressions

Through the Grades		
Kindergarten	**Grade 1**	**Grade 2**
• Compare the measurable attributes of two objects. • Solve addition and subtraction word problems within 10.	• Organize data into categories. • Compare data. • Use data to ask and answer questions. • Solve addition and subtraction word problems within 20. • Solve addition word problems with three addends.	• Create picture graphs and bar graphs. • Use bar graphs to solve put-together, take-apart, and compare problems. • Solve addition and subtraction word problems within 100. • Solve one- and two-step word problems.

	Through the Chapter				
Standard	**11.1**	**11.2**	**11.3**	**11.4**	**11.5**
1.MD.C.4 Organize, represent, and interpret data with up to three categories; ask and answer questions about the total number of data points, how many in each category, and how many more or less are in one category than in another.	●	●	●	●	★
1.OA.A.1 Use addition and subtraction within 20 to solve word problems involving situations of adding to, taking from, putting together, taking apart, and comparing, with unknowns in all positions, e.g., by using objects, drawings, and equations with a symbol for the unknown number to represent the problem.					★
1.OA.A.2 Solve word problems that call for addition of three whole numbers whose sum is less than or equal to 20, e.g., by using objects, drawings, and equations with a symbol for the unknown number to represent the problem.					★

Key: ▲ = Preparing ● = Learning ★ = Complete

Laurie's Overview

About the Math

Chapter 11 introduces new ideas and representations to students involving data. Students' work with data in the elementary grades lays the foundation for future studies in statistics and probability. In first grade, students sort items (the data) into groups with a defining characteristic. Each characteristic becomes a category that is represented in a table or graph. Students can ask and answer questions about the data, bringing their understanding of addition and subtraction into a real-world data context.

This chapter introduces the following foundational big ideas about data and statistics:

- There is a four-step process for statistics: asking a question, collecting data, analyzing data, and interpreting data.
- Data are organized to answer questions.
- Different types of data representations can more easily provide different kinds of information.
- Different models can show how place value and addition work together. These models can be used interchangeably.

In kindergarten, students worked with measurement data, comparing lengths or weights of objects. In first grade, students work with categorical data, organize it into representations, and answer addition and subtraction questions from the data. The context from which the data is gathered is important.

The chapter opens with students organizing items—forming categories. Students have had experience sorting objects from kindergarten, and it is recommended to continue sorting activities during station time or other flexible times. Defining the characteristic on which items have been sorted, or categorized, is an essential skill in working with data.

Once students have sorted the items into categories, they record the number of items in each category by making a tally mark for each one. This one-to-one recording system, a tally chart, is the most concrete representation of data. After making tally charts, students make picture graphs. In first grade, the symbol on a picture graph will always represent one item. The third representation students will work with is a bar graph. This is the most abstract representation, as a continuous bar indicates a quantity, not a one-to-one correspondence such as tallies or pictures. The progression of representations moves from most concrete to most abstract in Lessons 11.1, 11.2, and 11.3. Each representation is explained in greater detail.

Representations

- **Tally Charts:** One way to introduce students to the tally system is to have them sort items (buttons, linking cubes, color tiles, etc.) into categories. First-grade students work with up to three categories. As students pick up one of the items, they draw a tally mark next to the category name. Tell students a tally looks like a simple 1 and represents one thing in the category. Students learn to make a diagonal tally through four tallies to signify a group of 5. This can be explicitly modeled, or show the need for this notation with a long line of tallies: |||||||||||||||||||||||||. Ask students how many tallies there are. Counting will be tricky. Next show the groupings of 5 and ask how many are there: 𝍸 𝍸 𝍸 𝍸 𝍸. Have students count by fives, then by ones to review counting strategies.

Buttons	
Red	𝍸 II
Green	𝍸
Blue	IIII

- **Picture Graphs:** Picture graphs (also called *pictographs*) use a symbol to represent a quantity of items. In first grade, the picture or symbol will always represent 1. The symbol used does not have to be a picture. We use circles or smiley faces in our lessons. The graph names the category, then has a row in which the symbols are placed. The graph looks like a grid in which a symbol is placed in each cell. You can make a class picture graph and let students place a sticker to represent themselves in their category.

Pets										
🐱 Cat	🐱	🐱	🐱	🐱	🐱	🐱	🐱	🐱		
🐶 Dog	🐶	🐶	🐶	🐶	🐶	🐶	🐶	🐶	🐶	🐶
🐟 Fish	🐟	🐟								

- **Bar Graphs:** Bar graphs are the representation that will carry on throughout students' mathematics career. In upper grades, bar graphs form the basis of histograms and other representations. Instead of having a key like a picture graph to indicate quantity, a bar graph has the numbers along the bottom to show the quantity. One way to transition from a picture graph to a bar graph is to have students use a sticky note to represent themselves in a picture graph. Place the sticky notes so close together that visually they form a bar. Ask students if they think they could draw a bar to a certain number faster than drawing pictures or smiley faces. Both picture graphs and bar graphs can be made vertically as well as horizontally.

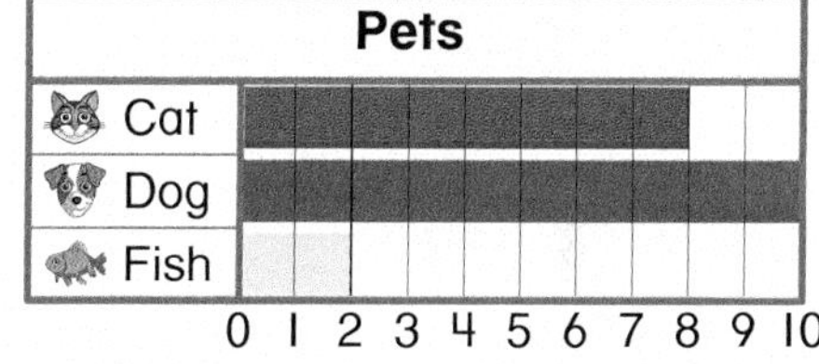

Throughout the lessons, students will both make and analyze the data representations. Perhaps the most important learning in the chapter however, is asking and answering questions. Students should begin by telling what they notice. This can be as simple as naming the categories, or explaining which category has the most or the least. Students will progress to answering more complex two-step questions involving addition and subtraction, as well as asking their own questions about data.

Understanding data is an ever-increasing important skill in our technological world. This chapter connects understanding the representation of data to using addition and subtraction in context.

Check out the
virtual manipulatives.
BigIdeasMath.com

Chapter Materials and Resources

The primary materials and resources needed for this chapter are listed below. Other materials may be needed for the additional support ideas provided throughout the chapter.

Classroom Materials	Chapter Opener	11.1	11.2	11.3	11.4	11.5	Connect and Grow
scissors	•						*
buttons		+	+				
tape			•				
linking cubes					*		
chart paper					+		
color tiles					•		
whiteboards					•	•	•
spinner							•
crayons							*
counters							*
dominoes							•

Instructional Resources	Chapter Opener	11.1	11.2	11.3	11.4	11.5	Connect and Grow
Vocabulary Cards	•	+	+	+			
Picture Graph Pets			+				
Spin and Graph Questions							*
Tally Mark Dominoes							*
Graph-Tac-Toe							*

• class set + teacher only * per pair/group

Suggested Pacing

Day 1	Chapter Opener	Performance Task Preview		Vocabulary			
Day 2	Lesson 11.1	Warm-Up	Dig In	Explore	Think	Apply: Practice	Think: Modeling Real Life
Day 3	Lesson 11.2	Warm-Up	Dig In	Explore	Think	Apply: Practice	Think: Modeling Real Life
Day 4	Lesson 11.3	Warm-Up	Dig In	Explore	Think	Apply: Practice	Think: Modeling Real Life
Day 5	Lesson 11.4	Warm-Up	Dig In	Explore	Think	Apply: Practice	Think: Modeling Real Life
Day 6	Lesson 11.5	Warm-Up	Dig In	Explore	Think	Apply: Practice	Think: Modeling Real Life
Day 7	Connect And Grow	Performance Task			Activity	Chapter Practice	
Day 8		Centers					
Day 9	Chapter Assessment	Chapter Assessment					

Year-to-Date: 124 Days

Laurie's Notes

Mathematical Practices

Students have opportunities to develop aspects of the mathematical practices throughout the chapter. Here are some examples.

1. **Make Sense of Problems and Persevere in Solving Them**
   11.5 Explore and Grow, *p. 565*
2. **Reason Abstractly and Quantitatively**
   11.1 Apply and Grow: Practice Exercise 3, *p. 543*
3. **Construct Viable Arguments and Critique the Reasoning of Others**
   11.3 Practice, *p. 558*
4. **Model with Mathematics**
   Performance Task Exercise 1, *p. 571*
5. **Use Appropriate Tools Strategically**
   11.4 Practice, *p. 563*
6. **Attend to Precision**
   11.2 Apply and Grow: Practice Exercise 3, *p. 549*
7. **Look for and Make Use of Structure**
   11.1 Think and Grow, *p. 542*
8. **Look for and Express Regularity in Repeated Reasoning**
   11.1 Think and Grow: Modeling Real Life, *p. 544*

Performance Task Preview

- Preview the page to gauge students' prior knowledge about eye color. In first grade science, students learn how parents and their children are similar and different.

? "What color are your eyes?"

? "Do any of your friends or family members have the same color eyes as you?" Students will be excited to share their eye color with you. Some students may share that they get their eye color from someone in their family.

- In the Performance Task at the end of the chapter, students will represent and interpret data by surveying the students in their class about their eye color.

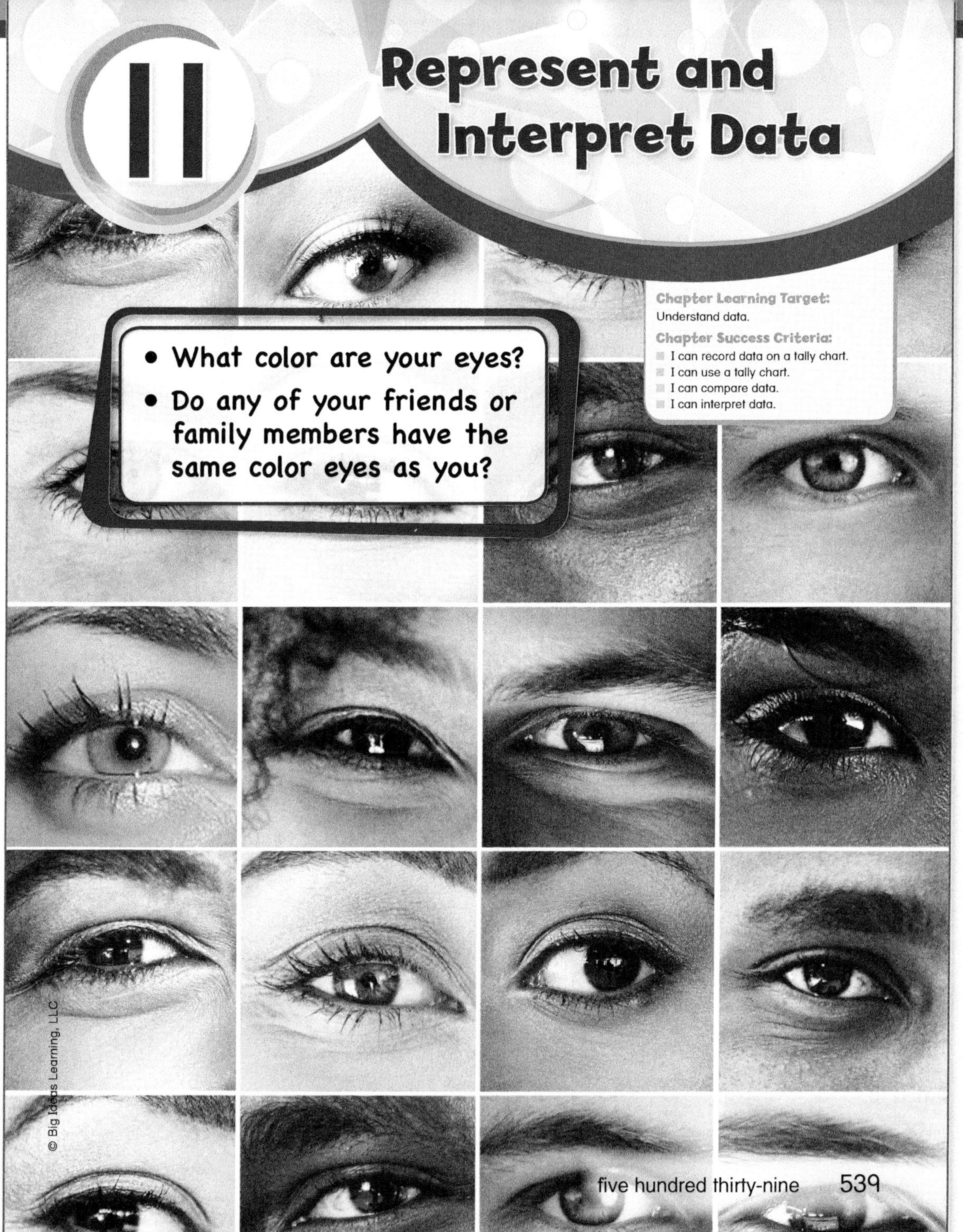
11
Represent and Interpret Data
Chapter Learning Target:
Understand data.
Chapter Success Criteria:
I can record data on a tally chart.
I can use a tally chart.
I can compare data.
I can interpret data.
• What color are your eyes?
• Do any of your friends or family members have the same color eyes as you?
five hundred thirty-nine 539

Check out the
digital flash cards.
BigIdeasMath.com

Laurie's Notes

ELL Support

Explain that in this chapter students will record and interpret data. Data are statistics, facts, figures, records, and numbers that provide information. Often to record data, a graph or a chart is used. The words *graph* and *chart* can be used to name the type of record (as a noun) or to describe the action of recording the data (as a verb).

Vocabulary Review

- ? **Preview:** "What information do you see?" *Sample answer:* crayons being sorted
- Have students say each review word out loud. Have students explain how the words are related.
- ? "Which part of the chart shows categories? Which part of the chart shows the crayons being classified?" Have students label each part.
- Direct students to the lower half of the page. Have students use their vocabulary cards to identify the words being modeled.
- **Extension:** Have students discuss what is being shown in the graphs.

Chapter 11 Vocabulary

Activity

- **Word/Picture Toss:** Lay out all of the cards on the floor with the word side up. Students take turns gently tossing a counter onto cards. You read the word on the card that the counter landed on and students repeat the word. A student turns over the card to see the definition and shows it to the class. Repeat this process until all of the cards show the definition side.
- **Supporting Learners:** Limit the amount of cards the students lay out in front of them.

Newton & Descartes's Math Musicals

with Differentiated Rich Math Tasks

Newton and Descartes team up in these educational stories and songs to bring mathematics to life! Use the Newton and Descartes hand puppets to act out the stories. Encourage students to sing the songs to take full advantage of the power of music to learn math. Visit *www.MathMusicals.com* to access all the adventures, songs, and activities available!

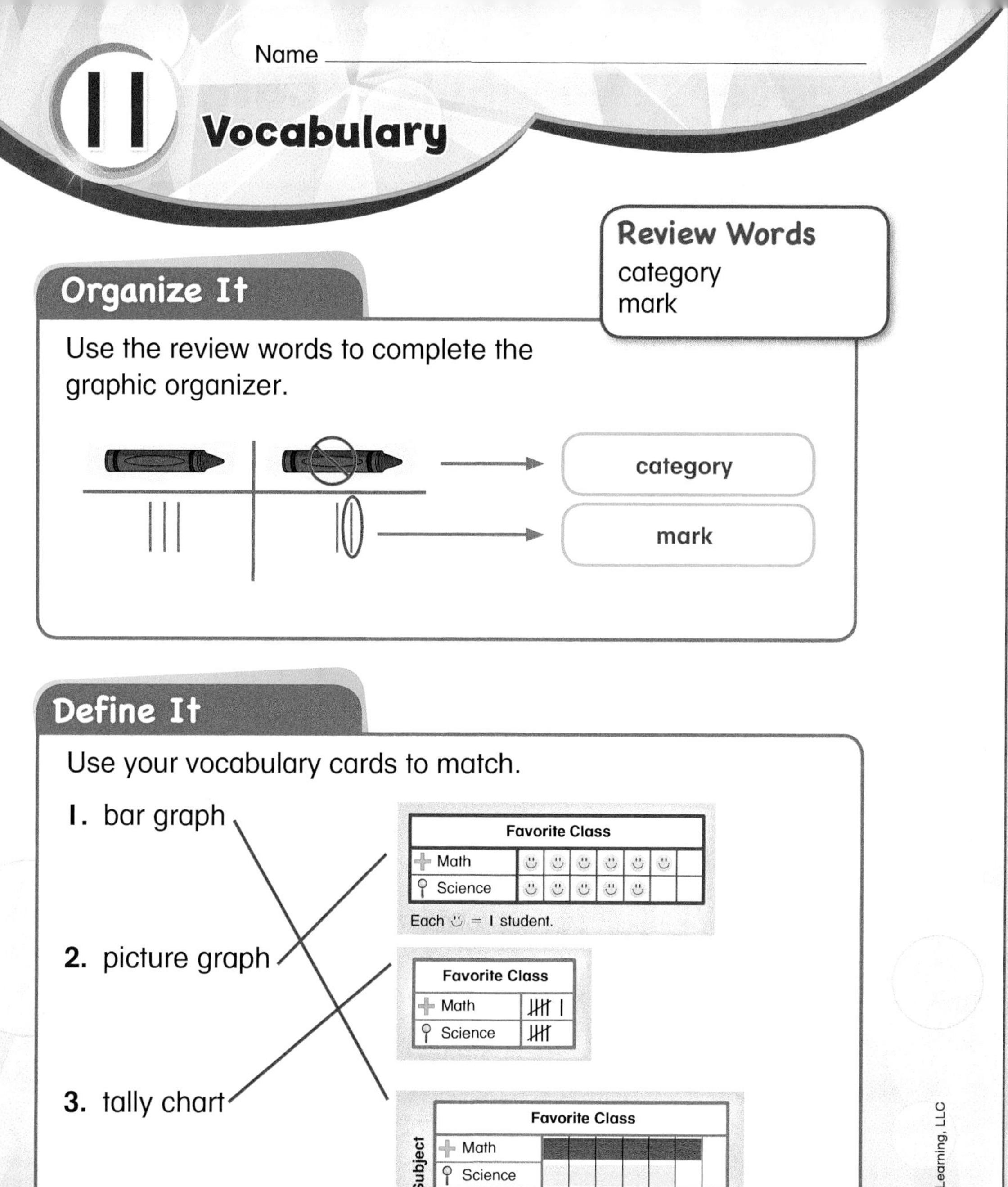

Name ________________________

11 Vocabulary

Review Words
category
mark

Organize It

Use the review words to complete the graphic organizer.

Define It

Use your vocabulary cards to match.

1. bar graph
2. picture graph
3. tally chart

Favorite Class

Math	☺	☺	☺	☺	☺	☺	
Science	☺	☺	☺	☺	☺		

Each ☺ = 1 student.

Favorite Class

Math	𝍸 |
Science	𝍸

Favorite Class

Chapter 11 Vocabulary Cards

bar graph	data
picture graph	tally chart
tally mark	

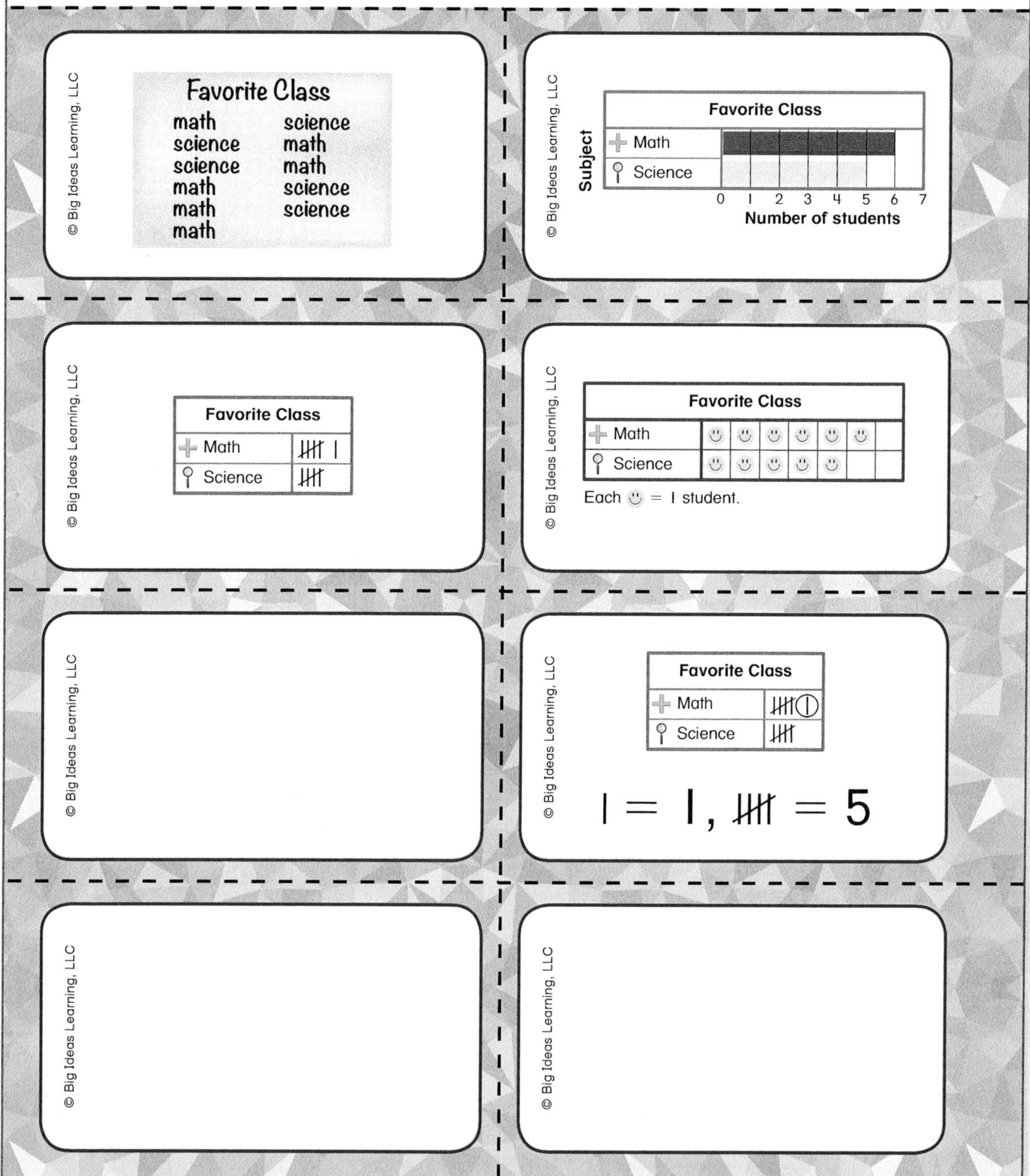
© Big Ideas Learning, LLC
Favorite Class
math
science
science
math
math
math
science
math
math
science
science
Favorite Class
Subject
Math
Science
0 1 2 3 4 5 6 7
Number of students
Favorite Class
Math
Science
Favorite Class
Math
Science
Each = 1 student.
Favorite Class
Math
Science
| = 1, 𝍸 = 5

Check out the
Dynamic Classroom.
BigIdeasMath.com

Laurie's Notes

COMMON CORE

STATE STANDARDS
1.MD.C.4

Learning Target

Make a tally chart to organize and understand data.

Success Criteria

- Record data in a tally chart.
- Use a tally chart to answer questions.

Warm-Up

Practice opportunities for the following are available in the Resources by Chapter or at *BigIdeasMath.com*.

- Daily skills
- Vocabulary
- Prerequisite skills

ELL Support

Explain that a tally chart is a visual record of counting objects. The word *tally* means to count, compute, or keep score. When you make a tally chart, you make a mark for each object you count. In Explore and Grow you can count the objects in different ways—by color (green, yellow, or blue) or by type of object (pencil, crayon, or marker). When you count by color or type you sort and organize objects into different categories.

Preparing to Teach

Students can naturally describe objects and group things that are alike. They might say to their friends, "We all have blue shirts on!" In today's lesson, students will learn about categories and how to use a tally chart to show how many are in each category.

Materials

- buttons

Dig In (Circle Time)

Students will be introduced to sorting by categories by describing how objects are sorted. They will group themselves in a variety of ways to determine categories for sorting. They will learn how to draw tally marks to tell how many are in each category.

- Pour the collection of buttons (or other sortable objects) out for students to see. Sort them in one way (round, square, other; color; size). Ask students how they think you sorted them.
- "Today, we are going to sort things! Usually a group of objects can be sorted in different ways. If we were going to sort us into groups, what kinds of things might we sort by?" *Sample answers:* eye color; hair color "The *thing* by which we sort is called a category."
- Select a group of 8 to 10 students to stand in the center of the circle. Ask students how they can group themselves. Have students form groups and tell their category. Have other students stand and sort themselves another way.
- Go back to the collection of buttons. Sort a group of buttons using three categories, such as by color, with more than 5 buttons in at least one group.

- Have students tell the categories that were used to sort the objects and how many are in each category.
- "There is a way to show how many buttons are in each category other than writing numbers called tallies. Has anyone seen or used tallies? A tally mark looks almost like a 1 because each tally shows one object. It is a helpful system if you are counting large groups because you can make a tally mark for each item you see."
- ◉ Show students how to make tally marks based on the number of buttons in each group. Show how to tally four and then cross through them for the fifth item.
- ◉ Ask a few questions about the chart, such as, "How many more red buttons than blue buttons are there?"
- ◉ "Today, we are going to use tally charts to show how many are in a group and to answer questions."

Buttons	
Red	卌 ||
Green	卌
Blue	||||

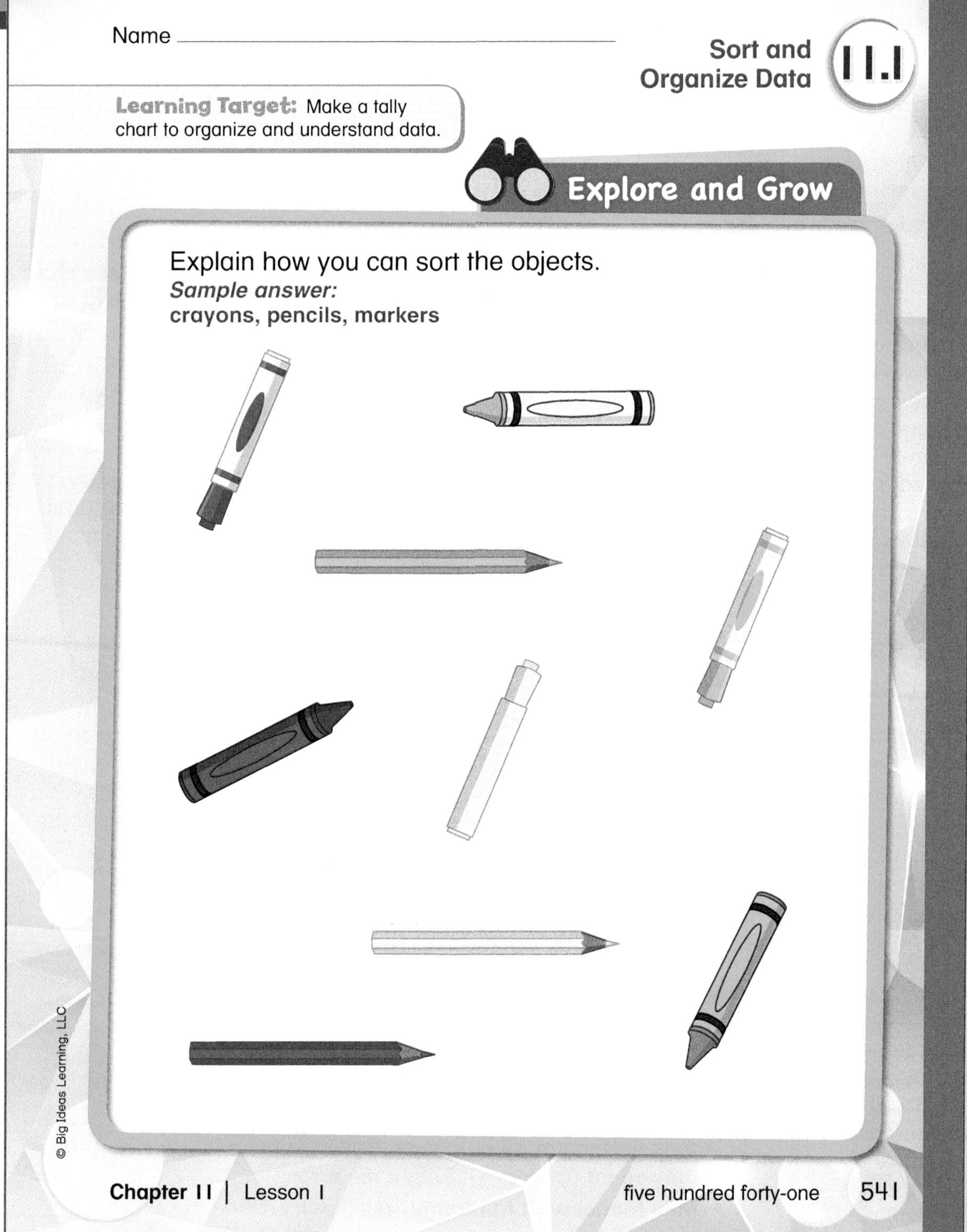

Name
Sort and Organize Data
11.1
Learning Target: Make a tally chart to organize and understand data.
Explore and Grow
Explain how you can sort the objects.
Sample answer:
crayons, pencils, markers
© Big Ideas Learning, LLC
Chapter 11 | Lesson 1
five hundred forty-one
541

Explore and Grow

- If you have spent time in the circle talking about the Dig In, this page could be done orally or you may want to move on to the Think and Grow page.
- Students can compare ways to sort the objects.
- Students can circle the groups if they desire. Name each category for the different sorts.

Laurie's Notes

ELL Support

Discuss the example. Point out the information given by Newton and Descartes. Have students work in groups as they practice language. Review the names of items pictured if necessary. Have groups discuss the following questions: "How many tally marks are needed for each item? Are there groups of five? How many? How many individual marks are there?" Monitor discussion and expect students to perform as described.

Beginner students may provide one-word answers.
Intermediate students may answer with phrases, such as, "one group of five."
Advanced students may describe the actions needed and answer with sentences, such as, "When we count buckets, there is one group of five."

Think and Grow

Getting Started

- Introduce the vocabulary terms **data**, **tally mark**, and **tally chart**. "The information we put into a chart are called data. Data can be things, numbers, or other information. Point to the tally chart. Point to the tally mark."
- Students may ask why they should use tallies when they can write the numbers. Explain that the tally system allows you to record items as you are sorting them. You don't have to sort first and then count. If the buttons were mixed up and you knew you wanted to record the number of red, green, and blue buttons, then each time you picked up a button you would make a tally and put it aside.

Teaching Notes

- ? **Model**: "Notice the title of the tally chart. It says Medals. Tally charts will always have a title to tell you what you are sorting. Read the chart. What types of medals are there?"
- ◉ **Model**: "One way we could tally the medals would be to count each type and then fill in the chart. But, we might miss one or miscount. Instead, we will make a tally for each medal as we work across the rows. The first medal is gold. Fill in one of the tallies in the gold. Do not fill in the diagonal tally. Why not?" It shows 5 medals.
- Finish going through the rows and tallying the medals with students. The gold and bronze medals may be a little hard to differentiate.
- ? "Notice that Newton reminds us what the tally marks mean. How many gold medals are there? silver? bronze?"
- Students can complete Exercise 1. They can either count the types of stickers and make tallies, or tally one by one.
- **Supporting Learners:** Students may lose track of whether or not they have counted an object. Have them cross off each item as they count or record it with a tally.
- **MP4 Model with Mathematics:** "Look around the room and create a tally chart for some of the objects you see."

Think and Grow

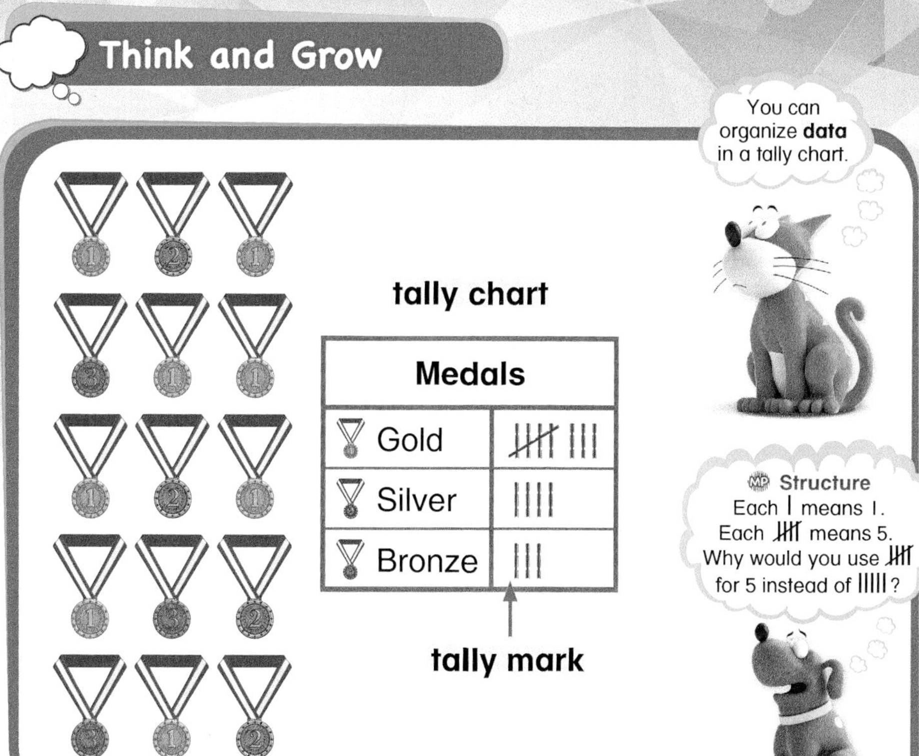

Medals	
Gold	𝍸 |||
Silver	||||
Bronze	|||

Show and Grow *I can do it!*

1. Complete the tally chart.

Stickers	
Umbrella	||||
Bucket	𝍸
Crab	𝍸	

Scaffold instruction to support all students in their learning. Learning is individualized and you may want to group students differently as they move in and out of these levels with each skill and concept. Student self-assessment and feedback help guide your instructional decisions about how and when to layer support for all students to become proficient learners.

Meeting the needs of all learners.

Laurie's Notes

Apply and Grow: Practice

SCAFFOLDING INSTRUCTION

Exercise 2 continues having students make a tally chart. Exercise 3 changes to see if students can correctly interpret a tally chart, and answer questions based on it.

EMERGING students may have difficulty counting the items from the picture and keeping track of the corresponding tallies. If this is their first experience with tallies, they may not remember the meaning of the diagonal tally. Remind students that it means you can count by 5 when they see it or make it.

- **Exercise 2:** If students have difficulty keeping track of the balls and writing tally marks, have them go one-by-one with each ball: make the tally, cross off the ball. At the end, count all of the balls and see if your chart shows the same total number of balls as by counting the tallies.
- **Exercise 3:** Students need to understand how to read the tallies to determine how many there are of each stuffed animal. They should look at each sentence, then look at the chart and decide if the sentence is true or not. Let students know there is more than one correct answer.

PROFICIENT students will be able to count the types of objects, but they may need practice making tallies as this is their first experience. Watch to see that they know when to make the diagonal tally and when not to.

- **Exercise 2:** Students may miss one of the balls or count the same ball twice and become confused.
- **Exercise 3:** Students should consider each sentence and then look at the chart to determine if it is correct or not.

Extension: Adding Rigor

- Have students make up their own sentences about the stuffed animals for a partner to determine if it is correct or not.

Name ___

Apply and Grow: Practice

2. Complete the tally chart.

Balls	
Football	𝍸 III
Soccer ball	𝍸
Basketball	III

3. **Reasoning** Which sentences are correct?

Stuffed Animals	
Tiger	𝍸 𝍸
Fox	𝍸 II
Raccoon	𝍸 II

There are 7 tigers.

The numbers of foxes and raccoons are the same.

There are 7 foxes.

There are 3 raccoons.

Chapter 11 | Lesson 1 543

ELL Support

Check for understanding of Lesson 11.1. Allow students time to familiarize themselves with each tally chart. Then ask the following questions and have students answer by holding up the appropriate number of fingers or a thumbs up/down signal to answer yes/no.

1. How many sunny days are there?
2. Is the number of cloudy days greater than the number of rainy days?
3. How many sunflowers are there?
4. Is the number of roses less than the number of daisies?

Laurie's Notes

Think and Grow: Modeling Real Life

These application problems allow students to show their understanding of tally charts. They can determine the number in each category from the tallies and use the chart to answer questions.

? **Preview:** "What do you see on this page? What are the charts comparing?" If you keep track of the weather on a calendar during morning meeting, you could make your own class tally chart like the example.

- Remind students that they count tallies like they count with ten frames. "Let's count the number of sunny days. 5, 6, 7, 8. Fill in 8 days. Let's count the number of cloudy days. 1, 2, 3, 4. Now the rainy days. 1, 2, 3. Is the number of cloudy days greater or less than the number of rainy days? Tell your partner."
- **MP8 Look for and Express Regularity in Repeated Reasoning:** Read Descartes's thought bubble. You want students to realize that more tally marks means more of that category. Have students use this strategy to help check their work.
- Review the directions with students for Exercise 4. Have them tell their partners what they are trying to decide to be sure they understand the directions.
- **MP3 Construct Viable Arguments and Critique the Reasoning of Others:** Ask different students to share if the number of roses is greater than or less than the number of daisies. Have them explain how they know. Ask other students to agree or disagree, and how they know.

◉ "You have sorted and counted objects. You have recoded the number of objects in a category with tally marks. The chart that you make is called a tally chart. Can you explain to your partner how a tally chart is helpful? How do you read tallies?" Students might say it is easier to use tallies than having to work with the objects or that tallies are easy to count.

Closure

- Show students a tally chart that you have made based on your own students, or use the one shown.
- Have students ask each other questions from the chart and call on another student to answer.

Pets	
Dogs	卌 卌 ||
Cats	卌 卌 ||||
None	卌

Think and Grow: Modeling Real Life

Weather	
Sunny	𝍸 III
Cloudy	IIII
Rainy	III

Repeated Reasoning Do you need to count the tally marks to compare? Explain.

How many sunny days are there? 8 days

Is the number of cloudy days greater than or less than the number of rainy days?

(greater than) less than

Show and Grow 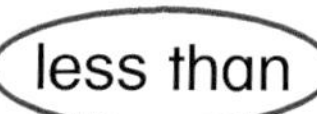 I can think deeper!

4.

Flowers in a Garden	
Rose	𝍸 I
Sunflower	II
Daisy	𝍸 II

How many sunflowers are there? 2 sunflowers

Is the number of roses greater than or less than the number of daisies?

greater than (less than)

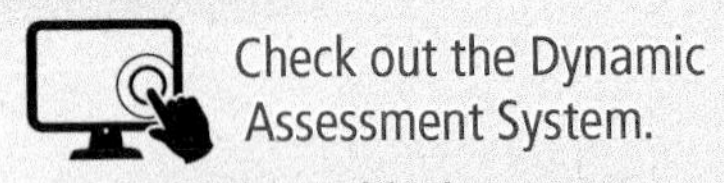
Check out the Dynamic Assessment System.
BigIdeasMath.com

Scaffold assignments to support all students in their learning progression. Revisit with spaced practice to move every student toward proficiency.

Connect and Extend Learning

Practice Notes

- Remind students how to make and count tally marks.
- **Exercise 1:** Go over the names of the insects.

Prior Skills

- **Exercises 5–7:** Grade 1, Comparing Numbers Using Symbols

Cross-Curricular Connections

Art

- Put a collection of three different types of stickers together for each student. Have students sort the stickers and then create a tally chart showing the types of stickers using cotton swabs, toothpicks, or craft sticks.

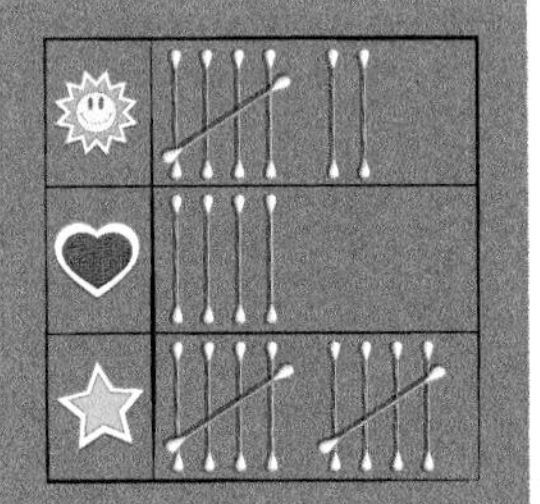

Name ______________________

Learning Target: Make a tally chart to organize and understand data.

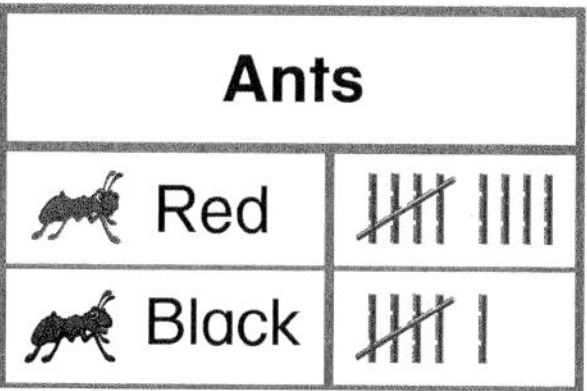

Ants	
Red	𝍸 IIII
Black	𝍸 I

1. Complete the tally chart.

Insects	
Caterpillar	𝍸 II
Fly	𝍸 III
Ladybug	II

2. MP **Reasoning** Which sentences are correct?

Favorite Movie	
Superhero	𝍸
Princess	𝍸 IIII
Mystery	𝍸

9 students like princess movies.

4 students like superhero movies.

Princess movies are the most favorite.

Connect and Extend Learning

Extend Student Learning

Bodily Kinesthetic

- Have students make a tally chart with the numbers 1 to 6 as the categories. Then have students roll a die and keep track of how many times they roll each number on the tally chart. Once they have rolled 12 times, have them write a sentence about their chart. It can describe which number was rolled the most or which number was rolled the least.

Lesson Resources	
Surface Level	**Deep Level**
Resources by Chapter • Extra Practice • Reteach Differentiating the Lesson Skills Review Handbook Skills Trainer	Resources by Chapter • Enrichment and Extension Graphic Organizers Dynamic Assessment System • Lesson Practice

3. **Modeling Real Life** Use the tally chart.

Favorite Breakfast	
Yogurt	卌
Fruit	||||
Cereal	卌 |

How many students chose fruit? 4 students

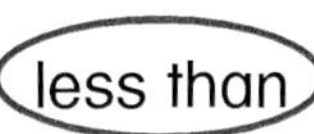

Is the number of students who chose yogurt greater than or less than the number of students who chose cereal?

greater than (less than)

4. **DIG DEEPER!** Complete the tally chart.

There are more ● than ■.

There are fewer ■ than ▲.

There are fewer ▲ than ●.

Sample answer:

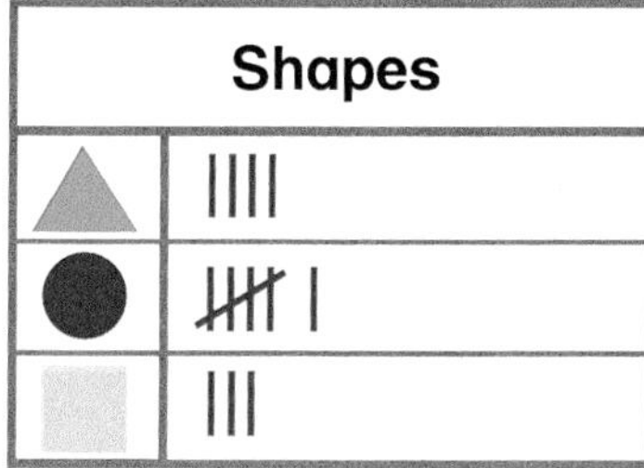

Shapes	
▲	||||
●	卌 |
■	|||

Review & Refresh

Compare.

5. 45 (<) 55

6. 74 (>) 47

7. 22 (=) 22

11.2

Laurie's Notes

Check out the
Dynamic Classroom.

BigIdeasMath.com

COMMON CORE STATE STANDARDS 1.MD.C.4

Learning Target

Understand the data shown by a picture graph.

Success Criteria

- Read the data in a picture graph to answer questions.
- Compare the data in a picture graph.

Warm-Up

Practice opportunities for the following are available in the Resources by Chapter or at *BigIdeasMath.com.*

- Daily skills
- Vocabulary
- Prerequisite skills

ELL Support

Point out that the instructions ask students to compare graphs. Explain that the tally chart is one of the graphs they are comparing. The other is a picture graph. The words *chart* and *graph* are often used interchangeably.

Preparing to Teach

Students have now experienced categorizing data, organizing it into a chart, and using tally marks to show how many are in each category. Today, we show another organizing tool: *picture graphs.* In later years, a picture may represent more than one item, usually 5, 10, 100, etc., but in first grade each picture will represent one data point.

Materials

- Picture Graph Pets*
- tape
- buttons

**Found in the Instructional Resources*

Dig In (Circle Time)

Students will vote for their favorite pet from a list of cat, dog, or fish. A tally chart of their answers is made, followed by a picture graph with students putting their picture on the graph for their choice. Cut out Picture Graph Pets and arrange in three piles by pet.

- "I'm wondering how many of you have pets? I wonder what our class's favorite pet is. I love both cats and dogs, but if I had to choose only one type of pet, I would choose a cat." Hold up the paper cut out of a cat.
- "We have three choices for favorite pet, and each of you can share your choice. You can choose a cat (hold up cat), a dog (hold up dog), or a fish (hold up fish)."
- Set up a chart with the three options. Have students raise their hands for each choice, and fill in the chart with a tallies as a review from yesterday's lesson. Ask which pet is most popular.

Pets	
Cat	𝍸 III
Dog	𝍸 𝍸
Fish	II

◉ "Today, we are going to learn another way to categorize and organize information. It is called a picture graph. A picture graph shows categories just like the tally chart. Instead of making a tally, a picture is shown."

- Create another chart with the same categories. Have all students who chose cat come up and tape a paper cat in the "cat" row. Follow with dog and fish. Be careful that students don't change their vote! Keep this graph for Lessons 11.3 and 11.5.

Pets										
Cat	🐱	🐱	🐱	🐱	🐱	🐱	🐱	🐱		
Dog	🐶	🐶	🐶	🐶	🐶	🐶	🐶	🐶	🐶	🐶
Fish	🐟	🐟								

? "Do the tally chart and picture graph show the same number of favorite pets in each category? Remember that each paper pet represents one vote. What is the most preferred pet in our class?"

◉ "Today, we are going to use picture graphs to show how many are in a group and to answer questions."

Name ______________________

Read and Interpret Picture Graphs 11.2

Learning Target: Understand the data shown by a picture graph.

Explore and Grow

How are the graphs similar? How are they different?

Sample answer:

Both graphs show that there are 6 red counters and 4 yellow counters; One graph uses tallies and the other uses pictures.

My Counters	
Red	卌 I
Yellow	IIII

My Counters							
Red	○	○	○	○	○	○	
Yellow	○	○	○	○			

Each ○ = 1 counter.

Explore and Grow

- Students discuss similarities and differences of the two representations with a partner. Have several students share their observations. "Notice the key at the bottom of the picture graph. That tells how many each circle represents."
- "We can answer questions from either representation. Some questions are easier with tallies, like how many are there, and some easier with pictures, like how many fewer yellows are there. Why are tallies easier for how many questions? Why are pictures easier for comparison questions? Which do you like best so far and why?"

ELL Support

Discuss the example. Make sure students understand the meaning behind the visuals and names in each picture graph. Have students work in groups as they practice language while completing Exercises 1 and 2. Have groups discuss the following questions: "How many of each are there? Which has the most? Which has the least? What are the answers to the questions?" Monitor discussion and expect students to perform as described.

Beginner students may provide one-word answers.
Intermediate students may answer with simple sentences, such as, "three chose a banana."
Advanced students may with detailed sentences, such as, "Apples are the most favorite fruit of all the students."

Laurie's Notes

Think and Grow

Getting Started

- Introduce the vocabulary term **picture graph**. Review the term *data*. "Who can remind us what *data* means? Who can tell us something about a picture graph?" Be sure that students point out the key. If they do not, ask them why it is there. Tell them that every picture graph will have a key to show how many things each picture represents.

Teaching Notes

◉ **Model**: "Notice that the pictures used in the Favorite Fruit picture graph are smiley faces, and not pictures of fruit. It does not matter if they showed bananas, apples, and oranges, or if they used a smiley face to show each student. Tell your partner how many students chose each type of fruit. How did you know? Fill in the number of bananas."

- **Model**: "How would you know which fruit is the most favorite?" most votes "How can you tell from the graph which is the most favorite without counting?" graph goes the farthest out

◉ Point out to students that a picture graph is easy to use to make comparisons. To find out how many more students preferred apples to oranges, they see two spaces open in oranges that are filled in for apples. Draw arrows to show the comparison. Repeat for comparing bananas to apples.

- Students can complete Exercise 1. Be sure that they pay attention to the question that asks for the least favorite, not most favorite, school trip. If there is an error for the number of students who chose the museum, see if it is a counting error or a misconception.
- **Supporting Learners:** Watch as students count the pictures. Where does the error occur?
- **Supporting Learners:** Have students tell what you would look for in the picture graph for "most" or for "least." They can answer these questions without counting.
- **Extension:** Have students answer additional questions such as how many students voted? How many more chose the zoo than a play? How many fewer students chose the play than the museum?

Think and Grow

picture graph

Favorite Fruit								
Banana	☺	☺	☺					
Apple	☺	☺	☺	☺	☺	☺	☺	
Orange	☺	☺	☺	☺	☺			

Each ☺ = 1 student.

How many students chose banana? 3

Which fruit is the most favorite?  

Show and Grow *I can do it!*

1.

Favorite School Trip									
Museum	☺	☺	☺	☺	☺	☺	☺	☺	
Zoo	☺	☺	☺	☺	☺	☺			
Play	☺	☺							

Each ☺ = 1 student.

How many students chose museum? 8

Which trip is the least favorite?   

Laurie's Notes

Scaffold instruction to support all students in their learning. Learning is individualized and you may want to group students differently as they move in and out of these levels with each skill and concept. Student self-assessment and feedback help guide your instructional decisions about how and when to layer support for all students to become proficient learners.

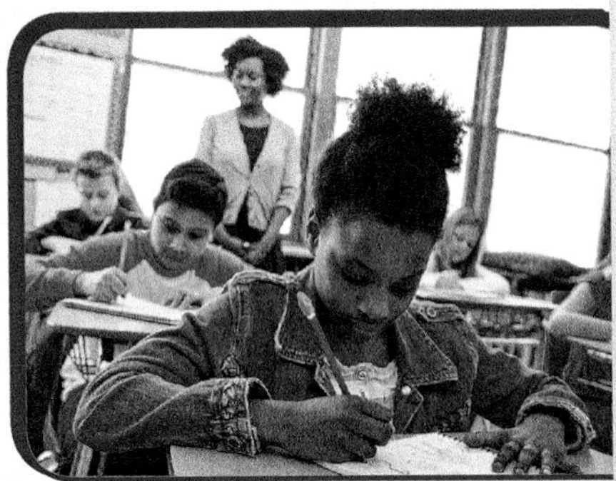

Meeting the needs of all learners.

Apply and Grow: Practice

SCAFFOLDING INSTRUCTION

Students continue to read a picture graph and answer questions. They will need to write an explanation for how they determined the answer for one question, so be sure to have students practice telling their partners how they know the answer to each of the questions in Exercise 2.

EMERGING students may only reason by counting each picture in the graph. For determining the number in each category, this makes sense. This will work when answering most or least questions, but it does not show sophisticated reasoning.

- **Exercise 2:** Have students explain how they found their answers to a partner. Have them explain how they know the least favorite lunch. Encourage two ways of knowing: counting the numbers of each category and looking at the category with the shortest row. The numbers will confirm the visual representation.
- **Exercise 3:** Students write their explanation for determining the favorite lunch. Any viable explanation is accepted as students will write in their best possible manner.

PROFICIENT students will be able to count the types of objects and reason about the relative length of rows of pictures for most or least.

- **Exercise 2:** Have students explain how they found their answers.
- **Exercise 3:** Students can list any method, but most will cite the length of the rows.

Additional Support

- Students can place markers on top of the pictures and count to show quantities. Ask students what the "most" number of pictures and the "least" number of pictures mean.

Extension: Adding Rigor

- Have students make up their own questions to answer from the picture graph in Exercise 2.

Name ______________________________

Apply and Grow: Practice

2.

Favorite Lunch									
Pasta	☺	☺	☺	☺	☺				
Soup	☺	☺	☺						
Taco	☺	☺	☺	☺	☺	☺	☺	☺	

Each ☺ = 1 student.

How many students chose pasta? 5

How many students chose soup? 3

Which lunch is the least favorite? 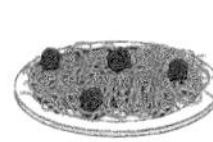  

---

3. MP **Communicate Clearly** In Exercise 2, how do you know which lunch is the most favorite?

Sample answer: **The most favorite lunch has the greatest number of smiley faces.**

Laurie's Notes

ELL Support

Check for understanding of Lesson 11.2. Allow students time to familiarize themselves with each picture graph. Then ask the following questions and have students answer using a thumbs up or down signal to answer *yes* or *no*.

1. Is the number of students who prefer rides less than the number of students who prefer animals?
2. Is the number of students who prefer bears greater than the number of students who prefer frogs?

Think and Grow: Modeling Real Life

These applications allow students to show their understanding of picture graphs. They can read and interpret the graphs to answer questions. In answering these applications, students will not need to count any category. They should be able to look and reason about the answers. The applications review greater than, less than, and equal to.

? **Preview:** "What do you notice about the picture graph at the top of the page?" Have students read the question they are to answer.

? **MP7 Look for and Make Use of Structure:** "What does a category that is greater than another look like on a picture graph? What does a category that is less than another look like on a picture graph? What does a category that is equal to another look like on a picture graph? Tell your partner your strategy for answering the question."

- Exercise 4 has the same directions as the example. Have students tell their partners what they are trying to decide and their strategy before completing the exercise.
- **MP3 Construct Viable Arguments:** Ask different students to share which way they prefer to organize data and answer questions: tally chart or picture graph, and why.

◉ "Take turns telling your partner something you know about a picture graph. Alternate saying things until you have said everything you know."

◉ "Use your thumb signals to say how you are doing with today's learning. How are you at reading a picture graph? How are you at finding the category with the most items from a picture graph? at finding the category with the least items?"

Closure

- Show two equal groups of equal buttons (e.g. round and square) or some other grouping of items. Ask students to tell their partner how their rows would compare on a picture graph.
- Take two of the items away from one of the groups. How would the rows compare now?

Think and Grow: Modeling Real Life

Favorite Activity at the Fair							
Rides	☺	☺	☺	☺	☺		
Animals	☺	☺					
Games	☺	☺	☺	☺			

Each ☺ = 1 student.

Is the number of students who chose rides greater than, less than, or equal to the number of students who chose animals?

(greater than) less than equal to

Show and Grow *I can think deeper!*

4.

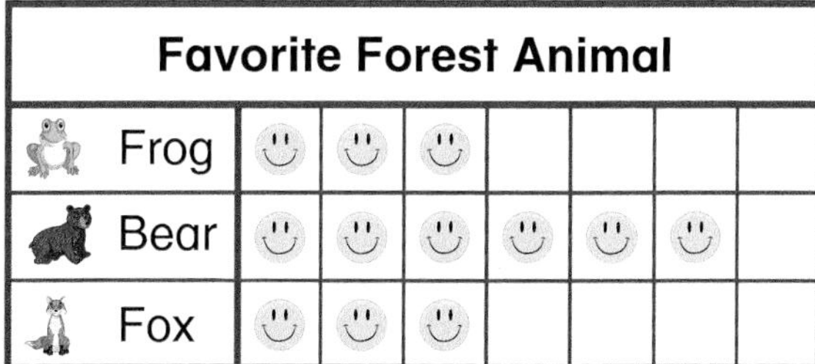

Favorite Forest Animal							
Frog	☺	☺	☺				
Bear	☺	☺	☺	☺	☺	☺	
Fox	☺	☺	☺				

Each ☺ = 1 student.

Is the number of students who chose frog greater than, less than, or equal to the number of students who chose bear?

greater than (less than) equal to

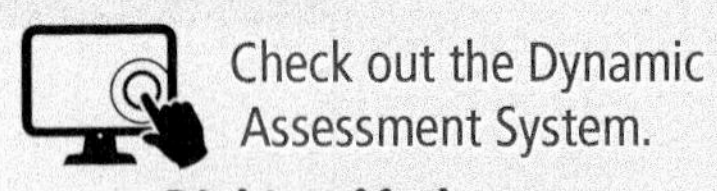
Check out the Dynamic
Assessment System.
BigIdeasMath.com

Scaffold assignments to support all students in their learning progression. Revisit with spaced practice to move every student toward proficiency.

Connect and Extend Learning

Practice Notes

- **Exercise 2:** Remind students how to write an explanation for their answer.

Prior Skills

- **Exercises 5 and 6:** Grade 1, Adding Tens to a Number

Cross-Curricular Connections

Language Arts

- *Let's Make a Picture Graph* by Robin Nelson; Read the book aloud to students. Discuss with students different kinds of apples. Focus on three kinds. Then have students take a survey of at least ten students and ask about their favorite apple out of the three kinds. Have them create a picture graph that shows the results.

What is your favorite kind of apple?

Name ____________________

Practice 11.2

Learning Target: Understand the data shown by a picture graph.

Favorite Snack							
Pretzels	☺	☺	☺	☺	☺	☺	
Apple	☺	☺	☺				

Each ☺ = 1 student.

Which snack is the most favorite?  

1.

Favorite Season									
Spring	☺	☺	☺						
Summer	☺	☺	☺	☺	☺	☺	☺		
Fall	☺	☺	☺	☺					
Winter	☺								

Each ☺ = 1 student.

How many students chose summer? 7

How many students chose fall? 4

Which season is the least favorite?   

Chapter 11 | Lesson 2 551

Connect and Extend Learning

Extend Student Learning

Interpersonal

- Have students survey at least ten other students about their favorite sport, class, or animal. Gather simple stamps for students to use as their pictures in a picture graph of the results. Have them label the title, categories, and key on their picture graph.

Lesson Resources	
Surface Level	**Deep Level**
Resources by Chapter • Extra Practice • Reteach Differentiating the Lesson Skills Review Handbook Skills Trainer	Resources by Chapter • Enrichment and Extension Graphic Organizers Dynamic Assessment System • Lesson Practice

2. **Communicate Clearly** How do you know which category has the least when looking at a picture graph?

The category with the least is the one with the fewest pictures.

3. **Modeling Real Life** Use the picture graph.

Favorite Drink at Lunch									
Milk	☺	☺	☺						
Water	☺	☺	☺	☺					
Juice	☺	☺	☺	☺					

Each ☺ = 1 student.

Is the number of students who chose water greater than, less than, or equal to the number of students who chose juice?

greater than less than equal to

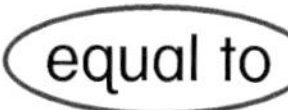

4. **DIG DEEPER!** In Exercise 3, four more students choose their favorite drink. Is it possible for the picture graph to show the same number of students in each category? Explain.

Yes No **Each of the drink types could have 5 students.**

Review & Refresh

5. $31 + 40 = $ 71

6. $62 + 20 = $ 82

Laurie's Notes

Learning Target

Understand the data shown by a bar graph.

Success Criteria

- Read the data in a bar graph to answer questions.
- Compare the data in a bar graph.

Warm-Up

Practice opportunities for the following are available in the Resources by Chapter or at *BigIdeasMath.com*.

- Daily skills
- Vocabulary
- Prerequisite skills

ELL Support

Point out that in this lesson students will read and interpret bar graphs. They may know the word *interpret* as the use of one language to explain the meaning of another language. Explain that when you interpret a graph, you explain in words what the graph shows by using visuals. So instead of interpreting from one language to another, you are interpreting visuals by using language.

Preparing to Teach

Students have now experienced two representations for organizing data and answering questions from them. Today, we show another representation that is one of the most commonly used, and will be used throughout the rest of their mathematics career: bar graphs.

Dig In (Circle Time)

Students will create a bar graph based on yesterday's tally chart and picture graph.

- "We've learned about tally charts and picture graphs to show data. Share what you think is good or not as good about each."
- ◉ "Today, we are going to learn about and use another graph called a bar graph. It is almost like a combination of both: it tells the number in each category like a tally chart, and it shows comparisons and rows like a picture graph."
- ◉ Display the tally chart and picture graph from Lesson 11.2. "This is our tally chart and picture graph from yesterday. To make it a bar graph, you color in a row to make it look like a bar to show how many there are. Instead of having a key like the picture graph, you have the numbers on the bottom. Let's make a bar graph from our class data." Note: Keep this bar graph for Lesson 11.5.

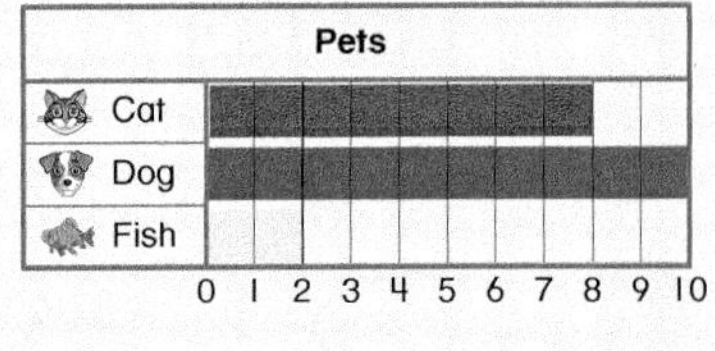

- ? "As you look at the three representations, how are they alike? How are they different? What else do you notice?"
- "Which graph would you use to tell how many people like dogs? Which graph would you use to tell how many more people like cats than fish? Why?"
- ◉ Ask a few questions about the charts such as, "how many more people prefer ___ than ___?"
- ◉ "One more thing about a bar graph: bars can go across or horizontally, or up and down or vertically. Let me show you. Tell how the two bar graphs are alike and how they are different. It doesn't matter which one you look at, they work the same way."
- Ask students one more opinion question with three answer options and create a bar graph. Have students pose questions to the group to answer.
- ◉ "Today, we are going to use bar graphs to show how many are in a group and to answer questions."

? Teaching Prompt ◉ Learning Target

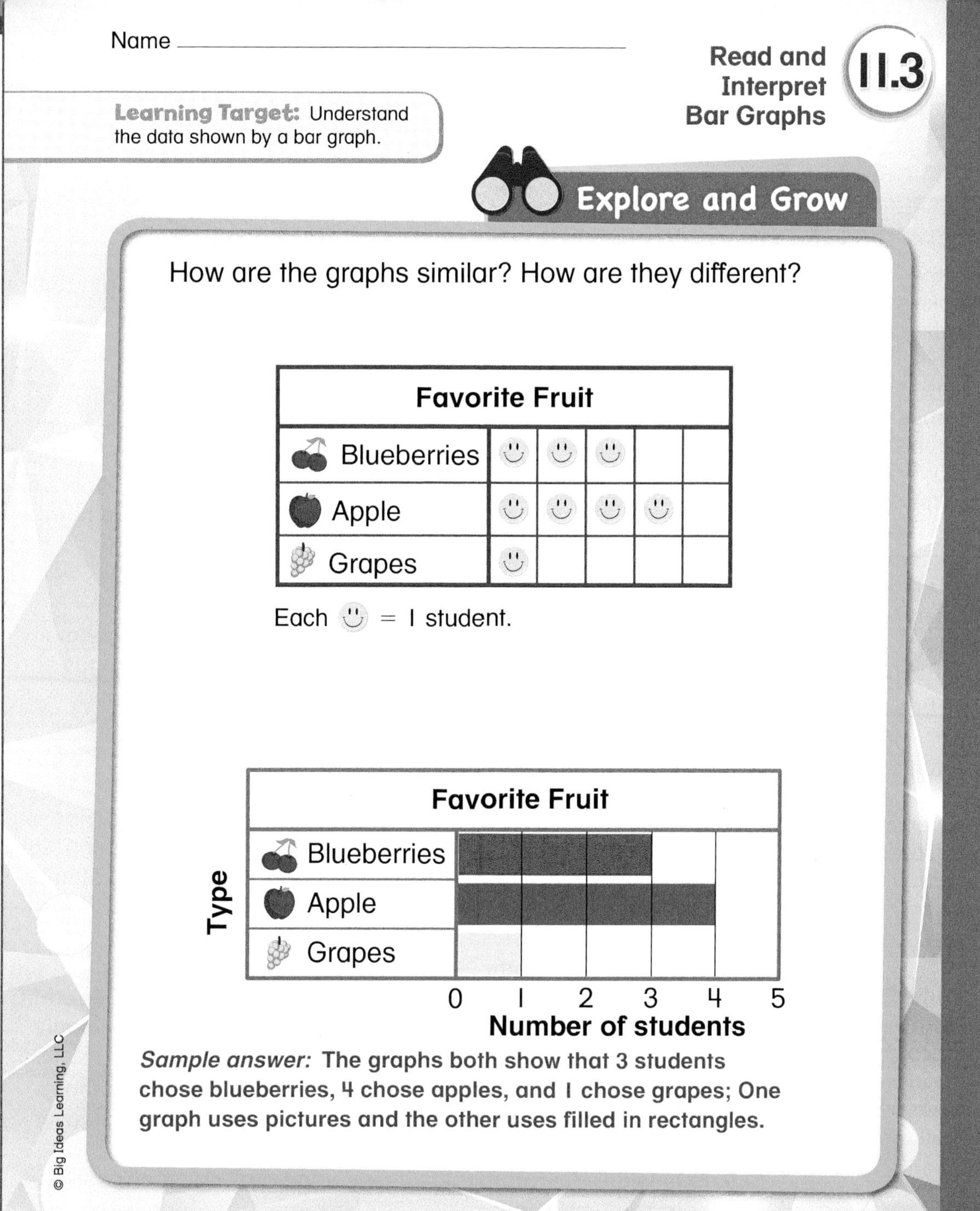

Name ____________________

Read and Interpret Bar Graphs **11.3**

Learning Target: Understand the data shown by a bar graph.

Explore and Grow

How are the graphs similar? How are they different?

Favorite Fruit					
Blueberries	☺	☺	☺		
Apple	☺	☺	☺	☺	
Grapes	☺				

Each ☺ = 1 student.

Sample answer: **The graphs both show that 3 students chose blueberries, 4 chose apples, and 1 chose grapes; One graph uses pictures and the other uses filled in rectangles.**

Explore and Grow

- If you have spent time in the circle talking about the Dig In, this page could be done orally or you may want to move on to the Think and Grow page.
- Students discuss similarities and differences of the two representations with a partner. Have several students share their observations.
- "We can answer questions from either representation. One advantage of a bar graph is that the numbers are given along the bottom, or up the side if the bar graph is vertical."

ELL Support

Work through the example as a class. Make sure students understand the meaning behind the visuals and names in each bar graph. Have students work in pairs as they practice language. Have one student ask another, "How many students prefer each object? Which is the most (or least) favorite?" Then have them alternate roles.

Beginner students may provide one-word answers.
Intermediate students may answer with simple sentences, such as, "Seven chose the lion."
Advanced students may answer with detailed sentences, such as, "Lions are the most favorite zoo animal of all the students."

Laurie's Notes

Think and Grow

Getting Started

- Introduce the vocabulary term **bar graph**. "Who can remind us what *data* means?

Teaching Notes

◉ **Model**: "We have a bar graph of favorite zoo animals. Tell your partner what your favorite animal at the zoo is. The first question asks how many students chose an elephant. Find the elephant category. Now trace along the bar until the yellow bar ends. Follow down the line at the end of the bar. Tell the number you see. 5 students chose an elephant. Fill in 5."

? **Model**: "How would you know which animal is the most favorite? Which animal has the longest bar? The lion is the most chosen animal. Circle the lion. Can you tell me how many students chose lion? Follow the lion bar across until it ends and then follow the line at the end down to find the number."

- **MP2 Reason Abstractly and Quantitatively**: Tell your partner how answering questions with a bar graph is like answering questions with a picture graph.
- Students complete Exercise 1. Students may answer 7 coins instead of 6 because they follow the bar to the end of the graph, and not the end of the actual bar. Be sure that they pay attention to the question that asks for the least favorite, not most favorite, object to collect.
- **Supporting Learners**: Watch as students follow the length of the bar. Do they stop and follow straight down for the number that is at the end of the bar, or do they move off course/diagonally and get a different number than the intended?
- **Supporting Learners**: Have students tell what you would look for in the bar graph for "most" or for "least." They can answer these questions without finding specific numbers.

? **Extension**: Have students answer additional questions such as how many students answered? How many students answered stickers and rocks? How many more students answered the favorite object to collect than the least favorite object?

Think and Grow

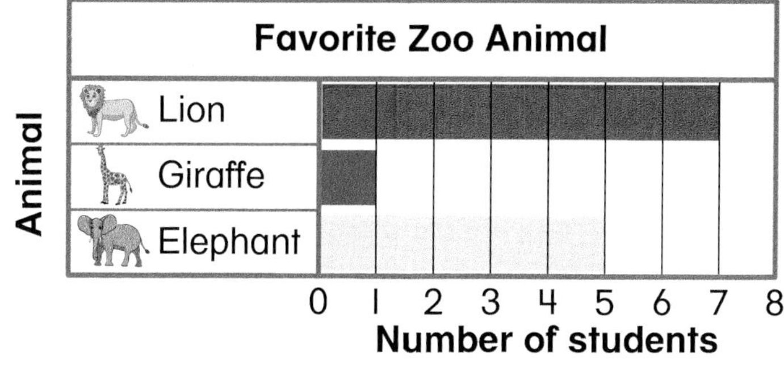

How many students chose elephant? 5

Which animal is the most favorite?   

Show and Grow *I can do it!*

1.

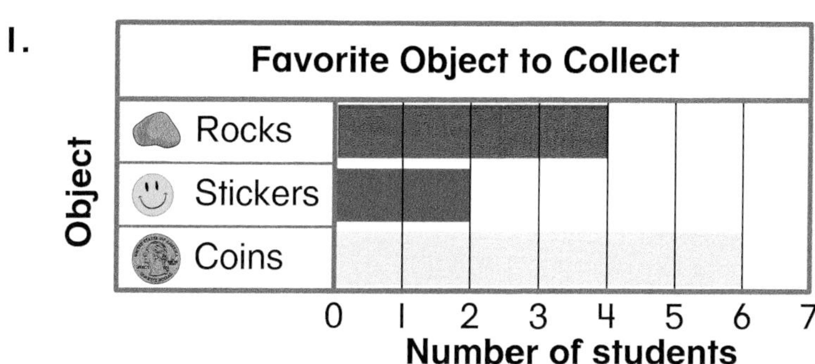

How many students chose coins? 6

Which object is the least favorite?   

Scaffold instruction to support all students in their learning. Learning is individualized and you may want to group students differently as they move in and out of these levels with each skill and concept. Student self-assessment and feedback help guide your instructional decisions about how and when to layer support for all students to become proficient learners.

Meeting the needs of all learners.

Laurie's Notes

Apply and Grow: Practice

SCAFFOLDING INSTRUCTION

Students continue to interpret a bar graph and answer questions. They encounter a vertical bar graph on this page.

EMERGING students may not recognize how a bar can represent a quantity. They are used to a one-to-one correspondence such as with tallies or pictures. Help students trace the ends of the bar to see the number it represents, whether horizontal or vertical.

- **Exercise 2:** This bar graph is in the vertical format. This may cause confusion. Show students how to find the end of a bar, and move across to the left to find the number. Remind students that this graph works very much like the picture graph, especially when finding the most favorite or least favorite.
- **Exercise 3:** Be sure students order all three options from greatest to least.

PROFICIENT students will be able to read the bar graph. They may need to be reminded of how to find the numbers with the vertical format, and then they will answer the questions easily.

- **Exercise 2:** Have students explain how they found their answers.
- **Exercise 3:** Be sure students order all three options.

Additional Support

- Have students count across or up the numbers to see how the bars match with numbers.

Extension: Adding Rigor

- Have students make up their own questions to stump their partner based on the bar graph in Exercise 2.

Name ______________________

Apply and Grow: Practice

2\.

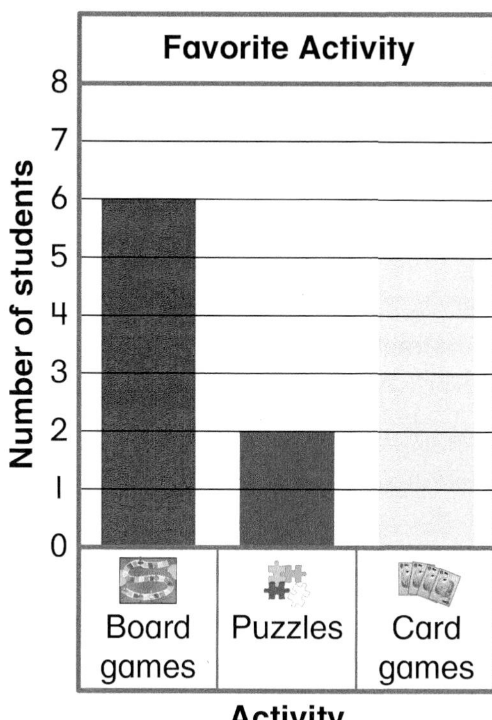

How many students chose card games?

5

How many students chose board games?

6

Which activity is the most favorite?

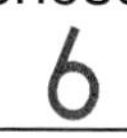

3\. DIG DEEPER! Order the activities in Exercise 2 from the most favorite to the least favorite.

Board games, Card games, Puzzles

ELL Support

Check for understanding of Lesson 11.3. Read each question aloud as students follow along. Clarify unknown vocabulary if necessary. Allow them time to interpret the data. Then ask the questions and have them answer using a thumbs up, down, or sideways signal for greater than, less than, or equal to.

Laurie's Notes

Think and Grow: Modeling Real Life

These applications allow students to show their understanding of bar graphs. They can read and interpret the graphs to answer questions. These applications will not require students to find the exact number of any category. They should be able to look at the graph and reason about the relationships among the categories.

? **Preview:** "Look at the community helpers. If you could be one of these, which would you be?"

- **MP2 Reason Abstractly and Quantitatively:** "What does a category that is greater than another look like on a bar graph? What does a category that is less than another look like on a bar graph? What does a category that is equal to another look like on a bar graph? Tell your partner your strategy for finding how the number of students who chose firefighters compares to the number of students who chose doctor."
- Exercise 4 has the same directions as the model. Have students tell their partners what they are trying to decide and their strategy before completing the exercise.
- **MP3 Construct Viable Arguments:** Ask different students to share which way they prefer to organize data and answer questions: Tally chart, picture graph, or bar graph, and why.

◉ "Take turns telling your partner something you know about a bar graph. Include how it is like a picture graph and tally chart, and how it is different. Alternate saying things until you have said everything you know." Have several students share ideas, especially about the comparison with other representations.

◉ "Use your thumb signals to say how you are doing with today's learning. How are you at reading a horizontal bar graph? vertical bar graph? How are you at finding the most from a bar graph? at finding the least?"

Closure

- Show three groups of objects. Make a bar graph with an error in one of the groups. For example, if the blue group has 4 items, graph it as 5 items.
- "There is a mistake in this bar graph. Tell your partner what the mistake is. Fix the graph."

Think and Grow: Modeling Real Life

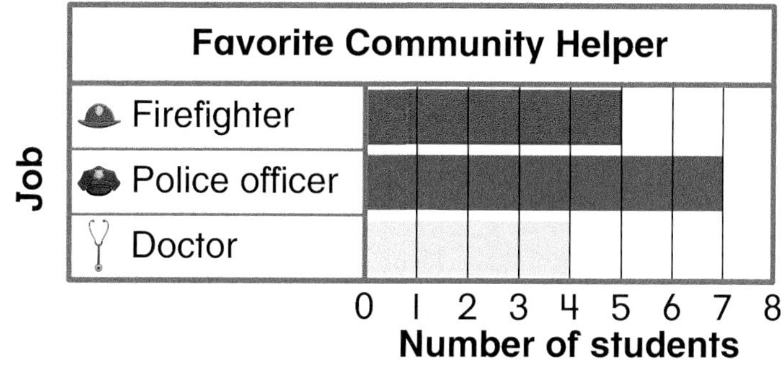

Is the number of students who chose firefighter greater than, less than, or equal to the number of students who chose doctor?

(greater than) less than equal to

Show and Grow *I can think deeper!*

4.

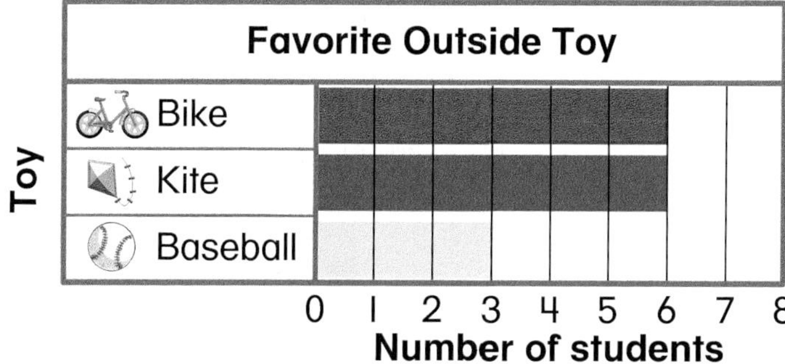

Is the number of students who chose bike greater than, less than, or equal to the number of students who chose kite?

greater than less than (equal to)

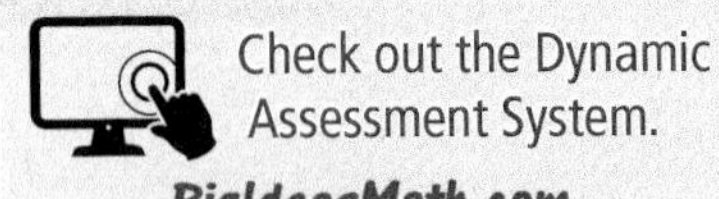

Scaffold assignments to support all students in their learning progression. Revisit with spaced practice to move every student toward proficiency.

Connect and Extend Learning

Practice Notes

- **Exercises 1 and 3:** Remind students that they can trace the ends of the bar and move down to find the numbers on these graphs.

Prior Skills

- **Exercises 5 and 6:** Grade 1, Adding Three Numbers

Cross-Curricular Connections

Science

- Discuss the characteristics of three planets with students. Then ask students what their favorite planet is. Record their results by graphing them in a bar graph on the board, or have students come up one at a time to fill in part of the bar that reflects their choice.

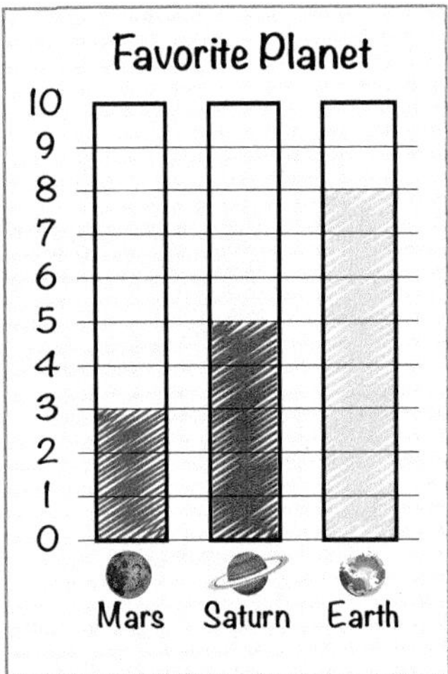

Name ______________________

Practice 

Learning Target: Understand the data shown by a bar graph.

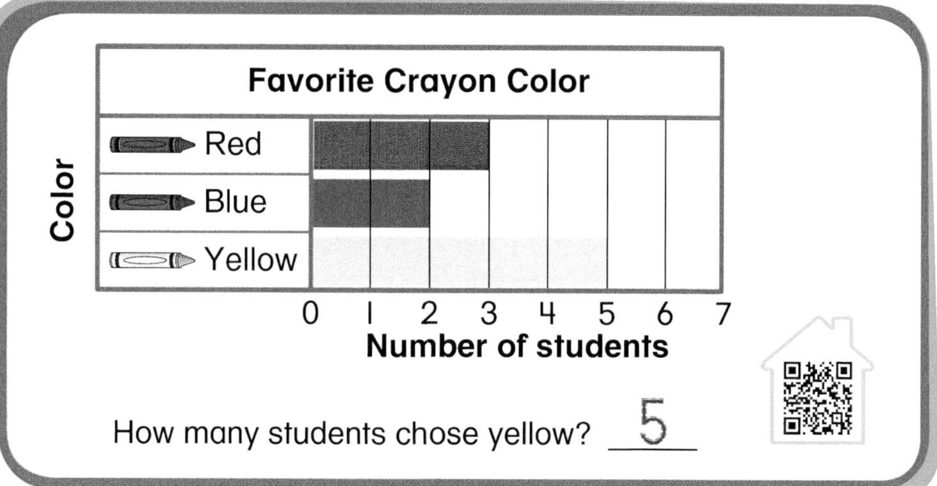

How many students chose yellow? 5

I.

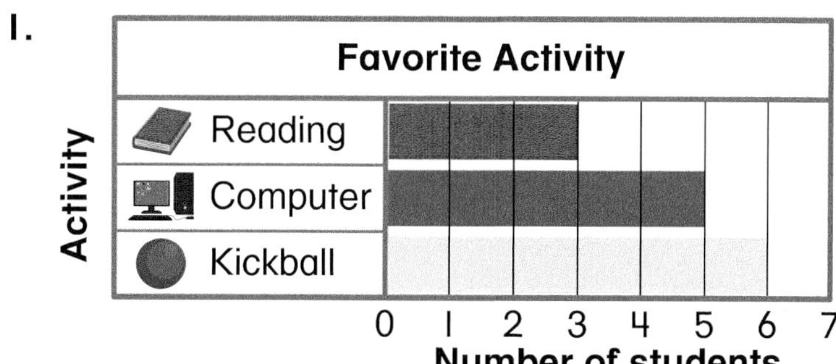

How many students chose reading? 3

How many students chose kickball? 6

Which activity is the least favorite? 

Chapter 11 | Lesson 3 557

Connect and Extend Learning

Extend Student Learning

Bodily-Kinesthetic

- Create a human bar graph with students. Make category labels for the graph have different actions on them and tape them on the floor. Such actions can be jump, stretch, skip, or jog. Ask students, "Which of these actions is your favorite?" Students will answer the question one at a time, do the action, and then lay down in the category that they chose. If another student is already there, they can lie side-by-side or head-to-toe to form bars.

Lesson Resources	
Surface Level	**Deep Level**
Resources by Chapter • Extra Practice • Reteach Differentiating the Lesson Skills Review Handbook Skills Trainer	Resources by Chapter • Enrichment and Extension Graphic Organizers Dynamic Assessment System • Lesson Practice

2. Communicate Clearly How do you know which category has the most when looking at a bar graph?

The category with the longest bar will have the most.

3. Modeling Real Life Use the bar graph.

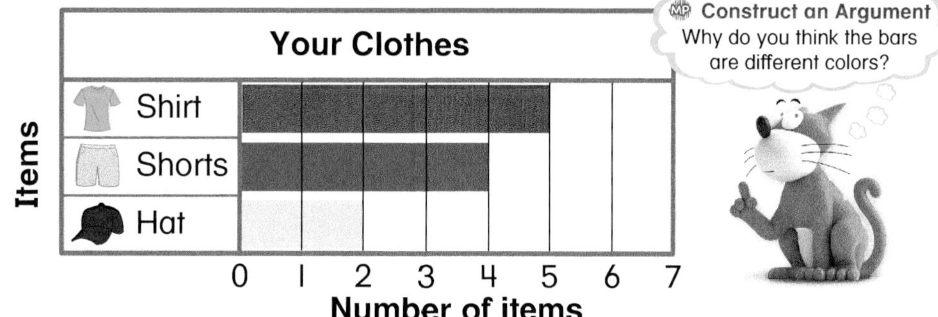

Is the number of pairs of shorts greater than, less than, or equal to the number of shirts?

greater than 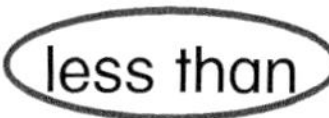 equal to

4. DIG DEEPER! In Exercise 3, how many more shirts do you have than hats?

3 shirts

Review & Refresh

5. 9 + 1 + 7 = 17

6. 6 + 3 + 6 = 15

11.4

Laurie's Notes

Check out the
Digital Flash Cards.

BigIdeasMath.com

COMMON CORE STATE STANDARDS
1.MD.C.4

Learning Target

Make picture graphs and bar graphs.

Success Criteria

- Count the tally marks in each category.
- Represent the data using a tally chart.
- Represent the data using a picture graph or bar graph.

Warm-Up

Practice opportunities for the following are available in the Resources by Chapter or at *BigIdeasMath.com.*

- Daily skills
- Vocabulary
- Prerequisite skills

ELL Support

Explain that in this lesson, instead of reading and interpreting data, they will be given data that they must then represent using picture and bar graphs. Explain that the word *represent* can mean "show, signify, exemplify, or express." They may want to add these words to their vocabulary notebooks.

Preparing to Teach

Students have learned the three representations for organizing data and showing how many are in each category. Students have answered questions based on the information in the chart or graphs. Today students will make their own graphs to organize data.

Materials

- linking cubes
- chart paper
- color tiles
- whiteboards

Dig In (Circle Time)

Students will work in groups of three. Students will look at a tally chart, a picture graph, and a bar graph of three colors (white, blue, green), and as a team build linking cubes to match the representation. Prepare the chart and graphs on chart paper in advance to show students.

- "We have been working with data. Tell your partner what data is. We've also been working with how to show data in different ways. Tell your partner the 3 ways we have shown data."
- "We are going to work with white, blue, and green linking cubes. Decide with your partners which color each of you will work with. I will show you a chart or graph, and you will build towers that have that many cubes."
- ◉ Show a tally chart of the three colors. Be sure that at least 2 colors have five or more, and the third has less than 5. Students build the color towers to match. Have students hold their towers up in the circle, one color at a time, to compare. Have students tell their partners how they knew how many cubes to use. Discuss with students what a picture graph of the same data would look like.
- ◉ Repeat this process with a picture graph. Use circles to represent the cubes in the picture graph. For this chart, have a different color have the most, middle, and least number of cubes as compared to the tally chart. Discuss with students what a bar graph of the same data would look like. Sketch it as students describe.
- ◉ Repeat a final time with a bar graph. Again, have different colors have the most, middle, and least number of cubes as compared to the others. This allows each student to build the most cubes.
- ? Ask questions about the charts such as, "Which was easiest to find out how many were in each linking cube tower? Which was most difficult? Why?"
- ◉ "Today, you will draw tally charts, picture graphs, and bar graphs."

? Teaching Prompt ◉ Learning Target

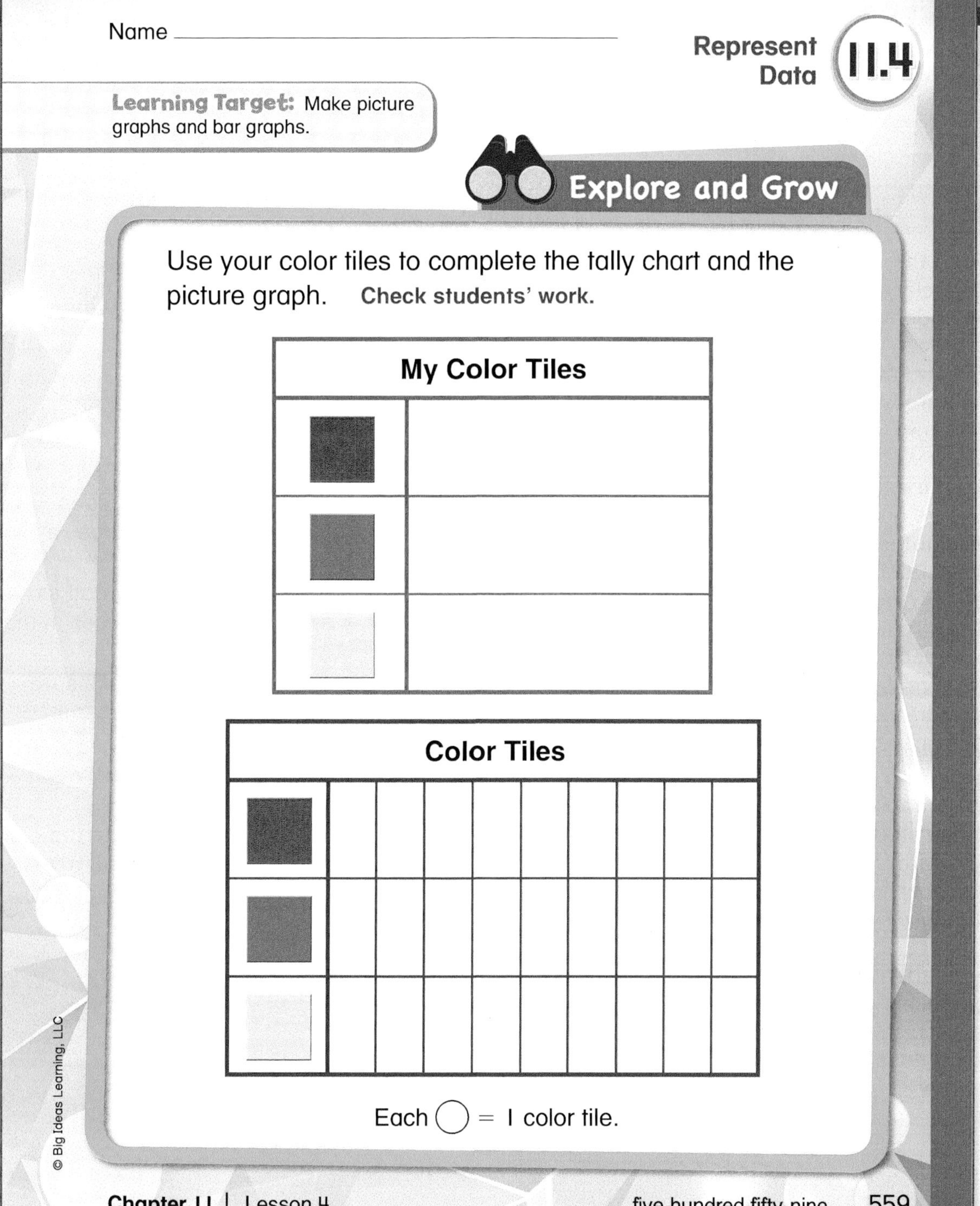
Name

Represent Data 11.4

Learning Target: Make picture graphs and bar graphs.

Explore and Grow

Use your color tiles to complete the tally chart and the picture graph. **Check students' work.**

My Color Tiles	
[red tile]	
[blue tile]	
[yellow tile]	

Color Tiles									
[red tile]									
[blue tile]									
[yellow tile]									

Each ◯ = 1 color tile.

Explore and Grow

- Provide students with sets of red, blue, and yellow color tiles. Be sure at least one of the colors has more than 5 tiles, and no color has more than 9.
- Students make a tally chart of their tiles and show a partner to check each other's work.
- Students fill in the picture graph using circles to represent each tile.
- ? "The key on the picture graph said to use a circle for each tile. Is it ok to use a circle when tiles are square? What does the key mean?"

ELL Support

Work through the example as a class. Make sure students understand the meaning behind the visuals and names in each tally chart. Have students work in pairs as they practice language. Have one student ask another, "How many students prefer each toy? How many pictures must be drawn for each toy?" Then have them alternate roles.

Beginner students may answer using numbers or phrases.
Intermediate students may answer with simple sentences, such as, "Draw four pictures."
Advanced students may with detailed sentences, such as, "To represent dolls you must draw four pictures."

Laurie's Notes

Think and Grow

Getting Started

- Review key vocabulary *data, tally mark, tally chart, picture graph*, and *bar graph*. Highlight the differences among the three representations.

Teaching Notes

- **Model:** "Look at the tally chart of favorite toys. Tell your partner the three choices for favorite toy. Would one of these be your choice for your favorite toy?"
- **Model:** "Below the tally chart is a picture graph. What does the key say to use as a picture for each student who chose a favorite toy?"
- ◉ **Model:** "Tell your partner how many students chose a doll as their favorite toy. In the picture graph draw 4 smiley faces in the doll row." Repeat for car and blocks.
- **MP6 Attend to Precision:** "Tell your partner how to make sure your picture graph is correct based on the tally chart." same number of tallies and pictures in each category
- Students complete Exercise 1. Discuss the difference between making a bar graph and making a picture graph.
- **Supporting Learners:** Students may not pay attention to the numbers in the bar graph, and instead just color the full rows. Remind students that they are to use the tally chart of colors to fill in the bar graph. Have students show you where the numbers are in the bar graph to show how many students chose each color.
- **Extension:** Have students make a bar graph of the toy data and/or a picture graph of the color data.

Think and Grow

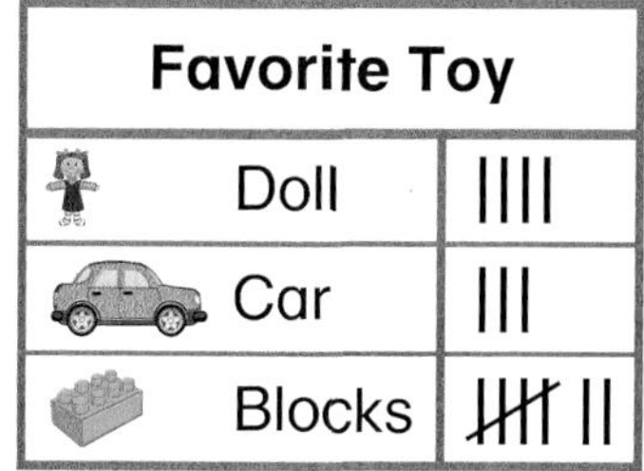

Favorite Toy	
Doll	||||
Car	|||
Blocks	~~||||~~ ||

Favorite Toy								
Doll	☺	☺	☺	☺				
Car	☺	☺	☺					
Blocks	☺	☺	☺	☺	☺	☺	☺	

Each ☺ = 1 student.

Show and Grow *I can do it!*

1. Complete the bar graph.

Favorite Color	
Blue	~~||||~~ |
Pink	~~||||~~
Yellow	||

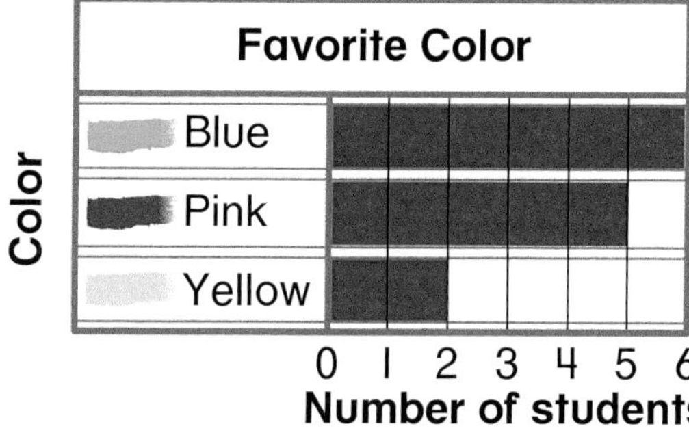

Scaffold instruction to support all students in their learning. Learning is individualized and you may want to group students differently as they move in and out of these levels with each skill and concept. Student self-assessment and feedback help guide your instructional decisions about how and when to layer support for all students to become proficient learners.

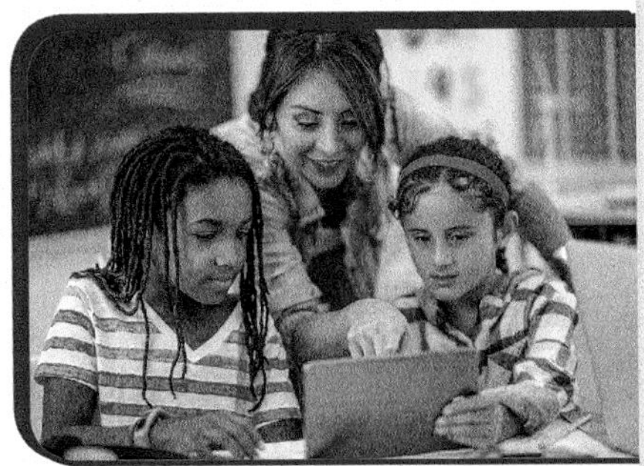

Meeting the needs of all learners.

Laurie's Notes

Apply and Grow: Practice

SCAFFOLDING INSTRUCTION

Students continue to interpret data in a tally chart to make a picture graph and a bar graph.

EMERGING students may need a reminder of how to count the tally marks. Some students may still have difficulty with the one-to-one correspondence involved. Do not let fine motor skills and messy drawings overshadow correct concepts.

- **Exercise 2:** Students use smiley faces to represent each student in a picture graph as in the example on Think and Grow.
- **Exercise 3:** Students make a bar graph in the same way as Exercise 1.

PROFICIENT students will be able to read the tally charts and make the picture and bar graphs. They understand the differences in the representations and how to make each type, but may have messy work due to still developing fine muscle skills.

- **Exercise 2:** Have students defend why their picture graph is correct.
- **Exercise 3:** Students compare their bar graphs with a partner to check each other's work.

Additional Support

- **Picture Graph:** Have students count tallies out loud, and then count each smiley face out loud as they make it. Have them go back and check the tally count and then the picture count after completing the picture graph.
- **Bar Graph:** After students count the tallies, have them locate that number on the bar graph and trace up the line to the correct category. Place a dot or mark on the cell, and then draw the bar.

Extension: Adding Rigor

- Have students ask friends their favorite farm animal among pig, cow, or horse. Have them make their own tally chart, picture graph, and bar graph.

Name ____________________

Apply and Grow: Practice

2. Complete the picture graph.

Favorite Farm Animal	
Pig	||||
Cow	~~||||~~ |
Horse	~~||||~~

Favorite Farm Animal							
Pig	☺	☺	☺	☺			
Cow	☺	☺	☺	☺	☺	☺	
Horse	☺	☺	☺	☺	☺		

Each ☺ = 1 student.

3. Complete the bar graph.

Favorite Sport	
Swimming	||||
Karate	||
Soccer	~~||||~~

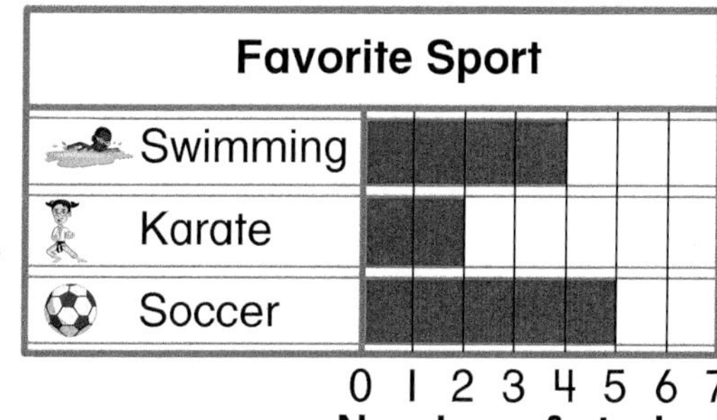

Chapter 11 | Lesson 4 **561**

ELL Support

Check for understanding of Lesson 11.4. Read each description aloud. Allow students time to think through the answers. Then ask the following questions and have students answer by holding up the appropriate number of fingers.

1. How many pictures do you draw to represent right-handed students?
2. How many units do you color the bar graph to represent students who prefer the slide?

Laurie's Notes

Think and Grow: Modeling Real Life

The application stories today have students interpret a graph, and then use addition to determine how to complete the rest of graph.

? **Preview:** "What does it mean to be right-handed or left-handed? How many of you are right-handed? left-handed?"

? **MP2 Reason Abstractly and Quantitatively:** "If 10 students are asked if they are left- or right-handed, and 2 students are left-handed, how can you determine how many students are right-handed?"

- Students can subtract or add using a missing addend. Have students share their strategies for determining how many students are right-handed, and tell their partners how many students are right-handed.

◉ **MP1 Persevere in Solving Problems:** "Now that we know there are 8 students who are right-handed, how do we finish the picture graph? What symbol do we use? How many do I draw?"

- Exercise 4 has the same directions as the example except students will draw a bar graph. Have students tell their partners what they are trying to find and their strategy for finding the number of students who prefer the slide. Have them complete the bar graph.
- **MP5 Use Appropriate Tools Strategically:** Ask different students to share which graph they prefer to make and why. "What are the advantages or disadvantages to each?"

◉ "Use your thumb signals to say how you are doing with today's learning. How are you at making a picture graph? How are you at making a bar graph?"

Closure

- Show 2 towers of linking cubes. Students draw a picture graph on whiteboards to show the colors. Once their picture graphs are compared and discussed, have them erase and draw a bar graph.

Think and Grow: Modeling Real Life

You ask 10 students whether they are right-handed or left-handed. 2 are left-handed. The rest are right-handed. Complete the picture graph.

How We Write									
Right-handed	☺	☺	☺	☺	☺	☺	☺	☺	
Left-handed	☺	☺							

Each ☺ = 1 student.

Show and Grow *I can think deeper!*

4. You ask 11 students whether they like the swings or the slide. 5 like the swings. The rest like the slide. Complete the bar graph.

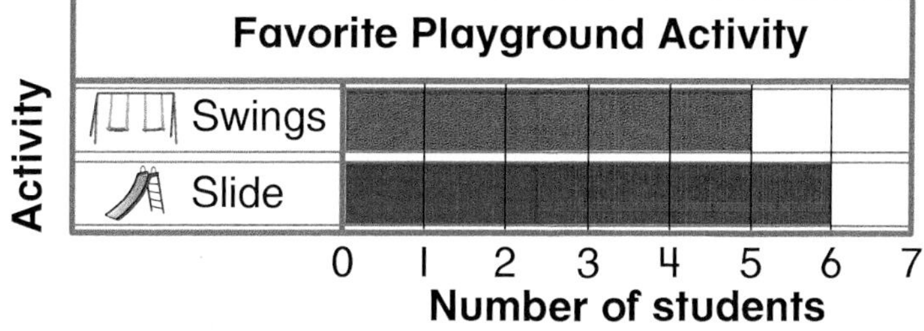

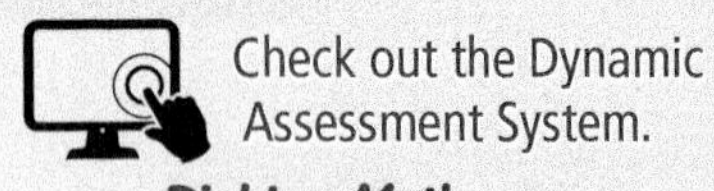

Scaffold assignments to support all students in their learning progression. Revisit with spaced practice to move every student toward proficiency.

Connect and Extend Learning

Practice Notes

- Discuss with students the differences between tally charts, bar graphs, and picture graphs.

Prior Skills

- **Exercise 5:** Grade 1, Adding in Any Order to Find a Sum

Cross-Curricular Connections

Language Arts

- Provide students with 3 spelling or sight words on the board. Have them roll a die for each word to determine how many times they will write that word on a sheet of paper. Make sure students write the words in a scattered arrangement. Then have students trade their paper with a partner. The partner first tallies how many times each sight word is written and then they create a bar graph of the results.

Name ______________________

Practice 11.4

Learning Target: Make picture graphs and bar graphs.

Favorite Socks	
Black	𝍸
Red	I
Stripes	𝍸

Favorite Socks						
Black	☺	☺	☺	☺	☺	
Red	☺					
Stripes	☺	☺	☺	☺	☺	

Each ☺ = 1 student.

1. Complete the bar graph.

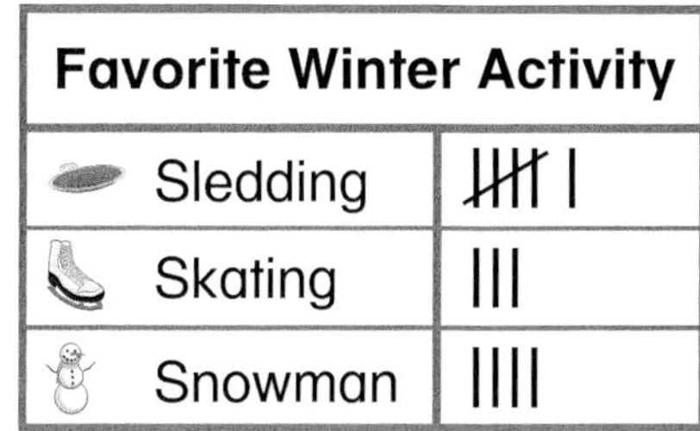

Favorite Winter Activity	
Sledding	𝍸 I
Skating	III
Snowman	IIII

Favorite Winter Activity							
Sledding	■	■	■	■	■	■	
Skating	■	■	■				
Snowman	■	■	■	■			

Activity (vertical axis); Number of students (horizontal axis): 0 1 2 3 4 5 6 7

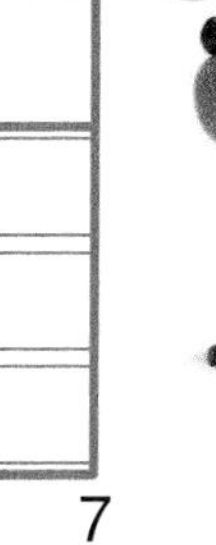

Choose Tools
What tools can you use to represent the bars in the bar graph?

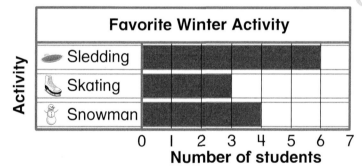

Connect and Extend Learning

Extend Student Learning

Visual-Spatial

- Have students draw three different shapes in a design or pattern. Each shape cannot be drawn more than 10 times. Once the drawings are complete, students will trade with a partner. Then they will keep track of how many times each shape was drawn by using a tally chart. Students will then graph the shapes using a bar graph or picture graph. Alternatively, have students use three colors to draw shapes and have partners track how many shapes there are of each color.

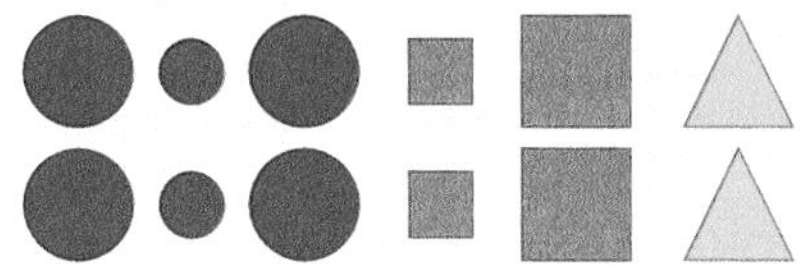

Lesson Resources	
Surface Level	**Deep Level**
Resources by Chapter • Extra Practice • Reteach Differentiating the Lesson Skills Review Handbook Skills Trainer Math Musicals	Resources by Chapter • Enrichment and Extension Graphic Organizers Math Musicals Dynamic Assessment System • Lesson Practice

2. Complete the picture graph.

Balloons	
Blue	𝍸
Red	II

Balloons						
Blue	○	○	○	○	○	
Red	○	○				

Each ○ = 1 balloon.

3. **DIG DEEPER!** In a picture graph, each ☺ represents 5. How can you find the total number of students the picture graph represents?

Sample answer: **Count by fives for every smiley face.**

4. **Modeling Real Life** You ask 8 students whether they buy or pack their lunches. 6 students buy. The rest pack. Complete the picture graph.

Lunch Choices							
Buy	☺	☺	☺	☺	☺	☺	
Pack	☺	☺					

Each ☺ = 1 student.

Review & Refresh

Find the sum. Then change the order of the addends. Write the new equation.

5. $2 + 6 =$ 8   6 + 2 = 8

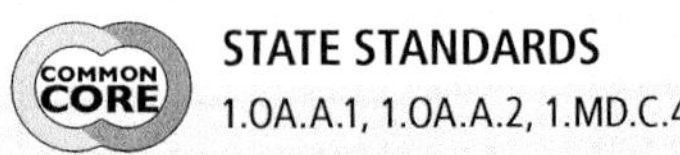

Laurie's Notes

COMMON CORE STATE STANDARDS
1.OA.A.1, 1.OA.A.2, 1.MD.C.4

Learning Target

Use data from graphs to answer questions.

Success Criteria

- Read different types of graphs.
- Compare amounts in each category.
- Write a question that reading a graph will answer.

Warm-Up

Practice opportunities for the following are available in the Resources by Chapter or at *BigIdeasMath.com*.

- Daily skills
- Vocabulary
- Prerequisite skills

ELL Support

Point out that the Explore and Grow asks students to write a question about their graphs. Review with students how questions are written. Remind them that a question begins with a word that has its first letter capitalized and ends with a question mark. Provide possible question starters, such as, "Which toy...?" and, "How many...?"

Preparing to Teach

Students have had quite a bit of experience with interpreting data representations and answering questions. Today, students will answer questions that incorporate operations.

Materials

- whiteboards

Dig In (Circle Time)

Students will pose and answer questions based on the data in the Favorite Pet picture graph (Lesson 11.2) and bar graph (Lesson 11.3).

- "We are becoming experts with data. A very important part of working with data is being able to answer questions about it. Today, we will answer all kinds of questions from data graphs." Show the Favorite Pet picture and bar graphs.
- "Here are our Favorite Pet graphs. How many students voted for a pet? Write an equation on your white boards to show how you would find out. Solve your equation."

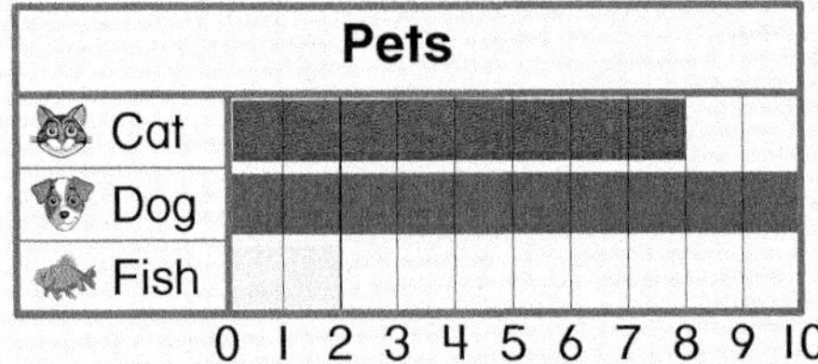

Pets										
Cat										
Dog										
Fish										

- Ask one or two additional questions that can be answered from the data, such as "how many fewer ____ than ____," etc. Students can use their whiteboards to show equations or to model to find answers as needed.
- Have students talk to their partners and think of a question that can be answered from the data. Have partners volunteer to ask their questions. If a question cannot be answered from the data, discuss why it cannot be answered with the class. This is also important learning.
- "Today, we will be looking at data and answering all kinds of questions."

? Teaching Prompt   ◉ Learning Target

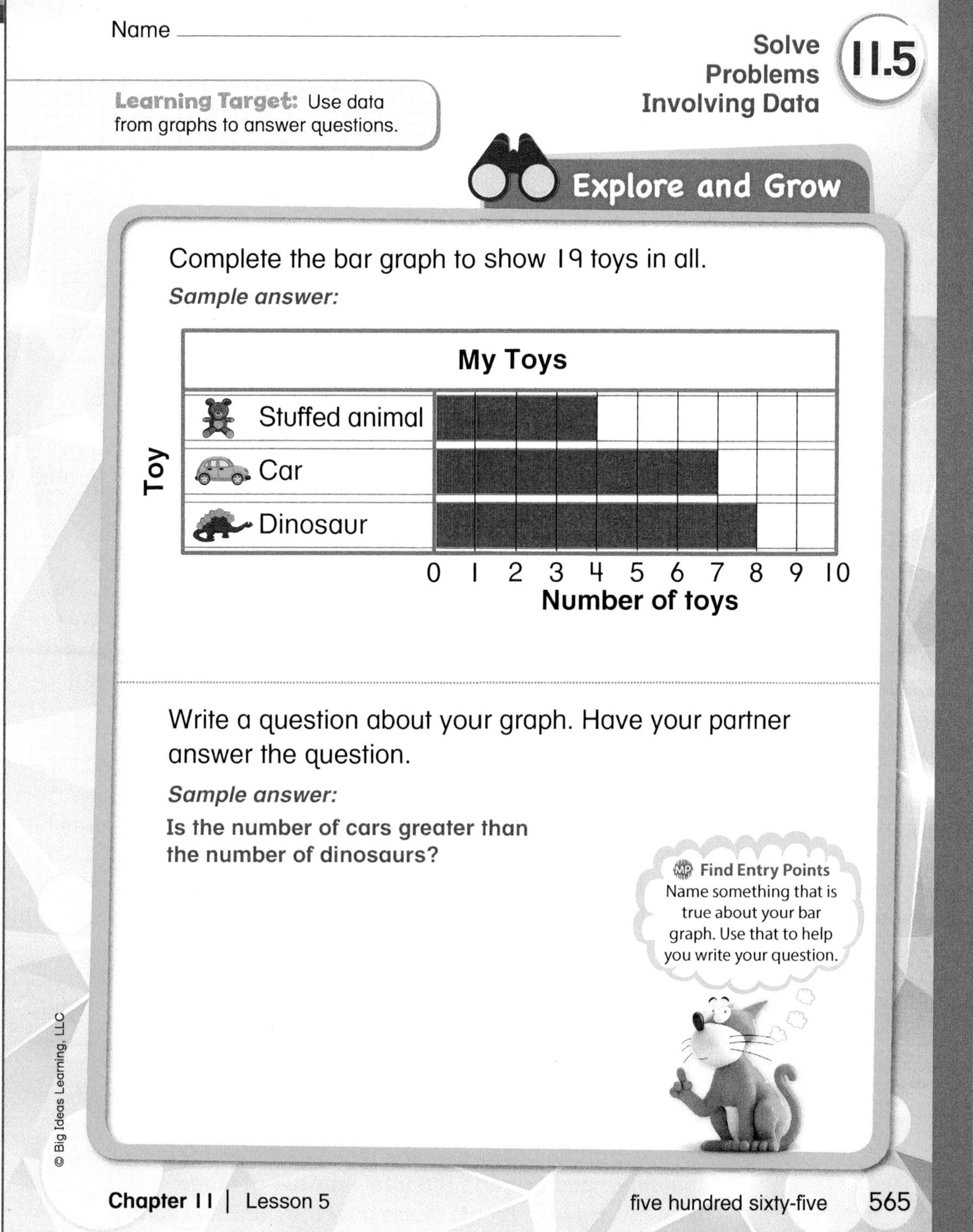

Name ______________________

Learning Target: Use data from graphs to answer questions.

Solve Problems Involving Data **11.5**

Explore and Grow

Complete the bar graph to show 19 toys in all.

Sample answer:

My Toys

Toy	Number of toys
Stuffed animal	4
Car	7
Dinosaur	8

Write a question about your graph. Have your partner answer the question.

Sample answer:

Is the number of cars greater than the number of dinosaurs?

Find Entry Points
Name something that is true about your bar graph. Use that to help you write your question.

Explore and Grow

- This is the first time students create data. You may need to explain that there needs to be 19 toys in all, it doesn't matter how the 19 is split up among the three toys. Students may show 10 of one toy, 9 of another, and 0 of the third.
- Discuss with students the type of graph they are to make. They will not be using symbols in each cell, but drawing a bar.
- Have students write a question that can be answered by their graph. Have them trade with a partner to answer questions. Have several students share their questions.

Laurie's Notes

ELL Support

Review the example. Then have students work in groups to complete the exercise. Have each group discuss the following questions: "How many of each are there? Which has the most? Which has the least? What is the equation? What are the answers to the questions?" Monitor discussion and expect students to perform as described.

Beginner students may provide one-word answers.
Intermediate students may answer with phrases, such as, "nine more students."
Advanced students may answer with sentences, such as, "Nine more students ride a bus than walk."

Think and Grow

Getting Started

- Students continue to answer questions from the data representations.
- Students write equations during the modeling on this page. It is not required that students write the equations to answer questions, but it is an explicit connection to the required mathematical reasoning. For example, instead of comparing pictures and counting blank spaces to find how many more, students could write a subtraction equation. It is also a reminder of their prior learning.

Teaching Notes

- **Model:** "Look at the tally chart of How You Get to School. We want to know how many more students ride a bus than walk. Tell your partner how you would figure that out from the tally chart. What would an equation look like?"
- Have students discuss how they would determine the difference. Some students may say that they would subtract, especially since that is the equation provided. They might also say they could use a missing addend equation. This is also correct. You can also show this equation, although students fill in the subtraction equation.
- **Model:** "Tell your partners how you can find out how many students were asked. Tell what that equation would be. Fill in the equation."
- Ask students how they will add 10 + 1 + 3. Do they add in order? Do they add in a different order, adding 1 + 3 and then 10 + 4? Do they count on? This will review addition strategies they have not used recently.
- Students complete Exercise 1. They can write equations, if it is helpful. The first question can be answered more easily by comparing the pictures in the two categories and counting the difference. Finding the total number of students requires a strategy. Have students share how they find the sum. Are they counting all the pictures? Are they adding using a strategy? If they counted, have students tell a partner what equation would show their count. What strategy could they have used? *Make a 10* would work with this data.
- **Supporting Learners:** Have students say what they are trying to find. What does that look like on the graph? Suggest strategies such as writing an equation or counting blank areas.
- **Extension:** Ask your partner other questions, such as how many students answered either bird or bat, etc.

Think and Grow

How You Get to School	
Bus	~~||||~~ ~~||||~~
Walk	|
Car	|||

How many more students ride a bus than walk?

10 ⊖ 1 = 9   9 students

How many students were asked?

10 + 1 + 3 = 14   14 students

Show and Grow *I can do it!*

1.

Favorite Animal That Flies								
Bird	☺	☺	☺	☺	☺	☺		
Bat	☺	☺	☺	☺				
Butterfly	☺	☺	☺	☺	☺	☺	☺	

Each ☺ = 1 student.

How many more students like butterflies than birds?

7 − 6 = 1   1 students

How many students were asked?

6 + 4 + 7 = 17   17 students

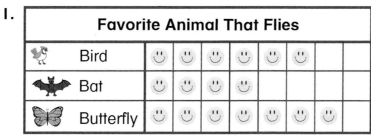

Scaffold instruction to support all students in their learning. Learning is individualized and you may want to group students differently as they move in and out of these levels with each skill and concept. Student self-assessment and feedback help guide your instructional decisions about how and when to layer support for all students to become proficient learners.

Meeting the needs of all learners.

Laurie's Notes

Apply and Grow: Practice

SCAFFOLDING INSTRUCTION

Students continue to answer questions from picture or bar graphs.

EMERGING students may need help understanding what the questions are asking, or connecting the question to a mathematical operation. The questions do not need an equation and can be answered from counting on the graph. Encourage students to think about the operation (addition or subtraction) that would be used to answer the question.

- **Exercise 2:** The use of the word *or* in this question may cause confusion. Most students do not realize they need to add the quantities when talking about *or*. Explain to students that they are finding how many students chose square and how many chose triangle. They want to find how many chose either the square or the triangle, so they need to combine them.
- **Exercise 3:** This is a two-step question. Help students recognize that they will need to find how many students have already answered, and then how many more need to answer for a total of 9 students.

PROFICIENT students can read the graphs and understand how to answer the questions. They may need support in thinking of the steps in a multi-step question.

- **Exercise 2:** The use of the word *or* in this exercise may cause confusion. Most students think to subtract rather than add. Explain that students are finding how many students chose square and how many chose triangle. They want to find how many chose either the square or the triangle, so they need to combine them.
- **Exercise 3:** Have students explain their solution process with a partner.

Additional Support

- Have students write the number of responses for each category next to the name of the category. This may help speed their solution process as they will not need to recount.

Extension: Adding Rigor

- Have students write the equations that would solve each of the questions.

Name ____________________

Apply and Grow: Practice

2.

Favorite Shape								
Square	☺	☺	☺	☺	☺	☺	☺	
Circle	☺	☺	☺	☺	☺			
Triangle	☺	☺	☺	☺	☺	☺	☺	

Each ☺ = 1 student.

How many fewer students chose circle than square?

7 − 5 = 2

2 fewer students

How many students chose square or triangle?

14 students

---

3. DIG DEEPER! You ask 9 students to name their favorite rainy-day activity. Complete the bar graph to show how many chose reading. Think: How do you know? 3 + 1 = 4   9 − 4 = 5

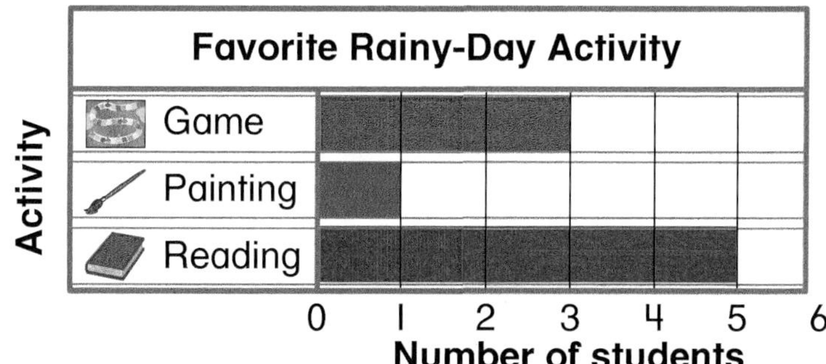

Chapter 11 | Lesson 5 567

ELL Support

Check for understanding of Lesson 11.5. Read each direction aloud. Allow students time to write questions and answers. When they have finished, have them share their question with another student and come to an agreement if they disagree on the answer. Provide support as needed.

Laurie's Notes

Think and Grow: Modeling Real Life

The applications today give students another chance to ask and answer their own question about data.

- ? **Preview**: "What do you think the data in this graph shows? What game do you think you, Newton, and Descartes are playing?"
- "Tell what you notice about the data. We are going to write and answer our own question. Discuss with your partner a question we could ask and answer."
- Have several students suggest questions, and let the class vote on the question to ask. You can list questions for students to look at for Exercise 4 as well. Write in the selected question and discuss how to find the answer.
- Exercise 4 has the same directions as the example. Students work from a tally chart. Encourage all students to ask questions that are more complex than "how many laps did Newton run?" You might tell students that they need to use at least two of the categories in their question.
- Students can compare and share their questions, or challenge each other with their questions. "Whose question is trickiest?"
- ◉ "Use your thumb signals to show how you did today with our learning. How did you do with answering questions from the data? How did you do with asking questions?"
- ? "Were there any types of questions that were easy for you to answer? Were there any questions that were a little harder for you to answer?"

Closure

- Give students any graph of data to look at. If you have a class set of data that hasn't been used often, use that.
- Ask your partner a question to answer from the data. Now trade roles.
- Have students share something they will remember about using a data graph.

Think and Grow: Modeling Real Life

Write and answer a question using the bar graph.

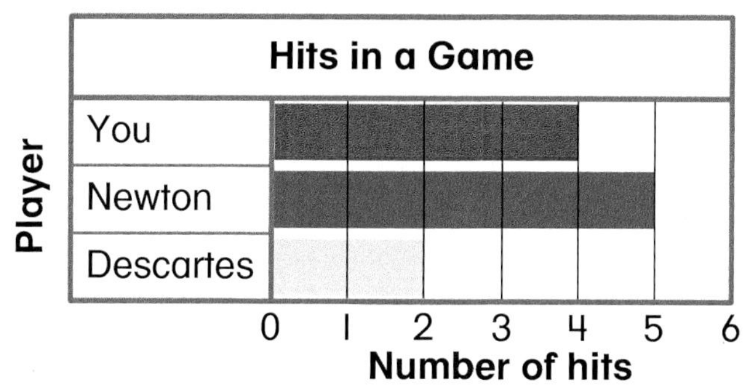

Sample answer: How many more hits did Newton get than Descartes? Newton got 3 more hits.

Show and Grow *I can think deeper!*

4. Write and answer a question using the tally chart.

Laps Run	
You	||
Descartes	~~||||~~
Newton	|

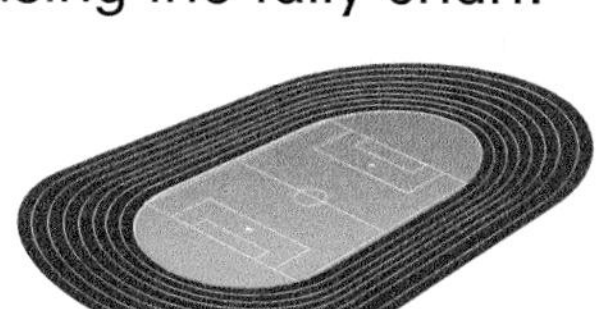

Sample answer: Who ran the most laps?

Descartes ran the most laps.

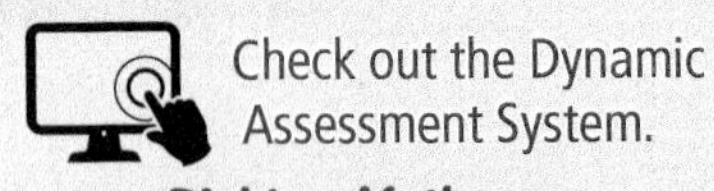
Check out the Dynamic
Assessment System.
BigIdeasMath.com

Scaffold assignments to support all students in their learning progression. Revisit with spaced practice to move every student toward proficiency.

Connect and Extend Learning

Practice Notes

- If students are having difficulties, remind them to think about the operation (addition or subtraction) that would be used to answer each question.

Prior Skills

- **Exercises 4 and 5:** Grade 1, Adding Tens and Ones

Cross-Curricular Connections

Social Studies

- Divide a map of the United States into three shaded regions. Have students create a tally mark chart to keep track of the number of states in each region. Then have them create a bar graph or picture graph. Finally, have them write a question about the graph and include its answer.

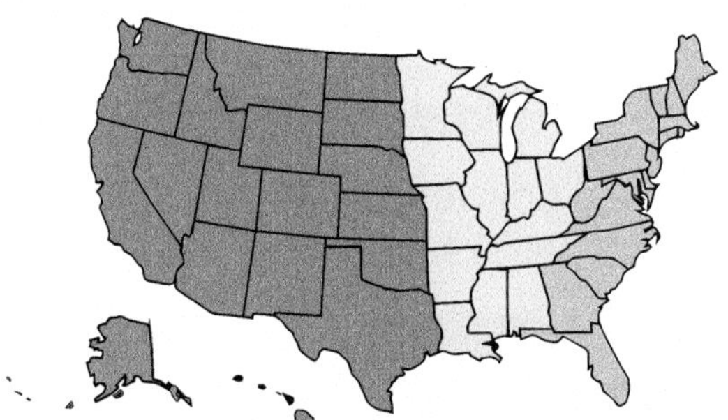

Name ______________________

Practice 11.5

Learning Target: Use data from graphs to answer questions.

My Writing Tools						
Marker	◯	◯	◯	◯		
Pencil	◯	◯	◯	◯	◯	

Each ◯ = 1 writing tool.

How many writing tools do you have?

4 + 5 = 9   9 writing tools

1.

Stuffed Animals

Animal	Number of stuffed animals
Bear	7
Penguin	2
Dog	5

Number of stuffed animals: 0 1 2 3 4 5 6 7 8

How many more dogs are there than penguins?

5 − 2 = 3   3 more dogs

How many bears and dogs are there in all?

7 + 5 = 12   12 bears and dogs

Connect and Extend Learning

Extend Student Learning

Interpersonal

- Create a class bar graph on a topic that interests students. Examples can include favorite class, lunch, recess toy, or book. Have students choose their favorite category and color in part of the bar graph that you created. Finally, have students write a question about the graph and trade it with another student. Then they can answer each other's questions, and trade them back to check that they are correct.

Lesson Resources	
Surface Level	**Deep Level**
Resources by Chapter • Extra Practice • Reteach Differentiating the Lesson Skills Review Handbook Skills Trainer	Resources by Chapter • Enrichment and Extension Graphic Organizers Dynamic Assessment System • Lesson Practice

2. **DIG DEEPER!** You ask 19 students to name their favorite fruit. Complete the tally chart to show how many chose apples. Explain how you know.

Favorite Fruit	
Apple	𝍸 𝍸
Banana	𝍸 ॥
Orange	॥

There are 9 students who named banana or orange as their favorite fruit. So 10 students named apple.

3. **Modeling Real Life** Write and answer a question using the bar graph.

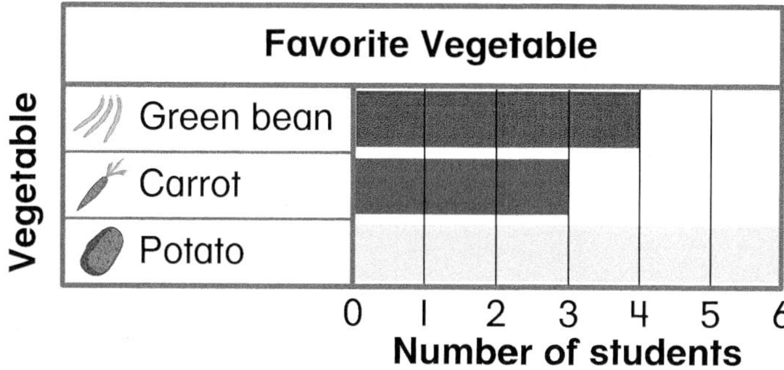

Sample answer: How many more students like potatoes than green beans? 2 more students like potatoes.

Review & Refresh

4. 51 + 40 = 91

5. 76 + 3 = 79

ELL Support

Have students practice verbal language by working on the Performance Task in groups. To make the task more manageable, have two groups work together to only collect data from their own groups. Circulate to monitor their language. Have each group discuss the following questions: "How many students have each eye color? How long is each bar? How do you determine the total number of students asked? What is your question and answer?" Expect students to perform according to their proficiency level.

Beginner students may use single words or short phrases.
Intermediate students may answer using phrases or simple sentences.
Advanced students may answer using detailed sentences and help guide the process used to find answers.

Laurie's Notes

Performance Task

In this task, students will represent and interpret data by surveying students in their class about their eye color. Gauge the differences in eye colors within the classroom and choose the three colors that students will use for their chart and graph. Have students color the inner circle of each eye in the tally chart and the bar graph. In Exercise 2, students may need help labeling their graph. Use student responses to gauge their understanding about representing and interpreting data.

- Decide ahead of time whether students will be working independently, in pairs, or in groups.
- Pause between direction lines for students to complete each step.
- Have students share their work and thinking with others. Discuss as a class.

Exercise	Answers and Notes	Points
1	Check students' work.	3
2	Check students' work.	4
3	Count the tallies. Find the sum of the bar lengths for all the colors.	3
4	*Sample answer:* Which eye color does the greatest number of students have? Most of the students have brown eyes.	2
	Total	12

Name ______________________________

Performance Task 11

1. **Graph Data** Ask your classmates about their eye colors. Use your data to complete the tally chart.

Check students' work.

Eye Color	

2. Use your tally chart to complete the bar graph.

Check students' work.

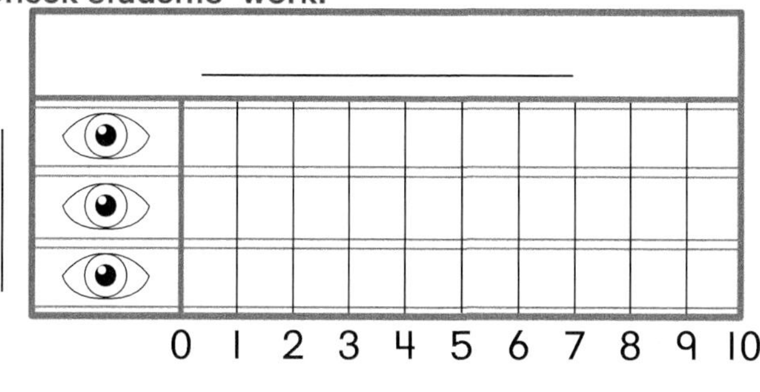

3. Describe two ways to tell how many students you asked.

Count the tallies.

Find the sum of the bar lengths for all the colors.

4. Write and answer a question about your graphs.

Sample answer: **Which eye color does the greatest number of students have? Most of the students have brown eyes.**

Check out the interactive version in the Game Library.
BigIdeasMath.com

Laurie's Notes

Spin and Graph

Materials

- 1 spinner per student
- 1 copy of Spin and Graph Questions* per pair

**Found in the Instructional Resources*

Spin and Graph takes students through creating, representing, and explaining data. This will allow you to assess where students excel and have difficulties with data.

? "What do you notice about the spinner, tally chart, and the bar graph?" *Sample answer:* The same colors are used on all of them. "What do you think we are going to do with the spinner?" *Sample answer:* graph the spins

- "Today, you are going to create and represent data using the colors on the spinner."
- Review the directions while modeling how to complete the chart.
- Explain that they will spin 10 times and then answer the questions on the Spin and Graph Questions page.
- **Note:** Students can do this independently, or with a partner.
- While students work, look for students who are answering the questions by counting and those who are using addition and subtraction to answer.
- **Extension:** Have students spin 10 times again and create another tally chart and bar graph for this data. Students can compare the two graphs.
- When students are finished, discuss the strategies students used to answer the questions.

Closure

? **Exit Ticket:** Display a graph created during a Dig In, or one made by a student. Ask, "Which group has the most? How many more does this group have than the other two groups?"

Spin and Graph

To Play: Spin 10 times. Complete the tally chart. Then complete the bar graph. Answer the Spin and Graph Questions about your graph.

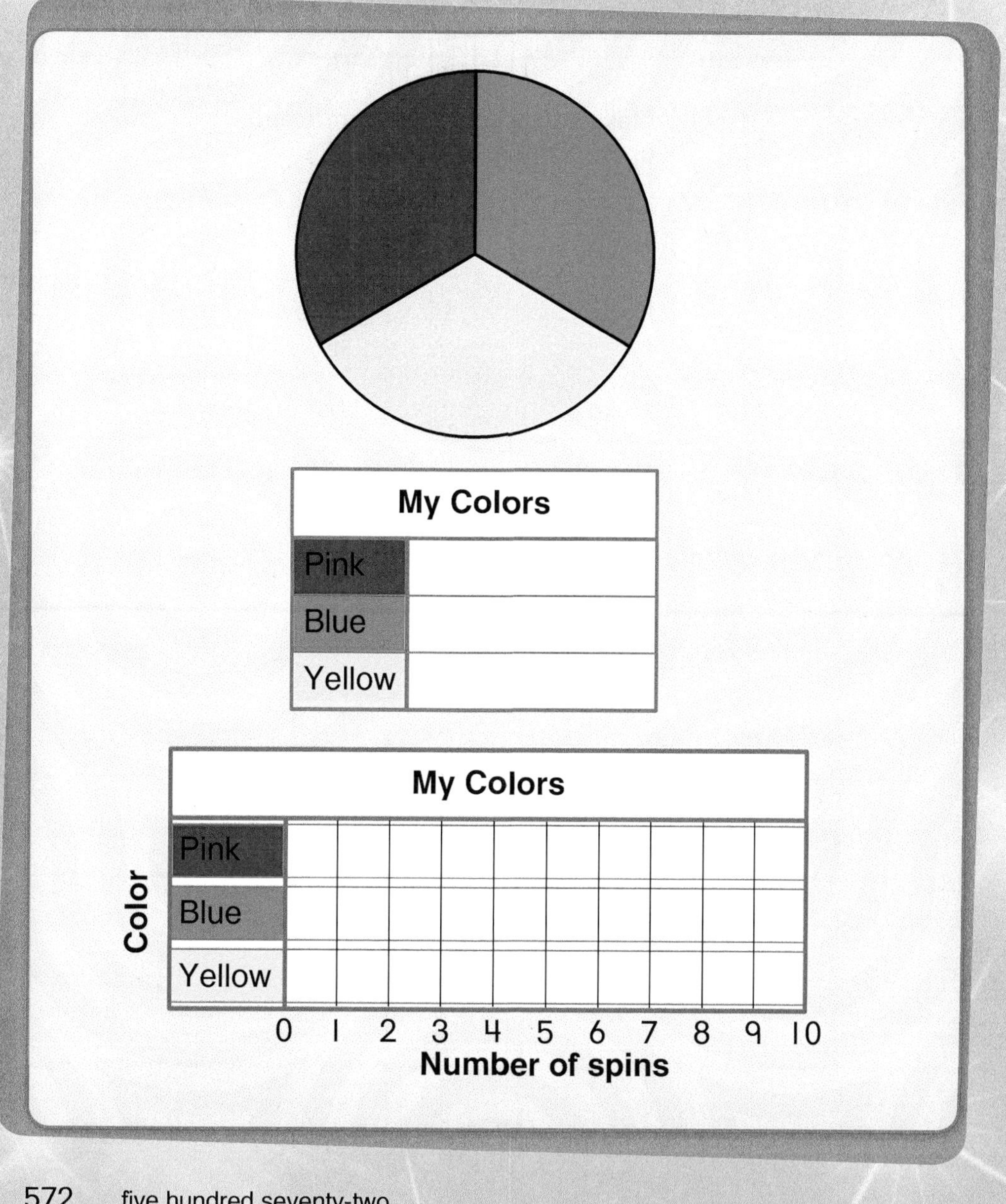

My Colors	
Pink	
Blue	
Yellow	

Learning Target Correlation

Lesson	Learning Target	Exercises
11.1	Make a tally chart to organize and understand data.	1, 2
11.2	Understand the data shown by a picture graph.	3
11.3	Understand the data shown by a bar graph.	4
11.4	Make picture graphs and bar graphs.	5, 6
11.5	Use data from graphs to answer questions.	7, 8

Name ____________________

Chapter 11 Practice

11.1 Sort and Organize Data

Complete the tally chart.

1.

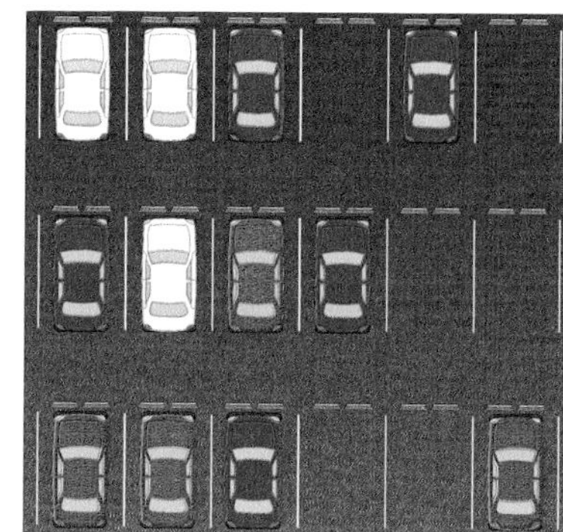

Cars	
Red	||||
White	|||
Blue	~~||||~~

2.

Pets	
Cat	||||
Dog	||
Fish	~~||||~~ |||

Chapter Resources

Surface Level	Deep Level	Transfer Level
Resources by Chapter • Extra Practice • Reteach Differentiating the Lesson Skills Review Handbook Skills Trainer Game Library Math Musicals	Resources by Chapter • Enrichment and Extension Graphic Organizers Game Library Math Musicals	Dynamic Assessment System • Chapter Test Assessment Book • Chapter Tests A and B

11.2 Read and Interpret Picture Graphs

3.

Favorite School Subject							
Art	☺	☺	☺	☺	☺		
Math	☺	☺	☺	☺	☺	☺	
Science	☺	☺	☺	☺			

Each ☺ = 1 student.

How many students chose science? 4

Which subject is the least favorite?  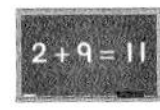 

11.3 Read and Interpret Bar Graphs

4.

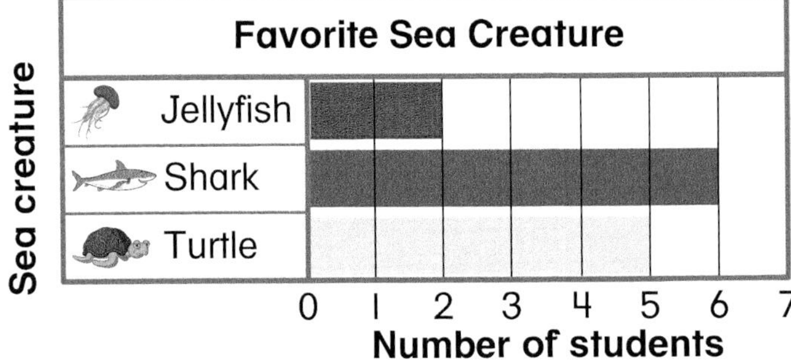

How many students chose turtle? 5

Which is the most favorite sea creature?   

11.4 Represent Data

5. Complete the bar graph.

Beads	
Blue	𝍸
Red	||
Yellow	||||

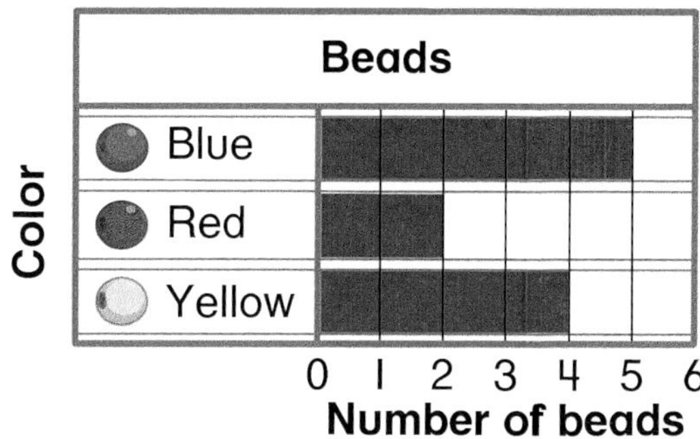

---

6. **Modeling Real Life** You ask 13 students whether they like volleyball or basketball. 7 like volleyball. The rest like basketball. Complete the picture graph.

Favorite Sport								
Volleyball	☺	☺	☺	☺	☺	☺	☺	
Basketball	☺	☺	☺	☺	☺	☺		

Each ☺ = 1 student.

11.5 Solve Problems Involving Data

7.

Favorite Color	
Purple	𝍸 ||||
Green	𝍸
Orange	||

How many fewer students chose green than purple?

$9 - 5 = 4$ 4 fewer students

How many students were asked?

$9 + 5 + 2 = 16$ 16 students

---

8. **Modeling Real Life** Write and answer a question using the bar graph.

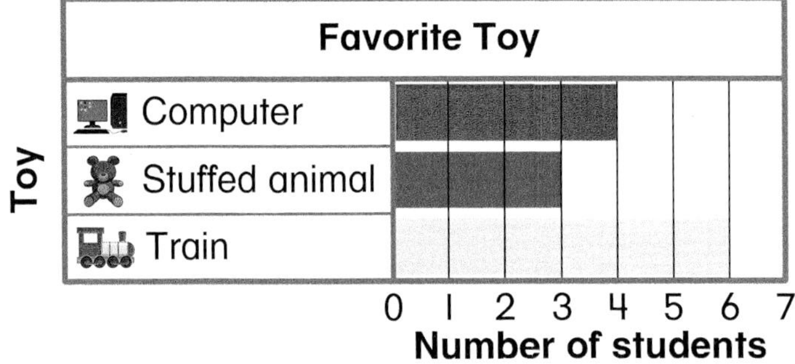

Sample answer: Is the number of students who choose computers or stuffed animals greater than the number of students who choose trains? Yes, $4 + 3 = 7$ and $7 > 6$.

Centers

Center 1: Spin and Graph

Materials: 1 spinner per student, 1 copy of Spin and Graph Questions* per pair

Have students complete the activity. See page T-572 for the directions.

Center 2: Skills Trainer

Materials: computers or devices with Internet access

Have students go to *BigIdeasMath.com* to access the Skills Trainer.

Center 3: Tally Mark Dominoes

Materials per pair: Tally Mark Dominoes*, scissors, crayons

Have students cut out and shuffle the Tally Mark Dominoes. One domino is set on the table to start and the remaining dominoes are divided up equally (13 for each student). Students take turns placing one of their dominoes by matching a number and set of tally marks. You may want to have each student color their dominoes a different color to keep track of how many of their cards are on the table.

Center 4: Graph-Tac-Toe

Materials per pair: Graph-Tac-Toe*, counters

Students take turns choosing a space on the board, reading the question about the graph and answering it. If the student is correct, they put a counter on the space. If the student is not correct, then the other student takes their turn. Play until someone gets three spaces in a row or the whole board is covered.

Center 5: Graph Dominoes

Materials: dominoes, whiteboards

Have students select twenty dominoes. Students look at the sides of each domino and decide if the number is greater than 5. Have students create a graph using a whiteboard titled "Greater Than 5" and write the categories 0 sides, 1 side, and 2 sides on the graph. Students will place each domino in a category on the graph based on how many sides have numbers greater than 5. Students continue until all the dominoes are used. Encourage students to ask a partner a question about the graph they have made.

**Found in the Instructional Resources*

Chapter Assessment Guide

Chapter tests are available in the Assessment Book. An alternative assessment option is listed below.

Visual-Spatial

Prepare ahead of time 3 different color pieces of confetti. Have each student grab a handful of confetti and count how many of each color they have. Hand out posters for students to divide into thirds. On the first part of their poster, students create a tally chart showing how many confetti pieces they have of each color. On the second part, students create a picture graph. Students create a bar graph on the third part. Finally, have students write and answer one question about each graph in the corresponding part of the poster.

Task	Points
Tally chart	2 points
Picture graph	2 points
Bar graph	2 points
1 question and correct answer about each graph	6 points
Total	12 points

My Thoughts on the Chapter

What worked...

Teacher Tip

Not allowed to write in your teaching edition? Use sticky notes to record your thoughts.

What did not work...

What I would do differently...

Learning Target Correlation

Item	Section	Learning Target
1	7.6	Identify numbers that are 1 more, 1 less, 10 more, and 10 less than a number.
2	9.3	Make a 10 to add a one-digit number and a two-digit number.
3	10.1	Order objects by length.
4	11.1	Make a tally chart to organize and understand data.
5	4.3	Use the *count on* strategy to find a sum.
6	8.2	Use mental math to subtract 10.
7	7.2, 7.4	Compare two numbers within 100. Use symbols to compare two numbers within 100.
8	9.6	Solve addition word problems.
9	10.3	Use like objects to measure length.
10	8.5	Subtract tens.
11	11.3	Understand the data shown by a bar graph.
12	2.5	Use the *doubles plus 1* and *doubles minus 1* strategies to find a sum.

Name ______________________________

Cumulative Practice 1–11

1. Match each number on the left with a number that is 10 more.

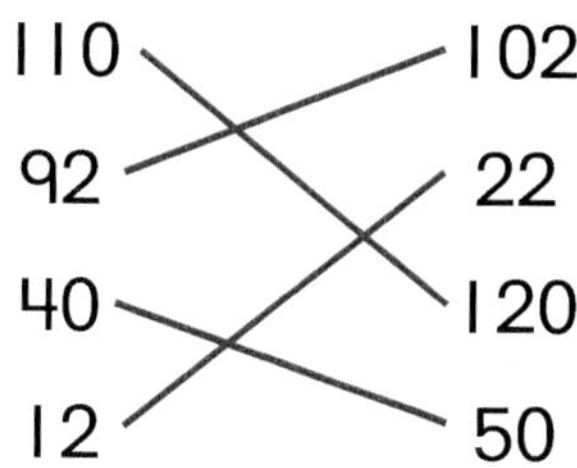

110	102
92	22
40	120
12	50

2. Complete.

56 + 6

56 + (4) + (2)

60 + (2)

56 + 6 = 62

3. Order from shortest to longest.

blue

yellow

red

yellow, blue, red

4. Shade the circle next to the number that tells how many horns there are.

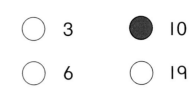

Instruments	
Drum	|||
Horn	𝍸 𝍸
Bell	𝍸 |

○ 3  10

○ 6 ○ 19

---

5. Shade the circle next to the sum.

12 + 5 = _____

○ 15  17

○ 16 ○ 7

---

6. There are 85 pages in a book. You read 10 of them. How many pages are left?

○ 95 ○ 85

 75 ○ 80

7. Is each sentence true?

52 is greater than 36.	(Yes)	No
100 < 90	Yes	(No)
75 is less than 57.	Yes	(No)
89 > 81	(Yes)	No

8. You collect 22 cans for a food drive. Your friend collects 36. How many cans do you and your friend collect in all?

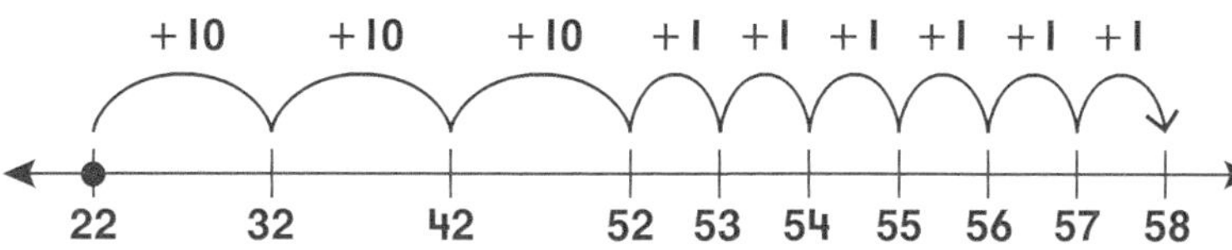

58 cans

9. Measure.

about 4 color tiles

10. Shade the circles next to the choices that match the model.

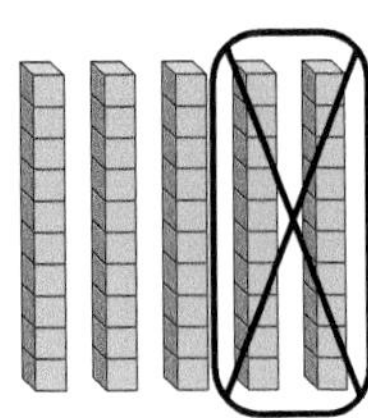

- ○ 50 − 30
- ● 5 tens − 2 tens
- ● 50 − 20
- ○ 3 tens − 2 tens

11.

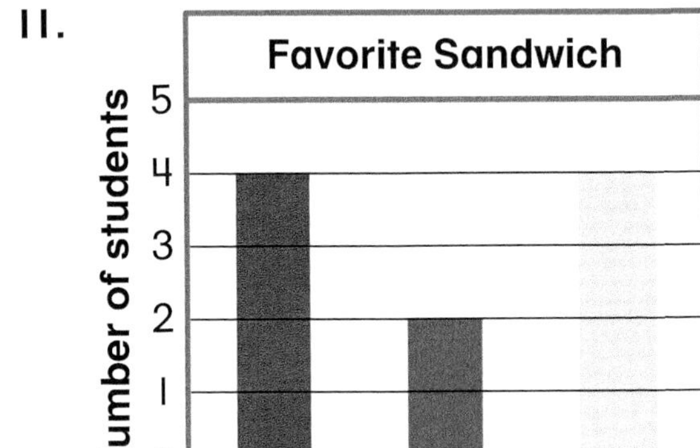

How many students chose ham? 2

Which sandwich is the least favorite?

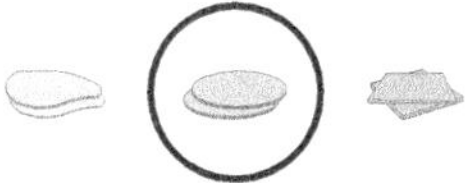

12. Use each card once to write an addition equation.

3 5 2

3 + 2 = 5

12 Tell Time

Chapter Overview

Lesson	Learning Target	Success Criteria
12.1 Tell Time to the Hour	Use the hour hand to tell time to the hour.	• Tell what number the hour hand is pointing to. • Explain how to tell time to the hour. • Draw to show the time to an hour. • Tell what one hour earlier or later is.
12.2 Tell Time to the Half Hour	Use the hour hand to tell time to the half hour.	• Tell what numbers the hour hand is pointing between. • Explain how to tell time to the half hour. • Draw to show the time to the half hour.
12.3 Tell Time to the Hour and Half Hour	Use the hour and minute hands to tell time to the hour and half hour.	• Tell where the hour and minute hands are pointing. • Write and tell the time in two ways. • Draw to show the time to the hour or half hour.
12.4 Tell Time Using Analog and Digital Clocks	Use analog and digital clocks to tell time.	• Read and write hours and half hours on analog and digital clocks. • Tell when analog and digital clocks are the same. • Tell and draw what one hour earlier or later is.

Chapter Learning Target:
Understand time.

Chapter Success Criteria:
- Identify numbers on a clock.
- Explain how to tell time to the hour.
- Compare different times on the clock.
- Draw to show the time.

Progressions

Through the Grades		
Kindergarten	**Grade 1**	**Grade 2**
• Write numbers from 0 to 20.	• Tell time to the hour and half hour using an analog clock. • Tell time to the hour and half hour using a digital clock.	• Tell time to the nearest five minutes on analog and digital clocks. • Tell time to the nearest five minutes using A.M. and P.M.

	Through the Chapter			
Standard	**12.1**	**12.2**	**12.3**	**12.4**
1.MD.B.3 Tell and write time in hours and half hours using analog and digital clocks.	●	●	●	★

Key: ▲ = Preparing ● = Learning ★ = Complete

Laurie's Overview

About the Math

Students have had many adults or older siblings talk to them about time. They hear "five more minutes" or "at 6 o'clock." However, most first grade students do not have any notion of time. They do not understand how long an hour is, or what 3:00 means. To help students get a sense of time, set alarms or timers to alert you on the hour for Lesson 12.1 and half hour for Lesson 12.2. You can point out the hands on the clock in your room when the alarm sounds. It will also start to help students develop a sense of units of time – how long an hour or half hour is.

Some students may have familiarity with a digital clock. For example, they know when 8:00 is showing on the digital clock, it is bedtime. In this chapter, students learn about telling time to the hour and half hour.

This chapter introduces the following foundational big ideas about time:

- Time is a measureable period described by units. In first grade, the units are an hour, half hour or minute.
- Time is shown on two types of clocks: analog and digital. Both clocks show the hour and minutes.
- Minutes are smaller units that make up a half hour (30 minutes) or an hour (60 minutes).

In first grade, students will tell time to the hour and half hour. They use the phrases *o'clock* and *half past* to describe the time until the final lesson, when digital time is taught.

The analog clock can be a challenge to learn to read. With the proliferation of digital technology, many students and even some adults do not read analog clocks today. Yet the advantage to being able to read an analog clock over a digital clock is showing "close to" times. Students who see the analog clock showing 3:55 realize that it is almost 4:00 from the position of the hands. With a digital clock, students would need to recognize that there are 60 minutes in an hour, and 60 − 55 is 5 minutes which is not very long. In third grade, clocks are often used to make sense of fractions.

The lessons begin with students working with one-handed clocks. They recognize that time to the hour means that the hour hand will point directly at a number, and time that is half past an hour means that the hour hand will be halfway between two numbers. It is not until the third lesson that students begin to work with the minute hand. They learn that the minute hand pointing to the top of the clock (12) means no minutes have passed and it would be "on the hour" or "o'clock." At half past, the minute hand has moved halfway around the clock and points to the 6. The final lesson brings together the digital clock and the analog clock.

Representations

- Students will work with their analog clocks to move hands and model times. For the first two lessons, only the hour hand is used. Students are directed to leave the minute hand pointing up to the 12 and ignore it from there in Lesson 12.1, learning *o'clock.* In Lesson 12.2 students are directed to leave the minute hand pointing down at the 6 while learning *half past* an hour.

- Digital clocks are drawn in this chapter. If you have digital clocks, a smart phone, digital watch, etc. it will be helpful to show students on the hour and half hour.

Many of the application stories involve having students reason about an hour earlier or later than a given time, and half an hour after a given time. These applications involve students telling the beginning time, reasoning about the passing of time, and then showing the resulting time on a clock.

Continue to reinforce time and the passing of time with students throughout each day for the rest of the year. Learning to read time is a skill that can be taught, but having a sense of time and the passing of time is much more difficult.

Check out the
virtual manipulatives.
BigIdeasMath.com

Chapter Materials and Resources

The primary materials and resources needed for this chapter are listed below. Other materials may be needed for the additional support ideas provided throughout the chapter.

Classroom Materials	Chapter Opener	12.1	12.2	12.3	12.4	Connect and Grow
scissors	•					•
student clocks		•	•	•	•	*
demonstration clock		+	+	+	+	+
whiteboards					*	•
tape						*
index cards						*

Instructional Resources	Chapter Opener	12.1	12.2	12.3	12.4	Connect and Grow
Vocabulary Cards	•	+	+	+	+	
Time Flip and Find Cards						•
Time Cube						*

• class set + teacher only * per pair/group

Suggested Pacing

Day 1	Chapter Opener	Performance Task Preview		Vocabulary			
Day 2	Lesson 12.1	Warm-Up	Dig In	Explore	Think	Apply: Practice	Think: Modeling Real Life
Day 3	Lesson 12.2	Warm-Up	Dig In	Explore	Think	Apply: Practice	Think: Modeling Real Life
Day 4	Lesson 12.3	Warm-Up	Dig In	Explore	Think	Apply: Practice	Think: Modeling Real Life
Day 5	Lesson 12.4	Warm-Up	Dig In	Explore	Think	Apply: Practice	Think: Modeling Real Life
Day 6	Connect And Grow	Performance Task			Activity	Chapter Practice	
Day 7		Centers					
Day 8	Chapter Assessment	Chapter Assessment					

Year-to-Date: 132 Days

Mathematical Practices

Students have opportunities to develop aspects of the mathematical practices throughout the chapter. Here are some examples.

1. **Make Sense of Problems and Persevere in Solving Them**
   12.3 Explore and Grow, *p. 595*
2. **Reason Abstractly and Quantitatively**
   12.4 Practice Exercise 9, *p. 606*
3. **Construct Viable Arguments and Critique the Reasoning of Others**
   12.3 Apply and Grow: Practice Exercise 13, *p. 597*
4. **Model with Mathematics**
   12.2 Practice Exercise 8, *p. 594*
5. **Use Appropriate Tools Strategically**
   12.3 Think and Grow: Modeling Real Life, *p. 598*
6. **Attend to Precision**
   12.1 Apply and Grow: Practice Exercise 13, *p. 585*
7. **Look for and Make Use of Structure**
   12.1 Explore and Grow, *p. 583*
8. **Look for and Express Regularity in Repeated Reasoning**
   12.2 Apply and Grow: Practice, *p. 591*

Laurie's Notes

Performance Task Preview

- Preview the page to gauge students' prior knowledge about going on a field trip and telling time.
- ? "Have you ever been on a field trip?" Students will be excited to share the different places they have visited on a field trip. They may even share another activity the class experienced within the school's property.
- ? "Where would you like to go? How long does it take to get there?"
- In the Performance Task at the end of the chapter, students will tell time using a field trip schedule.

12 Tell Time

Chapter Learning Target:
Understand time.

Chapter Success Criteria:
- I can identify numbers on a clock.
- I can explain how to tell time to the hour.
- I can compare different times on the clock.
- I can draw to show the time.

- Have you ever been on a field trip?
- Where would you like to go? How long does it take to get there?

Check out the digital flash cards.
BigIdeasMath.com

Laurie's Notes

Vocabulary Review

- ? **Preview:** "What do you see on the page?" bird, boy, grass, ball
- Have students say each review word out loud. Have students discuss how the words are related.
- ? "Where is the bird located? _____ the boy?" above "Where is the ground or grass? _____ the boy?" below
- Direct students to the lower half of the page. Have students use their vocabulary cards to go over the new words.
- **Extension:** Have students relate the review words to the position of the numbers on the clock.

Chapter 12 Vocabulary

Activity

- **Echo:** Say a vocabulary word and then pass an "echo ball" to a student. The student echos, or repeats, the word and then passes the echo ball back to you. Students need to listen carefully to repeat the word correctly. Consider challenging the students by having them define the words after they echo them.
  Teaching Tip: Decide how you are going to have your students pass the ball before you begin. Silent and gentle hand passes are recommended.
  Note: Many of these terms are brand new to students. Consider showing a visual of each vocab word or using a clock manipulative for certain words.

ELL Support

Discuss the two types of clocks that people use to tell time—analog and digital. Show examples of each. Explain that digital clocks tell time by showing only numbers, while analog clocks use moving arrows known as hands. Explain that a timepiece worn on the wrist is called a watch, while other types of timepieces are called clocks. In some languages, such as Spanish, the same word is used to describe both a clock and a wristwatch.

Newton & Descartes's Math Musicals

with Differentiated Rich Math Tasks

Newton and Descartes team up in these educational stories and songs to bring mathematics to life! Use the Newton and Descartes hand puppets to act out the stories. Encourage students to sing the songs to take full advantage of the power of music to learn math. Visit *www.MathMusicals.com* to access all the adventures, songs, and activities available!

Name ______________________

12 Vocabulary

Review Words
above
below
next to

Organize It

Use the review words to complete the graphic organizer.

above

next to

below

Define It

Use your vocabulary cards to identify the word.

1. 

analog clock

2. 

digital clock

3. 

hour hand

4. 

minute hand

Chapter 12 Vocabulary Cards

analog clock	digital clock
half hour	half past
hour	hour hand
minute	minute hand

3:00
half past 3
A half hour is 30 minutes.
An hour is 60 minutes.
60 minutes is 1 hour.

Chapter 12 Vocabulary Cards

© Big Ideas Learning, LLC
© Big Ideas Learning, LLC
3 o'clock
© Big Ideas Learning, LLC
© Big Ideas Learning, LLC
© Big Ideas Learning, LLC
© Big Ideas Learning, LLC
© Big Ideas Learning, LLC
© Big Ideas Learning, LLC

12.1

Check out the
Dynamic Classroom.

BigIdeasMath.com

Laurie's Notes

COMMON CORE STATE STANDARDS
1.MD.B.3

Learning Target

Use the hour hand to tell time to the hour.

Success Criteria

- Tell what number the hour hand is pointing to.
- Explain how to tell time to the hour.
- Draw to show the time to an hour.
- Tell what one hour earlier or later is.

Warm-Up

Practice opportunities for the following are available in the Resources by Chapter or at *BigIdeasMath.com*.

- Daily skills
- Vocabulary
- Prerequisite skills

ELL Support

Most students will be familiar with the word *hand* from talking about parts of the body, so they may find talking about telling time with an analog clock somewhat confusing at first. Explain that when they look at an analog clock, there are two arrows known as hands, an hour hand and a minute hand. Draw a clock and point out the short hour hand and longer minute hand.

Preparing to Teach

Students have heard about time and the language of time. Most students do not understand time or know how to tell time on an analog clock. In this lesson, students are introduced to telling time to the hour. They learn about the hour hand and telling time as o'clock.

Materials

- student clocks
- demonstration clock

Dig In (Circle Time)

Students have a lot of vocabulary to learn and practice during the Dig In. They will compare an analog clock with two hands to practicing with a one-handed clock. They will describe what they see on the clock. Students experience "o'clock" and the meaning of the hour hand.

- Distribute student clocks.
- "We talk about time a lot. Tell me some things you know about time and clocks. What words do you hear that mean time?"
- "When we talk about time we often say things like, dinner will be ready at six o'clock. When we say o'clock that means 6 is the hour. Today we are going to only talk about hours and we will use the phrase o'clock to mean the time to the hour."
- "Let's look at our clocks. What do you notice?" Students point out the numbers and two hands. Tell students the name of the hands, but let them know that today we are only going to work with the hour hand. Have them point the minute hand to the 12 and leave it there.
- ◉ "We start school at about 9 o'clock. To show 9 o'clock, the hour hand points to the 9. Show 9 o'clock on your clocks."
- ◉ "Every time the hour hand points to a number, that is the time in o'clock. I will show you time on my clock, and you tell your partner what time it is."
- ? Practice several different times with you showing the time on the demonstration clock and students telling you what time it is. Ask, "To what number is the hour hand pointing? What time is it?"
- ◉ "This time I will tell you a time, and you show me the time on your clocks." Give several times for students to model.
- ◉ "Today we will learn how to tell time to the hour. Tell your partner one thing you already know."

? Teaching Prompt ◉ Learning Target

Name
Tell Time to the Hour
12.1
Learning Target: Use the hour hand to tell time to the hour.
Explore and Grow
Write the missing numbers.
1 2 3 4 5 6 7 8 9 10 11 12
12
11
1
10
2
9
3
8
4
7
5
6
Structure
How do the numbers help you know which way the clock hands move?
© Big Ideas Learning, LLC
Chapter 12 | Lesson 1
five hundred eighty-three
583

Explore and Grow

- "We have worked with number lines. Our first number lines started at 0 and went up to 10. Look at the number line at the top of the page. It starts at 1. What number do you think it went to before two of the numbers were moved?"
- Tell students that they are going to put the numbers from the number line in order around the clock in a circle. Have them tell their partners where they think the number 1 belongs.
- **MP7 Look for and Make Use of Structure:** Students write the numbers in the boxes around the clock. "Tell your partner what you notice about the numbers on the clock."

ELL Support

Explain that the clocks shown here only have an hour hand. When the time is exactly on an hour, the term *o'clock* is used. The example shows two o'clock. After completing the example, have students work in pairs to complete Exercises 1–6. Have one student ask another, "What time is it?" Have them alternate roles for each exercise.

Beginner students may provide one-word answers, such as "two." **Intermediate** students may answer with phrases, such as, "two o'clock." **Advanced** students may answer with sentences, such as, "It's two o'clock."

Laurie's Notes

Think and Grow

Getting Started

- Introduce the vocabulary terms **analog clock**, **hour**, **hour hand**, and **o'clock**. Use the pictures of the analog clock showing 3:00. Let students know that they will be learning about the analog clock, and to begin they will only use one of the hands called the hour hand.
- Students begin to form hour concepts. Set a timer for the day to remind you to show students your classroom clock on the hour. Not only will this point out the hour hand on the clock, but it will also start to give them a sense of how much time passes in an hour.

Teaching Notes

- **Model**: "Newton is looking at the clock. The shorter hand on a clock is called the *hour hand*. It points to the number for the hour. When you put the numbers around the clock during the Explore and Grow, you were writing in the hours we use to tell time. Notice what Newton is saying. When the hour hand moves from one number to the next, an hour has gone by."
- **Model**: "Look at the clock by Newton. To what number is the hour hand pointing? When the hour hand points right at a number, we say it is o'clock. So, since the hour hand is pointing to 2, we say it is 2 o'clock. Fill in the 2 for 2 o'clock."
- Tell your partner what number the hour hand is pointing to in Exercise 1. Now tell your partner what time the clock shows. Write it in."
- Watch as students fill in the remaining times on Exercises 2–6. Have them say the time as they fill in each number.
- **Supporting Learners:** Have students extend the hour hand to find the number to which it is pointing.
- **Extension:** "Look at our classroom clock. Tell your partner which hand is the hour hand. To what number is it most closely pointing? Is it between two numbers? Which ones?"

Think and Grow

analog clock

An **hour** passes when the **hour hand** moves from one number to the next.

It is 2 **o'clock**.

Show and Grow *I can do it!*

Write the time shown by the hour hand.

1.

3 o'clock

2.

7 o'clock

3.

1 o'clock

4.

9 o'clock

5.

6 o'clock

6.

11 o'clock

Scaffold instruction to support all students in their learning. Learning is individualized and you may want to group students differently as they move in and out of these levels with each skill and concept. Student self-assessment and feedback help guide your instructional decisions about how and when to layer support for all students to become proficient learners.

Meeting the needs of all learners.

Laurie's Notes

Apply and Grow: Practice

SCAFFOLDING INSTRUCTION

The first exercises continue having students identify the time as in Exercises 1–6. They progress to drawing in the hour hand. This may be difficult at first. Remind students that the hour hand is short, so they should not draw the hand all the way to the number. If students become used to drawing a long hour hand, they will be confused when the minute hand is added to the clock.

EMERGING students may have some difficulty determining the exact number the hour hand is pointing to because it does not go all the way to the number. Students can use their fingers to trace the hour hand to the number, or draw a light line to the number. They should not have difficulty telling the time once they have the correct number. Some students may need to be reminded how to say "o'clock."

- **Exercises 10–12:** Students may need to be shown how to draw from the center toward the number. The way the hour hand points is most important, but when the minute hand is added to the clock, we do not want students to be used to drawing a long hour hand.

PROFICIENT students will be able to tell the number and the time based on the hour hand. Students should continue to say the time out loud.

- **Exercises 10–12:** Watch as students draw the hour hands. Notice the precision with which they point at the number and the length of the hour hand.
- **Exercise 13:** Have students say the time for all three clocks, and then select the correct clock.

Additional Support

- Students can use a straight edge to see the number to which the hour hand is pointing.
- Let students work with student clocks and move the hands for clarity.

Name ____________________

Apply and Grow: Practice

Write the time shown by the hour hand.

7.

8 o'clock

8.

12 o'clock

9.

4 o'clock

Draw the hour hand to show the time.

10. 5 o'clock

11. 10 o'clock

12. 2 o'clock

13. **Precision** You wake up at 7 o'clock. Which clock shows the time you wake up?

ELL Support

Check for understanding of Lesson 12.1. Read each story aloud as students follow along. Ask the following questions and have students hold up the appropriate number of fingers to answer.

1. What time do you eat dinner?
2. What time does math class start?

Laurie's Notes

Think and Grow: Modeling Real Life

The applications require students to not only recognize the time on a clock, but also reason about an hour before and an hour later. This should be related to adding or subtracting 1 to a number, for in fact it is adding or subtracting one hour.

- **Preview**: "Does anyone know what time they usually eat dinner? People eat at various times... some families eat early around 5:00. Some families eat late, around 7:00. Families in other countries eat dinner very late – around 10:00 at night!" Discuss the story with students.
- "If you eat dinner 1 hour later than your friend, we need to know what time your friend eats. Tell your partner what time your friend eats dinner."
- **MP4 Model with Mathematics**: "If you eat 1 hour later, that is like adding one hour. Your friend eats at 5:00. Tell your partner what time an hour later is." Model drawing the hour hand for 6:00 and fill in 6 in the blank.
- **MP1 Make Sense of Problems**: Review the directions with students in Exercise 14. Ask if 1 hour earlier would add or subtract an hour from the time science class starts. You can say that math class begins 1 hour before science and relate it to the number line.
- **MP3 Construct Viable Arguments**: Explain why an hour later would add 1 hour and an hour earlier would subtract 1 hour.
- ◉ "We have just begun to think about and tell time. So far we have only looked at telling time to the hour with the hour hand. Use your thumb signals to show how well you can tell time to the hour by looking at the hour hand."

Closure

- "Alternate with a partner telling one thing you know about telling time so far. Go back and forth until you run out of things to say."

Think and Grow: Modeling Real Life

You eat dinner 1 hour later than your friend. Show and write the time you eat dinner.

Friend

You

6 o'clock

Show and Grow *I can think deeper!*

14. Math class starts 1 hour earlier than science class. Show and write the time math class starts.

Science Class

Math Class

9 o'clock

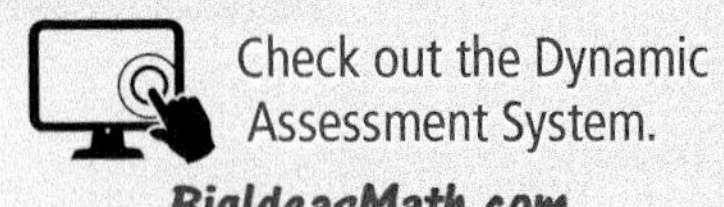
Check out the Dynamic
Assessment System.
BigIdeasMath.com

Scaffold assignments to support all students in their learning progression. Revisit with spaced practice to move every student toward proficiency.

Connect and Extend Learning

Practice Notes

- **Exercises 4–6:** Remind students that the hour hand points directly at the hour given.
- **Exercise 8:** Remind students that 1 hour later means the hour hand moves from one number to the next.

Prior Skills

- **Exercises 10 and 11:** Grade 1, Mental Math: Finding 10 More

Cross-Curricular Connections

Language Arts

- *What Time Is It, Mr. Crocodile?* by Judy Sierra; Read the book aloud to students. Every time Mr. Crocodile does a new activity, read the time to the students. Have each student show that time using their clocks.

Name ______________________

Practice 

Learning Target: Use the hour hand to tell time to the hour.

An hour passes
when the hour hand
moves from one number
to the next.

__3__ o'clock.

Write the time shown by the hour hand.

1.

__10__ o'clock

2.

__5__ o'clock

3.

__1__ o'clock

Draw the hour hand to show the time.

4. 4 o'clock

5. 12 o'clock

6. 8 o'clock

Chapter 12 | Lesson 1 **587**

Connect and Extend Learning

Extend Student Learning

Bodily-Kinesthetic

- Hand each student a clock. Describe a typical day for a student by hours, and have students show each time on their clocks. For example, wake up at 7:00, start school an hour later, etc.

Lesson Resources	
Surface Level	**Deep Level**
Resources by Chapter • Extra Practice • Reteach Differentiating the Lesson Skills Review Handbook Skills Trainer	Resources by Chapter • Enrichment and Extension Graphic Organizers Dynamic Assessment System • Lesson Practice

7. **Precision** You eat a snack at 2 o'clock. Which clock shows the time you eat a snack?

8. **Modeling Real Life** Your friend gets on the bus 1 hour later than you. Show and write the time your friend gets on the bus.

You

Friend

8 o'clock

9. **DIG DEEPER!** In Exercise 8, your cousin wakes up 2 hours before your friend gets on the bus. Write the time your cousin wakes up.

6 o'clock

Review & Refresh

Use mental math.

10. $60 + 10 =$ 70

11. $23 + 10 =$ 33

Check out the
Dynamic Classroom.
BigIdeasMath.com

Laurie's Notes

COMMON CORE
STATE STANDARDS
1.MD.B.3

Learning Target

Use the hour hand to tell time to the half hour.

Success Criteria

- Tell what numbers the hour hand is pointing between.
- Explain how to tell time to the half hour.
- Draw to show the time to the half hour.

Warm-Up

Practice opportunities for the following are available in the Resources by Chapter or at *BigIdeasMath.com.*

- Daily skills
- Vocabulary
- Prerequisite skills

ELL Support

Emphasize that when the hour hand is between two numbers, the time is past the hour. When it is halfway between two numbers, it is half past the earlier number. Draw several examples of half past the hour on the board, and have the class chorally state the time aloud to verify that they understand the concept.

Preparing to Teach

Students worked yesterday with the hour hand to tell time to the hour. Today, we continue using a one-handed clock to tell time to the half hour.

Materials

- student clocks
- demonstration clock

Dig In (Circle Time)

Students will work in the same style as in yesterday's Dig In, learning that when the hour hand points between two numbers, we say it is half past the hour. Students will put their minute hand on the six and leave it there for the Dig In.

- Distribute student clocks.
- "Yesterday we used the hour hand only to tell time to the hour. To review, show where the hour hand would be to show 8 o'clock."
- "We learned yesterday that each number on the clock represents an hour. When the hour hand moves from one number to the next, an hour has gone by. My alarm went off yesterday every hour to show us how long an hour is!"
- ◉ **Model**: "Today, we are going to think about another time that is not o'clock. When the hour hand moves from one number to the next, it does not jump. It does not jump from 4 to 5." Show the hour hand on the demonstration clock move very quickly from 4 to 5. "I can't make it jump. It moves very slowly between the numbers. When it is halfway between two numbers, we say it is *half past an hour*." Move the hour hand to halfway between 4 and 5. "We say it is *half past 4* when the hour hand is here. That is because it is past the 4, but not yet to the 5."
- ◉ Practice several half past times. Show the hour hand between two numbers. Students tell their partner the time as "half past ____."
- ◉ "This time I will tell you a time, and you show the time on your clocks. Remember to leave the minute hand down pointing at the 6 and only move your hour hand." Give students several times to practice.
- ◉ "Today we are continuing to learn about time. Tell your partner where the hour hand points if it is 5 o'clock. Tell where the hour hand points if it is half past 5. Tell your partner what is the difference in the hour hand between a time that is o'clock and a time that is half past."

? Teaching Prompt ◉ Learning Target

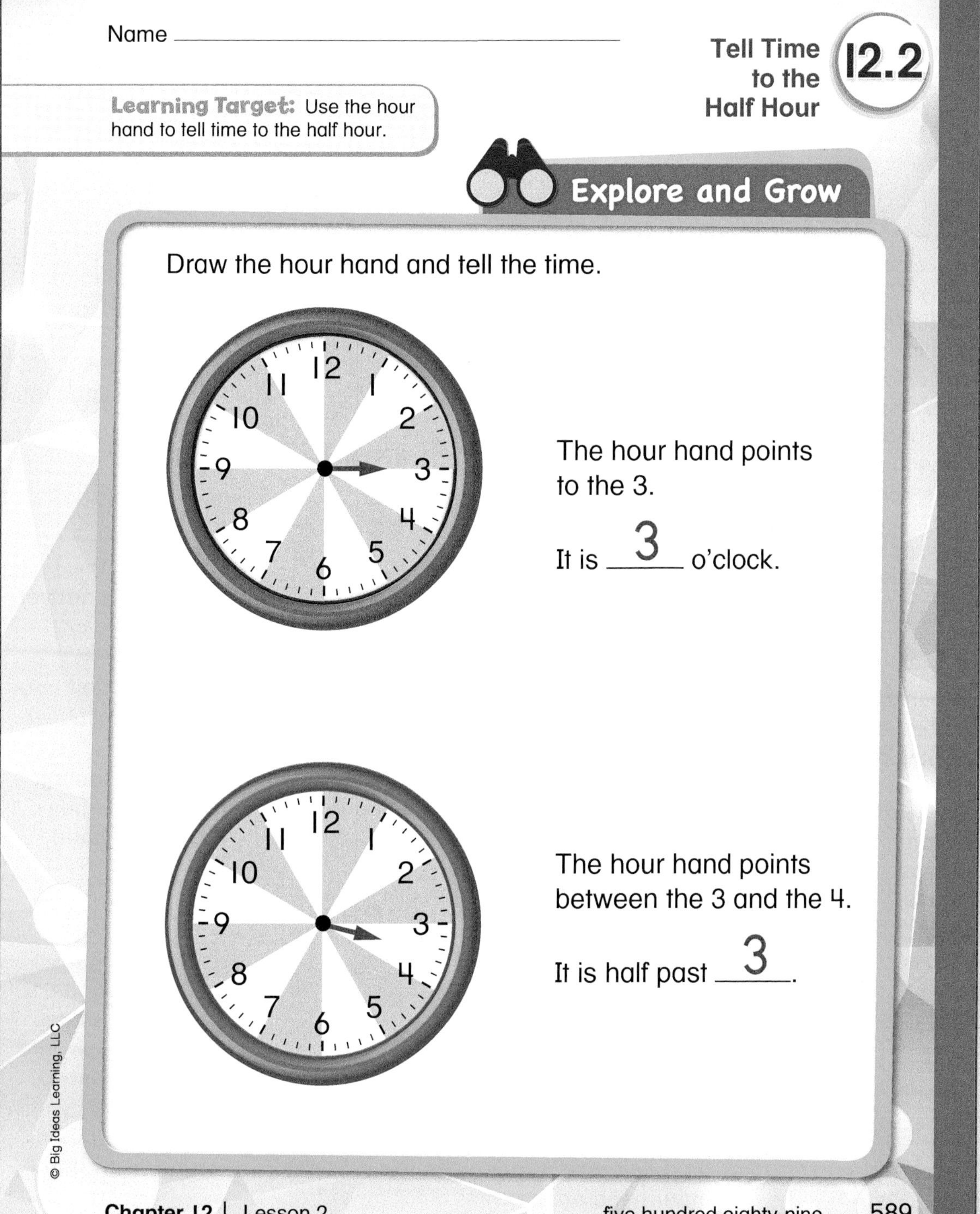

Name
Learning Target: Use the hour hand to tell time to the half hour.
Tell Time to the Half Hour
12.2
Explore and Grow
Draw the hour hand and tell the time.
The hour hand points to the 3.
It is 3 o'clock.
The hour hand points between the 3 and the 4.
It is half past 3.
© Big Ideas Learning, LLC
Chapter 12 | Lesson 2
five hundred eighty-nine 589

Explore and Grow

- Have students complete the top clock and tell their partner how they know they are correct.
- Have students draw the hour hand for the bottom clock. They should tell their partner what time they think it is.
- Observe how students are drawing the hour hands. Are they extending it too far? Is it pointing to the 3 for 3:00 and halfway between numbers for 3:30?

◉ **MP2 Reason Abstractly and Quantitatively:** "Tell you partner why the time on the blue clock is half past 3 and not half past 4."

Laurie's Notes

ELL Support

Explain that the clocks shown here only show the hour hand. Each hour hand is halfway between two numbers. The example shows half past one. After completing the example, have students work in pairs to complete Exercises 1–6. Have one student ask another, "What time is it?" Have them alternate roles for each exercise.

Beginner students may provide phrases, such as, "half past one." **Intermediate** and **Advanced** students may answer with sentences, such as, "It's half past one."

Think and Grow

Getting Started

- We continue telling time to the half hour by noticing that the hour hand is halfway between two numbers. This signifies that it is past the first hour, but not yet to the second hour. Set a timer to go off on the half hour. This will let students look at the clock to see the position of the hour hand. It also gives students a feel for how much time half an hour is.
- Introduce the vocabulary terms **half past** and **half hour**. Review *analog clock* and *hour hand*.

Teaching Notes

- **Model:** "Notice that the hour hand is halfway between the 1 and the 2. That means it has already been 1 o'clock. It is not yet 2 o'clock. That means it is half past 1."
- **Model:** "Descartes says that when the hour hand moves halfway to the next number, a half hour has passed. A half hour also passes when the hour hand moves from halfway between numbers to the next number."
- **MP8 Look for and Express Regularity in Repeated Reasoning:** Watch as students record the times in Exercise 1–6. Are they recognizing the two numbers between which the hour hand is pointing? Do they recognize the time as half past the first number?
- If students are having difficulty identifying the time, have a small group meet for re-teaching with Exercises 3 and 4, then they complete Exercises 5 and 6.
- **Supporting Learners:** Students say out loud the numbers between which the hour hand points. In Exercise 1, they would say, "the hour hand is between 10 and 11. So it is half past 10."

? **Extension:** "Look at our classroom clock. Tell your partner which hand is the hour hand. Is the hour hand closer to an *o'clock* or to a *half past*? What is the closest time you can tell from the hour hand on the class clock now?"

Think and Grow

The hour hand is halfway between the 1 and the 2.

So, it is **half past** 1.

A **half hour** passes when the hour hand moves halfway to the next number.

Show and Grow *I can do it!*

Write the time shown by the hour hand.

1. 
half past 10

2. 
half past 8

3. 
half past 5

4. 
half past 3

5. 
half past 12

6. 
half past 2

Scaffold instruction to support all students in their learning. Learning is individualized and you may want to group students differently as they move in and out of these levels with each skill and concept. Student self-assessment and feedback help guide your instructional decisions about how and when to layer support for all students to become proficient learners.

Meeting the needs of all learners.

Laurie's Notes

Apply and Grow: Practice

SCAFFOLDING INSTRUCTION

The first exercises continue having students identify the time as in Exercises 1–6. They progress to drawing in the hour hand to show half past an hour. This may continue to be difficult. Not only do they have to be careful with the length of the hour hand, they also have to show it pointing between the two hour numbers.

EMERGING students may have some difficulty determining where the hour hand is pointing. Students can use their fingers or a straight edge to determine between which two numbers the hour hand is pointing.

- **Exercises 10–12:** Students now draw in the hour hand to show the time. The way the hour hand points is most important, but allow some flexibility as students are developing their fine motor skills. Have students tell you where the hour hand should be pointing if you are unclear whether they understand or not.
- **Exercise 13:** Students select the correct numbers between which the hour hand points. This may be confusing if they read the hand from the top of the clock, and think the hand is pointing between 12 and 11. If they think in terms of counterclockwise, they will choose recess.

PROFICIENT students will be able to tell between which numbers the hour hand points and the time.

- **Exercises 10–12:** Watch as students draw the hour hands. Notice the precision with which they draw the hour hand.
- **Exercise 13:** Have students explain how they know if it is time for lunch or recess.

Additional Support

- Trace the movement of the hour hand with a clock. Show a clockwise direction (students do not need to know that term) to help determine which hour it is half past.
- Let students work with student clocks and move the hands for clarity.

Extension: Adding Rigor

- Have students use their clocks to show time to the hour or half hour with the hour hand. They quiz their partner for the time and then trade roles.

Name ______________________

Apply and Grow: Practice

Write the time shown by the hour hand.

7. 

half past 7

8. 

half past 4

9. 

5 o'clock

Draw the hour hand to show the time.

10. half past 6

11. 1 o'clock

12. half past 9

13. DIG DEEPER! Is it time for lunch or recess?

MP Repeated Reasoning
Where does the hour hand point when it is half past 11? half past 12?

(Lunch) Recess

ELL Support

Check for understanding of Lesson 12.2. Read each story aloud as students follow along. Ask the following questions and have students write the answers on whiteboards and hold up for your review.

1. What time does soccer practice end?
2. What time does the show end?

Laurie's Notes

Think and Grow: Modeling Real Life

The applications require students to not only recognize the time on a clock, but also reason about half an hour after a given start time. This will be more difficult than yesterday when students added or subtracted a full hour as that was the same as adding or subtracting 1. Remind students of Descartes's observation that a half hour passes when the hour hand moves from a number halfway to the next number, or from between two numbers to the next number.

- Discuss the story. "Soccer practice lasts half an hour. Tell your partner what time practice starts. Notice where the hour hand is pointing. If a half hour goes by, where will the hour hand point?"
- "Draw in the hour hand for when practice ends. Remember it is half an hour – not a whole hour."
- "Which phrase is the correct ending time? Circle it."
- Introduce Exercise 14. Have students tell what time the TV show starts. "Where will the hour hand point after a half hour moves? Sketch your hour hand. Circle the correct time."
- ◉ "Today, we learned that not all time is on the hour. We learned about half hours today. Use your thumb signals to show how you are doing with telling time to the half hour. How are you at telling the hour it is half past from the hour hand? How are you at drawing in the hour hand for half past an hour?"

Closure

- Students will show times on their students clocks. Give them several times, including o'clock and half past an hour times.

Think and Grow: Modeling Real Life

Soccer practice lasts a half hour. Show and circle the time practice ends.

Start

End

half past 3   5 o'clock   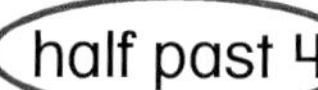 half past 4

Show and Grow *I can think deeper!*

14. A television show lasts a half hour. Show and circle the time the show ends.

Start

End

7 o'clock   half past 7   6 o'clock

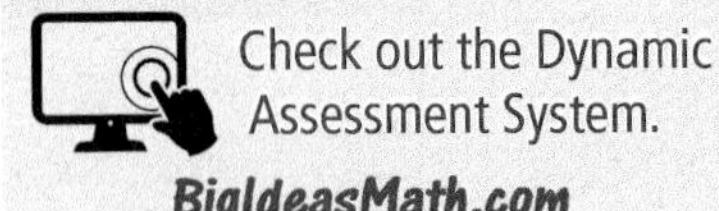
Check out the Dynamic Assessment System.
BigIdeasMath.com

Scaffold assignments to support all students in their learning progression. Revisit with spaced practice to move every student toward proficiency.

Connect and Extend Learning

Practice Notes

- **Exercises 4–6:** Remind students that when it is half past an hour, the hour hand should be halfway between the hour and the next hour.

Prior Skills

- **Exercise 9:** Grade 1, Solving Comparison Word Problems When Given How Many Fewer

Cross-Curricular Connections

Language Arts

- Show students an example of a television schedule. Ask them to look for a half-hour show and model the times it begins and ends on clocks. Then have students make their own television schedule. Students record the day, channel, and time, and draw clocks indicating when a show begins and ends.

Name ____________________

Practice  12.2

Learning Target: Use the hour hand to tell time to the half hour.

half past 3

Write the time shown by the hour hand.

1. 

half past 1

2. 

half past 5

3. 

half past 12

Draw the hour hand to show the time.

4. half past 9

5. half past 2

6. 10 o'clock

Connect and Extend Learning

Extend Student Learning

Bodily-Kinesthetic

- Write times, such as half past 1, on several index cards. Draw clocks showing the times on separate index cards or use student clocks to model. Hand out one index card or clock to each student. Have the students walk around the room and find a partner who has the same time.

Lesson Resources	
Surface Level	**Deep Level**
Resources by Chapter • Extra Practice • Reteach Differentiating the Lesson Skills Review Handbook Skills Trainer	Resources by Chapter • Enrichment and Extension Graphic Organizers Dynamic Assessment System • Lesson Practice

7. **DIG DEEPER!** Is it time for art class or math class?

Art class: half past 9
Math class: half past 10

(Art class) Math class

8. **Modeling Real Life** Your music class lasts a half hour. Show and circle the time your music class ends.

Start

End

half past 12 (half past 1) 2 o'clock

Review & Refresh

9. Your friend has 9 peanuts. You have 2 fewer than your friend. How many peanuts do you have?

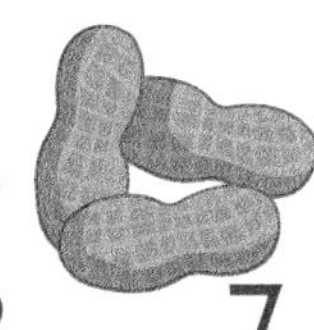

Sample answer:

Friend: 9

You: 7 | 2

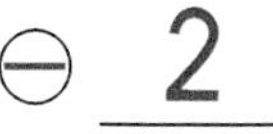

9 − 2 = 7

7 peanuts

Laurie's Notes

BigIdeasMath.com

STATE STANDARDS
1.MD.B.3

Learning Target

Use the hour and minute hands to tell time to the hour and half hour.

Success Criteria

- Tell where the hour and minute hands are pointing.
- Write and tell the time in two ways.
- Draw to show the time to the hour or half hour.

Warm-Up

Practice opportunities for the following are available in the Resources by Chapter or at *BigIdeasMath.com.*

- Daily skills
- Vocabulary
- Prerequisite skills

ELL Support

Explain that when telling time, students will always use a sentence that begins with *It is*, or *It's*. For example, you can say, "It is two o'clock." or "It's two o'clock." You can also say, "It is half past one." or "It's half past one." In many languages telling time switches from singular to plural when changing from the one o'clock hour to any other hour. Explain that it always stays the same in English.

Preparing to Teach

Students have worked with the hour hand to tell time to the hour and half hour. Today, we address the minute hand and the concept of one minute versus an hour or half hour.

Materials

- student clocks
- demonstration clock

Dig In (Circle Time)

Today, students will model time to the hour and half hour with both the hour and minute hands on their clocks. Students will discuss the difference between an hour, a half hour, and a minute by building a chart that describes what can be done in each time category.

- Distribute student clocks.
- "We have been telling time to the hour and to the half hour. Two days ago, we set a timer and had it go off every hour. Describe about how long an hour seemed to you. What are some things it takes about an hour to do?" Begin a chart of things done in an hour, a half hour, and a minute.
- "Yesterday the timer went off every half hour. What are some things it takes about an hour to do?" Add to the chart.
- ◉ **Model:** "Today we are going to tell time and learn about the longer hand on the clock. It is called a minute hand. The short hand is the hour hand, and it tells you the hour of the day. The minute hand tells you how many minutes in the hour have gone by. Let's see how long a minute is." Set a timer for one minute or watch a second hand for 1 minute. "What do you think can be done in a minute?"

Hour	Half Hour	Minute
Math	TV show	Whisper to your partner
Cook Dinner	Eat dinner	Chew
Gymnastics	Recess	Wash my hands
Karate	A puzzle	Sing the ABCs
Long car ride	Clean my room	Tic-tac-toe game
T-ball		

- ◉ "When we told time before, we only used the hour hand. The minute hand tells us how many minutes. When we are on the hour, the hour hand is pointing right at the number. If you remember, I had you put the minute hand on the 12 and leave it there when we practiced. That is where it will be for o'clock." Have students tell the time that you show on the demonstration clock, then show times you say with their clocks.
- "At half past an hour, the hour hand was between two numbers. If you remember, I had you put the minute hand on the 6 and leave it there when we practiced. That is where it will be for half past." Draw a clock and shade the right half. Explain that half an hour is half of the clock. Move the minute hand from the 12 to the 6 to show half past.
- ◉ Practice having students tell the time with "half past." Then have students show a "half past" time that you say on their clocks.
- ◉ "Today, we will show the time with both hands on the clock."

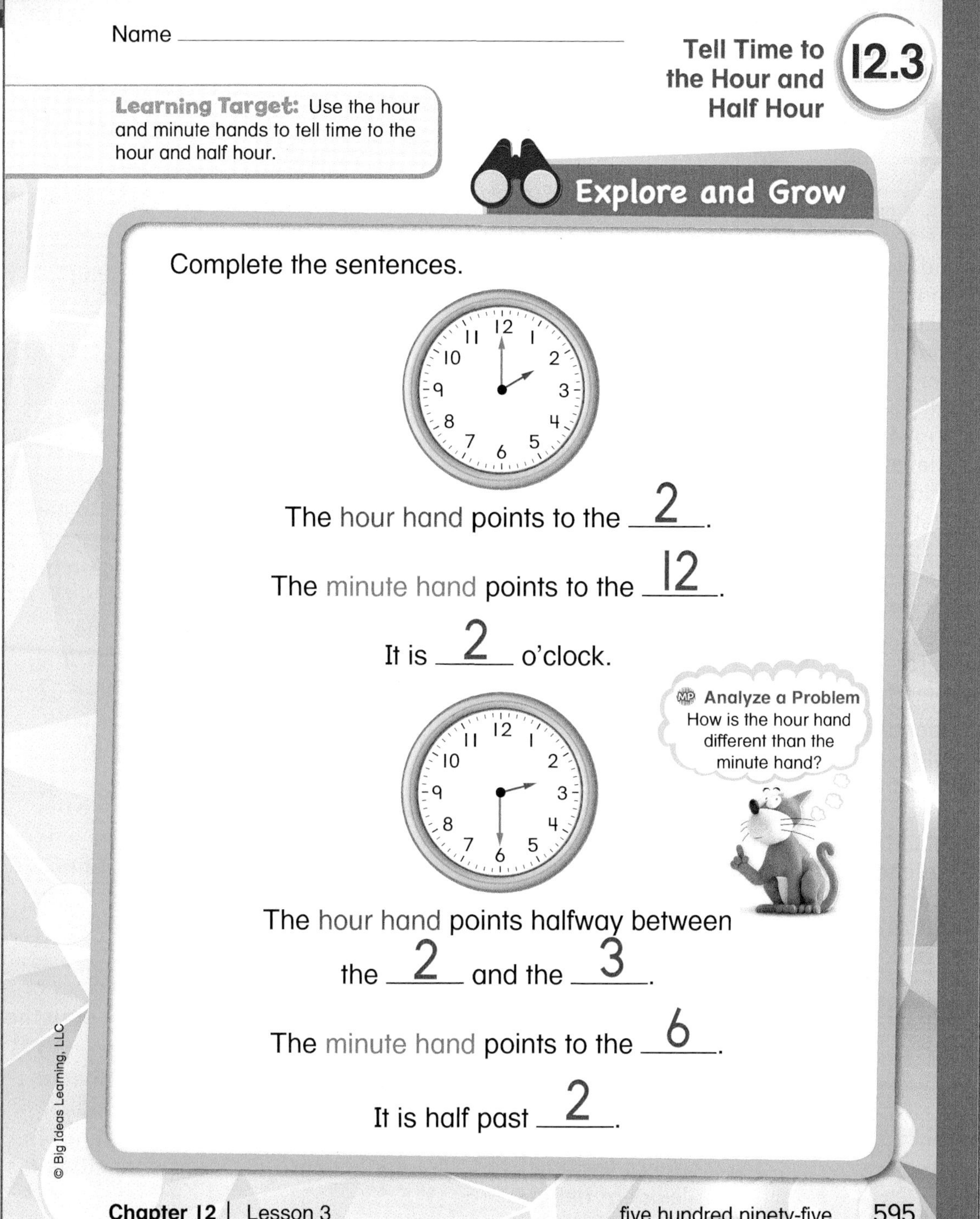

Name
Learning Target: Use the hour and minute hands to tell time to the hour and half hour.
Tell Time to the Hour and Half Hour
12.3
Explore and Grow
Complete the sentences.
The hour hand points to the 2.
The minute hand points to the 12.
It is 2 o'clock.
Analyze a Problem
How is the hour hand different than the minute hand?
The hour hand points halfway between the 2 and the 3.
The minute hand points to the 6.
It is half past 2.
© Big Ideas Learning, LLC
Chapter 12 | Lesson 3
five hundred ninety-five 595

Explore and Grow

- Have students complete where the hands are pointing on the top. Check to see that they correctly identified the hour and the minute hands.
- Students tell their partners what time it is. If they agree, they fill in the time. If not, they check with another pair of students.
- Complete the bottom clock in the same manner
- **MP2 Reason Abstractly and Quantitatively:** "In our clocks the hour and minute hands are color coded. Tell your partner how you can tell the difference between the two hands if they did not have color. Which determines the hour?"

ELL Support

Explain that the clocks shown here show both the hour hand and the minute hand. The example shows four o'clock and half past four. After completing the example, have students work in pairs to complete Exercises 1–3. Have one student ask another, "What time is it?" Have them alternate roles for each exercise.

Beginner students may provide phrases, such as, "half past four."
Intermediate and **Advanced** students may answer with sentences, such as, "It is half past one."

Laurie's Notes

Think and Grow

Getting Started

- Students will write the time as shown by the clocks. In this lesson, students will still write o'clock or half past.
- Introduce vocabulary terms **minute** and **minute hand**.

Teaching Notes

- **Model:** "Newton is reminding us about the hands on the clock. He says the minute hand is longer than the hour hand. Partner A, point to the minute hand on the first clock. Partner B, point to the minute hand on the second clock. The minute hand shows the minutes. Next year you will learn more about the minute hand. This year we are only thinking about time on the hour, or o'clock, and half past the hour."

? **Model:** "Look at the first clock. Tell your partner where the minute hand is pointing. Based on this, do you think the time will be o'clock or half past? Where is the hour hand pointing? Should that be o'clock or half past? Is what you said for both the minute and hour hands the same? What time does the clock show?"

? **Model:** "Look at the second clock. Tell your partner where the minute hand is pointing. Based on this, do you think the time will be o'clock or half past? Where is the hour hand pointing? Should that be o'clock or half past? Is what you said for both the minute and hour hands the same? What time does the clock show?"

- Have students say out loud whether the time will be o'clock or half past in Exercises 1–3. Have them explain based on both the minute and hour hands how they know.
- Watch as students fill in the time in Exercises 1–6. If students are confused by what time the clock shows, gather a small group and help them review that the hour hand determines the hour of the time, and the minute hand can confirm whether it is o'clock or half past.
- **Supporting Learners:** Cover the minute hand for a given clock and ask students what time the hour hand shows. Then reveal the minute hand and confirm that the way the minute hand points agrees with what they said for the time.
- **Extension:** Have students use their clocks to show time to the hour or half hour with the both clock hands. They quiz their partner for the time and then trade roles.

Think and Grow

4 o'clock

half past 4

The **minute hand** is longer than the hour hand. It shows the **minute**.

Show and Grow *I can do it!*

Write the time.

1.

7 o'clock

2.

2 o'clock

3.

half past 9

4.

8 o'clock

5.

half past 12

6.

half past 1

Scaffold instruction to support all students in their learning. Learning is individualized and you may want to group students differently as they move in and out of these levels with each skill and concept. Student self-assessment and feedback help guide your instructional decisions about how and when to layer support for all students to become proficient learners.

Meeting the needs of all learners.

Laurie's Notes

Apply and Grow: Practice

SCAFFOLDING INSTRUCTION

Students now draw in the hands on their clock for a specific time.

EMERGING students may mix up the minute and hour hands. They are likely to determine the time based on the number to which the minute hand is pointing rather than the hour. This is most likely a matter of needing more practice and reminding students to look at the hour hand first when determining the time. Students should exaggerate the difference in the length of the hands to be sure they know which hand is which.

- **Exercises 7–12:** Students should draw the hour hand first as they have had more experience with it and to tie the learning from the previous lessons to this lesson.
- **Exercise 13:** Students may not realize that both hands are pointing to the six. "Where should the minute hand point for half past? Where should an hour hand point for half past 6?"

PROFICIENT students will be able to tell time with both hands. They may not draw the hands accurately.

- **Exercises 7–12:** Watch as students draw the hands on the clock. Notice the precision with which they draw the hands. This will more than likely be the main area for improvement.
- **Exercise 13:** Students will need to pay attention to both hands to determine Newton's precision.

Additional Support

- Have students model the time on their clocks first, and then draw in the hands. They should be careful to remember which hand is the minute and which is the hour, and exaggerate the difference in length when drawing in the hands.

Extension: Adding Rigor

- Tell students, "The minute hand will tell many different times that you will learn next year. One of the times you can say with the minute hand is to say it is 'quarter past' when the minute hand points to the 3." Have students work in pairs and model on their clock o'clock, quarter past, and half past times for their partners to say out loud. Then trade roles.

Name ______________________________

Apply and Grow: Practice

Draw to show the time.

7. half past 5

8. 6 o'clock

9. half past 10

10. 3 o'clock

11. 11 o'clock

12. half past 4

13. MP YOU BE THE TEACHER Newton shows half past 6. Is he correct? Explain.

no ; The hour hand should point halfway between 6 and 7.

Laurie's Notes

ELL Support

Check for understanding of Lesson 12.3. Read each story aloud as students follow along. Ask the following questions and have students write the answers on whiteboards and hold up for your review.

1. What time do you leave the park?
2. What time do you finish your homework?

Think and Grow: Modeling Real Life

The applications require students to not only recognize the time on a clock, but also reason about an hour and half an hour after a given start time. This parallels the applications we have had each day so far. Today, students draw both hands to tell the ending times.

? **Preview:** "How long do you like to play outside? How long do you usually get to play outside?"

- Discuss the story. "You will spend an hour at the park. Tell your partner what time you get to the park (arrive). You play for one hour. Tell your partner the time it will be when you need to leave."
- Draw in the hands for when you leave the park. Compare with your partner. Write the time on the blank.
- Introduce Exercise 14. Have students tell what time they start homework. Have them say what time it will be when they finish homework. Draw in hands and write the time.

◉ "Today, we learned about the long hand on the clock. Tell your partner what that hand is called. Now tell where it will point if it is o'clock. Tell where it points at half past."

◉ "Use your thumb signals to show how you are doing with telling time. How are you at telling the time using both clock hands?"

Closure

- Students will show time on their clocks. Give them several times, including o'clock and half past an hour times.

Think and Grow: Modeling Real Life

You spend an hour at the park.
Show and write the time you leave.

Arrive

Leave

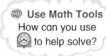

Use Math Tools
How can you use to help solve?

12 o'clock

Show and Grow I can think deeper!

14. You spend a half hour on your homework.
Show and write the time you finish.

Start

Finish

half past 3

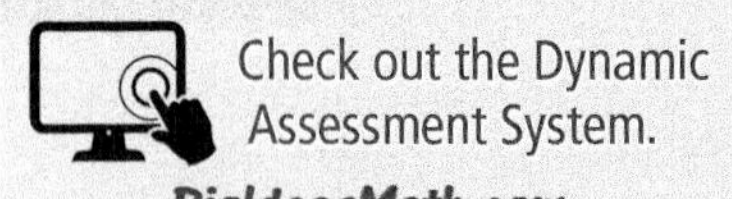

Scaffold assignments to support all students in their learning progression. Revisit with spaced practice to move every student toward proficiency.

Connect and Extend Learning

Practice Notes

- **Exercises 5 and 6:** Remind students that when showing half past an hour, the hour hand should be half way between that hour and the next hour.

Prior Skills

- **Exercise 10:** Grade 1, Counting to 120 by Ones

Cross-Curricular Connections

Art

- Show students pictures of cuckoo clocks. Then have students draw their own cuckoo clock. Provide students a time to show on their clock.

Name ___________________

Practice 12.3

Learning Target: Use the hour and minute hands to tell time to the hour and half hour.

8 o'clock

half past 8

Write the time.

1. 

half past 11

2. 

3 o'clock

3. 

1 o'clock

Draw to show the time.

4. 5 o'clock

5. half past 7

6. half past 2

Connect and Extend Learning

Extend Student Learning

Bodily-Kinesthetic

- Draw a large clock on the board. Have students stand in front of the clock and model times with their hands, or have the entire class model a given time with their arms.

<table>
<tr><th colspan="2">Lesson Resources</th></tr>
<tr><th>Surface Level</th><th>Deep Level</th></tr>
<tr><td>Resources by Chapter
• Extra Practice
• Reteach
Differentiating the Lesson
Skills Review Handbook
Skills Trainer
Math Musicals</td><td>Resources by Chapter
• Enrichment and Extension
Graphic Organizers
Math Musicals
Dynamic Assessment System
• Lesson Practice</td></tr>
</table>

7. YOU BE THE TEACHER Descartes shows 12 o'clock. Is he correct? Explain.

yes; Both the hour and minute hand are pointing to 12.

8. Modeling Real Life You play tag for an hour. Show and write the time you stop playing tag.

Start

Stop

10 o'clock

9. DIG DEEPER! You play hide-and-seek for one and a half hours. Show and write the time you stop playing hide-and-seek.

Start

Stop

11:30

Review & Refresh

Count by ones to write the missing numbers.

10. 43, 44, 45, 46, 47, 48

Check out the
Dynamic Classroom.

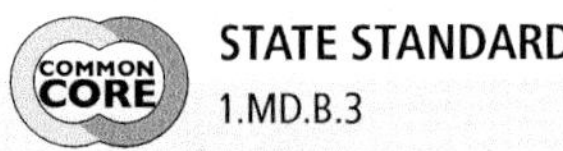
BigIdeasMath.com

12.4

Learning Target

Use analog and digital clocks to tell time.

Success Criteria

- Read and write hours and half hours on analog and digital clocks.
- Tell when analog and digital clocks are the same time.
- Tell and draw what one hour earlier or later is.

Warm-Up

Practice opportunities for the following are available in the Resources by Chapter or at *BigIdeasMath.com*.

- Daily skills
- Vocabulary
- Prerequisite skills

ELL Support

Explain that there are different ways to tell time to the half hour. For example, if it is a half hour past one o'clock, you can tell time by using the phrase *one-thirty* or the phrase *half past one*. Both phrases mean the same thing.

Laurie's Notes

COMMON CORE STATE STANDARDS
1.MD.B.3

Preparing to Teach

Today we introduce how to read a digital clock. This will lead to writing times. Students will learn that there are 60 minutes in one hour and 30 minutes in half an hour.

Materials

- student clocks
- demonstration clock
- whiteboards

Dig In (Circle Time)

Today students will show time on their student clocks based on time shown from a digital clock.

- Distribute student clocks.
- "We have been telling time with our analog clocks. Let's review how to tell time with an analog clock."
- Review the names of the hands, how to tell the hands apart, and where the hands will point for o'clock and for half past.
- ? "Who has seen another type of clock that doesn't have hands at all? These clocks only show numbers. Where have you seen one of these clocks?"
- "This type of clock is called a digital clock." Hold up a picture of a clock with 10:00 showing. "Tell your partners what you notice about the time on this clock."
- "You have noticed that there are two sets of numbers and a colon on the digital clock. The first set of numbers is for the hour. Those numbers go with what the hour hand shows. After the colon are the minutes. Those numbers go with what the minute hand shows."
- ◉ Hold up the demonstration clock showing 10:00. "Both clocks are showing 10:00. When we say 'o'clock,' we mean on the hour, or there are no extra minutes. That is why the minute hand points at the top of the clock at 12. The digital clock shows no minutes, or 00 after the colon."
- ◉ Show various digital o'clock times and have students show the same time on their clocks.
- ◉ "We also know that when the time is half past an hour, the minute hand has moved halfway around the clock and is pointing at the 6. There are a total of 60 minutes in one hour, so when the minute hand is halfway around, it has moved 30 minutes. Half an hour is the same as 30 minutes." Have students show 2:30 on their clocks and write the digital 2:30 to discuss "half past 2."
- ◉ Show various digital *half past* times and have students show the same time on their clocks.
- ◉ "Clocks that show the digits of the time are called digital clocks. Our clocks with hands are called analog clocks. Today we will read digital clocks and show the same time on analog clocks."

? Teaching Prompt ◉ Learning Target

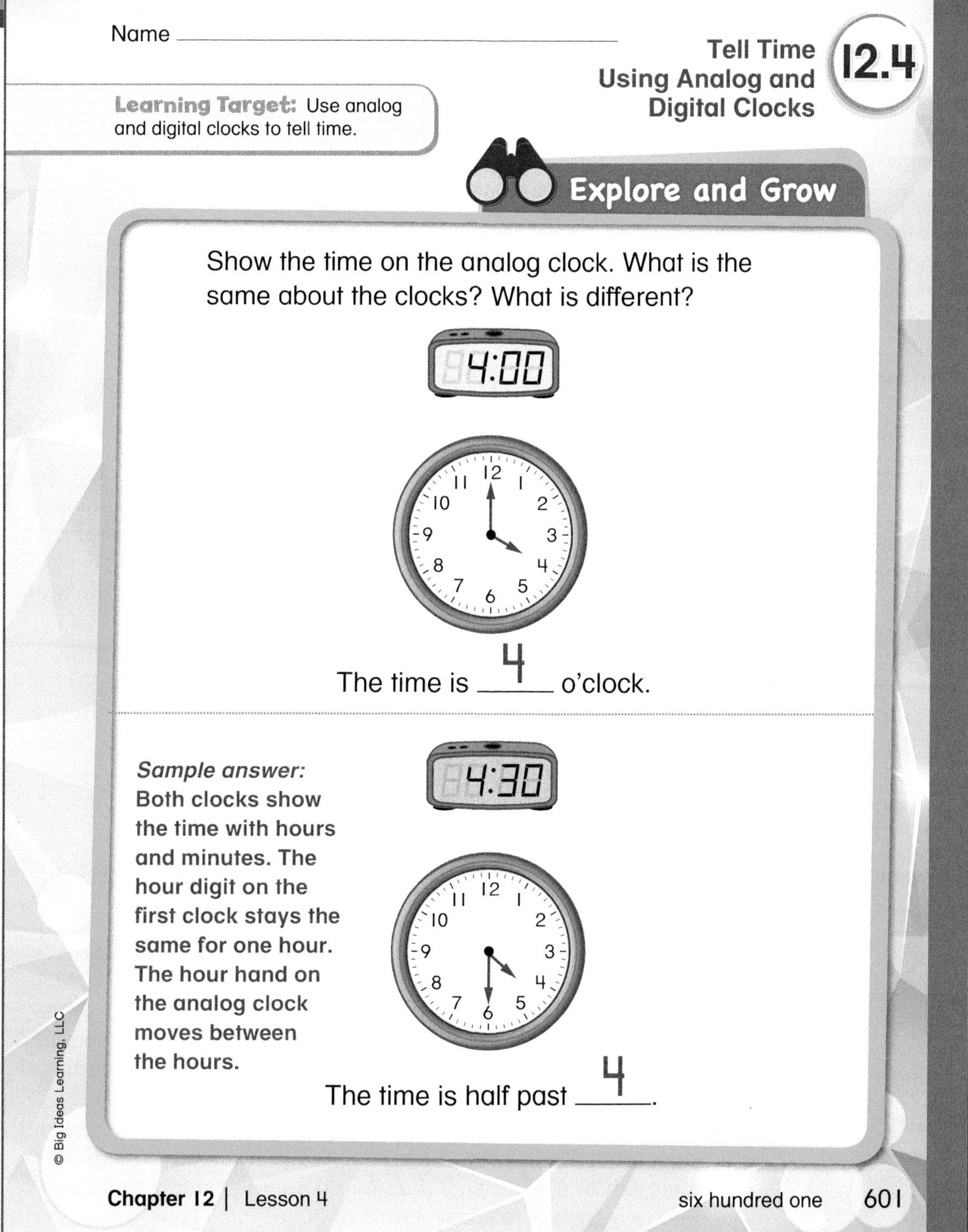

Name
Tell Time Using Analog and Digital Clocks
12.4
Learning Target: Use analog and digital clocks to tell time.
Explore and Grow
Show the time on the analog clock. What is the same about the clocks? What is different?
4:00
The time is 4 o'clock.
Sample answer: Both clocks show the time with hours and minutes. The hour digit on the first clock stays the same for one hour. The hour hand on the analog clock moves between the hours.
4:30
The time is half past 4.
© Big Ideas Learning, LLC
Chapter 12 | Lesson 4
six hundred one 601

Explore and Grow

- Have students tell the time on the first digital clock. Remind students of the meaning of :00 when telling time.
- Students draw in the hands on the clock and fill in the blank for the time.
- Repeat with the bottom clocks. Remind students that there are 60 minutes in one hour. Half an hour is 30 minutes. When they see :30, they know it is *half past*.

? **MP6 Attend to Precision**: "Work with a partner. What is the same and what is different about the clocks?" both show hours and minutes; one has hands to show, the other uses digits and a colon to separate; digital always has hours then minutes, etc.

ELL Support

After completing the example, have students work in pairs to complete Exercises 1–4. Have one student ask another, "What time is it?" Have them alternate roles for each exercise. You may want to circulate and monitor how they are writing digital time.

Beginner students may provide phrases, such as, "five thirty." **Intermediate** and **Advanced** students may answer with sentences, such as, "It is five thirty."

Laurie's Notes

Think and Grow

Getting Started

- Students will write digital times as shown by the analog clock.
- Introduce the vocabulary term **digital clock**.

Teaching Notes

- **Model:** "Look at the first clock and tell your partner the time. What is the hour? The hour is the first number before the colon on a digital clock. Write in the 5."
  - "It is 5 o'clock. That means that no minutes have passed. On a digital clock the numbers after the colon are the minutes. We always show two digits for minutes. Write two zeros following the colon."
- **Model:** "Look at the second clock and tell your partner the time. What is the hour? Write in the 5."
  - "It is half past 5. Notice that half the clock is shaded showing that half an hour has passed since the first clock at 5:00. We are reminded that a half hour is 30 minutes. That means that 30 minutes have passed. Write 30 following the colon to show the minutes."
- **Model:** "Look at the last clock and tell your partner the time. What is the hour? Write in the 6."
  - "It is 6 o'clock. Notice that the whole clock is shaded showing that an hour has passed since the first clock at 5:00. We are reminded that an hour is 60 minutes. We don't write a 60 following the colon because we are now at the next hour. Instead, we write 00 to show that we are starting the next hour. Fill in the minutes."
- Watch as students write the time in Exercises 1–4. Do students write the hour first followed by the minutes? Are they writing 00 for on the hour and 30 for half past?
- **MP5 Use Appropriate Tools Strategically:** Show on the hundred chart where 60 is and where 30 is. Have students explain why 30 is half of 60. Or use 6 rods for 60 minutes and divide them into two groups to show 3 rods or 30 minutes is half.
- **Supporting Learners:** Determine if the error comes from telling time on the analog clock incorrectly or if students are confusing how to write time digitally. If the confusion is with the analog clock, review the hour and minute hand positions. If it's with digital time, refer students to the model clocks to compare.
- **Extension:** Have students count by fives around the numbers on the clock, beginning with 1 as "5" and ending on 12, to see 30 minutes in the half hour (when they reach 6) and 60 minutes in one hour.

Think and Grow

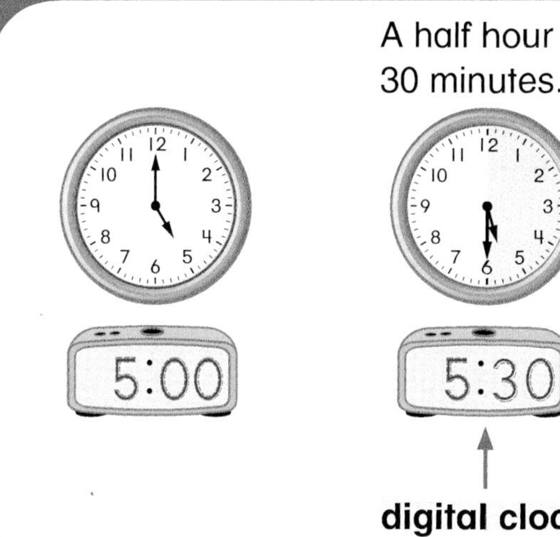

A half hour is 30 minutes.

An hour is 60 minutes.

digital clock

Show and Grow *I can do it!*

Show the time.

1. 

2. 

3. 

4. 

Scaffold instruction to support all students in their learning. Learning is individualized and you may want to group students differently as they move in and out of these levels with each skill and concept. Student self-assessment and feedback help guide your instructional decisions about how and when to layer support for all students to become proficient learners.

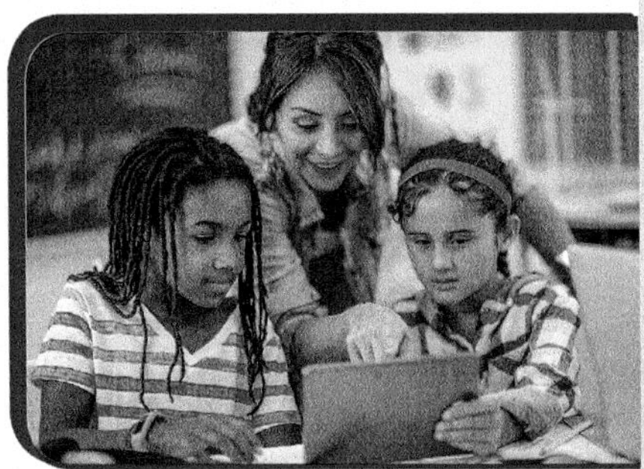

Meeting the needs of all learners.

Laurie's Notes

Apply and Grow: Practice

SCAFFOLDING INSTRUCTION

Students progress from writing digital times, as in the previous exercises, to drawing hands on the analog clock to match the digital, to filling in parts on each clock to make the clocks tell the same time.

EMERGING students are still working to keep all the elements of time and their representations straight. Time is still abstract – an hour and half hour may still be arbitrary to them. They are working to master the hands on the analog clock, and may confuse which numbers represent hour and minutes on the digital clock.

- **Exercises 5 and 6:** These exercises continue from the previous page. Exercise 6 could be used for re-teaching and Exercise 7 as a check for understanding.
- **Exercises 9 and 10:** These exercises may confuse students. Point out that one of the clocks shows the hour and the other shows the minutes. See if this gives enough information for them to complete both clocks.
- **Exercise 11:** Have students say the time out loud for each representation. Have them tell a partner which one does not mean the same thing.

PROFICIENT students will be able to tell time on both clocks. They may need brief review of one clock or the other.

- **Exercises 5–8:** Students are able to move between the clock types.
- **Exercises 9 and 10:** Have students tell what part of the time, hour or minute, each clock is showing.
- **Exercise 11:** Students explain to a partner how they found the one that does not belong.

Additional Support

- Have students use their clocks to show time before drawing the hands.

Extension: Adding Rigor

- If students worked with 'quarter past' yesterday, have them tell how many minutes that would be from a hundred chart or thinking half of 30. Have students model quarter after times on both clocks.

Name

Apply and Grow: Practice

Show the time.

5.  

6.  

Draw to show the time.

7.  

8.  

DIG DEEPER! Complete the clocks to show the same time.

9.  

10.  

11. **Which One Doesn't Belong?** Which time does not belong with the other three? Think: How do you know?

   half past 3

This clock shows 4:30, not 3:30.

ELL Support

Check for understanding of Lesson 12.4. Read each story aloud as students follow along. Ask the following questions and have students write the answers on whiteboards and hold up for your review.

1. What time does the play start?
2. What time does tumbling start?

Laurie's Notes

Think and Grow: Modeling Real Life

The application continue the same reasoning about an hour and half an hour after a given start time. Today, students show the end times on both types of clocks and circle the time in words.

- "Our story tells us that the play starts an hour later than the movie. Tell your partner what time the movie starts. The play is one hour later. Tell your partner time the play starts."
- "Write in the digital time for the start of the play. Compare with your partner. Circle the phrase that has the correct time."
- Introduce Exercise 12. Have students tell what time dance starts. Have them say what time tumbling starts. Draw in the hands on the analog clock and circle the phrase with the correct time.

? "Today, we learned about the digital clock. Time on the digital clock is usually how we write time. Tell your partner what you know about telling time on the digital clock. What does it look like? What do the numbers mean? Why is there a colon?"

◉ "Use your thumb signals to show how you are doing with telling time. How are you at matching time on both types of clocks?"

Closure

- Students will have a student clock and a whiteboard for each partner. The teacher will say a time, and one partner will show the time on the analog clock and the other partner will write the digital time on the whiteboard. Partners check each other's times. Switch roles.

Think and Grow: Modeling Real Life

A play starts 1 hour later than a movie. Show and circle the time the play starts.

Movie

Play

half past 2 | half past 4 | 3 o'clock | 4 o'clock

Show and Grow *I can think deeper!*

12. Tumbling starts a half hour later than dance. Show and circle the time tumbling starts.

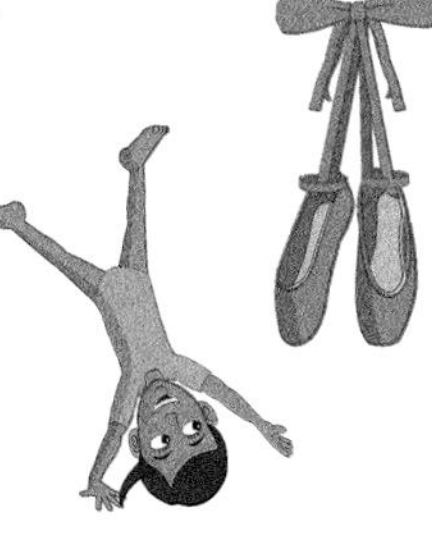

Dance

Tumbling

half past 5 | 4 o'clock | 6 o'clock | half past 4

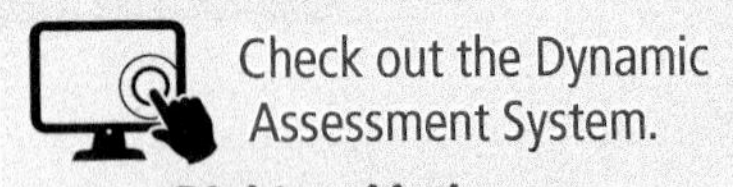
Check out the Dynamic Assessment System.

BigIdeasMath.com

Scaffold assignments to support all students in their learning progression. Revisit with spaced practice to move every student toward proficiency.

Connect and Extend Learning

Practice Notes

- **Exercises 4 and 6:** Remind students that when it is half past an hour, the hour hand should be halfway between the hour and the next hour.

Prior Skills

- **Exercise 10:** Kindergarten, Identifying Cones and Cylinders

Cross-Curricular Connections

Science

- Complete a dying flowers science experiment. Place white flowers, such as chrysanthemums, into water with food coloring. Have students draw what the flowers look like each half hour. Under their drawing, have the students draw and write the time.

Name ______________________

Practice 

Learning Target: Use analog and digital clocks to tell time.

Show the time.

1.

2.

3.

Draw to show the time.

4. 12:30

5. 11:00

6. 4:30

Chapter 12 | Lesson 4 **605**

Connect and Extend Learning

Extend Student Learning

Linguistic

- Show students a time. Have them tell you what the time would be one hour later or one hour earlier. Have all students find the same time, or divide the class into two groups and have one group find each time. You can also have students draw digital or analog clocks showing the time.

Lesson Resources	
Surface Level	**Deep Level**
Resources by Chapter • Extra Practice • Reteach Differentiating the Lesson Skills Review Handbook Skills Trainer	Resources by Chapter • Enrichment and Extension Graphic Organizers Dynamic Assessment System • Lesson Practice

7. Which One Doesn't Belong? Which time does not belong with the other three? Think: How do you know?

half past 6

This clock shows 7:30, not 6:30.

---

8. Modeling Real Life Bowling starts 1 hour later than ice skating. Show and circle the time bowling starts.

Ice Skating

Bowling

half past 5    5 o'clock   half past 4   3 o'clock

---

9. Reasoning As the minute hand moves from the 12 to the 6, how much time passes?

30 minutes

Review & Refresh

10. Circle the cone. Draw a rectangle around the cylinder.

ELL Support

Have students work in groups to complete the Performance Task. Have Intermediate and Advanced students alternate reading sentences aloud as the group discusses how to complete the schedule. Monitor discussion. Expect students to perform according to their language proficiency level.

Beginner students may provide phrases, such as, "twelve thirty." **Intermediate** students may provide simple sentences, such as, "Recess is at half past twelve." **Advanced** students may explain the logic of figuring out the schedule using detailed sentences, such as, "If lunch is at twelve, and recess starts a half hour after lunch, then recess starts at half past twelve."

Laurie's Notes

Performance Task

In this task, students will tell time using a field trip schedule. In Exercises 2 and 3, students will write the time in different ways using a digit clock and an analog clock respectively. Use student responses to gauge their understanding about telling time.

- Decide ahead of time whether students will be working independently, in pairs, or in groups.
- Pause between direction lines for students to complete each step.
- Have students share their work and thinking with others. Discuss as a class.

Exercise	Answers and Notes	Points
1a	Pond Study written at 11:30	2
1b	Wildlife Walk written at 9:30	2
1c	10:30 written at Scavenger Hunt	2
1d	Recess written at 12:30	2
1e	2:00 written at Leave	2
2	12:30 written on the digital clock	2
3	1:00 drawn on the analog clock	2
	Total	14

Name ____________________

Performance Task 12

1. Your class is on a field trip to a nature center. Complete the schedule.

a. The Pond Study starts at the time shown.

b. The Wildlife Walk starts at half past 9.

c. The Scavenger Hunt starts 1 hour after the Wildlife Walk starts.

d. Recess starts a half hour after lunch.

e. You leave 1 hour before 3:00.

Field Trip Schedule	
Activity	**Time**
Arrive	9:00
Wildlife Walk	9:30
Scavenger Hunt	10 : 30
Pond Study	11:30
Lunch	12:00
Recess	12:30
Live Animal Show	1:00
Leave	2 : 00

2. Lunch lasts a half hour. Write the time that lunch ends.

3. Draw the time the Live Animal Show starts.

Check out the interactive version in the Game Library.

BigIdeasMath.com

Laurie's Notes

Time Flip and Find

Materials

- a copy of Time Flip and Find Cards* per student
- scissors
- demonstration clock

* *Found in the Instructional Resources*

Time Flip and Find allows students to tell time to the hour and half past the hour on an analog clock, digital clock, and in written form.

? "What do you notice about the Time Flip and Find Cards?" *Sample answer:* The times are different on some of the cards. Some cards have the same times but show it in a different way.

- Explain that they will need to match the two times that are the same.
- Read the directions at the top of the page. Model what a turn looks like when finding a match and when not finding a match.
- Have students work with a partner or in groups.
- While students play, circulate and listen to student discussions. Students should be discussing how to read time to the hour and half past the hour on an analog clock, digital clock, and in written form.
- **MP6 Attend to Precision:** "As you played the game, how did you know when you found a match?" *Sample answer:* The times were the same.
- **Supporting Learners:** Have students work with student clocks to help practice telling time on an analog clock.

Closure

- Show different times to the hour and half past the hour on a demonstration clock. Ask students, "What time is it?" Students can show their answers on a whiteboard by writing the time in digital or in words.

Time Flip and Find

To Play: Place the Time Flip and Find Cards facedown in the boxes. Take turns flipping 2 cards. If your cards show the same time, keep the cards. If your cards show different times, flip the cards back over. Play until all matches are made.

Learning Target Correlation

Lesson	Learning Target	Exercises
12.1	Use the hour hand to tell time to the hour.	1–3
12.2	Use the hour hand to tell time to the half hour.	4–7
12.3	Use the hour and minute hands to tell time to the hour and half hour.	8–11
12.4	Use analog and digital clocks to tell time.	12–14

Name ______________________

Chapter 12 Practice

12.1 Tell Time to the Hour

Write the time shown by the hour hand.

1.

__1__ o'clock

2.

__11__ o'clock

3.

__8__ o'clock

12.2 Tell Time to the Half Hour

Draw the hour hand to show the time.

4. half past 9

5. 2 o'clock

6. half past 5

7. MP **Precision** Is it time to brush your teeth or go to bed?

Brush teeth: half past 7
Go to bed: half past 8

(Brush teeth) circled

Go to bed

Chapter Resources		
Surface Level	**Deep Level**	**Transfer Level**
Resources by Chapter • Extra Practice • Reteach Differentiating the Lesson Skills Review Handbook Skills Trainer Game Library Math Musicals	Resources by Chapter • Enrichment and Extension Graphic Organizers Game Library Math Musicals	Dynamic Assessment System • Chapter Test Assessment Book • Chapter Tests A and B

12.3 Tell Time to the Hour and Half Hour

Write the time.

8. 

6 o'clock

9. 

half past 10

10. 

half past 3

11. Modeling Real Life You read for a half hour. Show and write the time you stop reading.

Start

Stop

half past 4

12.4 Tell Time Using Analog and Digital Clocks

Complete the clocks to show the same time.

12. 

1:30

13. 

14. 

12:30

Centers

Center 1: Time Flip and Find

Materials: Student Edition page 608, Time Flip and Find Cards*, scissors, demonstration clock

Have students complete the activity. See page T-608 for the directions.

Center 2: Skills Trainer

Materials: computers or devices with Internet access

Have students go to *BigIdeasMath.com* to access the Skills Trainer.

Center 3: Race to Noon

Materials per group: Time Cube*, student clocks, scissors, tape

Have students assemble the Time Cube or prepare them for students. Each student starts with a clock set to 12 o'clock. Students take turns rolling the Time Cube and moving the hands on their clock accordingly. Play continues until someone moves all the way around the clock back to 12 o'clock.

Center 4: Time Heads Up

Materials per pair: student clocks, index cards, tape

Write different times, such as 9:00 and 4:30, down on index cards for each pair. One student picks up a card and tapes it to their forehead without looking at the time. The other student describes the time to the student. They can say things such as it is half past an hour, and the hour hand should be between 4 and 5. The first student shows the time on a clock. The other student checks their answer. Students switch roles and repeat.

**Found in the Instructional Resources*

Chapter Assessment Guide

Chapter tests are available in the Assessment Book.
An alternative assessment option is listed below.

Logical-Mathematical

Have students identify what time it is when shown a clock of 8:00 and 3:30. Have students draw the hands on an analog clock and write the time on a digital clock for 9:00 and half past 2.

Task	Points
Identify 8:00.	1 point
Identify 3:30.	1 point
Draw 9:00 on a clock.	1 point
Write 9:00 on a digital clock.	1 point
Draw half past 2 on a clock.	1 point
Write half past 2 on a digital clock.	1 point
Total	6 points

My Thoughts on the Chapter

What worked...

Teacher Tip

Not allowed to write in your teaching edition? Use sticky notes to record your thoughts.

What did not work...

What I would do differently...

13 Two- and Three-Dimensional Shapes

Chapter Overview

Lesson	Learning Target	Success Criteria
13.1 Sort Two-Dimensional Shapes	Sort two-dimensional shapes.	• Use a sorting rule to identify shapes. • Explain different ways to sort two-dimensional shapes.
13.2 Describe Two-Dimensional Shapes	Describe two-dimensional shapes.	• Draw two-dimensional shapes. • Identify the number of straight sides. • Identify the number of vertices. • Identify a shape from given information.
13.3 Combine Two-Dimensional Shapes	Join two-dimensional shapes to make another shape.	• Join shapes to make another shape. • Tell how many of each shape I used.
13.4 Create More Shapes	Join two-dimensional shapes to make a new shape. Use the new shape to make a larger shape.	• Join shapes to make a new shape. • Tell how many of each shape I used. • Use the new shape to make a larger shape.
13.5 Take Apart Two-Dimensional Shapes	Take apart two-dimensional shapes.	• Tell what shapes make up a given shape. • Draw a line to show the parts of a given shape.
13.6 Sort Three-Dimensional Shapes	Sort three-dimensional shapes.	• Use a sorting rule to identify shapes. • Explain different ways to sort three-dimensional shapes.
13.7 Describe Three-Dimensional Shapes	Describe three-dimensional shapes.	• Make three-dimensional shapes. • Identify the number of flat surfaces, vertices, and edges. • Identify a shape from given information.
13.8 Combine Three-Dimensional Shapes	Join three-dimensional shapes to make another shape.	• Join shapes to make another shape. • Tell which shape I used.
13.9 Take Apart Three-Dimensional Shapes	Take apart three-dimensional shapes.	• Tell what shapes make up a given shape. • Show the parts of a given shape.

Chapter Learning Target:
Understand two- and three-dimensional shapes.

Chapter Success Criteria:
- Identify shapes.
- Describe two- and three-dimensional shapes.
- Compare shapes.
- Create shapes.

Progressions

Through the Grades		
Kindergarten	**Grade 1**	**Grade 2**
• Classify objects into categories. • Analyze shapes and their attributes. • Build and draw shapes. • Put shapes together to make a new shape.	• Understand the difference between defining attributes of shapes and non-defining attributes of shapes. • Build and draw shapes with given attributes. • Put together shapes to make a new shape. Then use the new shape to make a larger shape.	• Identify and draw shapes with given attributes. • Identify triangles, quadrilaterals, pentagons, hexagons, and cubes.

	Through the Chapter								
Standard	**13.1**	**13.2**	**13.3**	**13.4**	**13.5**	**13.6**	**13.7**	**13.8**	**13.9**
1.G.A.1 Distinguish between defining attributes (e.g., triangles are closed and three-sided) versus non-defining attributes (e.g., color, orientation, overall size); build and draw shapes to possess defining attributes.	●	●				●	★		
1.G.A.2 Compose two-dimensional shapes (rectangles, squares, trapezoids, triangles, half-circles, and quarter-circles) or three-dimensional shapes (cubes, right rectangular prisms, right circular cones, and right circular cylinders) to create a composite shape, and compose new shapes from the composite shape.			●	●	●			●	★

Key: ▲ = Preparing ● = Learning ★ = Complete

Laurie's Overview

About the Math

Look around – our world is described by shapes! Even the earth is a sphere. Everything we see or touch can be described by its shape, the shapes that make it, or dimensions. Chapter 13 continues to develop students' spatial reasoning and vocabulary around geometric shapes, both two-dimensional and three-dimensional. Depending upon the toys or materials students have played with, their spatial development may be quite varied from other students. Much research suggests that a student's level of geometric development is a matter of experience and not chronological age, therefore it is important for all students to have access to a variety of spatial experiences. These experiences began in kindergarten by naming basic shapes, exploring some of their attributes, and seeing how these shapes might fit together to make new shapes.

In this chapter students continue to work with shapes from kindergarten, including triangles, rectangles, squares, hexagons, circles, cubes, spheres, cones and cylinders. We add to this list rhombi (plural of rhombus), trapezoids and rectangular prisms. Students experience and classify shapes with greater precision, including describing two-dimensional shapes as open or closed and continuing recognizing the number of sides and vertices. With three-dimensional figures, students add descriptions of surfaces as curved or flat, and describe edges and vertices. Students continue to determine what makes a defining attribute (number of sides or types of surface for example) as opposed to non-defining attributes (color, orientation, size). Additionally, we try to change the orientation of shapes and show various types of triangles beyond equilateral.

Many shapes share attributes. For example, a square, rectangle, rhombus and trapezoid all have four sides. In fact, a square is a type of rectangle and a type of rhombus. A cube is a type of rectangular prism. The overlaps and classifications of shapes is usually developed in fifth grade. With that in mind, it is tricky to count an answer of a rectangle as incorrect when it should most accurately be a square. Let students know a square is a type of rectangle, but square is a more precise answer which is what we are looking for.

One challenge with students learning about shape is that often we rely on a two-dimensional drawing to represent three-dimensional shapes. Often these drawings are based on experience… for example a ball can look like a circle as a picture if I'm not familiar with the type of ball. This is why it is important for students to hold and view solids from different perspectives. Helping students develop an "eye" for dimension in drawings and pictures is part of their developmental progress. Young students have not had sufficient spatial experiences to recognize the image they are looking at.

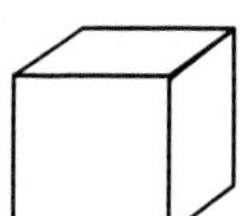 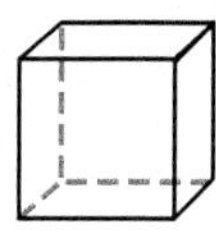 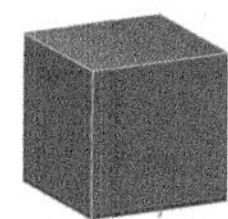 

For example, dotted lines that represent the hidden edges of a cube or rectangular prism are not understood at this age. The red cube is shaded and that helps student distinguish the image as a cube. An image of a real-life object that students are familiar with can be interpreted immediately. They see the blocks and the context helps them know that it is a three-dimensional solid. The same spatial challenge is true for spheres, cones, and cylinders.

Anchor Chart

It is recommended to keep an anchor chart of shapes for this chapter. You can combine all shapes in one, or create one chart for two-dimensions and one for three-dimensions. Include the shape name, an image of the shape, the number of sides or surfaces, the number of vertices, and any other information students may need to reference in this chapter.

Several lessons in the chapter have students compose and build new shapes from shapes that they know. This means they join two or more simple shapes to make a larger shape. An example would be putting two squares together to make a rectangle or stacking two cubes to make a rectangular prism. This is a natural experience for students who have played with blocks, tried to build towers, or used shape tiles to make designs and pictures. Students also work to decompose shapes, recognizing the simple shapes that have combined to make the more complex. Composing and decomposing shapes is comparable to joining and separating number with addition and subtraction contexts. It also lays the foundation for studies in perimeter, area, and volume in later grades.

Models

- Pattern blocks are used heavily throughout the chapter. If possible, students will benefit from having the blocks and use the Pattern Blocks Instructional Resource to send home.
- Geometric solids are also used in the last four lessons of the chapter. Blocks or a collection of objects of the shape, such as a can for a cylinder, are needed as models. Ideally students will be able to work with a collection of blocks individually or with a partner. A note home that you are looking for used toy blocks might be a way to acquire a sufficient collection so that all students can be holding a cylinder or cone when it is time for that lesson.

Geometry is often one of students' favorite topics because of its hands-on nature and applicability to the world around us. Enjoy!

Check out the
virtual manipulatives.
BigIdeasMath.com

Chapter Materials and Resources

The primary materials and resources needed for this chapter are listed below. Other materials may be needed for the additional support ideas provided throughout the chapter.

Classroom Materials	Chapter Opener	13.1	13.2	13.3	13.4	13.5	13.6	13.7	13.8	13.9	Connect and Grow
scissors	•	*					*				
glue		*					*				
two-dimensional shapes		*									
attribute blocks			•								
pattern blocks				•	•	•					•
straws			•			•					
shape cut outs				•	•	•					
composite outlines						•					
three-dimensional shapes							+	+	•	•	
materials to build three-dimensional shapes								*			
file folder										*	
die											•
counter											•
whiteboards											•
spinner											•
centimeter cubes									•		
modeling clay											•

Instructional Resources	Chapter Opener	13.1	13.2	13.3	13.4	13.5	13.6	13.7	13.8	13.9	Connect and Grow
Vocabulary Cards	•	+	+				+	+			
Shape Sort Cards		•									
Three-Dimensional Shape Cards							•				
Shape Dominoes											*
Shape Roll and Graph Board											*
Shape Roll and Graph Recording Sheet											*
Shape Castle Map											•

• class set   + teacher only   * per pair/group

Suggested Pacing

Day 1	Chapter Opener	Performance Task Preview		Vocabulary			
Day 2	Lesson 13.1	Warm-Up	Dig In	Explore	Think	Apply: Practice	Think: Modeling Real Life
Day 3	Lesson 13.2	Warm-Up	Dig In	Explore	Think	Apply: Practice	Think: Modeling Real Life
Day 4	Lesson 13.3	Warm-Up	Dig In	Explore	Think	Apply: Practice	Think: Modeling Real Life
Day 5	Lesson 13.4	Warm-Up	Dig In	Explore	Think	Apply: Practice	Think: Modeling Real Life
Day 6	Lesson 13.5	Warm-Up	Dig In	Explore	Think	Apply: Practice	Think: Modeling Real Life
Day 7	Lesson 13.6	Warm-Up	Dig In	Explore	Think	Apply: Practice	Think: Modeling Real Life
Day 8	Lesson 13.7	Warm-Up	Dig In	Explore	Think	Apply: Practice	Think: Modeling Real Life
Day 9	Lesson 13.8	Warm-Up	Dig In	Explore	Think	Apply: Practice	Think: Modeling Real Life
Day 10	Lesson 13.9	Warm-Up	Dig In	Explore	Think	Apply: Practice	Think: Modeling Real Life
Day 11	Connect And Grow	Performance Task		Activity		Chapter Practice	
Day 12		Centers					
Day 13	Chapter Assessment	Chapter Assessment					

Year-to-Date: 145 Days

Laurie's Notes

Mathematical Practices

Students have opportunities to develop aspects of the mathematical practices throughout the chapter. Here are some examples.

1. **Make Sense of Problems and Persevere in Solving Them**
   13.1 Practice, *p. 618*
2. **Reason Abstractly and Quantitatively**
   13.9 Practice Exercise 5, *p. 666*
3. **Construct Viable Arguments and Critique the Reasoning of Others**
   13.1 Explore and Grow, *p. 613*
4. **Model with Mathematics**
   13.2 Think and Grow: Modeling Real Life, *p. 622*
5. **Use Appropriate Tools Strategically**
   13.3 Apply and Grow: Practice Exercise 9, *p. 627*
6. **Attend to Precision**
   13.2 Apply and Grow: Practice Exercise 11, *p. 621*
7. **Look for and Make Use of Structure**
   13.6 Practice Exercise 4, *p. 648*
8. **Look for and Express Regularity in Repeated Reasoning**
   13.7 Practice Exercise 8, *p. 654*

Performance Task Preview

- Preview the page to gauge students' prior knowledge about two- and three-dimensional shapes.
- ? "Have you ever built a sandcastle?" Listen for students to tell you about their experiences building sandcastles.
- ? "What shapes do you see?" squares, triangles, rectangles
- In the Performance Task at the end of the chapter, students will identify, count, and draw two- and three- dimensional shapes to complete a sandcastle.

13 Two- and Three-Dimensional Shapes

- Have you ever built a sandcastle?
- What shapes do you see?

Chapter Learning Target:
Understand two- and three-dimensional shapes.

Chapter Success Criteria:
- I can identify shapes.
- I can describe two- and three-dimensional shapes.
- I can compare shapes.
- I can create shapes.

Check out the digital flash cards.
BigIdeasMath.com

ELL Support

Students may be familiar with the word *surface* from everyday life. If not, run your hand along the top of a desk and say "The flat top of the desk is its surface." Explain that surfaces are the outermost area of an object, and they are often flat, but sometimes are not. For example, the surface of a ball is curved.

Laurie's Notes

Vocabulary Review

- ? **Preview:** "What do you see at the top of the page?" *Sample answer:* shapes
- Have students say each review word out loud. Have students explain how the words are related.
- Have students label the shapes as hexagons or squares.
- Direct students to the lower half of the page. Review how to find the words in the word search.
- Have students use their vocabulary cards to identify the words being modeled.
- **Extension:** Challenge students to find additional vocabulary words. The words *edge, face,* and *vertex* are present.

Chapter 13 Vocabulary

Activity

- **Show and Tell:** Have students lay out their vocabulary cards in front of them with the picture side facing up. Say the word on the vocabulary card, show the word, and describe the picture definition to students. Have students find the corresponding card. Have students take turns showing the card and telling a partner about the word and its picture definition.
- **Supporting Learners:** Limit the amount of cards the students lay out in front of them.

Newton & Descartes's Math Musicals

with Differentiated Rich Math Tasks

Newton and Descartes team up in these educational stories and songs to bring mathematics to life! Use the Newton and Descartes hand puppets to act out the stories. Encourage students to sing the songs to take full advantage of the power of music to learn math. Visit *www.MathMusicals.com* to access all the adventures, songs, and activities available!

Name ______________________

13 Vocabulary

Review Words
hexagon
square

Organize It

Use the review words to complete the graphic organizer.

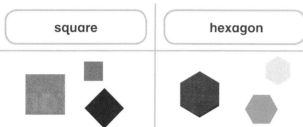

square	hexagon

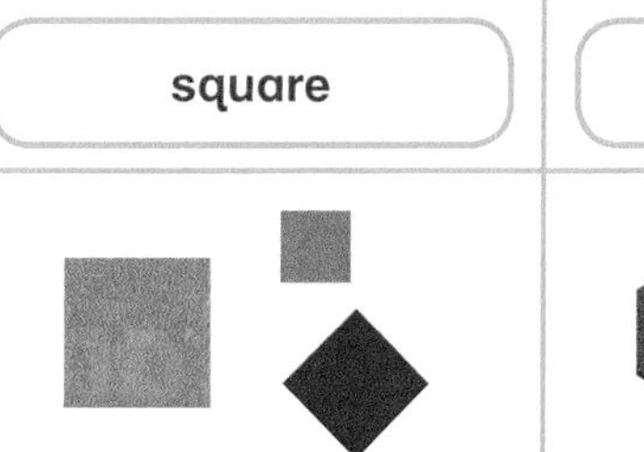

Define It

Use your vocabulary cards to identify the words. Find each word in the word search.

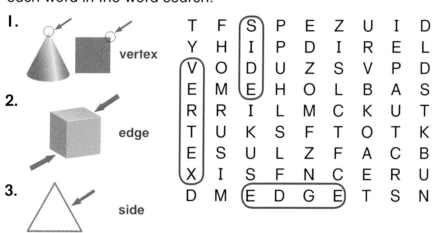

1.

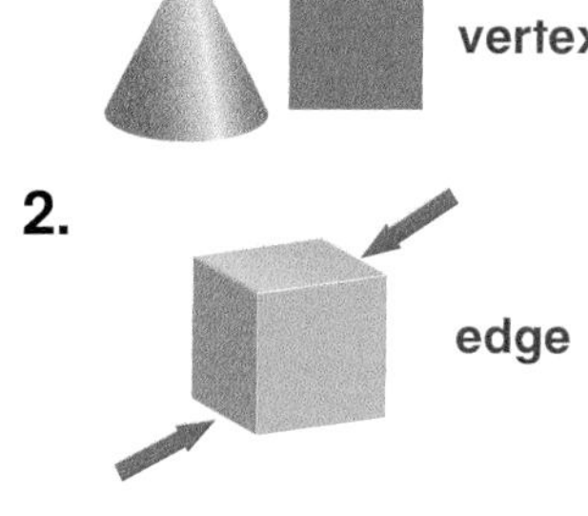

vertex

2. edge

3. side

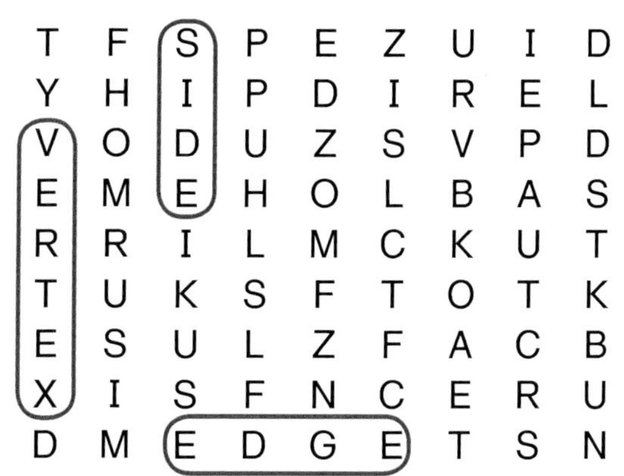

Chapter 13 Vocabulary Cards

curved surface	edge
flat surface	rectangular prism
rhombus	side
three-dimensional shape	trapezoid

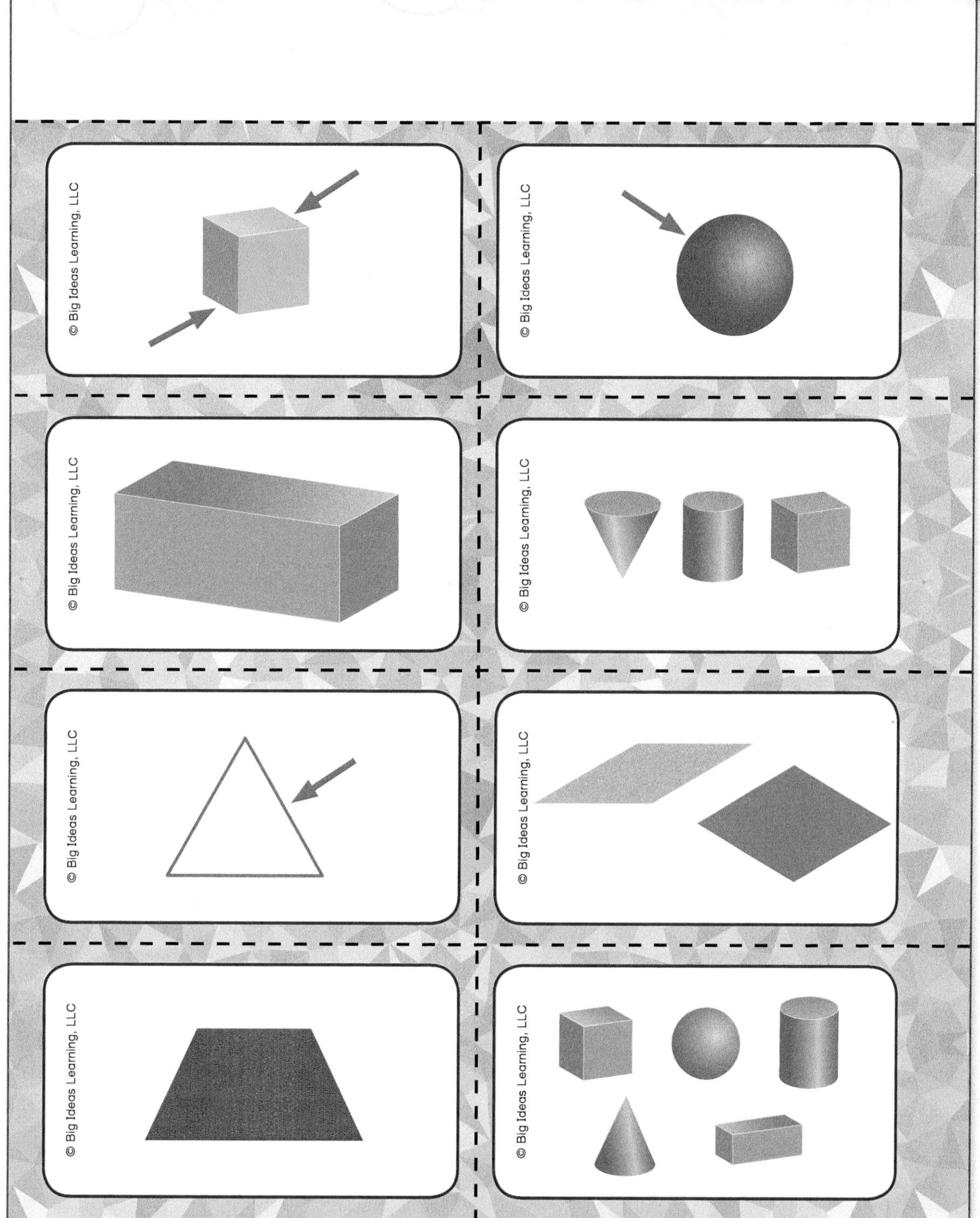
© Big Ideas Learning, LLC
© Big Ideas Learning, LLC
© Big Ideas Learning, LLC
© Big Ideas Learning, LLC
© Big Ideas Learning, LLC
© Big Ideas Learning, LLC
© Big Ideas Learning, LLC
© Big Ideas Learning, LLC

Chapter 13 Vocabulary Cards

two-dimensional shape

vertex

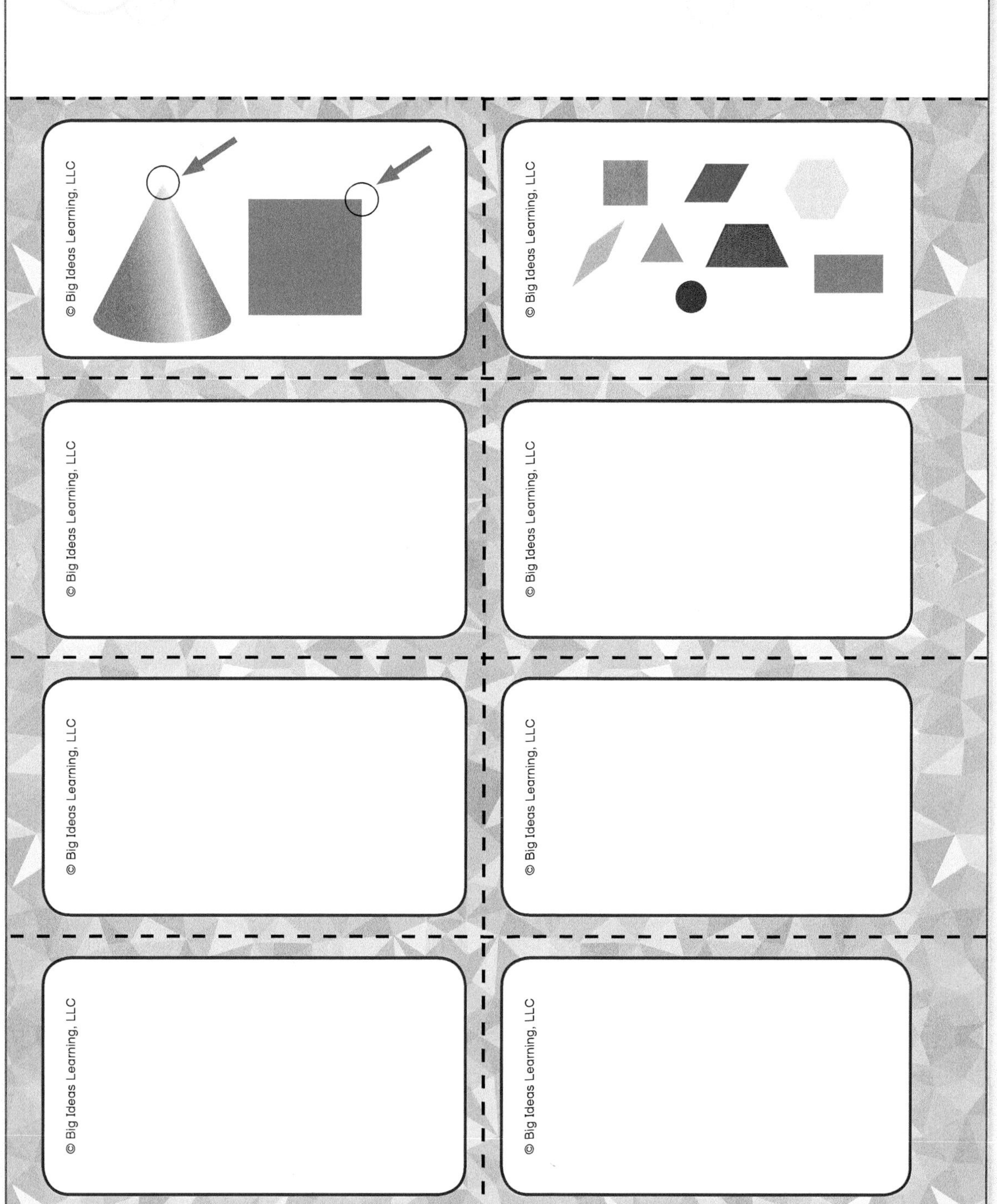
© Big Ideas Learning, LLC
© Big Ideas Learning, LLC
© Big Ideas Learning, LLC
© Big Ideas Learning, LLC
© Big Ideas Learning, LLC
© Big Ideas Learning, LLC
© Big Ideas Learning, LLC
© Big Ideas Learning, LLC

Check out the
Dynamic Classroom.

BigIdeasMath.com

Laurie's Notes

STATE STANDARDS
1.G.A.1

Learning Target

Sort two-dimensional shapes.

Success Criteria

- Use a sorting rule to identify shapes.
- Explain different ways to sort two-dimensional shapes.

Warm-Up

Practice opportunities for the following are available in the Resources by Chapter or at *BigIdeasMath.com.*

- Daily skills
- Vocabulary
- Prerequisite skills

ELL Support

Students may know the word *sort* as meaning "type." Explain that it also describes the action of putting things into groups or categories. When you sort, you group things according to attributes. For example, you may sort by color, size, or shape. Color, size, and shape are all attributes.

Preparing to Teach

This chapter extends learning on two-dimensional and three-dimensional shapes from kindergarten. Today's lesson reviews previous vocabulary and attributes of shapes. Students also define open and closed shapes as a defining attribute.

Materials

- two-dimensional shapes
- Shape Sort Cards*
- scissors and glue

**Found in the Instructional Resources*

Dig In (Circle Time)

A variety of objects and drawings are used to help students distinguish between various two-dimensional shapes. This is discussion time to hear student's thoughts on geometric shapes.

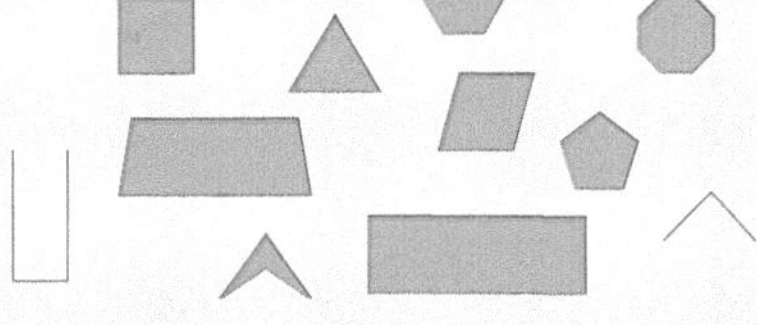

- Place a collection of two-dimensional objects or drawings in the circle or give one to every 2–3 students. Be sure to include drawings of open shapes as shown. "Tell your partner what you know about the object(s)." Provide time for students to share out loud. You want to hear the distinguishing feature such as 3 versus 4 sides, rectangle versus square, 3 versus 4 vertices, straight edges versus curved sides.
- ? Focus on two objects, such as an index card and a fact family card (triangle). "How are these alike? How are they different?" If students compare the size or color, agree with the distinction, but ask if color or size would change the type of shape. This is a difference between distinguishing features and non-distinguishing features.
- Compare a square with a drawing of an open square with only 3 sides drawn. Tell them shapes are called open if the sides or curves do not all meet. There will be an *open* space in the shape. Have students identify all the open shapes in the circle.
- Continue comparing shapes. Students can select any two or three from the circle and ask their classmates to make comparisons.
- ◉ Suggest a rule to sort the shapes, such as "open or closed" or "types of sides." Have students tell which category the shapes would belong in.
- ◉ Ask students to determine a rule by which the shapes could be sorted. It is okay if some shapes do not get included.
- ◉ "Today we will be sorting shapes in all kinds of ways."

? Teaching Prompt ◉ Learning Target

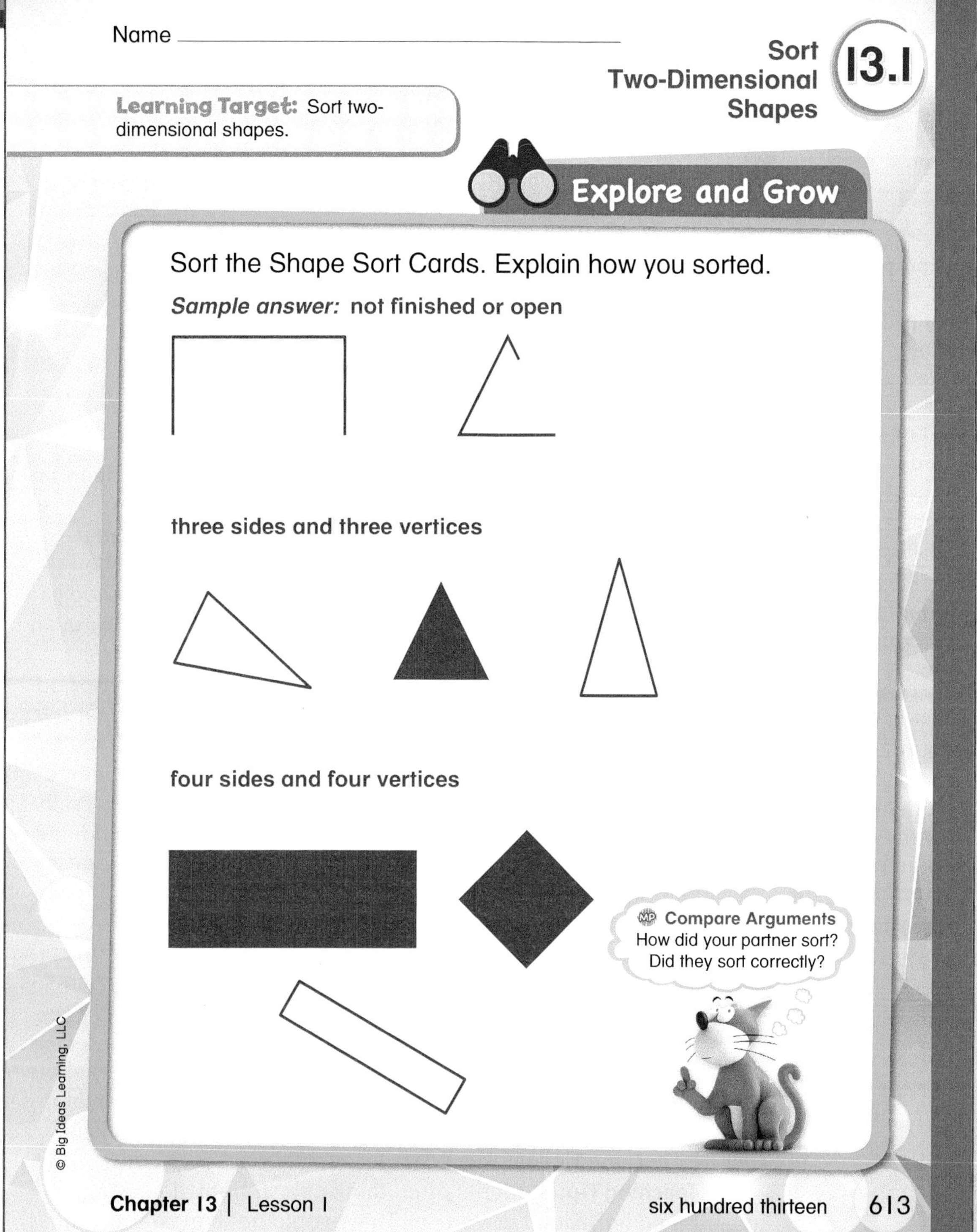

Name
Learning Target: Sort two-dimensional shapes.
Sort Two-Dimensional Shapes
13.1
Explore and Grow
Sort the Shape Sort Cards. Explain how you sorted.
Sample answer: not finished or open
three sides and three vertices
four sides and four vertices
Compare Arguments
How did your partner sort? Did they sort correctly?
© Big Ideas Learning, LLC
Chapter 13 | Lesson 1
six hundred thirteen
613

Explore and Grow

- Each partner pair can share scissors and glue. Students cut out the Shape Sort Cards. Have them sort in various ways before deciding which way they want to sort.
- Students should glue their sorted cards to the page and title each by how they sorted.
- "Tell your partner how you sorted the cards. If any shapes were left out, tell why."

ELL Support

Discuss the example. Have students work in groups as they practice language while completing Exercises 1 and 2. Monitor discussion and provide support as needed. Expect students at different language levels to perform as described.

Beginner students may use single words or simple phrases. **Intermediate** students may answer with longer phrases or simple sentences. **Advanced** students may answer with sentences and help direct the discussion.

Laurie's Notes

Think and Grow

Getting Started

- Students will use specific attributes to sort shapes. This will demonstrate an understanding of the vocabulary.
- Introduce the vocabulary cards **side**, **vertex**, and **two-dimensional shape**.

Teaching Notes

- There are three different ways to sort in the example and two groupings within each sort. Take time with each one to talk about all of the shapes within the groupings.
- **Model:** "Look at the first sentence." Have a student read it. "Tell your partner what a two-dimensional shape is. When we sort two-dimensional shapes, there are many ways we can do it. We will look at three examples and you will sort by even more ways."
- **Model:** "Let's look at how the first group of shapes are sorted. It says to sort by closed or open shapes. Remind your partners what a closed shape is. Remind them what an open shape is."
- **MP6 Attend to Precision:** "Explain why each shape under closed is really closed. Now tell why each shape under open is really open." Hold up an open shape from the Dig In. Have students tell whether it would be in the closed or open group. Repeat with a closed shape.
- Repeat this process with sorting by the number of sides and vertices. Be sure students can point to and explain the meaning of a side and a vertex. Tell students that one of the "corners" is a vertex. Two or more (the plural) are vertices.
- Discuss which attributes students will circle in Exercise 1. If students circle a shape that does not belong, have them explain their reasoning. Spatial abilities and comprehension develop at different times. Listening to students' misconceptions is important. Repeat this process with Exercise 2.
- **Teaching Tip:** Students often think of a straight side as only being horizontal or vertical. They would not consider the sides of a trapezoid or a rhombus to be straight because they "slant." Watch for this misconception in Exercise 2.

? **Supporting Learners:** Ask students to describe each shape. "Is it open or closed? Does it have straight sides or is it curved?" Have students trace the shapes with their fingers. For Exercise 1, do students hit any open spaces? For Exercise 2, is it smooth and continuous, or do they hit a corner?

- **Extension:** Find other shapes around the room to fit the categories.

◉ "Tell your partner how you know if the shape is open or closed. Tell how you know if it has a curve or straight sides."

You can sort **two-dimensional shapes** in many ways.

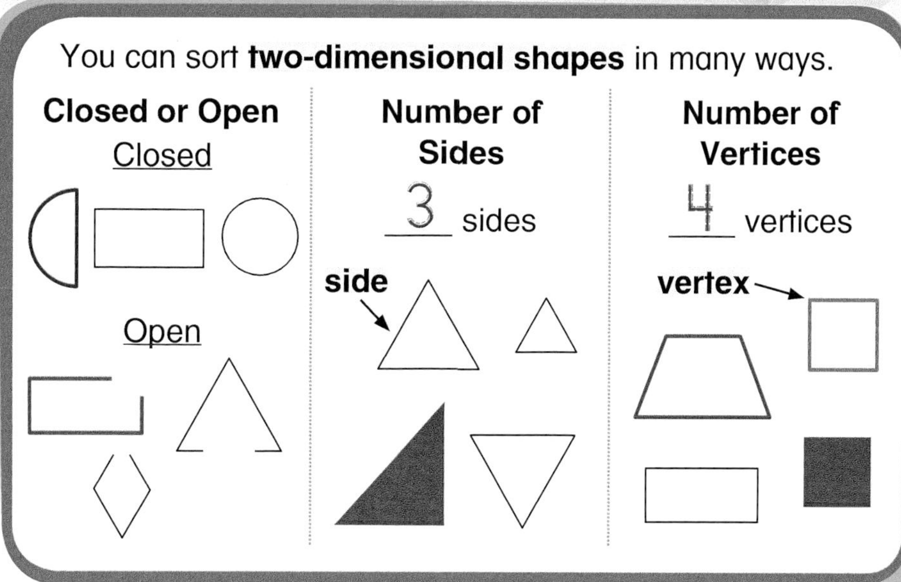

Show and Grow *I can do it!*

1. Circle the closed shapes with 4 vertices.

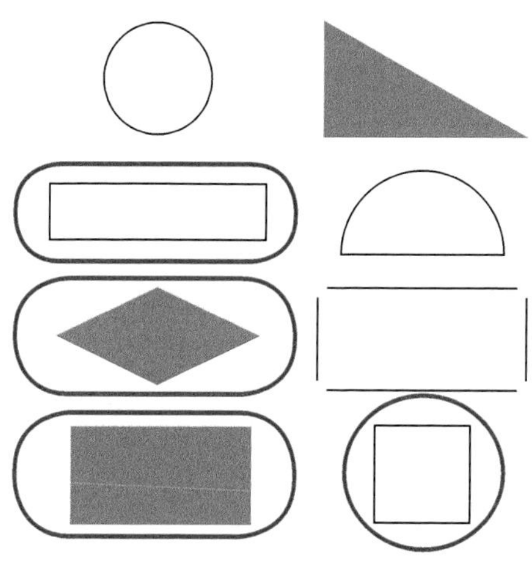

2. Circle the closed shapes with no straight sides.

Scaffold instruction to support all students in their learning. Learning is individualized and you may want to group students differently as they move in and out of these levels with each skill and concept. Student self-assessment and feedback help guide your instructional decisions about how and when to layer support for all students to become proficient learners.

Meeting the needs of all learners.

Laurie's Notes

Apply and Grow: Practice

SCAFFOLDING INSTRUCTION

Each exercise on the page is different, requiring students to pay attention to each set of directions. Discussion about each exercise is valuable and will give you insights into your students' learning. Listen to see how students are finding open or closed shapes, counting the sides or vertices, or inspecting the types of vertices.

EMERGING students may have difficulty distinguishing between fine attributes of shapes. They have difficulty identifying vertices if they are not really 'pointy,' meaning very acute, or recognizing what an "L-shaped" vertex means. They may not consider a side to be straight if it is not horizontal or vertical.

- **Exercise 3:** Students may choose only colored-in shapes as they are closed, but miss the directions of 3-vertices. They may miss the uncolored triangles as well.
- **Exercise 4:** Hold up an envelope or piece of paper and point out the right angle. Tell students this is the type of vertex they are looking for. You can give the mathematical vocabulary of right angle, but students do not need to know the term.
- **Exercise 5:** When looking for shapes that have *more than 4 straight sides*, students hear only the number 4. Emphasize more than 4.
- **Exercise 7:** Students may need help thinking of two shapes to draw. Point out squares, rectangles, trapezoids, and rhombi on the page.

PROFICIENT students are generally accurate in distinguishing two-dimensional shapes and specific attributes.

- **Exercises 3 and 4:** Students need to pay attention to two criteria. They may only look at one or the other.
- **Exercise 7:** Notice if students draw two shapes with right angles, such as a square and a rectangle. Challenge them to draw a shape without "L-shaped" vertices.

Additional Support

- Use highlighters to accentuate the desired attributes. Use a different highlight to accentuate an undesired attribute (such as open when looking for closed) when appropriate.

Extension: Adding Rigor

- Ask if students know the names of all the shapes on this page.

Name ________________________________

Apply and Grow: Practice

3. Circle the closed shapes with only 3 vertices.

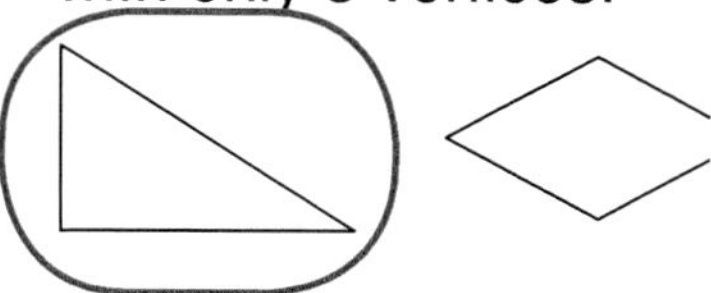

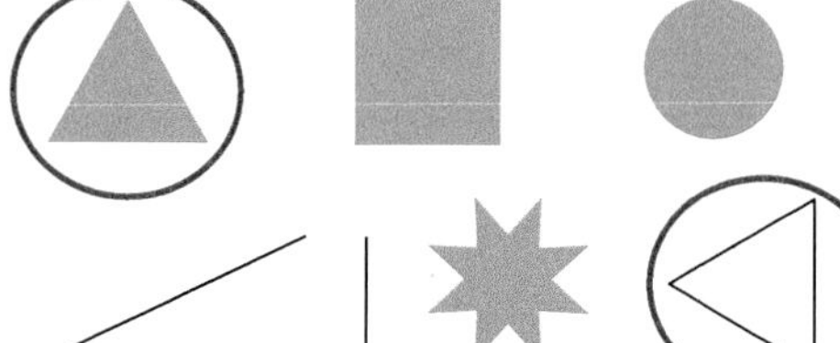

4. Circle the closed shapes with only L-shaped vertices.

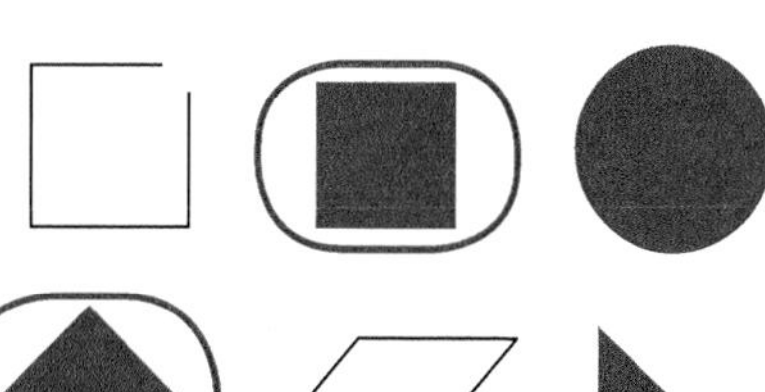

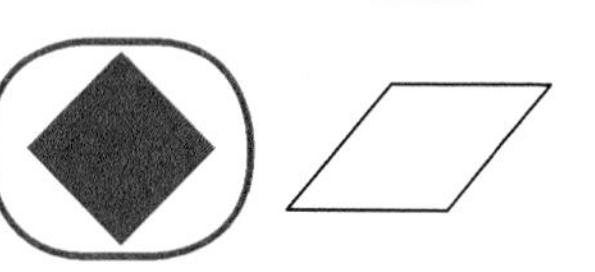

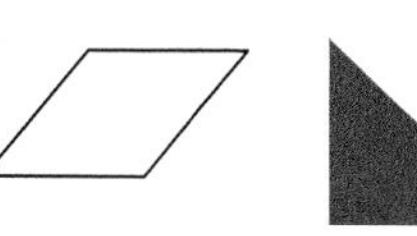

5. Circle the shapes with more than 4 straight sides.

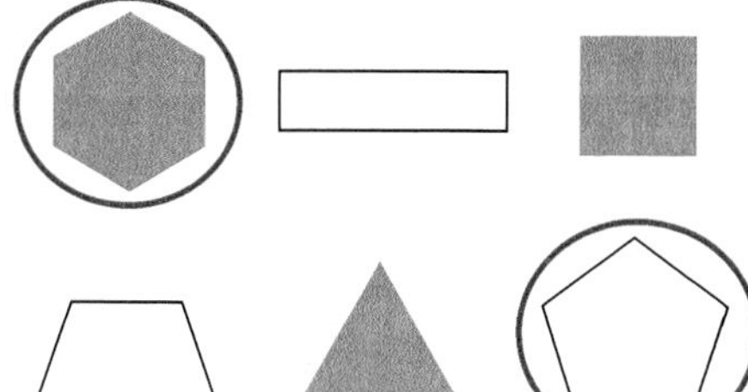

6. Circle the shapes with 6 straight sides.

7. DIG DEEPER! Draw 2 different two-dimensional shapes that have only 4 straight sides.

Sample answer:

ELL Support

Check for understanding of Lesson 13.1. Read the direction lines as students follow along. Have students draw each of the following and hold up for your review.

1. a green shape with only three vertices
2. an orange shape with only L-shaped vertices
3. a blue shape with four straight sides and no L-shaped vertices
4. a yellow shape with six straight sides

Laurie's Notes

Think and Grow: Modeling Real Life

These applications allow students to show their understanding of two-dimensional shapes. They can distinguish between curved shapes and straight edges and they can identify the number of sides and vertices.

? **Preview:** "What do you see on this page? Do any of them look familiar?" Students may see shapes that make a picture (a snake and a flower). They may also mention the names of the shapes, the colors, and even the directions of what they will do.

- Go through the example instructions one at a time. After each instruction, have students find one of the shapes and color it that color. For the yellow instruction, ask students what kinds of shapes have no straight sides. Once students have colored one of each shape, they color the rest of the snake.
- Introduce Exercise 8. Repeat the procedure with the directions as in the example. Students may miss the rectangular stem.

◉ Students have sorted two-dimensional shapes by various attributes. "Show me with your thumb signals how confident you are in describing two-dimensional shapes. Tell your partner what you have learned today." Have several students share out what they have learned, calling on students at random and not raised hands. Listen for the number and types of sides, vertices, and open and closed in particular.

Closure

- Hold up some of the objects from the Dig In. Have students describe the characteristics of the shape to a partner.

Think and Grow: Modeling Real Life

Use the clues to color the picture.

Only 3 straight sides: **blue** Only 4 straight sides: **green**

No straight sides: **yellow** More than 4 vertices: **red**

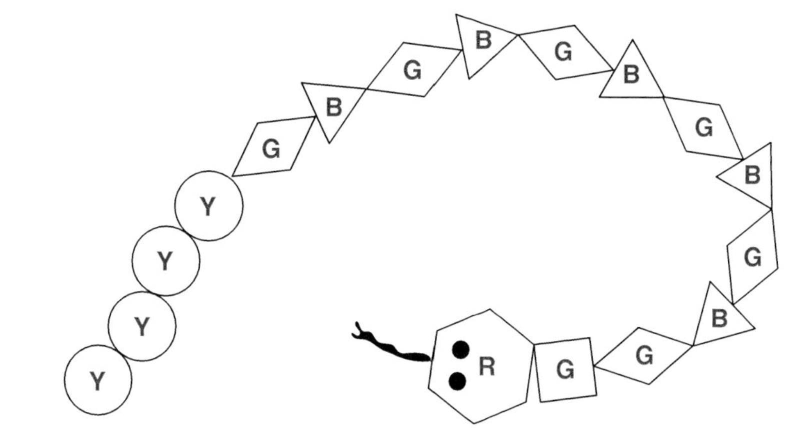

Show and Grow *I can think deeper!*

8. Use the clues to color the picture.

Only 3 vertices: **green**

All L-shaped vertices: **orange**

Only 4 straight sides and no L-shaped vertices: **blue**

6 straight sides: **yellow**

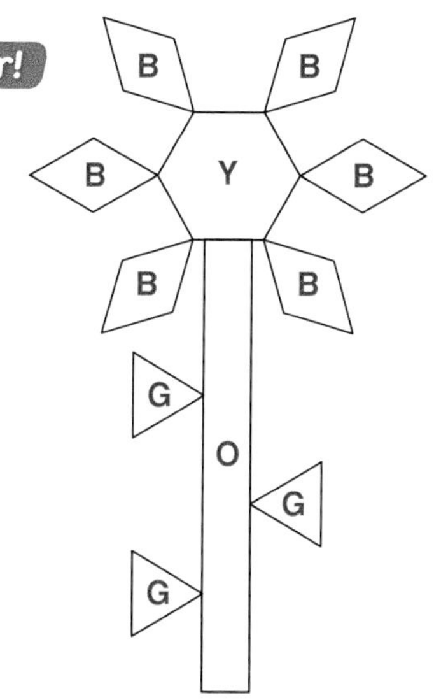

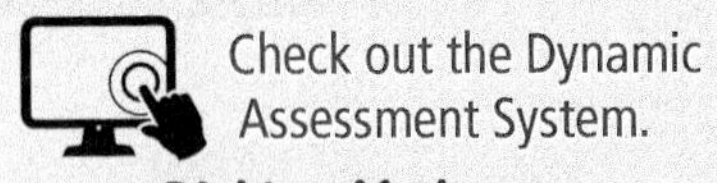
Check out the Dynamic Assessment System.
BigIdeasMath.com

Scaffold assignments to support all students in their learning progression. Revisit with spaced practice to move every student toward proficiency.

Connect and Extend Learning

Practice Notes

- Remind students what closed or open shapes look like along with how to count sides and vertices.
- **Exercise 5**: Discuss with students shapes that have two long straight sides and two short straight sides.

Prior Skills

- **Exercise 7**: Grade 1, Comparing Lengths Indirectly

Cross-Curricular Connections

Physical Education

- Make different shapes that students have learned on the floor in a scattered arrangement or patterned array. Use shape printouts, tape, or draw the shapes with chalk outside. Have students take turns sorting the shapes by jumping on the same kind of shape. Assign another student to sort by jumping on a different shape. Students can put markers such as bean bags or counters down on the shapes they have already jumped on. Play until everyone gets at least one turn.

Name ______________________

Practice 

Learning Target: Sort two-dimensional shapes.

You can sort two-dimensional shapes in many ways.

Closed or Open

Closed Open

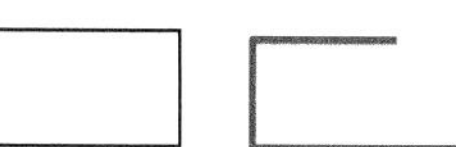

Number of Sides

4 sides

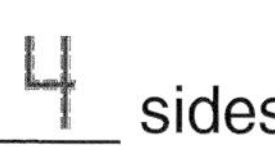

Number of Vertices

3 vertices

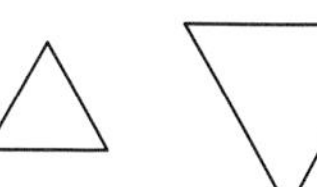

1. Circle the closed shapes with no straight sides.

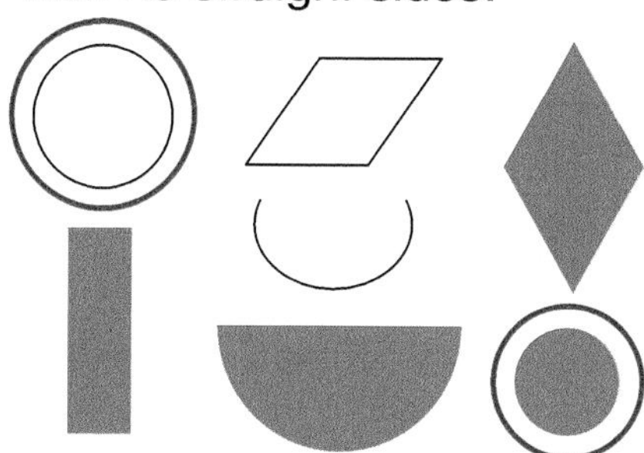

2. Circle the closed shapes with 4 sides of the same length.

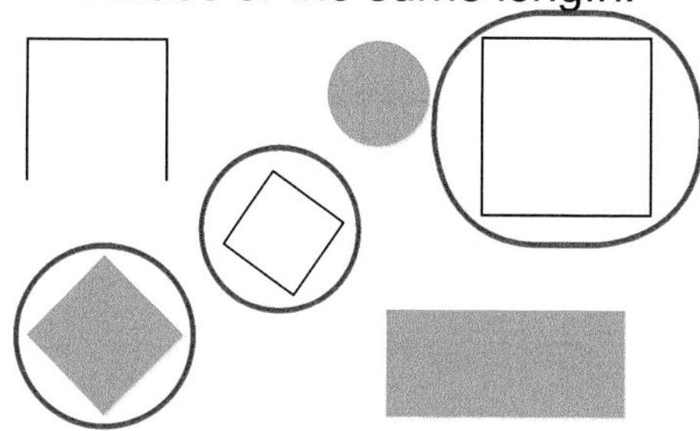

3. Circle the shapes with no vertices.

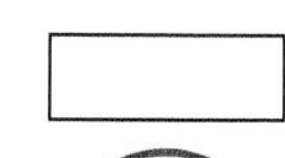

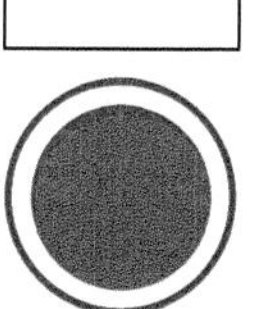

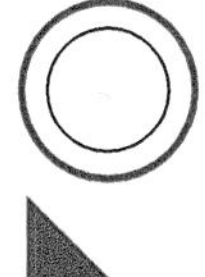

4. Circle the shapes with more than 4 vertices.

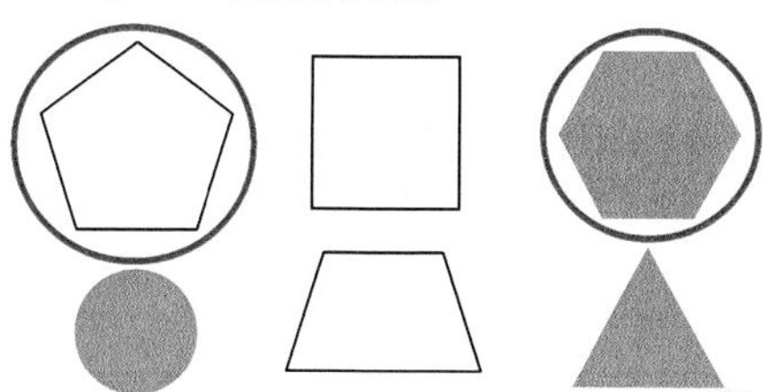

Connect and Extend Learning

Extend Student Learning

Visual-Spatial

- Draw a shape collage on the board, or create one on poster board with shape cut outs. Have students keep track of the shapes they see in a tally chart. Go over the number of shapes that are in the collage with students. Then have them create their own shape collages.

Lesson Resources	
Surface Level	**Deep Level**
Resources by Chapter • Extra Practice • Reteach Differentiating the Lesson Skills Review Handbook Skills Trainer	Resources by Chapter • Enrichment and Extension Graphic Organizers Dynamic Assessment System • Lesson Practice

5. **DIG DEEPER!** Draw 2 different two-dimensional shapes with 2 long straight sides and 2 short straight sides.

Sample answer:

6. **Modeling Real Life** Use the clues to color the picture.

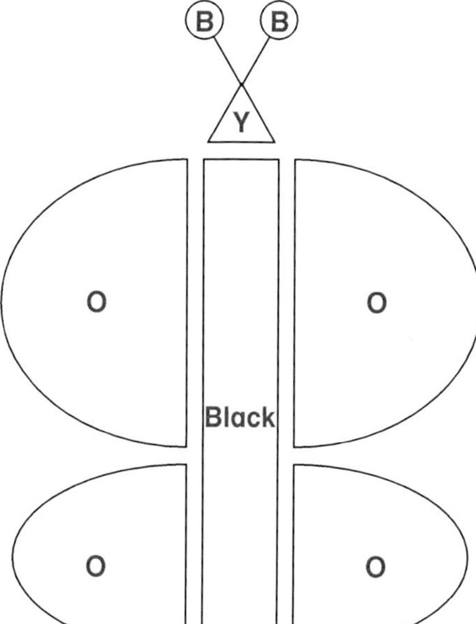

Only 3 vertices: **yellow**

Only 4 sides: **black**

Only 1 straight side: **orange**

No straight sides: **blue**

Check Your Work
How can you work backward to check your work?

7. Circle the longer object.

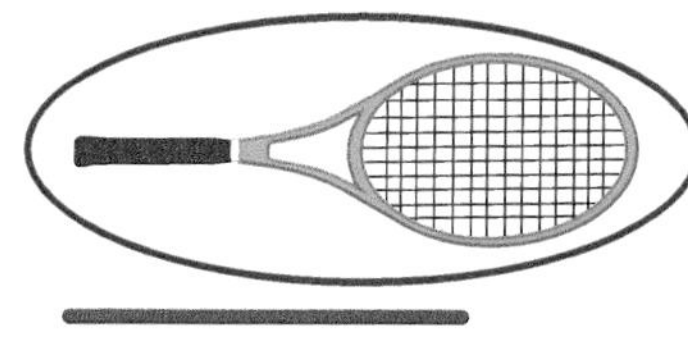

13.2

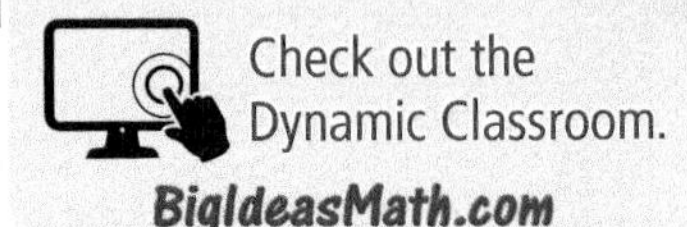
Check out the
Dynamic Classroom.

BigIdeasMath.com

Laurie's Notes

STATE STANDARDS
1.G.A.1

Learning Target

Describe two-dimensional shapes.

Success Criteria

- Draw two-dimensional shapes.
- Identify the number of straight sides.
- Identify the number of vertices.
- Identify a shape from given information.

Warm-Up

Practice opportunities for the following are available in the Resources by Chapter or at *BigIdeasMath.com.*

- Daily skills
- Vocabulary
- Prerequisite skills

ELL Support

Explain that length, width, and height are all dimensions. When an object only has two dimensions, it is flat and only has length and width. You may want to model these dimensions by pointing them out using two-dimensional cutouts, such as squares and rectangles.

Preparing to Teach

Students have worked with triangles, rectangles, squares, hexagons, and circles in kindergarten. Students are introduced to a rhombus and a trapezoid. The trapezoids are all isosceles trapezoids which means the "slanted" sides are of equal length.

Materials

- attribute blocks
- straws

Dig In (Circle Time)

Students are given six shapes. They will compare and describe the shapes in order to define them by their attributes. They will play a "Guess My Shape" game.

- Give students a triangle, rectangle, square, trapezoid, rhombus, and hexagon attribute block. "Many of these shapes should be familiar to you. Choose a shape. Name it. Tell everything you can about it. Take turns saying things about the shape until you've said everything you can. Choose another shape."
- Review the familiar shapes: triangle, rectangle, square, and hexagon. Remind students of their attributes. A square and rectangle all have four sides and four L-shaped vertices, but all sides of a square are the same length. A triangle has three sides and the lengths do not matter. Hexagons have six sides.

? "Today we have two new shapes." Hold up a rhombus. "This shape is called a rhombus. The plural is rhombi." Have students repeat the words. "It has four sides. Which other shapes have four sides? Like a square, a rhombus has four sides that are the same length. It does not have to have L-shaped vertices. Do you see any rhombi in the room?"

? "We have another new shape." Hold up a trapezoid. "How many sides does it have? What do you notice about a trapezoid?" Describe the two parallel sides of the trapezoid, called bases, as best you can for students. The other two sides can connect in any manner.

- Play "Guess my shape." Give clues to a specific shape. Students hold up their attribute block as soon as they know. Point out that some shapes have the same attributes as 4 sides. Play some rounds with 4 sides for multiple answers, and others with more specificity.

◉ "Today we will be describing two-dimensional shapes."

? Teaching Prompt ◉ Learning Target

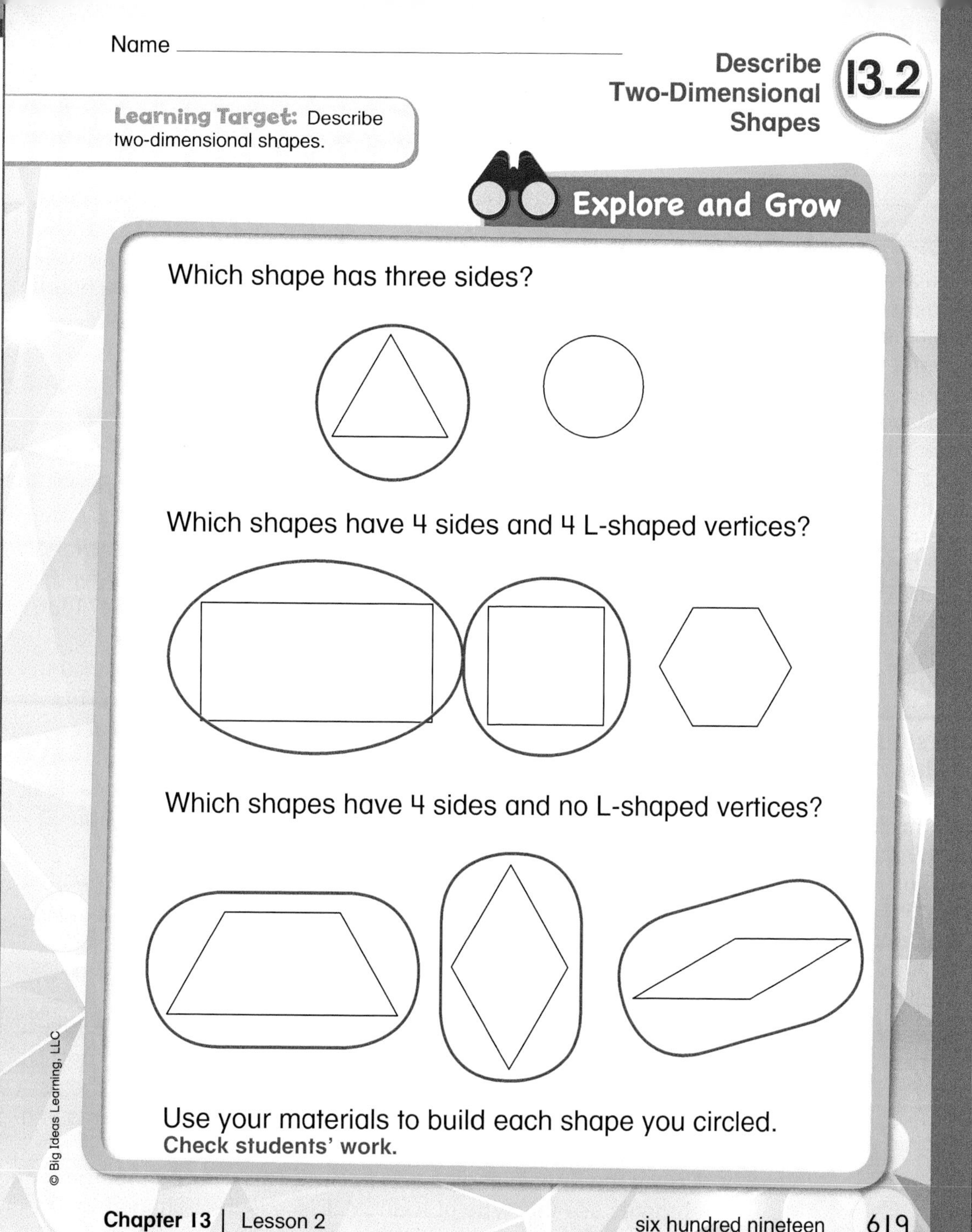

Name
Describe Two-Dimensional Shapes 13.2
Learning Target: Describe two-dimensional shapes.
Explore and Grow
Which shape has three sides?
Which shapes have 4 sides and 4 L-shaped vertices?
Which shapes have 4 sides and no L-shaped vertices?
Use your materials to build each shape you circled.
Check students' work.
© Big Ideas Learning, LLC
Chapter 13 | Lesson 2
six hundred nineteen 619

Explore and Grow

- Students circle the shapes as described. Students will see that more than one type of shape may share certain attributes. That is why some of the questions have more than one answer.
- Once students select the shapes, they will build the shape with straws. You can use toothpicks or another substitute. If they do not have materials to build the shapes, they can draw their own shapes of different sizes.
- **Extension:** "Are there other shapes that would also fit the description? Draw some."

ELL Support

Discuss the examples. Then have students work in pairs as they practice language while completing Exercises 1–4. Have one student ask the other, "How many straight sides are there? How many vertices?" Then have them alternate roles for the other exercises.

Beginner students may answer with numbers.
Intermediate students may answer with simple sentences, such as, "There are three."
Advanced students may answer with compound sentences, such as, "There are three straight sides and three vertices."

Laurie's Notes

Think and Grow

Getting Started

- Introduce the vocabulary cards **trapezoid** and **rhombus**. Remind students of the vocabulary cards *edge, side vertex*, and *two-dimensional shape*.
- If you have been building an anchor chart, add the two new shapes.

Teaching Notes

? "Look at our six shapes. What do they all have in common? What are some differences?"

? **Model:** Hold up a triangle from Dig In. "Let's look at the triangle. How many sides does it have? Trace them with your finger. Fill in the number of sides. How many vertices does it have? Touch each one with your finger. Fill in the number of vertices."

- Repeat this process with the rectangle, square, and hexagon.

? **Model:** Hold up a trapezoid. "Let's look at the trapezoid. This is a new shape for us. How many sides does it have? Trace them with your finger. What do you notice about the sides of a trapezoid? Fill in the number of sides. How many vertices does it have? Touch each one with your finger. Fill in the number of vertices."

? **Model:** "Let's look at the rhombus. This is our other new shape. How many sides does it have? Trace them with your finger. Fill in the number of sides. How many vertices does it have? Touch each one with your finger. Fill in the number of vertices. A rhombus has sides that are the same length, just like a square. But a rhombus doesn't have to have L-shaped vertices."

- **MP6 Attend to Precision:** "Our vocabulary word is *side*, not straight side. Remember that all sides are straight. This helps us as we are learning that sides are straight line segments and not curves."
- Notice the right triangle in Exercise 3. This may be the first time students see this type of triangle. Discuss the L-shaped vertex in the triangle to show it can be in other shapes besides rectangles and squares.
- Students will trace each shape and fill in the number of sides and vertices. Have students trace the sides and point to the vertices with their fingers.

? **MP8 Look for and Express Regularity in Repeated Reasoning:** "What do you notice about the number of sides and vertices for each shape?"

- **Supporting Learners:** Students have the shapes from the Dig In. They can rotate the physical shapes to match the orientation on the page, especially the trapezoid in Exercise 2.
- **Extension:** Find other shapes around the room to fit the categories.

Think and Grow

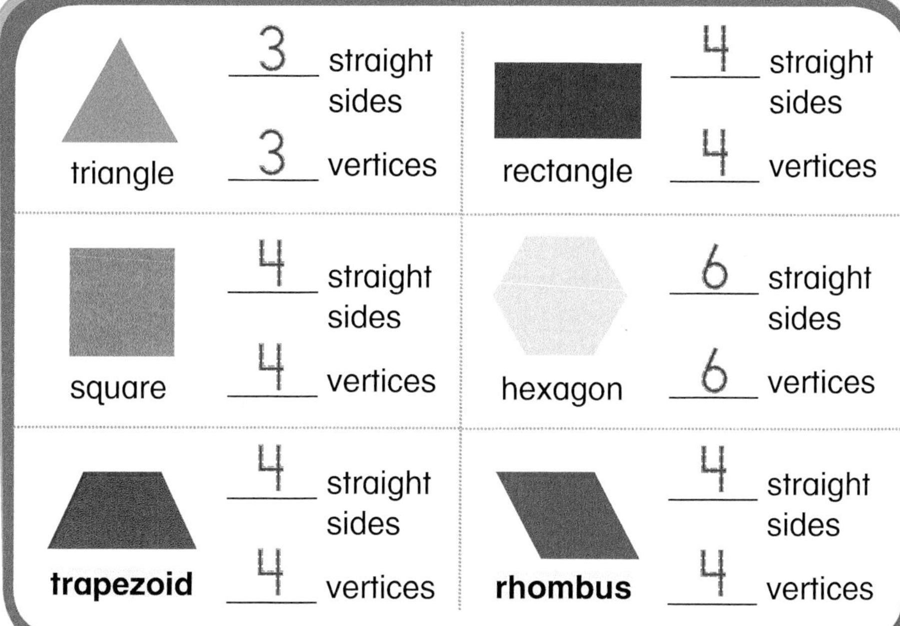

Show and Grow *I can do it!*

1. 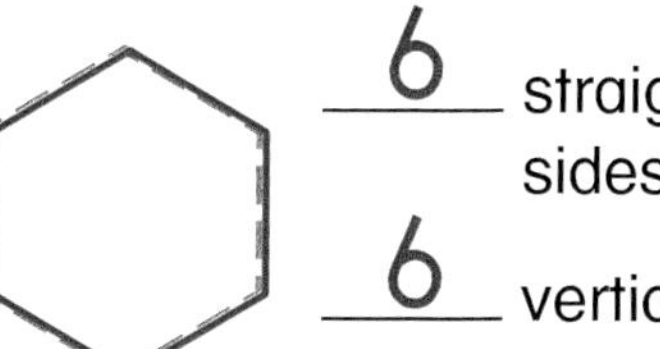

   6 straight sides

   6 vertices

2. 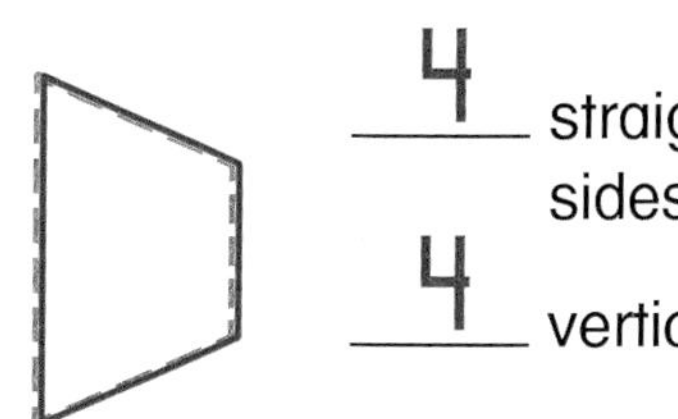

   4 straight sides

   4 vertices

3. 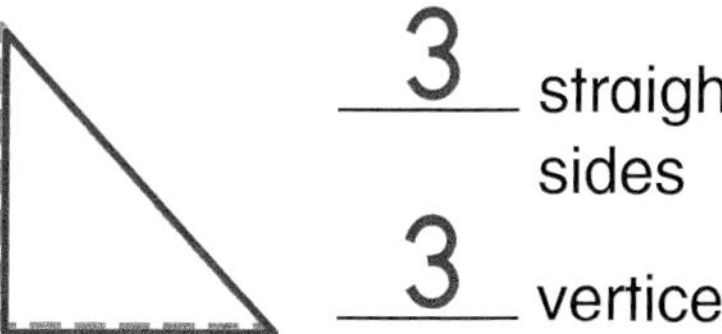

   3 straight sides

   3 vertices

4. 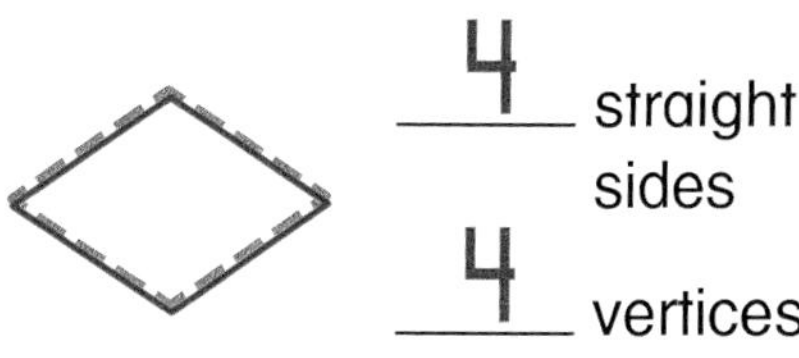

   4 straight sides

   4 vertices

Scaffold instruction to support all students in their learning. Learning is individualized and you may want to group students differently as they move in and out of these levels with each skill and concept. Student self-assessment and feedback help guide your instructional decisions about how and when to layer support for all students to become proficient learners.

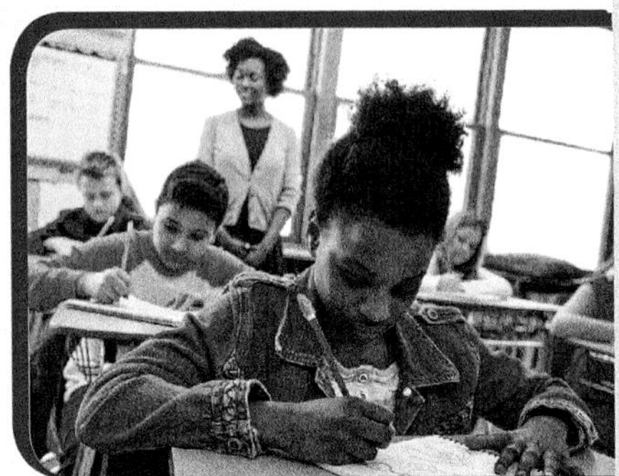

Meeting the needs of all learners.

Laurie's Notes

Apply and Grow: Practice

SCAFFOLDING INSTRUCTION

Students continue to identify the number of sides and vertices for shapes. They progress to selecting the correct attributes from a list without the shape drawn for them.

EMERGING students may know the differences between sides and vertices. They are not consistent with identifying sides and vertices without seeing the shape. They still may not consider a side to be a side if it is not horizontal or vertical.

- **Exercises 5–8:** Students continue tracing shapes and counting sides and vertices. Have students say the name of the shapes.
- **Exercises 9 and 10:** Students select the attributes for a shape from a list. Students will benefit from being able to look at the shapes from the Dig In to help them select the correct attributes.
- **Exercise 11:** Students match the shape with one of the attribute descriptors. Students may only think of circles as a curved shape, and not connect that to not having vertices. Remind students that as they trace the edge of a circle they do not ever hit a corner of any kind.

PROFICIENT students can identify the number of sides and vertices for all shapes.

- **Exercises 5–8:** Students continue as with the previous exercises. Have students write the name of each shape below the shape.
- **Exercises 9 and 10:** Students choose the correct attributes for the shapes. Have students name the shape to which the attributes that are not selected belong.

Additional Support

- Provide students with additional experiences seeing and holding the six shapes. They should be as flat as possible, meaning it can be confusing to students to ask them to think about a two-dimensional shape within a three-dimensional shape (such as bases or faces of a pyramid). Any pictures you find that show the shapes can be shown to students.

Extension: Adding Rigor

- Have students name other attributes for the shapes in Exercise 11 that are not given.

Name ___

Apply and Grow: Practice

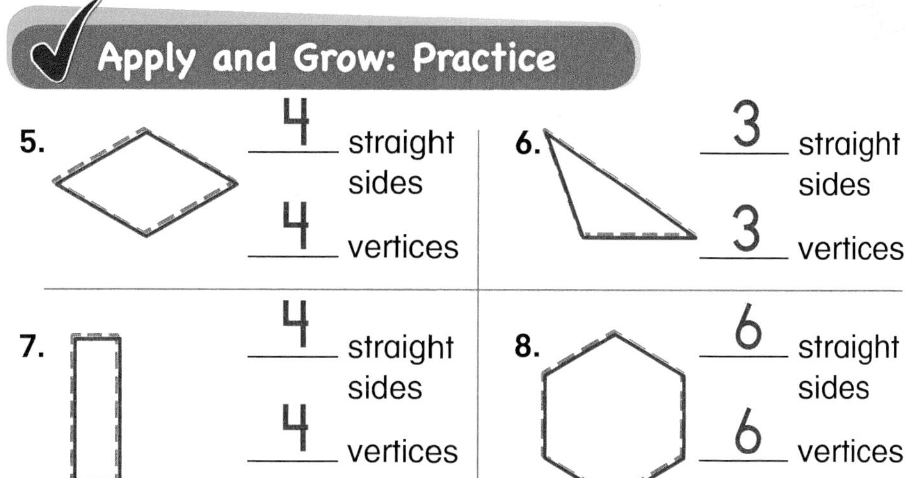

Circle the attributes of the shape.

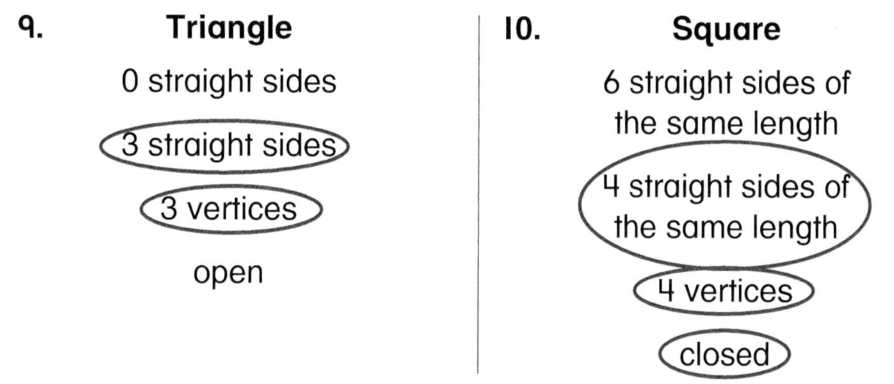

9. Triangle
0 straight sides
3 straight sides
3 vertices
open
10. Square
6 straight sides of the same length
4 straight sides of the same length
4 vertices
closed

11. **Precision** Match each shape with an attribute that describes it.

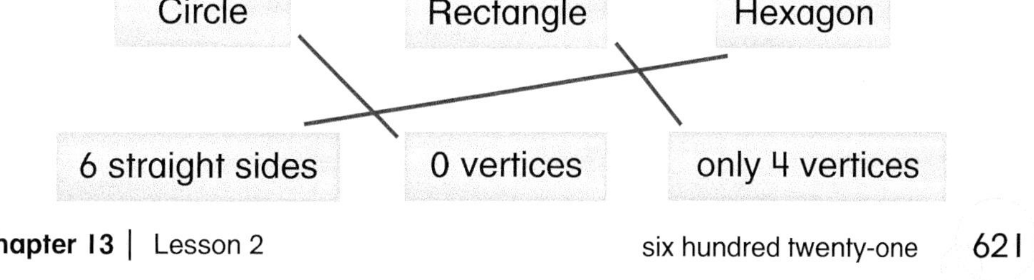

ELL Support

Check for understanding of Lesson 13.2. Read each story aloud as students follow along. Clarify unknown vocabulary if necessary. You may want to discuss experiences with board games if students are unfamiliar with them. Have students draw shapes and write names on a whiteboard and hold up for your review.

Laurie's Notes

Think and Grow: Modeling Real Life

These applications allow students to demonstrate their ability to identify and draw different two-dimensional shapes.

- ? **Preview**: "What games do you like to play? What shapes are part of your game–either on the board or as playing pieces? Our applications today have you finding out the types of shapes involved with two different games."
- Read the description for the board game. Have students tell their partners what shapes have 4 sides and 4 L-shaped vertices. Once students agree on the two shapes, have them circle the names, and then draw the square and the rectangle.
- Have students show their drawing to a partner. Do the square and rectangle look different? At this stage, students will not learn that a square is also a rectangle and we expect their shapes to look different.
- Introduce Exercise 12. Repeat the procedure with the directions as in the example. Have students tell their partners the two shapes that qualify and circle the names. Watch as students draw the trapezoid and rhombus as these may be more challenging to draw.
- **Supporting Learners:** Allow students to trace the shapes onto the exercises. Have attribute blocks for students to trace.
- ◉ Students have described shapes by the number of sides and vertices. "Show me with your thumb signals how confident you are in describing two-dimensional shapes. How are you at counting sides and vertices of a shape? How are you at naming the shape from a number of sides or vertices?"

Closure

- Play "Guess My Shape" from the Dig In.

Think and Grow: Modeling Real Life

A board game has 4 sides and 4 L-shaped vertices. Name and draw two shapes for the board game.

Circle: Square   Hexagon   Trapezoid   Rectangle

Draw shapes:

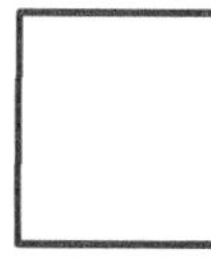

Show and Grow *I can think deeper!*

12. A board game has 4 sides and no L-shaped vertices. Name and draw two shapes for the board game.

Circle: Triangle    Trapezoid   Rhombus   Square

Draw shapes:

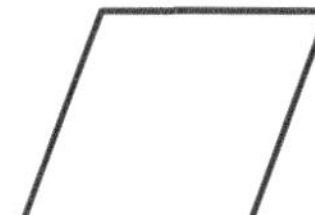

Modeling Real Life Describe the shape of your favorite board game to a partner.

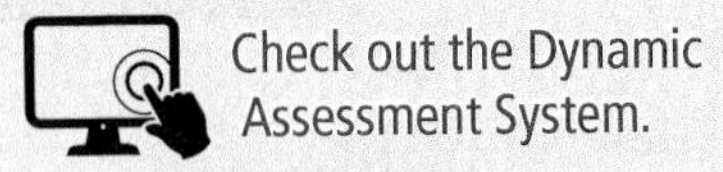
Check out the Dynamic Assessment System.
BigIdeasMath.com

Scaffold assignments to support all students in their learning progression. Revisit with spaced practice to move every student toward proficiency.

Connect and Extend Learning

Practice Notes

- Remind students what the word attribute means.

Prior Skills

- **Exercise 10:** Grade 1, Sorting and Organizing Data

Cross-Curricular Connections

Language Arts

- Go over descriptions of the different shapes with students. Have each student pick a shape, draw or trace it using a pattern or attribute block, and write a caption or short poem about it. Look for students to be detailed and creative.

What am I?
I have 4 sides that are the same
With 4 square corners
That will never change
4 sides, 4 vertices, do you dare...
Call me a square?

Learning Target: Describe two-dimensional shapes.

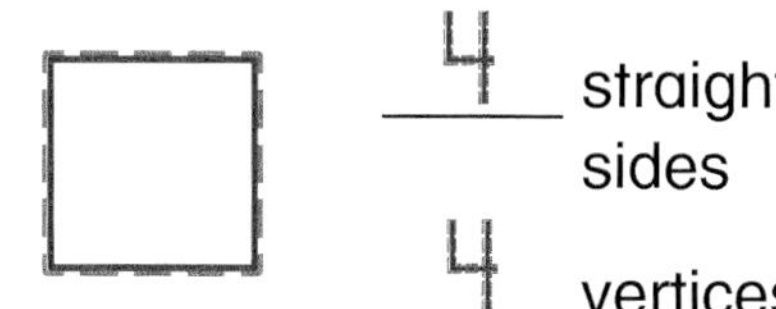

4 straight sides

4 vertices

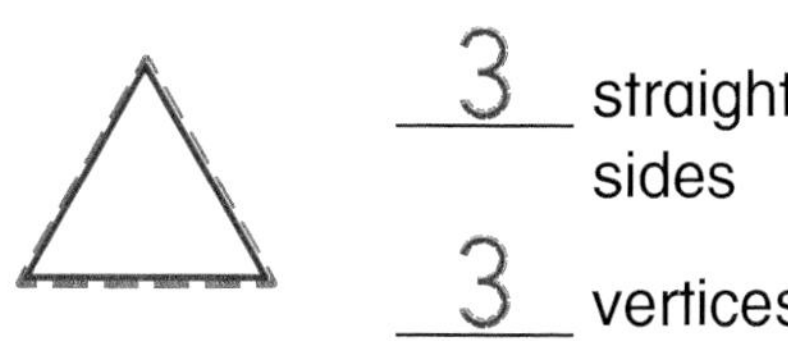

3 straight sides

3 vertices

1. 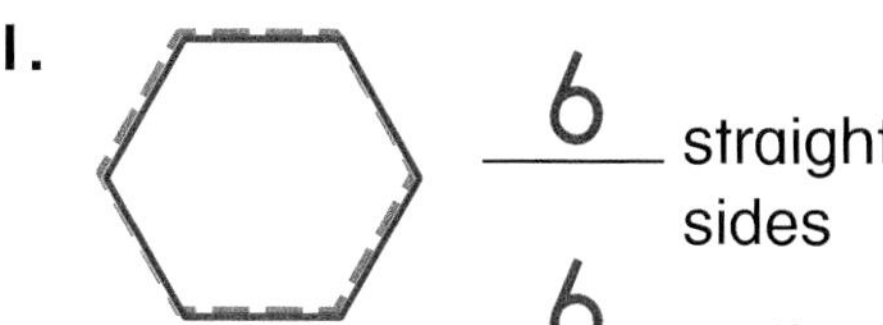

6 straight sides

6 vertices

2. 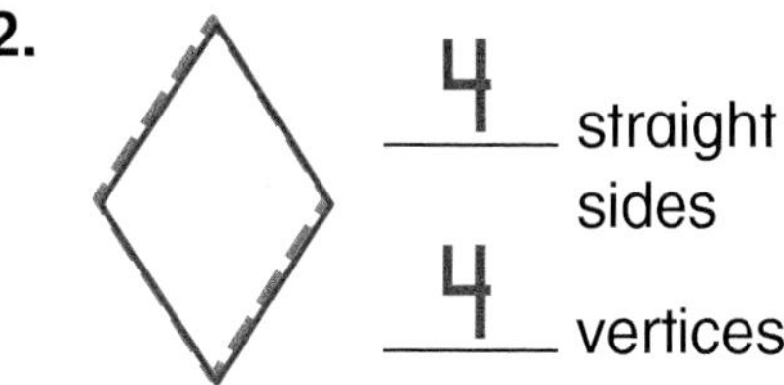

4 straight sides

4 vertices

3. 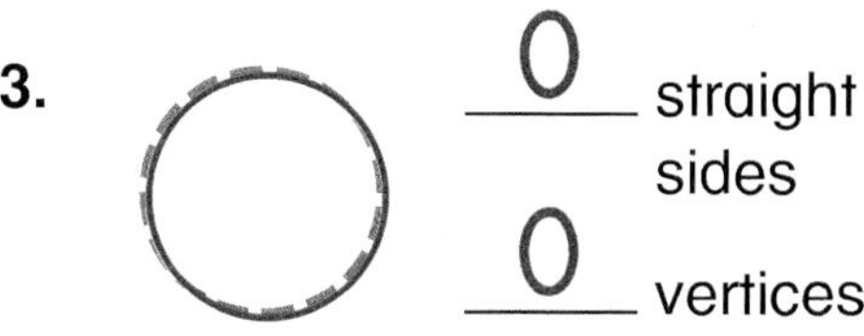

0 straight sides

0 vertices

4. 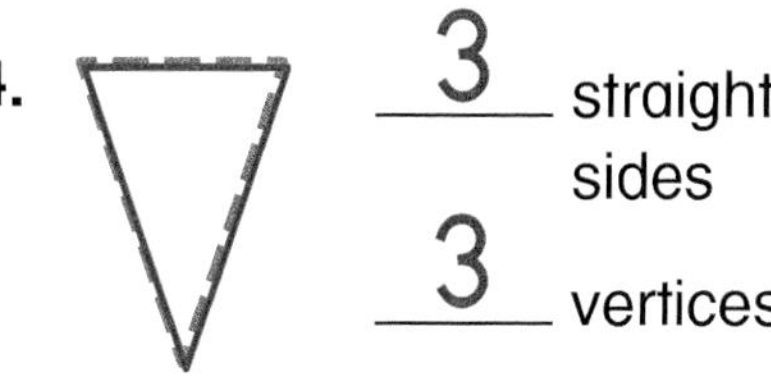

3 straight sides

3 vertices

Circle the attributes of the shape.

5. **Trapezoid**

(4 straight sides)

6 straight sides

5 vertices

(closed)

6. **Rectangle**

(4 straight sides)

0 vertices

(4 vertices)

open

Connect and Extend Learning

Extend Student Learning

Bodily-Kinesthetic

- Assign different shapes to students and have them walk around the room one at a time in an outline of their shape. Have other students guess what shape the student just outlined while walking. You can have other students walking behind the outline leader so they get a feel for what shape the leader is creating.

Lesson Resources	
Surface Level	**Deep Level**
Resources by Chapter • Extra Practice • Reteach Differentiating the Lesson Skills Review Handbook Skills Trainer Math Musicals	Resources by Chapter • Enrichment and Extension Graphic Organizers Math Musicals Dynamic Assessment System • Lesson Practice

7. **Precision** Match each shape with an attribute that describes it.

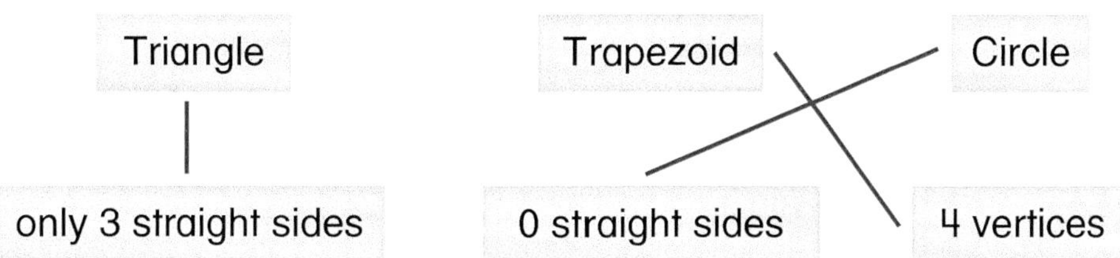

8. **Modeling Real Life** A photograph has 4 straight sides of the same length and 4 vertices. Draw and name two possible shapes for the photograph.

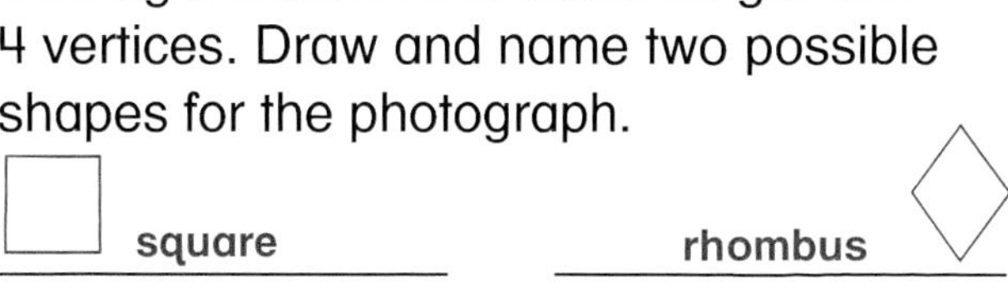

9. **DIG DEEPER!** Draw three triangles that are not touching. How many vertices are there in all? Write an equation to match.

Sample answer:

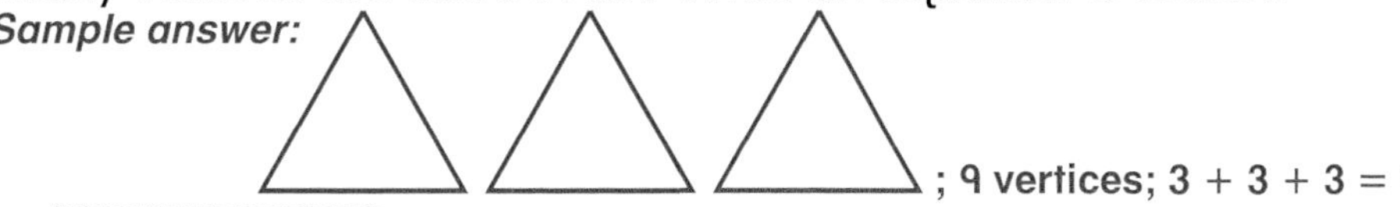

; 9 vertices; $3 + 3 + 3 = 9$

Review & Refresh

10. Complete the tally chart.

Milk Choice	
Chocolate	|||
Strawberry		
White	𝍸

13.3

Check out the
Dynamic Classroom.
BigIdeasMath.com

Laurie's Notes

Learning Target

Join two-dimensional shapes to make another shape.

Success Criteria

- Join shapes to make another shape.
- Tell how many of each shape I used.

Warm-Up

Practice opportunities for the following are available in the Resources by Chapter or at *BigIdeasMath.com.*

- Daily skills
- Vocabulary
- Prerequisite skills

ELL Support

Students will make shapes in this lesson. Remember that many non-native speakers confuse the use of the words *make* and *do*, as they are often the same word in other languages. There is no easy rule for using them correctly. Remind students that in general *make* is used when something is created and *do* is used for tasks and activities.

COMMON CORE

STATE STANDARDS
1.G.A.2

Preparing to Teach

Students love to be creative with pattern block pieces or any geometric shapes that can be put together to make a picture. In this lesson it is really helpful for students to have the pieces to manipulate, turn, move, and so on. To make it manageable, put a collection of the pieces in a zipped baggie for each pair or group of students to share. These can be pattern blocks or the Pattern Blocks Instructional Resource cut from heavy paper. The minimum amount needed per student is six triangles, two trapezoids, two squares, one rectangle, three rhombi, and one hexagon. Cut two semi-circles and two right triangles made by cutting a diagonal of the rectangle for the bag.

Materials

- pattern blocks
- shape cut outs

Dig In (Circle Time)

Students explore shapes and patterns with a random collection of pattern blocks. The goal is for students to notice what new shapes can be made when combining two shapes.

- Give each pair of students a collection of pattern blocks. Let students play with the shapes and make any pictures they want.
- One observation that is quite common is that students will make a shape or design that is symmetric. That is not a goal of the lesson, but you might comment how one side looks like the other.
- "Use just one type of shape and make a design. Also, I want the whole sides to touch in your design." Demonstrate what this means by holding two squares or triangles.

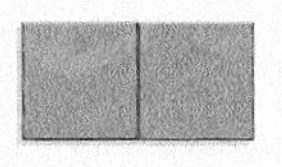

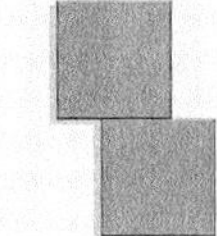

- Using only squares you might see rectangles, squares, or a something else. Using only triangles you might see a parallelogram, trapezoid, triangle, hexagon, or something else.

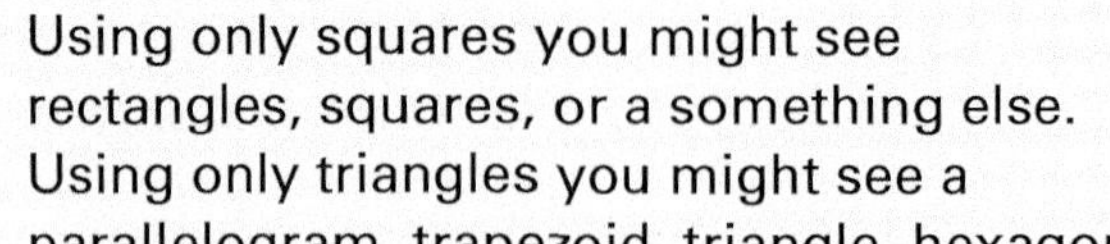

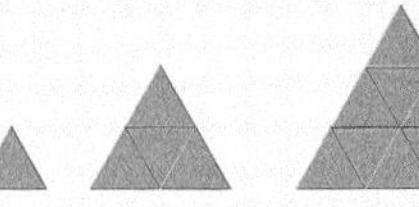

◉ Explain that today they are going to join shapes to make a larger shape. "Some of you used two squares. What do two squares make? Some of you made shapes with triangles. What shapes did you make? What other shapes did you make?"

? Teaching Prompt ◉ Learning Target

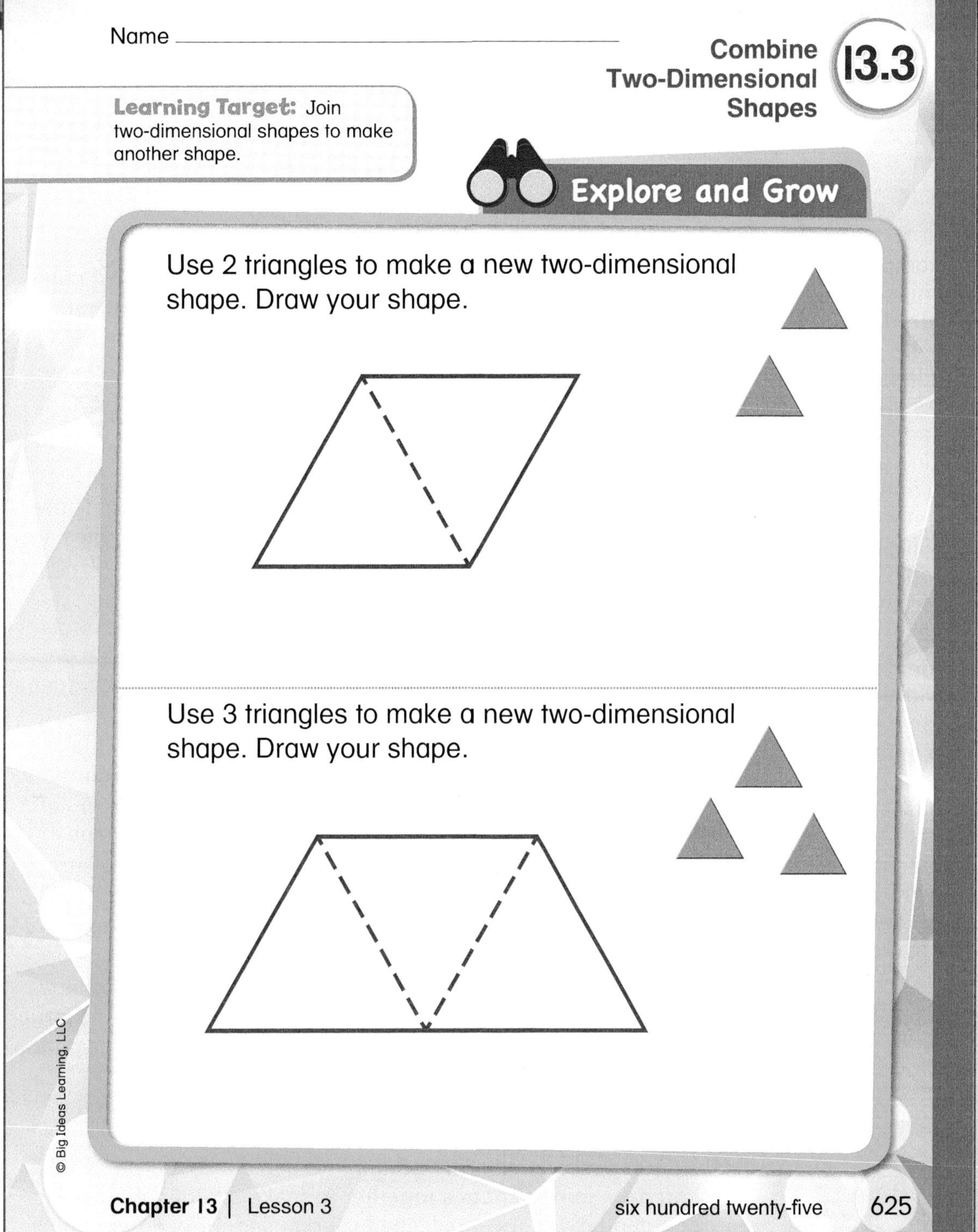

Name
Combine Two-Dimensional Shapes
13.3
Learning Target: Join two-dimensional shapes to make another shape.
Explore and Grow
Use 2 triangles to make a new two-dimensional shape. Draw your shape.
Use 3 triangles to make a new two-dimensional shape. Draw your shape.
© Big Ideas Learning, LLC
Chapter 13 | Lesson 3
six hundred twenty-five
625

Explore and Grow

- Each student will need three pattern block triangles.
- "I want you to start with two triangles. Put them together to make a new shape." Wait for students to complete. "What shape did you make? Trace your shape."
- "Now use three triangles to make a different shape." Wait for students to complete. "What shape did you make? Trace your shape."
- ◉ "You joined shapes to make a larger shape. What shapes could you make with 2 triangles? with three triangles? "

ELL Support

Discuss the example. Review the names of shapes pictured in Exercises 1–4. Then have students work in pairs as they practice language while completing each exercise. Have one student ask another, "How many triangles make a hexagon?" Have them alternate roles for each exercise.

Beginner students may answer with a number.
Intermediate students may answer with phrases, such as, "six triangles."
Advanced students may answer with sentences, such as, "Six triangles make a hexagon."

Laurie's Notes

Think and Grow

Getting Started

- Each student will need a bag of pattern blocks from circle time. If students shared with a partner, they can continue to work with a partner and share the bag of shapes.

Teaching Notes

- There are four problems, each with the same direction line. Make clear that when joining shapes they should share an entire side, not just a portion of a side.
- ? **Model**: "Look at the green shape. What do you notice?" There are six triangles all pointing in. "How many small triangles are joined to make the larger shape?" 6 "Write the number 6. What shape did we make?"
- **MP5 Use Appropriate Tools Strategically**: "In the next exercises see if you can join the shapes to make the new shape shown." Manipulating the smaller shapes helps students develop spatial reasoning skills.
- In these exercises, the shapes to join and the shape to make are shown. Some students may try to visualize and fill in numbers. Do not let them do that. It is important for them to manipulate the pieces and see how they join to make the larger shape.
- Watch as students manipulate the smaller shapes to be sure they are aligning sides completely.
- Review how many of each smaller shapes are needed to make the larger. Have students show how they made the shapes.
- **Supporting Learners:** Students should join the smaller shapes on top of the larger shape rather than trying to match the larger shape. For example, they arrange the two right triangles on top of the rectangle for Exercise 4.
- **Extension:** Have students trace or draw how they made the larger shapes from smaller in the space in the exercise.
- ◉ "You have been working on the first two success criteria. You have joined shapes together to make a larger shape. You counted how many small shapes you used. How do you think you are doing with your learning?"

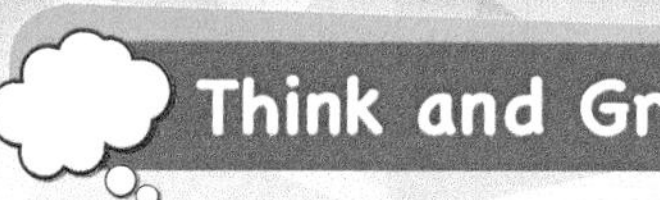

Think and Grow

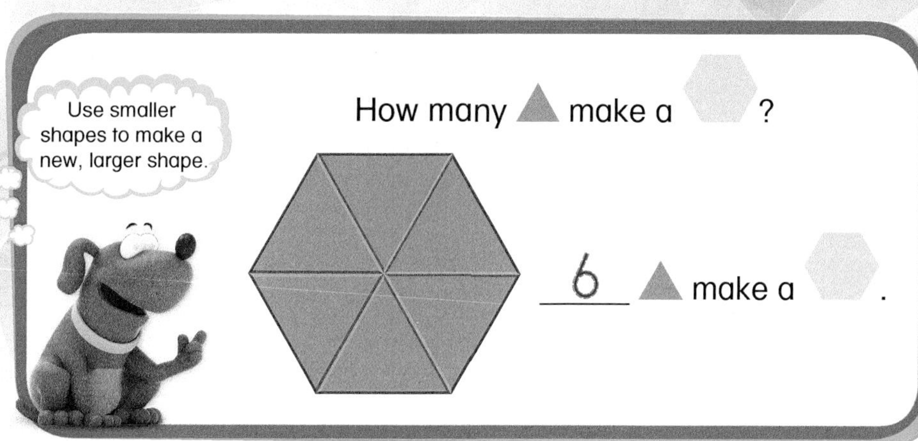

Use smaller shapes to make a new, larger shape.
How many make a ?
6 make a .

Show and Grow I can do it!

1. How many make a ?

2 make a .

2. How many make a ?

3 make a .

3. How many make a ?

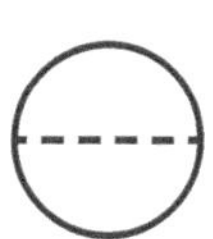

2 make a .

4. How many make a ?

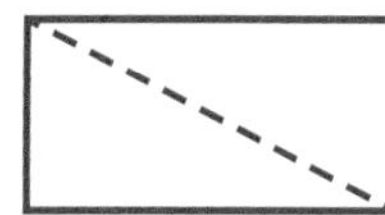

2 make a .

Scaffold instruction to support all students in their learning. Learning is individualized and you may want to group students differently as they move in and out of these levels with each skill and concept. Student self-assessment and feedback help guide your instructional decisions about how and when to layer support for all students to become proficient learners.

Meeting the needs of all learners.

Laurie's Notes

Apply and Grow: Practice

SCAFFOLDING INSTRUCTION

The exercises on this page continue to have students make large shapes from smaller ones. They progress from being told the shapes to use, to the number of shapes needed and they determine which shape will work.

EMERGING students may not understand what it means for shapes to be joined along their sides. They do not always see this as necessary when they fit shapes together and the design ends up with gaps in it. They may not focus on the spatial clues about what can fit. They may not think to rotate shapes.

- **Exercises 5 and 6:** These exercises continue the same directions as Exercises 1–4.
- **Exercises 7 and 8:** Students need to find the shape that will fill the hexagon based on the number of times the shape is used. This will be trial and error for many students. When they find the correct shape, they draw it in the exercise space.
- **Exercise 10:** Students build the shape in two different ways. Students do not need to use only one shape as they build. For example, students can use a triangle and a square as one way.

PROFICIENT students have developed spatial skills that enable them to look at the outline of a figure and note the key attributes that help them join smaller shapes to make the larger shape.

- **Exercises 7 and 8:** Students may need to use trial and error to find the correct pieces.
- **Exercise 10:** Students can use different shapes in how they make the shape.

Additional Support

- There are online supports for students to have additional practice joining shapes to make a larger shape.

Extension: Adding Rigor

- Create a shape made with 3 or 4 other shapes. Trace the outline. Have your partner fill in the outline to see if they can find your shapes.

Name

Apply and Grow: Practice

5. How many  make a 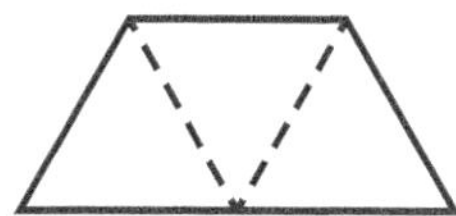?

3 make a .

6. How many make a 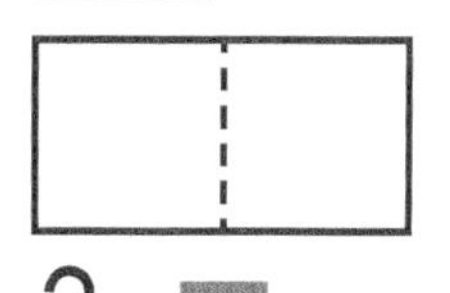?

2 make a .

7. Draw the shape you can use 2 times to make a .

8. Draw the shape you can use 3 times to make a .

9. Choose Tools Which shape can you use 2 times to make a ?

10. DIG DEEPER! Draw to show 2 different ways you can use pattern blocks to make the shape.

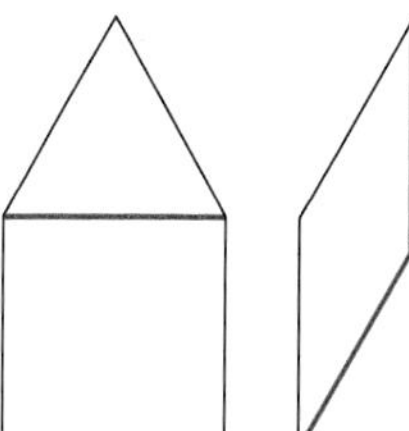

ELL Support

Check for understanding of Lesson 13.3. Read each question aloud as students follow along. Ask how many of each shape is used in Exercise 11 and have students answer by holding up the correct number of fingers for your review.

Laurie's Notes

Think and Grow: Modeling Real Life

The exercises on this page may remind students of working with tangrams. The outline of a shape is given and they need to decide what shapes are used to cover the outline. There are not gaps or overlap of pieces when they finish. The shapes available to use for each design are shown. The number of each shape to use is not known. Observe what shapes students use to fit in the corners of the shape. Do they sense the size of the piece, or attend to the angle that is needed to fit in the outline of the shape?

? **Preview:** "What do you see in the picture? What shapes do you think were used to make the picture?" Students will be excited to use their shapes to cover the picture.

? **MP1 Make Sense of Problems:** "What shapes are we going to use to make the fish in Newton's sign?" Give time for students to observe the shapes at the bottom. "In the first sign, you can only use three shapes. In the second sign you can only use four shapes. Do you know how many we need of each?" no "Are you already thinking about where some of the pieces will go?" yes

- Have students try to fit shapes into the outlines. Circulate and observe as students place their pieces.
- The first sign will be easier to fill because it uses three of the same shape. Finding a way to fill with four pieces is more challenging. If students see to use a trapezoid and hexagon, ask what three shapes will fill a hexagon.
- **Supporting Learners:** Provide the pattern blocks they will need and have them arrange them.

◉ "You have joined shapes together to make larger shapes and you have used your shapes to make a picture. Tell your partner how you are doing with your learning today."

Closure

- "You have done well today joining shapes to make a larger shape. I want you to use five or more shapes to make a picture that your partner will recognize. Show your partner when you finish." This is an open-ended problem.

Think and Grow: Modeling Real Life

Use the number of pattern blocks to fill the shape on the sign. How many of each block do you use? Draw to show your work.

3 blocks:
Sample answer:

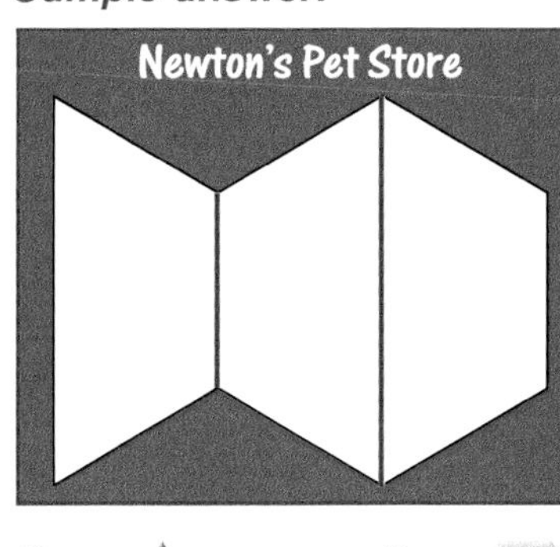

0 triangle 0 hexagon
3 trapezoid 0 rhombus

4 blocks:
Sample answer:

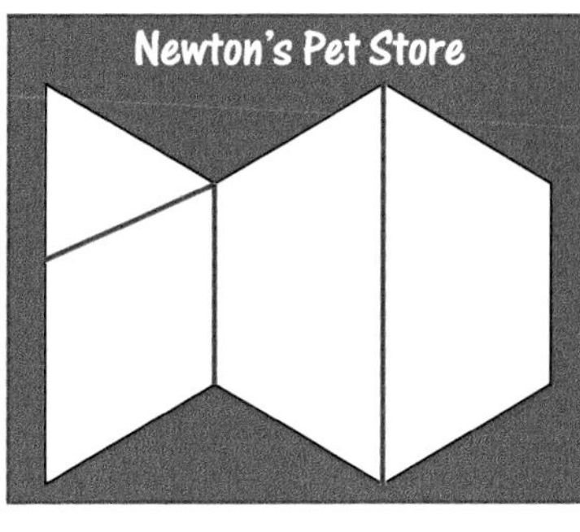

1 triangle 0 hexagon
2 trapezoid 1 rhombus

Show and Grow *I can think deeper!*

11. Use 3 pattern blocks to fill the shape on the sign. How many of each block do you use? Draw to show your work.
Sample answer:

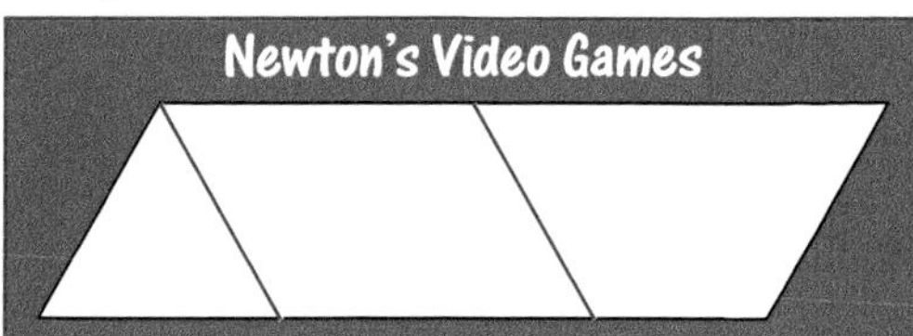

1 triangle
0 hexagon
1 trapezoid
1 rhombus

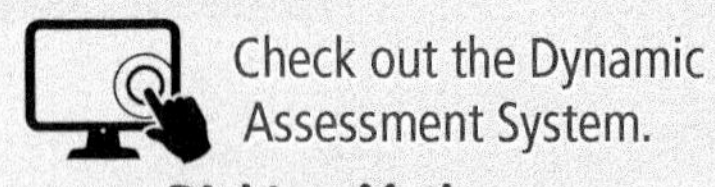
Check out the Dynamic Assessment System.
BigIdeasMath.com

Scaffold assignments to support all students in their learning progression. Revisit with spaced practice to move every student toward proficiency.

Connect and Extend Learning

Practice Notes

- Remind students what it means to join shapes along their sides.

Prior Skills

- **Exercises 8 and 9:** Grade 1, Telling Time to the Hour and Half Hour

Cross-Curricular Connections

Art

- Have students use pattern blocks to join shapes and then trace them. They can then make designs or pictures of their shapes using crayons, colored pencils, or paint.

Name ____________________

Practice 13.3

Learning Target: Join two-dimensional shapes to make another shape.

How many ◆ make a ⬡?

3 ◆ make a ⬡.

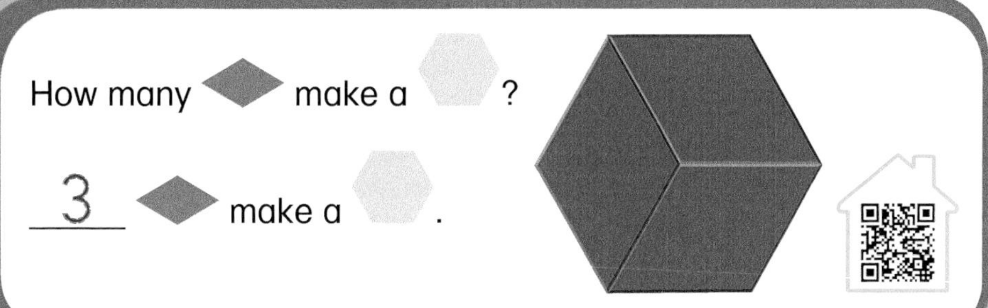

1. How many ▲ make a ◆?

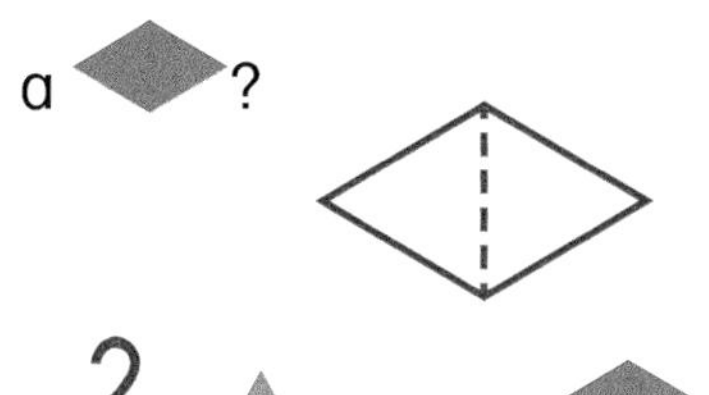

2 ▲ make a ◆.

2. How many ▱ make a ❮?

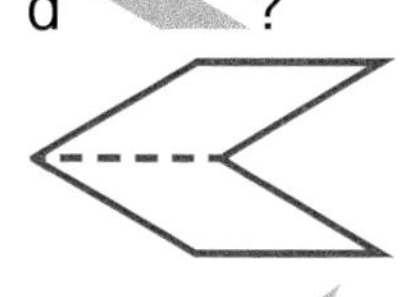

2 ▱ make a ❮.

3. How many ▲ make a ⬡?

6 ▲ make a ⬡.

4. How many ◗ make a ◡?

2 ◗ make a ◡.

Connect and Extend Learning

Extend Student Learning

Visual-Spatial

- Have students play "Teacher Says" and list descriptions to draw about shapes that are created from other shapes without giving the larger shaper away. For example the teacher can say, "Teacher says to draw three shapes that all have four sides and four square corners. Attach them to make a larger shape. The new shape still has four sides, however, the sides are not all the same length. What is this larger shape?" Use pattern blocks for students to trace.

Lesson Resources	
Surface Level	**Deep Level**
Resources by Chapter • Extra Practice • Reteach Differentiating the Lesson Skills Review Handbook Skills Trainer	Resources by Chapter • Enrichment and Extension Graphic Organizers Dynamic Assessment System • Lesson Practice

5. **Choose Tools** Which 2 pattern blocks can you use to make the shape?

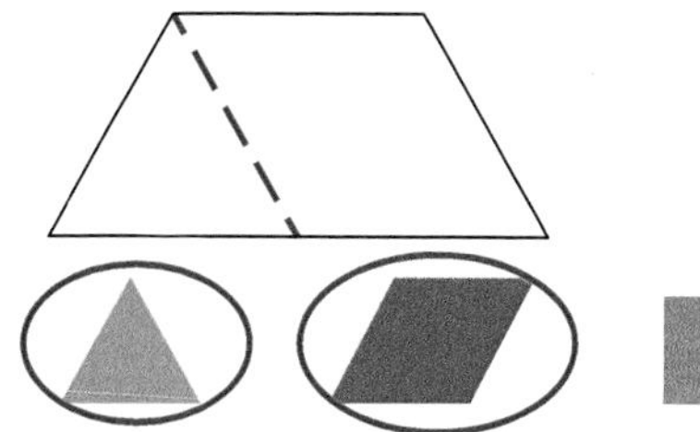

6. **DIG DEEPER!** Draw to show 2 different ways you can use pattern blocks to make a larger △. ***Sample answers:***

7. **Modeling Real Life** Use 5 pattern blocks to fill the shape on the sign. How many of each block do you use? Draw to show your work.

3 (triangle) 2 (square)

0 (trapezoid) 0 (rhombus)

Review & Refresh

Write the time.

8. 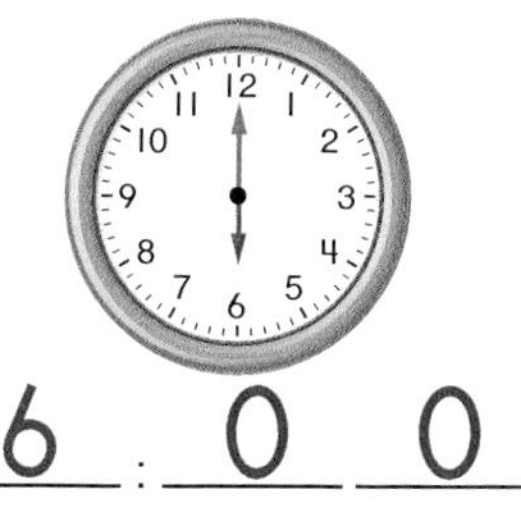

6 : 0 0

9.

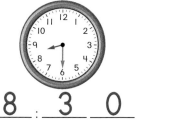

8 : 3 0

13.4

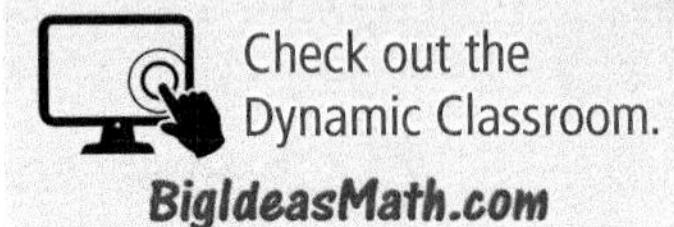
Check out the
Dynamic Classroom.

BigIdeasMath.com

Laurie's Notes

COMMON CORE STATE STANDARDS
1.G.A.2

Preparing to Teach

Today students have even more fun with shapes. They will use small shapes to build a larger shape as in the previous lesson, and then use that new shape to build pictures and other larger shapes. Use the shape cut outs from yesterday and add four quarter circles and four right triangles. This lesson is very much like filling in tangram pictures.

Materials

- pattern blocks
- shape cut outs

Dig In (Circle Time)

Students explore with pattern blocks to make pictures. They first build a new shape using two or three pieces. They trade their shapes with a partner, and add on to the shapes to make even larger shapes or pictures.

- Give each pair of students a collection of pattern blocks. Let students play with the shapes and make any pictures they want.
- ◉ "Yesterday we used our shapes to make new shapes. Today we will continue making new shapes by combining even more shapes together. To begin, choose two of the same shape and put them together to make a new shape."
- "Exchange the shape you just made with your partner. Now add between two and five more shapes to make a new picture."
- Be sure students remember that when joining shapes the entire sides needs to match. There should be no spaces or gaps in the design.
- Let students continue to build shapes or pictures in two steps. They can continue to trade with their partner, or they can build their own in two stages.
- ◉ Explain that today they are going to join shapes to make a larger shape. They will use the larger shape with another to make a third shape.

Learning Target

Join two-dimensional shapes to make a new shape. Use the new shape to make a larger shape.

Success Criteria

- Join shapes to make a new shape.
- Tell how many of each shape I used.
- Use the new shape to make a larger shape.

Warm-Up

Practice opportunities for the following are available in the Resources by Chapter or at *BigIdeasMath.com*.

- Daily skills
- Vocabulary
- Prerequisite skills

ELL Support

Point out that in this lesson, students will create more shapes. Say that when one creates something, one makes, forms, or produces it. Explain that these words are synonyms of *create* and they may want to note them in a vocabulary notebook to help build their vocabulary.

? Teaching Prompt ◉ Learning Target

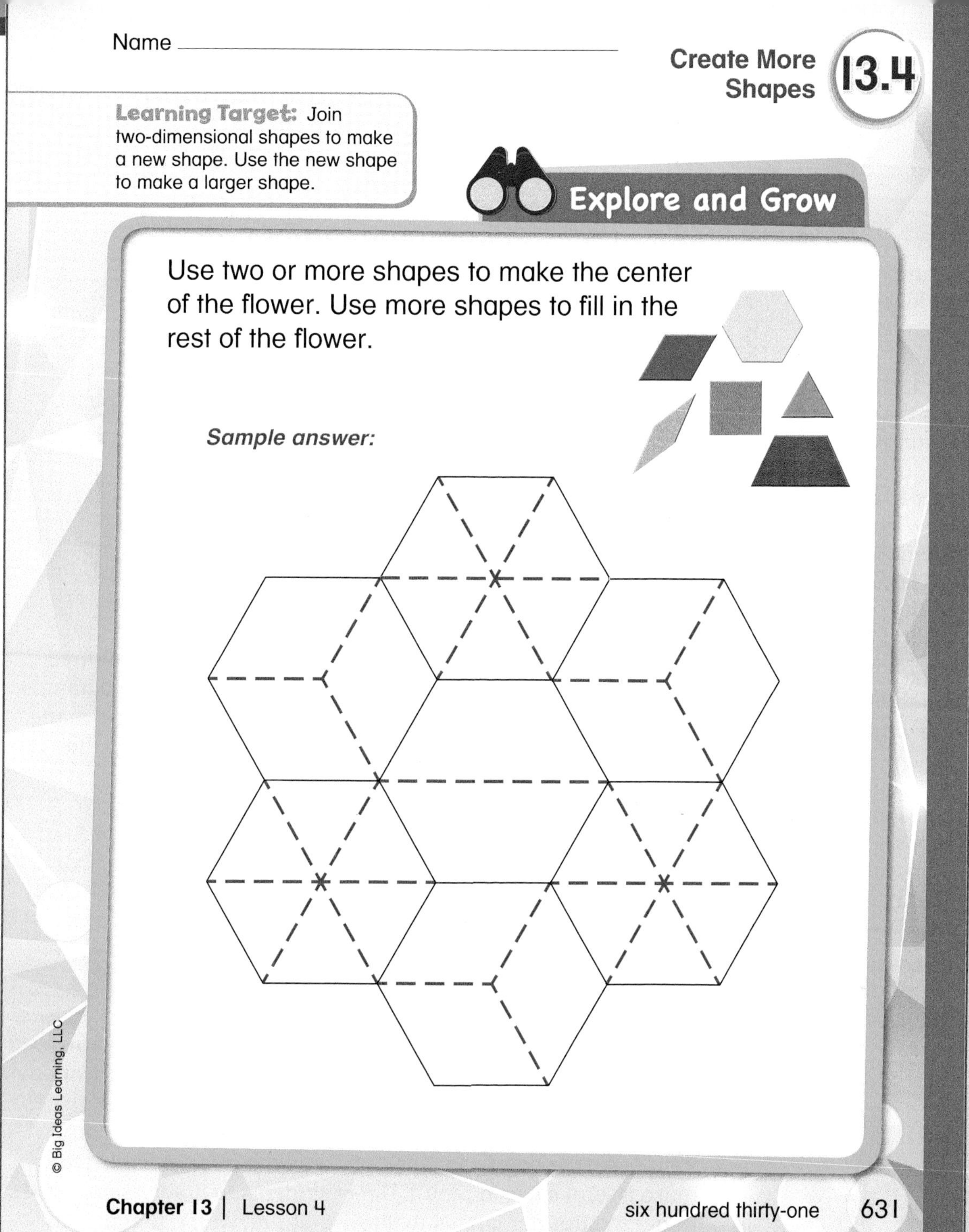

Name
Create More Shapes
13.4
Learning Target: Join two-dimensional shapes to make a new shape. Use the new shape to make a larger shape.
Explore and Grow
Use two or more shapes to make the center of the flower. Use more shapes to fill in the rest of the flower.
Sample answer:
© Big Ideas Learning, LLC
Chapter 13 | Lesson 4
six hundred thirty-one
631

Explore and Grow

- Students explore with pattern blocks to make pictures.
- There is no correct answer for making the flower. Students should use two or more shapes for the center, but they can use hexagons for the petals if they want.
- Set a time limit for filling in the flower, as some students might want to take the entire class time to make different types of hexagons.
- "You joined shapes to make a larger shape. What different ways could you make hexagons?

ELL Support

Review the example. Then have students practice verbal language in groups using Exercise 1. Have groups discuss the following questions: "Which shape do we use? How many shapes do we use? How do we arrange them?" Monitor discussion and expect students to perform according to their proficiency level.

Beginner students may use single word answers.
Intermediate students may use phrases and simple sentences.
Advanced students may use detailed sentences.

Laurie's Notes

Think and Grow

Getting Started

- Students will make new shapes from smaller shapes using a two-step process. In the directions students will see the pattern piece they are to use and the final shape they will make.
- Students will benefit from having shapes to manipulate and then sketch in how the shapes fit to make the final shape. The shapes added to the bags will enable students to have all the needed shapes.

Teaching Notes

- There are two problems, each with the same type of directions. Students will show how to make the first shape in step 1, then use two of the shapes just made to make the final shape in Step 2.
- **Model:** "Look at the directions. We are going to use L-shaped triangles to make a square. The first step is to make a rectangle with two L-shaped triangles." Use the two right triangles made from the rectangle from the original bag of shapes, not the triangles added for today.
- "Tell your partner how the triangles fit together to make a rectangle. Draw in the edge where they meet to show in Step 1."
- "Now we have a rectangle from the two triangles. If we use another rectangle, we can put them together to make a square. Draw in the two rectangles. How will they come together to make a square? Draw in the side where the rectangles meet in Step 2."
- **MP5 Use Appropriate Tools Strategically:** "In the next exercises, see if you can join the shapes to make the new shape shown." Manipulating the smaller shapes helps students develop spatial reasoning skills.
- In Exercise 1, students will trace the two quarter circles and then draw the common side that joins the quarter circles to make a semi-circle in Step 1. Direct students to draw 2 semi-circles under the quarter circles to show that they come together to make a circle. Draw in the common edge to show how semi-circles come together to make the circle.
- **Supporting Learners:** Students will benefit from working with the shapes and not just drawing. They may need help learning how to show the shapes in each step.
- ◉ "You have been working on two of our success criteria. You have joined shapes together to make a larger shape, and used that shape to make a final shape. What is going well? What is still tricky?"

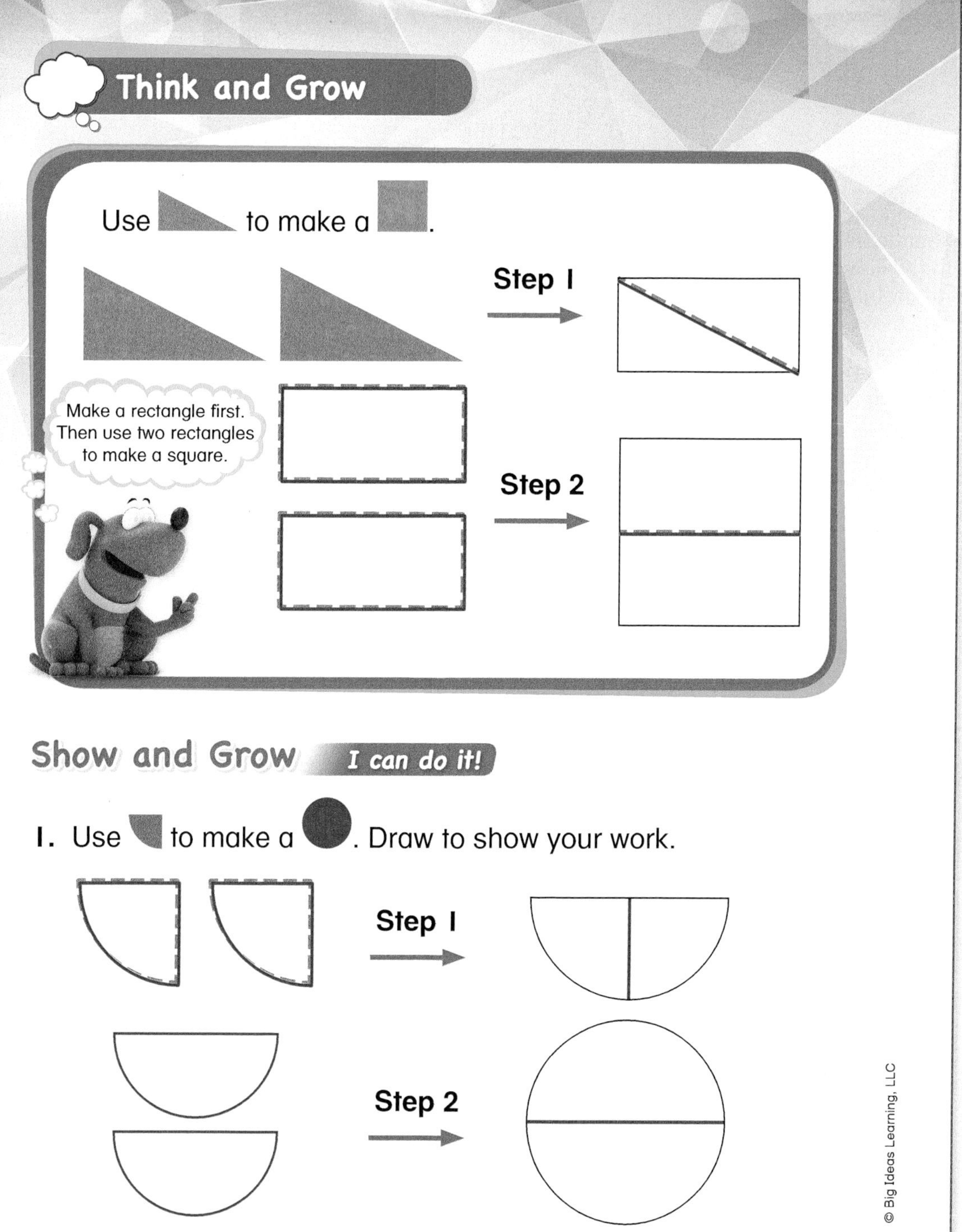

Think and Grow
Use to make a .
Step 1
Make a rectangle first. Then use two rectangles to make a square.
Step 2

Show and Grow I can do it!

1. Use to make a . Draw to show your work.

Step 1

Step 2

Scaffold instruction to support all students in their learning. Learning is individualized and you may want to group students differently as they move in and out of these levels with each skill and concept. Student self-assessment and feedback help guide your instructional decisions about how and when to layer support for all students to become proficient learners.

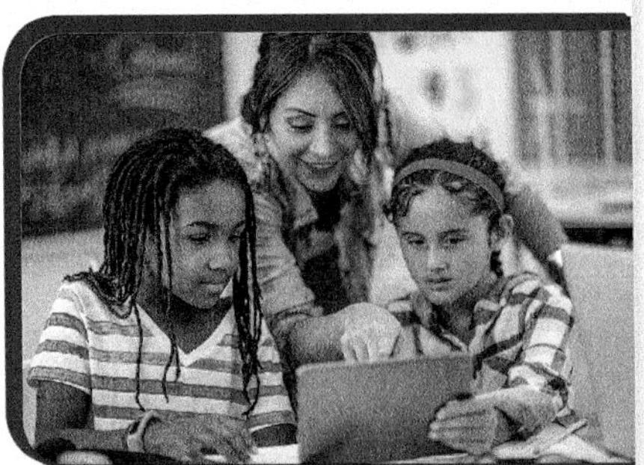

Meeting the needs of all learners.

Laurie's Notes

Apply and Grow: Practice

SCAFFOLDING INSTRUCTION

The exercises on this page continue the two-step process of making a final large shape from and intermediate and original smaller shapes. Students record how the shapes come together at each stage.

EMERGING students may have difficulty with these exercises. Spatial reasoning develops at very different times. Working with the shapes will help all students with this reasoning.

- **Exercise 2:** This is like the example on theThink and Grow. Use the new right triangles to build a square, and two squares to build the rectangle.
- **Exercise 3:** Put the small triangle on top of the trapezoid to make the larger triangle.Two larger triangles with one inverted make the rhombus.
- **Exercise 4:** Students should see the three quarter circles that will make the shape
- **Exercise 5:** Four equilateral triangles can be arranged with three on the bottom, the center triangle inverted, and one on the top.
- **Exercise 6:** The rectangle can be used as the horizontal piece or vertical piece.The two triangles come together to make the remaining square.

PROFICIENT students will have fun figuring out how to manipulate the shapes to form the shapes.They should still use the shapes before drawing. Drawing the steps may be challenging for students.

Additional Support

- Provide pattern blocks for students to use.

Extension: Adding Rigor

- Make up a two-step puzzle for your partner.

Name ______________________________

Apply and Grow: Practice

2. Use [triangle] to make a [rectangle]. Draw to show your work.

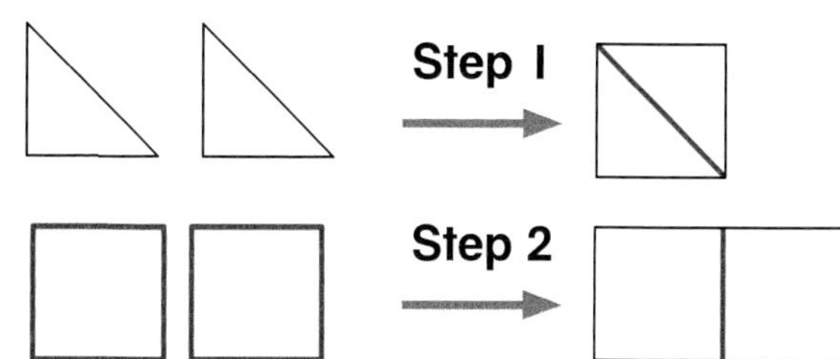

3. Use [triangle] and [trapezoid] to make a [parallelogram]. Draw to show your work.

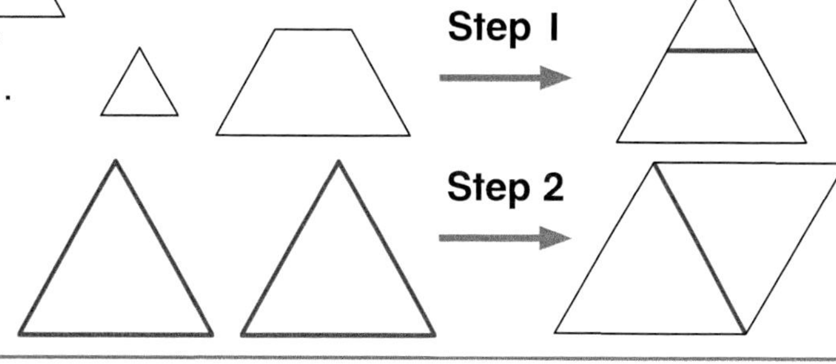

4. Draw the shape you can use 3 times to make a [circle shape].

5. Draw the shape you can use 4 times to make a [triangle].

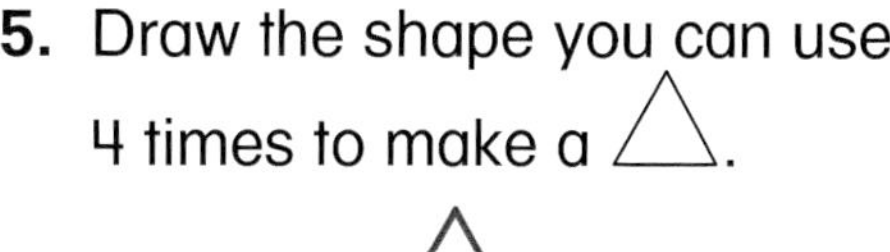

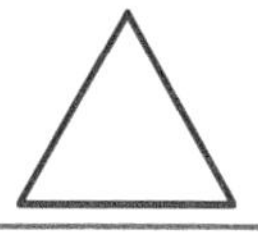

6. **DIG DEEPER!** Draw to show two different ways you can join the shapes on the left to make the larger shape.

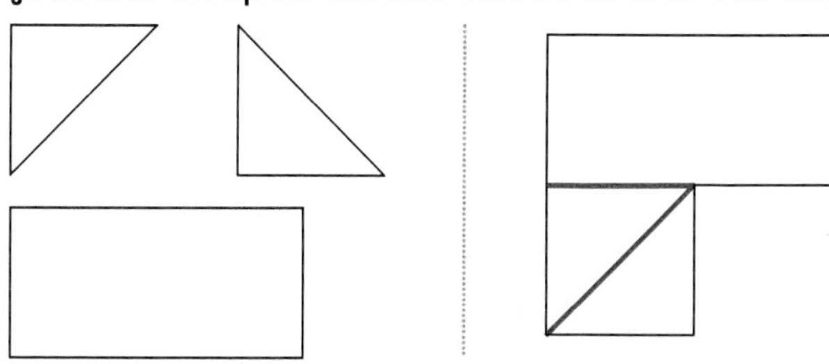

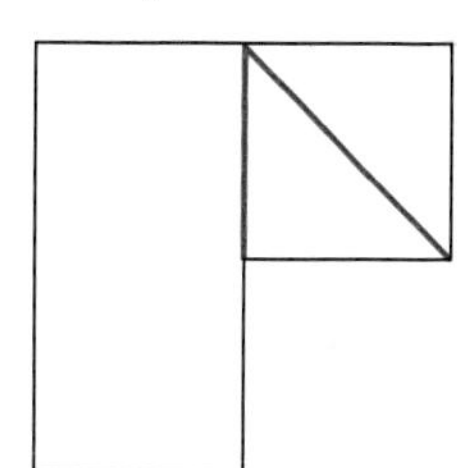

ELL Support

Check for understanding of Lesson 13.4. Read each exercise aloud as students follow along. Ask how many of each shape is used in Exercise 7 and have students answer by holding up the correct number of fingers for your review. Have them create their drawings on a whiteboard or a large piece of paper and hold up for your review.

Laurie's Notes

Think and Grow: Modeling Real Life

The exercises on this page are shape puzzles. The outline of a shape is given and they need to decide what shapes are used to cover the outline. Students will need to use pattern blocks on top of the outline. Once the outline is filled, they count and fill in how many of each pattern block they used.

- ? **Preview:** "What do you see in the picture? What shapes do you think were used to make the picture?"
- Have students try to fit shapes into the outlines. Circulate and observe as students place their pieces.
- Once students fill in the top shape, they can do the same with Exercise 7.
- **Supporting Learners:** Have students notice some of the obvious pieces like the tan rhombus.
- **Supporting Learners:** Provide the pieces they will need and have them arrange them.
- ◉ "You have joined shapes together to make intermediate shapes, and used those shapes to make larger shapes. We have used our shapes to make pictures. Use your thumb signals to show how you are doing with your learning today."

Closure

- "Alternate telling your partner everything you know about two-dimensional shapes."
- Have students name shapes, number of sides and vertices, and how some of the specific shapes can come together to make other specific shapes (e.g. triangles to make a square or hexagon).

Think and Grow: Modeling Real Life

Use pattern blocks to complete the puzzle. How many of each block do you use? Draw to show your work.

Sample answer:

4 

0 

2 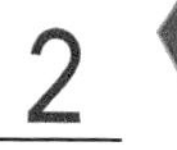

2 

1

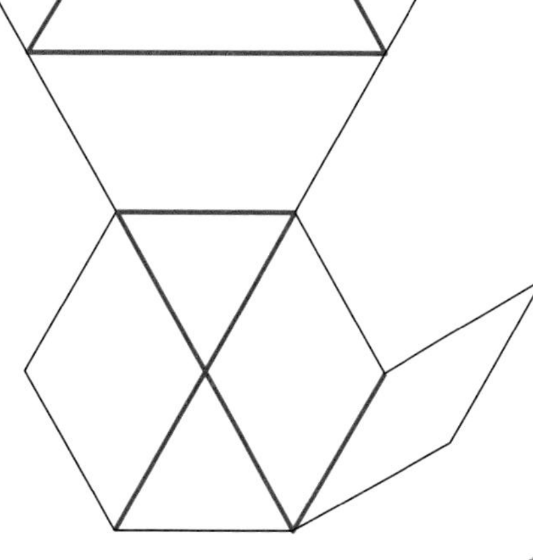

Show and Grow *I can think deeper!*

7. Use pattern blocks to complete the puzzle. How many of each block do you use? Draw to show your work.

Sample answer:

6 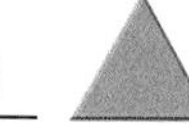

0 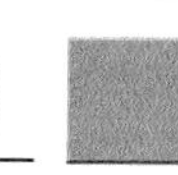

0 

4

1 

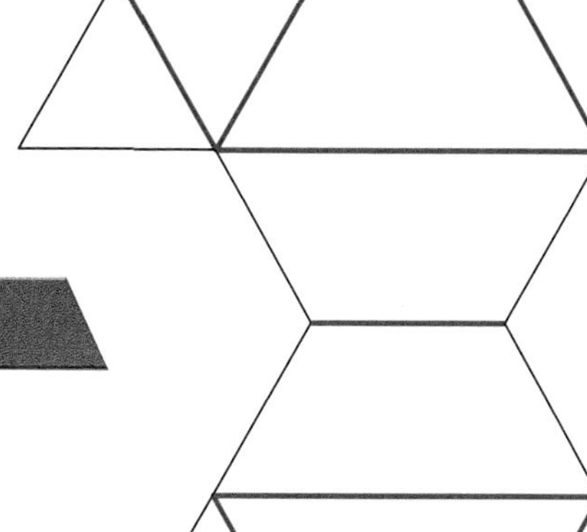

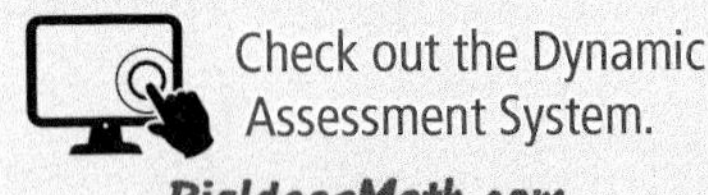
Check out the Dynamic Assessment System.
BigIdeasMath.com

Scaffold assignments to support all students in their learning progression. Revisit with spaced practice to move every student toward proficiency.

Connect and Extend Learning

Practice Notes

- Provide cut out shapes similar to ones on the page for students to use.

Prior Skills

- **Exercises 5 and 6:** Grade 1, Comparing Numbers 11 to 19

Cross-Curricular Connections

Language Arts

- Have students draw a shape and then cut it into two other shapes. They can write a story about how the shapes met and became a new shape once they got together. Have them decorate the shapes with faces and other details.

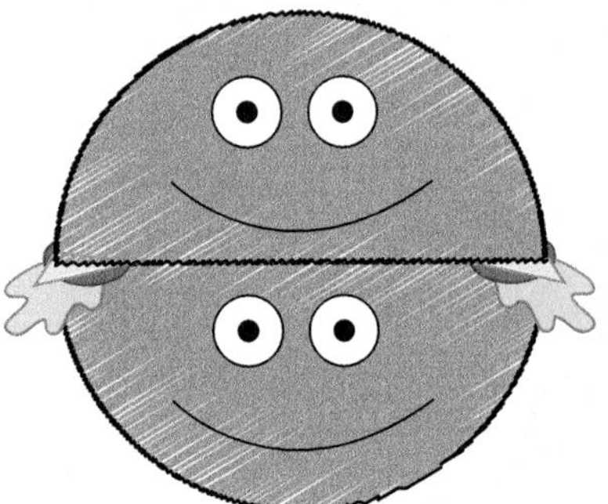

Name ____________________

Practice 13.4

Learning Target: Join two-dimensional shapes to make a new shape. Use the new shape to make a larger shape.

Use △ to make a ▱. Draw to show your work.

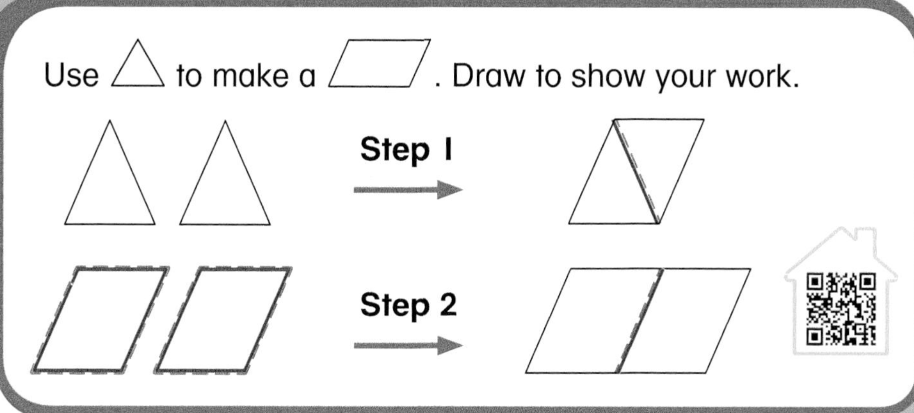

1. Use □ to make a larger □. Draw to show your work.

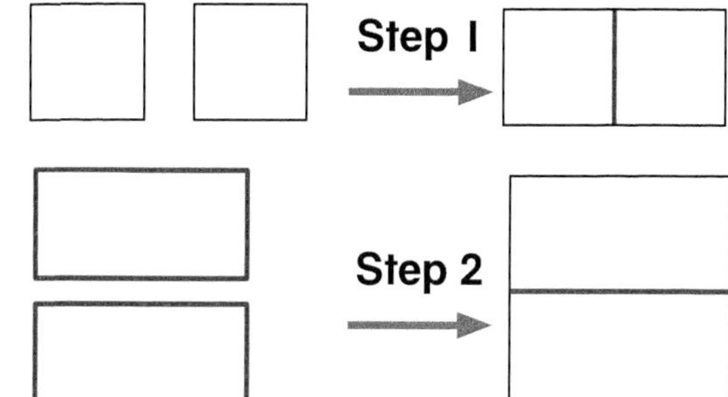

2. Use ◺ to make a ◇. Draw to show your work.

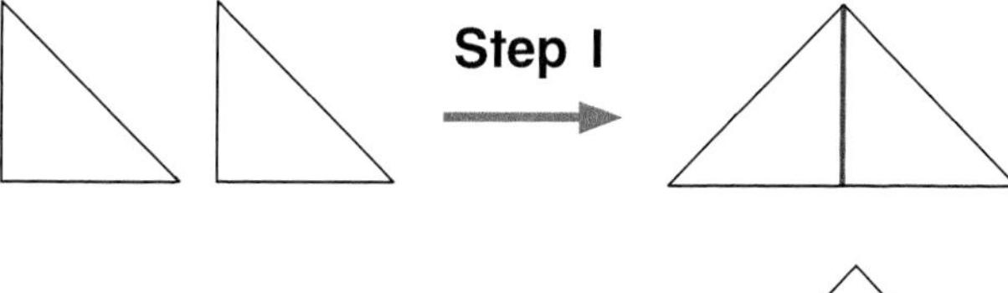

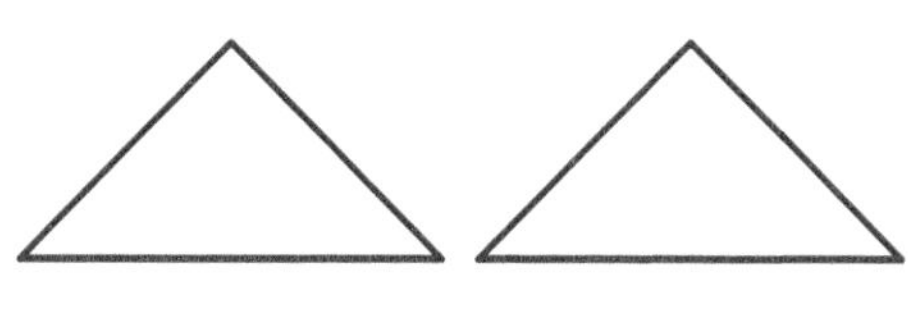

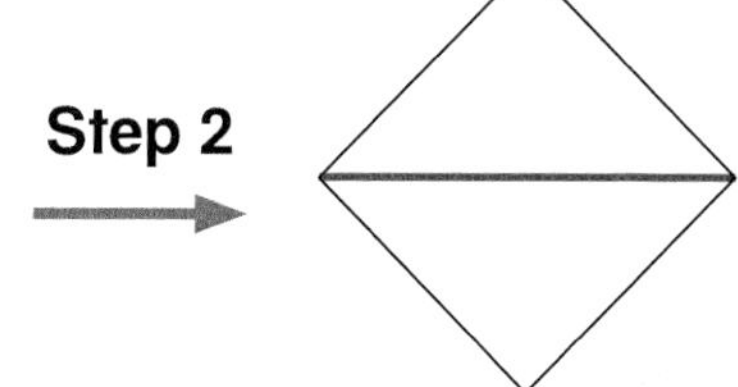

Connect and Extend Learning

Extend Student Learning

Musical

- Pass out different shapes to students. Then have them sit in the circle. Sing the following song with students and let one person at a time decide on the shape that is to be called. Once students' shapes are called, have them follow the directions of the song below. All students stand up, align or join together with at least one other student, and create a new shape. At the end of the song, students can trade their shapes with a partner and sing again.

  If you're holding a __(name of shape)___, please stand up
  If you're holding a __(name of shape)___, please stand up
  Now join together and align
  Now join together and align
  Look what you made, bow, and sit down
  Look what you made, bow, and sit down

<table>
<tr><th colspan="2">Lesson Resources</th></tr>
<tr><th>Surface Level</th><th>Deep Level</th></tr>
<tr><td>Resources by Chapter
• Extra Practice
• Reteach
Differentiating the Lesson
Skills Review Handbook
Skills Trainer</td><td>Resources by Chapter
• Enrichment and Extension
Graphic Organizers
Dynamic Assessment System
• Lesson Practice</td></tr>
</table>

3. **DIG DEEPER!** Draw to show two ways you can combine the 3 shapes on the left to make the larger shape.

4. **Modeling Real Life** Use pattern blocks to complete the puzzle. How many of each block do you use? Draw to show your work. ***Sample answer:***

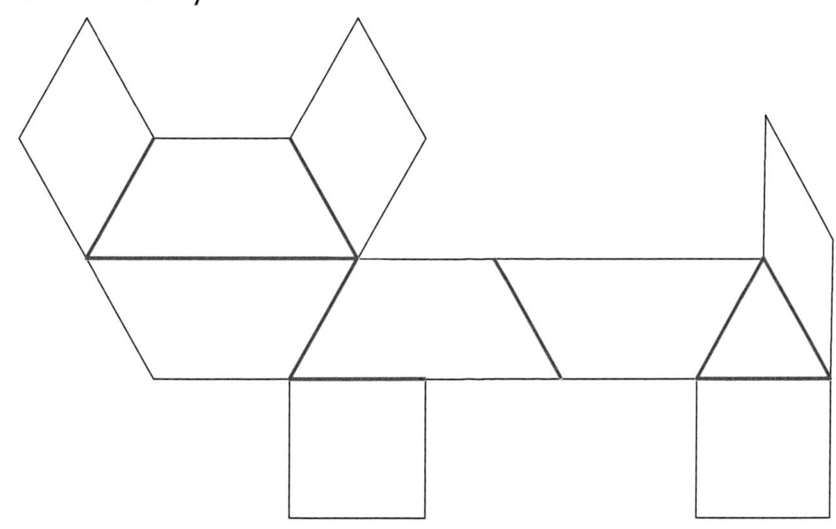

triangle: 1 square: 2 rhombus: 2 trapezoid: 4 thin rhombus: 1

Review & Refresh

5. 17 is greater than / (is less than) 19.

6. 12 (is greater than) / is less than 11.

13.5

Laurie's Notes

Check out the
Dynamic Classroom.

BigIdeasMath.com

Learning Target

Take apart two-dimensional shapes.

Success Criteria

- Tell what shapes make up a given shape.
- Draw a line to show the parts of a given shape.

Warm-Up

Practice opportunities for the following are available in the Resources by Chapter or at *BigIdeasMath.com.*

- Daily skills
- Vocabulary
- Prerequisite skills

ELL Support

Explain that the two words *take apart* function as one phrasal verb or action. *Take apart* means to deconstruct. Using a phrasal verb can be tricky, as it may or may not be possible to separate its words. *Take apart* may be used both ways: "We will take apart the figures. We will take the figures apart." The meaning and use of each phrasal verb must be learned.

COMMON CORE STATE STANDARDS
1.G.A.2

Preparing to Teach

Students have been working with shapes and combining shapes to make new shapes. Today students will take composite shapes and break them apart into basic pattern block shapes.

Materials

- pattern blocks
- shape cut outs
- composite outlines
- straws

Dig In (Circle Time)

Students will be shown an outline of a composite shape and build it with their pattern blocks. Students will then see how lines can be drawn on the outline to show the individual blocks, thus taking apart the composite shapes.

- ◉ "We have been doing a lot of work with shapes. The past two days we took our shapes, put them together, and made new shapes. Today we will start with the bigger shapes, and take them apart to find the smaller shapes."
- Show students the outline of the hexagon. Tell students that they have put together shapes to make a hexagon before. Students build a hexagon any way they want. They tell their partners what shapes they used to make the hexagon.
- Use the outline of the hexagon to show how lines can be drawn to show the shapes. This can be repeated to show various divisions.
- Repeat this process of showing an outline of a house, followed by an outline of a castle. Students will build them with shapes, followed by dividing the outline into the individual shapes. You can continue to divide the shape or have students volunteer to come up and show how to divide the shape.

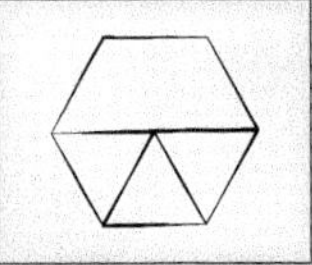

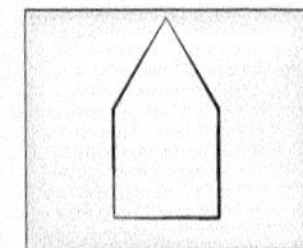

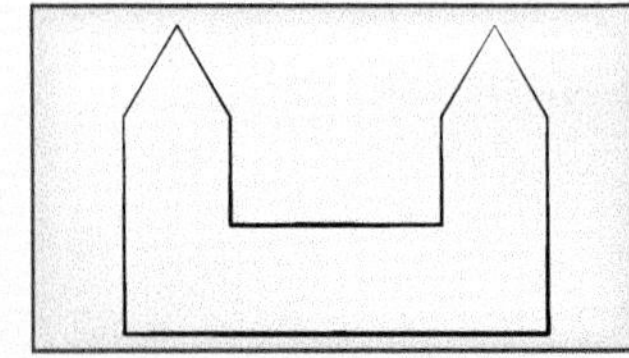

- ◉ Explain that today they are going to divide large shapes to show the smaller shapes. They will be told which shapes to find within the big shapes.

? Teaching Prompt ◉ Learning Target

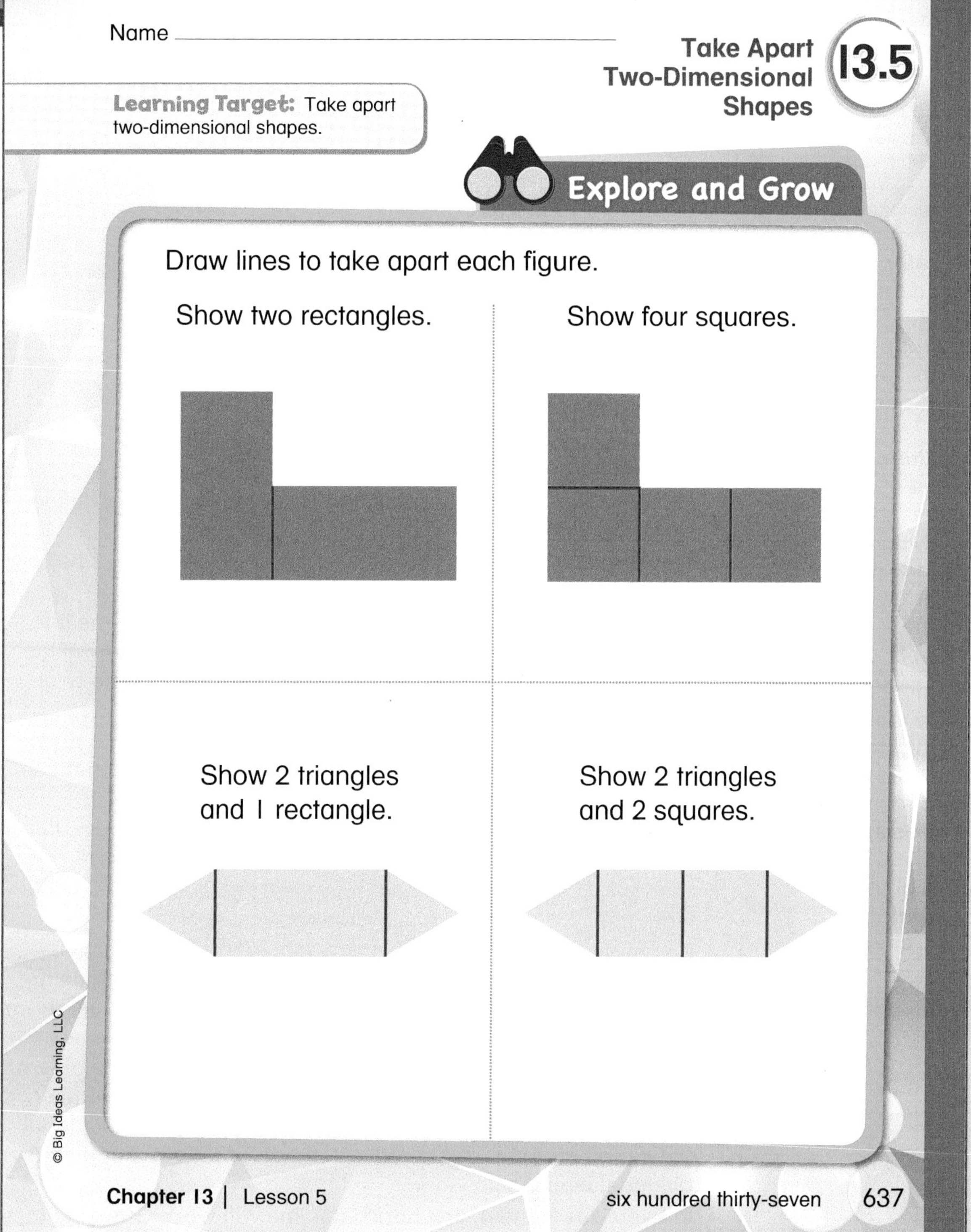

Name
Learning Target: Take apart two-dimensional shapes.
Take Apart Two-Dimensional Shapes
13.5
Explore and Grow
Draw lines to take apart each figure.
Show two rectangles.
Show four squares.
Show 2 triangles and 1 rectangle.
Show 2 triangles and 2 squares.
© Big Ideas Learning, LLC
Chapter 13 | Lesson 5
six hundred thirty-seven 637

Explore and Grow

- Students draw lines to show the specific shapes.
- **Supporting Learners:** If students have difficulty seeing the individual shapes, let them build the larger shape with the pieces first, and then draw the lines.
- ? **MP3 Construct Viable Arguments:** "Explain how to find specific shapes within the large shapes. Is there something you look for first that helps?"

ELL Support

Review the example. Then have students practice verbal language in groups using Exercises 1–4. Have groups discuss the following questions: "Where do we draw the lines? How does the shape look?" Monitor discussion and expect students to perform according to their proficiency level.

Beginner students may use single word answers or indicate by drawing.
Intermediate students may use phrases and simple sentences.
Advanced students may use detailed sentences and direct the activities.

Laurie's Notes

Think and Grow

Getting Started

- Students will divide the shapes with one line to form two specific shapes.
- Students will benefit from having shapes to manipulate and then sketch in how the shape is divided.

Teaching Notes

- There are four exercises, each with the same direction line. Students will show how to make the first shape in step 1, then use two of the shapes just made to make the final shape in step 2.
- **Teaching Tip:** Give students a straw to divide the shapes before drawing lines.
- ◉ **Model:** "Look at the directions. We are going to draw one line to divide the rectangle into two rectangles. We can draw a line horizontally through the middle of the rectangle to form two rectangles."
- ? **Model:** "Descartes says that there are two more ways to divide the rectangle. Tell your partner if Descartes is correct. Do those lines also show two rectangles?"
- ? **MP7 Look for and Make Use of Structure:** "Are there more lines than these that could be drawn to make two rectangles?"
- Students may debate whether a vertical line down the center would be correct. This would form two squares. That is mathematically correct as a square is a type of rectangle. If this comes up, do not let the misconception that you could not use two squares be accepted. Tell them a square is a type of rectangle, so it would be okay.
- In Exercises 1 and 2 there are two diagonals that can be drawn. Most students will probably draw from the upper left vertex to the lower right. See if any students draw the other diagonal (lower left to upper right vertices). If not, point out that the other diagonal would also work.
- In Exercises 3 and 4, any horizontal line will work. Students may have more of a challenge seeing the two trapezoids in Exercise 3 than the triangle and trapezoid in Exercise 4.
- **Supporting Learners:** Students will benefit from working with the shapes to clearly see how to divide the shape on the page.
- ◉ "You have been working on our learning target! How is it going so far? Can you see the smaller shapes within the big shape before knowing what shapes to make?"

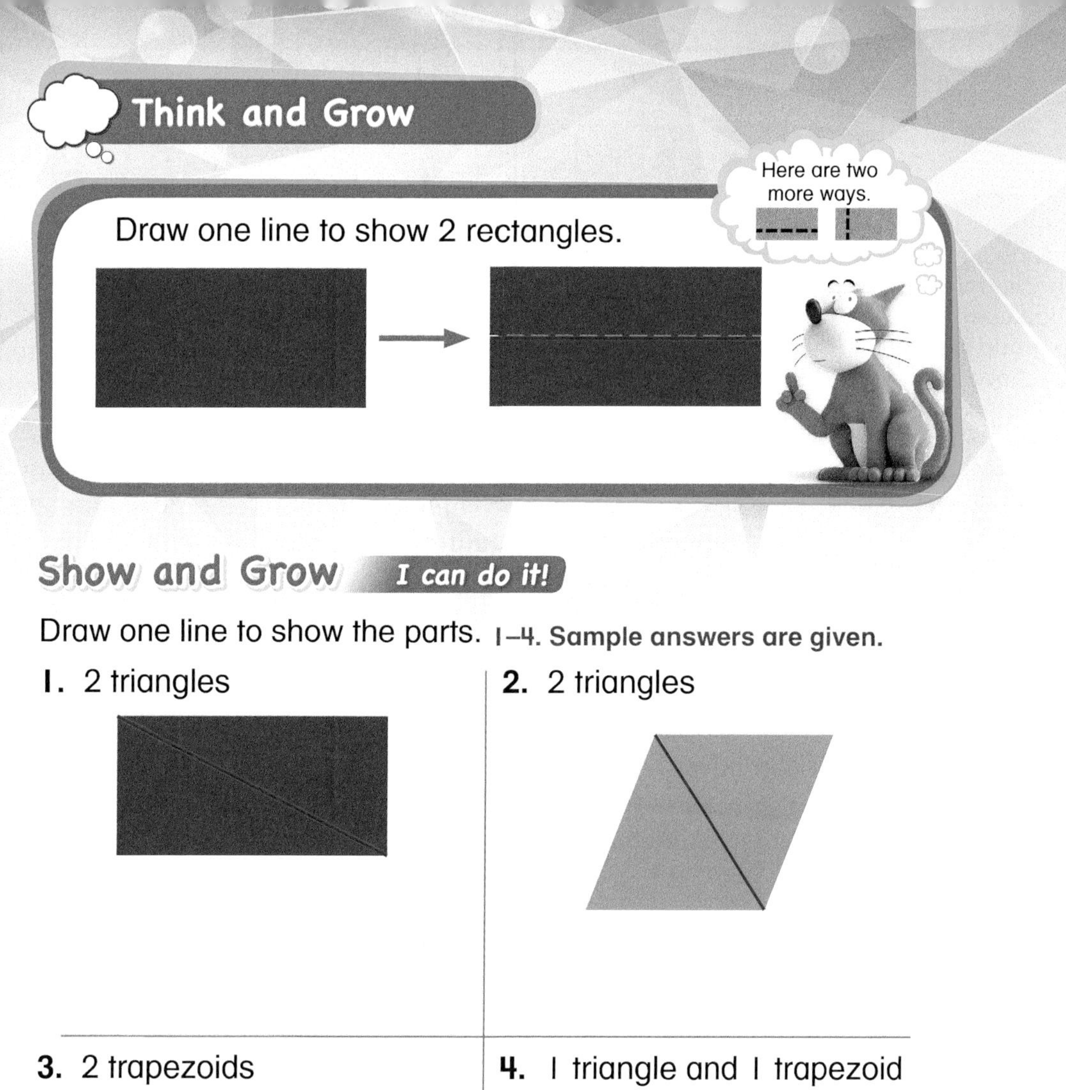

Think and Grow
Draw one line to show 2 rectangles.
Here are two more ways.

Show and Grow I can do it!

Draw one line to show the parts. **1–4. Sample answers are given.**

1. 2 triangles

2. 2 triangles

3. 2 trapezoids

4. 1 triangle and 1 trapezoid

Scaffold instruction to support all students in their learning. Learning is individualized and you may want to group students differently as they move in and out of these levels with each skill and concept. Student self-assessment and feedback help guide your instructional decisions about how and when to layer support for all students to become proficient learners.

Meeting the needs of all learners.

Laurie's Notes

Apply and Grow: Practice

SCAFFOLDING INSTRUCTION

The exercises on this page continue dividing a given shape to form specific smaller shapes. Students will progress from drawing one line to divide, to two lines, to multiple lines.

EMERGING students may have difficulty with these exercises. Spatial reasoning can be challenging for even adults. Working with the shapes will help all students with this reasoning.

- **Exercise 5:** Students may not think about any kind of triangle other than an equilateral as shown. Remind them or show the "L-Shaped" triangle (right triangle) that they have used.
- **Exercise 9:** Tell students to build the hexagon with two trapezoids or three rhombi and then substitute one shape with triangles.
- **Exercise 10:** Have students start with the semi-circle and determine how many semi-circles are needed for the circle. Then look at the quarter-circles.

PROFICIENT students understand what they are trying to do, but may be very challenged with some of these shapes! If needed, give a hint as to where to start drawing a line.

Additional Support

- Students take out the shapes from the bag and build the composite shape first.

Extension: Adding Rigor

- Build a picture or shape with your pattern blocks. Trace the outline. Write how many of each shape you used. Give your puzzle to a partner to solve.

Name ______________________________

Apply and Grow: Practice

Draw one line to show the parts.

5. 2 triangles

Sample answer:

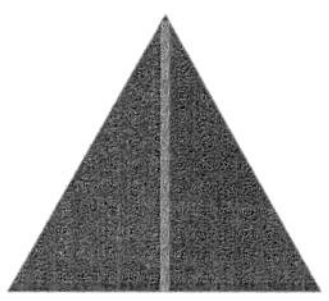

6. 2 squares

Draw two lines to show the parts.

7. 2 triangles and 1 trapezoid

Sample answer:

8. 2 triangles and 1 rectangle

9. **Reasoning** Show how to use the shapes to make the hexagon. *Sample answer:*

1 

3 

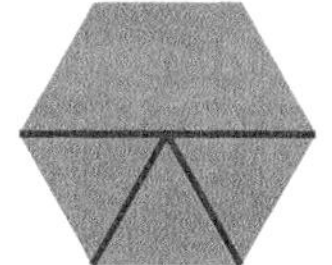

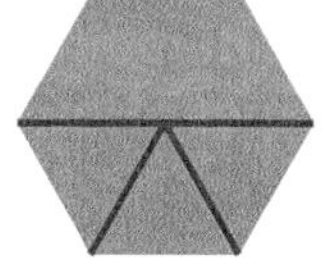

Sample answer:

2 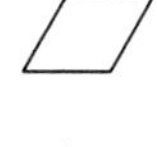

2

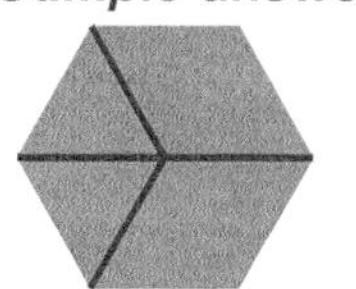

10. **Reasoning** Show how to use the shapes to make a circle. How many of each shape do you use?

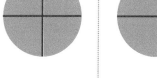

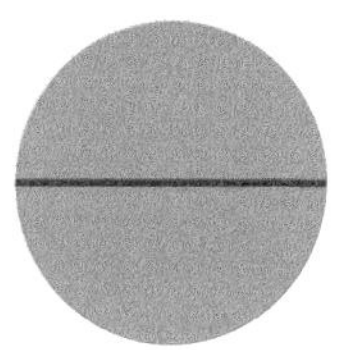

4

2

ELL Support

Check for understanding of Lesson 13.5. Read each direction aloud as students follow along. Have students respond to the questions by writing the answers on a whiteboard and holding them up for your review. If there is confusion you may want to review how answers are found.

Laurie's Notes

Think and Grow: Modeling Real Life

The exercises on this page ask students to find how many squares are in a design.

? **Preview:** "What do you see in the picture? Have you played Four Square?"

- Students will see the four colored squares in the example. They may not see the larger square formed by the colored squares, outlined in white. Some students may look at the shadowed grey cement area and count that as a square. If only looking at the Four Square court, the answer is 5. If including the grey shadow, the answer is 6.
- Exercise 11 is more difficult. Students will see the 10 squares (9 individual and the 3-by-3 outer square), but will probably miss the four squares that can be formed inside by squares 2, 7, 9 and 5; 7, 6 5 and 1; 9, 5, 4 and 3; and 5, 1, 3 and 8. Total squares are 14. Point out the square formed by 2, 7, 9 and 5 and see if students find the other three.
- **Extension:** Exercise 11 is a magic square, which means every row, column, and diagonal have the same sum. "What is the sum? Is it correct?"

◉ "You have been separating shapes into smaller shapes. Use your thumb signals to show how you did with your learning today. How are you at understanding that larger shapes can be divided into smaller shapes? How did you do with finding the smaller shapes?"

Closure

- "Tell your partner which exercises were easy to do. Tell your partner which exercises were a challenge to do. Tell why some were easier than others."

Think and Grow: Modeling Real Life

How many squares can you find on the Four Square court?

5 squares

Show and Grow *I can think deeper!*

11. How many squares can you find on the magic square?

2	7	6
9	5	1
4	3	8

14 squares

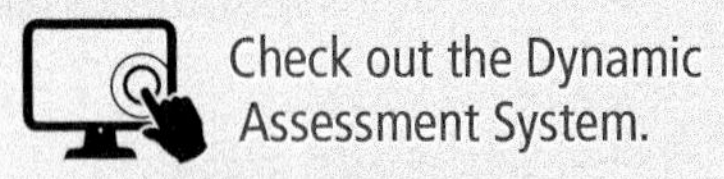
Check out the Dynamic Assessment System.

BigIdeasMath.com

Scaffold assignments to support all students in their learning progression. Revisit with spaced practice to move every student toward proficiency.

Connect and Extend Learning

Practice Notes

- Support students by offering pattern blocks or other shape cut outs to recreate the shapes that they take apart.

Prior Skills

- **Exercise 8:** Grade 1, Identifying Two-Dimensional and Three-Dimensional Shapes

Cross-Curricular Connections

Physical Education

- Tape down large shapes to the floor. Have students decide how to draw a line to show two shapes within that shape. Students can do this by laying down string or tape to show the shapes. Then have students walk on the new line(s) of the shape.

Name ______________________

Practice 13.5

Learning Target: Take apart two-dimensional shapes.

Draw one line to show 2 triangles.

Draw one line to show the parts. **1–4. Sample answers are given.**

1. 2 trapezoids

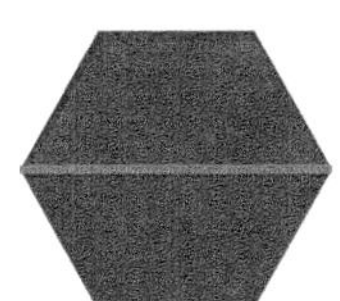

2. 1 rectangle and 1 square

Draw two lines to show the parts.

3. 3 triangles

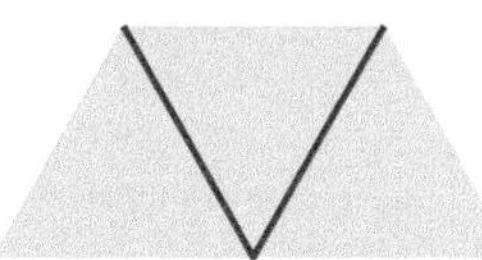

4. 1 rectangle and 2 triangles

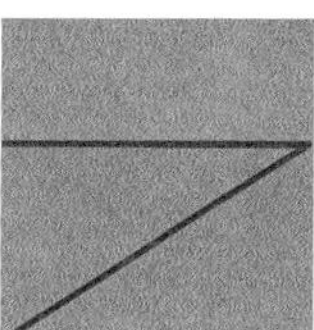

Connect and Extend Learning

Extend Student Learning

Visual-Spatial

- Provide students with toothpicks or craft sticks and modeling clay. Then have them create shapes that can be taken apart into more shapes. Have them exchange shapes with a partner and then take the shapes apart. They can do this by adding more materials such as toothpicks to separate the different shapes.

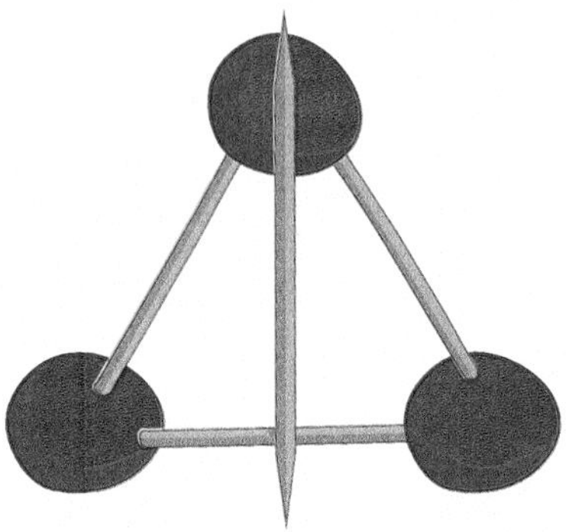

Lesson Resources	
Surface Level	**Deep Level**
Resources by Chapter • Extra Practice • Reteach Differentiating the Lesson Skills Review Handbook Skills Trainer	Resources by Chapter • Enrichment and Extension Graphic Organizers Dynamic Assessment System • Lesson Practice

5. **Reasoning** Show how to use the shapes to make the ▰.

Sample answer:

1 ▱

2 △

1 ⏢

Sample answer:

1 △

6. **DIG DEEPER!** You take apart a shape. You are left with a trapezoid and 3 triangles with equal side lengths. Write the name of the shape you started with.

Sample answer: **hexagon**

7. **Modeling Real Life** How many triangles are in Descartes's design?

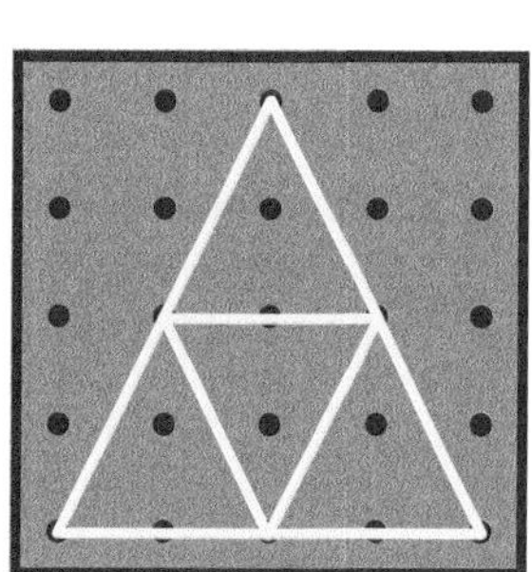

5 triangles

Review & Refresh

8. Circle the three-dimensional shapes. Draw rectangles around the two-dimensional shapes.

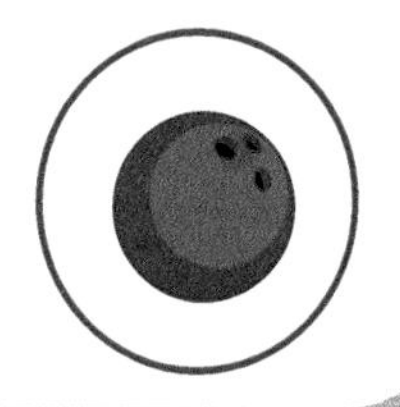

13.6

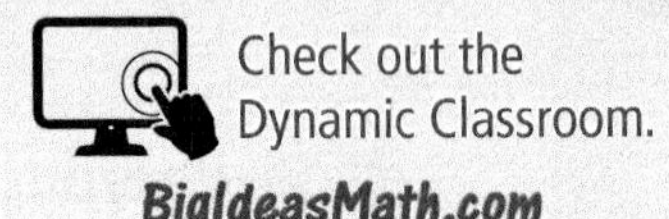
Check out the
Dynamic Classroom.

BigIdeasMath.com

Learning Target

Sort three-dimensional shapes.

Success Criteria

- Use a sorting rule to identify shapes.
- Explain different ways to sort three-dimensional shapes.

Warm-Up

Practice opportunities for the following are available in the Resources by Chapter or at *BigIdeasMath.com.*

- Daily skills
- Vocabulary
- Prerequisite skills

ELL Support

Explain that when an object only has two dimensions, it is flat and only has length and width. When it has three dimensions, it has length, width, and height. You may want to model the three dimensions by using objects in the classroom such as books or bookcases.

Laurie's Notes

COMMON CORE STATE STANDARDS
1.G.A.1

Preparing to Teach

We now move to working with three-dimensional shapes. This lesson follows Lesson 13.1, sorting two-dimensional shapes. It also builds on the foundation from kindergarten.

Materials

- three-dimensional shapes
- Three-Dimensional Shape Cards*
- scissors and glue

**Found in the Instructional Resources*

Dig In (Circle Time)

A variety of three-dimensional solids are placed, one at a time, in a bag. A volunteer describes what the object feels like, and whether it will roll or not. Use simple shapes from the building toys collection or similar geometric solids. Do not use an action figurine, hairbrush, or other odd shapes.

- Place the collection of three-dimensional objects in the circle. "Tell your partner what you know about the object(s). Tell what makes these objects different from the shapes we have been working with. Predict which shapes will roll, which will roll on certain parts, and which will not roll at all." Provide time for students to share out. You want to hear distinguishing feature such as three-dimensions or solids, shapes that make up the solid, and possibly flat or curved surfaces.
- Hold the bag in front of you. "I have put a shape from our collection in this bag. I want someone to put their hand in the bag and feel the solid. Describe what it feels like. Tell if it will roll or not. Do not give the name of the solid even if you know it. I want everyone to guess what the shape is."
- Shapes to explore: cone, sphere, cube, cylinder, rectangular prism. Review the difference between two-dimensional and three-dimensional shapes. Students can explain the difference in their own words. Show the difference between a flat and curved surface. Curved surfaces will roll and flat surfaces will not.
- Suggest a rule to sort the objects, such as "has a curved surface." Students select the objects that would belong to the category.
- ◉ Ask students to determine a rule by which the objects could be sorted, and then sort the objects that way. It is okay if some objects are not get included because they do not meet the category.
- ◉ "Today we will be sorting three-dimensional objects in all kinds of ways."

? Teaching Prompt ◉ Learning Target

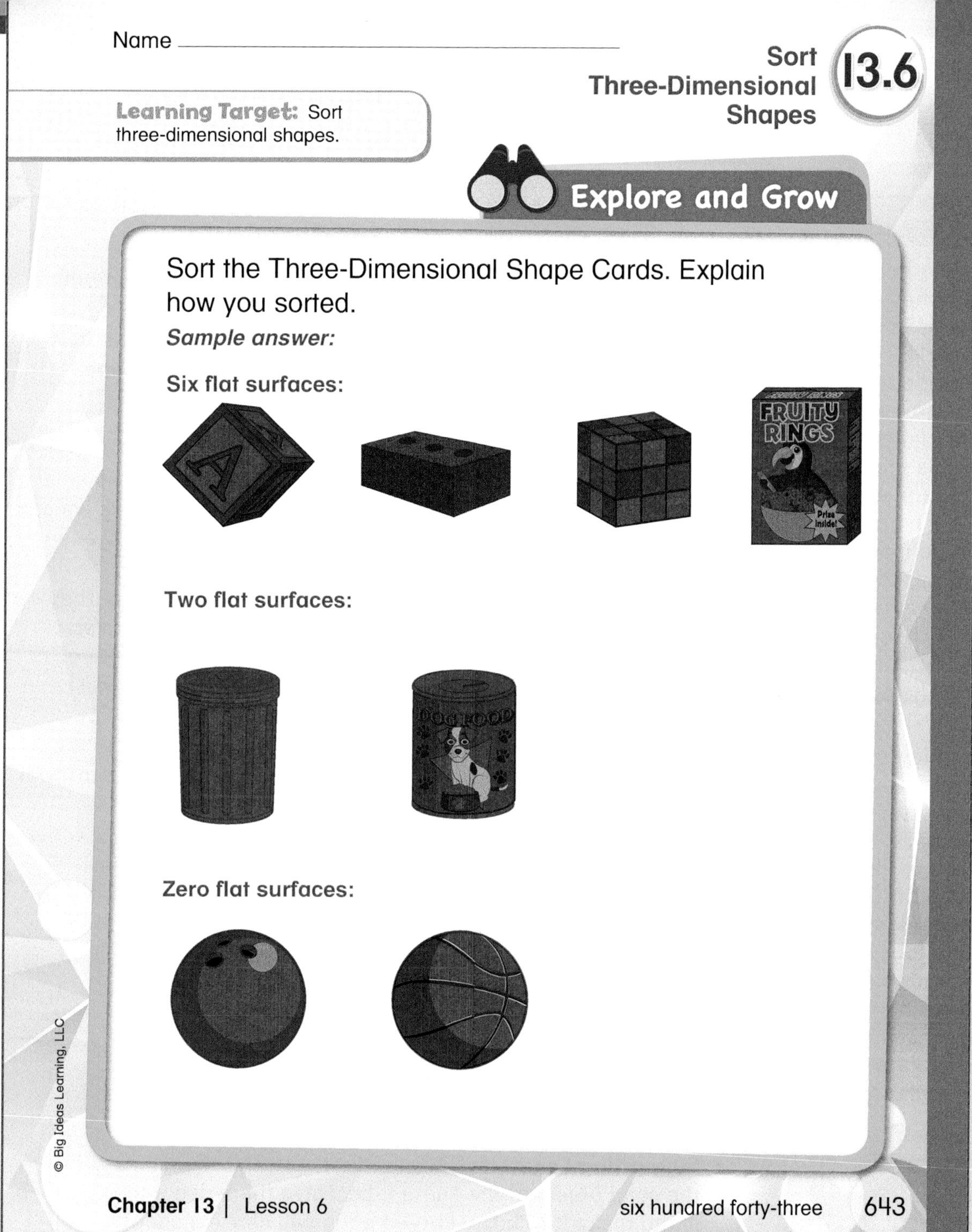

Name
Learning Target: Sort three-dimensional shapes.
Sort Three-Dimensional Shapes
13.6
Explore and Grow
Sort the Three-Dimensional Shape Cards. Explain how you sorted.
Sample answer:
Six flat surfaces:
FRUITY RINGS
Prize Inside!
Two flat surfaces:
DOG FOOD
Zero flat surfaces:
© Big Ideas Learning, LLC
Chapter 13 | Lesson 6
six hundred forty-three
643

Explore and Grow

- Each partner pair can share scissors and glue. Students cut out the Three-Dimensional Shape Cards to sort. Have them sort in various ways before deciding which way they want to sort.
- Students should glue their cards to the page and title each by how it was sorted.
- "Tell your partner how you sorted the shape cards. If any shapes were left out, tell why."

ELL Support

Discuss the example. Review the names of the attributes in Exercises 1 and 2, such as flat and curved surfaces and circles. Then have students work in pairs as they practice language while completing each one. Have one student ask the other, "How many shapes did you circle? Which ones?" Then have them alternate roles for the other exercises.

Beginner students may answer with a number or by indicating visually.
Intermediate students may answer with simple sentences, such as, "There are four."
Advanced students may answer with detailed sentences, such as, "There are four objects with only flat surfaces."

Laurie's Notes

Think and Grow

Getting Started

- Students will use specific attributes to sort shapes. This will demonstrate an understanding of the vocabulary.
- Introduce the vocabulary cards **edge**, **rectangular prism**, **vertex**, **flat surface**, **curved surface**, and **three-dimensional shape**.

Teaching Notes

- **Model:** "Look at the first sentence." Have a student read it. "Tell your partner what a three-dimensional shape is. When we sort three-dimensional shapes, there are many ways we can do it. We will look at two examples, and you will sort by even more ways."
- The example shows students to sort shapes by whether they only have *flat surfaces* or if they only have a *curved surface*. Have students point out objects in the room that only have flat surfaces. "These will never roll. They will slide if you push them."
- **Model:** "Let's look at the second group of shapes. It says the shapes only have a curved surface. Find this shape in our room. Tell your partners what these shapes remind you of."
- "Look at the shapes in Exercise 1. Tell your partner if you know any of the names of the shapes." Discuss which attributes students will circle for Exercise 1. If students circle a shape that does not belong, have them explain their reasoning. Students may confuse a sphere, which is round, with the flat circle of a cylinder.
- Repeat this process with Exercise 2.
- **Teaching Tip:** If you have cylinders, cubes, spheres, and cones, display them in a place where all students can see them. You can also use the common objects from the Dig In for the display.
- **Supporting Learners:** Have students match the picture with the solid object of the same type. Have them see if they can tap it and make it roll. The curved edge will cause a shape to roll with just a push, as opposed to "rolling a die" which is a cube. If you set a die on a surface and push it, it does not roll. If you put a cone, cylinder, or sphere on its curved surface and push it, it will roll.
- **Extension:** Find other shapes around the room to fit the categories.

◉ "Tell your partner how you know if the shape has curved or flat surfaces."

Think and Grow

You can sort **three-dimensional shapes** in many ways.

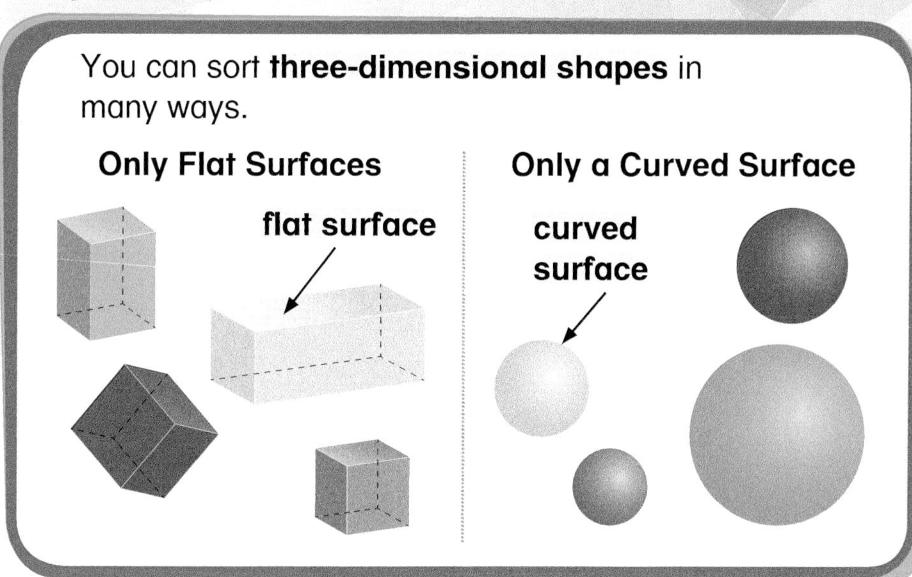

Show and Grow I can do it!

1. Circle the shapes with flat surfaces that are circles.

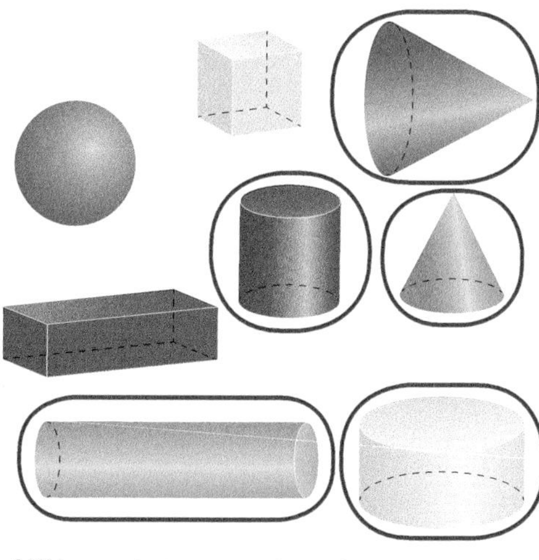

2. Circle the shapes with both flat and curved surfaces.

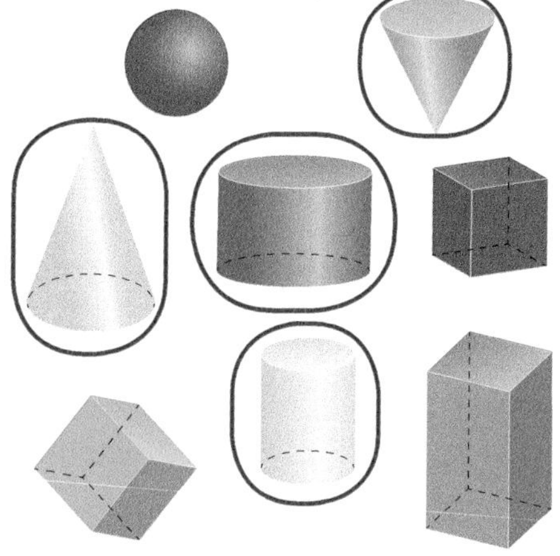

Scaffold instruction to support all students in their learning. Learning is individualized and you may want to group students differently as they move in and out of these levels with each skill and concept. Student self-assessment and feedback help guide your instructional decisions about how and when to layer support for all students to become proficient learners.

Meeting the needs of all learners.

Laurie's Notes

Apply and Grow: Practice

SCAFFOLDING INSTRUCTION

Each exercise on the page is different, requiring students to pay attention to each set of directions. Discussion about each exercise is valuable and will give you insights into your students' learning. Listen to see how students are finding the types and numbers of surfaces.

EMERGING students may have difficulty distinguishing a circle as a flat surface and a curved surface. They may think of a circle as a sphere instead of a two-dimensional flat figure.

- **Exercise 3:** Clarify what "one or more" flat surfaces means.
- **Exercise 4:** Watch to see if students choose the cylinder and cones as well as the spheres.
- **Exercise 5:** This calls for exactly two flat surfaces as compared to Exercise 3.
- **Exercise 6:** This exercise allows students to sort shapes another time by looking at curved and flat surfaces.

PROFICIENT students are generally accurate in distinguishing three-dimensional shapes and the type of surfaces.

- **Exercises 3–5:** Students need to pay attention to two criteria. They may only look at one or the other.
- **Exercise 6:** Be sure students assign all shapes to one of the categories, not just find one shape for each category.

Additional Support

- Students may need to hold and feel actual objects to determine the types of surfaces they have. If you have blocks in the room, students can have some on their desk to look at to see and experiment with flat and curved surfaces.

Extension: Adding Rigor

- Ask if students know the names of all the shapes on this page.

Name ______

Apply and Grow: Practice

3. Circle the shapes with 1 or more flat surfaces.

4. Circle the shapes with a curved surface.

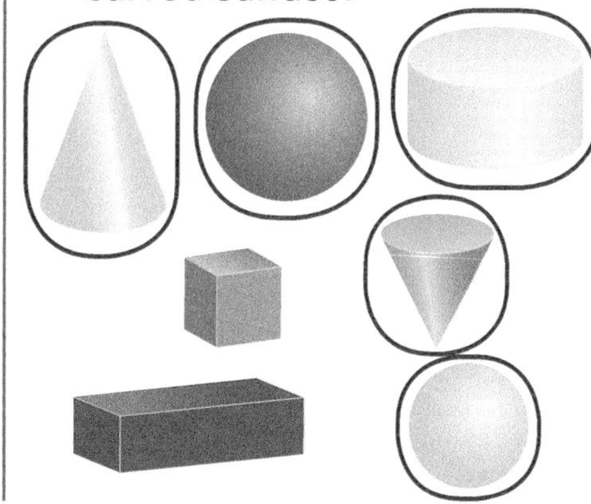

5. Circle the shapes with only 2 flat surfaces.

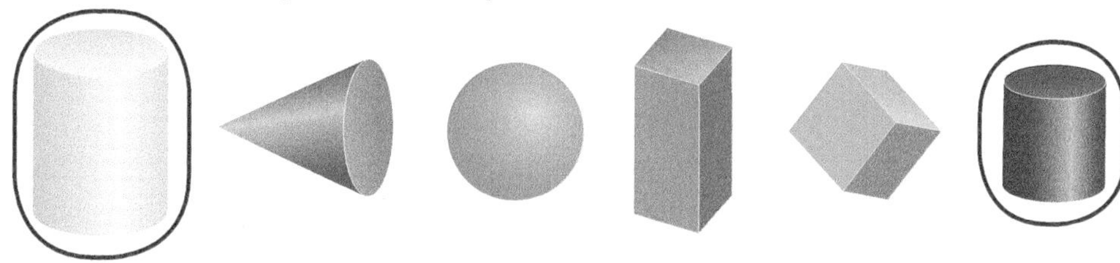

6. MP **Structure** Match each shape to its group.

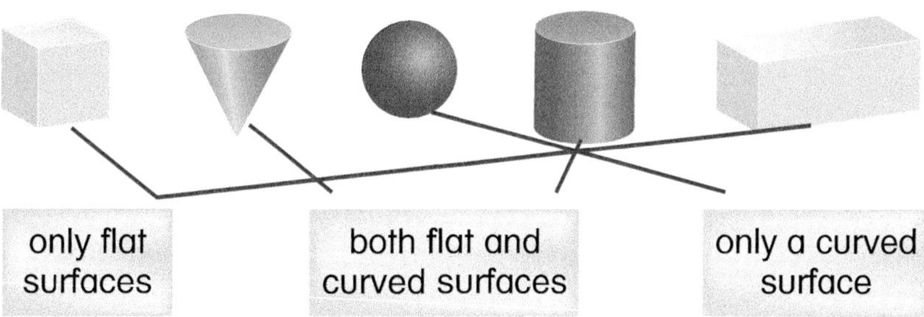

only flat surfaces | both flat and curved surfaces | only a curved surface

ELL Support

Check for understanding of Lesson 13.6. Review the names of the items pictured in Exercise 7. If students are unfamiliar with some, you may want to discuss what each is. Read aloud as students follow along. Ask if they have circled each item (marble, block, eight ball, drum, cylinder, cereal box, kaleidoscope, ice cream cone) and have them answer using a thumbs up or thumbs down signal for *yes* or *no*.

Laurie's Notes

Think and Grow: Modeling Real Life

These applications allow students to show their understanding of the surfaces of three-dimensional shapes. They can distinguish between curved and flat surfaces.

? **Preview**: "Describe the shapes you see on the page. Have you ever gone on a scavenger hunt? A scavenger hunt gives you a list of things to collect. Sometimes it is specific, like a blue rubber band, but sometimes it is a description for which many things could work. Our applications today ask you to select objects for a scavenger hunt that would match a clue."

? **MP2 Reason Abstractly and Quantitatively**: Go through the example instructions. "If an object has no flat surfaces, what kind of surface must it have?"

- Have students circle the objects that will fit the first scavenger hunt clue.
- Introduce Exercise 7. Remind students that the object needs to have exactly two flat surfaces.
- **MP4 Model with Mathematics**: Have students find other objects around the room that they could use for the scavenger hunt.

⦿ Students have sorted three-dimensional shapes based on their surfaces. "Show me with your thumb signals how confident you are in describing three-dimensional surfaces. Tell your partner what you have learned today." Have several students share what they have learned, calling on students at random and not raised hands. Do students recognize the two types of surfaces, and that objects can have different combinations of surfaces?

Closure

- Hold up some of the objects from circle time. Have students describe the surfaces of the shape to a partner.

Think and Grow: Modeling Real Life

You need to find an object that has no flat surfaces for a scavenger hunt. Circle the objects you can use.

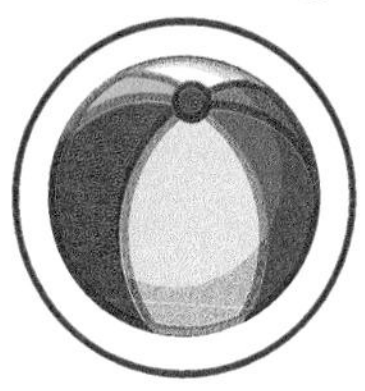

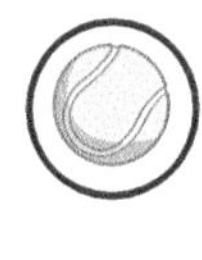

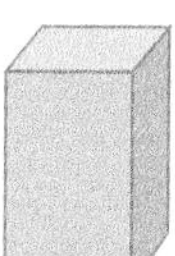

Show and Grow *I can think deeper!*

7. You need to find an object that has only two flat surfaces for a scavenger hunt. Circle the objects you can use.

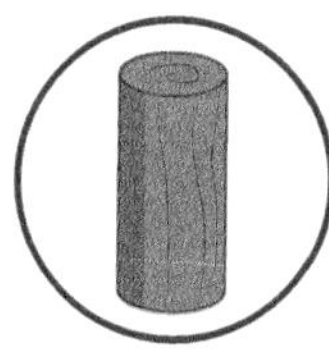

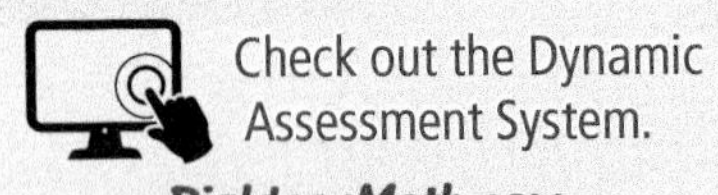
Check out the Dynamic Assessment System.

BigIdeasMath.com

Scaffold assignments to support all students in their learning progression. Revisit with spaced practice to move every student toward proficiency.

Connect and Extend Learning

Practice Notes

- Tell students to pay close attention to each set of directions.
- **Exercise 5:** Remind students that the objects they circle have to have both a flat and curved surface.

Prior Skills

- **Exercises 7 and 8:** Grade 1, Adding Tens

Cross-Curricular Connections

Art

- Bring in empty cans and other items that are three-dimensional shapes such as tissue boxes, food boxes, balls, and cones. Have students put together an art piece with these different shaped items. Then have a partner look at the art piece and record how many of each shape there is in a tally chart. Then they can graph their results.

SOUP
Quick
RICE

Name ______________________

Practice 13.6

Learning Target: Sort three-dimensional shapes.

You can sort three-dimensional shapes in many ways.

Flat Surfaces that are Rectangles	**Flat Surfaces that are Circles**

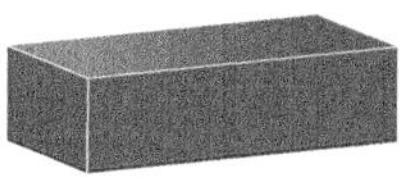

1. Circle the shapes with no flat surface.

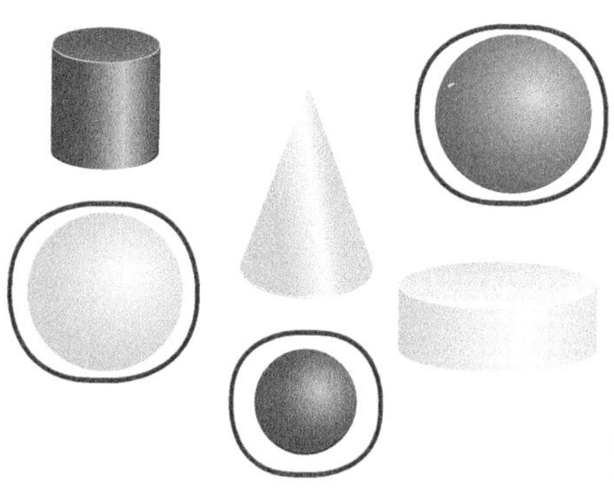

2. Circle the shapes with flat surfaces that are rectangles.

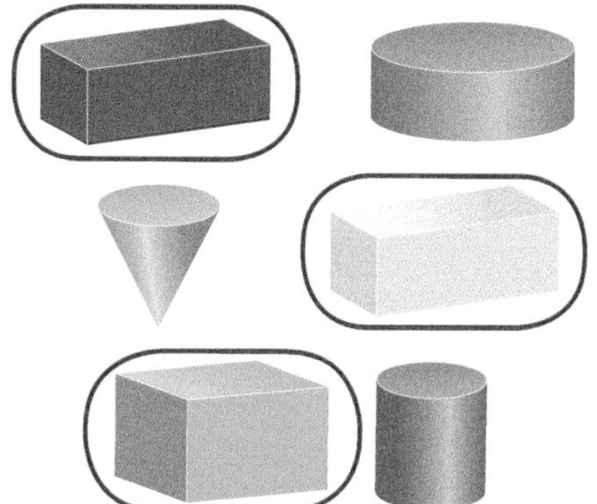

3. Circle the shapes with more than 2 flat surfaces.

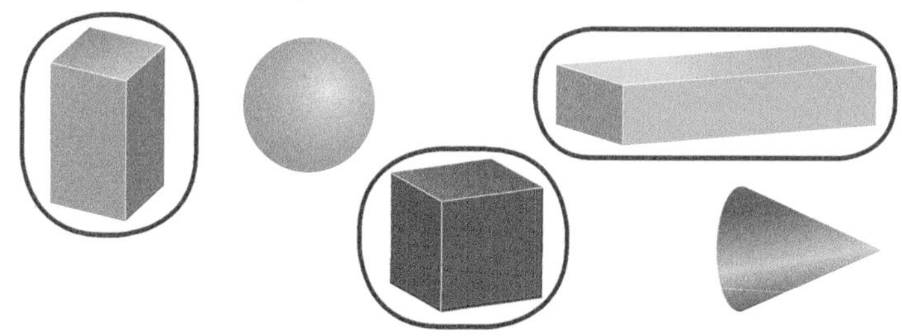

Connect and Extend Learning

Extend Student Learning

Bodily-Kinesthetic

- Have students act out the different ways they can sort shapes. Assign each student a three-dimensional shape. Have them decide how they would like to represent their shape through body movement and words. Put them into groups and have them create a skit about how to sort their shapes. For example, one student can be the sorter and say, "I sort the shapes that have flat surfaces." All of the shapes with flat surfaces will demonstrate how they are flat by possibly laying down or jumping on two feet (to show stacking). For curved surfaces, students can roll or do a somersault (if appropriate).

Lesson Resources

Surface Level	Deep Level
Resources by Chapter • Extra Practice • Reteach Differentiating the Lesson Skills Review Handbook Skills Trainer	Resources by Chapter • Enrichment and Extension Graphic Organizers Dynamic Assessment System • Lesson Practice

4. **Structure** Match each shape to its group.

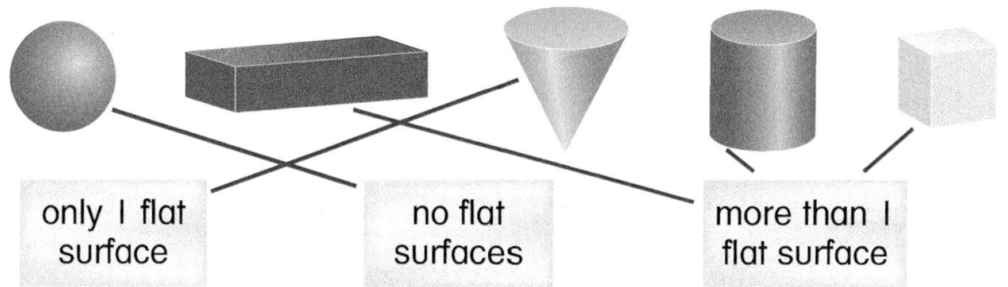

only 1 flat surface | no flat surfaces | more than 1 flat surface

5. **Modeling Real Life** You need to find an object that has both flat and curved surfaces for a scavenger hunt. Circle the objects you can use.

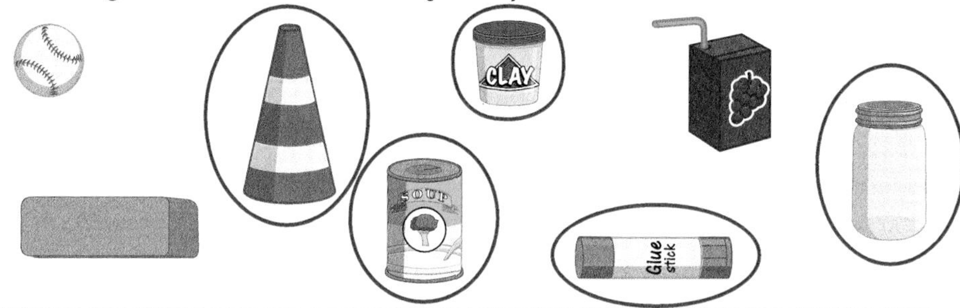

6. **DIG DEEPER!** Compare the shapes. How are they the same? How are they different?

Sample answer:

Same: Both shapes have flat and curved surfaces.

Different: Cylinders have 2 flat surfaces and cones have 1 flat surface.

Review & Refresh

7. 30 + 30 = 60

8. 60 + 20 = 80

Check out the
Dynamic Classroom.

BigIdeasMath.com

13.7

Laurie's Notes

COMMON CORE STATE STANDARDS
1.G.A.1

Learning Target

Describe three-dimensional shapes.

Success Criteria

- Make three-dimensional shapes.
- Identify the number of flat surfaces, vertices, and edges.
- Identify a shape from given information.

Warm-Up

Practice opportunities for the following are available in the Resources by Chapter or at *BigIdeasMath.com*.

- Daily skills
- Vocabulary
- Prerequisite skills

ELL Support

The Explore and Grow asks that students to build a three-dimensional shape. Explain that *build* may be considered another synonym for *make*. Suggest that students add it to their vocabulary notebooks.

Preparing to Teach

The Explore and Grow in today's lesson is very open-ended in terms of the materials you select to use. The goal is to make three-dimensional shapes from materials on hand such as coffee stirrers, pipe cleaners, popsicle sticks, toothpicks, clay, marshmallows, and so on. These materials form the edges and vertices of the solid or perhaps the entire solid if you are using modeling clay. Student will describe three-dimensional shapes in terms of the number and type of surfaces, vertices, or edges it has.

Materials

- three-dimensional shapes
- materials to build three-dimensional shapes

Dig In (Circle Time)

Students are given a picture of a three-dimensional shape. They will compare and describe the shapes in order to define them by their attributes. They will play a "Stand Up, Sit Down" game based on the attributes of their shapes.

- "Yesterday we started looking at three-dimensional shapes and the surfaces they have. We sorted by whether they had a curved surface, a flat surface, or both."
- Review the familiar objects. Pick up a sphere. "Who knows the name of this? Spheres look like balls. Do they have a vertex? Do they have a flat surface? Spheres are all curved surface. If you have a picture of a sphere, stand up."
- Repeat this process with a cone. Point out the flat surface which is a circle. It has a curved surface. It has one vertex (review vocabulary). Have students stand up if they have a picture of a cone.
- Repeat this process with a rectangular prism. Point out the flat surfaces (6 total) which are all rectangles. It does not have a curved surface. It has 8 vertices. It has *edges* where the flat surfaces meet. Have students stand up if they have a picture of a rectangular prism.
- Play "Stand Up, Sit Down." Give clues to a specific shape. Students stand up if their shape fits the description. If you want everyone to stand, say "It is a three-dimensional shape." If you want no one to stand, say "It is a two-dimensional shape." Otherwise, use clues such as "one vertex, many edges, only a curved surface, etc."
- Discuss what materials students will use to build solids. Review proper use and clean up procedures for the Explore and Grow.
- ◉ "Today we will be building and describing three-dimensional shapes."

? Teaching Prompt ◉ Learning Target

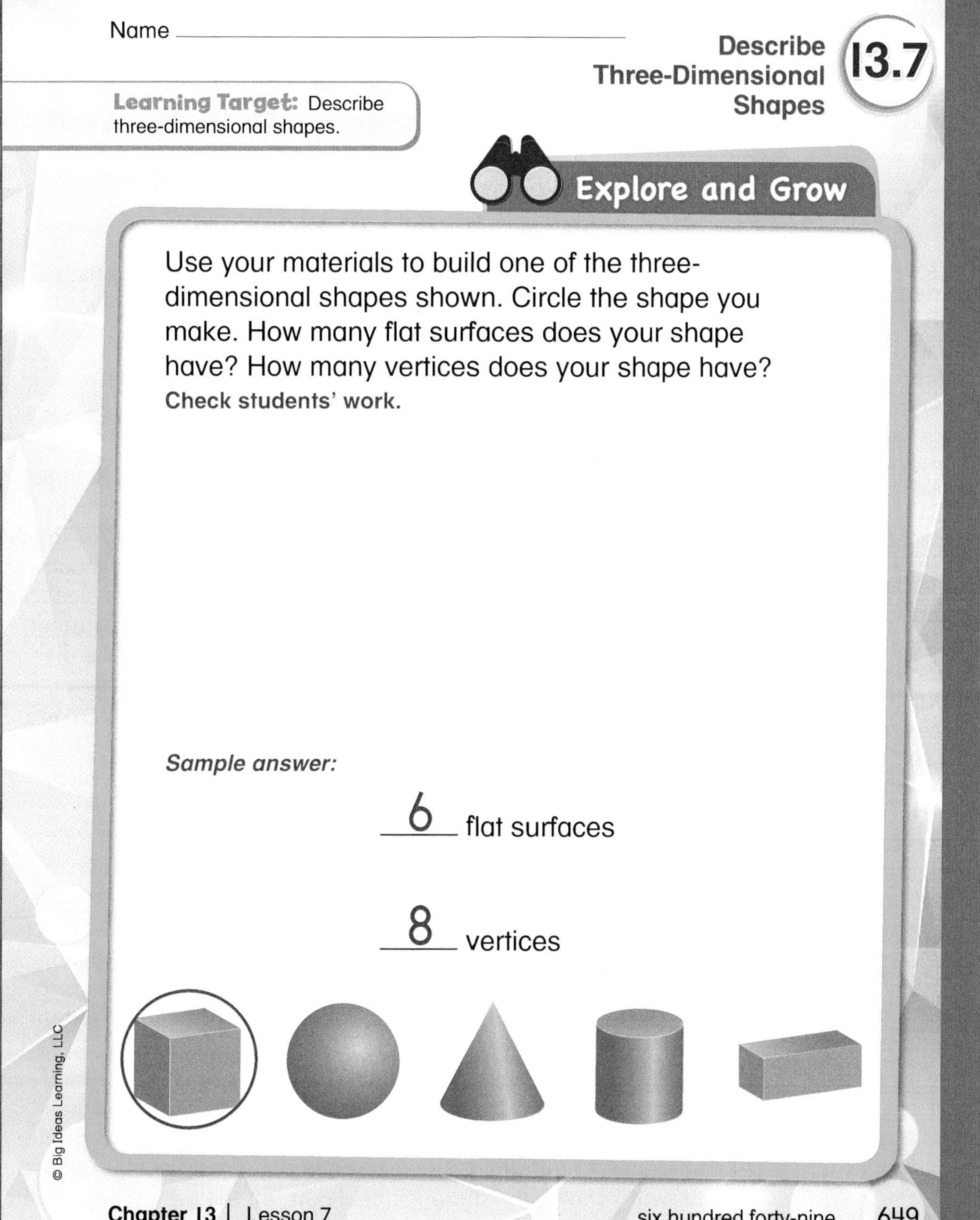

Name ______________________

Describe Three-Dimensional Shapes **13.7**

Learning Target: Describe three-dimensional shapes.

Explore and Grow

Use your materials to build one of the three-dimensional shapes shown. Circle the shape you make. How many flat surfaces does your shape have? How many vertices does your shape have?

Check students' work.

Sample answer:

<u>6</u> flat surfaces

<u>8</u> vertices

Explore and Grow

- The materials you have may not allow for all of the solids to be made.
- Make the materials available to each group. Read the directions. "You are going to make just one shape. When you finish, circle the shape you made."
- When students have finished, do a *poster walk* so that students can observe the work of others.
- Discuss any interesting work that students comment on.

ELL Support

Discuss the examples. Then have students work in pairs to practice language. Have one student ask the other, "How many flat surfaces are there? How many vertices? How many edges?" Then have them alternate roles.

Beginner students may answer with a number.
Intermediate students may answer with simple sentences, such as, "There are six."
Advanced students may answer with detailed sentences, such as, "There are six flat surfaces."

Laurie's Notes

Think and Grow

Getting Started

- Introduce the vocabulary cards **edge** and **rectangular prism**. Remind students of the vocabulary cards *thee-dimensional, vertex, flat surface*, and *curved surface*.

Teaching Notes

? "Look at our three-dimensional shapes. What do they all have in common? What are some differences?"

- **Model:** Hold up a cube from the Dig In. "Let's look at the cube. How many flat surfaces does it have? Touch each face. Fill in the number of flat surfaces. How many vertices does it have? Touch each one with your finger. Fill in the number of vertices. Look at what is formed in a three-dimensional shape when flat surfaces come together. It forms an edge. Each time flat surfaces meet, it is called an edge. How many edges does it have? Trace the edges with your finger. Fill in the number of edges."
- Repeat this process with the rectangular prism, cylinder, cone, and sphere.
- Notice that when a curved surface meets a flat surface, such as with the cylinder or cone, it is not called an edge. The mathematical definition of an edge is a line segment that joins two vertices. That is why a cylinder or cone does not have one. A side of a two-dimensional shape can also be called an edge.
- Students will record the number of flat surfaces, vertices, and edges in a rectangular prism. They should trace, describe, or point to where each are located. If possible, let every student or pair of students have a solid (block, tissue box, etc.) to touch and count so as not to be dependent on the picture.
- **Teaching Tip:** Three-dimensional drawings are very abstract and often difficult for students to reason with. For example, the green sphere will appear to be a circle to many first-grade students. Continue to show the solid object and explain how the drawing shows the dimensions. Point out the dotted lines in the other shapes indicating depth and the other edges, etc.
- **Supporting Learners:** Students have the shapes to touch and count. Not only will having the shape to touch to determine the number of flat surfaces, curved surfaces, vertices, and edges help students fill in quantities, but tracing and touching the various attributes will also reinforce the vocabulary. For example, as students run their finger along an edge, they count the edge and reinforce the definition of edge kinesthetically.
- **Extension:** Find other examples of three-dimensional shapes around the room to fit the categories. "Can you find any three-dimensional shapes that do not match the shapes on this page?"

Think and Grow

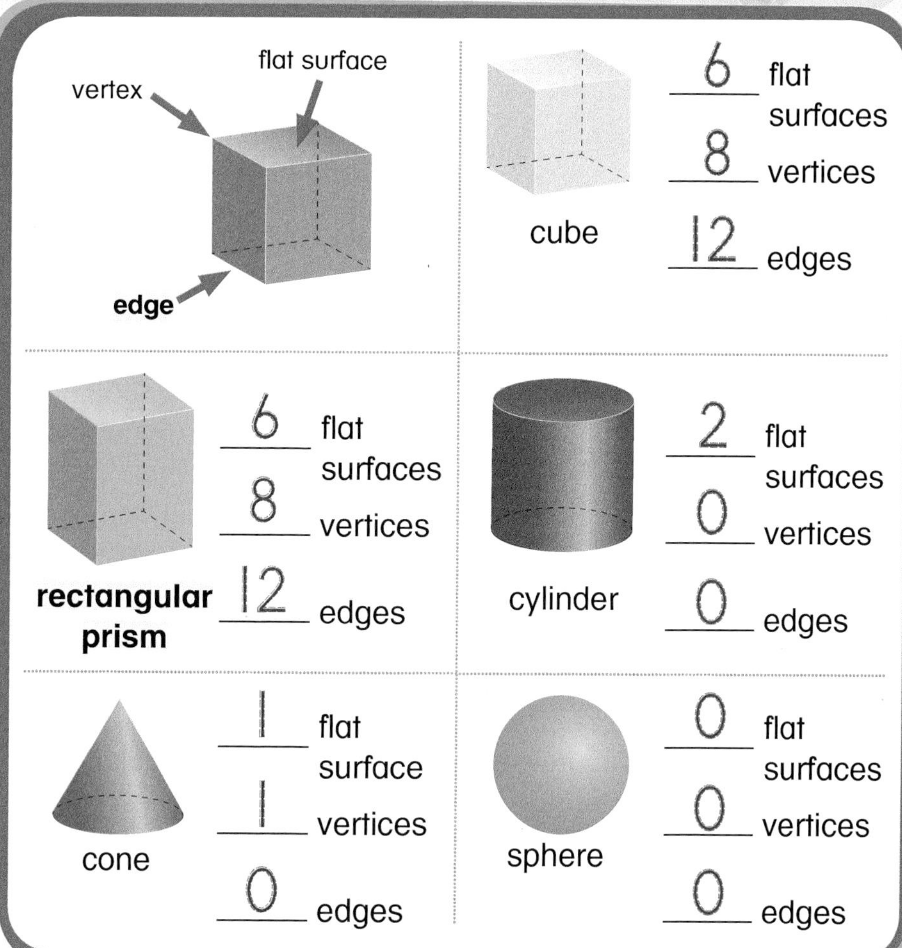

Show and Grow *I can do it!*

1. 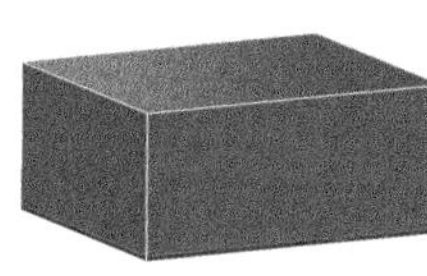

6 flat surfaces 8 vertices

12 edges

Scaffold instruction to support all students in their learning. Learning is individualized and you may want to group students differently as they move in and out of these levels with each skill and concept. Student self-assessment and feedback help guide your instructional decisions about how and when to layer support for all students to become proficient learners.

Meeting the needs of all learners.

Laurie's Notes

Apply and Grow: Practice

SCAFFOLDING INSTRUCTION

Students continue to identify the number of flat surfaces, vertices, and edges for specific three-dimensional shapes. They progress to selecting the correct attributes from a list without the shape drawn for them and finally solving shape riddles for any three-dimensional shape.

EMERGING students may struggle with three-dimensional drawings. They are not consistent with identifying all the sides and vertices, especially without seeing the shape. Some students may not realize the "point" of a cone is the same as a vertex on prisms.

- **Exercises 2 and 3:** Students continue tracing counting the flat surfaces, vertices, and edges. Students may say that a cylinder has two edges, describing where the curved and flat surfaces meet. Remind students that edges are always between two vertices. A cylinder does not have any vertices, so it cannot have an edge.
- **Exercises 4 and 5:** Students select the attributes for a shape from a list. Students will benefit from being able to look at the shapes.
- **Exercises 6 and 7:** These riddles involve a different kind of thinking and may be more challenging than describing a given shape. They should see the shapes to solve the riddles. They can also look back at Think and Grow if needed. If so, students should defend why the shape they choose is described correctly rather than simply matching the attributes.

PROFICIENT students can identify the attributes for all shapes.

- **Exercises 4 and 5:** Students choose the correct attributes for the shapes. Have students name the shape to which the attributes that are not selected belong.

Additional Support

- Provide students with additional experiences seeing and holding the five shapes. They should make their own comparisons among the shapes.

Extension: Adding Rigor

- Have students create their own riddles for two- or three-dimensional shapes.

Name

Apply and Grow: Practice

2. 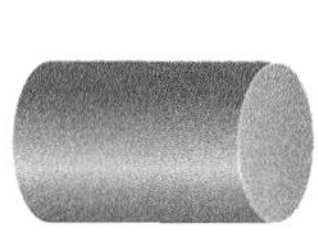

2 flat surfaces

0 vertices

0 edges

3. 

6 flat surfaces

8 vertices

12 edges

Circle the attributes of the shape.

4. **Cone**

1 flat surface

0 vertices

slides

two-dimensional

5. **Cube**

6 flat surfaces

12 vertices

12 edges

rolls

6. I am a three-dimensional shape that has no flat surfaces, no vertices, and no edges. What am I?

sphere

7. I am a three-dimensional shape that has 1 flat surface, 1 vertex, and no edges. What am I?

cone

8. **DIG DEEPER!** Newton buys an item that has 2 more flat surfaces than edges. Which item does he buy?

ELL Support

Check for understanding of Lesson 13.7. Review the names of the items pictured in Exercise 9. If students are unfamiliar with some, you may want to discuss what each is. Read aloud as students follow along. Ask if they have circled each item. Then ask if they have drawn a line through each item. Have them answer using a thumbs up or thumbs down signal for *yes* or *no*.

Laurie's Notes

Think and Grow: Modeling Real Life

These applications allow students to demonstrate their ability to identify real-world shapes that meet given attributes.

? **Preview**: "What do you see in these pictures? What are some of the shapes you notice the objects have?" For example, a globe is a sphere and the thermos is a cylinder.

- Read the description for the objects in the first table. Have students tell their partners what shape has no vertices. Once students agree on the type of shape, have them circle the basketball below the table (instead of the globe). If students mention the globe, agree that it is a sphere, but it is not below the table.
- Repeat the process with a shape that has 12 edges (rectangular prism). Have students practice saying, "rectangular prism" instead of calling the shape a box. Circle the tissue box on the table.
- Students can work together on Exercise 9. Students may not realize that the floor of the tepee is a flat surface for the cone.
- **Supporting Learners:** Point out three-dimensional objects in the classroom. Ask students to tell what shape it is. For example, a water bottle is a cylinder. Our cubbies are cubes. The dice are cubes, etc.

◉ Students have described three-dimensional shapes by their attributes. "Tell your partner how well you can count flat surfaces. Tell your partner how well you can count vertices. Tell your partner what an edge is. Tell your partner how well you can count edges."

Closure

- Play "Stand Up Sit Down" from the Dig In. Or, describe the attributes of a three-dimensional shape. Students stand up when they know what shape it is. When several students are standing up, randomly call on a student to tell which shape.

Think and Grow: Modeling Real Life

Circle the object below the table that has 0 flat surfaces. Draw a line through the object above the basketball that has 12 edges.

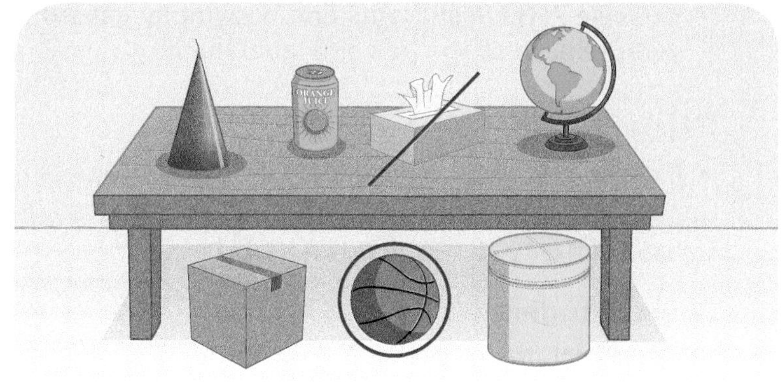

Show and Grow *I can think deeper!*

9. Circle the object in front of the campers that has more than 2 flat surfaces. Draw a line through the object behind the logs that has 1 vertex and 1 flat surface.

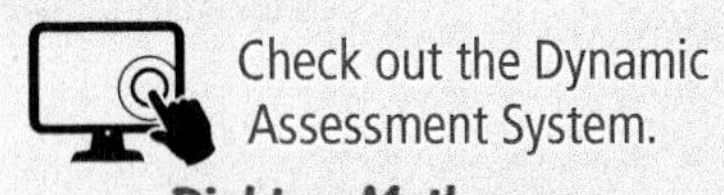
Check out the Dynamic
Assessment System.
BigIdeasMath.com

Scaffold assignments to support all students in their learning progression. Revisit with spaced practice to move every student toward proficiency.

Connect and Extend Learning

Practice Notes

- If students are having difficulty, provide them with the three-dimensional shapes to hold on to and observe.
- **Exercise 7:** Have students find how many flat surfaces and vertices each shape has and label them.

Prior Skills

- **Exercises 10 and 11:** Grade 1, Adding Two-Digit Numbers

Cross-Curricular Connections

Social Studies

- Show pictures of cities and ask students what shapes they see. Focus on different three-dimensional shapes like rectangular prisms, cubes, cones, and cylinders. Have students create their own map of a city with different three dimensional shapes. They can create each shape using craft sticks and clay, folding paper, or by drawing the flat surfaces of each shape on the paper and labeling them. Be sure students provide a map key.

Name ____________________

Practice 13.7

Learning Target: Describe three-dimensional shapes.

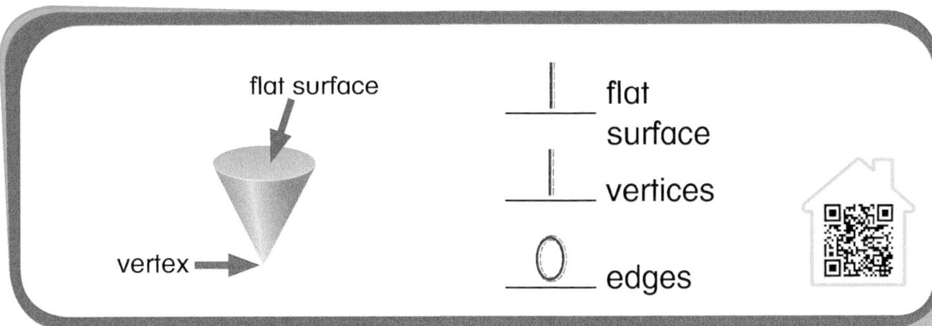

1 flat surface

1 vertices

0 edges

1. 0 flat surfaces

0 vertices

0 edges

2. 

6 flat surfaces

8 vertices

12 edges

3. Circle the shape that has the same number of vertices as edges.

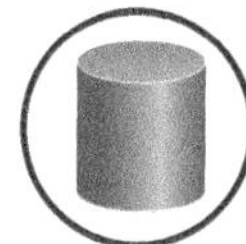  

4. Circle the shape that has the same number of flat surfaces as vertices.

Circle the attributes of the shape.

5. Cylinder

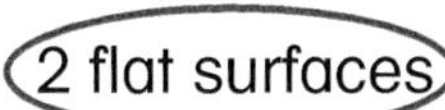
2 flat surfaces

3 flat surfaces

2 vertices

stacks

6. Rectangular Prism

8 flat surfaces

12 edges

slides

three-dimensional

Connect and Extend Learning

Extend Student Learning

Linguistic

- Have students think of a shape and write down clues such as the number of flat surfaces, vertices, edges it has along with whether it rolls, stacks, or slides. Each student will work with a partner and tell their partner one clue at a time about their shape. Provide materials for the partner to use to create the shape to guess. Once the partner guesses the correct answer, the two students switch roles and play again.

Lesson Resources	
Surface Level	**Deep Level**
Resources by Chapter • Extra Practice • Reteach Differentiating the Lesson Skills Review Handbook Skills Trainer	Resources by Chapter • Enrichment and Extension Graphic Organizers Dynamic Assessment System • Lesson Practice

7. **DIG DEEPER!** Descartes buys an item that has 2 fewer flat surfaces than vertices. Which item does he buy?

8. **MP Repeated Reasoning** What other shape has the same number of surfaces, vertices, and edges as a rectangular prism? How is that shape different from a rectangular prism?

cube; A cube is made up of flat surfaces that are all squares.

9. **MP Modeling Real Life** Circle the object next to the hat that has 6 square flat surfaces. Draw a line through the object in front of the hat that has 0 edges and 1 vertex.

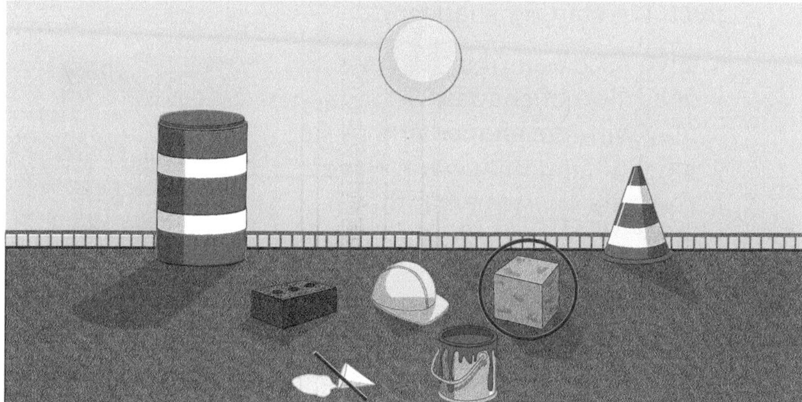

Review & Refresh

10. 20 + 18 = 38

11. 40 + 25 = 65

13.8

Check out the
Dynamic Classroom.
BigIdeasMath.com

Laurie's Notes

COMMON CORE

STATE STANDARDS
1.G.A.2

Learning Target

Join three-dimensional shapes to make another shape.

Success Criteria

- Join shapes to make another shape.
- Tell which shapes I used.

Warm-Up

Practice opportunities for the following are available in the Resources by Chapter or at *BigIdeasMath.com.*

- Daily skills
- Vocabulary
- Prerequisite skills

ELL Support

Explain that *join* and *combine* are used as synonyms and mean "connect."

Preparing to Teach

Students love to build with blocks. In this lesson, students will recognize what can be built if you put three-dimensional shapes together. It is helpful for students to have the shapes with which to build. Students will need multiple cubes for this lesson.

Materials

- three-dimensional shapes
- centimeter cubes

Dig In (Circle Time)

Students explore building with three-dimensional shapes. The goal is for students to notice what new shapes can be made when you put two shapes together, and what would not be possible to make given the starting shapes.

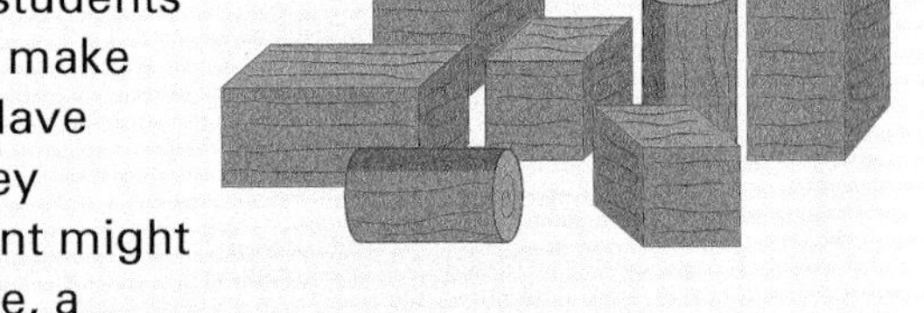

- Give each pair of students a collection of shapes. Let students play with the shapes and make any building they want. Have students explain what they stacked together. A student might say, "My tower has a cube, a rectangular prism, and a cylinder."

◉ "Just like we joined two-dimensional shapes to make a new shape, we can also join three-dimensional shapes. You have just done that with your buildings. Today we will decide if a shape can be formed from two others or not. Let's try some."

- Show a rectangular prism with a cylinder on top. "If you think I can make this with all cubes show thumbs up. If you don't think cubes could make this, show thumbs down."
- Show a picture of an ice cream cone (single scoop). "If you can make this with a sphere and a cone, show thumbs up. If not, show thumbs down."

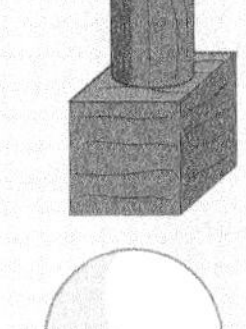

? "Can I make a snowman from a sphere and a cylinder?" Repeat with other examples that can and cannot be completed.

◉ Explain that today they are going to decide what can and cannot be made by putting three-dimensional shapes together.

? Teaching Prompt ◉ Learning Target

Name ______________________

13.8 Combine Three-Dimensional Shapes

Learning Target: Join three-dimensional shapes to make another shape.

Explore and Grow

Which three-dimensional shapes can you make using cubes? Build one of the shapes.

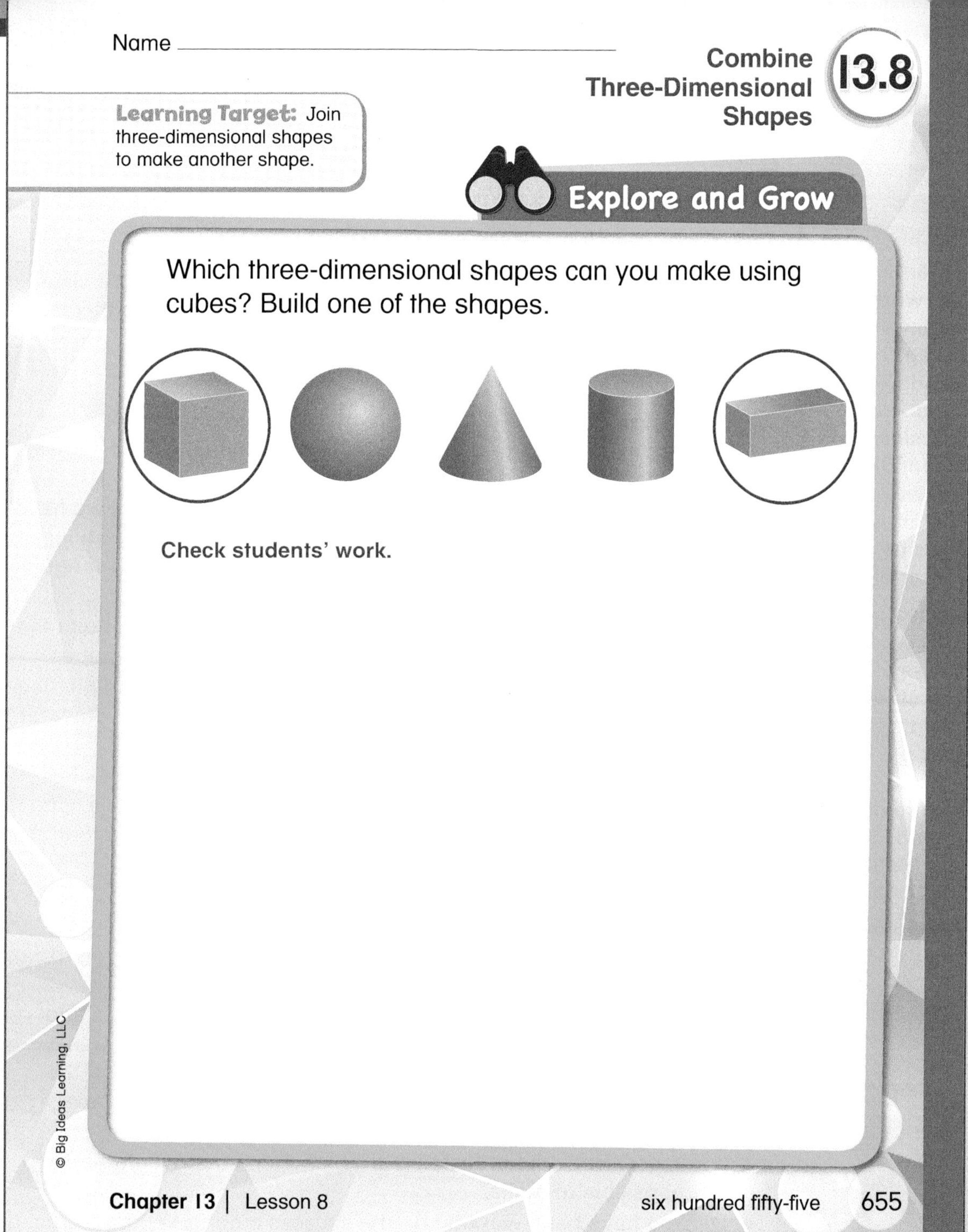

Check students' work.

Explore and Grow

- Each student will need centimeter cubes.
- "You are trying to build as many of the shapes on this page using only cubes. See which ones you can build and which you cannot."
- "Which shapes could you build?" cube and rectangular prism
- "Which shapes could you not build? Why couldn't they be built?" Have students refer to shapes by name.
- "You decided what could and could not be built based on cubes. You will continue deciding which shapes can or cannot be made from two other shapes."

Laurie's Notes

ELL Support

Discuss the example. Have students work in groups as they practice language while completing Exercises 1 and 2. Monitor discussion and provide support as needed. Expect students at different language levels to perform as described.

Beginner students may use single words or simple phrases. **Intermediate** students may answer with longer phrases or simple sentences. **Advanced** students may answer with sentences and help direct the discussion.

Think and Grow

Getting Started

- Most students will not need shapes to answer these exercises. Having blocks available will help students who have difficulty determining what shapes are being shown.

Teaching Notes

- There are two exercises, each with the same direction line. Remind students that they are considering what would a tower or putting the shapes together look like.
- ? **Model**: "Look at the green shapes. Newton tells us that we have two rectangular prisms. If you put them together, what shape would you get? Which one came from Newton's two rectangular prisms? How do you know?"
- **MP5 Use Appropriate Tools Strategically**: Students can build the different towers as desired based on the starting two shapes.
- In these exercises, the shapes to join are given first and divided. The combined shapes from which students choose the one that could be made are given on the right.
- Remind students that shapes can be turned on different sides for the new shape. For example, in Exercise 1 the cone is lying on its side. It can be turned to be placed on the flat side. Same idea with the rectangular prism in Exercise 2.
- Watch to see if students can imagine using the shapes, or if they need to use the concrete blocks.
- Have students tell the names of the shapes they are using to start and the names of the shapes in the two new shapes.
- **Supporting Learners:** Have students take the two shapes and try to build the two different new shapes. Which one can they make? Why can't they make the other? They can cross off the shape that makes it impossible to build the incorrect shape.
- **Extension:** Have students create new shapes from three other shapes. Have them describe another shape that would be impossible to make.
- ◉ "You have been working on the success criteria. You have joined shapes together to make a larger shape. You have told which shapes you used. How do you think you are doing with your learning so far?"

Think and Grow

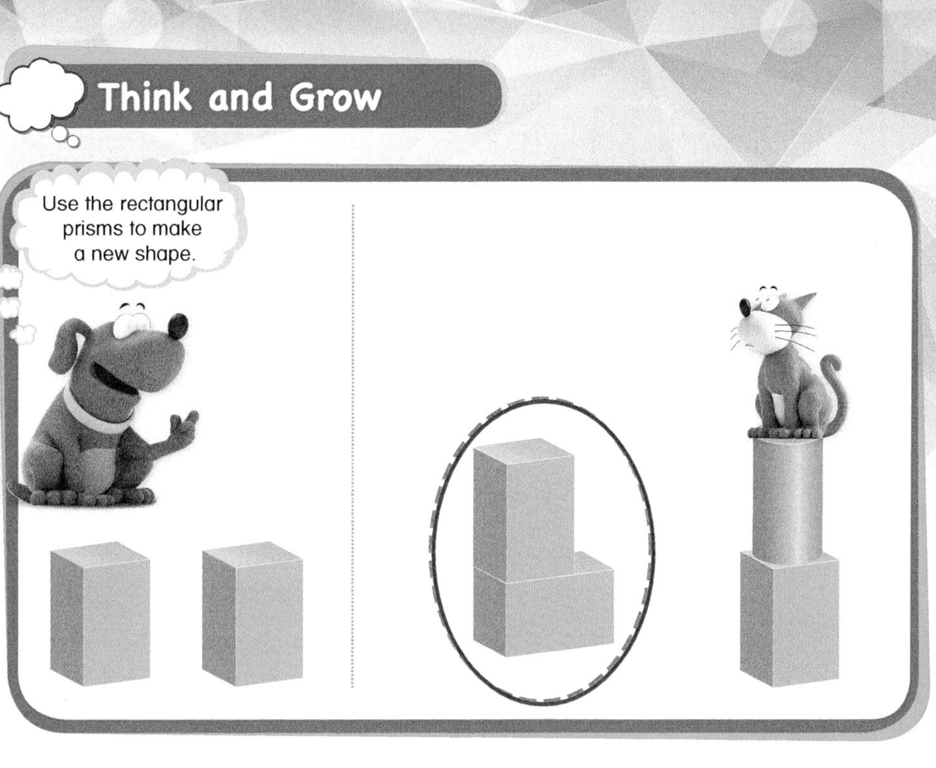

Use the rectangular prisms to make a new shape.

Show and Grow *I can do it!*

Circle the new shape that you can make.

1.

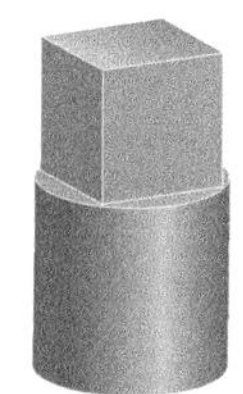
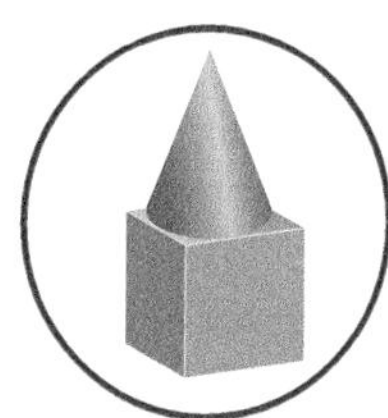

2.

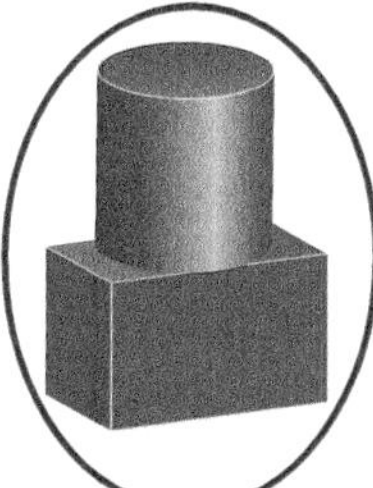

Scaffold instruction to support all students in their learning. Learning is individualized and you may want to group students differently as they move in and out of these levels with each skill and concept. Student self-assessment and feedback help guide your instructional decisions about how and when to layer support for all students to become proficient learners.

Meeting the needs of all learners.

Laurie's Notes

Apply and Grow: Practice

SCAFFOLDING INSTRUCTION

The exercises on this page continue to have students choose the new shape that can be made from the original two shapes. They are challenged by the final exercise to recognize a pattern with cubes.

EMERGING students may recognize one of the beginning shapes in a new shape and assume that the new shape is correct. Students need to consider that both of the shapes that are given at the beginning must be in the final new shape.

- **Exercises 3–5:** These exercises are similar to Exercises 1 and 2.
- **Exercise 6:** Students will need to build the next shape and count the cubes. They will need support for seeing how the pattern is changing to build the next shape.

PROFICIENT students have developed spatial skills that enable them to look at the shapes and envision how they might be put together.

- **Exercise 6:** This is a complex reasoning exercise. Students may need to build the next shape and count the cubes. They might be able to see an addition pattern from shape to shape. Have students explain how they "see" the next shape, and how they determined the number of cubes.

Additional Support

- Allow students to build shapes.

Extension: Adding Rigor

- Build a tower of 3 to 4 shapes. Hide your tower behind a file folder. Describe your tower to a partner and see if he or she can build the same thing.

Name ______________________________

Apply and Grow: Practice

Circle the new shape that you can make.

3.

   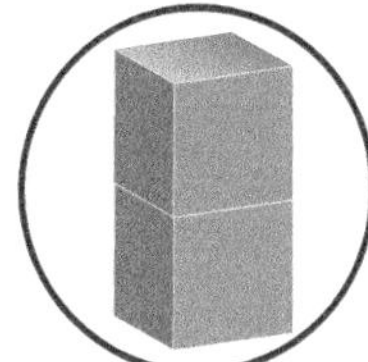

4.

5.

   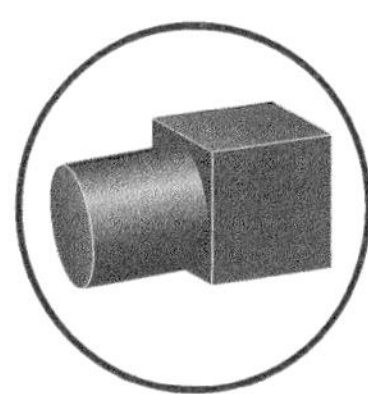

6. DIG DEEPER! How many cubes do you need in all to make the next shape?

   ?

9 cubes

Chapter 13 | Lesson 8 **657**

ELL Support

Check for understanding of Lesson 13.8. Read each story aloud as students follow along. Clarify any unknown vocabulary. Allow time to complete each exercise. Ask the following questions and have students indicate the answers by holding up the appropriate number of fingers.

1. How many more cubes do you use than your friend?
2. How many more cubes does your friend use than you?

Laurie's Notes

Think and Grow: Modeling Real Life

Today's applications involve multiple steps. Students will build two walls of cubes and determine the difference in the total number of cubes between the two walls. Students are asked to draw pictures. More than likely students cannot draw a cube. They should draw a "math picture" as we have done in addition and subtraction lessons. They can use squares to show the walls.

- ? **Preview**: "Have you ever seen a wall made with bricks or blocks? In our applications today, we will think about building walls with cubes. We want to compare the number of cubes needed to build the different walls."
- "We want to build a wall that is 5 cubes long and 2 cubes tall." Have a student build the wall as an example. "We can draw the wall by using squares. How many cubes does our wall take to build?" Fill in 10 under you. "Our friend builds a wall that is 4 cubes long and 2 cubes tall." Have another student build that wall, and show the sketch. "How many cubes does our friend's wall need?" Fill in 8 below friend.
- ? "We need to figure out how many more cubes we used than our friend. What equation will help us find out?" $10 - 8 =$ ____ or $8 +$ ___ $= 10$ "Fill in how many more cubes we used than our friend."
- Introduce Exercise 7. The exercise follows the same process as the example. Watch as students determine the total number of cubes and how they set up an equation.
- **Supporting Learners**: Provide the cubes for them to build the wall. A drawing of squares might be the easiest way to find the number of cubes for each wall, as they do not have to worry about the wall falling over.
- ◉ "We have been determining what shapes can be made by joining three-dimensional shapes. Use your thumb signals to show how you are doing at knowing what shapes can be made. Use your thumb signals to show how well you can recognize a shape that cannot be made."

Closure

- Show a drawing or a block tower made of three shapes. "Tell your partner what shapes were used to make my tower. Name one shape that I did not use."

Think and Grow: Modeling Real Life

You build a wall. It is 5 cubes long and 2 cubes tall. Your friend builds a wall. It is 4 cubes long and 2 cubes tall. How many more cubes do you use than your friend?

Draw pictures: You Friend

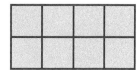

Equation:

$10 - 8 = 2$

2 more cubes

Show and Grow *I can think deeper!*

7. You build a wall. It is 3 cubes long and 3 cubes tall. Your friend builds a wall. It is 5 cubes long and 3 cubes tall. How many more cubes does your friend use than you?

Draw pictures: You Friend

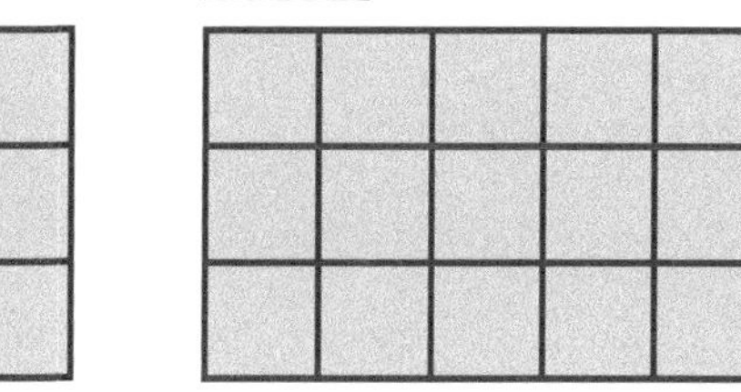

Equation:

$15 - 9 = 6$

6 more cubes

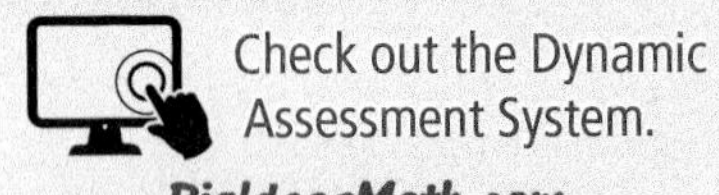
Check out the Dynamic Assessment System.
BigIdeasMath.com

Scaffold assignments to support all students in their learning progression. Revisit with spaced practice to move every student toward proficiency.

Connect and Extend Learning

Practice Notes

- Provide three-dimensional shapes for additional support.

Prior Skills

- **Exercise 5:** Grade 1, Ordering Objects by Length

Cross-Curricular Connections

Language Arts

- Create a story problem with missing numbers, words, and three-dimensional shapes, or use the one below.

  The Prince builds a wall. It is ___(a)___ cubes long and ___(b)___ cubes tall. The Princess builds a wall that is ___(c)___ cubes long and ___(d)___ cubes tall. They both want to protect their castles from the ____(e)____ ___(f)___. Who uses the most cubes to build their wall?

  Have students decide what to put in the blanks. Ask students for (a) a number within 5 and (b) another number within 5. For (c) and (d) ask students to provide numbers that are different than (a) or (b) but still within 5. For (e) have students provide an adjective and then for (f) a singular noun.

  A complete example is then "The Prince builds a wall. It is 4 cubes long and 2 cubes tall. The Princess builds a wall that is 5 cubes long and 3 cubes tall. They both want to protect their castles from the terrible wolf. Who uses the most cubes to build their wall?" Have students solve the problem, and then start over with new responses.

Name ______________________

Practice 13.8

Learning Target: Join three-dimensional shapes to make another shape.

Circle the new shape that you can make.

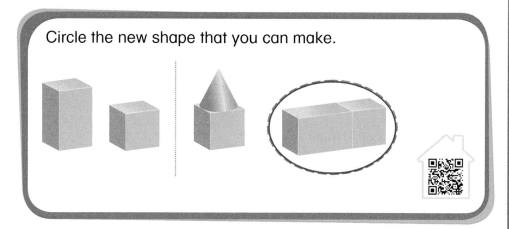

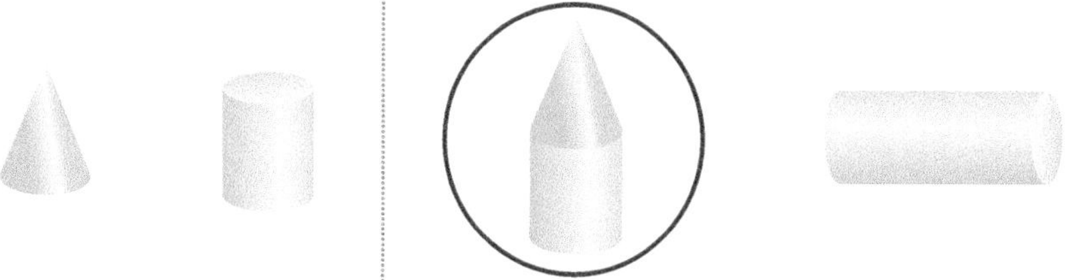

Circle the new shape that you can make.

1.

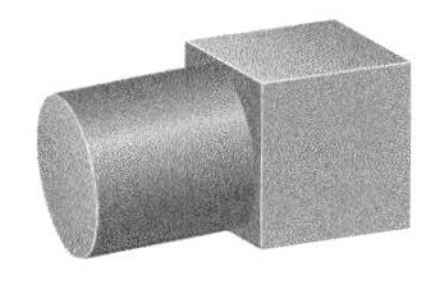
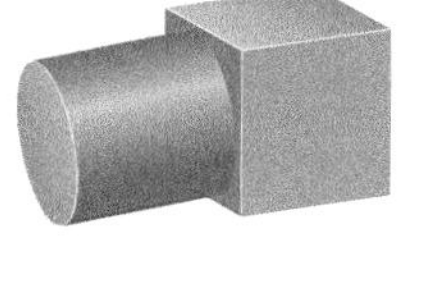
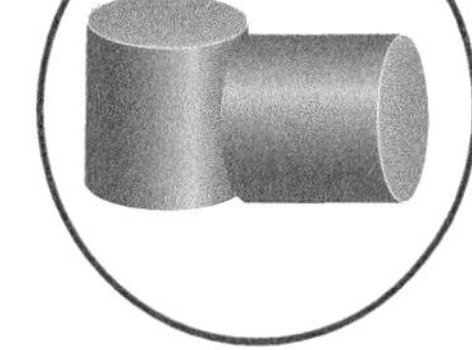

2.

Connect and Extend Learning

Extend Student Learning

Visual-Spatial

- Divide the class into groups of three students. Provide each group with twenty cubes. Partner A and B will build two separate walls without Partner C watching. Partner C will then examine both walls, create an equation on a whiteboard, and determine which partner used more cubes. This activity can be repeated by rotating which two partners build and which partner creates an equation.

Lesson Resources	
Surface Level	**Deep Level**
Resources by Chapter • Extra Practice • Reteach Differentiating the Lesson Skills Review Handbook Skills Trainer	Resources by Chapter • Enrichment and Extension Graphic Organizers Dynamic Assessment System • Lesson Practice

3. **DIG DEEPER!** How many cubes do you need in all to make the next shape?

?

13 cubes

---

4. **Modeling Real Life** You build a wall that is 2 cubes long and 4 cubes tall. Your friend builds a wall that is 4 cubes long and 3 cubes tall. How many more cubes does your friend use than you?

You:

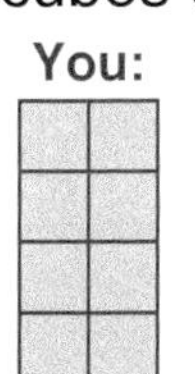

Friend:

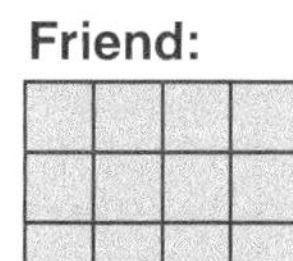

12 − 8 = 4

4 more cubes

Review & Refresh

5. Order from shortest to longest.

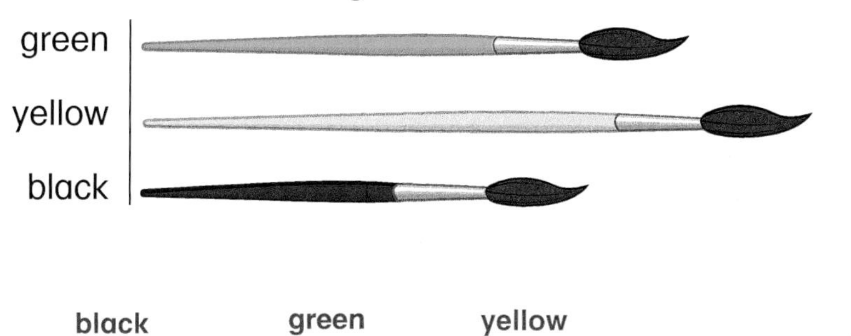

black, green, yellow

Check out the
Dynamic Classroom.

BigIdeasMath.com

13.9

Laurie's Notes

Learning Target

Take apart three-dimensional shapes.

Success Criteria

- Tell what shapes make up a given shape.
- Show the parts of a given shape.

Warm-Up

Practice opportunities for the following are available in the Resources by Chapter or at *BigIdeasMath.com.*

- Daily skills
- Vocabulary
- Prerequisite skills

ELL Support

Review the names of each shape. Provide a word bank with the names of the shapes shown: cone, rectangular prism, cylinder, cube, sphere. Read each name aloud and have students repeat. Present one of the shapes to the class or point to a representation in the book. Have them chorally name the shape.

COMMON CORE **STATE STANDARDS**
1.G.A.2

Preparing to Teach

Students have been working with three-dimensional shapes and combining them to make new shapes. Today students will take composite shapes and buildings and identify the basic three-dimensional shapes used to make it.

Materials

- three-dimensional shapes
- file folder

Dig In (Circle Time)

Students will be shown a tower, shape, or building made from three-dimensional shapes. Students will name the individual blocks used to make it. They will play "Master Builder" in partners to build and take apart shapes.

- ⊙ "We have been doing a lot of work with shapes. Yesterday we took our solids, put them together, and made new shapes. Today we will start with the bigger shapes, and take them apart to find the specific shapes used to make it."
- Show students a building made from shape blocks or a picture of one. Students should take turns with their partners naming the three-dimensional shapes in the building.
- ⊙ Have different partners share one of the shapes they named, and where it can be seen.
- Repeat with another shape.
- Model "Master Builder." Set up a file folder to block students from seeing what you build. Build a simple building with 5 or less blocks. Describe your building to the students. They try to build it as you describe it. When finished, remove the file folder to show your building. How did the students do?
- Have students play two rounds with a partner. Each partner should have a chance to build and describe.
- ⊙ Explain that today they are going to find the three-dimensional shapes that were used to make a bigger object or building.

? Teaching Prompt ⊙ Learning Target

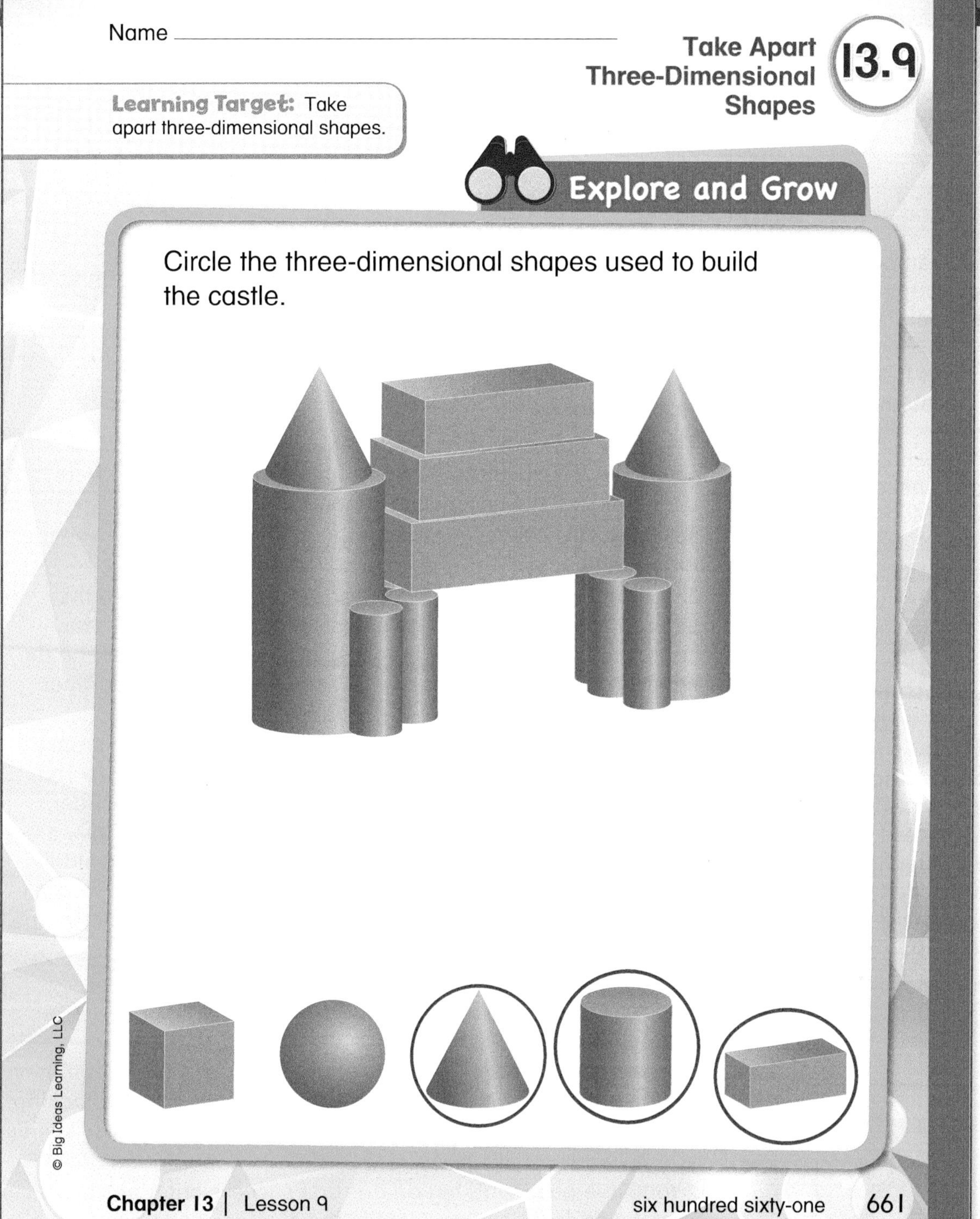

Name
Take Apart Three-Dimensional Shapes
13.9
Learning Target: Take apart three-dimensional shapes.
Explore and Grow
Circle the three-dimensional shapes used to build the castle.
© Big Ideas Learning, LLC
Chapter 13 | Lesson 9
six hundred sixty-one
661

Explore and Grow

- Students identify the shapes used to build the castle, and circle the shapes at the bottom of the page.
- **Supporting Learners:** If students have difficulty seeing the individual shapes, point to each shape individually. Remind students that they are looking at the type of shape, not the exact dimensions or size to match.
- **Extension:** Have students write the number of specific shapes used in the castle, for example two cones.

ELL Support

Review the example. Then have groups work together to complete Exercises 1–4. Have groups discuss the following questions as they apply to each exercise: "Which shapes do we need? How many?" Monitor discussion and expect students to perform according to their language proficiency level.

Beginner students may state one-word answers.
Intermediate students may state phrases and simple sentences.
Advanced students may state detailed sentence and help guide discussion.

Laurie's Notes

Think and Grow

Getting Started

- Students will circle the specific shapes that make up the design or building.
- Students will benefit from having the shapes to look at or manipulate.

Teaching Notes

- There are four exercises, each with the same direction line. Students will circle the three-dimensional shapes that were used to make the composite shape.
- **Teaching Tip:** Shapes are colored to enable students to see the different shapes.
- **Teaching Tip:** Many rectangular prisms are thinner than the sample at the bottom of the exercise to be circled. This may confuse students. Remind them that the shapes will not be the same size, thickness, length, etc. That is not what determines the shape.
- ? **Model:** "We need to find out what shapes were used to make the yellow and red design. Tell your partner what pattern you see. What are they yellow shapes called? Circle the cylinder. What are the red shapes called?" Students may think they are rectangular prisms. Point out that there is a line in the middle showing that two red shapes are stacked together. We want to be as accurate as possible, so the cube is the most exact shape. "Circle the cube."
- Students identify the shapes that were used to build the structure. Let students know that each type of shape is a different color in each of the structures.
- **Supporting Learners:** Students should compare the shape they are determining with the actual solid model. If they are looking at the green cone in Exercise 1, seeing a cone turned on its side will help.
- ⦿ "You have been working on our first success criteria! How is it going so far? Can you identify the shapes used to make the big shape?"

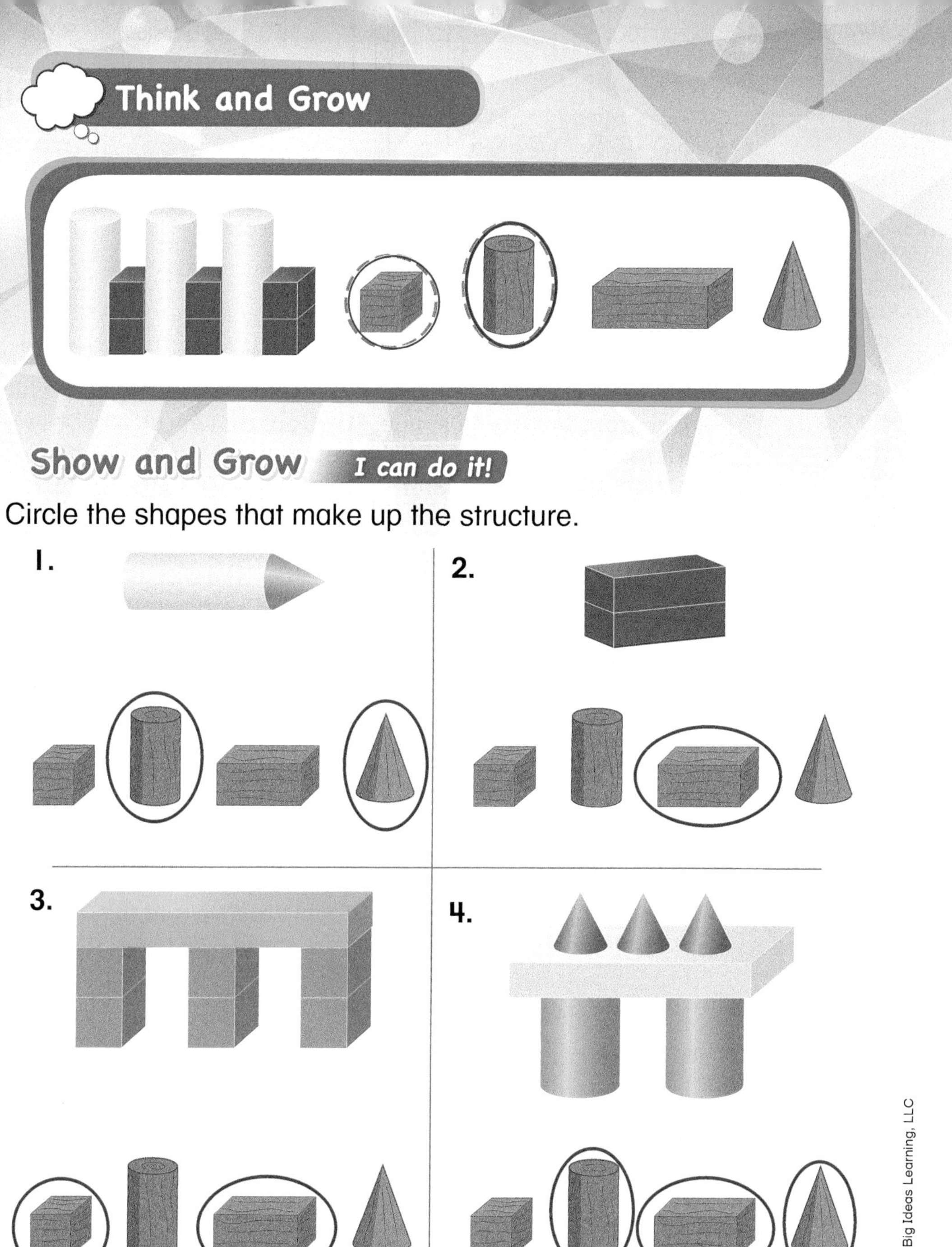

Think and Grow

Show and Grow *I can do it!*

Circle the shapes that make up the structure.

1.

2.

3.

4.

Scaffold instruction to support all students in their learning. Learning is individualized and you may want to group students differently as they move in and out of these levels with each skill and concept. Student self-assessment and feedback help guide your instructional decisions about how and when to layer support for all students to become proficient learners.

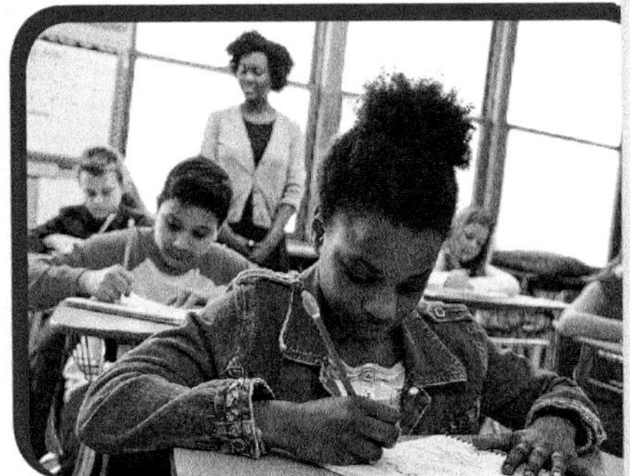

Meeting the needs of all learners.

Laurie's Notes

Apply and Grow: Practice

SCAFFOLDING INSTRUCTION

The exercises on this page continue identifying the specific smaller three-dimensional shapes within the larger structures.

EMERGING students may have difficulty separating individual shapes from the whole shape. Point out that each color shows a different type of shape. They should not pay attention to the orientation of the shape in the building as compared to the shapes at the bottom of the exercise from which they will circle.

- **Exercises 5–8:** Students follow the same process as in Exercises 1–4. Each structure becomes slightly more complex.
- **Exercise 7:** Students may not recognize the yellow shapes as cylinders as they are not "tall" like most of the cylinders we have used. If you have cylinders that look like this, for example a breath mint container, show students that cylinders can look like this or like a soup can. The red shapes might be squares, or they might be rectangular prisms. We cannot really tell how deep they are. Most students will say cubes, but it is not worth arguing about. Accept both answers.
- **Exercise 8:** This is the only structure that uses all shapes.
- **Exercise 9:** There are three possible answers to this exercise. No two structures are equally the same. However, the green and orange both have the same size and shape. The red and orange both use cubes and rectangular prisms.

PROFICIENT students can identify the shapes within the structures easily.

Additional Support

- Have students consider the options of shapes at the bottom of each exercise and see if it is in the structure, rather than trying to see the shapes within the structure. For example, consider the square first for Exercise 5. Are there any squares? Where? Then look for cylinders, etc.

Extension: Adding Rigor

- Build a picture or shape with your pattern blocks. Trace the outline. Write how many of each shape you used. Give your puzzle to a partner to solve.

Name ______________________________

Apply and Grow: Practice

Circle the shapes that make up the structure.

5.

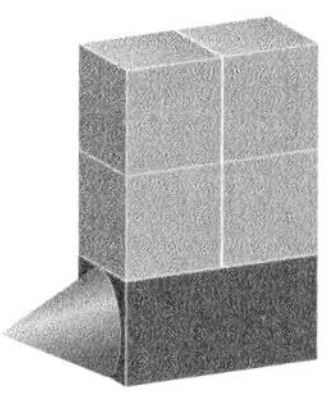

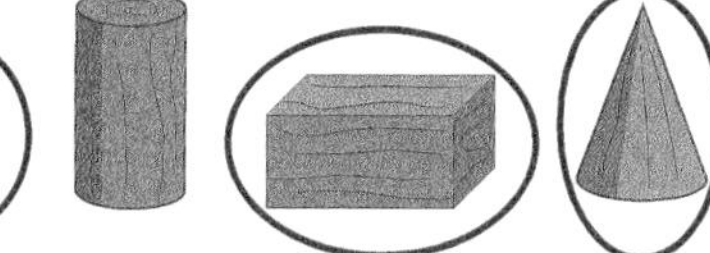

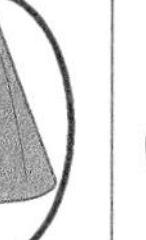

6.

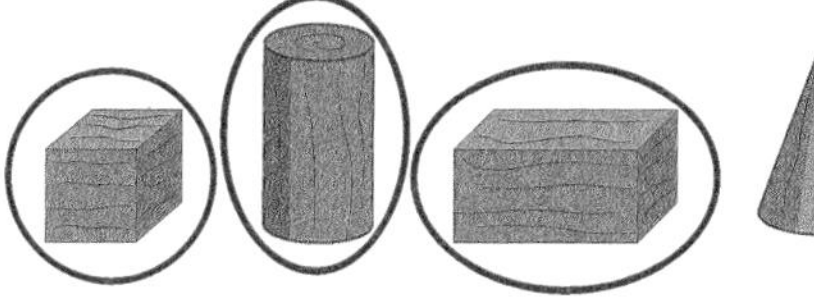

7.

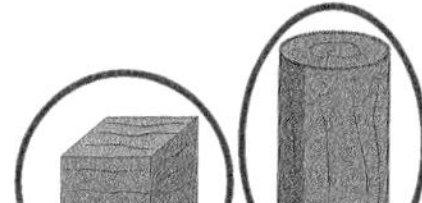

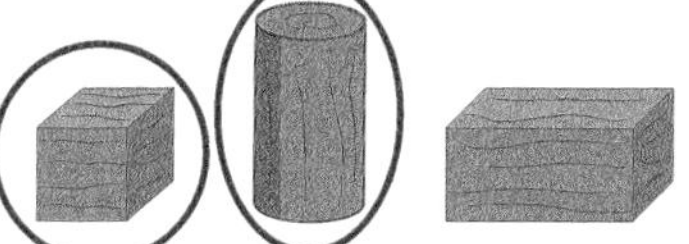

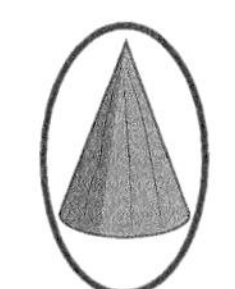

8.

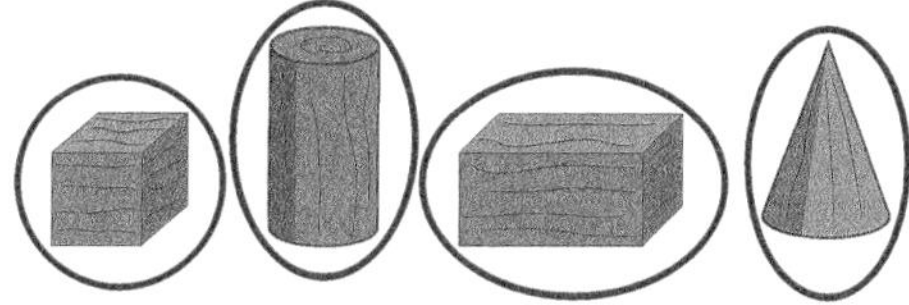

9. **Reasoning** Which two structures are the same?

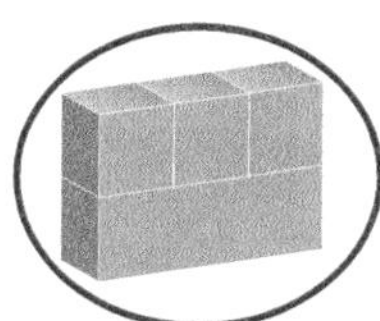

ELL Support

Check for understanding of Lesson 13.9. Read each question aloud. Allow students time to complete each problem. Have students respond to the following questions for each shape by holding up the appropriate number of fingers.

1. How many cubes are there?
2. How many rectangular prisms are there?
3. How many cylinders are there?
4. How many cones are there?

Laurie's Notes

Think and Grow: Modeling Real Life

The exercises on this page ask students to find how many of each three-dimensional shape are in a building. This should remind students of building in the block center.

? **Preview**: "Who has seen colored blocks like these before? Do you like building with them?"

? **Model**: "Let's look at the building at the top of the page. Describe what you see to your partner. Let's count and see what it took to make up the structure. Do you see any cubes?" No "Fill in zero cubes. Do you see any rectangular prisms? Where are they? How many?" 7; red, green, and yellow "Do you see any cylinders? Where? How many?" 4; 2 thin red stacked on top of each green rectangular prism "Do you see any cones? Where? How many?" 2 blue at the top

- The yellow rectangular prism and the red cylinders may still confuse students because they are very thin as compared to the cylinders and rectangular prisms that are typically used.
- Discuss Exercise 10. This structure only uses cubes and rectangular prisms.
- **Teaching Tip**: Perspective drawing and seeing three-dimensions from a two-dimensional drawing is difficult. Many adults do not possess this ability. Build structures that model the pictures when possible. Point to the depth of the shapes on the picture to help students the ability to see the perspective in the pictures.

◉ "Use your thumb signals to show how you are doing with recognizing three-dimensional shapes within bigger structures? How are you doing at naming them? How are you doing with seeing the shapes in a picture?"

Closure

- "Tell your partner which exercises were easy to do. Tell your partner which exercises were a challenge to do. Tell why some were easier than others."
- If time, play "Master Builder" as a class or in partners.

Think and Grow: Modeling Real Life

How many of each shape make up the gate?

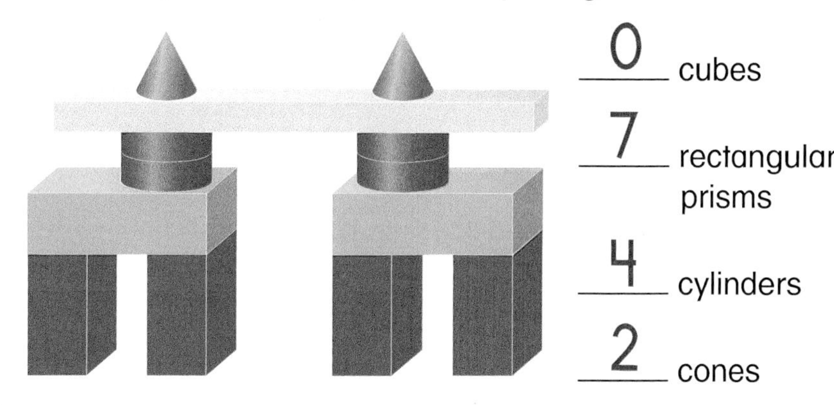

0 cubes

7 rectangular prisms

4 cylinders

2 cones

Show and Grow *I can think deeper!*

10. How many of each shape make up the bridge?

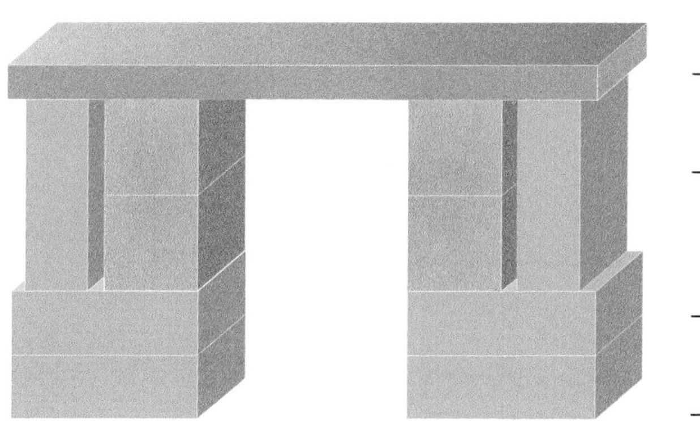

4 cubes

7 rectangular prisms

0 cylinders

0 cones

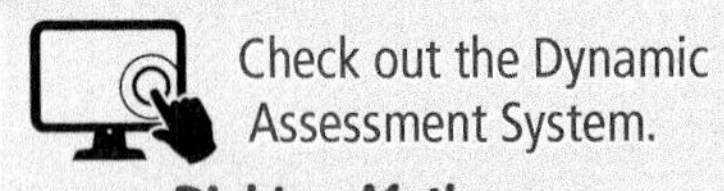
Check out the Dynamic
Assessment System.
BigIdeasMath.com

Scaffold assignments to support all students in their learning progression. Revisit with spaced practice to move every student toward proficiency.

Connect and Extend Learning

Practice Notes

- If students are having difficulty, provide them with the three-dimensional shapes or blocks to create the pictures of the structures.

Prior Skills

- **Exercises 8 and 9:** Grade 1, Practicing Addition Strategies

Cross-Curricular Connections

Science

- Introduce different science tools that can be used to conduct experiments. Focus on a simple microscope or whatever kind you have available. Study the parts of the microscope and have students identify any three-dimensional shapes they see. Discuss each part's importance and then give an opportunity for students to use the microscope.

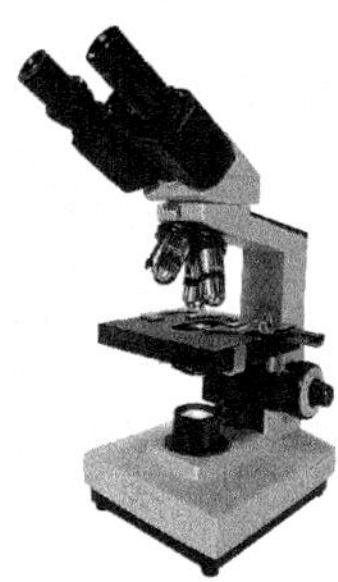

Name ______________________

Practice 13.9

Learning Target: Take apart three-dimensional shapes.

Circle the shapes that make up the structure.

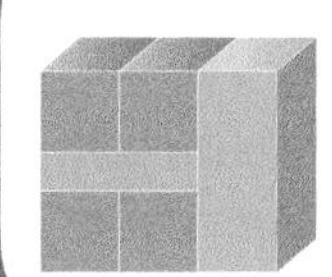  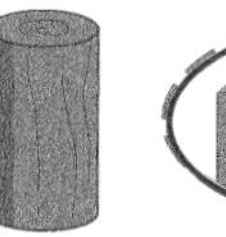 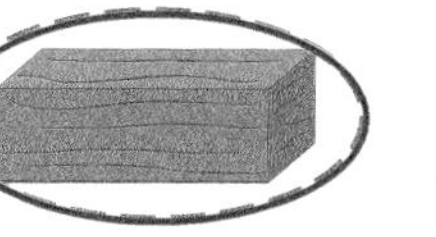  

Circle the shapes that make up the structure.

1.

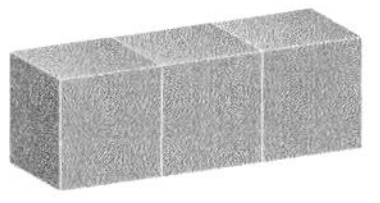

2.

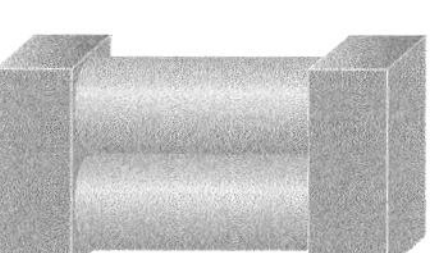

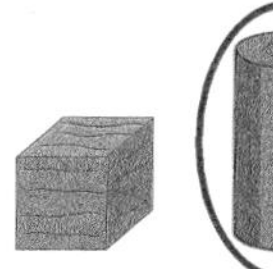 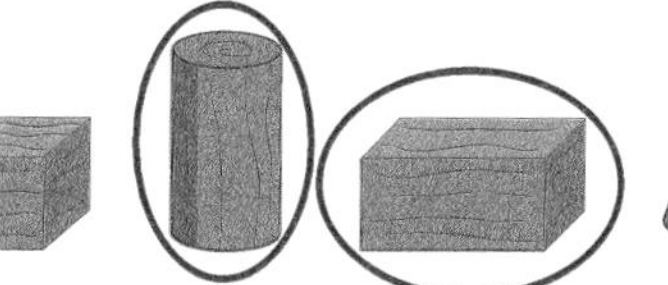 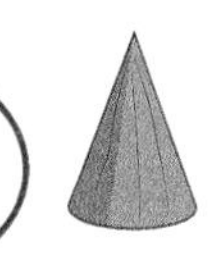

3.

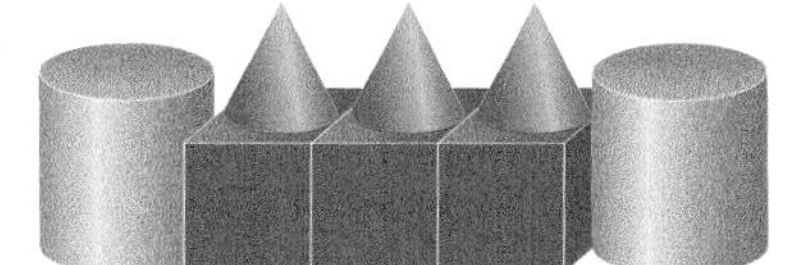

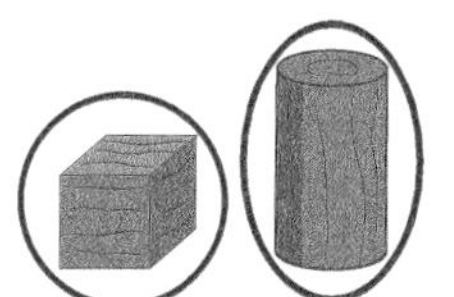  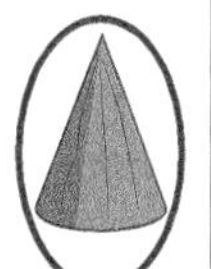

4.

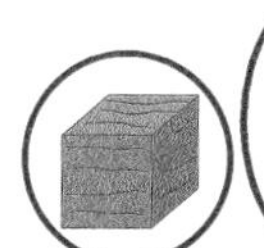 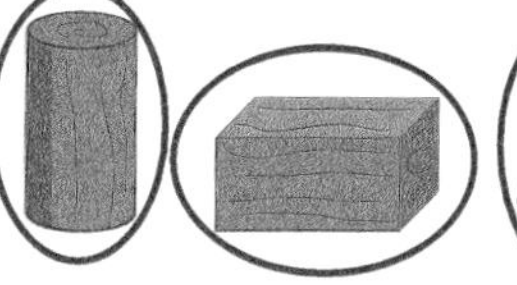 

Connect and Extend Learning

Extend Student Learning

Bodily-Kinesthetic

- Provide students with three-dimensional shape blocks. Students work with a partner. Partner A has their back turned while Partner B builds. Partner A then turns around and names all the shapes used to make Partner B's structure. Then they switch roles.

Lesson Resources	
Surface Level	**Deep Level**
Resources by Chapter • Extra Practice • Reteach Differentiating the Lesson Skills Review Handbook Skills Trainer	Resources by Chapter • Enrichment and Extension Graphic Organizers Dynamic Assessment System • Lesson Practice

5. **Reasoning** Which two structures are the same?

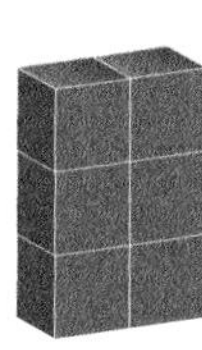

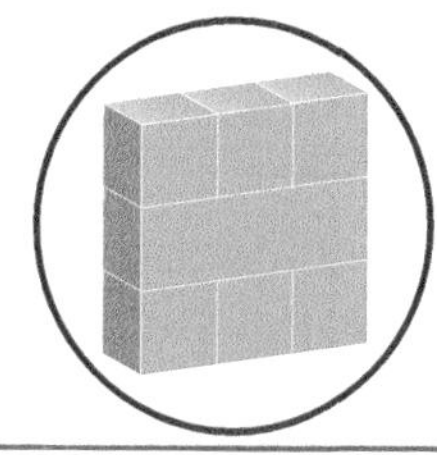

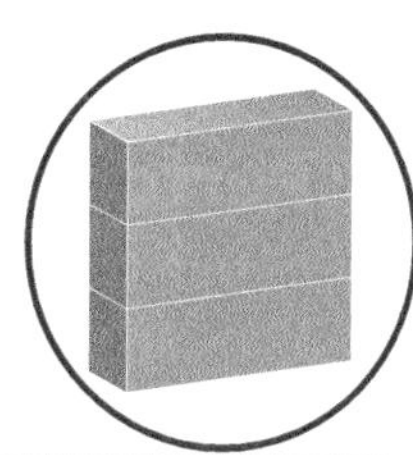

6. **Modeling Real Life** How many of each shape make up the castle?

6 cubes

5 rectangular prisms

8 cylinders

4 cones

7. **DIG DEEPER!** Circle the names of the shapes that do *not* make up the desk.

sphere rectangular prism

cylinder cone

Review & Refresh

8. 12 + 7 = 19

9. 42 + 14 = 56

Laurie's Notes

ELL Support

Have students work in groups to complete the Performance Task. Have Intermediate and Advanced students alternate reading sections aloud as the group discusses the answers. Monitor discussion. Expect students to perform according to their language proficiency level.

Beginner students may indicate answers visually or provide single words.
Intermediate students may provide phrases or simple sentences.
Advanced students may guide others to complete the exercises and answer with sentences.

Performance Task

In this task, students will identify attributes, describe, and draw two- and three-dimensional shapes. Encourage students who have trouble locating or counting vertices to highlight these on each shape. Use student responses to gauge their understanding about two- and three-dimensional shapes.

- Decide ahead of time whether students will be working independently, in pairs, or in groups.
- Pause between direction lines for students to complete each step.
- Have students share their work and thinking with others. Discuss as a class.

Exercise	Answers and Notes	Points
1	Students will draw the following: Triangle flag Square shovel handle Hexagon window Half of a square door	8
2a	Cone is circled	2
2b	Top of center cylinder is colored	2
	Total	12

Name ______________________________

Performance Task 13

1. Use the clues to finish the two-dimensional sand castle drawing.

- The flag on the castle is a closed shape with only 3 straight sides.
- The handle of the shovel is a closed shape with L-shaped vertices and 4 sides of the same length.

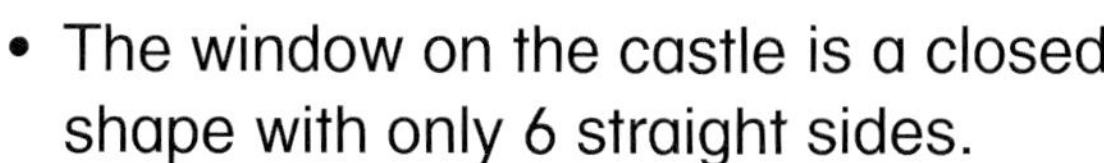

- The window on the castle is a closed shape with only 6 straight sides.
- The door on the castle is a closed shape with 4 sides that you can use 2 times to make a square.

---

2. You are building a sand castle using these three-dimensional shapes.

- 4 shapes that have square flat surfaces
- 5 shapes that have 2 flat surfaces and no vertices
- 3 shapes that have the same number of flat surfaces as vertices

a. Which shape is missing from the sand castle?

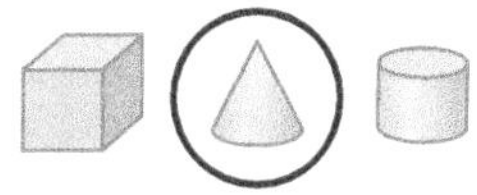

b. Color a flat surface to show where you would stack the missing shape to complete the sand castle.

Check out the interactive version in the Game Library.

BigIdeasMath.com

Laurie's Notes

Shape Roll and Build

Materials

- 1 die per student
- pattern blocks

Shape Roll and Build reviews two-dimensional shapes students worked with in this chapter. Students will locate the given shapes to create a butterfly.

? "What do you see on the page?" *Sample answers:* shapes, pattern blocks "What object is made from the shapes?" butterfly

- "Today you are going to build the butterfly using pattern blocks."
- Review the directions while modeling how to relate the dice roll to the correct pattern block.
- **Teaching Tip**: Students may roll shapes that have all been covered. Decide if students are able to use this shape to build other shapes that have not been covered yet.
- **Note**: This can be done independently, or students can race to build the butterfly within their groups.
- **Supporting Learners**: Some students may have difficulty keeping the pattern blocks in place. Allow students to color the shapes as they roll.
- When students are finished, discuss what shapes can be used to make other shapes.

Closure

- Prompt students to create an object using pattern blocks. Have students share their object and identify the shapes they used to create it.

Shape Roll and Build

To Play: Roll a die to choose a pattern block. Cover a shape in the picture. Keep rolling until all shapes have been covered.

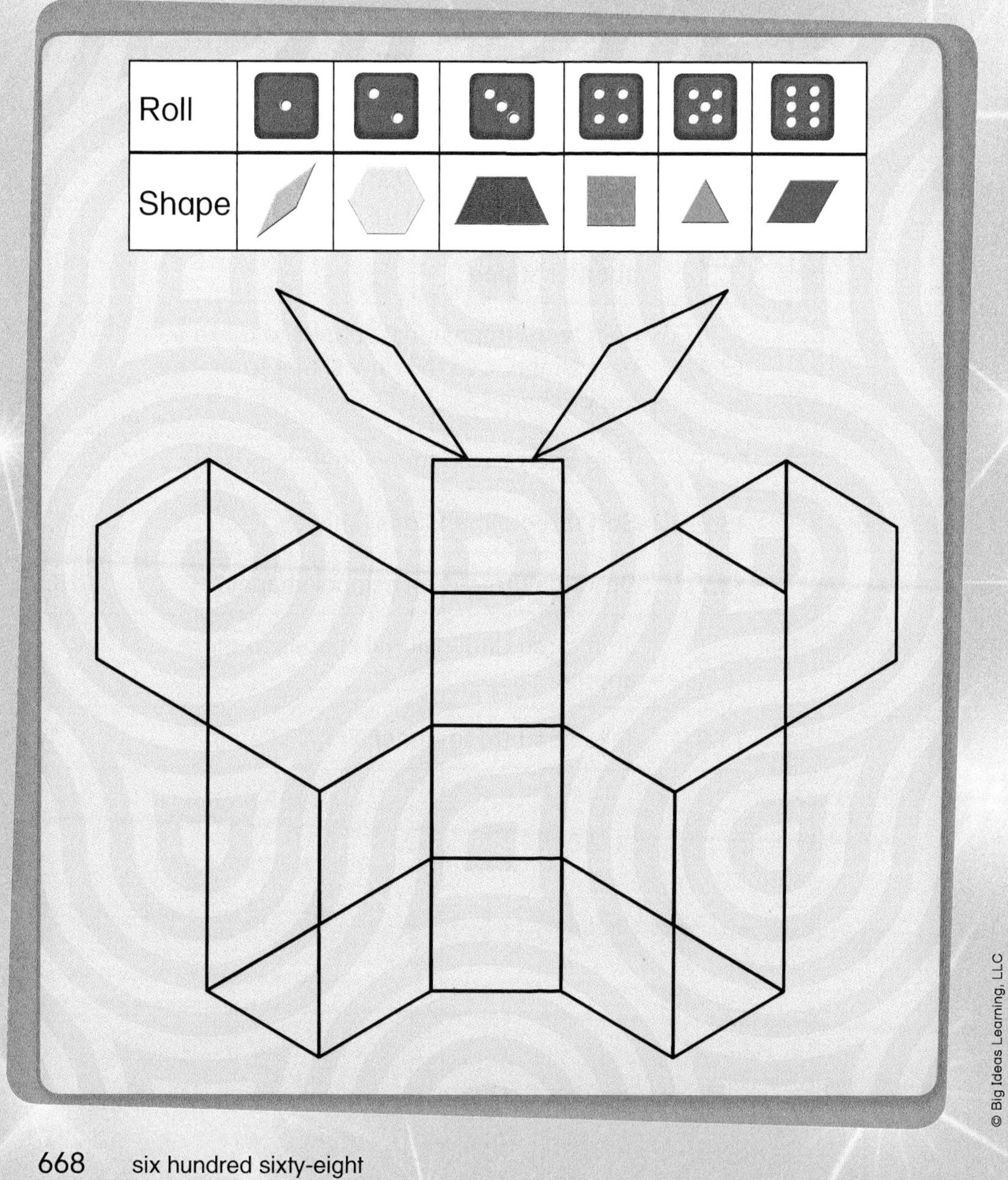

Learning Target Correlation

Lesson	Learning Target	Exercises
13.1	Sort two-dimensional shapes.	1, 2
13.2	Describe two-dimensional shapes.	3, 4
13.3	Join two-dimensional shapes to make another shape.	5, 6
13.4	Join two-dimensional shapes to make a new shape. Use the new shape to make a larger shape.	7, 8
13.5	Take apart two-dimensional shapes.	9, 10
13.6	Sort three-dimensional shapes.	11, 12
13.7	Describe three-dimensional shapes.	13, 14
13.8	Join three-dimensional shapes to make another shape.	15
13.9	Take apart three-dimensional shapes.	16

Name ___________________________

Chapter 13 Practice

13.1 Sort Two-Dimensional Shapes

1. Circle the closed shapes with only 3 straight sides.

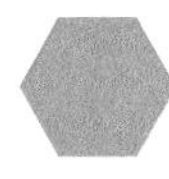  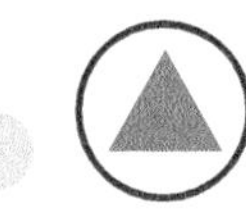 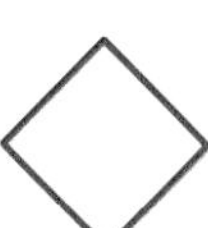  

---

2. **Structure** Draw 2 different two-dimensional shapes that have 1 or more L-shaped vertices.
Sample answer:

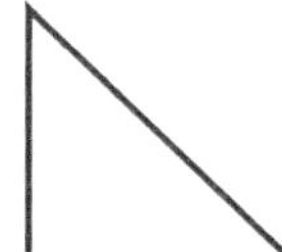 

13.2 Describe Two-Dimensional Shapes

Circle the attributes of the shape.

3. **Hexagon**	4. **Rhombus**
(6 straight sides)	(4 straight sides)
8 straight sides	(4 vertices)
8 vertices	6 vertices
(closed)	open

Chapter Resources		
Surface Level	**Deep Level**	**Transfer Level**
Resources by Chapter • Extra Practice • Reteach Differentiating the Lesson Skills Review Handbook Skills Trainer Game Library Math Musicals	Resources by Chapter • Enrichment and Extension Graphic Organizers Game Library Math Musicals	Dynamic Assessment System • Chapter Test Assessment Book • Chapter Tests A and B

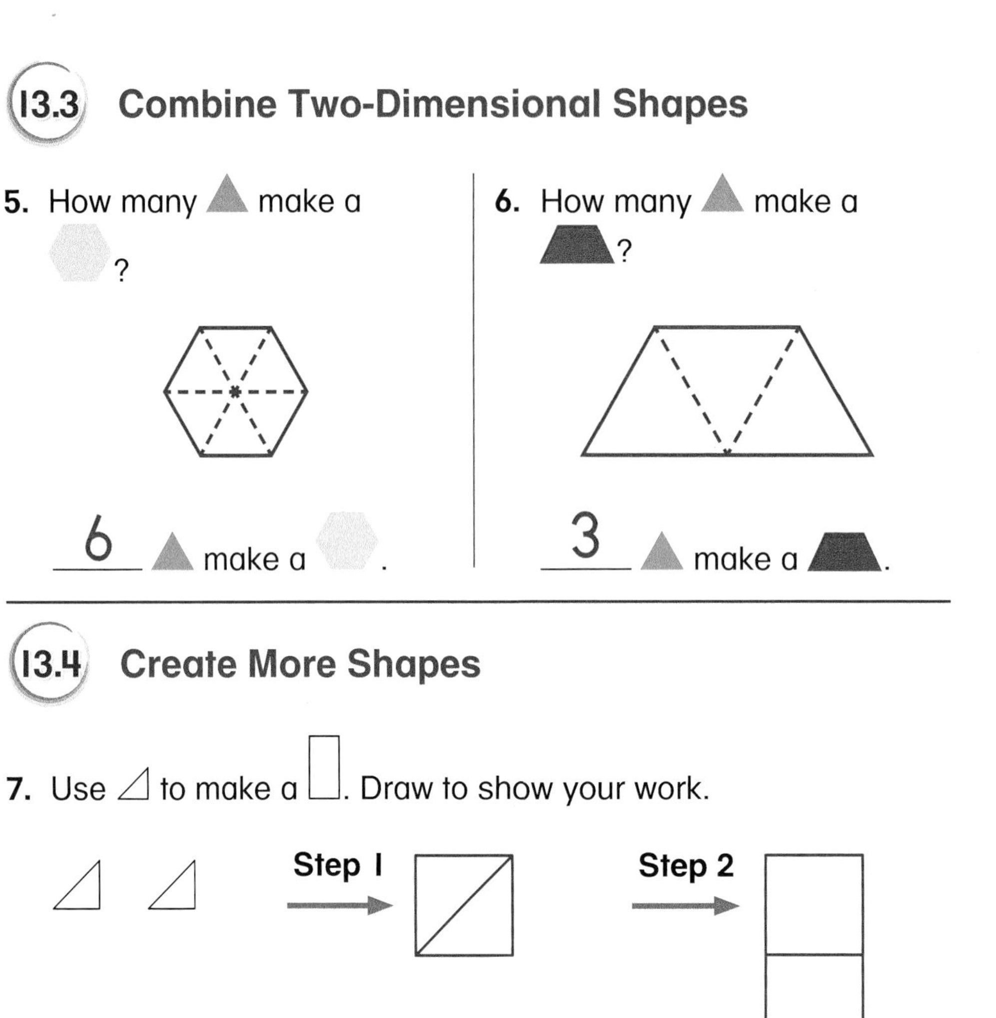

13.3 Combine Two-Dimensional Shapes

5. How many ▲ make a ⬢?

6 ▲ make a ⬢.

6. How many ▲ make a trapezoid?

3 ▲ make a trapezoid.

13.4 Create More Shapes

7. Use ◺ to make a ▯. Draw to show your work.

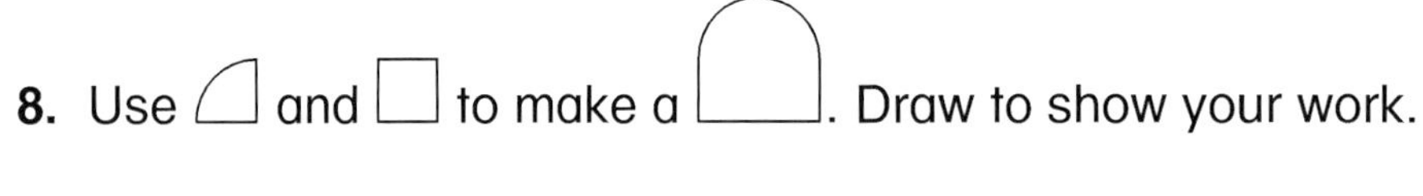

8. Use the quarter-circle shape and □ to make the arch shape. Draw to show your work.

13.5 Take Apart Two-Dimensional Shapes

Draw two lines to show the parts.

9. 1 square and 2 triangles

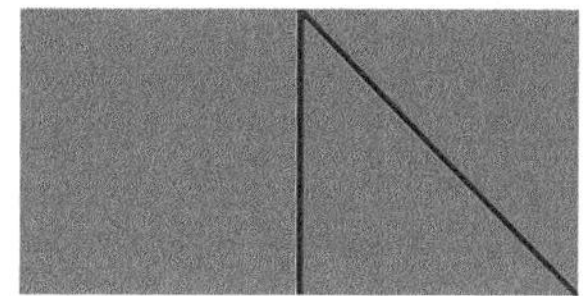

10. 2 triangles and 1 square

13.6 Sort Three-Dimensional Shapes

11. Circle the shapes with flat surfaces that are all squares.

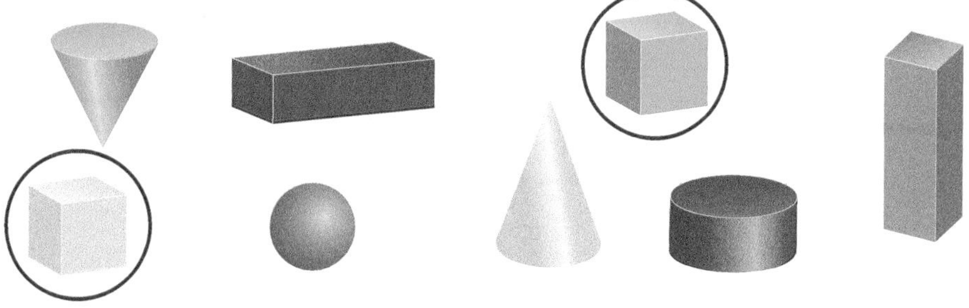

12. **Modeling Real Life** You need to find an object that has only flat surfaces for a scavenger hunt. Circle the objects you can use.

13.7 Describe Three-Dimensional Shapes

Circle the attributes of the shape.

13. Rectangular Prism

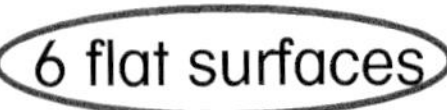

6 flat surfaces

12 vertices

12 edges

two-dimensional

14. Sphere

0 flat surfaces

1 flat surface

0 edges

rolls

13.8 Combine Three-Dimensional Shapes

15. Circle the new shape that you can make.

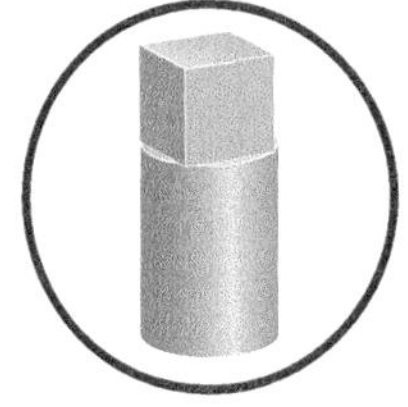

13.9 Take Apart Three-Dimensional Shapes

16. Circle the shapes that make up the structure.

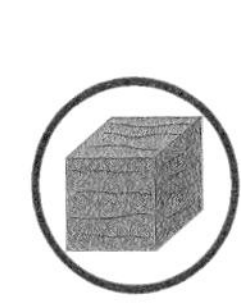

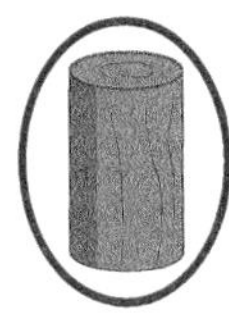

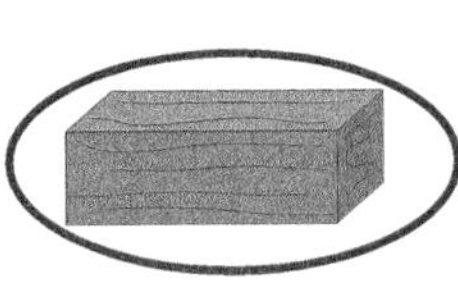

Centers

Center 1: Shape Roll and Build

Materials per student: Student Edition page 668, 1 die, pattern blocks

Have students complete the activity. See page T-668 for the directions.

Center 2: Skills Trainer

Materials: computers or devices with Internet access

Have students go to *BigIdeasMath.com* to access the Skills Trainer.

Center 3: Shape Dominoes

Materials per pair: Shape Dominoes*

Students shuffle the cards and hand them out to one another so that each person gets 13. The remaining card is placed on the table. Students take turns matching the side of the card that shows the two-dimensional shapes to the words that describe them. Play until one person is out of cards.

Center 4: Shape Roll and Graph

Materials per pair: Shape Roll and Graph Board*, Shape Roll and Graph Recording Sheet*, die, counter, whiteboards

Students take turns rolling a die to move their playing piece on the board. Whatever shape they land on, they keep track of in a tally chart on a whiteboard. Once students have made it to the finish line, they graph their tallies on the Shape Roll and Graph Recording Sheet. Students can play multiple rounds or until one of their shapes reaches 9 on their graph.

Center 5: Shape Castle Map

Materials: Shape Castle Map*, spinner, modeling clay

Students use a spinner to see which three-dimensional shape they will find on the board. They create that three-dimensional shape using modeling clay and cover one of its matching spots. They spin and create until the whole board is covered. Then have students focus on two different shapes from the spinner and compare how many times they have made each on the board. Have them provide an equation to show how many more times the greater number of shapes was made compared to the lesser number of shapes. Be sure students show their work on paper.

Note: If students spin a three-dimensional shape that has already been covered, then they can spin again.

**Found in the Instructional Resources*

Chapter Assessment Guide

Chapter tests are available in the Assessment Book.
An alternative assessment option is listed below.

Interpersonal

Have a pile of two-dimensional and three-dimensional shapes for each pair. Have each partner take a turn closing their eyes while the other partner takes a shape and hides it in their hands. The partners will sit back-to-back from each other. They will write at least three questions to ask one another in order to determine the other person's shape. The first question should address whether the shape is two-dimensional or three-dimensional. If the shape is two-dimensional, then the questions can be about the number of sides, vertices, or whether the shape is open or closed. Three-dimensional shape questions can address the flat surfaces, vertices, edges, or whether it rolls, stacks, or slides. Partners ask the questions and then make a guess at identifying the shape. Partners should play at least two rounds. They will pick a two-dimensional shape for the first round and a three-dimensional shape for the second.

Task	Points
At least three questions and answers about the two-dimensional shape	6 points
Identified the two-dimensional shape	1 point
At least three questions and answers about the three-dimensional shape	6 points
Identified the three-dimensional shape	1 point
Total	14 points

My Thoughts on the Chapter

What worked...

Teacher Tip

Not allowed to write in your teaching edition? Use sticky notes to record your thoughts.

What did not work...

What I would do differently...

Equal Shares

Chapter Overview

Lesson	Learning Target	Success Criteria
14.1 Equal Shares	Identify equal shares in two-dimensional shapes.	• Identify shapes that show equal shares. • Explain how I know the shares are equal. • Tell how many equal shares are in the shape.
14.2 Partition Shapes into Halves	Identify shapes that show halves.	• Tell whether there are two equal shares. • Use *halves* to name the shares. • Draw to show halves.
14.3 Partition Shapes into Fourths	Identify shapes that show fourths.	• Tell whether there are four equal shares. • Use *fourths* or *quarters* to name the shares. • Draw to show fourths.

Chapter Learning Target:
Understand equal shares.

Chapter Success Criteria:
- Identify shapes that show equal shares.
- Explain which shapes are equal.
- Compare shares.
- Draw to show shares.

Progressions

Through the Grades		
Kindergarten	**Grade 1**	**Grade 2**
• Build and draw shapes. • Put shapes together to make a new shape.	• Partition circles and rectangles into two and four equal shares. • Describe equal shares as halves, fourths, and quarters. • Describe equal shares using the phrases half of, fourth of, and quarter of. • Understand that the more equal shares, the smaller the share.	• Partition circles and rectangles into two, three, or four equal shares. • Describe equal shares as halves, thirds, fourths, and quarters. • Describe equal shares using the phrases half of, third of, fourth of, and quarter of. • Describe a whole as two halves, three thirds, or four fourths. • Understand that equal shares do not need to have the same shape.

	Through the Chapter		
Standard	**14.1**	**14.2**	**14.3**
1.G.A.3 Partition circles and rectangles into two and four equal shares, describe the shares using the words halves, fourths, and quarters, and use the phrases half of, fourth of, and quarter of. Describe the whole as two of, or four of the shares. Understand for these examples that decomposing into more equal shares creates smaller shares.	●	●	★

Key: ▲ = Preparing ● = Learning ★ = Complete

Laurie's Overview

About the Math

"It's not fair. My piece is smaller than his!" These words will ring true with many students... and many teachers. Students have a sense of dividing shapes evenly, especially when it comes to food.

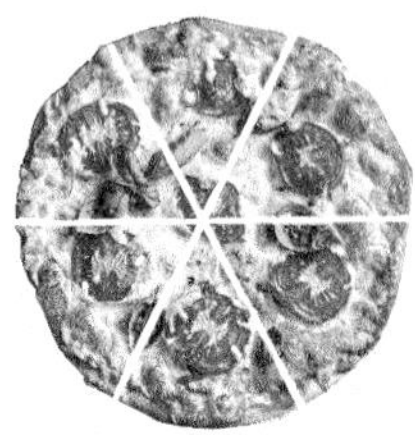

In this chapter students begin to think about fractional parts, although the word *fraction* is never used or discussed. Developmentally, the first goal is for students to develop the idea of dividing a shape to result in equal-sized pieces. Sometimes these pieces have been referred to as a "fair share." It has been found that in some cultures this can cause a misconception because a "fair share" means everyone gets what they need rather than everyone getting the same amount. For example, a "fair share" may mean that adults get larger portions. We refer to the equal-sized pieces as *equal shares* or *equal parts.* In the first lesson students identify *equal shares* and *unequal shares.*

We work with the initial concepts of fractions by using an area model. This model for fractions divides shapes as opposed to dividing a number line or set of objects. The process of dividing a shape in mathematics is referred to as *partitioning*, but this is certainly not a term students need to hear. This is a natural transition from Chapter 13 where students have worked extensively with shapes. In the first lesson, students will progress from determining if these familiar shapes have been divided into equal or unequal parts to dividing shapes themselves. The next lesson introduces the names and concept of *half of* and dividing into *halves.* The final lesson explores *fourths* or *quarters.*

Students come to recognize two important concepts related to fractional parts. The first is that the parts must be the same size although not necessarily the same shape, and the second is that the number of the equal-sized parts determines the name of the part. In first grade we work only with halves and fourths, and work only with equal sizes and shapes of parts. The following all show fourths, but students will only work with examples of the first and second type.

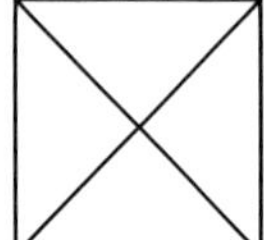

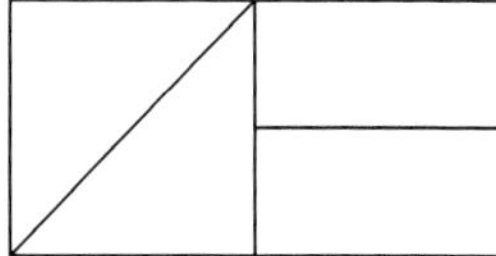

Students may need multiple examples to determine what is truly an equal part. Sometimes divisions can be drawn that are evenly spaced, and appear to create equal shares. However, the shape itself prevents the shares from being equal. An example is shown below.

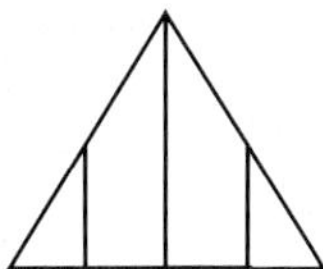

In first grade students work with the words for fractional parts, and not with numerical representations. It is not until third grade that the symbols for fractions and notation is introduced to students.

Models

- Pattern blocks and the Pattern Block Instructional Resource continue to be used to model equal parts. This is primarily shown by aligning pieces on top of hexagons.
- Students fold paper shapes to discover halves and fourths. They color the fractional parts and practice the vocabulary during Dig In activities in Lessons 14.2 and 14.3.

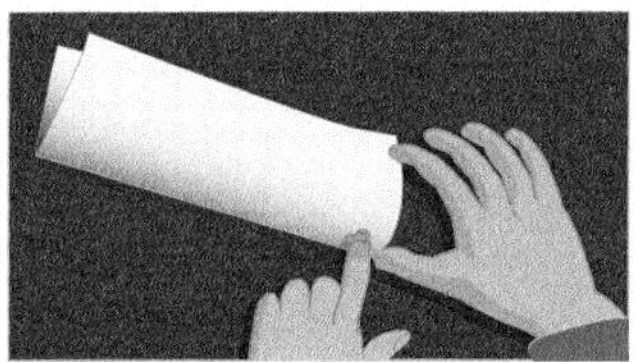

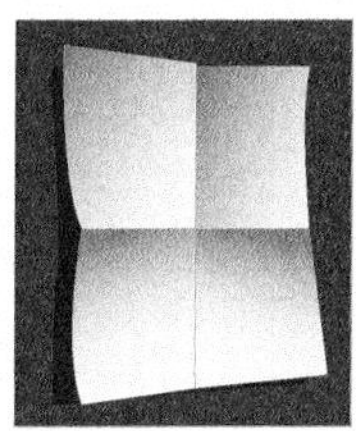

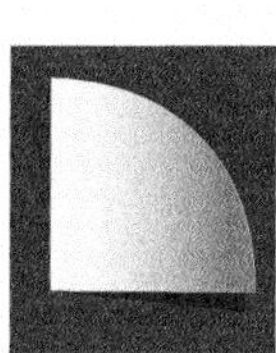

Students' introduction to fractions builds foundational concepts by working with the shapes with which they are familiar. To make learning the fractional names and concepts more natural, point out every time something is divided in half or in fourths throughout the day. Of course, cutting treats into halves or fourths to share with the class will always be a favorite example!

Chapter Materials and Resources

Check out the
virtual manipulatives.
BigIdeasMath.com

The primary materials and resources needed for this chapter are listed below. Other materials may be needed for the additional support ideas provided throughout the chapter.

Classroom Materials	Chapter Opener	14.1	14.2	14.3	Connect and Grow
scissors	•	*		*	•
pattern blocks		•	•		
bread or sandwiches		+			
whiteboards		•	•	•	
glue		*		*	
paper shapes			•	•	
crayons			•	•	•
spinners					•
counters	•				•
construction paper					•
tape					•

Instructional Resources	Chapter Opener	14.1	14.2	14.3	Connect and Grow
Vocabulary Cards	•	+	+	+	
Equal Shares Sort Cards		•			
2, 4, or Unequal Shares Sort Cards				•	
Coloring Shapes					•

• class set + teacher only * per pair/group

Suggested Pacing

Day 1	Chapter Opener	Performance Task Preview		Vocabulary			
Day 2	Lesson 14.1	Warm-Up	Dig In	Explore	Think	Apply: Practice	Think: Modeling Real Life
Day 3	Lesson 14.2	Warm-Up	Dig In	Explore	Think	Apply: Practice	Think: Modeling Real Life
Day 4	Lesson 14.3	Warm-Up	Dig In	Explore	Think	Apply: Practice	Think: Modeling Real Life
Day 5	Connect And Grow	Performance Task		Activity		Chapter Practice	
Day 6		Centers					
Day 7	Chapter Assessment	Chapter Assessment					

Year-to-Date: 152 Days

Laurie's Notes

Mathematical Practices

Students have opportunities to develop aspects of the mathematical practices throughout the chapter. Here are some examples.

1. **Make Sense of Problems and Persevere in Solving Them**
   14.2 Think and Grow: Modeling Real Life, *p. 684*
2. **Reason Abstractly and Quantitatively**
   14.3 Practice Exercise 7, *p. 692*
3. **Construct Viable Arguments and Critique the Reasoning of Others**
   14.1 Explore and Grow, *p. 675*
4. **Model with Mathematics**
   14.2 Practice Exercise 9, *p. 686*
5. **Use Appropriate Tools Strategically**
   14.2 Apply and Grow: Practice, *p. 683*
6. **Attend to Precision**
   14.3 Apply and Grow: Practice Exercise 8, *p. 689*
7. **Look for and Make Use of Structure**
   14.2 Apply and Grow: Practice Exercise 10, *p. 683*
8. **Look for and Express Regularity in Repeated Reasoning**
   14.3 Explore and Grow, *p. 681*

Performance Task Preview

- Preview the page to gauge students' prior knowledge about equal shares.

? "What is your favorite food? Is there a food you eat on a special day?" Listen for students to share their favorite foods with you and foods they eat during the holidays or their birthdays.

? "How can you cut a sandwich so the pieces are the same size?" Divide the sandwich in half or in quarters, so the pieces are in triangles or squares.

- In the Performance Task at the end of the chapter, students will divide food from a picnic into equal shares.

14 Equal Shares

• What is your favorite food?
• How can you cut a sandwich so the pieces are the same size?

Chapter Learning Target:
Understand equal shares.

Chapter Success Criteria:
- I can identify shapes that show equal shares.
- I can explain which shapes are equal.
- I can compare shares.
- I can draw to show shares.

Check out the
digital flash cards.
BigIdeasMath.com

ELL Support

Explain that when an area or group of objects is divided into equal parts, specific words describe the value of those parts. When divided into two, each part is one half. When divided into four, each part is one quarter. When a game is divided into two or four periods, the periods are called halves or quarters.

Laurie's Notes

Vocabulary Review

? **Preview:** "What do you see at the top of the page?" *Sample answer:* graphs

- Have students say each Review Word out loud. Have students explain how the words are related.
- Have students label the two graphs.
- **Extension:** Have students write two things they know to be true from the graphs.
- Direct students to the lower half of the page. Have students use their vocabulary cards to complete the crossword puzzle. Remind students that although there are spaces in some vocabulary words, they will skip the space when writing it in the crossword puzzle.
- **Note:** *Fourths* and *quarters*, as well as *fourth of* and *quarter of* have the same images on the vocabulary cards to show that they are synonyms. Remind students that the word needs to fit in the crossword puzzle.
- **Supporting Learners:** Some students may be overwhelmed by the boxes. Explain that they are able to compare the number of boxes to the number of letters in the word.

Chapter 14 Vocabulary

Activity

- **Word/Picture Toss:** Lay out all of the cards on the floor with the word side up. Students take turns gently tossing a counter onto cards. You read the word on the card that the counter landed on and students repeat the word. A student turns over the card to see the definition and shows it to the class. Repeat this process until all of the cards show the definition side.

Newton & Descartes's Math Musicals

with Differentiated Rich Math Tasks

Newton and Descartes team up in these educational stories and songs to bring mathematics to life! Use the Newton and Descartes hand puppets to act out the stories. Encourage students to sing the songs to take full advantage of the power of music to learn math. Visit *www.MathMusicals.com* to access all the adventures, songs, and activities available!

Name ____________________

Vocabulary

Review Words
bar graph
picture graph

Organize It

Use the review words to complete the graphic organizer.

bar graph

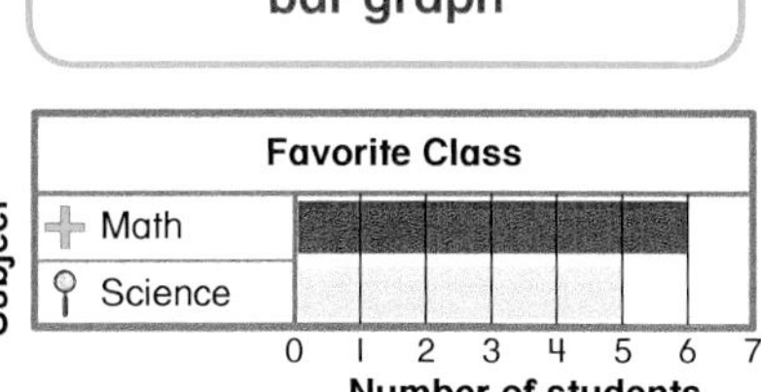

picture graph

Favorite Class							
Math	☺	☺	☺	☺	☺	☺	
Science	☺	☺	☺	☺	☺		

Each ☺ = 1 student.

Define It

Use your vocabulary cards to complete the puzzle.

Across

1. 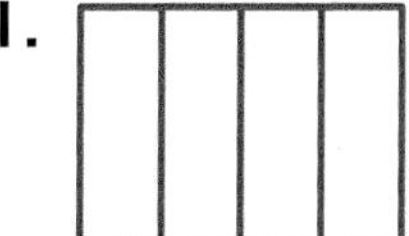

Down

2. 

3. 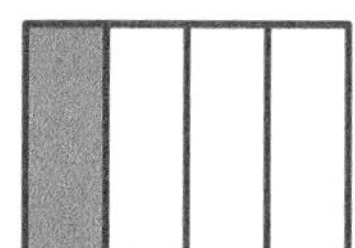

						3 f	
						o	
		2 h				u	
1 q	u	a	r	t	e	r	s
		l				t	
		v				h	
		e				o	
		s				f	

Chapter 14 Vocabulary Cards

equal shares	fourth of
fourths	half of
halves	quarter of
quarters	unequal shares

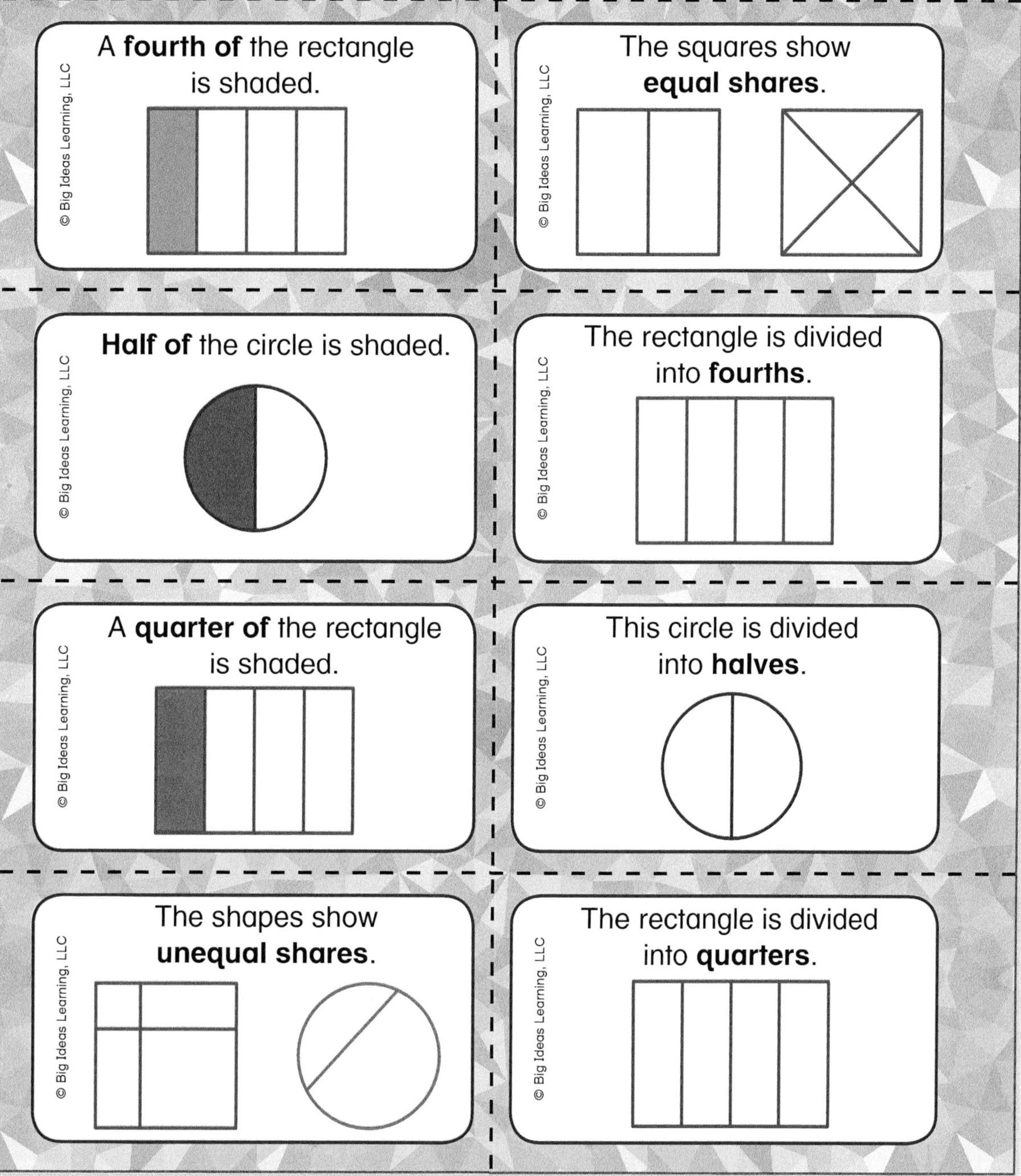
A **fourth of** the rectangle is shaded.
© Big Ideas Learning, LLC
The squares show **equal shares**.
© Big Ideas Learning, LLC
Half of the circle is shaded.
© Big Ideas Learning, LLC
The rectangle is divided into **fourths**.
© Big Ideas Learning, LLC
A **quarter of** the rectangle is shaded.
© Big Ideas Learning, LLC
This circle is divided into **halves**.
© Big Ideas Learning, LLC
The shapes show **unequal shares**.
© Big Ideas Learning, LLC
The rectangle is divided into **quarters**.
© Big Ideas Learning, LLC

14.1

Check out the
Dynamic Classroom.

BigIdeasMath.com

Laurie's Notes

COMMON CORE STATE STANDARDS
1.G.A.3

Learning Target

Identify equal shares in two-dimensional shapes.

Success Criteria

- Identify shapes that show equal shares.
- Explain how I know the shares are equal.
- Tell how many equal shares are in the shape.

Warm-Up

Practice opportunities for the following are available in the Resources by Chapter or at *BigIdeasMath.com*.

- Daily skills
- Vocabulary
- Prerequisite skills

ELL Support

Explain that a share is one part of a whole. Synonyms for the word *share* are *part, portion,* or *piece*. When shares are equal, it means that the whole is divided into parts that are all the same size. Explain that the word *share* can be used to name a portion (as a noun) or to describe the activity of sharing something (as a verb). When you give part of your lunch to someone, you share it.

Preparing to Teach

Today's lesson will most likely be students' first exposure to fraction concepts apart from their natural occurrence in life. Today students determine if a shape is divided into equal shares. For a first-grade student this will be shown by being the same size and shape. This is not a purely mathematical equivalence as shown by the fourths of the rectangle, but is the foundational understanding of an equal portion.

Materials

- pattern blocks
- bread or sandwiches
- whiteboards
- Equal Shares Sort Cards*
- scissors and glue

**Found in the Instructional Resources*

Dig In (Circle Time)

A variety of objects and drawings are used to divide into parts, or "shares". Some of the divisions will be equal and others will not. Students say if the parts are *equal* or *unequal*.

? "When we share food, sometimes it gets cut into pieces. Have you ever shared a sandwich? We cut it in half if we are sharing with a friend." Cut a piece of bread or sandwich equally in half. "Would my two friends be happy if each got one of these pieces? Why?"

- "We call these pieces *equal parts* or *equal shares* because they are the same amount."

? "What would happen if I cut it in two pieces like this?" Cut another piece of bread or sandwich unevenly "Would my two friends be happy if each got one of these pieces? Why?"

? "We can also share with 4 friends." Cut the equal halves into equal fourths. "Would my four friends be happy if each got one of these pieces? Why? These are *equal shares*."

◉ "Today we will decide if shapes are divided into *equal shares* or *unequal shares*."

- **MP5 Use Appropriate Tools Strategically**: Have students use the hexagon pattern block and cover it in various ways: 2 trapezoids, 1 trapezoid, 1 rhombus and 1 triangle; 3 rhombi; 2 rhombi and 2 triangles. Have students say if the parts are equal or not for each case.
- Model for students, and have them draw with you, a square on a whiteboard. Divide it into 2 equal parts. Check to see if students understand the concept. Next draw another square and divide it into two unequal parts. Have students draw shapes and divide them into either two or four equal or unequal parts.

◉ "Today we will tell if a shape is divided into equal or unequal shares."

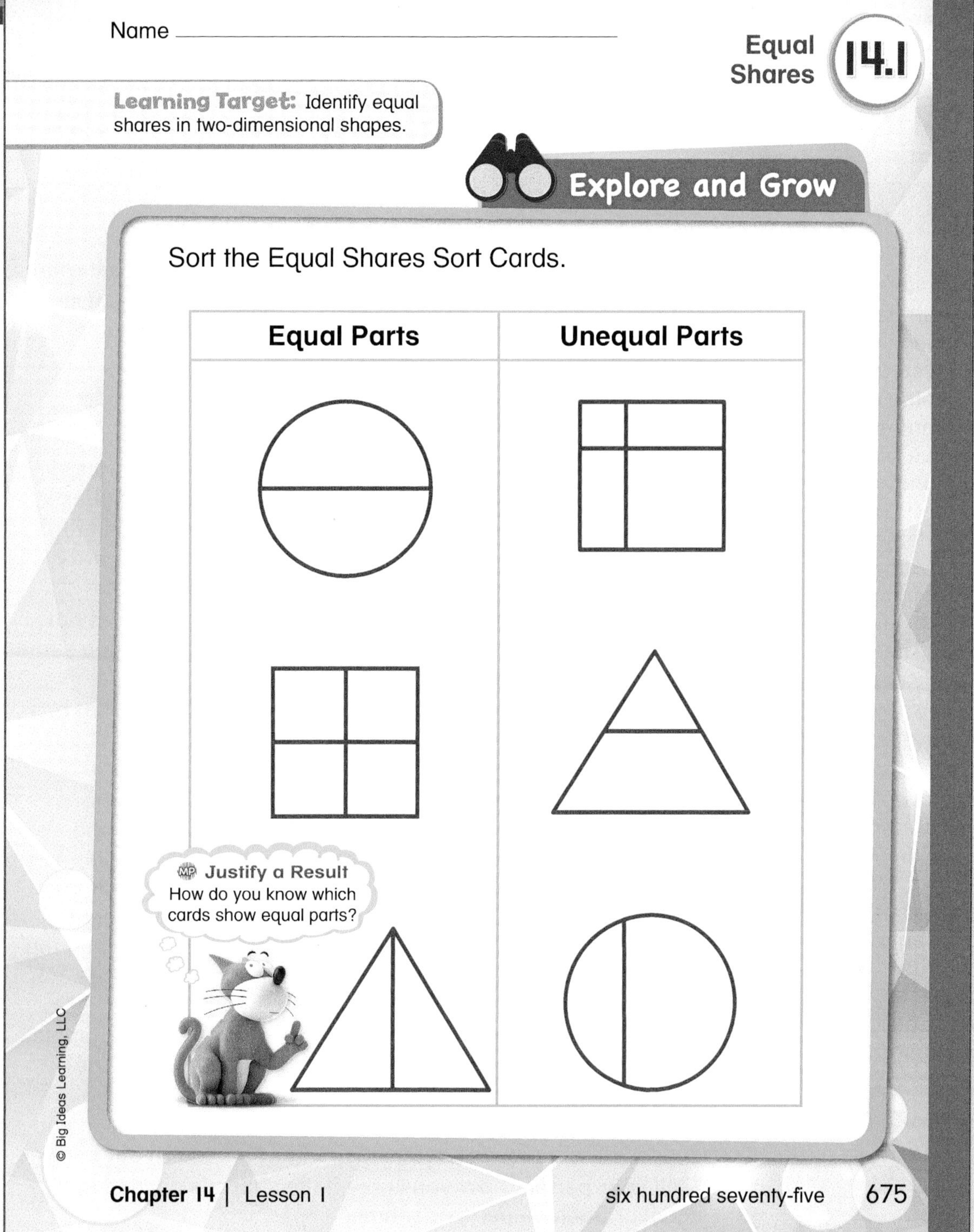

Name
Equal Shares
14.1
Learning Target: Identify equal shares in two-dimensional shapes.
Explore and Grow
Sort the Equal Shares Sort Cards.
Equal Parts
Unequal Parts
Justify a Result
How do you know which cards show equal parts?
© Big Ideas Learning, LLC
Chapter 14 | Lesson 1
six hundred seventy-five 675

Explore and Grow

- Each pair can share scissors and glue. Students cut out the Equal Shares Sort Cards to sort.
- Have students place their cards into the two columns and compare with a partner before gluing them down.

◉ "Tell your partner how you knew if the parts were equal or not."

ELL Support

After discussing the example, have students work in pairs to complete Exercises 1–4. Verify that students know the meaning of the words *left* and *right*. Draw two circles side by side and point to the left one and say, "This circle is on the left." Do the same for the right. Have one student ask another, "Which shows equal shares?" The partner will indicate left or right.

Beginner students may provide one-word answers, such as, "left." **Intermediate** students may answer with phrases, such as, "the left rectangle." **Advanced** students may answer with sentences, such as, "The left rectangle shows equal shares."

Laurie's Notes

Think and Grow

Getting Started

- Students will circle the shapes that are divided into *equal shares*.
- Introduce vocabulary cards for **equal shares** and **unequal shares** along with the picture of the square with equal shares and shapes that show unequal shares.

Teaching Notes

- **Model:** "Newton and Descartes have divided a rectangle into two parts. We need to decide if Newton's or Descartes's rectangle has equal shares. Tell your partner what you think."
- **Model:** "Descartes says that the parts of the rectangle on top have parts that are the same size. That means the parts are equal or that it has equal shares. Circle the top rectangle."
- **Model:** "Tell your partner why the bottom rectangle does not have equal shares. Newton says that the parts are not the same size. So the rectangle shows unequal shares."
- Have students discuss Exercise 1 and circle the shape that has equal shares. Check to see that students are reasoning about equal and unequal shares.
- Students continue with Exercises 2–4.

? **MP7 Look for and Make Use of Structure:** "Each of the shapes in Exercises 1–4 have the same type of cuts. For example, the squares in Exercise 1 have one vertical line. The circles in Exercise 4 have two lines that cross each other in the middle. How do you decide which shape shows equal shares when the types of cuts are the same?" Look at the size of the pieces, not the types of the lines or cuts

- **Supporting Learners:** Give students cut out squares, rectangles and circles that they can fold or cut to see if pieces are the same size.
- **Extension:** Use back-to-back whiteboards to draw a shape and divide it into equal or unequal parts. Turn and quiz your partner.

◉ "Tell your partner how you know if the shape is divided into equal or unequal parts or shares."

Think and Grow
Circle the shape that shows equal shares.
The parts are the same size. So, the rectangle shows equal parts, or **equal shares**.
The parts are not the same size. So, the rectangle shows unequal parts, or **unequal shares**.

Show and Grow *I can do it!*

Circle the shape that shows equal shares.

1.

2.

3.

4.

Scaffold instruction to support all students in their learning. Learning is individualized and you may want to group students differently as they move in and out of these levels with each skill and concept. Student self-assessment and feedback help guide your instructional decisions about how and when to layer support for all students to become proficient learners.

Meeting the needs of all learners.

Laurie's Notes

Apply and Grow: Practice

SCAFFOLDING INSTRUCTION

Students continue to select the shape that is divided into equal shares. Shapes are divided into two or four parts.

EMERGING students may have difficulty determining equal shares. They may look at the basic shape of a part, or the direction of the line or lines cutting the shapes rather than examining the pieces to determine equal shares.

- **Exercises 5 and 6:** Students should be able to see the equal parts easily.
- **Exercise 7:** Students may be confused by the heart as it is not one of the traditional shapes studied in the last chapter. They have probably folded a heart for Valentine's Day. This will help them see why it has equal parts. It should be clear that the rectangle has unequal parts.
- **Exercise 8:** The circle may be tricky. The divisions from the lines are evenly spaced, but the circle tapers at the top and bottom. Thus, the top and bottom sections are smaller than the center. Students may select the circle based on the spacing of the lines and the division of the square may not seem correct as it is positioned on a vertex rather than a side.
- **Exercises 9 and 10:** Students write in the number of equal parts. For Exercise 9, there are 2. For Exercise 10, there are 0.
- **Exercise 11:** The line divides the trapezoid horizontally through its center. However, the trapezoid is not a regular shape, so the parts are not equal. This is the same as the circle in Exercise 8.

PROFICIENT students are accurate in distinguishing equal and unequal parts. They may need to slow down to consider the heart, circle and trapezoid shapes.

- **Exercise 8:** The parts appear to be equal because the spacing of the lines is even.
- **Exercise 11:** This might be tricky for students because the parts appear even at first glance. Point out the difference in the two bases of a trapezoid and see if students catch on from that hint.

Additional Support

- Provide shape cut outs for students to fold or draw on to determine equal shares.
- Point at a shape. "Is it regular? That is, are all sides equal (Trapezoid)? Are some areas smaller than others (circle)?"

Name

Apply and Grow: Practice

Circle the shape that shows equal shares.

5.

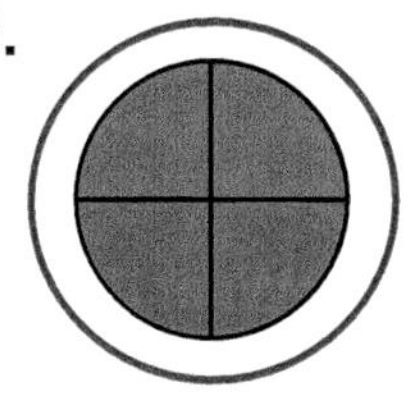

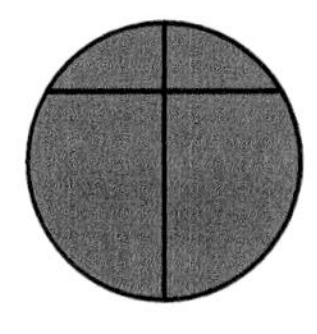

6.

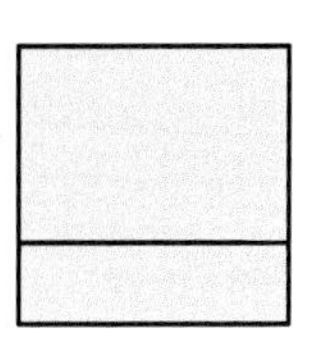

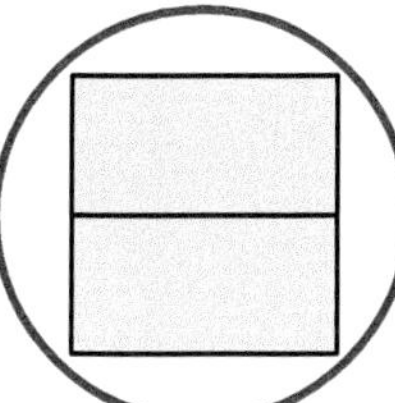

7.

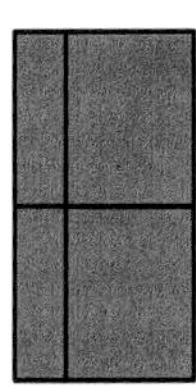

8.

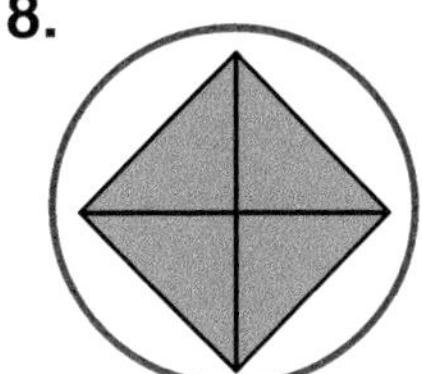

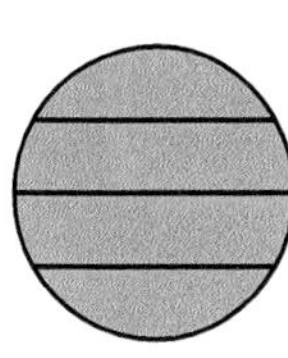

9.

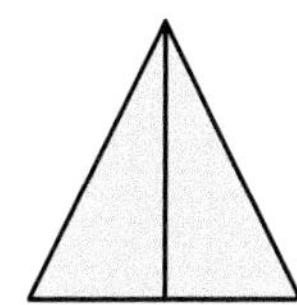

2 equal shares

10.

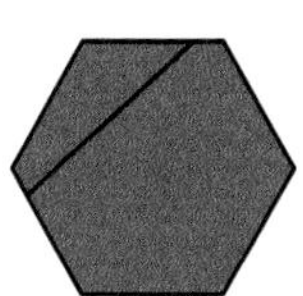

0 equal shares

11. YOU BE THE TEACHER Newton says the shape shows equal shares. Is he correct? Explain.

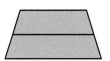

no; The parts are not the same size.

ELL Support

Check for understanding of Lesson 14.1. Read each story aloud as students follow along. Have students draw the figures indicated on whiteboards or sheets of paper and hold up for your review.

Laurie's Notes

Think and Grow: Modeling Real Life

This application allows students to show their understanding of equal and unequal parts. They divide shapes in two ways. Students should have fun and be given time to color the kites and posters.

? **Preview:** "Has anyone ever flown a kite? What do they look like?"

- Explain the directions for the kites. Students will divide their kite into two equal parts and their friend's kite into two parts that are unequal. Watch to see if anyone draws a horizontal line between the vertices as an equal division. This will seem like a natural place to draw a line, but it does not result in equal parts because the kite is not a rhombus. Do students think it is correct because both parts form triangles? Let students color the parts in two different colors. The only line of symmetry is vertically down the center.
- Introduce Exercise 12. Students now divide into four equal and unequal parts. Notice the order is reversed, and the first poster which is "your" poster has unequal parts. Allow students to color in the parts.

◉ "You have been determining whether a shape is divided into equal shares or unequal shares. Tell your partner what makes an equal share. Tell your partner how to recognize if shares are unequal. Use your thumb signal to show how well you can divide a shape into equal shares."

Closure

- "We are going to use thumb signals one final time. I am going to draw a shape on the whiteboard and divide it. Give me thumbs up if the shape has equal parts and thumbs down if it has unequal parts."

Think and Grow: Modeling Real Life

You and your friend each design a kite. Your kite has 2 equal shares. Your friend's has 2 unequal shares. Draw to show the parts.

Sample answer:

You

Friend

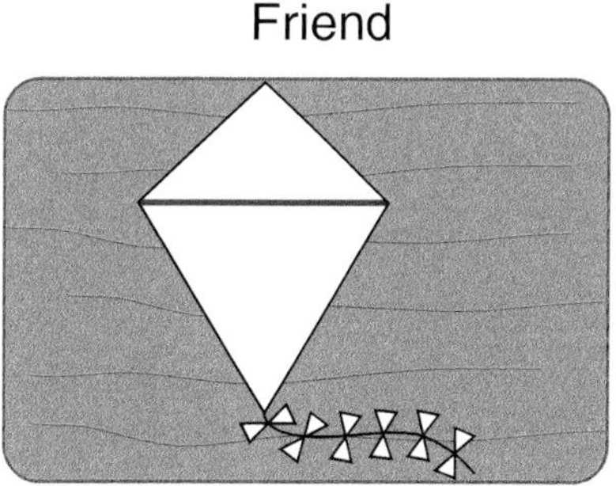

Show and Grow *I can think deeper!*

12. You and your friend each design a poster. Your poster has 4 unequal shares. Your friend's has 4 equal shares. Draw to show the parts.

Sample answer:

You

Friend

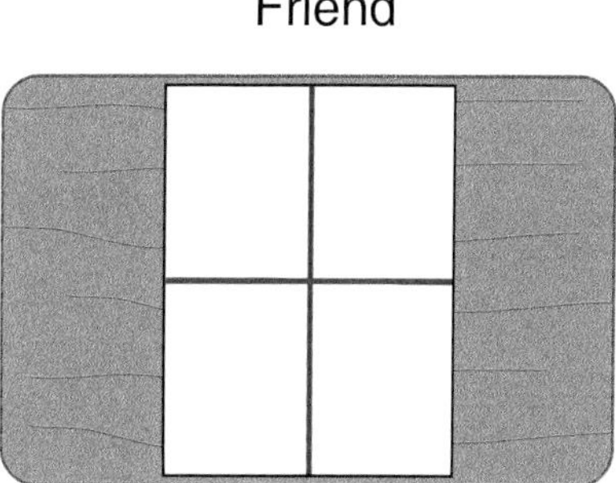

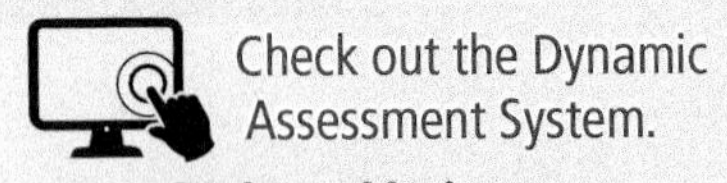
Check out the Dynamic
Assessment System.
BigIdeasMath.com

Scaffold assignments to support all students in their learning progression. Revisit with spaced practice to move every student toward proficiency.

Connect and Extend Learning

Practice Notes

- Remind students that each section of a shape has to be equal for it to show equal shares.

Prior Skills

- **Exercises 10 and 11:** Grade 1, Adding Two-Digit Numbers

Cross-Curricular Connections

Language Arts

- *Equal Schmequal* by Virginia Kroll; Read the book aloud to students. Pause at each scenario to allow students to explain why the groups are not equal.

Name ______________________

Practice **14.1**

Learning Target: Identify equal shares in two-dimensional shapes.

Equal Shares

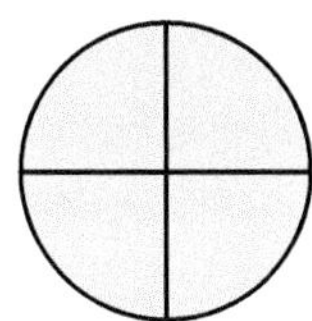

Unequal Shares

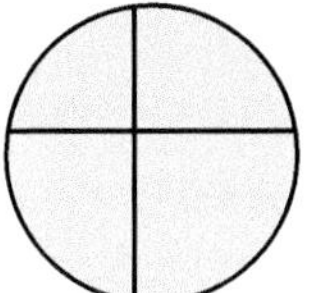

Circle the shape that shows equal shares.

1.

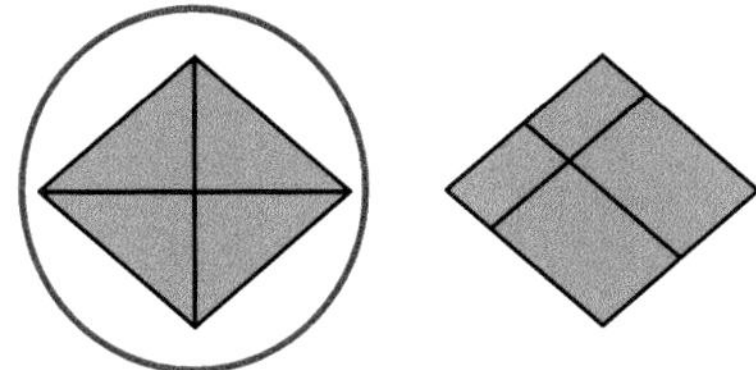

2.

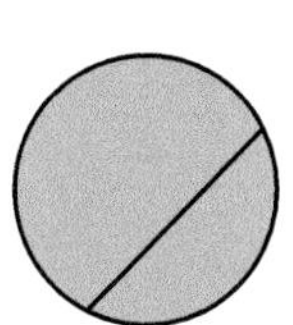

3.

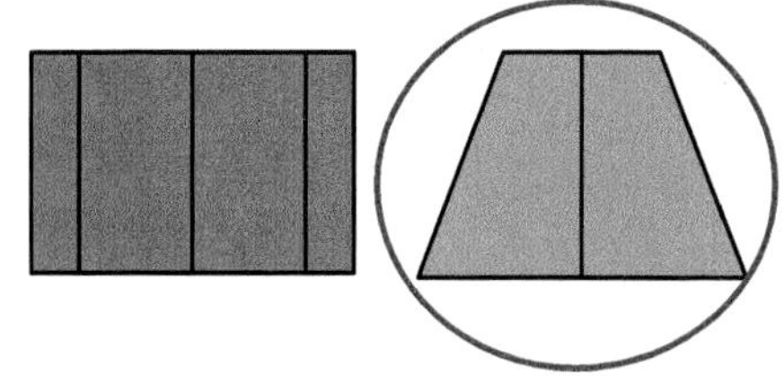

4.

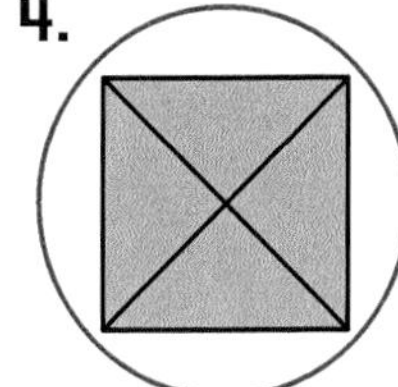

5.

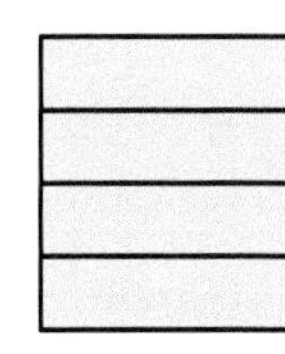

4 equal shares

6.

0 equal shares

Connect and Extend Learning

Extend Student Learning

Bodily-Kinesthetic

- Place pictures of shapes with equal and unequal shares face down on chairs or around the classroom. Have students walk around the chairs while music plays. Once the music stops, students find and flip over a picture. If the picture shows equal shares, students raise a hand. If the picture shows unequal shares, students sit down. Place all cards face down and repeat.

Lesson Resources	
Surface Level	**Deep Level**
Resources by Chapter • Extra Practice • Reteach Differentiating the Lesson Skills Review Handbook Skills Trainer	Resources by Chapter • Enrichment and Extension Graphic Organizers Dynamic Assessment System • Lesson Practice

7. **Precision** Descartes makes a thank you card with 4 equal shares. Which card does Descartes make?

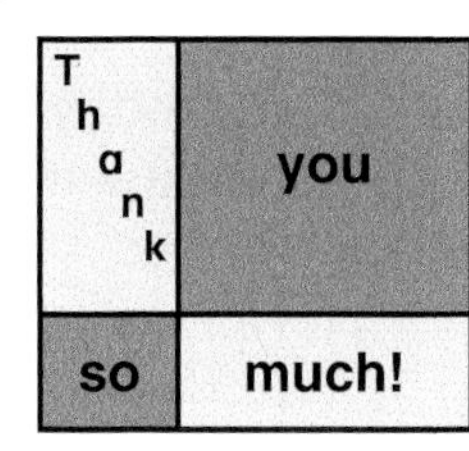

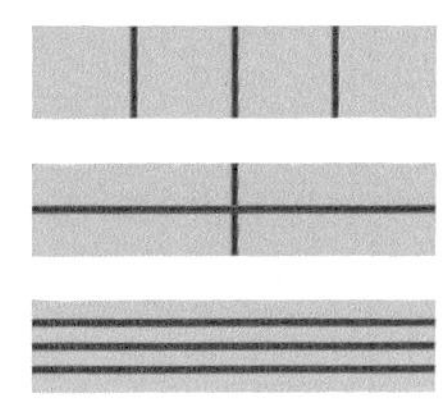

8. **DIG DEEPER!** Draw to show 4 equal shares in three different ways.

9. **Modeling Real Life** You and your friend each design a sticker. Your sticker has 2 unequal shares. Your friend's has 2 equal shares. Draw to show the parts.

Sample answer:

You

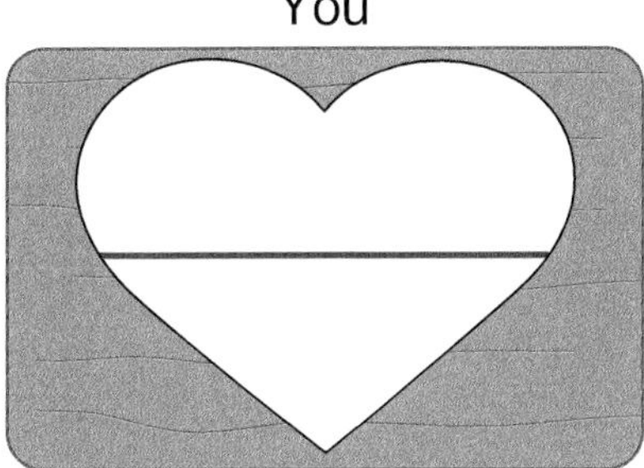

Friend

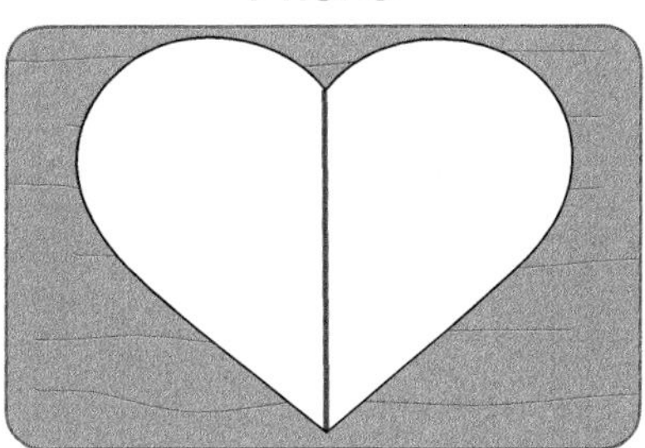

Review & Refresh

Make quick sketches to find the sum.

10. $\begin{array}{r} 32 \\ +\ 25 \\ \hline 57 \end{array}$

Tens	Ones
|||	••
||	•••••

11. $\begin{array}{r} 61 \\ +\ 15 \\ \hline 76 \end{array}$

Tens	Ones
||||||	•
|	•••••

Check out the
Dynamic Classroom.
BigIdeasMath.com

14.2

Laurie's Notes

STATE STANDARDS
1.G.A.3

Learning Target

Identify shapes that show halves.

Success Criteria

- Tell whether there are two equal shares.
- Use *halves* to name the shares.
- Draw to show halves.

Warm-Up

Practice opportunities for the following are available in the Resources by Chapter or at *BigIdeasMath.com*.

- Daily skills
- Vocabulary
- Prerequisite skills

ELL Support

Explain that when you partition something, you divide it. Point out that if you divide it in half, you have two halves. The word *half* has an irregular plural form. So when describing more than one half, instead of simply adding -*s* to the word, you must change the *f* to a *v* and add -*es*. Pronounce each word and have students repeat.

Preparing to Teach

We continue exploring fractions today by finding and dividing a shape into two equal shares. Students will practice using the vocabulary *half, half of*, and *halves*.

Materials

- paper shapes
- crayons
- pattern blocks
- whiteboards

Dig In (Circle Time)

Students will fold paper shapes, such as rectangles, hearts, squares, and circles, to show two equal parts. They will follow directions to color the halves in various colors and practice hearing and saying the correct terms.

- ◉ "Yesterday we talked about dividing shapes into equal parts or equal shares. When we divide a shape into equal parts, the parts have names based on how many there are. Today we will name two equal parts."
- Remind students of cutting the sandwich in two equal parts. What do we call one of the parts? Students will be familiar with saying "half a sandwich." Write the word *half* on chart paper.
- "When I have one of the two pieces of a sandwich, I say I have *half of* the sandwich. When I cut the sandwich, and have both pieces there, I can say that I cut the sandwich into *halves*. *Half* is one, *halves* are both."
- "We are going to fold shapes into two *halves*, and color each *half* a different color."
- Have students start with a rectangle. Have them fold it in half. Students may never have done this before so it may need to be modeled. There are two ways that students can fold, vertically or horizontally. Either is fine.
- ◉ Have students say that they folded the rectangle into *halves*. They color half of the rectangle one color, and the other half a different color. They tell their partners, "*Half of* my rectangle is (color 1) and the other *half* is (color 2)."

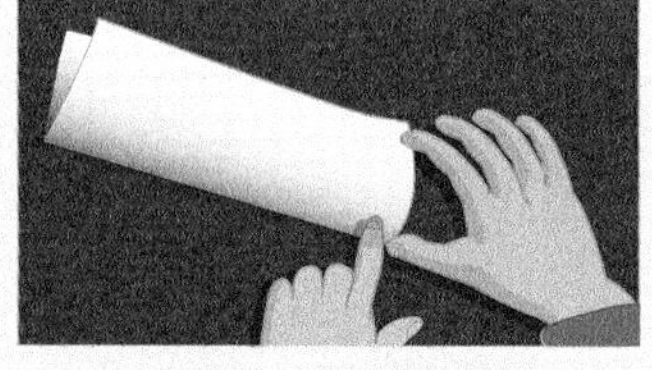

- Repeat with folding and coloring multiple shapes. Students practice using the vocabulary terms *half, half of*, and *halves*.
- **MP3 Construct Viable Arguments:** Show a square that is divided into two unequal parts, with one part colored. "Tell your partner if *half of* my square is colored. Why or why not?"

- ◉ "Tell your partners what we call two equal parts."

? Teaching Prompt ◉ Learning Target

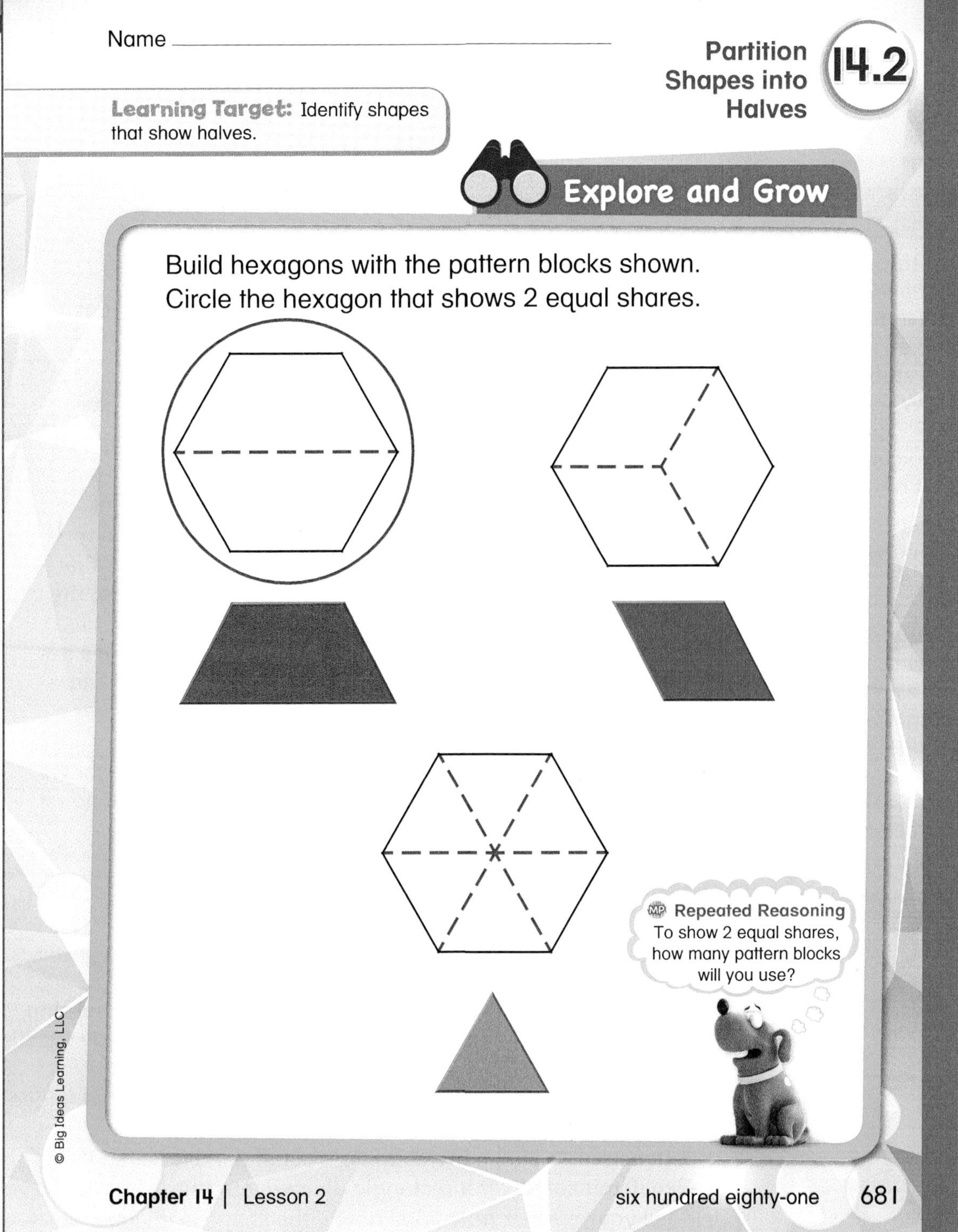
Name
Partition Shapes into Halves
14.2
Learning Target: Identify shapes that show halves.
Explore and Grow
Build hexagons with the pattern blocks shown.
Circle the hexagon that shows 2 equal shares.
Repeated Reasoning
To show 2 equal shares, how many pattern blocks will you use?

Explore and Grow

- Students use the pattern blocks to fill in the hexagons. They are to trace the shapes in the hexagon to show how they fit.
- Tracing the shapes will be hard for most first-graders. Show them how to put one of the trapezoids in the shape and draw the center line to "trace" the trapezoid. For the other shapes, show how to pick one shape up and draw the revealed edges. They pick up a different shape to draw the additional edges. Repeat as needed.
- "Tell your partner which hexagon had 2 equal shares, and how you knew. Tell what they are called."

ELL Support

After working through the example, have students work in pairs to complete Exercises 1–4. Have one student ask another, "Which shows halves?" The partner will indicate left or right, top or bottom.

Beginner students may provide one-word answers, such as, "bottom."
Intermediate students may answer with phrases, such as, "the bottom rectangle."
Advanced students may answer with sentences, such as, "The bottom rectangle shows halves."

Laurie's Notes

Think and Grow

Getting Started

- Students will circle the shapes that show halves.
- Introduce vocabulary cards for **half of** and **halves** along with the pictures of the circles divided into *halves* and having *half of* the circle shaded.

Teaching Notes

- **Model**: "Newton and Descartes have divided a rectangle into two parts. We need to decide if Newton's or Descartes's rectangle shows halves. Tell your partner what you think."
- **Model**: "Newton says that the parts of the rectangle on top have parts that are the same size. Since there are two equal shares, it means the parts are halves. Each of the parts is half of the rectangle. Circle the top rectangle."
- **Model**: "Tell your partner why the bottom rectangle does not show halves. Descartes says that the parts are not the same size. Even though there are two parts, they are not *halves* because they are not equal.
- Have students discuss Exercise 1 and circle the shape shows halves. Check to see that students are reasoning about equal and unequal parts in terms of halves.
- Students continue with Exercises 2–4.

? **MP6 Attend to Precision**: "Each of the shapes in Exercises 1–4 have the two parts. Why aren't they all *halves*? Exercise 4 has equal parts in both squares. Why isn't the square on the right showing *halves*?"

- **Supporting Learners**: Remind students of yesterday's learning on equal parts. If a shape shows *halves*, there have to be exactly two equal parts.
- **Supporting Learners**: Refer students to the paper shapes folded during the Dig In. Compare the colored *halves* to the pictures.
- **Extension**: "A shape divided into 3 equal parts is called thirds. See if you can draw a rectangle divided into thirds."

◉ "Tell your partner how you know if the shape is divided into *halves*."

Think and Grow

Circle the shape that shows halves.

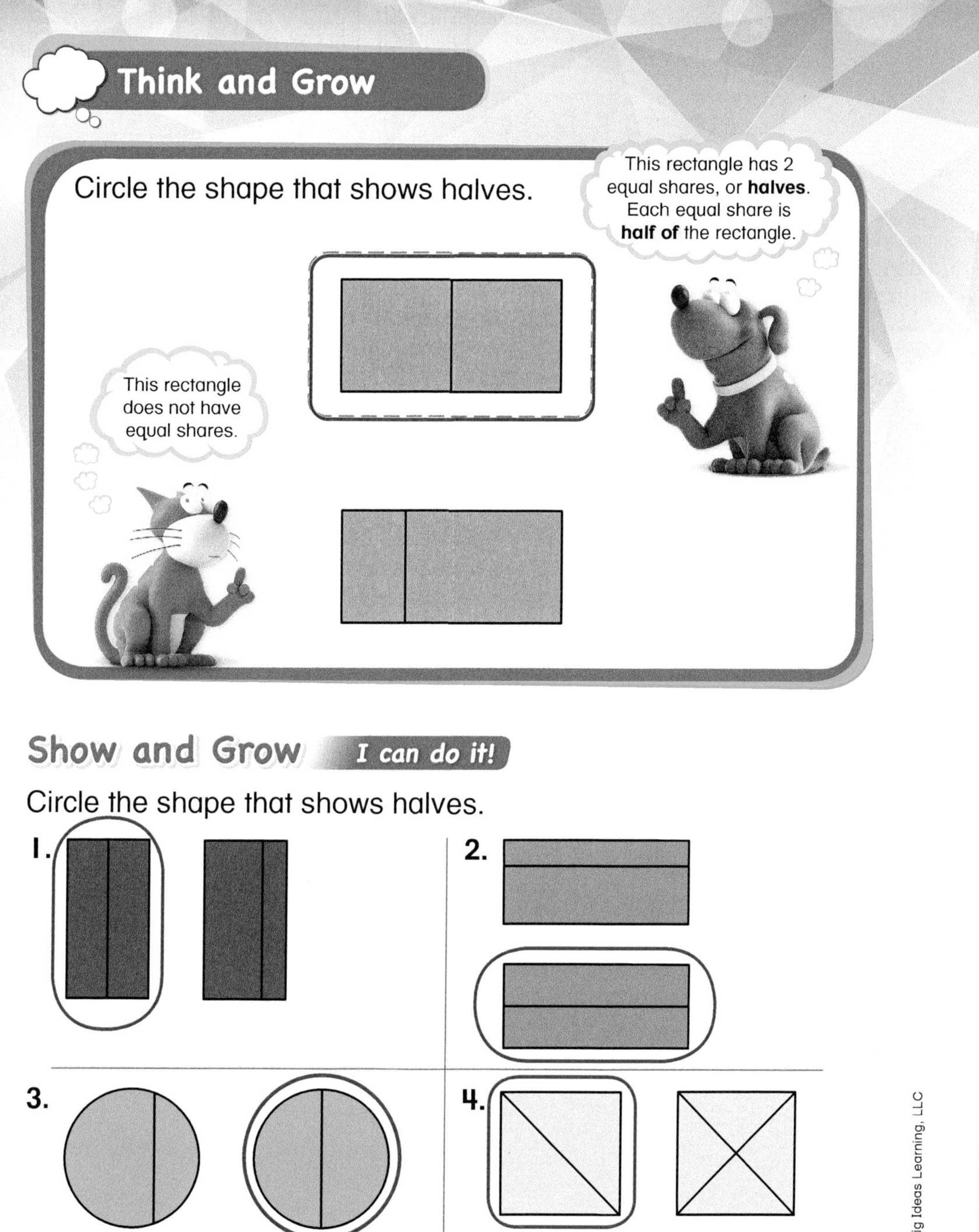

This rectangle has 2 equal shares, or **halves**. Each equal share is **half of** the rectangle.
This rectangle does not have equal shares.

Show and Grow *I can do it!*

Circle the shape that shows halves.

1.

2.

3.

4.

Scaffold instruction to support all students in their learning. Learning is individualized and you may want to group students differently as they move in and out of these levels with each skill and concept. Student self-assessment and feedback help guide your instructional decisions about how and when to layer support for all students to become proficient learners.

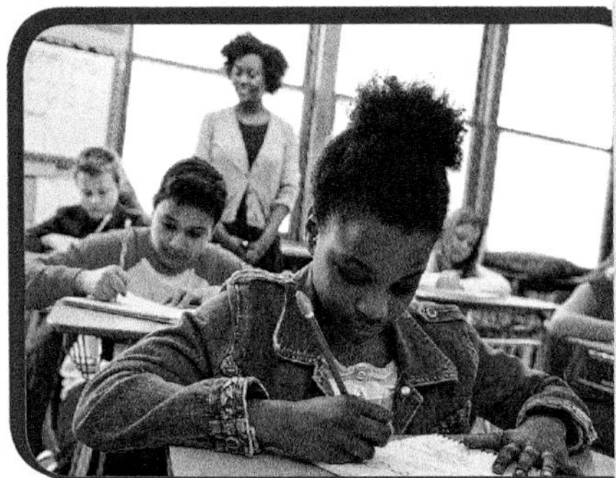

Meeting the needs of all learners.

Laurie's Notes

Apply and Grow: Practice

SCAFFOLDING INSTRUCTION

Students continue to identify halves and a half. The exercises on this page change direction lines, so students need to pay attention to them.

EMERGING students may still have difficulty determining equal shares, especially if the difference between the parts is subtle. Some students may assume that halves must be formed by horizontal and vertical lines.

- **Exercises 5 and 6:** Students need to choose all the shapes that are divided into halves. Remind students to look carefully at the two parts to see if they are equal.
- **Exercises 7–9:** Students need to color half of the shape. This is to understand the difference between *half of* and *halves*.
- **Exercise 10:** This exercise may take visualization that some students may not have developed. Suggest they divide the whole shape in half and see if they can match that way.

PROFICIENT students identify and use correct vocabulary involving halves.

- **Exercise 6:** Students may not select the red rectangle as showing halves because it could not be folded. If this is the case, cut the diagonal of a rectangle and show how they will lay on top of each other.
- **Exercise 10:** See if students recognize the difference of the square and rectangular halves and the shapes they will fit.

Additional Support

- Provide shape cut-outs for students to fold or draw on to determine equal shares.

Extension: Adding Rigor

- Give students outlines of rectangles and circles. See if they can divide the shapes into thirds, fourths, sixths, and eighths.

Name ______________________

Apply and Grow: Practice

Circle the shapes that show halves.

5.

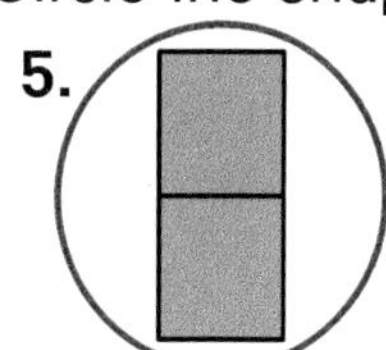 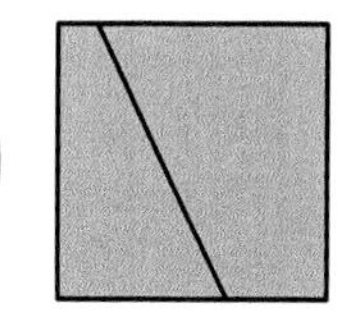  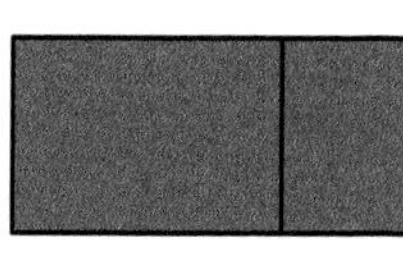

6.

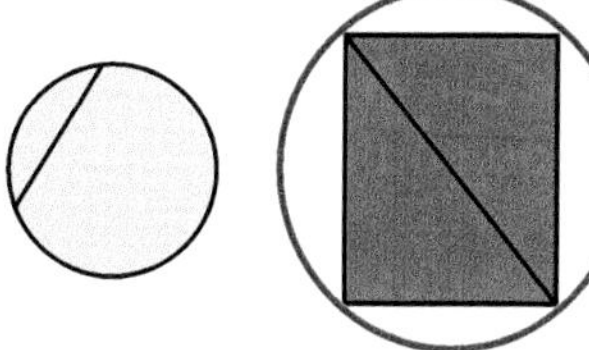 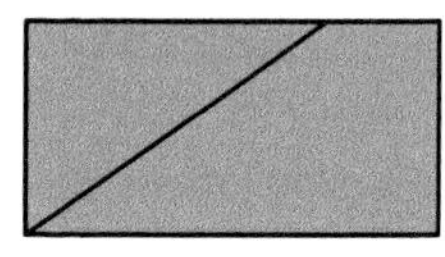 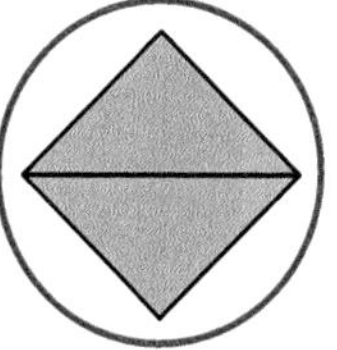

Color half of the shape.

7. 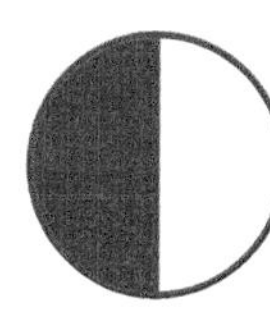

8. 

9. 

10. **Structure** Match each half with its whole.

Half

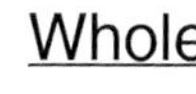

Whole

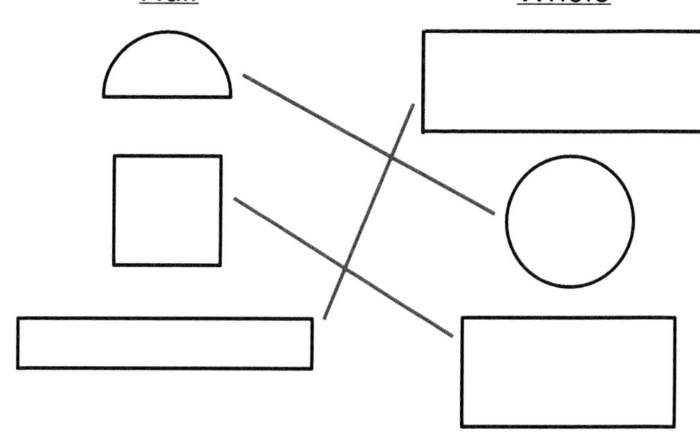

Use Math Tools
How can you use
paper shapes to
check your work?

ELL Support

Check for understanding of Lesson 14.2. Read each story aloud as students follow along. Have students draw the figures indicated on whiteboards or sheets of paper and hold up for your review.

Laurie's Notes

Think and Grow: Modeling Real Life

These applications allow students to show their understanding of halves. They divide the objects in three different ways to show halves.

- ? **Preview:** "What do you see on this page? Have you ever seen a block of cheese? Do you have a round rug?"
- "We want to show how we can cut the block of cheese in half. Draw lines to show how you could cut it."
- **MP1 Persevere in Solving Problems:** Discuss with students how they know that each part shows half of the cheese. They should notice that the halves are not the same shape, yet they are all half. Students tell their partners how they know each piece is half of the cheese.
- Introduce Exercise 11. Students show how to fold the rug in half. If the "fold" goes through the center of the circle, there are infinite ways to do this. This could be an interesting discussion with the students.
- ◉ "You have been determining whether a shape is divided into *halves*. Tell your partner what makes a *half*. Use your thumb signal to show how well you recognize halves. Use your thumb signal to show how well you can divide a shape into *halves*. Use your thumb signal to show how well you understand our vocabulary of *half* and *halves*."

Closure

- Tell students a shape to draw on their whiteboards. Have them color half of the shape. When students have had enough time, they turn and compare their drawings with a partner.

Think and Grow: Modeling Real Life

Show three ways to cut the cheese in half.

Sample answer:

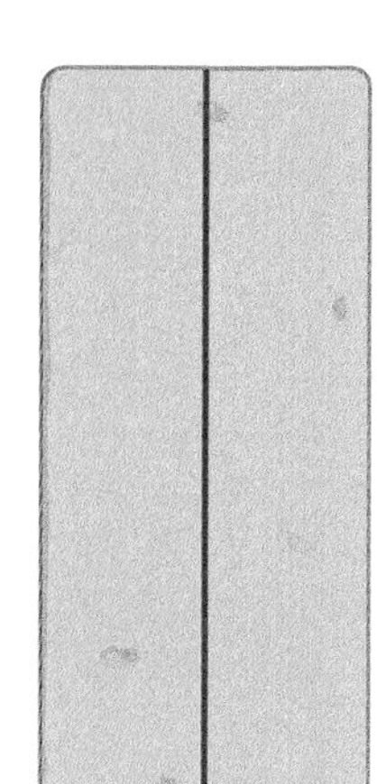

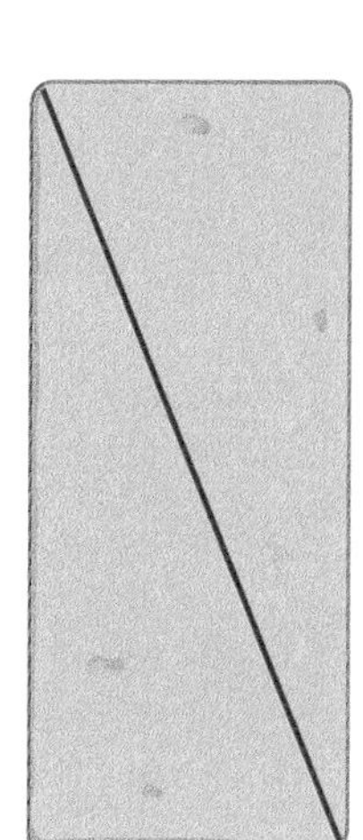

Check Your Work
If you cut along the lines you drew, what should be true about the shapes?

Show and Grow *I can think deeper!*

11. Show three ways to fold the rug in half.

Sample answer:

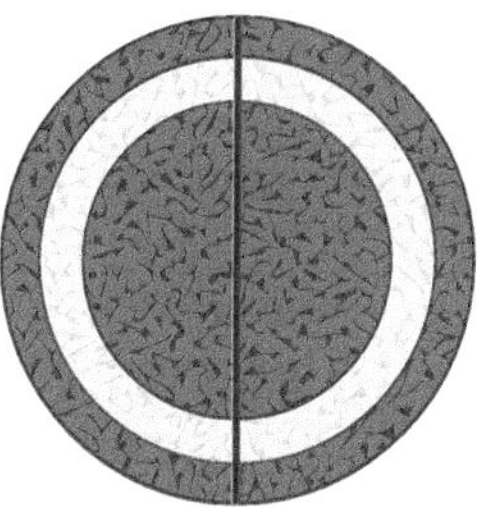

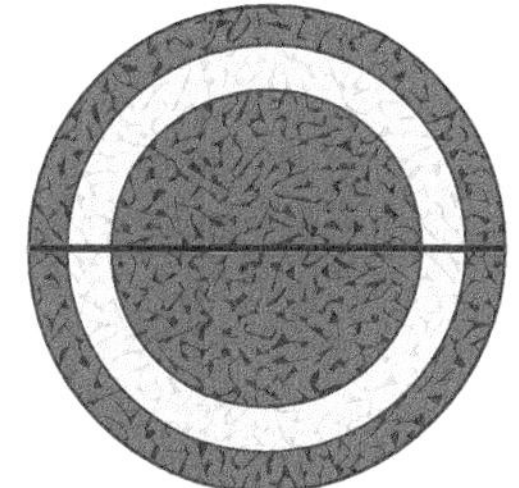

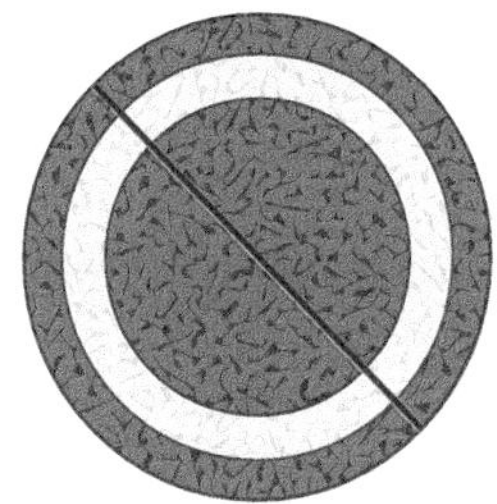

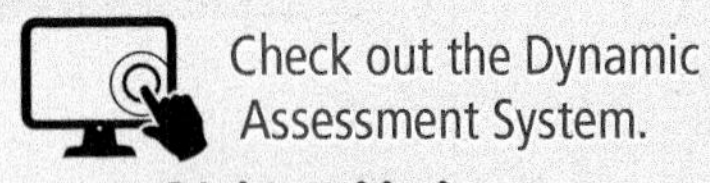
Check out the Dynamic Assessment System.
BigIdeasMath.com

Scaffold assignments to support all students in their learning progression. Revisit with spaced practice to move every student toward proficiency.

Connect and Extend Learning

Practice Notes

- Remind students that halves represent two equal shares.

Prior Skills

- **Exercise 10:** Grade 1, Sorting Three-Dimensional Shapes

Cross-Curricular Connections

Social Studies

- Display images of flags that show halves, such as the flag of Poland or the flag of Ukraine. Discuss these with students. Display other flags that show equal shares, such as the flag of Ireland or the flag of Jamaica, and ask students if the flags show halves or only equal shares.

Name ______________________

Practice  14.2

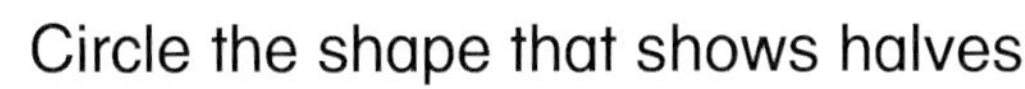
Learning Target: Identify shapes that show halves.

Circle the shape that shows halves.

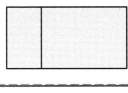

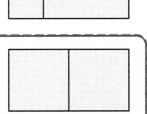

This rectangle has 2 equal shares, or **halves**. Each equal share is **half of** the rectangle.

Circle the shape that shows halves.

1. 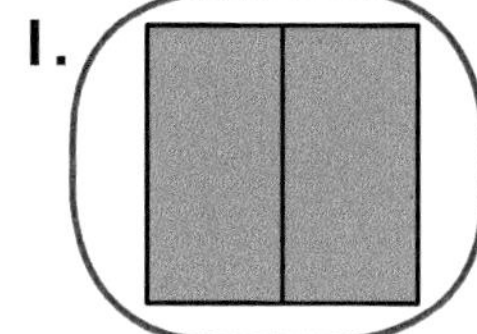 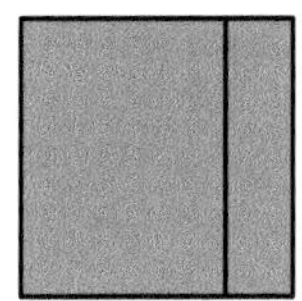

2. 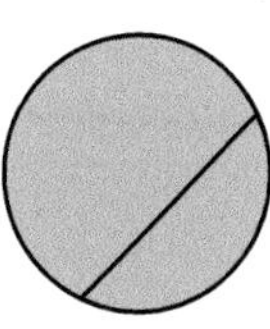

Circle the shapes that show halves.

3. 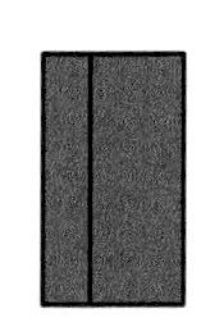 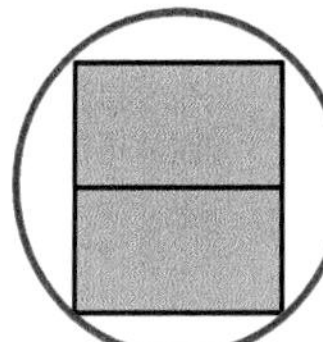 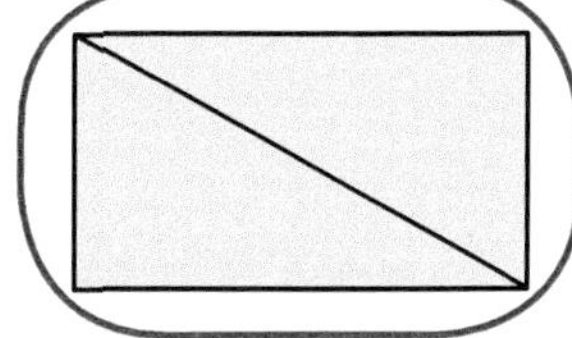 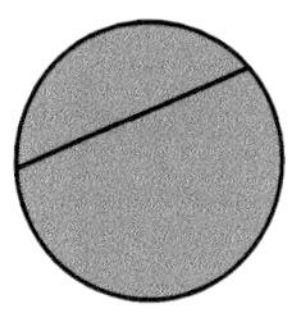

4. 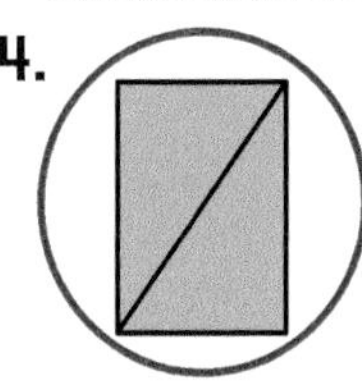  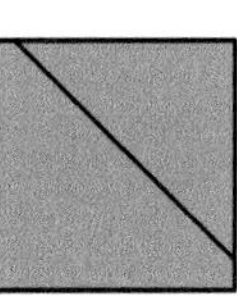 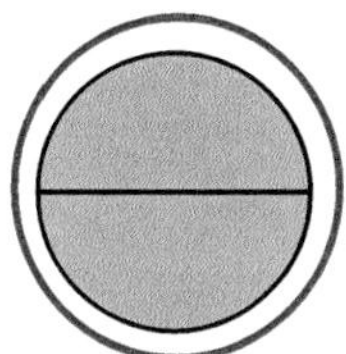 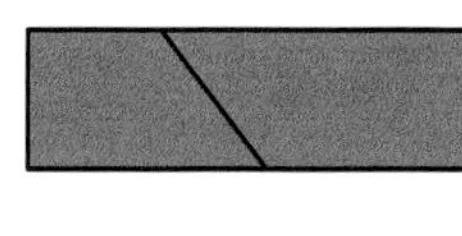

Connect and Extend Learning

Extend Student Learning

Visual-Spatial

- Have students make shapes out of clay. Then tell them to partition the shape into halves, pressing a pencil into the clay. Students can choose their own shapes or you can name a shape for students to make. Repeat with different shapes.

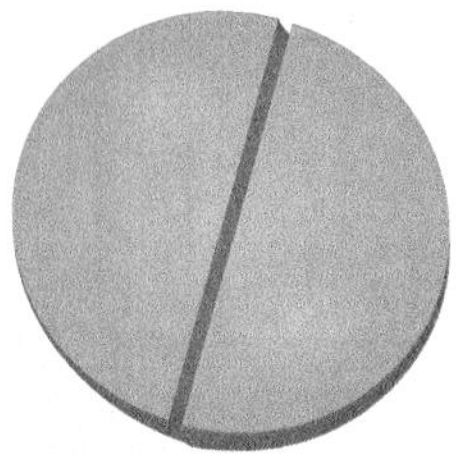

Lesson Resources	
Surface Level	**Deep Level**
Resources by Chapter • Extra Practice • Reteach Differentiating the Lesson Skills Review Handbook Skills Trainer Math Musicals	Resources by Chapter • Enrichment and Extension Graphic Organizers Math Musicals Dynamic Assessment System • Lesson Practice

Color half of the shape.

5. 

6. 

7. 

8. DIG DEEPER! Circle the shapes that show halves.

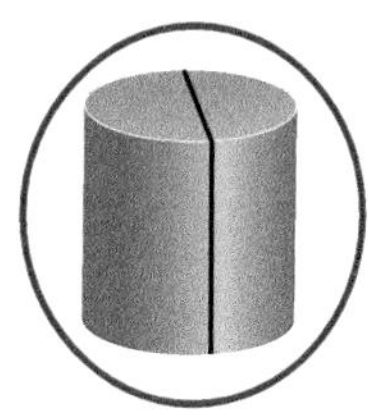

9. **Modeling Real Life** Show three ways to fold the bandana in half.

Sample answer:

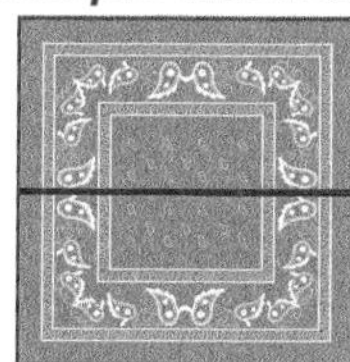

Review & Refresh

10. Circle the shapes that only have a curved surface.

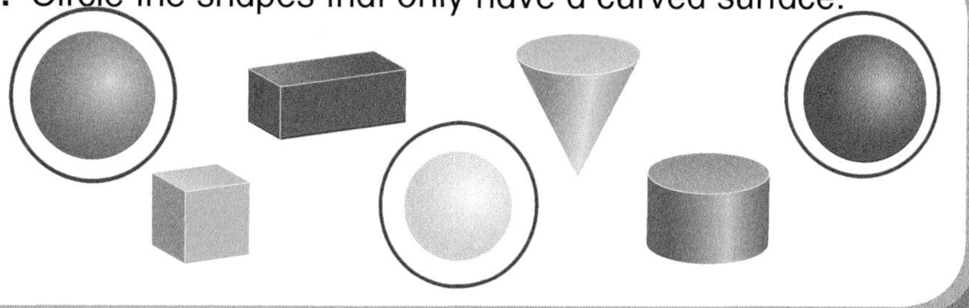

Check out the
Dynamic Classroom.

BigIdeasMath.com

Laurie's Notes

Learning Target

Identify shapes that show fourths.

Success Criteria

- Tell whether there are four equal shares.
- Use *fourths* or *quarters* to name the shares.
- Draw to show fourths.

Warm-Up

Practice opportunities for the following are available in the Resources by Chapter or at *BigIdeasMath.com.*

- Daily skills
- Vocabulary
- Prerequisite skills

ELL Support

The word *fourth* can be difficult for non-natives to pronounce, as the *th* sound is not found in many languages. Say the word and have students repeat. Then say the word *first* and have students repeat. Say the words together—*first/fourth*—and have students repeat, carefully distinguishing each word. You may want to write simple sentences on the board using these words and ask a student to read one aloud as others cover their eyes. The class will guess if the meaning is first or fourth by holding up one or four fingers.

COMMON CORE **STATE STANDARDS**
1.G.A.3

Preparing to Teach

We continue exploring fractions today by dividing a shape into four equal shares. This lesson directly parallels yesterday so that students can make the connection that the only difference between halves and quarters are the number of parts.

Materials

- paper shapes
- crayons
- 2, 4, or Unequal Shares Sort Cards*
- scissors and glue
- whiteboards

**Found in the Instructional Resources*

Dig In (Circle Time)

Students will fold paper shapes, such as rectangles, circles, and squares, to show four equal parts. They will follow directions to color the fourths in various colors to practice hearing and saying the correct terms.

- ◉ "Yesterday we talked about halves. Tell your partner how you know if a shape is divided into halves." Be sure that students state both conditions: two parts that are equal.
- "Today we are going to talk about dividing shapes into four equal pieces. Does anyone know what the parts will be called?"
- **MP4 Model with Mathematics:** Introduce the terms *fourths* and *quarters*. They mean the same thing. *Quarter* is like the coin because it takes four *quarters* to equal a dollar. Students will probably know about money, but may not know the name of a quarter or its value. It does not hurt to mention it for students who do know the coin.
- "We are going to fold shapes into four quarters and color each quarter a different color."
- ◉ Have students start with a rectangle. Have them fold it in half and then half again. Have students open the rectangle and count the sections. "How many sections are there? Are they equal? This means we have folded the rectangle into *fourths*. Color each *quarter* a different color. Tell your partner, 'One quarter of my rectangle is (color 1), a fourth of my rectangle is (color 2), another quarter of my rectangle is (color 3), and the last fourth is (color 4).' "This will probably need to be repeated phrase by phrase to practice.

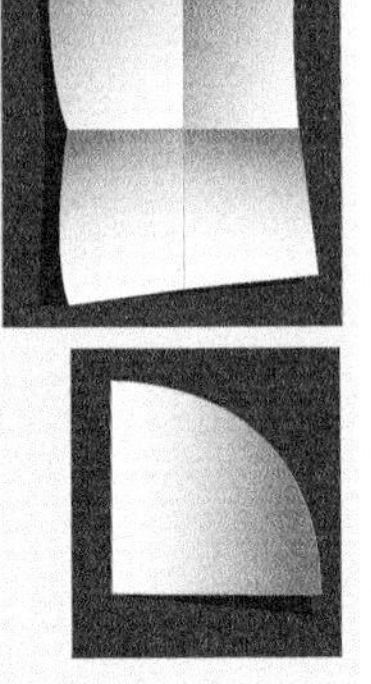

- Repeat with folding the circle and square.
- Show a triangle that is divided into four unequal parts, with one part colored. Tell your partner if *a quarter of* my triangle is colored. Why or why not?

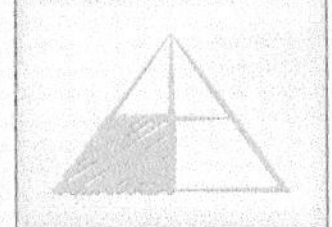

- ◉ "Tell your partners what we call four equal parts."

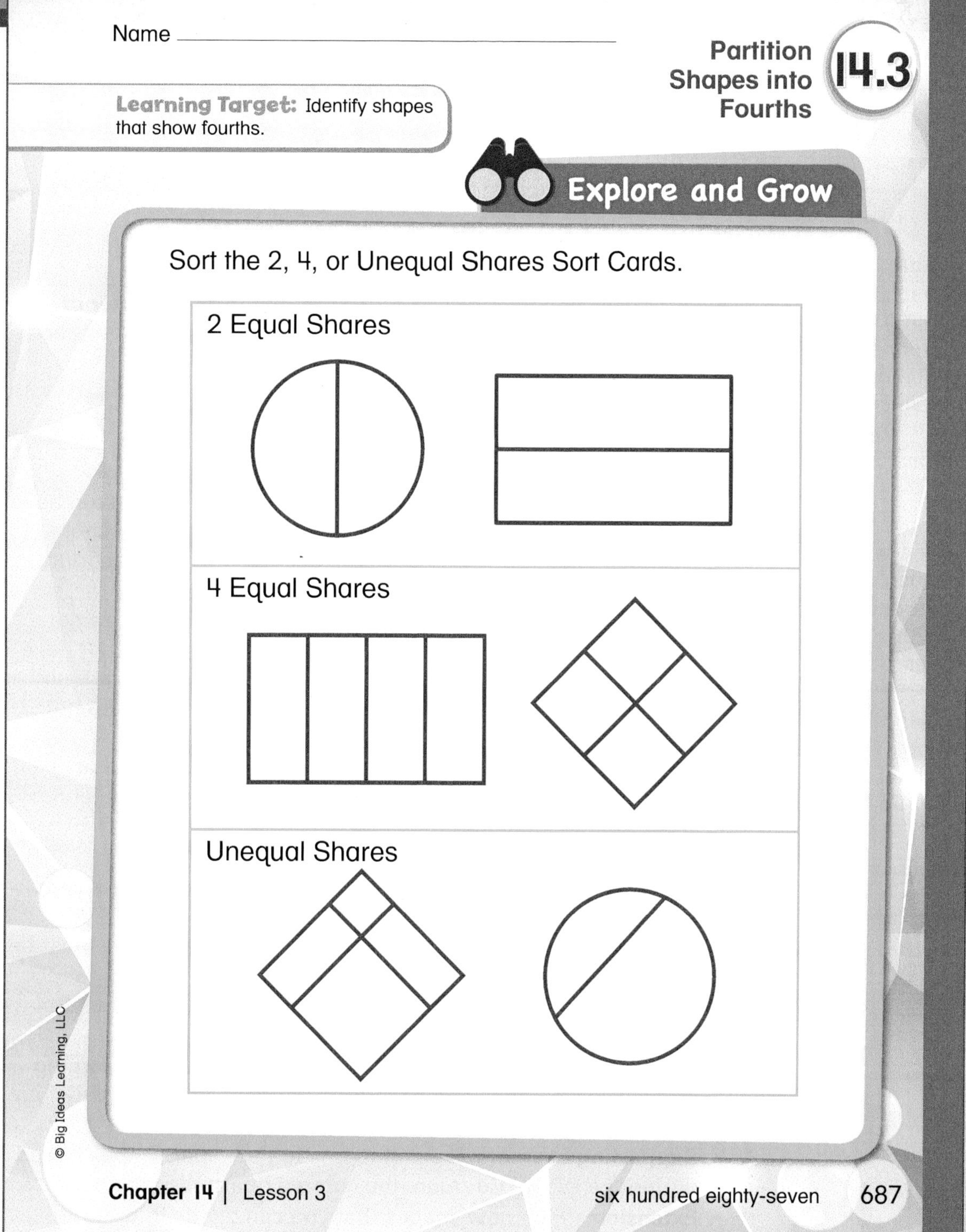
Name ______________________________

Partition Shapes into Fourths **14.3**

Learning Target: Identify shapes that show fourths.

Explore and Grow

Sort the 2, 4, or Unequal Shares Sort Cards.

2 Equal Shares

4 Equal Shares

Unequal Shares

Explore and Grow

- Each pair can share scissors and glue. Students cut out the 2, 4, or Unequal Shares Sort Cards to sort.
- Have students place their cards into the three rows and compare with a partner before gluing them down.
- "Tell your partner how you knew which cards fit in 2 equal shares, 4 equal shares, or unequal shares."

ELL Support

After working through the example, have students work in pairs to complete Exercises 1–4. Have one student ask another, "Which shows fourths?" The partner will indicate left or right.

Beginner students may provide one-word answers, such as, "left." **Intermediate** students may answer with phrases, such as, "the left rectangle." **Advanced** students may answer with sentences, such as, "The left rectangle shows fourths."

Laurie's Notes

Think and Grow

Getting Started

- Students will circle the shapes that show fourths.
- Introduce vocabulary cards for **fourth of**, **fourths**, **quarter of** and **quarters** along with the pictures showing fourths and quarters.

Teaching Notes

- **Model**: "Newton and Descartes have divided a rectangle into four parts. We need to decide if Newton's or Descartes's rectangle shows *fourths*. Tell your partner what you think."
- **Model**: "Newton says that the parts of the rectangle on top have parts that are the same size. Since there are four equal shares, they are called fourths or quarters. Each of the parts is a fourth of or a quarter of the rectangle. Circle the top rectangle."
- **Model**: "Tell your partner why the bottom rectangle does not show quarters. Descartes says that the rectangle does not have equal shares. Tell your partner what that means." parts are not the same size "Even though there are four parts, they are not fourths because they are not equal."
- Have students discuss Exercise 1 and circle the shape that shows fourths. Check to see that students are reasoning about equal and unequal parts.
- Students continue with Exercises 2–4.

? **MP8 Look for and Express Regularity in Repeated Reasoning:** "In order to show fourths, a shape must be divided into how many equal parts?" 4 "In order to show halves, a shape must be divided into how many equal parts?" 2

? **MP6 Attend to Precision**: "Each of the shapes in Exercises 1–4 have the four parts. Why aren't they all fourths?"

- **Supporting Learners:** Remind students of yesterday's learning on halves. If a shape shows fourths, there has to be exactly four equal parts.
- **Supporting Learners:** Refer students to the paper shapes folded during the Dig In. Compare the colored quarters to the pictures.
- **Extension**: "Find new shapes that you can divide into fourths. Is there a shape you can find that cannot be divided into *quarters*?"

◉ "Tell your partner how you know if the shape is divided into fourths."

Think and Grow

Circle the shape that shows fourths.

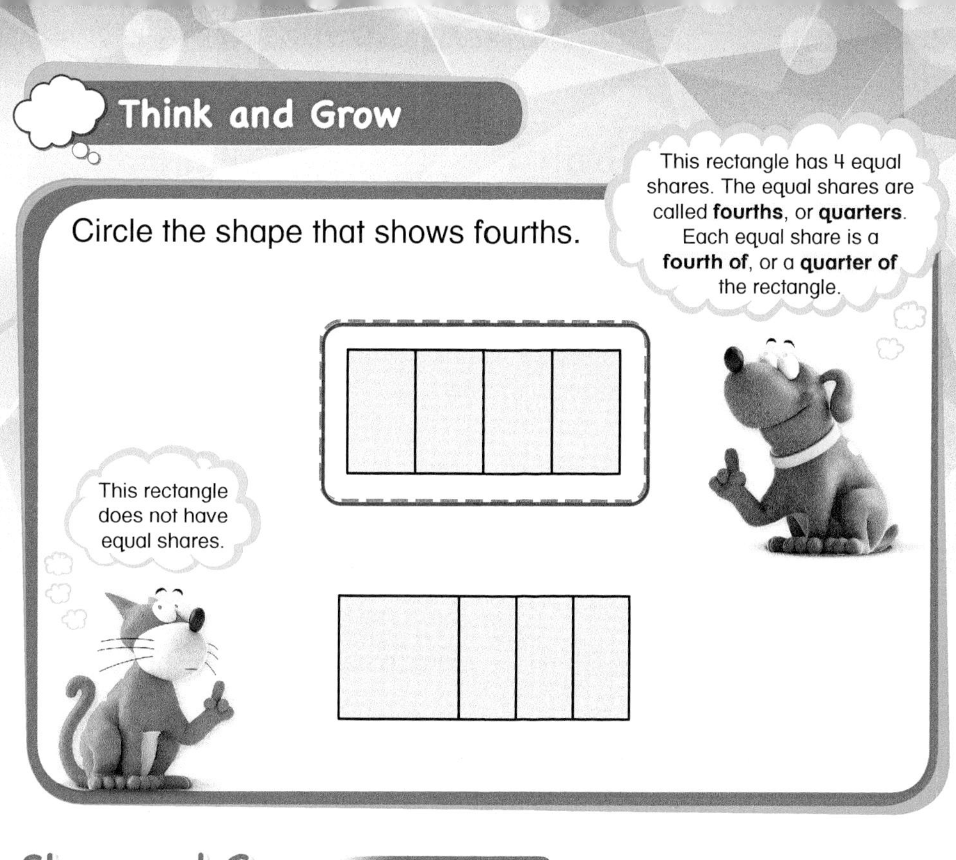

This rectangle has 4 equal shares. The equal shares are called **fourths**, or **quarters**. Each equal share is a **fourth of**, or a **quarter of** the rectangle.
This rectangle does not have equal shares.

Show and Grow *I can do it!*

Circle the shape that shows fourths.

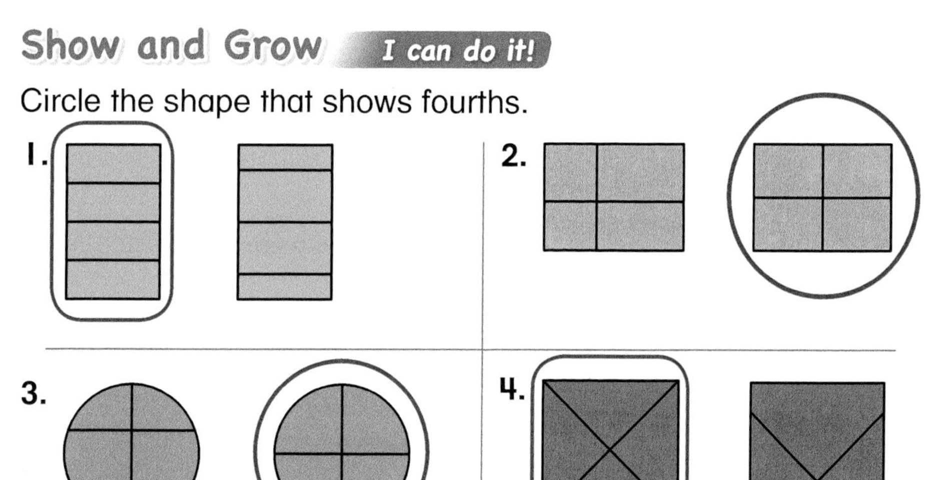

Scaffold instruction to support all students in their learning. Learning is individualized and you may want to group students differently as they move in and out of these levels with each skill and concept. Student self-assessment and feedback help guide your instructional decisions about how and when to layer support for all students to become proficient learners.

Meeting the needs of all learners.

Laurie's Notes

Apply and Grow: Practice

SCAFFOLDING INSTRUCTION

Students continue to identify quarters. The exercises on this page change direction lines, so students need to pay attention to them. They are the same types of exercises that they completed yesterday with halves.

EMERGING students may still have difficulty determining equal shares, especially if the type of divisions is new, such as in Exercise 7. Some students may assume that fourths must be formed by horizontal and vertical lines.

- **Exercise 5 :** Students need to choose all the shapes that are divided into *fourths*. There is more than one correct answer.
- **Exercises 6 and 7:** Students need to color a quarter of the shape.
- **Exercise 8:** This exercise requires students to think and visualize creatively. If they have difficulty, remind them of folding the square during the Dig In.
- **Exercise 9:** This exercise requires students to start making sense of relative sizes of pieces. This will become an important concept as they develop number sense with fractions. Provide two circles for students to divide to compare the size of the parts.

PROFICIENT students identify and use correct vocabulary involving fourths.

- **Exercise 8:** Students may visualize four smaller squares and draw those in. This will still lead to filling in the horizontal and vertical lines.
- **Exercise 9:** Have students explain how they know which piece is larger.

Additional Support

- Provide shape cut-outs for students to fold or draw on to determine equal shares.
- Use the folded shapes from the Dig In to remind students of fourths.

Extension: Adding Rigor

- Give students outlines of rectangles and circles. See if they can divide the shapes into thirds, sixths, and eighths.

Name

Apply and Grow: Practice

Circle the shapes that show fourths.

5.

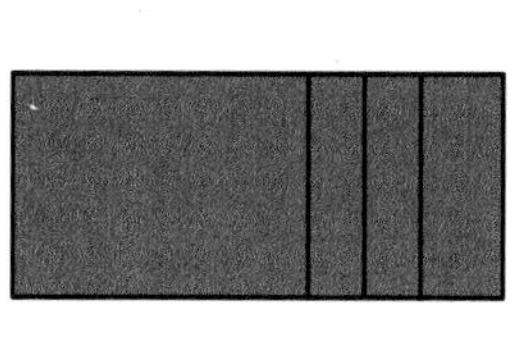

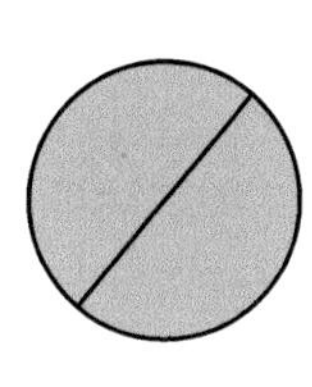

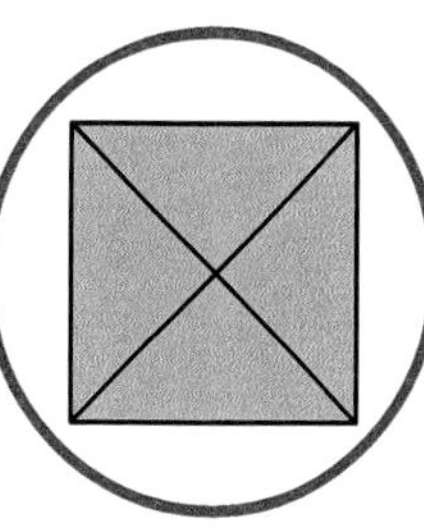

Color a quarter of the shape.

6.

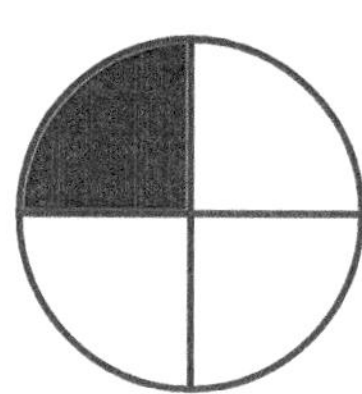

7.

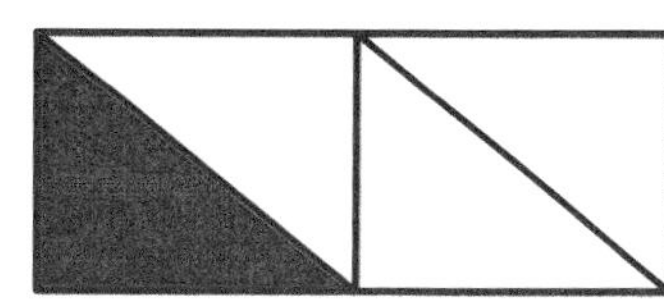

8. MP **Precision** Draw more lines to show fourths.

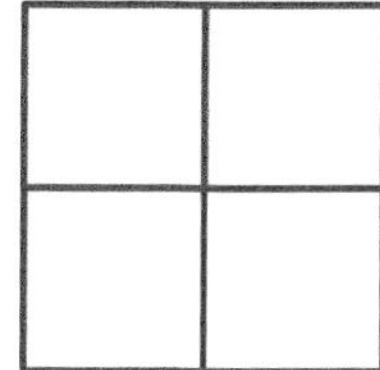

9. DIG DEEPER! You cut a circle into halves. Your friend cuts the same-sized circle into quarters. Who has the larger pieces? Think: How do you know?

You

Friend

Each of these pieces is half of a half.

ELL Support

Check for understanding of Lesson 14.3. Read each story aloud as students follow along. You may want to have students share their knowledge of the foods mentioned, or describe each. Allow time to complete the exercises. Ask the following questions and have students indicate the answers by holding up the appropriate number of fingers.

1. How many more friends could have a piece of pizza?
2. How many more friends could have a piece of the granola bar?

Laurie's Notes

Think and Grow: Modeling Real Life

These applications allow students to show their understanding of quarters. They reason about the number of pieces and that they can be subtracted.

- **Model**: "Look at the pizza. We are going to cut it into quarters. Draw lines to divide it into fourths." Check to see that students have divided it correctly.
- ? **Model**: "One of your friends eats one quarter. Cross out one of the quarters. How many pieces are left? How many friends can have a piece of pizza?" Student might say 2 friends and me. Either way, 3 people can still have a piece.
- **MP2 Reason Abstractly and Quantitatively**: "Who gets a smaller equal share, two friends who share the pizza or four friends who share the pizza? How do you know?" Four friends get a smaller share because their equal shares, quarters, are smaller than halves.
- Introduce Exercise 10. Students can follow the model by dividing the granola bar into quarters and crossing off two pieces. Watch to see how students divide the bar into fourths.
- ◉ "You have been determining whether a shape is divided into fourths or quarters. Tell your partner how to recognize a fourth. Use your thumb signal to show how well you can see quarters. Use your thumb signal to show how well you can divide a shape into fourths. Use your thumb signal to show how well you understand our vocabulary of fourth and quarter."

Closure

- Tell students a shape to draw on their whiteboards. Have them color a fourth of the shape. When students have had enough time, they turn and compare their drawings with their partner.

Think and Grow: Modeling Real Life

You cut a pizza into quarters. Your friend eats 1 quarter. How many more friends could have a piece of pizza?

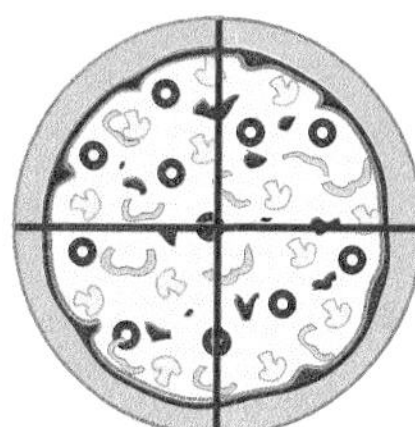

3 friends

Show and Grow I can think deeper!

10. You cut a granola bar into quarters. Your friend eats 2 quarters. How many more friends could have a piece of the granola bar?

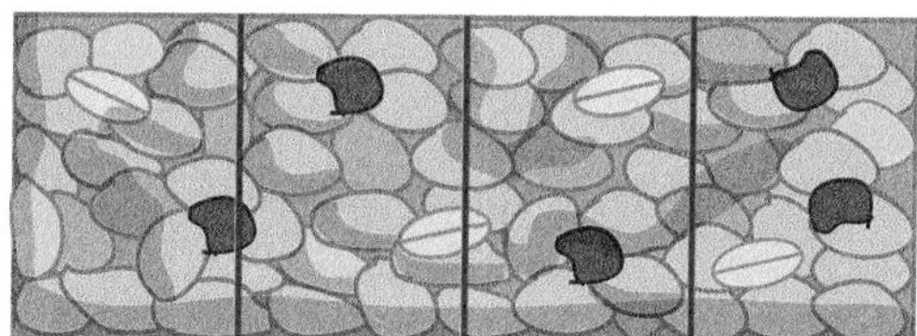

2 friends

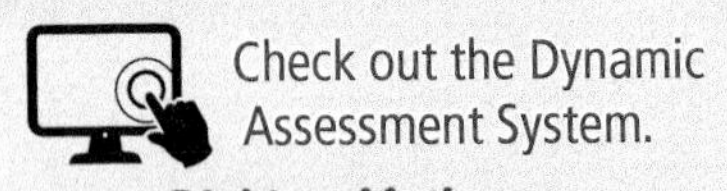

Check out the Dynamic Assessment System.

BigIdeasMath.com

Scaffold assignments to support all students in their learning progression. Revisit with spaced practice to move every student toward proficiency.

Connect and Extend Learning

Practice Notes

- Remind students that a quarter is another way to say fourths.

Prior Skills

- **Exercises 9 and 10:** Grade 1, Telling Time Using Analog and Digital Clocks

Cross-Curricular Connections

Art

- Show students how to make origami that involves folding into fourths, such as fortune tellers. Demonstrate for students or have each student follow along with their own. After each of the first three steps, ask students how many equal parts they see.

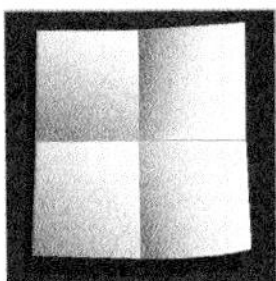

Step 1: Fold a square piece of paper in half left to right and unfold. Fold the paper in half again from top to bottom and unfold.

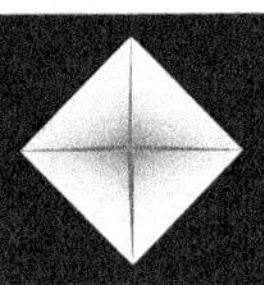

Step 2: Fold the 4 corners to the center.

Step 3: Turn the paper over and repeat.

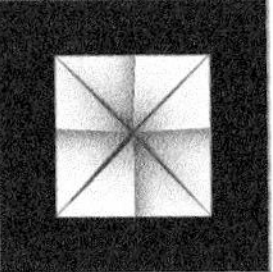

Step 4: Fold the paper in half left to right and unfold. Fold the paper in half again from top to bottom and unfold.

Step 5: Bring the four corners together.

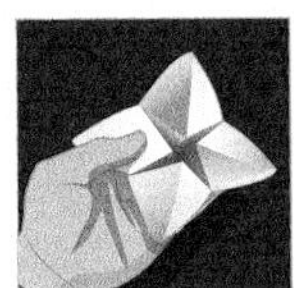

Step 6: Open the flaps.

Name ______________________________

Practice 

Learning Target: Identify shapes that show fourths.

Circle the shape that shows fourths.

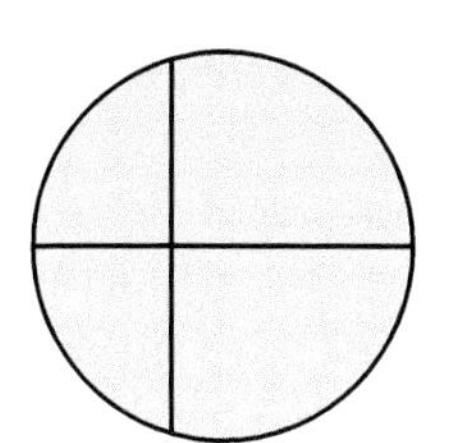 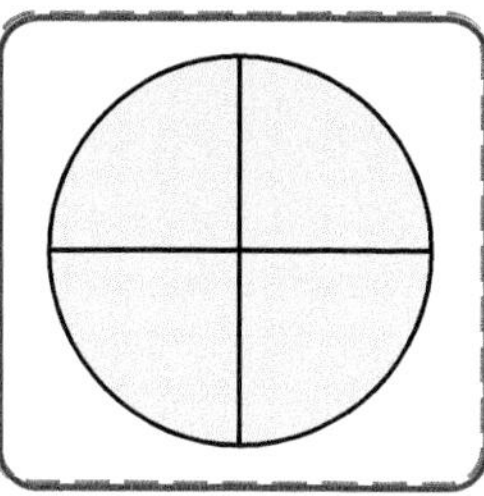

This circle has 4 equal shares. The equal shares are called fourths, or quarters.

Circle the shape that shows fourths.

1.  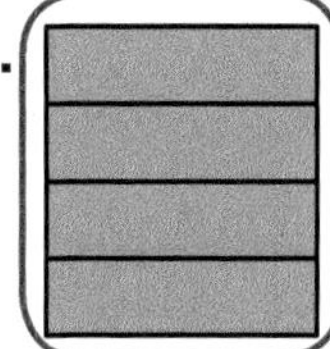 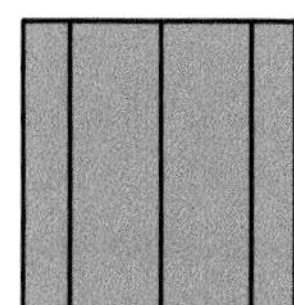

2. 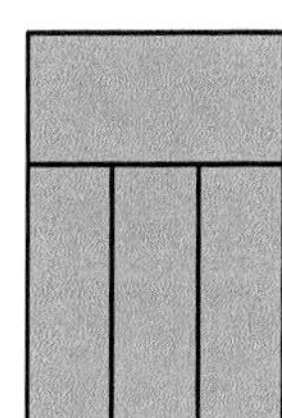 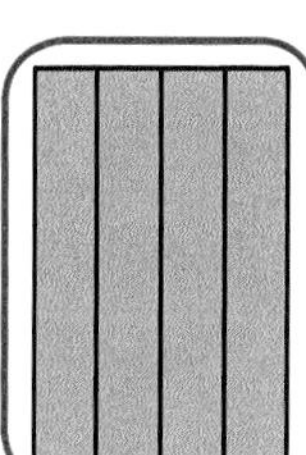

Circle the shapes that show fourths.

3. 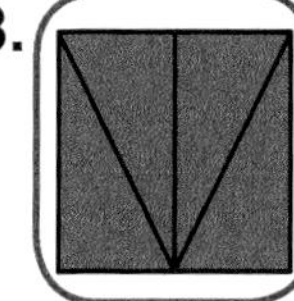 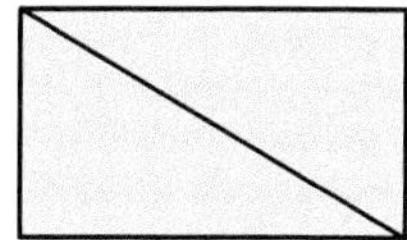  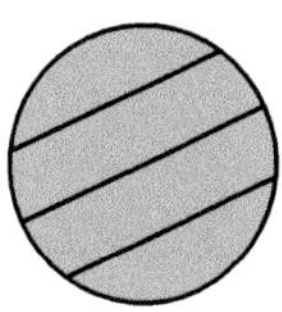

Color a quarter of the shape.

4. 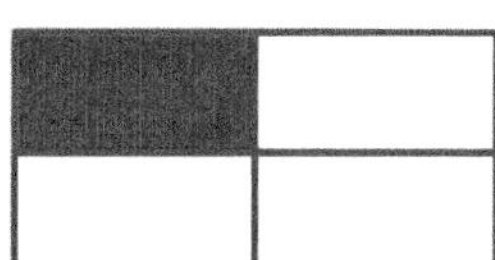

5. 

Connect and Extend Learning

Extend Student Learning

Bodily-Kinesthetic

- Use masking tape to split desks, shelves, windows, or other surfaces in the classroom into four equal parts or four unequal parts. Give each student a piece of paper and have them make two columns, one labeled Four Equal Parts and the other labeled Four Unequal Parts. Have students to go on a scavenger hunt looking for objects split into fourths. Students write down or draw a picture of the surfaces in the correct column.

Lesson Resources	
Surface Level	**Deep Level**
Resources by Chapter • Extra Practice • Reteach Differentiating the Lesson Skills Review Handbook Skills Trainer	Resources by Chapter • Enrichment and Extension Graphic Organizers Dynamic Assessment System • Lesson Practice

6. 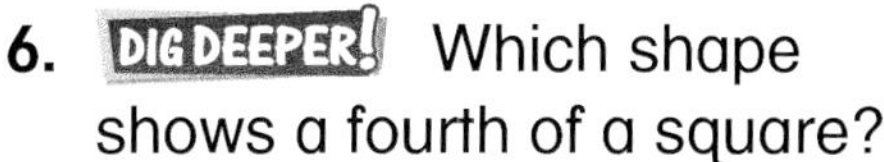 Which shape shows a fourth of a square?

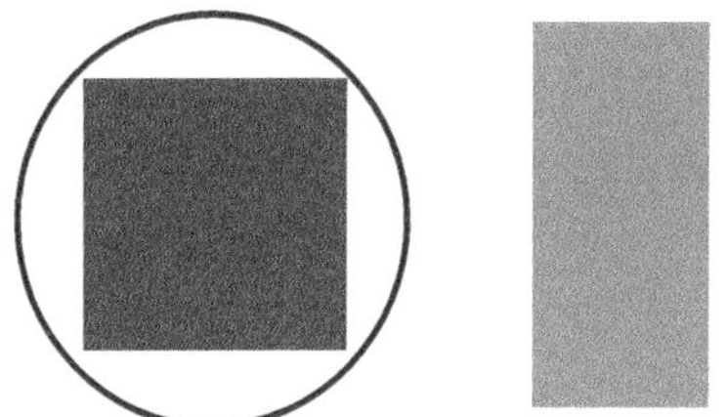

7. Reasoning Color half of the square. How many fourths did you color?

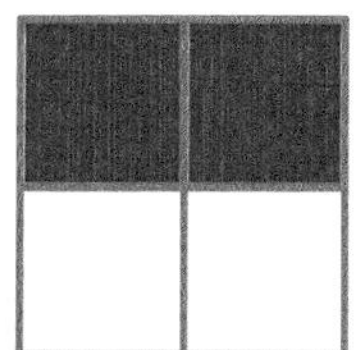

2 fourths

8. Modeling Real Life You cut a slice of bread into quarters. Your friend eats 3 quarters. How many more friends could have a piece of bread?

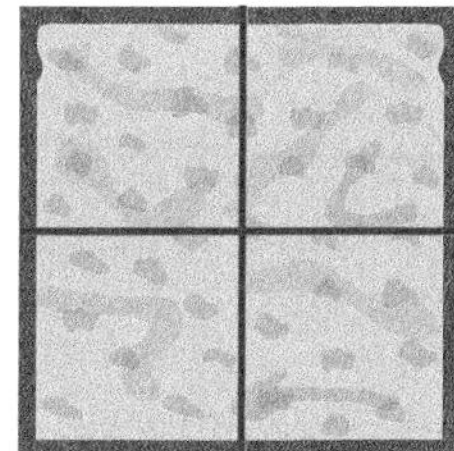

1 friend

Review & Refresh

Draw to show the time.

9.

10.

ELL Support

Have students work in groups to complete the Performance Task. Have Intermediate and Advanced students alternate reading sections aloud as the group discusses the answers. Monitor discussion. Expect students to perform according to their language proficiency level.

Beginner students may indicate answers visually or provide single words, such as, "four."
Intermediate students may provide phrases, such as, "four equal shares."
Advanced students may guide others to complete the exercises and answer with sentences, such as, "I have four equal shares of the apple."

Laurie's Notes

Performance Task

In this task, students will demonstrate their understanding of equal shares. In Exercise 1, look to see that students have drawn lines from person to their correct item. Use student responses to gauge their understanding about halves and quarters.

- Decide ahead of time whether students will be working independently, in pairs, or in groups.
- Pause between direction lines for students to complete each step.
- Have students share their work and thinking with others. Discuss as a class.

Exercise	Answers and Notes	Points
1	Students will draw lines from: You to the casserole dish Friend to the sandwich Cousin to the watermelon	3
2a	4 equal shares; Students will show their work, which may include drawing a circle partitioned into fourths	4
2b	3 shares	3
	Total	10

Name ______________________________

Performance Task

1. You, your friend, and your cousin are having a picnic. Use the clues to match each person with a food item.

- You bring an item that is cut into 4 unequal shares.
- Your friend brings an item that is cut into halves.
- Your cousin brings an item that is cut into quarters.

You Friend Cousin

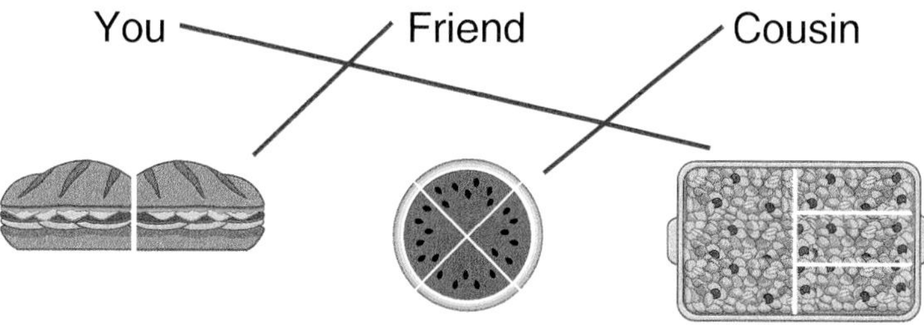

---

2. a. You cut an apple into 2 equal shares. You cut each share in half. How many equal shares do you have now?

4 equal shares

Show how you know:

b. You give your friend a fourth of the apple. How many shares do you have left?

3 shares

Check out the interactive version in the Game Library.

BigIdeasMath.com

Laurie's Notes

Three In a Row: Equal Shares

Materials

- spinners
- counters

Three In a Row: Equal Shares reviews equal and unequal shares, by having students to use their knowledge of *fourths, half of, halves*, and *quarter of* to match the vocabulary word to a model.

? "What do you remember about playing Three In a Row in Chapter 1?" *Sample answer:* We solved addition and subtraction problems to get three in a row.

- "Today you will be playing Three In A Row: Equal Shares using a spinner instead of cards."
- Review the directions with the class while modeling how to play.
- **Note:** Decide before playing whether students can bump a counter off the board or not.
- Partner students and distribute spinners. Have students begin playing.
- While students play, pay attention to whether students understand the difference between *half of* and *halves*.
- When students have finished Game A, they can move on to Game B.

Closure

- **Exit Ticket:** "Draw a rectangle. Divide the rectangle into fourths. Shade in a quarter of the rectangle."
- **Supporting Learners:** Some students may have difficulty making accurate fourths. Explain that as long as they are close to equal, that is fine. The goal of this Closure is for students to model what they know about equal shares, not their drawing abilities.

Three In a Row: Equal Shares

To Play: Players take turns. On your turn, spin the spinner. Cover a square that matches your spin. Continue playing until a player gets three in a row.

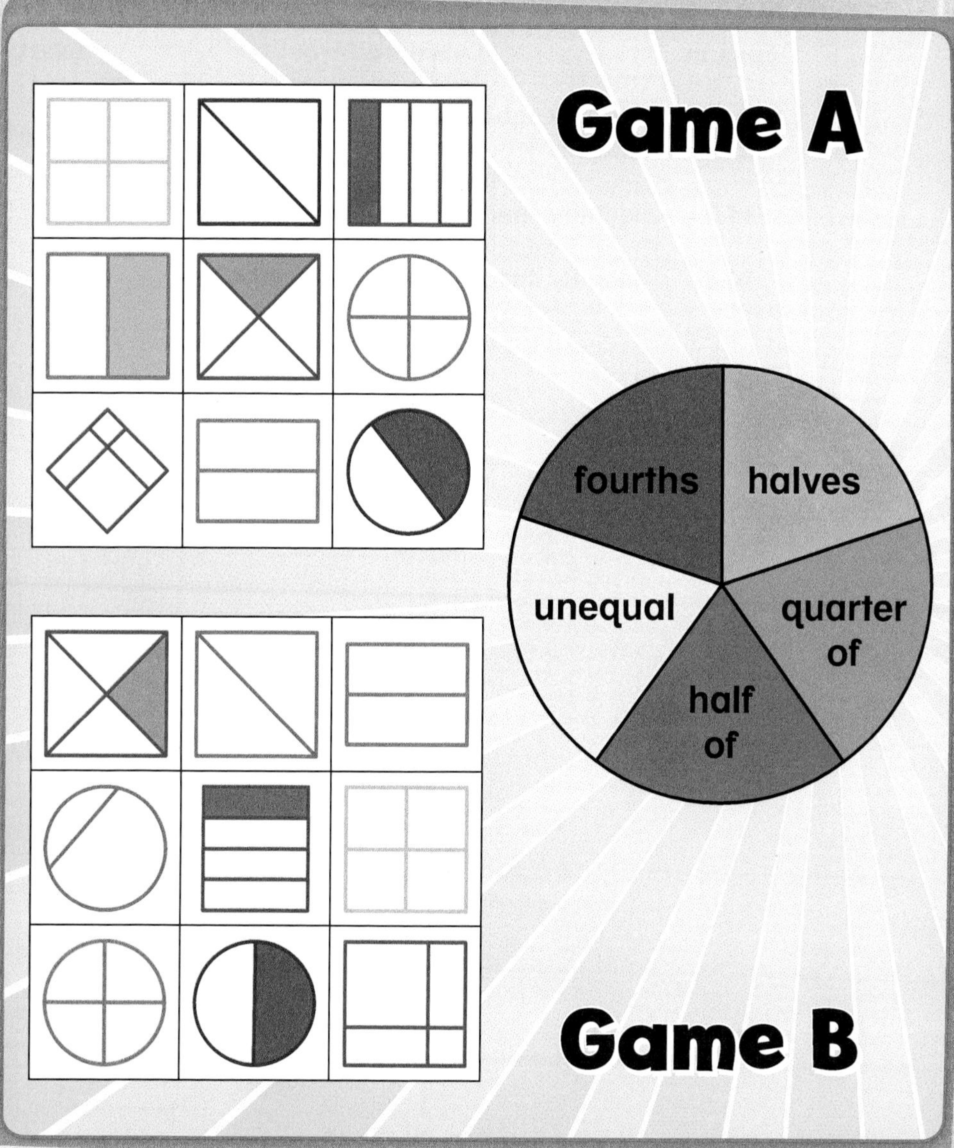

Learning Target Correlation

Lesson	Learning Target	Exercises
14.1	Identify equal shares in two-dimensional shapes.	1–3
14.2	Identify shapes that show halves.	4, 5
14.3	Identify shapes that show fourths.	6–8

Name ______________________

Chapter Practice

14.1 Equal Shares

1.

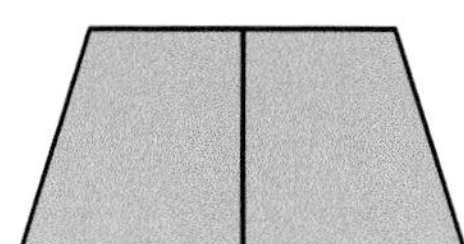

2 equal shares

2.

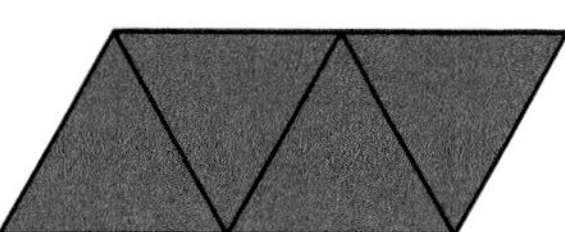

4 equal shares

3. Modeling Real Life Newton and Descartes each design a place mat. Newton's has 4 equal shares. Descartes's has 4 unequal shares. Draw to show the parts. *Sample answer:*

Newton  Descartes 

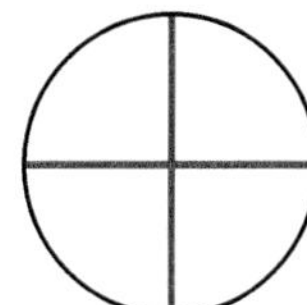

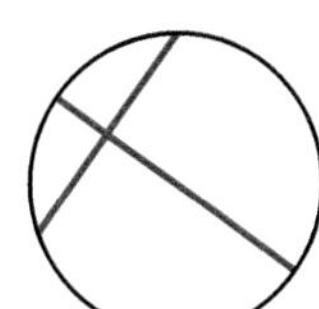

14.2 Partition Shapes into Halves

4. Circle the shapes that show halves.

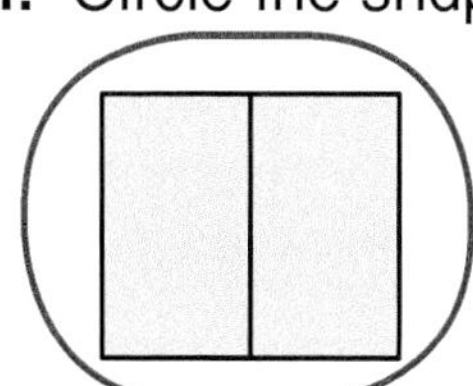

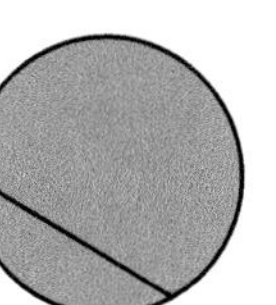

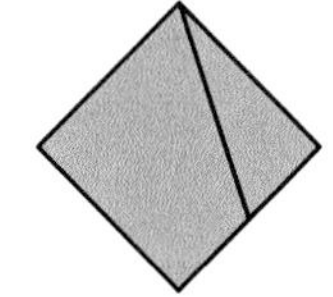

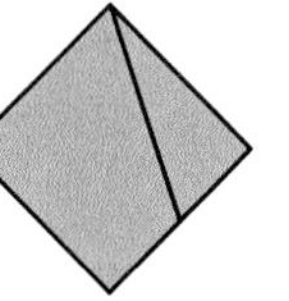

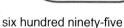

Chapter Resources		
Surface Level	**Deep Level**	**Transfer Level**
Resources by Chapter • Extra Practice • Reteach Differentiating the Lesson Skills Review Handbook Skills Trainer Game Library Math Musicals	Resources by Chapter • Enrichment and Extension Graphic Organizers Game Library Math Musicals	Dynamic Assessment System • Chapter Test Assessment Book • Chapter Tests A and B

5. **Structure** Match each half with its whole.

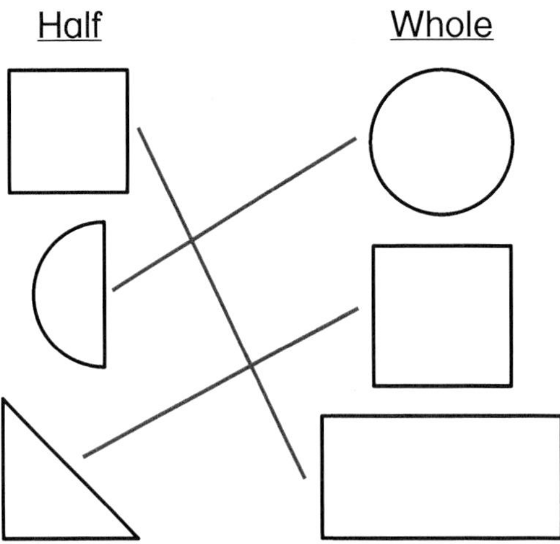

14.3 Partition Shapes into Fourths

6. Circle the shapes that show fourths.

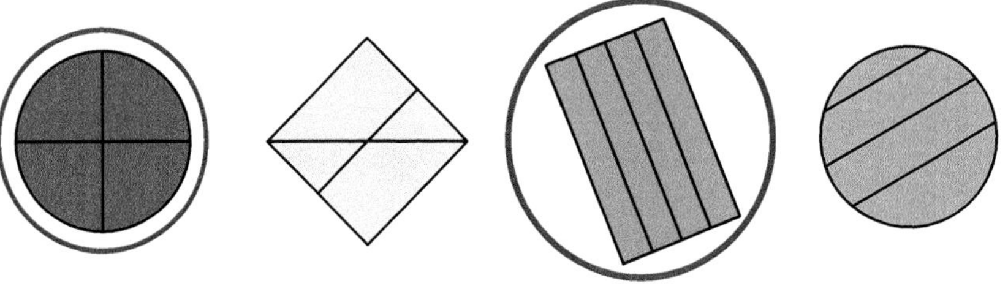

Color a quarter of the shape.

7.

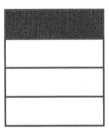

8.

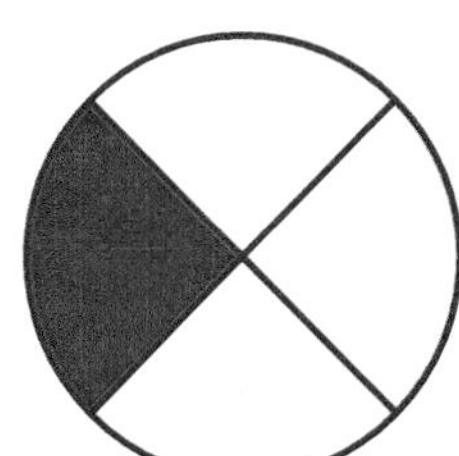

Centers

Center 1: Three In a Row: Equal Shares

Materials: Student Edition page 694, spinners, counters

Have students complete the activity. See page T-694 for the directions.

Center 2: Skills Trainer

Materials: computers or devices with Internet access

Have students go to *BigIdeasMath.com* to access the Skills Trainer.

Center 3: Coloring Shapes

Materials: Coloring Shapes*, crayons

Give each student a copy of the Coloring Shapes and three colors of crayons. Have students color shapes showing unequal groups one color, shapes showing halves a different color, and shapes showing quarters the third color.

Center 4: Making Partitioned Shapes

Materials: construction paper, scissors, tape

Set up three large pieces of paper, one labeled Unequal Parts, one labeled Halves, and one labeled Fourths. Give students construction paper and scissors. Have them create their own shapes partitioned into unequal groups, halves, or fourths. Have them use tape to attach their shapes to the correct paper.

**Found in the Instructional Resources*

Chapter Assessment Guide

Chapter tests are available in the Assessment Book. An alternative assessment option is listed below.

Logical-Mathematical

Show each student a picture of a shape with unequal parts, a shape split into halves, and a shape split into fourths. Have the student identity what the shape is showing. Show the student a blank rectangle. Have them split the rectangle into fourths. Show the student a blank circle. Have them split the circle in halves.

Task	Points
Identify unequal parts.	1 point
Identify halves.	1 point
Identify fourths.	1 point
Draw halves.	1 point
Draw fourths.	1 point
Total	5 points

My Thoughts on the Chapter

What worked...

Teacher Tip

Not allowed to write in your teaching edition? Use sticky notes to record your thoughts.

What did not work...

What I would do differently...

Learning Target Correlation

Item	Section	Learning Target
1	11.5	Use data from graphs to answer questions.
2	12.4	Use analog and digital clocks to tell time.
3	14.3	Identify shapes that show fourths.
4	13.1	Sort two-dimensional shapes.
5	5.1	Use the *count back* strategy to find a difference.
6	14.2	Identify shapes that show halves.
7	12.3	Use the hour and minute hands to tell time to the hour and half hour.
8	13.7	Describe three-dimensional shapes.
9	8.3	Add tens.
10	13.3	Join two-dimensional shapes to make another shape.
11	14.1	Identify equal shares in two-dimensional shapes.
12	3.3	Solve a subtraction equation to find the whole.
13	13.9	Take apart three-dimensional shapes.

Name ______________________

Cumulative Practice 1–14

1. Shade the circle next to the equation that tells how many fewer students chose manga comics than superhero comics.

Favorite Comics	
Science Fiction	𝍸
Superhero	𝍸 III
Manga	II

○ $5 + 8 + 2 = 15$

○ $8 - 5 = 3$

○ $8 + 2 = 10$

● $8 - 2 = 6$

2. Shade the circle next to the number that tells how many minutes are in a half hour.

○ 15  30  45 ○ 60

3. Shade the circle next to the shape that does *not* show fourths.

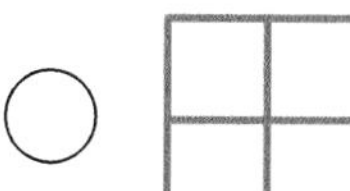

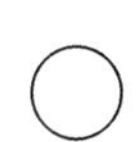 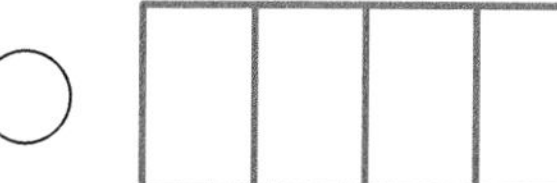

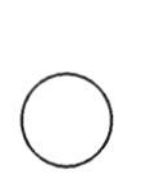 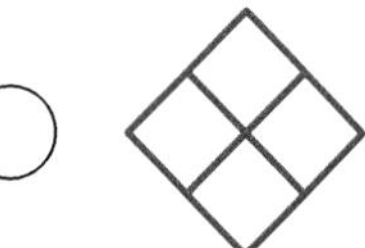

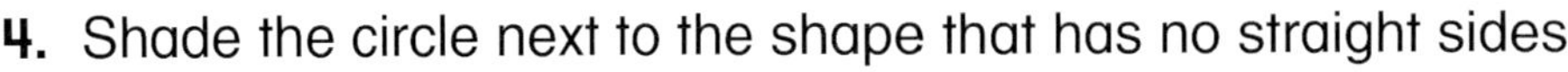

4. Shade the circle next to the shape that has no straight sides.

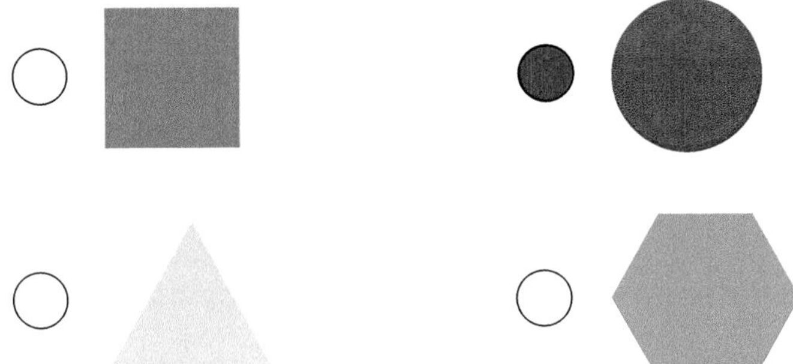

5. Shade the circle next to the difference.

17 − 8 = ____

6. Draw lines to show halves.

Sample answer:

7. Write the time on the clock two ways.

half past 8

8 : 30

8.

cube

6 flat surfaces

8 vertices

12 edges

9. Shade the circles next to the choices that match the model.

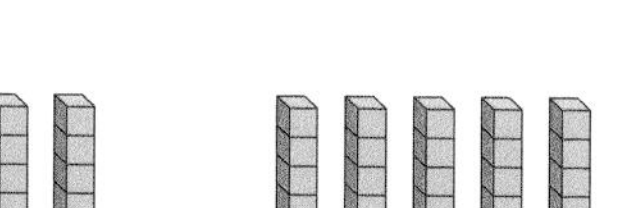

○ 7 ones

● 2 tens + 5 tens

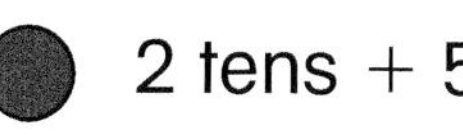

● 70

● 20 + 50

10. Shade the circles next to the choices that show the shapes you can use to make a .

○ 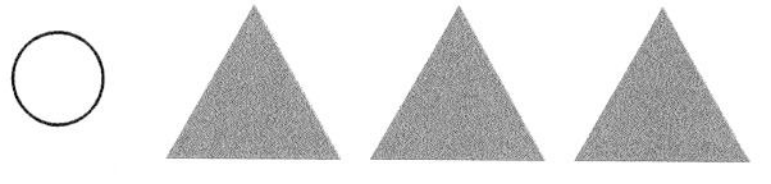

● 

● 

○ 

11. Tell how many equal shares.

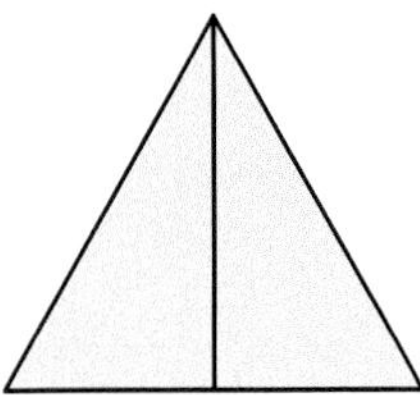

2 equal shares

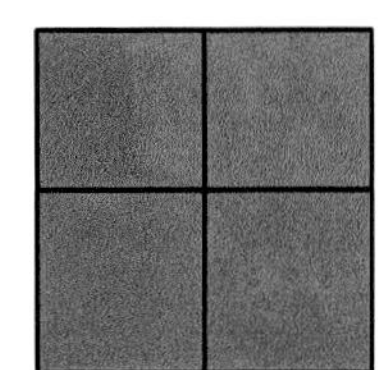

4 equal shares

12. A group of students are at a park. 2 of them leave. There are 4 left. How many students were at the park to start?

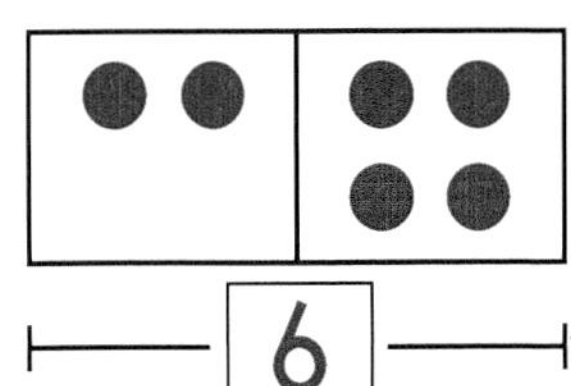

6 − 2 = 4

6 students

13. Circle the shapes that make up the structure.

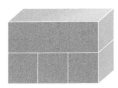

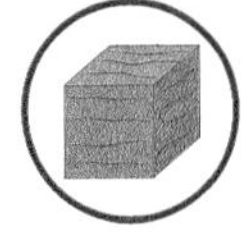  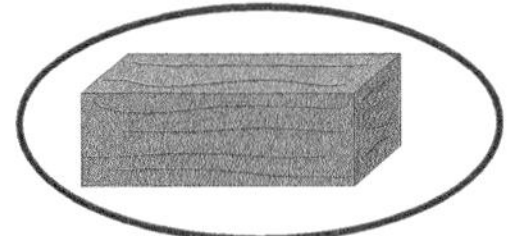 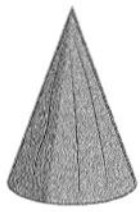

Newton & Descartes's Math Musicals:

Day at the Beach

Sheet Music

I See Seashells

Words and Music by
Michael Wiskar

A E
39
So ma-ny sea-shells here. How ma-ny have you got? Pick them up! How ma-ny have you got?
44
I've got three. You've got four. Three and four is se - ven. I've got
49
four. You've got four. Four and four is eight. Now I've got
A E B A
53
five. And you've got four. Five and four is nine. Now I've got five. You've got five.
E
59
Five and five is ten. How ma-ny have you got? I See sea - shells, So ma-ny sea-shells
64
on the beach. I see sea - shells, So ma-ny sea-shells here. How ma-ny have you
A E
69
got? Pick them up! How ma - ny have you got? How ma - ny have you
B A E
73
got? How-ma-ny have you got? Pick them up!

Cora's New Home

Words and Music by
Michael Wiskar

Dmi
I'm a lit-tle pick-y but I know what I like. Five sea shells, let's go! Let's find a home for me that's right.
Cma7
F(♭5)
7fr.
This one here, weighs too much. Five mi-nus one is four.
Emi
Dmi
These two here, not real-ly my style. Four mi-nus two is two. This one here, no win-dows at all.
Cma7
Two mi-nus one is one. Sor-ry, guys. And this last one It's just kind of ugly.
F(♭5)
7fr.
Emi
Ten mi-nus one is nine. Nine mi-nus two is se-ven Se-ven mi-nus two is five. Five mi-nus one is four.
Dmi
Cma7
Four mi-nus two is two. Two mi-nus one is one. So what else have you got?

100 Waves

Words and Music by
Michael Wiskar

E7 A E7
28
waves keep com-ing, se-ven-ty, eigh-ty, nine-ty, one hun-dred waves!
A7 E
33
Here we go swim-ming in the waves. One hun-dred waves com-ing our way. Don't
A7 E7 A G
37
want to be swim-ming here all day. Got to be home be-fore it gets too late. They go
A E7 A
41
splish splash, splish splash, splish splash, And the waves keep com-ing. They go splish splash,
E7 A
46
splish splash, splish splash, And the waves keep com-ing. ten, twen-ty,
E7 A
51
thir-ty And the waves keep com-ing, for-ty, fif-ty, six-ty And the
E7 A E7 A
56
waves keep com-ing, se-ven-ty, eigh-ty, nine-ty, one hun-dred waves!

Racing the Clock

Words and Music by
Michael Wiskar

F♯mi E F♯mi/A Emi/G C♯7
28
And the little hand's between two and three It's two thirty, but what does that mean? We've on-ly thir-ty min-utes un-
F♯mi
33
til it's three! We're ra-cing the clock Got to make it to the dock While the hands on the clock go
Bmi F♯mi
37
Tick tock tick tock! We're ra-cing the clock It's much too far to walk And we're in a state of shock.
DMA7 C♯ C♯mi D♯7 DMA7
41
Tick tock tick tock! When the big hand's on the twelve And the little hand is on the three
G♯ 4fr. C♯aug F♯mi
47
It's three o'clock. Time's up! Aaarg! We're ra-cing the clock Got to make it to the dock. We're
52
ra-cing the clock. Tick tock tick tock! We're ra-cing the clock We're in a state of shock. We're
F♯mi
56
ra - cing the clock Tick tock tick tock!

Best Friends
(I Get You and You Get Me)
Words and Music by
Michael Wiskar
♩ = 140
A wink, a nod, a
side-ways glance, a lit-tle el-bow to the ribs.
We speak a se - cret lan - guage and no one else
knows what it is.
You know me bet - ter than I ev - en know my-self.
It's a mu-tu-al con-nec - tion be-tween us and no one else.
You've got a
friend, When-ev-er you need a friend. You've got a friend, When-ev-er you need a friend. I can't pre-
tend there's an-y-where else I'd ra - ther be,
1st x to ⊕
2nd x to ⊕⊕
'Cause I get you and you
get me.
And ev - en when there's no -
Copyright © Big Ideas Learning, LLC

Best Friends (I Get You and You Get Me)
D/A F♯mi E A D/A
thing to do we're ne-ver feel-ing bored. We've had a thou-sand ad-ven-tures and we'll have
F♯mi E A/C♯ D F♯mi E
a thou-sand more. You make me laugh so hard I feel like I could cry.
A/C♯ D F♯mi E
And we pick each o-ther up when we're to-ge-ther, we don't ev-en have to try. You've got a
D.S. AL CODA
CODA
D/E A Emi7 A
you've got a friend in me. Yeah 'Cause I get you and you get me. 'Cause
Emi7 A Emi7 DMA9
9fr.
I get you and you get me. We're a spe-cial kind of fa-mi-ly.
F♯mi E G F♯mi
And ev-en if there's trou-ble brew-ing we al-ways know just what we're do-ing, 'Cause I've
B D/E E7
al-ways got your back and you've got mine. And ev-'ry-thing's fine. You've got a
D.S. AL CODA

CODA
D/E A D/G A D/G
I get you and you get me. 'Cause I get you and you get me. Need a friend. I can't pre-
When-ev-er you need a friend. When-ev-er you
F#mi A/C# Bmi D/E A
tend there's an-y-where else I'd ra - ther be. 'Cause you've got a friend in me. 'Cause
Emi7 A Emi7 A Emi7
I get you and you get me. 'Cause I get you and you get me. We're a spe-cial kind of fa -
Yeah, I get you. I think you get me too.
DMA9 A Emi7 A
9fr.
mi - ly. 'Cause I get you and you get me. 'Cause I get you and you
Let's sing it!
You've got a friend, when - ev - er you need a friend. You've got a friend, when - ev - er you
Emi7 A Emi7 Emi/D
1, 2. DMA9
get me. 'Cause I get you and you get me. We're a spe-cial kind of fa - mi-ly. 'Cause
need a friend. You've got a friend, when-ev-er you need a friend. We're a spe-cial kind of fa - mi-ly. You've got a
3. DMA9
A
mi - ly.

Glossary

add [sumar]

2 + 4 = 6

addend [sumando]

4 + 3 = 7

addition equation
[ecuación de adición]

4 + 5 = 9

analog clock [reloj analogo]

B

bar graph [gráfica de barras]

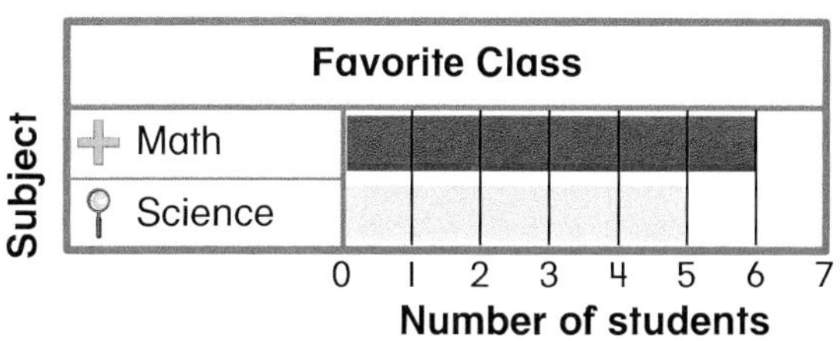

bar model [modelo de barra]

You: 5

Friend: 2 3

column [columna]

1	2	3	4	5	6	7	8	9	10
11	12	13	14	15	16	17	18	19	20
21	22	23	24	25	26	27	28	29	30
31	32	33	34	35	36	37	38	39	40
41	42	43	44	45	46	47	48	49	50
51	52	53	54	55	56	57	58	59	60
61	62	63	64	65	66	67	68	69	70
71	72	73	74	75	76	77	78	79	80
81	82	83	84	85	86	87	88	89	90
91	92	93	94	95	96	97	98	99	100
101	102	103	104	105	106	107	108	109	110
111	112	113	114	115	116	117	118	119	120

compare [comparar]

There are more red cubes than yellow cubes.

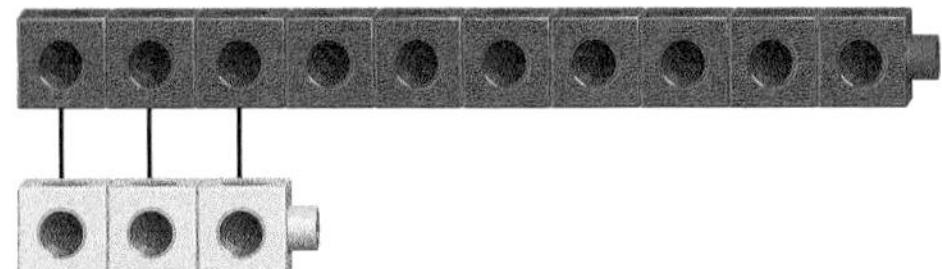

count back [contar hacia atrás]

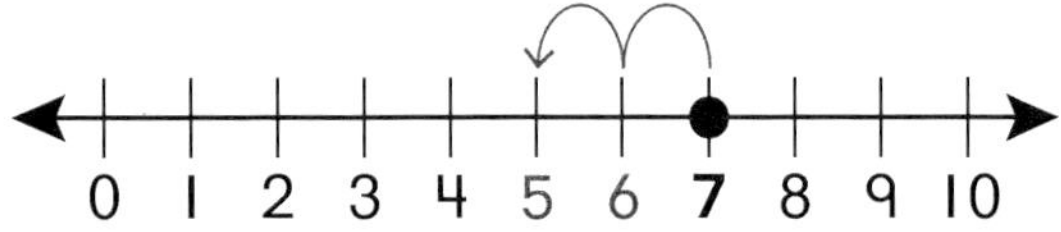

count on [contar hacia delante]

curved surface [superficie curva]

data [datos]

Favorite Class

math	science
science	math
science	math
math	science
math	science
math	

decade numbers [números de la década]

1	2	3	4	5	6	7	8	9	10
11	12	13	14	15	16	17	18	19	20
21	22	23	24	25	26	27	28	29	30
31	32	33	34	35	36	37	38	39	40
41	42	43	44	45	46	47	48	49	50
51	52	53	54	55	56	57	58	59	60
61	62	63	64	65	66	67	68	69	70
71	72	73	74	75	76	77	78	79	80
81	82	83	84	85	86	87	88	89	90
91	92	93	94	95	96	97	98	99	100
101	102	103	104	105	106	107	108	109	110
111	112	113	114	115	116	117	118	119	120

difference [diferencia]

$$8 - 3 = 5$$

digit [dígito]

The digits of 16 are 1 and 6.

16

digital clock [reloj digital]

doubles [dobles]

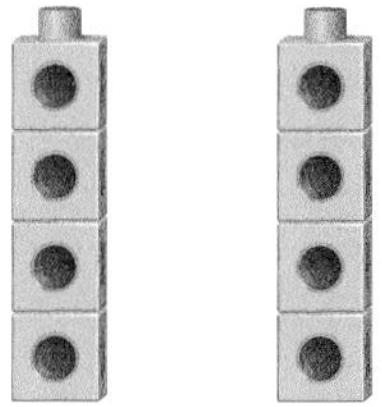

4 + 4 = 8

doubles minus 1
[dobles menos 1]

4 + 4 = 8, so 4 + 3 = 7

doubles plus 1
[dobles más 1]

4 + 4 = 8, so 4 + 5 = 9

edge [arista]

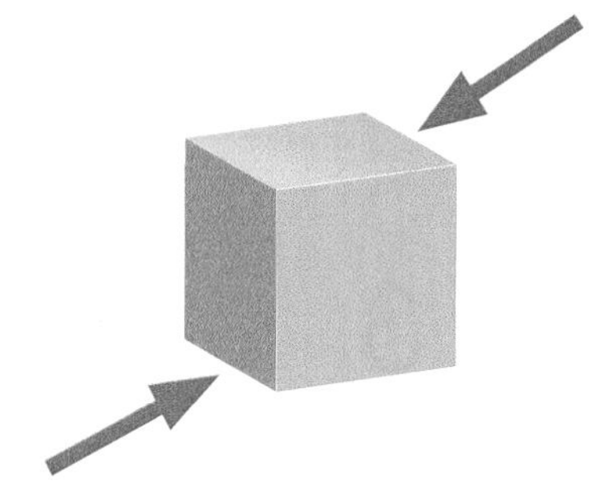

equal shares [partes iguales]

The squares show **equal shares**.

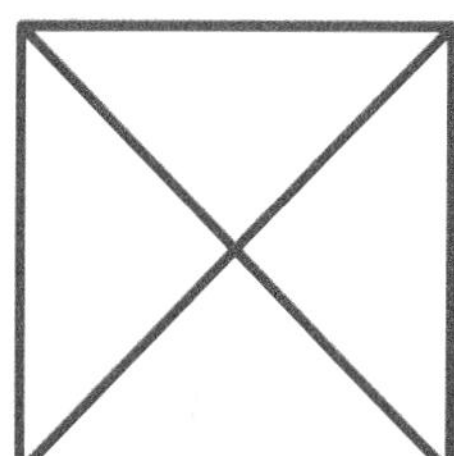

equals [igual]

8 + 2 = 10

8 plus 2 equals 10

fact family [hecho de la familia]

$2 + 3 = 5$
$3 + 2 = 5$
$5 - 2 = 3$
$5 - 3 = 2$

2	3

5

fewer [menos]

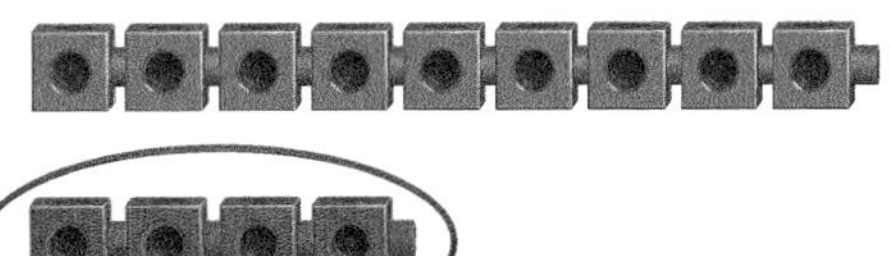

flat surface [superficie plana]

fourth of [cuarto de]

A **fourth of** the rectangle is shaded.

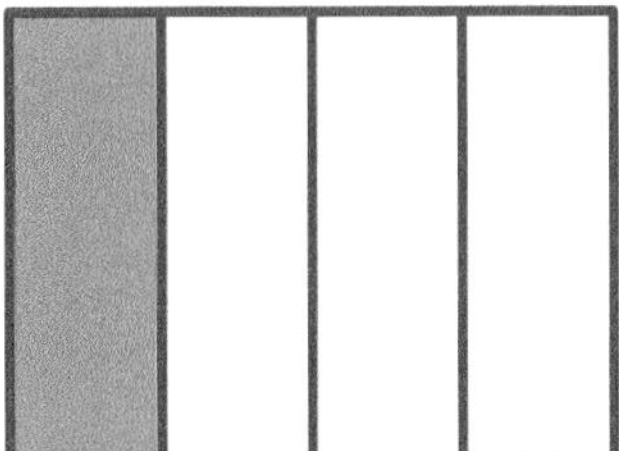

fourths [cuartos]

The rectangle is divided into **fourths**.

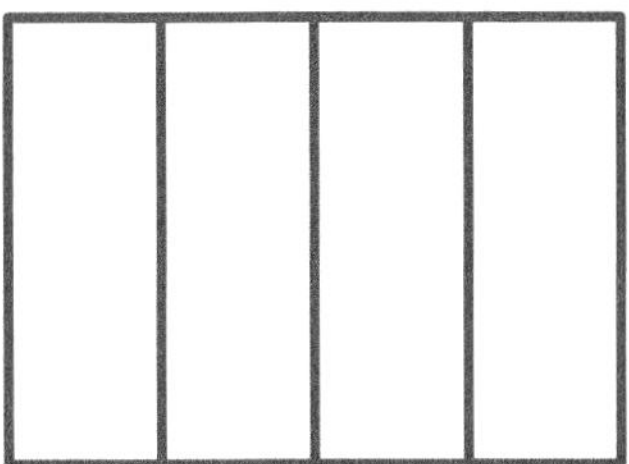

greater than [mayor que]

26 is greater than 23.

26 > 23

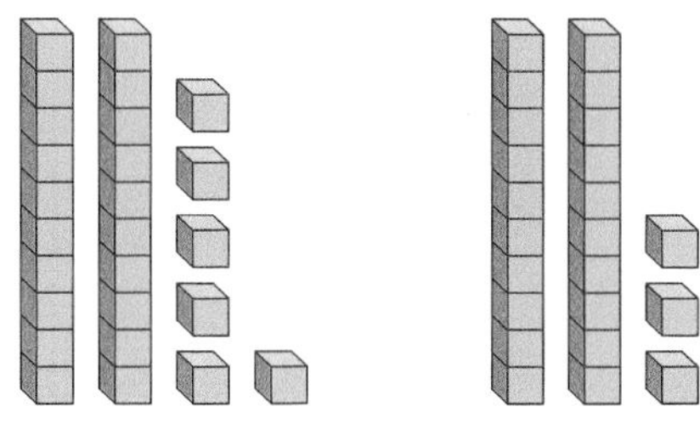

half hour [media hora]

A half hour is 30 minutes.

half of [mitad de]

Half of the circle is shaded.

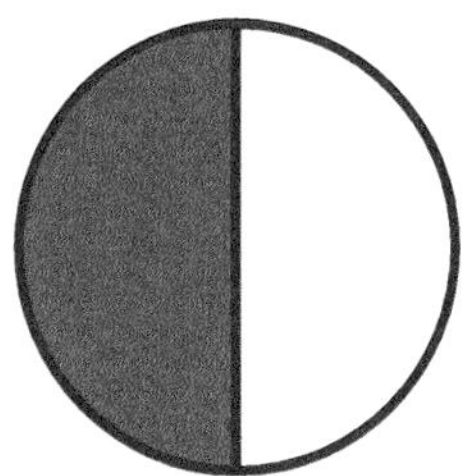

half past [y media]

half past 3

halves [mitades]

This circle is divided into **halves**.

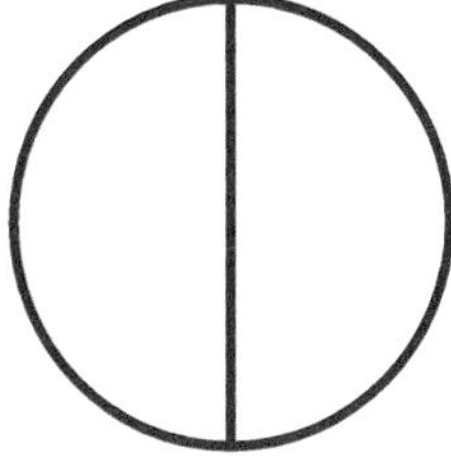

hour [hora]

An hour is 60 minutes.

hour hand [horario]

L

length [longitud]

length unit [unidad de longitud]

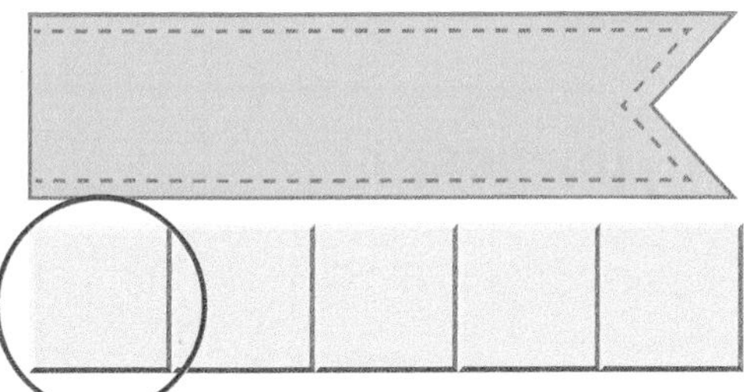

less than [menor que]

22 is less than 38.

22 < 38

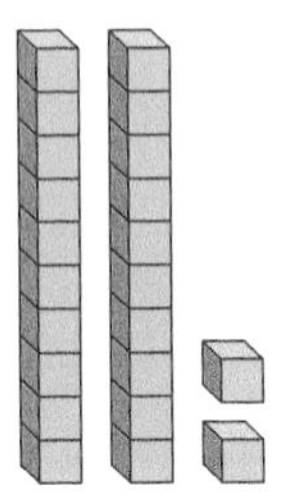
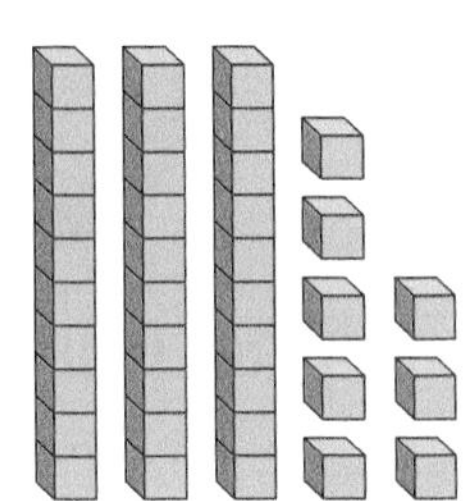

longest [más largo]

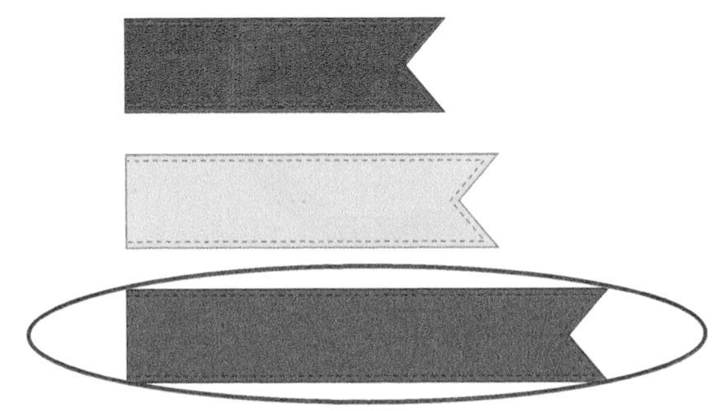

measure [medida]

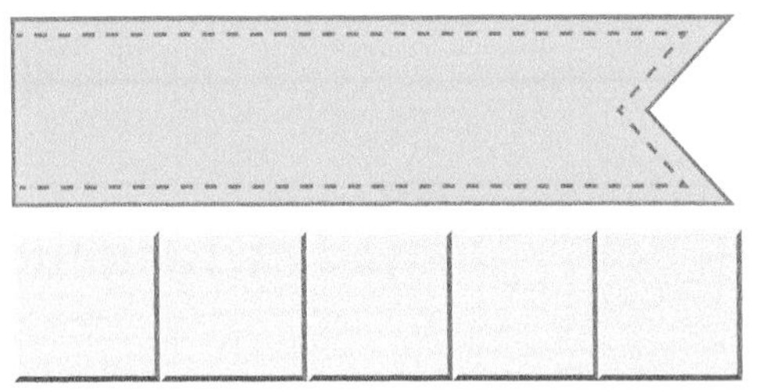

minus [menos]

3 – 1

3 minus 1

minute [minuto]

60 minutes is 1 hour.

minute hand [minutero]

more [más]

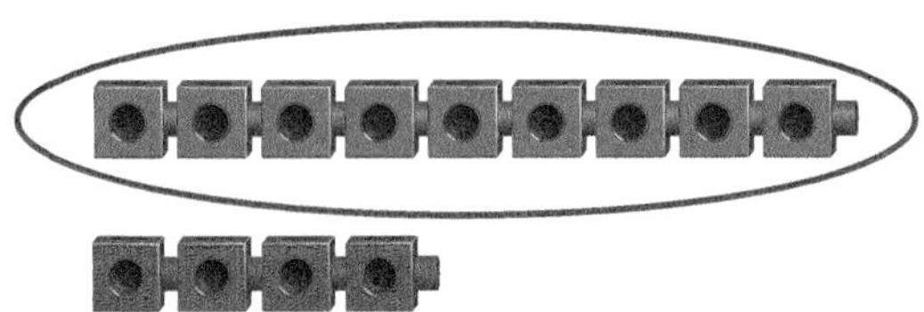

N

number line [numero de linea]

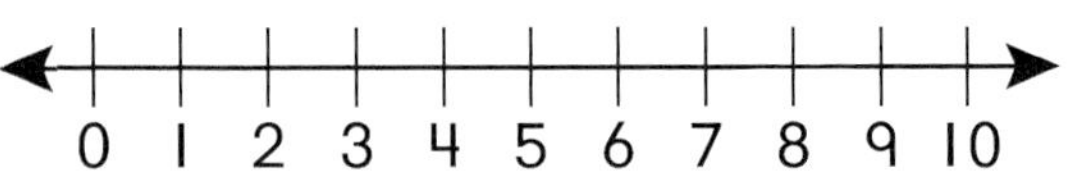

O

o'clock [en punto]

3 o'clock

120 chart [120 gráfico]

1	2	3	4	5	6	7	8	9	10
11	12	13	14	15	16	17	18	19	20
21	22	23	24	25	26	27	28	29	30
31	32	33	34	35	36	37	38	39	40
41	42	43	44	45	46	47	48	49	50
51	52	53	54	55	56	57	58	59	60
61	62	63	64	65	66	67	68	69	70
71	72	73	74	75	76	77	78	79	80
81	82	83	84	85	86	87	88	89	90
91	92	93	94	95	96	97	98	99	100
101	102	103	104	105	106	107	108	109	110
111	112	113	114	115	116	117	118	119	120

ones [unidades]

23 has 3 ones.

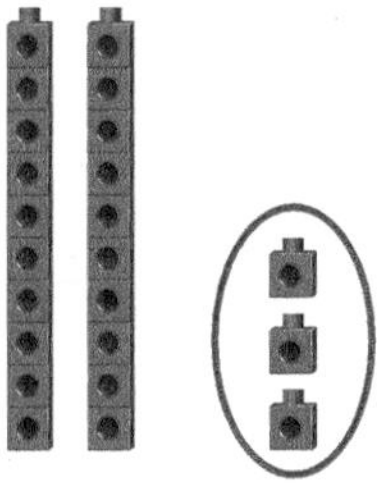

ones place [un lugar]

2<u>3</u>

open number line
[abrir la línea numérica]

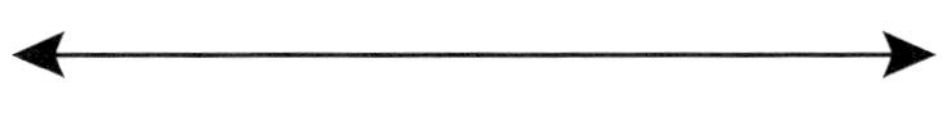

P

part [parte]

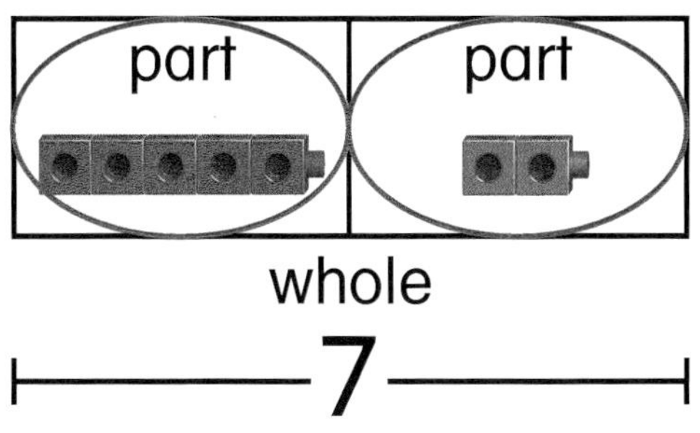

part-part-whole model
[modelo parte-parte-todo]

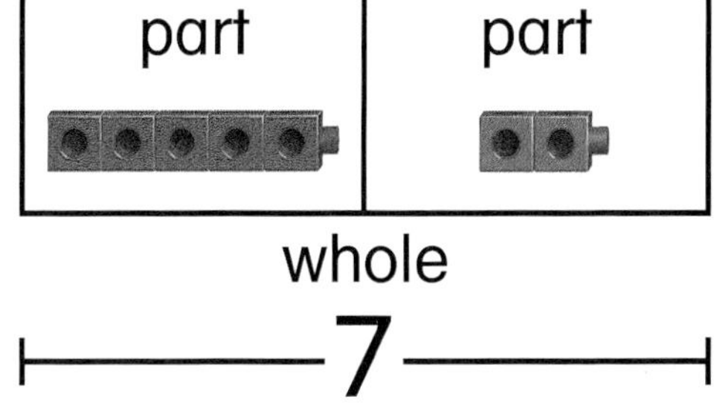

picture graph [gráfico de imagen]

Favorite Class							
Math	☺	☺	☺	☺	☺	☺	
Science	☺	☺	☺	☺	☺		

Each ☺ = 1 student.

plus [más]

2 + 1

2 plus 1

quarter of [cuarta parte de]

A **quarter of** the rectangle is shaded.

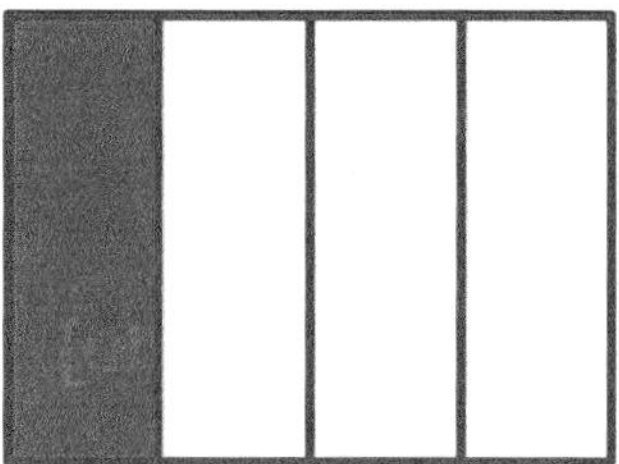

quarters [cuartas partes]

The rectangle is divided into **quarters**.

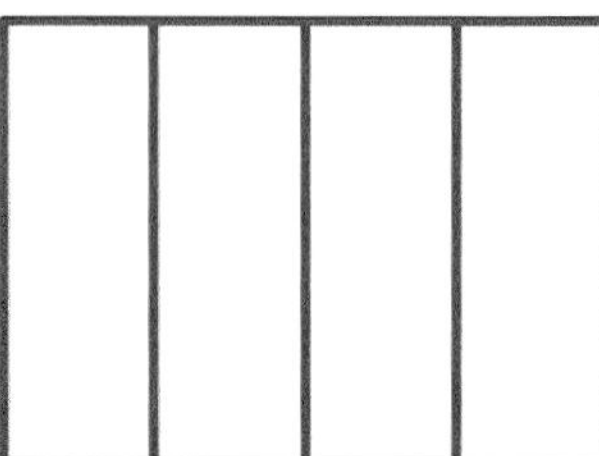

rectangular prism
[prisma rectangular]

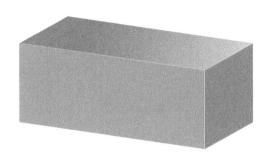

rhombus [rombo]

row [fila]

1	2	3	4	5	6	7	8	9	10
11	12	13	14	15	16	17	18	19	20
21	22	23	24	25	26	27	28	29	30
31	32	33	34	35	36	37	38	39	40
41	42	43	44	45	46	47	48	49	50
51	52	53	54	55	56	57	58	59	60
61	62	63	64	65	66	67	68	69	70
71	72	73	74	75	76	77	78	79	80
81	82	83	84	85	86	87	88	89	90
91	92	93	94	95	96	97	98	99	100
101	102	103	104	105	106	107	108	109	110
111	112	113	114	115	116	117	118	119	120

shortest [el más corto]

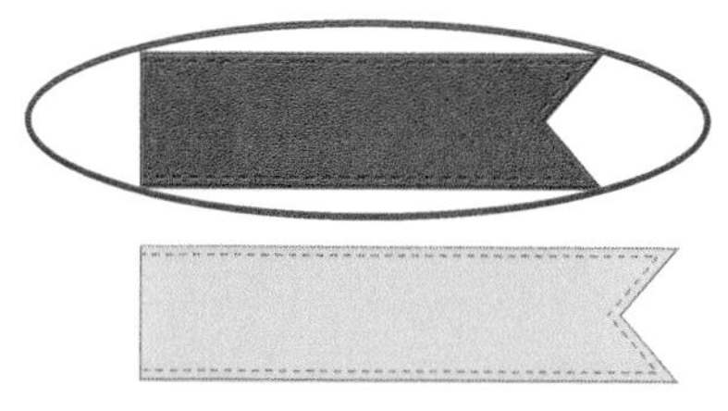

side [lado]

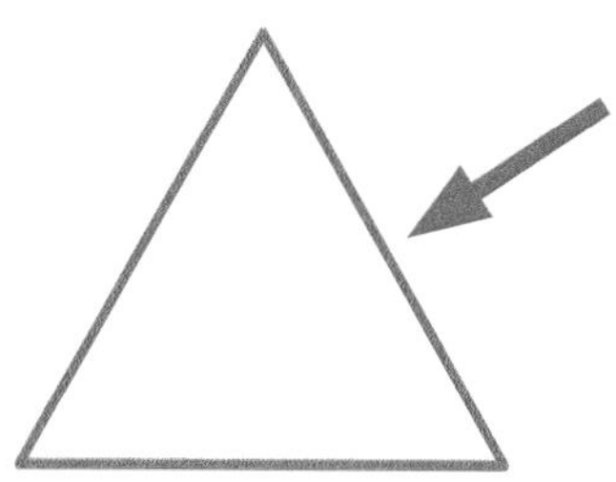

subtract [restar]

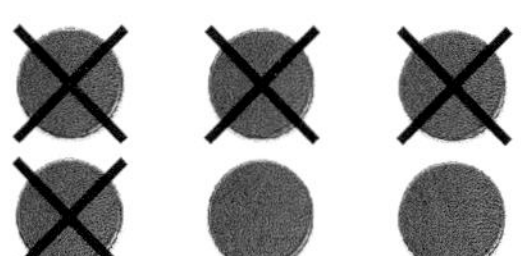

$$6 - 4 = 2$$

subtraction equation
[ecuación de resta]

$$9 - 5 = 4$$

sum [suma]

$$5 + 3 = 8$$

tally chart [tabla de conteo]

Favorite Class	
Math	卌 I
Science	卌

tally mark [marca de conteo]

Favorite Class	
Math	卌 (I)
Science	卌

I = 1, 卌 = 5

tens [decenas]

23 has 2 tens.

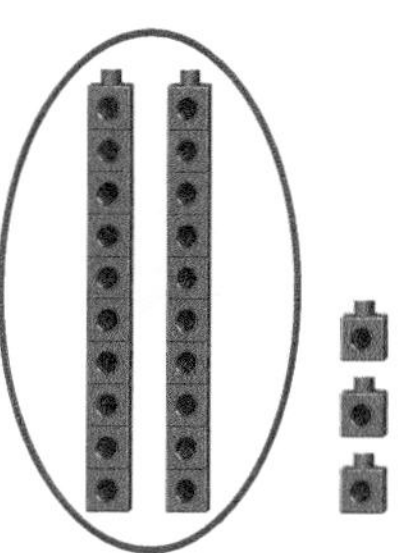

Glossary

tens place [lugar de decenas]

2̲3

three-dimensional shape [forma tridimensional]

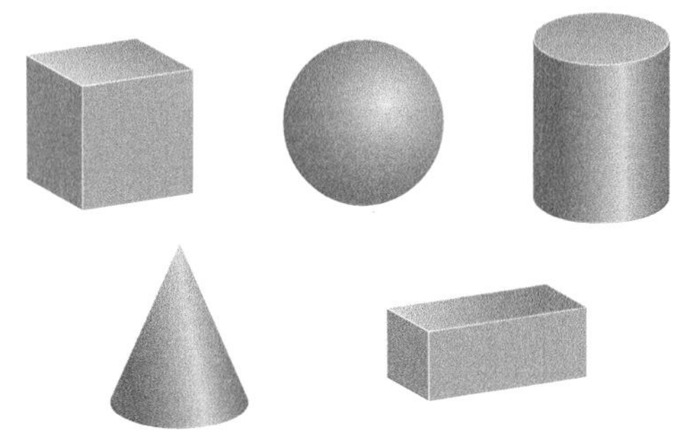

trapezoid [trapecio]

two-dimensional shape [forma bidimensional]

unequal shares [partes desiguales]

The shapes show **unequal shares**.

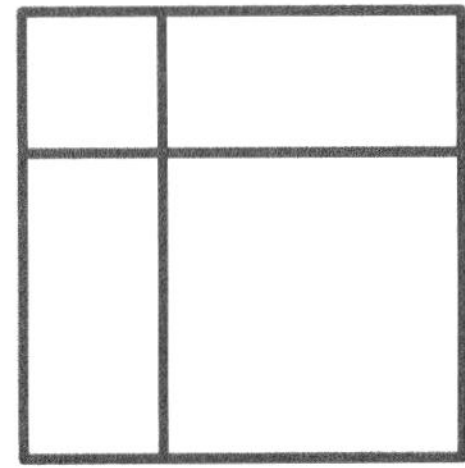

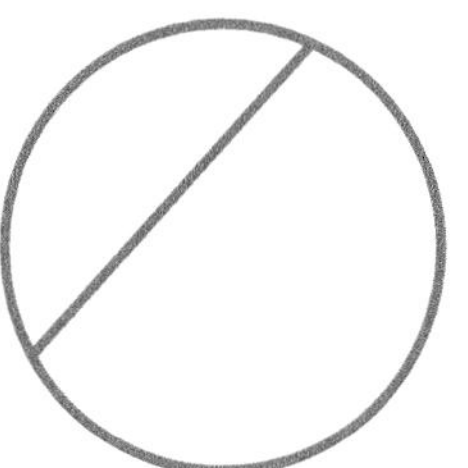

vertex [vértice]

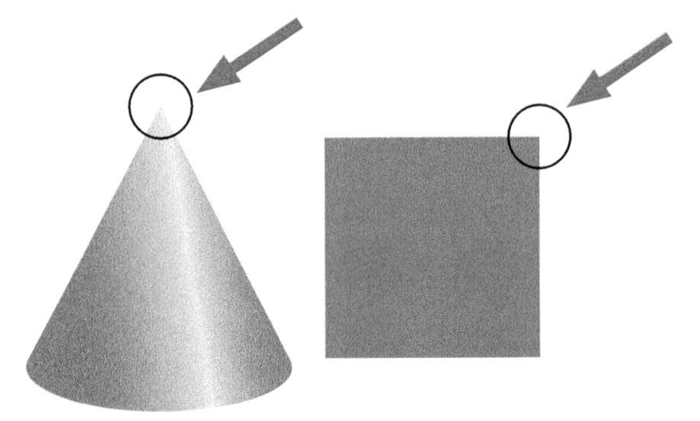

whole [todo]

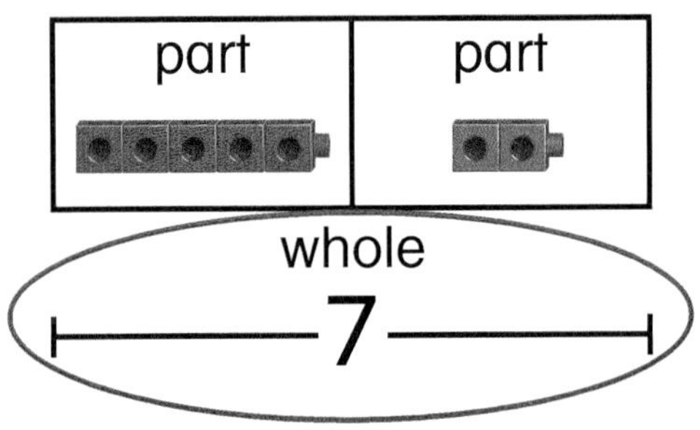

Index

A

B

C

D

E

F

G

H

Index

L

Index

O

Index

Q

R

S

Index

T

U

V

W

Y

Z

Reference Sheet

Symbols

+	plus
−	minus
=	equals
>	greater than
<	less than

Doubles

1 + 1 = 2	6 + 6 = 12
2 + 2 = 4	7 + 7 = 14
3 + 3 = 6	8 + 8 = 16
4 + 4 = 8	9 + 9 = 18
5 + 5 = 10	10 + 10 = 20

Equal Shares

fourths
quarters

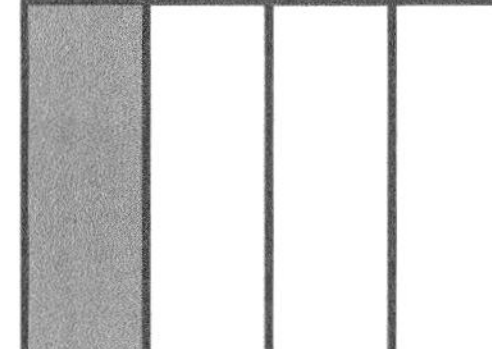

fourth of
quarter of

halves

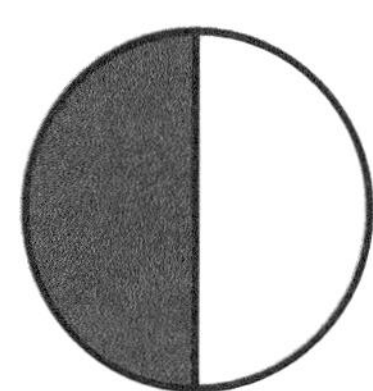

half of

Time

analog clock

digital clock

An hour is 60 minutes.

A half hour is 30 minutes.

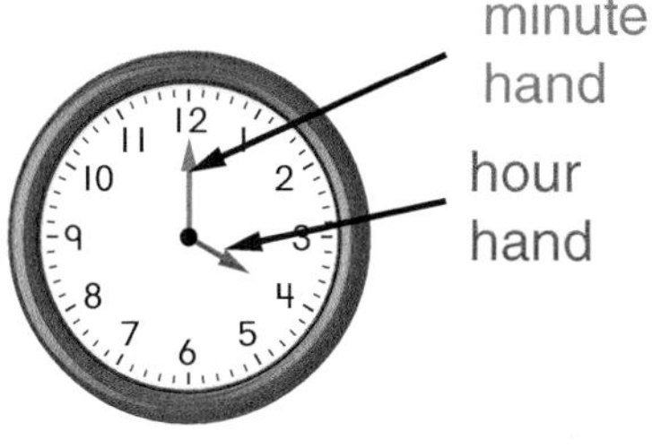

4 o'clock

half past 4

Two-Dimensional Shapes

triangle
3 straight sides
3 vertices

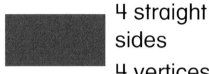

rectangle
4 straight sides
4 vertices

square
4 straight sides
4 vertices

hexagon
6 straight sides
6 vertices

trapezoid
4 straight sides
4 vertices

rhombus
4 straight sides
4 vertices

Three-Dimensional Shapes

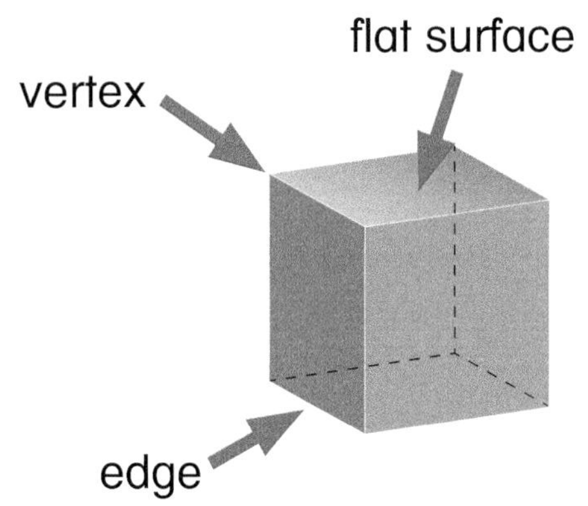

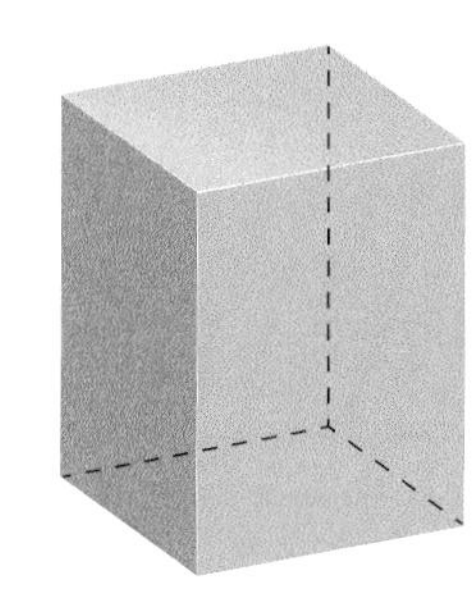
rectangular prism
6 flat surfaces
8 vertices
12 edges

cube
6 flat surfaces
8 vertices
12 edges

cone
1 flat surface
1 vertex
0 edges

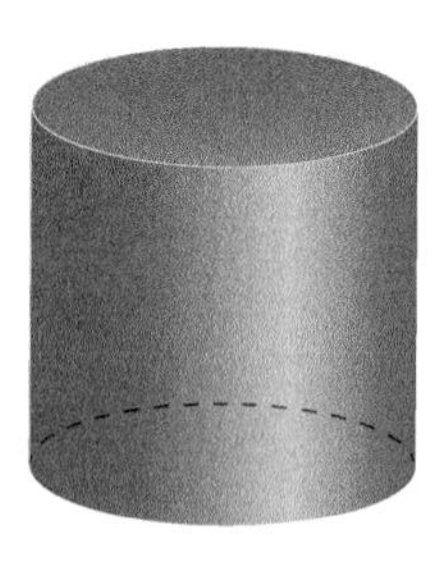
cylinder
2 flat surfaces
0 vertices
0 edges

sphere
0 flat surfaces
0 vertices
0 edges

Credits

Chapter 1
1 Rike_/iStock/Getty Images Plus; **T-20** TokenPhoto/E+/Getty Images

Chapter 2
63 Liliboas/E+/Getty Images; **80** Aratehortua/Shutterstock.com

Chapter 3
125 Nastco/iStock/Getty Images Plus, taratata/iStock/Getty Images Plus

Chapter 4
185 macrovector/iStock/Getty Images Plus

Chapter 5
241 DiyanaDimitrova/iStock/Getty Images Plus; **T-243** Zeljko Bozic/iStock/Getty Images Plus

Chapter 6
291 shutter_m/iStock/Getty Images Plus

Chapter 7
353 keita/iStock/Getty Images Plus; **T-378** joxxxxjo/iStock/Getty Images Plus

Chapter 8
401 PaulMichaelHughes/iStock/Getty Images Plus

Chapter 9
457 FatCamera/E+/Getty Images

Chapter 10
501 muchomor/iStock/Getty Images Plus

Chapter 11
539 PeopleImages/iStock/Getty Images Plus

Chapter 12
581 kali9/iStock/Getty Images Plus

Chapter 13
611 Jon (https://commons.wikimedia.org/wiki/File:Ultimate_Sand_Castle.jpg), „Ultimate Sand Castle", https://creativecommons.org/licenses/by/2.0/legalcode; **T-661** Comstock/Stockbyte/Getty Images

Chapter 14
673 mediaphotos/iStock/Getty Images Plus; **T-673C** *left* Mizina/iStock/Getty Images Plus; *right* underworld111/iStock/Getty Images Plus

Cartoon Illustrations: MoreFrames Animation
Design Elements: oksanika/Shutterstock.com; icolourful/Shutterstock.com; Valdis Torms; FatCamera/E+/Getty Images; gradyreese/E+/Getty Images